Organizational
Behaviour

To the memory of my mother
and to
Valerie, Jeffrey, Richard and Shona

Organizational Behaviour

John Martin
The University of Hull

INTERNATIONAL THOMSON BUSINESS PRESS
I T P® An International Thomson Publishing Company

London • Bonn • Boston • Johannesburg • Madrid • Melbourne • Mexico City • New York • Paris
Singapore • Tokyo • Toronto • Albany, NY • Belmont, CA • Cincinnati, OH • Detroit, MI

Organizational Behaviour

Copyright © 1998 John Martin

First published 1998 by International Thomson Business Press
I**T**P® A division of International Thomson Publishing Inc.
The ITP logo is a trademark under licence

British Library Cataloguing-in-Publication Data
A catalogue record for this book is available from the British Library

First edition 1998

Produced by Gray Publishing, Tunbridge Wells, Kent
Printed in the UK by Clays Ltd, St Ives plc

ISBN 1-86152-180-4

International Thomson Business Press
Berkshire House
168–173 High Holborn
London WC1V 7AA
UK

International Thomson Business Press
20 Park Plaza
14th Floor
Boston, MA 02116
USA

http://www.itbp.com

Contents

Contents

Preface

This preface places the book into the management and organizational context within which human behaviour takes place. It also provides an introduction to the key features and structure of the book, along with suggestions on how students and lecturers might make use of the content. Another important feature of this book available to both lecturers and students is the accompanying web site, also introduced later in this preface.

Organizational behaviour and management

Organizations in their many forms represent a fundamental part of the human experience. They provide the goods and services that form an essential part of human life in the late twentieth century. They also provide the employment from which individuals and families draw the money that allows them to acquire the goods and services essential for life. Organizations also pollute the world in which we and future generations live and cause untold harm to the people that work in them. They are a 'double-edged sword' in every sense of the term. In short, they are a fascinating social creation, both interesting to study and to work within.

Individuals who aspire to achieve success in the formal organization within which they seek to carve out careers need to develop an understanding of many specialist disciplines. There is a need to understand marketing, accounting and those aspects associated with product manufacture and service design and delivery. In addition to developing these technical skills, there is a need to develop competence in understanding how an organization functions as a collective endeavour. This is the realm of organizational behaviour.

There are many constituent parts of an organization. The individuals and groups that form the basis of human activity must have their behaviour directed and channelled if the organization is to stand any chance of achieving its objectives. This text attempts to tease out and illuminate the major forces that shape and control this dynamic activity. It is inevitable given the relatively brief history of the study of organizations and management that there is considerable argument and contradiction among all of the perspectives discussed in this book. At the moment there is no formula or 'one best way' of managing or organizing that will guarantee success. Real success in managing organizations comes from this recognition and through being equipped to understand the strengths, weaknesses and limitations of the many perspectives offered. The understanding and flexible adaptation of the perspectives offered represent the only path for those aspiring to run organizations effectively. The complexity of organizational behaviour demands nothing less.

Objectives of the book

It is human beings that design organizations and work within them. They determine both what is done and how it is achieved. The purpose of this book is to develop an understanding of the nature of individuality; the groups that carry out much of the work; the influence of technology on structure and work; the power, political and control dimensions. Specifically, this text sets out to achieve a number of objectives. To:

- Provide an introduction to organizational behaviour. Whilst offering an up-to-date and reflective perspective, the text does not seek to be of interest only to expert readers seeking to advance their already considerable knowledge. It is intended to be of interest to those readers who need to develop their breadth and depth of understanding of what makes an organization function.
- Include a critical perspective. In addressing the first objective the text goes beyond the purely descriptive and introduces a critical perspective to the material. However, it does not seek to become a critical text in its own right. The critical perspective suggests that knowledge as well as organizations are grounded in the social context that created them and any real understanding must take that into account. This text seeks to achieve that perspective whilst not losing sight of the other objectives.
- Demonstrate an applied relevance. To be of any value the study of organizational behaviour needs to retain a relevance to actual organizations and the experience of those within them. This is achieved in a number of ways, including the incorporation of applied research studies, the Management in Action Panels, and through some of the Research questions at the end of each chapter.
- Provide a basis for further study. The reference sources used as well as the Further and Key readings are intended to provide a basis for readers to take their interest in particular topics further.
- Provide a student-centred perspective. There are a number of student-centred devices that have been used in the text as an aid to encouraging learning. These include the Chapter summary and Learning objectives at the start of each chapter, frequent headings and key point markers in the text, the Management in Action panels and the Discussion and Research questions at the end of each chapter.
- Encourage students to develop research as well as practical and theoretical understandings. The use of Research questions as well as Discussion questions will encourage students to become actively involved in their own learning in relation to the subject matter. It will also help them to understand the difficulties of carrying out field and desk research as a necessary part of creating understanding.
- Interactive approach to learning. The use of group activities as part of the Research questions for each chapter allows students to develop collaborative skills in seeking to explore relevant features of the subject matter.
- Learning support. Through the *Lecturers' Resource Manual* and web site students and lecturers are encouraged to interact with other students, the world at large, the publishers and author in making the book a learning event for mutual benefit.

The audience

There are a number of groups for whom this book would be appropriate. Human behaviour occurs in every organization, irrespective of size, location and industry. There are many courses and degree programmes that contain aspects of management or perspectives on the people issues associated with running an organization. These can include undergraduate programmes in management and business studies, or those degrees with management as a minor component as well as postgraduate degrees and other post-experience qualifications such as the Diploma of Management Studies. These days such courses are invariably offered on a full and part-time basis, and many self-study or distance-learning approaches exist.

To cater for this breadth of audience the material is presented as both academic and practical in nature. It is also presented in a way which encourages students to interact with the material and to seek out applications from live organizations. For students studying alone, perhaps on a distance-learning programme, the web site should be particularly useful in helping to offset the feeling of isolation that often accompanies such study patterns.

The structure of the book

Each chapter is essentially self-contained, unless it specifically forms part of a sequence. However, it is inevitable that there is considerable interaction between the material. For example, the groups that form part of every organization are made up of individuals, are part of the organizational hierarchy and there will be some degree of organizational politics displayed within them. However, for ease of research, study and book organization these issues have to be compartmentalized. Students should recognize that much of the richness and complexity of organizational behaviour arises from the multiple elements active in any particular situation. This should become evident and be reinforced through the Management in Action Panels and the Research questions.

For a proper understanding of this subject it is necessary to reflect on the history of the material included as it did not arise within a vacuum. Many of the ideas currently used within modern organizations can trace their origins back many years, centuries in some cases. I have attempted to include a flavour of this evolutionary perspective, without allowing the text to become a historical review. Suggested further reading sources provide additional material in this respect.

Chapter 1 serves as an introduction and in so doing places the other chapters into a framework based on the:

- Individual.
- Groups.
- Organizational structure and design.
- The influence of technology.
- The management of organizations.
- Workplace dynamics.

Key features

- Chapter summary. Each chapter begins with a brief outline of the content which provides a clear indication of the range of material covered. It effectively sets the scene for study of the chapter content.
- Learning objectives. The learning objectives for each chapter provide a clear statement of what students should expect to master by the end of their work on that material.
- Key readings. At the end of each chapter a range of key readings is identified. These are all taken from the same book and are important, being extracts from the original work of leading thinkers.
- Further readings. These suggestions are intended to provide students with additional sources of material on aspects of the material discussed within each chapter.
- Discussion questions. A range of questions that could be used as the basis of discussion or essays is provided to allow students to test and further their understanding of the material covered.
- Research questions. These activities are designed to further student's understanding of the material through library and field research activities.
- Management in Action panels. These are included to provide an indication of aspects of organizational behaviour as experienced by managers in a real organizational context.
- Web site. This represents an innovative feature for this book, intended to allow students and lecturers to interact, together with enlarging and enriching their study of the material through the power of the Internet.

How to use the book

Everyone has their own preferred way of studying. Most courses differ in the way that they approach a topic and the emphasis given to particular perspectives. It is, therefore, difficult to offer precise advice on how to use this book and the available support material that would be applicable in every situation. Chapter 4 specifically addresses the subject of training and development and introduces a number of perspectives on different learning strategies. This material could usefully be reviewed as an aid to making the most of the material available to you.

There are, however, a number of general pointers that may be of use in seeking to gain maximum advantage from this book and your study of organizational behaviour. They include:

- Recognizing that this book is not attempting to provide you with a formula through which to manage other people or guarantee organizational success. That 'holy grail' does not exist; individuals and situations are too complex and dynamic for a simplistic approach to be credible.
- Evolution of knowledge is occurring all of the time. New ideas, perspectives and interpretations are emerging almost every day. The study of organizational behaviour is not a fixed event. It is for that reason that monitoring appropriate sections of the business press and the management journals and magazines pays dividends. This is also the value of the web site for this book.

- Resources exist to be used in support of your study. This book is not a novel, but it does represent a major resource for your journey of discovery in organizational behaviour. The learning objectives and chapter summaries are intended to guide you in your travels. Also the discussion questions, research questions, key and further reading act as pointers, maps and travel guides to help you gain the maximum benefit from the minimum effort on route. They are there as a help, not a hindrance or a chore, do use them. During your course you will be examined or tested in some way. The resources provided through this book are attempting to prepare you for that process as well as ensure a fuller understanding of the subject.

- Personal experience. Every student reader has had direct experience of organizational behaviour in some capacity. It may have been extensive through working in organizations as a paid employee or even a manager. It could also have been a vacation job as a student. However, it may also have been through school, or membership of a sports or youth club. The important thing to keep in mind throughout your study of this book is that you will have seen many of the concepts in practice, whether you realize it or not. Consider for a moment a primary school and the way that the total activity is organized (structure), the way that teachers lead the learning process (leadership, management and control) and the interpersonal behaviour of the children (individuals, groups, power, etc.). Reflect on your experience and its ability to enhance and illustrate this subject.

- Networking is an important aspect of any manager's experience. The same is true in your study of organizational behaviour. Every student will know many people who have been or are currently involved in organizations. Parents, grandparents, family members, friends, other students and lecturers are all likely to have had direct experience of a wide range of organizations across a considerable period of time. These are all valuable sources of material, examples and illustrations of organizational behaviour in practice. The research questions associated with each chapter should encourage you to begin to make effective use of these resources in support of your learning experience.

- When studying each chapter consider the integrated nature of human behaviour. It is not possible to consider each chapter as an isolated 'chunk' of material that can be ignored once it is finished. Look for and consider the links between ideas and concepts as you work through the book.

- Confidence in managing comes through experience and learning. Use the opportunities provided by the book and its treatment of organizational behaviour to experiment with ideas, test them out and to interact with other people to enable you to develop your own perspectives on human behaviour in a work context.

Support material

Accompanying text of key readings

Clark, H, Chandler, J and Barry, J (1994) *Organizations and Identities: Text and Readings in Organizational Behaviour*, International Thomson Business Press, London.

The text of key readings referred to at the end of each chapter is intended to support this book through the provision of a wide range of original sources. It is not often that students have the opportunity of reading such a diverse range of original material in one book. To search out appropriate material from each of the authors identified would take an inordinate amount of time and effort.

Lecturers' Resource Manual

This has been developed to ensure that lecturers adopting the book have an opportunity to co-ordinate their teaching with the content and structure of the material as presented. It is available free from the publisher to lecturers who adopt the text for their courses.

The *Lecturers' Resource Manual* contains a number of distinct features, including OHP masters (diagrams and text) and teaching notes for the material from each chapter. A number of case studies (and teaching notes) are included for use in seminar and small group activity. Outline answers for many of the discussion questions at the end of each chapter are also included.

Organizational Behaviour web site

Another innovative feature for this book is the creation of the *Organizational Behaviour web site*. This can be located at http://www.itbp.com. This resource is available to both lecturers and students and makes a considerable contribution to the study of organizational behaviour through the Internet. The web site contains material that would be useful in illustrating the subject matter as well as identifying links with other relevant sites. It also provides the opportunity for users of the book to communicate directly with the author and other users, and to receive updated information, new case studies and other learning materials as these become available. *Organizational Behaviour* is currently the only major book in this field to offer this important resource for its readers.

The web site is a totally optional resource. Use of the book is not dependent in any way on the web site. Full value can still be obtained through the many excellent features included the book and the more traditional *Lecturers' Resource Manual*. However, the Internet provides an opportunity to enhance the level of support and understanding in ways not available through the medium of the printed word. For example, the web site offers students the opportunity to explore the enormous potential of the World Wide Web in their study of organizational behaviour. The primary links have been selected because of their relevance to the subject matter and potential interest to readers. The web site resource will be regularly updated so that it retains its value to students and lecturers as the most appropriate starting point on the Internet for organizational behaviour topics.

A further benefit of the web site is the opportunity to update illustrative examples of organizational behaviour and learning materials after publication of the book. This will ensure that the book retains its currency and freshness throughout its life – a major benefit to both lecturers and students. Users can send comments back to the author about the book and the web site, as well as interesting examples of organizational behaviour in practice that they have encountered. There is also a new discussion group for lecturers which will serve as a forum for users to discuss ways of using the book and related materials on organizational behaviour and management courses, and to debate issues of current interest in the area of organizational behaviour. This resource will be particularly useful for users outside the UK and for distance or self-directed study courses.

The *Organizational Behaviour web site* is a valuable new resource which highlights the importance of *Organizational Behaviour* as a book and as a subject at the heart of the management of organizational endeavour. It also demonstrates the commitment to keep this book at the forefront of both teaching and debate in this area. Why not visit the web site and experience this for yourself!

Acknowledgements

Any organizational activity inevitably reflects the efforts of a great many people. Writing a book is no exception. It is not possible to specifically mention everyone who played a part in helping to create this text. The following people have been particularly generous with their time in reviewing material and offering advice on the content of the book:

- Professor Michael Brimm, Professor of Organizational Behaviour at INSEAD (Fontainebleau, France).
- Professor Gordon C Anderson, Principal of Caledonian College of Engineering, Sultanate of Oman and Visiting Professor of Business, The Philips College, Nicosia, Cyprus.
- Professor Derek Torrington, Emeritus Professor of Human Resource Management, UMIST.
- Professor Eugene McKenna, Professor Emeritus, University of East London, Chartered Psychologist and Director of Human Factors International Ltd.
- Professor Dave Tromp, Professor of Industrial Psychology and Chairperson of Industrial Psychology, University of Stellenbosch, South Africa.
- Dr Jim Barry, Reader in Organization Studies, University of East London.

The end result can only be described as a considerable improvement as a consequence of their efforts. The responsibility for any mistakes, errors and omissions remain, however, firmly my own.

At International Thomson Business Press a number of people have been supportive of the whole project and of invaluable help in attempting to steer the work in appropriate directions. Worthy of particular note in this context are Mark Wellings, who first persuaded me of the challenge in writing this book. Steven Reed and Jenny Clapham subsequently attempted to cajole and encourage me into producing the work in a reasonable time and of a high quality. Penny Grose was responsible for converting the final jottings into the finished text you see before you. Without them it would never have happened.

There are many academics, managers, bosses, subordinates and colleagues with whom I have had the pleasure and sometimes pain of working with over the course of my career. Individually and collectively these have all played a considerable role in shaping my fascination with, and views on, organizational life and behaviour. The benefits and effects of their impact on me are in no small way reflected in the views and perspectives offered in this book.

Finally, and by no means least, I would like to place on record the support and interest of my wife and family, who tolerated the time spent on the project as well as continually showing interest in how it was progressing.

Every effort has been made to identify and contact all copyright holders, but if any have been inadvertently omitted the publisher will be pleased to make the necessary arrangement at the earliest opportunity.

Part I

Management and organizational behaviour

1

Management and organizations

▤▤ browse this web site ▤▤

www.itbp.com

Chapter summary

This chapter introduces the concepts of organization and management. This is followed by consideration of research in the social sciences, how it differs from the natural sciences and the concept of an organization as a social construction. Management is then introduced as a specific category of activity within an organization. Organizational behaviour and other perspectives are also introduced. The chapter concludes with managerial perspectives on these topics.

Learning objectives

After studying this chapter and working through the associated Management in Action panels, discussion questions and research activities, you should be able to:

- Understand the evolution of organizations as social structures intended to contribute to human society.
- Describe the distinction between research in the natural and social sciences.
- Explain the particular difficulties involved in studying and developing theories in the area of management.
- Outline some of the ways in which organizations change and evolve over time.
- Assess the relative merits of the differing theoretical traditions in the study of organizations.
- Appreciate that the concept 'organization' incorporates many different forms.
- Discuss the nature of management and its relationship to the organization within which it is practised.
- Detail how the study of organizational behaviour can contribute to an understanding of management.

Introduction

Organizations are an inescapable feature of modern social experience for all human beings. From the remotest village high in the Himalayan foothills to life in a large metropolis, organizations impact on all aspects of the human experience. The work activities and responsibilities referred to as management are also inextricably linked to the functioning of organizations and form a parallel theme of study in this introduction.

A first look at organizations

When asked to describe what is meant by the term *organization* most people indicate the many public and private sector bodies that provide the goods and services necessary for life and employment. However, there are many bodies that bear strong similarity to commercial organizations but which are undeniably different in function or purpose. For example, is the Church of England (or any other religious grouping) an *organization* in the same way that IBM is? Is a trade union, a students union or a sports club an organization in the same sense of the term as a university or hospital?

No two commercial organizations are the same. Figure 1.1 identifies some of the major variables that influence the physical manifestation (profile) of individual organizations.

A number of the variables identified in Figure 1.1 are relatively obvious, others less so. Although there is a degree of interrelationship between the variables, there is scope for management choice. For example, it is not unusual for some owners to deliberately restrict the growth of their organization to retain direct involvement in running the business. Taking each variable in turn:

- ■ Size. The physical size of an organization is a major determinant of how it appears. The small corner shop selling a range of grocery items and sweets, employing two people would be vastly different in appearance to a large national supermarket chain with many thousands of employees. The size of an organization could also influence many of the other variables, such as the level of technology that it is able to support.
- ■ Age. There is an apparent stability and security that comes from the appearance of age – financial institutions deliberately create this image. The age of an organization could also be expected to impact on many structural and functional issues.
- ■ Industry. The nature of the product or service from which the organization derives its income is another primary determinant of its form. A company engaged in quarrying minerals would be expected to differ in many ways from a bank of roughly similar size and age.
- ■ Technology. The type and level of technology used by an organization is another variable that is both influenced by and influences the organization.

Figure 1.1 Determinants of organizational form.

The use of robotic assembly processes has reduced the human involvement in the assembly of products such as motor vehicle and other consumer goods, thereby driving up productivity as well as influencing the profile of the organization.

■ Management style. The dominant style of management within the organization also influences the appearance that it presents to the outside world. The use of hierarchical control through layers of supervision and management produces a tall, thin organizational form. This can be contrasted with the approach to management that relies on self-managed work teams and which would provide a flatter organization as a consequence.

■ Structure. The functional approach to organizational activity in which departments are *organized* around job expertise such as personnel, finance and production provides a very different appearance to one which is based upon product groupings with mixed operational teams.

■ Scope of operations. A wholesaler of children's toys is acting as a distributor within the supply chain. Such an organization would appear very different to another organization in the children's toy industry which made some toys and retailed a much wider range directly to customers.

■ Management preference. The application of the same set of principles across every organization is doomed to failure because of the *situational variety* experienced in practice. Managers exercise a degree of preference and choice in designing their organizations.

■ Profitability. The larger the monetary resource available the greater the degree of elaboration possible. The scale of finance available provides an opportunity to influence the form that individual organizations take.

■ Culture. Issues such as the degree of individuality and formality influence work preferences and the way that work is undertaken within an organization. There is an inevitable tension within large international organizations between the need for a global corporate identity and the dominant culture within local operating environments.

■ Location. There are cultural, legislative and dominant business practice issues that vary across the world and which shape organizations within each national border. Aspects such as communications and transportation also influence activities significantly. For example, mining operations are frequently carried out far from the location of the users of the extracted minerals and the company head office. Management in Action 1.1 demonstrates some of these issues as identified by a Japanese company setting up business in the UK.

Variables such as the type of people employed, job design, control processes and patterns of employment also influence how any specific organization will manifest itself.

So far the discussion has not provided a clear differentiation of the parameters of an *organization*. How can a commercial organization be differentiated from a social club? The ultimate answer is that there is no clear distinguishing criteria as all forms of social grouping contain elements of similarity in terms of purpose, structure, people and systems. A number of writers offer definitions of an organization that offer broad similarities, including:

A   'Organizations are collections of people working together in a coordinated and structured fashion to achieve one or more goals,' Barney and Griffin (1992, p 5).

Management in Action 1.1

Implementing Japanese management methods

Yuasa Battery was set up in the early 1980s in Wales to make sealed lead-acid batteries. It fell to the Japanese managing director, Kazuo Murata, to build and establish the factory as a viable operation. Two important lessons were learned from the experience of opening Yuasa Battery:

- Do the simple things right.
- Create conditions for improvement.

In seeking to establish the company a number of problems endemic to Western companies were identified. They included:

- Worker attitude to the wage – work bargain.
- Lack of the strict application of company rules.
- Workers not involved in determining improvements in productivity and working practice.
- Individualism emphasized within Western culture.

The managing director of Yuasa Battery, Kazuo Murata, began the process of unlearning the 'bad habits' and creating the improvement necessary. This included:

- Fairness. The strict application of rules, procedures and standards in a fair manner resulted from this strategy. Rules are intended to benefit the organization and they should be applied consistently and fairly if they are to have any value.
- Discipline. Consider a sports team or a military force. Each must exercise a disciplined approach to its task if it is to be successful. This implies a controlled approach to work and getting the basics right.
- Improvement. The two earlier points are the basics of good organization, but to become a world-class organization continuous improvement is also necessary. Everyone must feel challenged by this necessity every working day. This implies critical self examination and the development of better ways of working.

Based on: Harrison, A (1994) Implementing Japanese management methods. Professional Manager, *January, pp 10–12.*

B   'Organizations are social arrangements for the controlled performance of collective goals,' Huczynski and Buchanan (1991, p 7).
C   Organizations are ... 'consciously created arrangements to achieve goals by collective means,' Thompson and McHugh (1995, p 3).

Each of these definitions is able to differentiate the more obvious non-organizational forms such as friendship groups, but what of other organizations such as youth clubs? A club with specific goals for the social development of members could easily fall within these definitions and yet would be of little interest to management and organizational researchers. Yet to incorporate terms such as *profit*, *budget* or *commercial* into the definition would cut out many non-profit organizations that do form a legitimate focus of study. The short answer is that there is no single definition that tightly draws a boundary around the notion of an *organization*. Different research activity is addressed at aspects associated with slightly different categories of the concept. This is just one level of complexity in attempting to understand both organizations and the managers who run them.

A first look at management

Managers by definition are the individuals that organize and control the organizations that employ them. In a small company they may actually own the organization itself, but usually they run an organization on behalf of the people to whom the organization legally belongs. It is the task of the management of the organization to ensure that the objectives of the beneficial owners are achieved. They are required to *operationalize* the objectives of the beneficial owners. It is from that perspective that their decision-making function and power originates.

It is only over recent years with the delayering of organizations that managers have seen their own position come under threat. Prior to that form of cost cutting, managers tended to have a much higher degree of job security than other categories of employee. They also enjoyed higher pay, better benefits and career opportunities. As a consequence, their primary loyalty was to the absentee owner, from whom these benefits accrued. However, in the search for ever higher levels of productivity and cost efficiency senior managers (and owners) found that having reduced the numbers of employees significantly the only areas left within which to seek dramatic cuts in cost were the previously protected management areas. This *delayering* created a situation in which managers began to experience high levels of stress and job insecurity. The result being the emergence of feelings of alienation and an increase in trade union membership among managerial employees. In short, they were recognizing the need to find ways of looking after their own interests in response to the *employer* not being willing to do so.

Management is a strange type of work in that it is an activity in which an employee, no different in principle to any other employee, is expected to act *in loco parentis* for the owner. As such the manager should act in ways that may be to their own disadvantage in pursuit of the objectives of the owner. The *delayering* of organizations is a clear result of this requirement of managerial activity. It is because managers have traditionally become so personally and closely aligned with the objectives of the beneficial owner that the implications of delayering and related forms of cost saving have been such a traumatic shock. Managers are paid by the owners of the organization to act on their behalf; they forget that contractual relationship at their peril!

There is an inherent conflict of interest in terms of the expectations and requirements of the owners and those of the manager as an employee. In addition, management is not a homogeneous activity. The two major differences identifiable in management activity are:

- ■ Level. There are many different ways to describe the level of management activity, the most common being a reflection of seniority, director, senior manager, junior manager and supervisor. Whilst that approach provides a useful basic reference criterion, it also contains considerable ambiguity. For example, simply knowing that an individual was a chief executive provides no clue to the level of responsibility involved. The company might employ 10 people in one location or many thousands in locations throughout the world.
- ■ Job. The second major difference in managerial activity refers to the work of the individual. A manager might be responsible for the work of a personnel department, an engineering department, an accounting department, or

a production department. They might be a general manager, responsible for the work of several functions and having specialist managers reporting to them. In this later case the manager will be responsible for activities in which they have no direct experience, which in itself creates complexity.

Figure 1.2 reflects these two variables and their impact on jobs.

Figure 1.2 Major influences on management activities.

In addition to the two determinants of management activity described above, many of the variables described in Figure 1.1 also impact on management work. For example, the industry is a significant factor in this respect. Consider the very obvious differences between the job of a branch manager of a major bank and the job of a departmental manager in a manufacturing company. Both are responsible for the operational aspects within a defined part of the business, yet in other respects the jobs are very different as a result of the manufacturing/service nature of the organizations.

Management preference is another major influence on the actual job of a manager. In many management jobs there is a high level of opportunity to shape the actual work undertaken by the individual holding that position. A personnel manager has some degree of freedom to determine what tasks to delegate and which to retain for their personal attention. They also have considerable latitude to practise a style of management that they as individuals feel comfortable with, which can influence their own job activities and those of their subordinates.

The conclusion from this first look at management is that the practice of management reflects a complex process involving level, job, personal and professional variables. This process is carried out in a complex organizational environment. The result being that it is not possible to talk of either organization or management as single entities. Management in Action 1.2 reflects one person's view of the skills needed by future generations of managers.

Natural and social science research

The discussion so far has provided an introduction to the concepts of *organization* and *management* that suggests a high degree of complexity as well as high levels of interdependence. This provides a fertile basis for research activity as well as the opportunity for the parallel existence of competing explanations.

In attempting to understand organizations as entities in their own right and management as a human activity within that context, it is necessary to be able to offer explanations that stand up to critical evaluation and replication. The natural sciences have developed mechanisms over many centuries that are able to meet that need. However, the primary difficulty for organization or management research is that it is not possible to isolate the key variables and replicate organizational functioning in the laboratory. Study of these phenomena therefore rests firmly within the social science arena.

Management in Action 1.2

Survival skills for a new breed

The manager of the future will need different skills it was argued by Karen Clarke in the essay that won first prize in an Institute of Management competition.

The skills required of managers in the past were decision making, expert (in their field), boss and director. This is progressively being replaced by three roles as organizations prepare for the twenty-first century. They are:

■ Leader. The person setting the future direction for the business and concentrating on the wider picture (not day-to-day activity). The role of the leader becomes one of ensuring that progress towards the goal is maintained.

■ Coach. The job of a coach is one of encouragement and of ensuring that everyone is pulling in the same direction. It is a process which allows empowerment and change to flourish.

■ Facilitator. This is the process of identifying continuous improvement and encouraging a self-critical evaluation of work activity and performance.

It is argued by Clarke that it is now essential to achieve strategic positioning and operation of the business through the effort and ability of the staff employed within it. In order to achieve the world-class service and manufacturing levels increasingly necessary for survival, staff must be committed to meeting the needs of customers. Consequently, delegation and empowerment are key factors in employee work activities of the future. The desirability for managers to be the decision makers is increasingly being questioned. In the face of global competition there is simply not the time for employees to pass decisions back in the system for someone else considered more appropriate to determine. It is employees who are closest to the needs of customers and they must be allowed to operate as the customers representative within the organization.

Adapted from: Clarke, K (1993) Survival skills for a new breed. Management Today, *December, p 5.*

It is frequently suggested that the study of organizations and management provides many competing theories but is unable to offer clear guidance to practitioners. For example, there are many theories of motivation, but on what basis should a manager choose between them? It is only within the last 100 years that writings in management encompassed more than a reflection of the experience of practitioners offering their own recipes for success, or an intuitive analysis of organizational functioning. It is hardly surprising that the study of management and organizations is still comparatively unsophisticated and crude in its ability to offer comprehensive explanations.

The study of people and organizations is different to the study of the physical properties of metal or chemical reactions. However, that does not mean that it is impossible to apply the principles of scientific enquiry into social areas. For example, there are many psychologists working at the micro-level of human behaviour that provide *robust scientific explanations* for aspects of it. Theories developed in this way are frequently based on laboratory studies in which there is much care over the control of variables and other conditions. The difficulty comes from the need to extrapolate adequately from laboratory conditions to the *complexity* and *richness* of human experience within an organizational concept.

Consider as an example a laboratory experiment in which decision-making strategies among managers were to be investigated. The variables such as the decision-making topic; characteristics of the individuals concerned; restrictions on extraneous factors and time limits could all be accounted for. Equally, the measurement of the process could take a number of forms. For example, the actual decision made; time taken to reach a decision; individual interaction patterns and information used in the process. However, it is difficult to be certain what such an experiment indicates about decision making by *real* managers in *real* organizations in *real* time, and perhaps more importantly dealing with *real* problems with *real* outcomes. There are so many additional variables that can influence decision making in practice. Power, control, politics and the dynamics of organizational experience are not accounted for in a laboratory experiment.

The experience of the world around each and every human being is dependent upon their ability to undertake three activities:

■ Detect. It is first necessary to be aware of the objects and situations outside the individual that provide the form for *reality*. This requires the input of information to the individual through the senses of hearing, sight and so on. However, the human senses are not aware of all possible stimuli available. For example, we cannot detect radio waves or see very well in the dark.

■ Interpret. Having detected the existence of *things* around the individual it is then necessary to impose meaning onto them. As a simple example consider the act of seeing a motor car. The *reality* of it being a motor car comes from the ability of the individual to add meaning and significance to the visual image from past experience and learning. The problems and consequences of this inability to apply an existing *frame of reference* to reality has been the basis of many science fiction books and films.

■ Predict. Having perceived a motor car then it can be predicted (if the individual is attempting to cross a busy street) that it could harm them and so it is necessary to wait for a more appropriate time to cross. Without prior knowledge and experience of the object it would not be possible to accurately predict or develop an appropriate response.

From that basis it is clear that reality is not something that exists in a purely physical form outside the individual, but as a social construction experienced within the mind of each individual. The physical objects may be identical for all individuals in that situation, but their experience of them may be very different. Figure 1.3 illustrates this point by showing that two people looking at the same solid object will experience very different representations of it. Each person has only partial insight into the whole.

One of the most frequently referenced works in this field is that of Berger and Luckmann (1967) in which they explore the sociology of knowledge. Much of the possible variation in interpretation of stimuli is eliminated by the

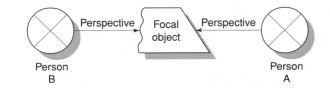

Figure 1.3 Different perceptions of the same focal object.

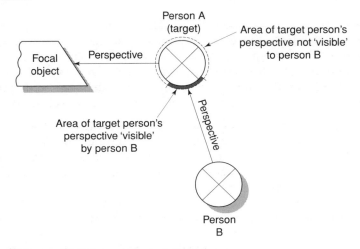

Figure 1.4   Understanding the perspectives of others.

education and socialization processes to which all human beings are subjected as they develop within a particular society. In effect, we are *conditioned* how to *see* and *interpret* the world around us. This forms the justification for induction courses which provide new employees with the *organization's preferred ways* of *seeing* the world.

When social scientists attempt to theorize about the world inhabited by human beings they are to a very real extent researching themselves as well. When attempting to understand an interpretation of the social world offered by a researcher it is important to consider their perspective in relation to it. But this is able to offer only a partial insight of the perspective of the individual in question. Figure 1.4 attempts to illustrate this phenomena by showing that it is never possible to fully understand another's perspective because in *observing* it only a partial view of the target person's perspective is provided.

The scientific process that forms the basis of the natural sciences is described in the following diagram, Figure 1.5 adapted from Wallace (1971). It demonstrates a circular process that allows for hypotheses to be developed from existing theory (or understanding of the world). In turn these must be operationalized and subjected to some form of testing in order to verify or

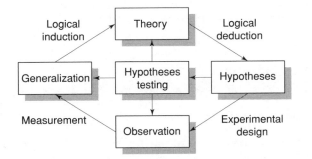

Figure 1.5   Scientific research processes (adapted from Wallace, W (1971) *The Logic of Science in Sociology,* Aldine-Atherton, Chicago).

refute the theory being examined. A cyclical process of identifying and testing hypotheses, leading to more generalizations about the world, leading to the development of more theory.

Another important feature of the social science research is the *level* at which it is being carried out. Essentially the level in this context can be described as a scale running from macro to micro issues. There are five levels as follows:

- Individual. This represents the micro level and takes as its focus of attention the individual within an organizational setting. This field is predominantly based on the work of psychologists. Issues such as perception, attitude formation, individual difference and motivation are common topics under this heading.
- Group. Most human behaviour within an organization takes place in a group. It is important therefore to understand how groups form and perform the work expected of them.
- Managerial. Managers are individuals, and they operate in groups just like other employees. However, there are a number of distinctive features associated with management activities that make it worthy of special categorization. For example, the nature, act and process of managing others are major areas of study.
- Organizational. Typically this would seek to address issues such as job design, the structural frameworks and technology.
- Societal. Issues such as power, control, politics, conflict and change fall under this umbrella heading. They represent part of the dynamic of the ways that organizations function as a small-scale version of society.

In addition to the obvious differences between the natural and social sciences there is the ethical issue of carrying out research on human subjects. Any of the research fields which involve human beings are faced with ethical problems. Chemists working in the field of new drug treatments invariably reach a point at which they must be tested on human beings.

There are research guidelines on how human beings should be studied and by which researchers must abide if they are to attract funding and recognition for their work. The primary difficulty presented by such requirements is that research subjects should knowingly participate and should not be subjected to risk, harm or damage in any way as a result of the process. The challenge for researchers under these conditions is to develop and test theory in such a way that it is not affected by the subjects knowing that they are being studied. The basic problem is how the behaviour of the subjects might have changed as a result of knowing that they were being studied.

The study of organizations

The evolution of organizations

Organizations have always existed in one form or another. When human beings began to develop collective activity as a means of improving their chances of survival and the quality of life, the basis of the social organization was formed. This form of activity is still evident today in the many thousands of small family businesses (Bork, 1986). There is evidence of early forms of organization not based upon the family unit being used by the Sumerian people who settled around the river Euphrates around 3500 years BC (McKelvey, 1982). Of course, many organizations during that period continued to be family run. For example, the leadership of the state was based upon dynastic family groupings. By the time of the Roman Empire (around 300 BC) there was a significant banking and insurance industry in existence to support international trade and commerce.

With the fall of the Roman Empire the large organizations that had existed to facilitate trade disappeared. Smaller organizations more local in focus emerged. During the Middle Ages the *Guild* became a significant force in controlling organizational activity. Craftsmen from a particular trade would band together and regulate entry to that trade, the number of people allowed to practise the craft and other aspects of the work such as pricing. In that sense they were the early forms of the trade unions and trade associations found today.

The emergence of the factory system during the Industrial Revolution again changed the nature of organizational activity. Large-scale factory-based production became the normal working experience for many people. The creation of factory-based systems of production required different types of job to be designed for the workers and the development of new forms of hierarchical management and technical specialism. This approach formed the basis for most modern large-scale organizations.

The *bureaucratic* approach to organizational activity emerged as a result of the need to have large-scale administrative structures to run both commercial and public sector organizations. This was necessary in the days before computer technology. The bureaucratic form of organization began to be expensive to run, slow to respond and unable to meet the needs of customers effectively. Consequently, over recent years many organizations have developed alternative structural forms in an attempt to make themselves cheaper to run and more responsive to ever changing consumer demand. This process is creating circumstances which allow small organizations to flourish, as large companies outsource much of their activity (Wood, 1989). However, some of the challenges facing small organizations in today's competitive world are outlined in Management in Action 1.3.

The distinction has already been made between family owned and commercial organizations. This is not the usual distinction that would be made between organizations. The main distinction that would be made between organizations would be between those in the *private* and *public* sectors. Private sector organizations are those that exist for the commercial benefit of their owners. The owners can be any group of individuals, a family, partnership or shareholders. Public sector organizations are not run directly as commercial organizations but are the public service and local government institutions that are necessary for the effective functioning of society.

Another way of classifying organizations is in relation to the *profit* or *non-profit* nature of their activities. Over the past few years there has been a significant development in non-profit organizations that either run on commercial lines or interest group organizations that exist on a network basis. An example of the former would be a co-operative. The latter a community group running an allotment and selling the produce to its members at cost price as a means of providing work experience and an interest for local people.

Management in Action 1.3

The big challenge facing small firms

About one-third of all jobs are in firms with fewer than 20 employees and one-half are in firms of less than 100 employees. However, many small firms have a relatively short lifespan. The Institute of Directors estimates that four out of five go under within six years.

In attempting to survive, small businesses are faced with many of the same requirements placed upon much larger organizations. There are requirements covering tax returns, employment legislation, health and safety requirements and local authority planning requirements to name just a few. These areas of demand on a company can make the difference between life and death for a small company who might not have the technical or financial capability to absorb the costs and time involved.

The abolition of maximum awards for compensation in sex and race discrimination cases could result in costs of £30,000 in some cases which would be difficult enough for most companies to absorb, but could result in the closure of a small one. The industrial tribunal system has become increasingly legalistic over the past few years and it is not uncommon to find both parties to an unfair dismissal claim being represented by a solicitor. Under these circumstances it is frequently cheaper for a company to settle out of court for (say) £400 rather than pay the legal costs even if the case is won. This sends a wrong signal to employees and can encourage frivolous claims with little of substance to support them.

Over recent years the development of national training and other initiatives such as National Vocational Qualifications and Investors in People have been introduced as a means of encouraging improvements in business. The schemes themselves frequently contain significant levels of bureaucracy (for a small firm) and they find it difficult to find the financial resources to pay for the introduction. However, evidence suggests that if undertaken effectively the changes that come about as a result of changes to communication and training of employees can help to reduce cost and encourage employee commitment to the survival of the business.

Based upon: Thatcher, M (1996) The big challenge facing small firms. People Management, *July, pp 20–5.*

The discussion so far has emphasized a Western perspective on organization and the developments in management. In the Asian world there were parallel developments from quite a different tradition. The Confucian perspective in China emerged around 500 BC and has produced a different basis for running organizations and society.

Challenges facing organizations

The world is constantly changing, some of this change is *evolutionary* and other *revolutionary*. For example, the development of computer technology is subject to continual refinement. This is something that is *evolutionary* in nature. A change process experienced as a series of small frequent (incremental) amendments to the existing situation. Considering this type of change on a daily basis would offer no noticeable difference, but over the period of years considerable change is achieved.

Revolutionary change by comparison is a sudden and dramatic process that fundamentally alters the situation. One example of this is the arrival of the out-of-town shopping and leisure complex. Over a relatively short period of time town centres have become deserted as people find it more convenient to be able to drive to one of these centres. The effect has been to force many town centre businesses to either relocate to a new complex or close down.

Change has always been part of life. It has been argued by many writers that the pace of change impacting on organizations is occurring at an ever more rapid rate. So much so that one catch-phrase over recent years has been an exhortation to innovate or die! Carrying the clear implication that unless change becomes institutionalized then the organization will not stay in business for long.

There is a counter argument to this view which suggests that by forcing change into an organization, managers are creating the very instability that can inhibit their ability to survive. Inevitably, change within an organization impacts on all the people within it. Managers themselves are no longer exempt from this, as Management in Action 1.4 demonstrates.

Management in Action 1.4

Metamorphosis of the manager

There has been a process of cutting-back, downsizing, delayering and rightsizing going on for many years now. It has had many titles, most have attempted to hide the brutality of the process – that of cutting thousands of jobs. For example, General Electric (GE) shed more than 100,000 jobs during the 1980s. However, a new phenomenon has been detected over recent years, that of title cuts, rather than job cuts.

A job cut simply means that human beings lose their jobs (perhaps in their thousands). This is a process largely separate to that of a consideration of the structure of the organization or the design of jobs within it. Factories can be closed and work reallocated without actually changing the nature of the jobs within the remaining parts of the business.

A title cut implies that the work of the organization is being reviewed and that as a result job design issues will be raised. The work being done within the organization will be reallocated and distributed differently from the past and so it is 'jobs' that become surplus to requirement. What happens to the people in those jobs then becomes the second phase of the process. Title cuts imply a fundamental review of the hierarchy, compartmentalization, structure and design of the way that the organization goes about its business. To indicate the significance of these ideas, GE 'promised' a third fewer managers by the year 2000.

Networking is the process being suggested as the management approach of the future in an attempt to eliminate titles and to transform organizations into the rapid-response, customer-sensitive entities necessary for global competition. There are many examples of these networks evolving in practice. For example, Du Pont removed four layers of management and gave employees more power to act faster and more decisively. Business managers were brought in lower down the organization in an attempt to provide hands-on managers with the opportunity to win orders. WT Gore & Associates abolished all job titles and termed everyone an associate, expected to work towards the best interests of the company. With Apple Computers speed of response and development is vital and managers must now seek out opportunities and then find the necessary support for their proposals.

Adapted from: Lester, T (1992) Metamorphosis of the manager. Management Today, *August, pp 72–5.*

There are many ways of categorizing change. Johnson and Scholes (1993) describe a *PEST* analysis process that provides a systematic basis for considering the environmental influences surrounding an organization:

■ Political/legal. Influences impacting on the organization from political and legislative sources.

■ Economic. These reflect the economic conditions and trends that can influence the environment within which the organization must operate.

■ Social/cultural. Changes to the populations (customer and workforce) surrounding the organization can also have a significant impact on its functioning. For example, in Europe there is an expectation among employees that they are entitled to increasing levels of involvement in company decision making.

■ Technological. The changes to the technology available to organizations affects both the products and services available and also the ways that companies operate.

Figure 1.6 is taken from the Johnson and Scholes (1993) text and identifies some of the more important PEST issues that present challenges to be addressed by the organization.

The factors identified in Figure 1.6 represent a very rational view of change as it influences organizations. In addition there are the political reasons that lead managers to seek change within their organizations. For example, new managers often seek to make change in order to demonstrate a break with what existed previously. Equally, managers can attempt to enhance their own career prospects by seeking to be regarded by senior managers as proactive in pursuing change.

People within organizations

Organizations do not *exist* in any real sense of the word. They might be described as legal and financial entities on paper, but it is the people within them that breathe life into the documents. Management in Action 1.5 illustrates some of these people perspectives in the context of the introduction of business process re-engineering.

---

1. **What environmental factors are affecting the organization?**
2. **Which of these are the most important at the present time? In the next few years?**

Political/legal
Monopolies legislation •
Environmental protection laws •
Taxation policy • Foreign trade
regulations • Employment law •
Government stability

Socio-cultural
Population demographics •
Income distribution • Social
mobility • Lifestyle changes •
Attitudes to work and leisure •
Consumerism • Levels of education

Economic
Business cycle • GNP trends • Interest
rates • Money supply • Inflation •
Unemployment • Disposable income
• Energy availability and cost

Technological
Government spending on research •
Government and industry focus of
technological effort • New
discoveries/development • Speed of
technology transfer • Rates of
obsolescence

Figure 1.6 'PEST' analysis (taken from Johnson, G and Scholes, K (1993) *Exploring Corporate Strategy*, 3rd edn, Prentice-Hall, Hemel Hempstead, Figure 3.3, p 82).

Management in Action 1.5

Cut out the middle men

The techniques and formulas that are used as the basis of seeking out the best way of working and the lowest cost of operation are often silent on the human impact of their activity. At best these approaches assume a rationality in the human dimension and imply that communication can overcome any unwillingness on the part of employees to accept the need to produce more for less.

Business process re-engineering is the latest in a long line of approaches to attempt to ensure that organizations become truly efficient. Michael Hammer is one of the leading gurus in this field and insists that it is a process that is about eliminating work, a process that should not be considered as the same as eliminating people (simple downsizing). The net result, however, is the same, but it is argued that by concentrating on the fundamental redesign of the business process an effective organization will then result and one into which the people can be accommodated. The major area of impact for this approach to efficiency is the middle

manager levels, what Hammer calls the 'death zone'. Re-engineering he describes as a process intended to replace the organizational forms that emerged during the industrial revolution when workers needed to be closely supervised for many reasons, including low levels of trust.

In the re-engineered company teams are essential and a customer rather than boss focus is required. This invariably leads to the notion of self-managed teams with a much reduced role for managers in the traditional sense of the job. Management becomes a role requiring lead-and-enable skills rather than those of command-and-control. It also reduces the ratio of managers required from approximately 1:7 to anything approaching 1:50. As an indication of the impact of re-engineering, Taco Bell moved from 350 area supervisors for its 1800 fast food outlets in 1988 to 100 market managers responsible for 2300 outlets a few years later. The effect on sales was an increase (on average) of 22% per year and profits by 31% per year.

Based on: Flood, G (1994) Cut out the middle men. Personnel Today, *22 March, p 36.*

The earlier discussion on management stated that the manager is acting on behalf of an absentee owner. This view is usually referred to as an *agency* perspective – the manager acting as an agent (on behalf of) of the owner. From a different perspective, as early as 1964, Cyert and March were writing about coalitions and Rhenman was writing about *stakeholders* in the running of organizations. Networks and coalitions formed between the many internal and external stakeholder groups linked with the organization is implied by these views. Figure 1.7 illustrates some of the primary stakeholder groups that can be identified.

Each one of the stakeholder groups identified in Figure 1.7 has an interest in some aspect of the focal organization. Owners are interested in a financial return for their money; employees might be interested in a secure and interesting job that pays a realistic wage; suppliers in the opportunity to create long-term strategic alliances for commercial benefit; and government as a source of employment and taxation. Internally some of the groups will be temporary and seek to achieve limited goals.

These stakeholder groups are essentially people oriented and so provide a basis for analysis. Human beings are complex as individuals and even more so in collective situations. Each person has many similarities with other humans, but, critically for organizational purposes, a great many differences. Personality factors differ as does the education level and life experience of each person.

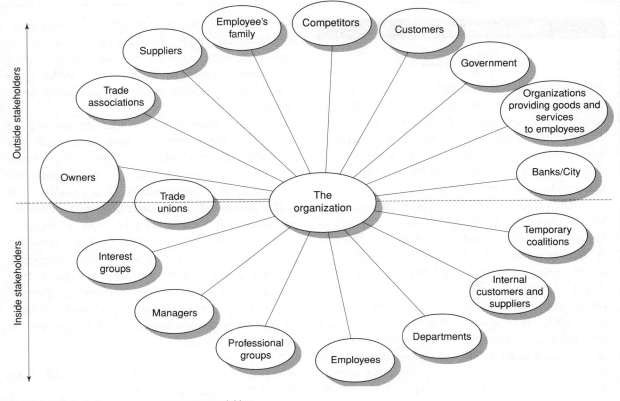

Figure 1.7 Major influences on management activities.

These form the basis of how individuals interpret and relate to the world in which they live. People can be unpredictable to an extent which makes consistency of behaviour in an organizational setting difficult to achieve. Illness, mood and temperament are just some of the variables that can affect how each person will behave on any particular day. This does not just affect employees, it affects managers as well. No individual can be expected to function consistently and at peak performance all day, every day.

It is the predictable consistency in operation provided by computer-based technology that makes it such an attractive option in most work settings. It is not possible for human beings to match the unfailing and relentless consistency of performance achieved by robots in a factory. However, human beings do have some advantages over computer technology. They are adaptable, flexible and can show initiative beyond that capable by any computer. Consequently there is still a need to employ, and a benefit to be gained from, that unpredictable but fascinating beast of burden – the human being. Management in Action 1.6 reflects some of the issues surrounding the introduction of teleworking – allowing individuals to work from home using computer technology.

It is people that create organizations, either as a source of income or in response to a perceived social, political or personal need. It is people who operate the organization, taking decisions and physically arranging to produce the products or services. It is yet more people who regulate the organization in

Management in Action 1.6

Flexible working with 'IT'

Estimates vary as to the level of teleworking that actually exists. One study by the Henley Centre for Forecasting suggests that around 1.2 million people are engaged in teleworking in the UK, which represents about 4% of the workforce. They also suggest that about 70% of large- and medium-sized organizations intend to introduce tele-working over the next few years.

The potential benefits to organizations can make the introduction of teleworking a very attractive option. The reduced costs of running company premises (heat, light, insurance, and so on); the reduced levels of stress and absence for staff who do not have to experience commuting each day; and the part-time employment of specialists who might otherwise need office accommodation being among the more obvious benefits. In addition, there can be the benefits for business as a result of the distributed nature of work and information. For example, if there were to be a serious fire in the head office, not all information and equipment would be lost and a rapid recovery would be more likely. For employees the reduced cost of work activity (travel, clothing, and so on) as well as the opportunity to be flexible when they actually perform the necessary tasks represent some of the potential benefits.

There are, however, a number of disadvantages. There is the reliability of technology to be considered; the security of sensitive or confidential data; employees may not work the hours expected of them; employees may not like to be isolated from co-workers all of the time or to be at home constantly. Equally, there are occasions when face-to-face contact is an important part of management and organizational functioning.

The use of teleworking has not developed as quickly as some writers anticipated but the use of technology to transfer work to remote locations is a trend likely to continue. Some companies have begun to relocate whole operations through the technology opportunities available. For example, London Underground has its timetables created by IT experts in Bangalore, India and American Airlines has moved its ticketing operations to Barbados.

Adapted from: Baron, A and Hutchinson, S (1995) Flexible working with IT. Consultants' Conspectus, January, p 31; and Littlefield, D (1995) Remote working has pleasures and perils. People Management, 30 November, p 13.

terms of safety, taxation, financial matters and fraud. Even more people are the suppliers and customers of the organization. Within the organization careers are worked out and living standards are determined, individuals seek to advance their own position and status at the expense of others. On occasions they also seek revenge for some real or imagined slight from the past. In short, the human aspect of organizations is the story of human life and experience plus that of society, albeit writ small!

Human behaviour also influences the perception and understanding of organizations themselves. Morgan (1986) and Gharajedaghi and Ackoff (1984) both describe organizational activity in terms of the differing *metaphors* that can be employed by people to understand it. They represent the ways that an individual interprets an organization, which determines the characteristics that will be attributed to it and assumptions about how it functions. For example, considering an organization in metaphorical terms as a brain or as a machine bestows on it qualities associated with those structures. It also conditions how individuals will assume that the organization works. The decisions and expectations of individuals in relation to the organization are also influenced by the metaphor adopted.

The study of organizations

The study of organizations as institutions takes many different forms. Accountants, lawyers, economists and strategists all have research interests in organizations. Marketing specialists, human resource management, operations management are all management disciplines that attempt to offer some insight into the functioning of organizations. Sociologists, psychologists and critical thinkers from various traditions also have an interest in attempting to theorize about organizations. It is difficult to be specific when describing what defines the study of organizations; it means many different things depending upon who uses the phrase.

However, simply because something is complex does not mean that it could not or should not be studied. Indeed, it is that very complexity that makes situations attractive from a research point of view. Thompson and McHugh (1995) provide a means of defining what they term as the *mainstream* and *critical* approaches to the development and interpretation of organizational theory. The main domain assumptions made in each tradition as identified in Table 1.1.

The assumptions identified in Table 1.1 from the mainstream approach to the study of organizations emphasize a very rational view of the attribution of qualities. In short, the application of scientific method in the search for explanation and a more valid *science of organizations*.

The critical tradition, in contrast, requires approaches to the study of organizations to be:

- **Reflexive.** This implies that any approach to the study of organizations should attempt to ensure that the values, practices, knowledge and expectations are not taken for granted.
- **Embedded.** This element insists that organizations need to be considered as one part of a total environment. They are *embedded* in a context, and that context needs to be understood and incorporated into any explanation.
- **Multi-dimensional.** The people dimension of an organization needs to be explained in terms of the multi-dimensional nature of human beings. Individual behaviour is embedded in a contextual and family setting.
- **Dialectical and contradictory.** There are many inherently contradictory and inconsistent patterns of organizational functioning. For example, control of operational activity is a necessary aspect of managerial activity. However this directly impacts on employee behaviour either in the form of work regulation or social control. In either case it is likely that employees will resist attempts to prescribe levels of control that they find unacceptable. This inevitably leads to attempts to increase the level of control and a cycle of reciprocal behaviours is set up.

Table 1.1
Domain assumptions of the mainstream and critical approaches to the study of organizations (taken from Thompson, P and McHugh, D (1995) *Work Organisations*, Macmillan, Chapter 1)

Domain assumptions of mainstream approaches	Domain assumption of critical approaches
Organizations as goal seekers	Reflexivity
Search for rational-efficiency based order and hierarchy	The embeddedness of organizations
Managerialism	Multi-dimensionality
Search for organizational science	Dialectics and contradiction
	Social transformation

■ Socially transforming. Critical theory is part of the creation of an attempt to *empower* all members of an organization. The beginnings of a notion (praxis) that individuals can be encouraged to see beyond the existing constraints and to be able to reflect on and engineer a reconstruction of their 'reality'.

The management of organizations

Why organizations need managers

Managers plan, organize and control the acquisition, disposal and application of resources within the organization in pursuit of the goals determined by the owners. That view reflects the classical model described by Fayol (1916). From that perspective management is a very rational process and one category of employment within the organization. It requires someone to undertake specific duties, just as a cleaner in a factory undertakes a particular job.

There are, however, fundamental differences between the jobs of managers and those of other employees. Most employees are engaged to undertake a range of duties associated with the creation of the product or service that forms the rationale for the existence of the organization. Even employees who act as a support to the creation process contribute in a very necessary way by preventing the waste of productive resource. Managers on the other hand do not do that. They are specifically tasked to direct, organize and control the activities of others. They represent the most indirect of all operational jobs. It is this remoteness from direct operational activity and their agency function that sets them apart from other employees.

The type of work expected of managers is different to other employees and the impact of their activities on other employees affects their relationship with other employees. For example, it is management that decides who to recruit and who to dismiss. The power to take away someone's job is a particularly powerful weapon, right or responsibility irrespective of how it is defined. It is such a potent tool that it is a right not given to every level of management. Managers are able to direct, channel and change the organizational experience for employees. Employees are not able to impact on managers in the same way. That is not to suggest, however, that employees are powerless.

Why managers need organizations

Perhaps a more interesting question to ask is why do managers need organizations? At first it would appear to be a nonsensical question based on the assumption that organizations created the need for managers. However, there are a number of issues that suggest that the relationship between management and organizations is more complex than would appear to be the case.

One joke suggests that there are only two skills in management. One is to create enough problems to justify the need for the job to exist. The second is not to create more problems than make for a comfortable life. This may be a cynical view of managerial activity but it does reflect aspects of the power and influence that managers have. This view of management can be reinforced by the shock that was experienced by many managers as organizations began to downsize and delayer. Up to that time redundancy was something that happened to other employees, not managers. The trauma experienced by many managers resulted in increased levels of alienation and lower levels of commitment. The justification being that employers (more senior managers) could not be trusted to consider individual managers or protect them from the effects of change.

So what are some of the factors that might create a reciprocal need between managers and organizations?

- Career. Individual managers expect to have a career. Organizations need managers for more senior positions. Performance appraisal systems, career development and succession planning all provide a basis for career development. However, there is a wide diversity of opportunity available within organizations as indicated in Management in Action 1.7.

Management in Action 1.7

Ticket to ride or no place to go?

In days gone by there was a degree of certainty in career path direction and development opportunities. It was rather like buying a ticket for a train journey. Once the journey was planned, the ticket could be bought and the ensuing ride would provide a predictable form of transport towards a known destination. The changes that are being experienced in many organizations these days has largely destroyed that certainty and introduced a need to identify alternative career development practices.

One early response to this was the attempt to introduce self-development and career planning. Early experience, however, tended to be disappointing with this approach for a number of reasons, including:

- Frequent changes to the career development process by HR departments.
- Small (and downsized) HR departments cannot sustain such initiatives over time.
- Limited scope and support for career development in totality. For example, comparatively limited capability to support lateral career moves.
- Limited ability of line managers to direct and manage career development programmes.
- General company processes. For example short-term

business objectives limit the scope for career planning to be taken seriously.

Research by the Institute for Employment Studies suggests that there is a trend back towards company involvement through a partnership approach to career development. The basis being the need for role adaptation, teamworking and lateral job movement rather than vertical job promotion. The intention being to create flexibility in the workforce and an ability to cope with continual change, supported by development. In achieving these ideals, three issues need to be addressed in order to give any career development strategy credibility:

- An appropriate and honest message. Any message from the organization about career development has to be credible in the eyes of those to whom it is intended to apply.
- Workable career development processes. Whatever the process of career development it has to add value to the experience and needs of the business.
- Real intention to deliver. It is also necessary to intend to deliver the career development promised and to follow through with the purposes behind it.

Adapted from: Hirsh, W and Jackson, C (1996) Ticket to ride or no place to go? People Management, *27 June, pp 20–5.*

- Status/power. With a managerial position comes status and power. The ability to have other people do what the individual manager wants is a heady wine! Being considered as a significant member of the local community can also reflect the status of a manager.
- Work preference. Being a manager gives the individual some degree of choice in their work activities. They can delegate aspects of their work. They are able to *shape* events and the direction of work under their control.
- Professionalization. There is an increasing trend to *professionalize* management. Increasingly, the professional associations to which managers belong and the educational establishments offering management training are making efforts to raise the status of the job.
- Self-interest. Management is a political process as much as it is a decision-making one. There are few managers who are as quick to take responsibility when something goes wrong as they are when accolades are being handed out. The question to be answered is not does self-interest feature in management practice but to what extent will a manager put self-interest ahead of other criteria in any given situation.
- Lifestyle. A higher salary, better benefit package, and so on, generate a whole range of lifestyle differences. Not that all managers earn more than those that they supervise. Frequently for first line managers the opposite is true. However, there are differences in the social groupings with which people mix and the leisure activities that they undertake that create a raft of lifestyle differences.
- Expectation. Individuals are conditioned to expect differences as a result of becoming a manager. They expect respect, a higher income and greater freedom to influence events around them. Consequently, having tasted these fruits the result is an expectation (and desire) that they continue, leading to a need to perpetuate such positions.

Many of the above issues are generalizations which interlink and reinforce each other. For example, career and expectation are strongly linked together, as are the status and lifestyle benefits that result from promotion. The line of argument here is not that management originally created organizations because they needed them but that once in existence management perpetuates a *need* for organizations to exist in order to continue to fulfil their needs.

The study of management

Prior to the twentieth century the management literature tended to be based around the writings of individuals who brought to the attention of a wider audience their own perspectives. For example, Babbage (1832), a mathematician by training, attempted to offer ideas on how to improve the efficiency of operational activity. One of the first teachers of management topics was one Andrew Ure who taught in Glasgow in the early seventeenth century (Wren, 1987). However, it was not until the beginning of the twentieth century that the study of management began to feature systematically as a major activity in its own right.

Just as with the study of organizations described above the study of management can be broken down into two broad classification types. They are the *mainstream perspectives* and the *critical perspectives* (Alvesson and Willmott, 1996). Griffin (1993) identifies a number of what could be described as the mainstream perspectives to management theory, see Table 1.2.

Table 1.2 Mainstream management perspectives (adapted from Griffin, RW (1993) *Management*, 4th edn, Houghton Mifflin, Boston, Chapter 2)

Classical perspectives
- Scientific management. concerned with the systematic evaluation of work and the search for higher productivity
- Administrative management. A forerunner of the systems approach, attempting to identify ways of managing the whole organization

Behavioural perspectives
- Human relations. An approach to management based upon the importance of groups and the social context
- Organizational behaviour. A holistic approach to managing organizations incorporating individual, group and organizational processes

Quantitative perspectives
- Management science. The development of mathematical models as the basis of decision making and problem solving
- Operations management. That area of management attempting to produce the goods or services more effectively

Integrating perspectives
- Systems theory. A range of approaches to the study of organizations and management that attempt to cast these issues as an interrelated set of elements which are able to function as a whole
- Contingency theory. An approach which views the behaviour in any given context as a function of a wide set of contingent factors acting upon that situation

Contemporary
- Popularism. This reflects the wide variety of fads and fashions that gain rapid credence and just as quickly fade into obscurity. Only a few approaches in this category ever last longer than a few years or become a sustainable basis for actual managerial behaviour.

Not every writer would agree with every entry in Table 1.2. For example, it could be argued that the inclusion of operations management is wrong because it represents a particular function within management – the management of production or service activities. Equally some systems theorists would argue that they go beyond the mainstream perspective and attempt to incorporate a critical perspective into their work.

Not every approach identified in Table 1.2 will be discussed in this book. Elements of those approaches appropriate to the study of organizational behaviour will be incorporated. The mainstream perspectives (Alvesson and Willmott, 1996, pp 10–11) are limited in their ability to offer a comprehensive explanation of management because they ascribe to it the qualities of a *technical activity* which underplays the *social relations* and *political dimensions* involved. They describe the critical perspective on the study of management as incorporating the following characteristics (pp 38 and 39):

- Management is a social practice. The evolution of management reflects a practice that emerged within a social, historical and cultural context. It cannot be separated from that context if it is to be understood properly.
- Tensions exist in management practice. The experienced reality of management as a political and social process is different from that postulated in the mainstream perspectives as a rational process seeking to apply impartial and scientific techniques to the problems of managing.

- Critical studies are themselves embedded. Although critical studies attempt to acknowledge the existence of the tensions inherent in management, they are themselves embedded in a particular context. Consequently they need to incorporate a measure of reflexivity in them.
- Critical studies seek to illuminate and transform power relations. Critical studies attempt to transform the practice of management as well as illuminate it.
- Critical theory contains an emancipatory intent. One of the purposes of critical theory is to provide a basis for individuals within organizations to become emancipated from the constrictions implicit in mainstream views.
- Critical analysis is concerned with the critique of ideology. It is implied that modern forms of domination are maintained through the theories and ideologies that underpin and inform the running of society and organizations. The questioning of received wisdom on how things should be provides a basis for liberation and emancipation.
- Critical theory implies more than a reconstruction of mainstream perspectives. Critical thinkers seek to achieve fundamental change in the essentially power-based nature of management.

The study of management is a complex process and there are many different perspectives that could be adopted towards it. Yet for all the research that has been undertaken into management we are no more able to practise it effectively than in years gone by. As Mant (1979) said, 'We do not, it seems to me, require one penny more spent on fundamental research into the "unknown", but to understand why we are so bad at putting to use what we already know' (p 207), quoted in Watson (1994, p 11).

The emergence of organizational behaviour

It is implied in Table 1.2 that *organizational behaviour* can be considered as providing a mainstream perspective on management. From that position it is clear that it has strong links with the human relations school which emerged after the *Hawthorne Studies* directed by Elton Mayo during the late 1920s and early 1930s. It was these studies that first highlighted the complexity of human behaviour in an organizational setting. This led to a recognition of the importance of the social context within which work occurred and of group dynamics as a significant influence on individuals.

However, organizational behaviour incorporates many more features than might be considered at first glance appropriate to a behavioural approach to human activity within an organization. The study of organizational behaviour involves two distinct features:

- Interdisciplinary. There are many areas of study that can be integrated into organizational behaviour. It involves aspects of psychology, sociology, anthropology, political science, philosophy, economics and the systems sciences. To this wealth of base material can be added a critical theory perspective on the embedded nature of much mainstream literature. Critical theory seeks to emancipate people from existing constraints and power relationships. Yet in so doing it invariably imposes another *reality*, albeit a different one, on the situation.

■ Explanatory. Organizational behaviour sets out to offer *explanations* of the relationships between variables. It does not provide an intention to *prescribe* the relationships or interactions between variables. When dealing with human behaviour at the macro level one is concerned with probability rather than certainty.

The study of organizational behaviour can be most easily reflected in a diagram (see Figure 1.8).

Each section within this book takes as its focus one aspect of organizational behaviour. Compartmentalization is a convenient means of considering complex material from a teaching perspective. However, the reality of organizational behaviour is that there are considerable and significant interdependencies and interrelationships between all of the topics discussed. Rather than make Figure 1.8 look a complete mess with lines going in every direction, this has been shown as two-way lines between individual boxes and the linking theme box of organizational behaviour.

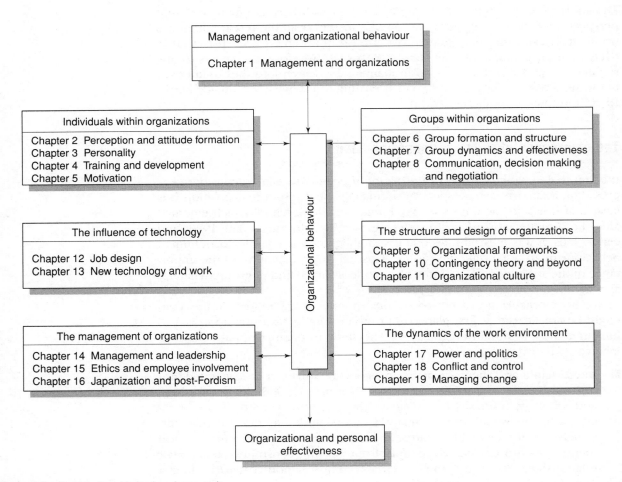

Figure 1.8   Organizational behaviour framework.

Management and organizations: a management perspective

Organizations are the entities that require the roles and skills that managers possess. Management can therefore be described in terms of three main functions:

■ Direction. Before any work can be done there is a need for a plan of action. It is necessary for management to decide what the organization should do and how it should achieve that objective. Once done at the level of the organization then this process can be broken down into the strategies and goals to be achieved by each sub-unit within the company. For example, once a chocolate manufacturer has decided that it will make Easter eggs in particular varieties and sizes, it is then the job of the various section managers to set about determining the production schedule and other operational parameters so that the sales objectives can be met.

   In practice, this *top-down* approach is much too simplistic as there may well be constraints in the system that limit the ability to achieve the overall objective. For example, the chocolate company may not have the warehouse capacity to store the volume of Easter eggs produced. So the development of strategy at any level of the organization is based on an iterative process and also contains elements of *bottom-up* determination.

■ Resources. Another important function of management is to provide the resources to enable the task to be achieved. There are many resources necessary, including money, organization structure, job design, technology, procedures, systems and appropriately skilled people.

■ People. In all but the very smallest of organizations managers do not physically make whatever it is they are responsible for. One way of conceptualizing management is to think of it as a series of sub-contracting arrangements. The Board of Directors is sub-contracted by the owners to run the company. The Board of Directors in turn sub-contract the departmental work to line managers. This process cascades down to the people who actually make the products. This demonstrates that managers achieve their objectives through the efforts of other people. Therefore in order to achieve their goals managers find themselves in the position of having to manage the people rather than the process.

Having determined that management can be considered as a set of functions it is necessary to consider how managers *manage* in that context. Recognizing the existence of *level* and *specialism* in management there are two variables in management activity:

■ Role. This view of management suggests that each manager adopts a particular *role* in performing the duties associated with their job. Just as an actor plays a part in a play and in doing so adopts appropriate behaviour patterns, managers are expected to adopt particular patterns of behaviour in doing their job. Mintzberg (1975) identified 10 management roles which he grouped into three categories. Figure 1.9 identifies each role.

   Role theory does not effectively explain all management activity as at any point in time a manager might be engaged in a number of roles at the same time. For example, at a meeting they might be a *spokesperson* in representing their department's view, *disturbance handler* by attempting to find a compromise between two opposing points of view and *leader* by seeking to provide direction and leadership to the meeting.

■   Skill. Over recent years there has been an emergence of the notion of competency as the basis of identifying the abilities needed to perform specific jobs (Armstrong, 1991). Katz (1987) provides one list of the management competencies necessary to undertake a job in this field (see Table 1.3).

Not all management jobs require equal measures of each of the three skill areas. It will vary with seniority and function. There are many other writers who have claimed to identify the competencies necessary for particular managerial jobs. For examples of other competency lists see Dulewicz (1989) and Woodruffe (1990). Management in Action 1.8 illustrates how the effectiveness of directors within the AA (Automobile Association) was improved using a competency based approach.

One of the other major aspects of organizational activity that managers are having to come to terms with is the effect of globalization. Even very small companies are experiencing some form of global activity. This might include selling products made by the company through a sales agent in another country. At the other end of the spectrum it could involve a very large organization operating across several national boundaries and with a truly multinational workforce and global perspective on its operations. Organizations need to develop an expertise in operating in locations that may have cultural and operating conditions very different to those prevailing at home. Individual managers need to develop the skills and ability to deal with governments, customers, suppliers, employees and colleagues from different countries.

Category	Role	Example
Interpersonal	Figurehead	Represent company on trade delegation
	Leader	Chair department meeting
	Liaison	Co-ordinate activities with another department
Informational	Monitor	Check weekly production figures from department
	Disseminator	Write report on monthly production for directors
	Spokesperson	Attend board meeting to speak about expansion plans
Decision-making	Entrepreneur	Design productivity improvement scheme
	Disturbance handler	Resolve argument with another department
	Resource allocator	Allocate budget to section heads
	Negotiator	Agree new budget with boss

Figure 1.9   Mintzberg's management roles.

Table 1.3 Management skills	Interpersonal skills	necessary to communicate with other people in such a way as to facilitate operations
	Conceptual skills	necessary to provide a basis to think in ways that solve problems creatively
	Diagnostic skills	necessary in identifying cause-and-effect relationships and problem solving

---

Management in Action 1.8

Tuning up for life in the fast lane

The AA (Automobile Association) is a diverse group providing a wide range of motoring services commercially and on behalf of its members. It is made up of six business areas covering commercial services, retail operations, membership services, insurance services, business services and financial services. Each business is headed by its own board of directors, which in turn report to the group board. Senior management development has long been a main board standing agenda item and one such discussion led to a consideration of the value of creating the role of internal non-executive directors.

Following the request by another group to allow one of the senior managers from the AA to become a non-executive director a review of company practice was undertaken. As a result, an opportunity to enhance both management development practices and performance of the separate businesses within the AA group was recognized. The creation of the role of internal non-executive director was a novel way of gaining multiple benefits. Retaining the talent of senior managers within the group was seen as one of the major benefits to be gained, along with the availability of more knowledgeable (in company terms) non-executive directors and the potential to develop board level skills among senior managers. The period of office for the non-executive director was set at a fixed two years. The aim of the role was to contribute to the business by:

■ Taking a strategic perspective and identifying issues and implications, applying past experience in a creative and constructive way.
■ Probing the facts, challenging assumptions and providing counter arguments, using the benefit of wider experience and knowledge.
■ Being alert to the need for change, and supporting new initiatives, policies and practices.
■ Helping to make sure that AA values are safeguarded.
■ Evaluating the performance of the business in wider context.
■ Acting as an adviser or sounding-board to the business.

Launched in the summer of 1994 initial reviews suggest that the process has benefited both the organization and the individuals involved. It led to the creation of business development opportunities between individual businesses and also opened up career moves for the individuals on the programme into areas of the business for which they have gained experience as internal non-executive directors.

Adapted from: Bennett, H (1996) Tuning up for life in the fast lane. People Management, *132, June, pp 34–5.*

There are recruitment and career pathing implications resulting from being involved with international operations that do not exist in single country situations. For example, in seeking to open up a new operation in a foreign country should the management team be recruited in that country and trained in company operations, or should they be company people that are sent on assignment to the new country? Only after the event when the success of the venture is being judged against the original plan can any evaluation of the original recruitment decision be made.

There are many ethical issues that arise as a result of operating globally. For example, business practice around the world varies in relation to the giving of gifts, provision of hospitality and the offering of inducements in order to acquire orders. Company policy is needed to provide guidance for employees at all levels in relation to dealing with these issues.

Some of the large multinational organizations are bigger in financial terms than many of the countries that they operate in. This gives them considerable power – in terms of the potential to be able to influence the economic health, political processes and legislation in those countries. Managers need to be able to deal with these situations and an understanding of organizational behaviour can assist with the development of appropriate competencies.

Managers have a clear self-interest in the study of both organizations and management itself. With increasing knowledge and understanding comes an increased ability to control. This oversimplifies the arguments involved as issues such as company politics, prestige and an ability to fight off competition and so remain in business are also part of the process. However, from a management perspective running an organization is not just about the technology or techniques. It is about the personal, interpersonal, social, power and political aspects associated with the process.

Conclusions

This chapter has introduced the concepts of both organization and management which form the basis of much of the emphasis in the rest of this book. It has also included some of the research orientations and approaches adopted to the study of these issues in the real world and by real people.

The purpose of this chapter is to set the scene for much of the later work in the book. It also sets out to provide readers with some background to the research issues and approaches that are used to inform thinking in this and other areas of the study of management and organizations.

Discussion questions

1 Define the following key terms used in this chapter:

PEST analysis	Organization	Guild
Agency	Management	Organizational behaviour
Stakeholder	Frame of reference	Bureaucracy
Embeddedness	Natural science	Critical theory
Metaphor	Social science	Professionalization

2 Should a company recruit locally or appoint a home country team to start up an operation in a new country? Justify your answer.
3 'It is not possible to generate robust social science theories because there are so many variables at work. It requires the development of a totally new science.' To what extent would you agree with this statement and why?
4 'There is no such thing as a typical organization or management job therefore it is pointless attempting to theorize about them.' To what extent would you agree with this view? Justify your answer.
5 'Managers need organizations.' To what extent do you agree with this view and why?
6 To what extent does critical theory offer an improved way of thinking and theorizing about organizations?
7 'Management decision making is a complex activity and differing rationalities can be applied to the expenditure of resources.' What do you think is meant by this phrase?

8   Why do you think that individual human beings seek out jobs as managers?
9   'The study of organizational behaviour enables managers to become more effective at their job.' Discuss this statement.
10 Change can be equated with challenges facing organizations and managers. Is this a valid comparison to make? Examine both sides of the argument and justify your own point of view.

Research questions

1   With a group, arrange to interview about 10 managers from a range of type and size of organization. Select managers from different job areas, different levels of seniority, of different ages and include both men and women. Find out why they became managers, how they learned what the job involved, what they consider the job to be about and how they define an organization. Compare the results from the different people in your sample with each other. What conclusions can you draw from your research and how does it compare and contrast with the material in this chapter?
2   Repeat Research Question 1, but this time interview a range of non-management employees and compare their views on management and organizations with those collected from among the management population. What differences and similarities between the two sets of responses emerge and why? What does this tell you about conducting research into management and organizational areas?
3   In the library use books, magazines, journals, newspapers and any other resource that you can find to identify as many different types of management job and type of organization. From this information (and by using your own knowledge) what distinguishes management from non-management jobs and what differentiates a social group from an organization? To what extent do you consider that these differences are meaningful from a research point of view?

Key reading

From Clark, H, Chandler, J and Barry, J (1994) *Organization and Identities: Text and Readings in Organizational Behaviour*. International Thomson Business, London:

■ Kumar, K: Specialization and the division of labour, p 13. This extract attempts to rationalize the transformations that took place during the industrial revolution.
■ Kumar, K: Secularization, rationalization, bureaucratization, p 17. This extract considers a number of organizational and work related changes in a broader social context.
■ Friedman, AL: Marx's framework, p 25. This article introduces the work of Marx on the capitalist system and its effects on society.
■ Foucault, M: Docile bodies and panopticism, p 35. This extract considers the nature of control and the role of surveillance in achieving it.
■ Foucault, M: The subject and power, p 43. This considers the nature of power in relation to organizational and social activity.
■ Campbell, B *et al.*: The manifesto for new times, p 49. This article suggests that change is not something from history and that society is in a continually evolutionary state.
■ Fundamental list: modern times and new times, p 57. This list provides a number of terms, people and products from the recent past and from more current times.

Further reading

Chisholm, A and Davie, M (1992) *Beaverbrook: A Life*, Hutchinson, London. This book reflects the life history of one of the more colourful characters and adventurers in the twentieth century. It reflects many facets of organization and management.

Clegg, SR and Palmer, G (eds) (1996) *The Politics of Management Knowledge*, Sage, London. This text explores the relationship between management knowledge, power and practice within an increasingly global organizational environment.

de la Billière, General Sir P (1994) *Looking For Trouble*, Harper Collins, London. An autobiography of a senior military officer, this book provides an insight into the nature of leadership as well as military organization.

Gunn, C (1993) *Nightmare on Lime Street*, 2nd edn, Smith Gryphon, London. This book provides a perspective on the possibility of malpractice in Lloyds of London. It reflects the possibility that not all employees can be trusted to act in the best interests of the owners.

MacGregor, I with Tyler, R (1986) *The Enemies Within*, Collins, London. This is the story of the miners strike in the British coalfields during 1984 and 1985 written from the perspective of the Chairman of the then National Coal Board.

McClintick, D (1982) *Indecent Exposure: A True Story of Hollywood and Wall Street*. Columbus Books, London. This book provides a number of insights into the way that some people operate in search of personal advantage within an organizational framework.

Mills, AJ and Murgatroyd, SJ (1991) *Organizational Rules*, Open University Press, Milton Keynes. This text introduces the existence of the formal and informal rule frameworks that guide much of the human activity within organizations.

Potter, J (1996) *Representing Reality*, Sage, London. This book provides a review of various *constructionist* views of scientific knowledge as well as providing examples from conversations and other interactions.

References

Alvesson, M and Willmott, H (1996) *Making sense of Management: A Critical Introduction*, Sage, London.

Armstrong, M (1991) *A Handbook of Personnel Management Practice*, 4th edn, Kogan-Page, London.

Babbage, C (1832) *On the Economy of Machinery and Manufactures*, Charles Knight, London.

Barney, JB and Griffin, RW (1992) *The Management of Organizations: Strategy, Structure, Behaviour*, Houghton Mifflin, Boston, MA.

Berger, P and Luckmann, T (1967) *The Social Construction of Reality*, Penguin, Harmondsworth.

Bork, D (1986) *Family Business, Risky Business*, AMACOM, New York.

Cyert, RM and March, JG (1964) *A Behavioural Theory of the Firm*, Prentice-Hall, New York.

Dulewicz, V (1989) Assessment centres as the route to competence. *Personnel Management*, November.

Fayol, H (1916) *General and Industrial Management* (trans C Storrs in 1949), Pitman, London.

Gharajedaghi, J and Ackoff, RL (1984) *Mechanisms, Organisms and Social Systems*. Reprinted in Tsoukas, H. (1994) *New Thinking in Organizational Behaviour*, Butterworth-Heinemann, Oxford.

Griffin, RW (1993) *Management*, 4th Edn, Houghton Mifflin, Boston, MA.

Huczynski, AA and Buchanan, DA (1991) *Organizational Behaviour*, 2nd edn, Prentice-Hall, Hemel Hempstead.

Johnson, G and Scholes, K (1993) *Exploring Corporate Strategy*, 3rd edn, Prentice-Hall, Hemel Hempstead.

Katz, RL (1987) The skills of an effective administrator. *Harvard Business Review*, September–October, pp 90–102.

References

Mant, A (1979) *The Rise and Fall of the British Manager*, Pan, London.

McKelvey, W (1982) The evolution of organizational form in ancient Mesopotamia. In *Organizational Systematics*, University of California Press, Los Angeles, CA, pp 295–335.

Mintzberg, H (1975) The manager's job: folklore and fact, *Harvard Business Review*, July–August, 49–61.

Morgan, G (1986) *Images of Organization*, Sage, Newbury Park, CA.

Rhenman, E (1964) *Industrial Democracy and Industrial Management*, Tavistock Institute, London.

Thompson, P and McHugh, D (1995) *Work Organizations: A Critical Introduction*, 2nd edn, Macmillan, Basingstoke.

Wallace, W (1971) *The Logic of Science in Sociology*, Aldine-Atherton, Chicago, IL.

Watson, TJ (1994) *In Search of Management*, Routledge, London.

Wood, S (1989) *The Transformation of Work*. In *The Transformation of Work* (ed S Wood), Unwin Hyman, London.

Woodruffe, C (1990) *Assessment Centres*, Institute of Personnel Management, London.

Wren, D (1987) *The Evolution of Management Theory*, 3rd edn, John Wiley, New York.

Part II

Individuals within organizations

2

Perception and attitude formation

browse this web site

www.itbp.com

Chapter summary

In this chapter we consider the concepts of perception and attitude. We begin by describing perception as a process and then review each of the stages in detail. This is followed by the introduction of attitudes as a basis of behaviour, also demonstrating the links with perception. An introduction to the topic of impression management follows, together with the organizational implications of perception. The chapter concludes with a review of the management perspectives on perception and attitude formation.

Learning objectives

After studying this chapter and working through the associated Management in Action panels, discussion questions and research activites, you should be able to:

- Describe the processes of perception and attitude formation.
- Detail the perceptual framework model.
- Explain the links between perception, attitude and subsequent behaviour in an organizational context.
- Understand what it is about perception and attitude formation that makes it difficult for managers to utilize them in managing people.
- Discuss the practical and ethical dilemmas facing managers in their attempts to shape perceptions and attitudes.
- Appreciate the links between perception, attitudes and other management activities.
- Outline the impression and image management concepts and their relationship with perception and attitude formation.
- Assess the significance of the behaviour of others being subject to interpretation through the perceptual filters within managers.

Introduction

Perception can be considered as a process of *simplification*. There are so many stimuli hitting our senses all the time, even when we sleep, that it is not possible for us to pay attention to every one and cope with the most simple of tasks. In addition, we need to be able to classify the sensations that we experience in order to make them meaningful to us.

In acting out their lives every human must become aware of what is *out there*; then decide what is significant, in what way 'it' is significant and then how to respond to 'it'. This is the basis of the process referred to as *perception*. Most of the time people are not aware of the psychological process of perception. They simply become aware of the things going on around them that attract their attention. The process is *sub-conscious*. Below are listed the five main *senses* as a guide to the areas in which perception occurs:

- Vision.
- Sound.
- Taste.
- Touch.
- Smell.

Management in Action 2.1

Attitudes and perceptions in times of change

The organization in question was going through a significant period of change. As part of this, the Personnel Department was expected to manage many aspects of the process and a number of new appointments were made in order to strengthen the ability of the function to achieve these objectives. This involved the recruitment of a number of experienced personnel specialists from outside the industry, training and industrial relations being two examples of the additional expertise sought.

The process also involved the re-allocation of a number of the existing personnel staff to new duties. One of the existing personnel staff perceived that the newly appointed specialists were a threat to their standing within the organization and began to engage in hostile behaviour towards them. The situation became extremely political, and resulted in many additional problems for the organization until the Personnel Director was able to stabilize the situation.

Interpretation of this story from an attitudes and perception perspective suggests several things:

- The existing personnel specialist held a number of attitudes that led him to perceive the new people from outside as having skills that were more valued by the organization. This led him to interpret this as a threat to his future career and position within the organization. This resulted in attitudes and behaviour that were openly hostile to the people involved and anything suggested by them.

- The new personnel specialists had been brought in to supplement the existing resources of the organization. They arrived with a set of attitudes that implied that the organization was not unique in the process that it was going through and that adopting their previously learned skills would enable it to achieve its objectives. Resistance from the established specialists was at first seen as a minor irritation and inevitable. However, the continued display of hostile behaviour led to a deterioration in the working relationship between the people involved. The new staff began to interpret this behaviour at a personal level, and as a slight on their skills. Consequently, the negative attitudes of the existing specialists produced an increasingly negative response from the new staff.

- In effect a 'doom loop' of deteriorating attitudes, fuelled by perceptions of other people's behaviour, was happening. This led to appeals to higher authority to resolve the perceived problems (by removing the 'other' people). Several conflict-resolving sessions were held and one or two of the new specialists left of their own accord. Some three years later the situation is not completely resolved and a form of uneasy truce exists between the individuals concerned.

This case study illustrates many different aspects of human behaviour in a work context, not just perception and attitudes. It can be interpreted from the perspectives of management control, politics, group dynamics and the management of change, for example. It is introduced here in order to illustrate the circular relationship between attitudes and perceptions.

There is a sixth sense, an ability to be aware of spatial relationships. For example, blindfolded you could probably find your way around your room without too much difficulty, a *mental map* exists in your head indicating where 'things' are normally found.

The significance of perception within organizational behaviour lies in the nature of it as the basis for action. For example, management may *perceive* the introduction of empowerment as the delegation of decision making as part of a job enrichment process. Employees, on the other hand, may *perceive* it as an attempt to reduce the number of jobs and to make remaining staff work harder.

The attitudes that people hold are formed throughout life as a result of *experience* and *socialization*. Some attitudes are deeply held, and probably difficult to change, whilst others are less entrenched and liable to change in line with experience. There are obvious and strong links between perception and the attitudes that people hold. Attitudes are formed on the basis of perceived information. Perceptions are interpreted in the light of experience and attitudes. Management in Action 2.1 provides examples of these links.

Perception as a process

Humans are constantly bombarded with stimuli from a variety of sources. It is a necessary part of survival that humans are able to differentiate between trivial and important events. Imagine attempting to cross a busy street whilst concentrating only on the insects that crawl on the surface of the road!

It is often assumed that as individuals we all perceive the 'reality' of the world around us in the same way. However, a glance at a range of newspapers covering political stories or industrial relations should provide adequate support for the view that there are always at least two points of view in any situation. This reflects something that has been acknowledged by psychologists for some considerable time. Look at Figure 2.1. What do you see? Now ask one or two of your friends.

Figure 2.1   Ambiguous figure (originally published by Hill, WE (1915) *Punch*, 6 November).

Do you see a young woman or an old woman in the picture? Does everyone that you ask see the same? It is the individual that interprets the 'raw material' serving as a stimulus, in the light of a range of internal and external influences. It is easier to illustrate the perceptual process using visual examples. Readers should understand that similar processes are at work in all of the senses.

A model of perception

Perception as a process can be described as a sequence of events from the receipt of a stimuli to the response to it (see Figure 2.2).

There is a process of learning built into this model of perception to account for the feedback in many experiences. Humans quickly learn to identify which sounds are the most significant in any particular context. Traffic sounds have a particular importance when attempting to cross the road and are therefore attended to, yet are often ignored when sitting at home.

In the following sections we will consider each of the elements from the model in Figure 2.2 in greater detail.

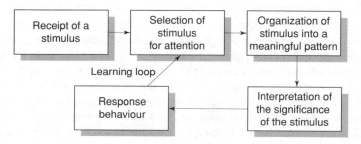

Figure 2.2   The perceptual process.

Receipt of a stimulus

Each of the human senses has its own mechanisms for the registration of stimuli. For example, Figure 2.3 illustrates an experiment in which a pair of coiled but separate tubes have cold water passed through one and warm water passed through the other. If the temperature of the cold water is between 0–5 degrees centigrade and the warm between 40–44 degrees centigrade a subject taking hold of the coil will experience a hot burning sensation. It is thought that the perception of this sensation occurs as the result of the simultaneous stimulation of warm and cold sensation receptors in the skin. This example illustrates a feature common to all sensory receptors: that raw data, or energy from the environment, impacts on one or more of our senses and stimulates a physical reaction within that particular location.

That the perceptions from our senses can play tricks on us has already been established in the experiment illustrated in Figure 2.3. This is more apparent in the world of visual illusion. Indeed magicians rely on just this phenomena to amaze audiences during stage and television performances. Another aspect of this is demonstrated in the impossible figure, which at one and the same time exists and yet cannot exist. Figure 2.4 is an example.

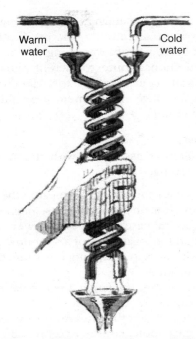

Figure 2.3 Perception of 'hot' as a result of the simultaneous stimulation of warm and cold sensation receptors (from Hilgard, ER, Atkinson, RC and Atkinson, RL (1971) *Introduction To Psychology*, 5th edn, Harcourt Brace Jovanovich, New York, p. 5.26).

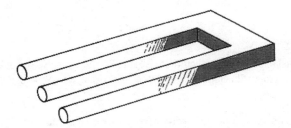

Figure 2.4 An impossible figure (from Hilgard, ER, Atkinson, RC and Atkinson, RL (1971) *Introduction To Psychology*, 5th edn, Harcourt Brace Jovanovich, New York, p. 6.11).

In this particular case, the difficulty lies with the ability of the eye to *see* two dimensions from the image presented and the *perceptual systems* ability to construct three dimensions from that data. In most instances the process works consistently, but in this particular example the two systems provide contradictory messages and *reality* breaks down.

Selection of stimuli for attention

The selection of which stimulus to pay attention to allows the individual to identify the most significant events. Those which need to be attended to, or those which are of most interest. This is a function of three main elements.

The circumstances

Circumstances can have a direct impact on the selection of the stimuli to which attention will be directed. Senior managers experiencing financial difficulties could be expected to pay more attention to the justification for every item of expenditure than when a healthy profit was being made.

Within the same organizational context different perceptions can operate. People in business suits walking around a factory can create a wide variety of rumours, whereas in a head office environment it would be people in boiler suits that would attract attention.

Factors external to the individual

There are a number of features associated with the stimuli themselves that influence the process, including:

- Repetition. The more often something is repeated the more likely it is that the message gets through to the level of consciousness. Advertising often applies this principle to increase awareness. However, repetition can lead to the senses turning off the awareness of a stimulus. This is called *habituation*. This can create hazards in a working environment, individuals ignoring warning signs for example.
- Size. It is perhaps obvious, but the larger a particular stimulus is, the more likely it is that it will attract attention.
- Contrast. The relative features of the foreground and background can influence a perception. For example, consider Figure 2.5.

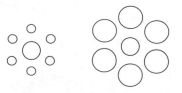

Figure 2.5 Contrast effect on perception (from Hilgard, ER, Atkinson, RC and Atkinson, RL (1971) *Introduction To Psychology*, 5th edn, Harcourt Brace Jovanovich, New York, p. 6.9A).

Do you see:
A Two figures, one a large circle surrounded by small ones, and a small circle surrounded by large ones, or,
B Two figures, each with a same size of circle in the centre, but surrounded by different sizes of circle?

Option B is a more accurate reflection of the two diagrams. The relationship between foreground and background influences the perception of the figures.

- Novelty. The unusual tends to attract attention. This aspect of perception is also used by marketing specialists in designing advertising campaigns.
- Intensity. The brighter or louder a particular stimulus the more likely it is to attract attention.
- Motion. Something which moves is more likely to attract attention than something which is stationary. Predatory animals use this in hunting their prey.
- Familiarity. Humans find it very easy to spot a familiar face in a crowd of strangers.

Factors internal to the individual

There are a range of internal factors that influence which stimuli are attended to (see Figure 2.6).

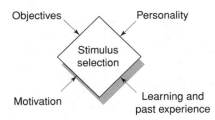

Figure 2.6   Internal factors influencing stimulus selection.

Taking each factor in turn:

- ■ Personality. The personality characteristics of individuals influences the way that they predispose themselves to seek information from the environment (Witkin *et al*., 1954).
- ■ Learning and past experience. Young children and animals become aware of relevant stimuli very early on. Figure 2.7 shows the hesitation of a toddler faced with a visual cliff. The same pattern is used for the 'ground' on both sides of the central island. Both sides are covered with thick glass, however, the 'cliff' side is much lower. Although it would be perfectly safe for the infant to crawl out over the 'cliff' it is reluctant to do so, yet it will crawl happily onto the 'shallow' side. This suggests that depth perception develops very quickly after the infant begins to move around (Gibson and Walk, 1960).

Figure 2.7   The visual cliff.

In an organizational context Oliver and Wilkinson (1992) provide a detailed review of Japanese management practices, including the emphasis on *socialization* and *training*. Employees are *tuned-into* the issues that management consider important. Their perceptions and attitudes are shaped by management.

- ■ Motivation. The needs (physical and social) that are influential for an individual at any point in time will affect the environmental stimuli to which attention will be given. An employee paid a bonus based on the number of units of output is likely to change their attitude to work and seek out ways of increasing production.
- ■ Objectives. People seek out those things and situations which are of value to them. Individuals have goals, intelligence and ability which they utilize

to advantage in interacting with their environment. Consequently, stimuli which offer a synergy, or which may be relevant to that framework will be scanned for relevance before being rejected or processed further.

Organization of stimuli into meaningful patterns

Infants are born with no direct experience of the world. Their experience is based on the genetic material which they inherit from their parents and their experience whilst in the womb. The process of grouping the stimuli from the environment into meaningful patterns is one that develops with experience. The most important aspects of this process appear to be:

■ The figure-ground principle. This principle is all about the process of perceiving a stimulus in a background context. Figure 2.8 illustrates the principle.

Do you see a chalice or two face profiles? It depends what you identify as background and what as foreground.

Figure 2.8 Reversible figures.

■ The principle of continuity. This relates to the tendency to detect continuous patterns in groups of individual stimuli. However, a row of numbers may be just that, they may not be related in a meaningful way. The daily sales returns from each of the outlets of a national company may not be related in any way, yet management frequently attempt to *identify* patterns from such data.

■ The principle of proximity. Proximity refers to the process of creating association simply on the basis of nearness. For example, Figure 2.9 indicates

The proximity of the lines that appear to be in pairs leads us to see three pairs and an extra line at the right.

The same lines as above, but with extensions, lead to opposite pairing: three broken squares and an extra line at the left.

Figure 2.9 The principle of proximity (from Hilgard, ER, Atkinson, RC and Atkinson, RL (1971) *Introduction To Psychology*, 5th edn, Harcourt Brace Jovanovich, New York).

how lines could be assumed to associated, yet with a little more information a different relationship is suggested.

■ The principle of closure. The principle of closure is all about making a whole out of the parts available. Figure 2.10 is a series of dark shapes, what does it suggest to you?

Figure 2.10 The closure principle (taken from Coon, D. Copyright © 1985, 1991. West Publishing Company. By permission of Brooks/Cole Publishing Company, Pacific Grove, CA. A division of Thomson Publishing Inc.).

Perhaps it appears as a dog? If it does then it is doing so not because of the actual drawing, but because your perceptual system is seeking to draw together the available information and close it into a known and familiar image.

■ The principle of similarity. This concept relates to the grouping together of stimuli on the basis of similar characteristics. For example all workers are lazy.

Interpretation of the significance of the stimulus

The significance of a particular stimulus will be judged against a range of criteria. For example it will depend upon the physical and mental state of the individual at the time and also as a result of prior experience. This can be thought of as a *filtering* mechanism, attempting to judge the significance of any particular stimulus. It is a process that is subjective and *goes beyond* the information contained in the stimulus. The result of this can include the following.

Perceptual errors

Mistakes in the process of making sense of perceptual information. They can be mistakes of judgement or in understanding. The major categories include:

■ The Halo Effect. This is the bias introduced when attributing all of the characteristics of a person (or object) from a single attribute. For example, a person who is a good timekeeper may be claimed to be a high performing employee in all other respects. The opposite of this phenomena is referred to as the *Horns Effect*. This attributes all negative attributes because of a single instance.

■ Stereotyping. This is the tendency to attribute everyone (or thing) in a particular category with the characteristics from a single example.

- Perceptual defence. This is a protection against information, ideas or situations that are threatening to an existing perspective. It is a process that encourages the perception of stimuli in terms of the known and familiar.
- Expectancy. The expectations that exist prior to an event can significantly influence behaviour relative to that event. Being told that a new boss is temperamental and a stickler for accuracy will lead to a different approach to being told that they are friendly with an informal style.
- Projection. Implies that others possess the same characteristics as ourselves. In other words we tend to assume that everyone thinks as we do. Also that they will behave in the way that we would.

Attributions

Attribution theory attempts to provide a model which accounts for the way that we make sense of other people's behaviour. Using the ideas outlined earlier in this chapter we attribute various characteristics to other people. We also interpret their behaviour in comparison with others and in terms of past experience. This forms the basis of attribution theory. It is about the causes of behaviour in others, as perceived by ourselves. Management in Action 2.2 illustrates these experiences in a newly appointed first-line manager.

What does this tale suggest in the context of attribution theory? It is clear that the new manager's manager adjusted his perception of the causes of staff behaviour in the department. This was the result of their complaints over his head to the director. Kelley (1973) is credited with developing the theory of attribution. The central principle is that of *covariation*. A causal relationship is said to exist between two events if they occur together. If a particular outcome only occurs when a specific situation exists, then the situation is said to *covary* with the effect. For example, on a car assembly-line good-quality output is observed to occur when supervisors are walking the line; it is also noted that when they are absent from the line (say at meetings) an increase in quality defects occurs. In this situation it would be natural to suggest (attribute) that close supervision is the cause of good quality output.

Kelley suggests that individuals attempt to identify covariance relationships through a number of devices. The criteria used include:

- Distinctiveness. If the particular event is not distinctive then it becomes pointless to imply a specific attribution as its cause. For example, a manager considered it her responsibility to improve the standard of English in reports produced by her staff. On one occasion a report was allowed to be issued without being vetted. That was distinctive behaviour in that context and therefore worthy of further consideration as to the cause by staff.
- Consensus. If the particular event produces the same effect on other people, then a degree of consensus is said to exist. If the manager who is always rude and bad tempered is suddenly friendly and if other people are more friendly than usual, then there is consensus between reactions. This implies that something common to both reactions exists.
- Consistency. The *sameness* of reaction and behaviour over time and situations. If a manager is always rude and bad tempered it would not seem to suggest anything unusual if they are abusive in a particular context. However, if the same manager were to praise, thank, or be pleasant on a particular occasion then it would become inconsistent behaviour and worthy of further consideration.

Management in Action 2.2

The new manager's tale

The manager had been in post for about three months at the time of the interview. He was in his early twenties and it was his first managerial appointment. He had been employed by the organization for about two years prior to the interview and had been working in an administrative capacity during that time. The individual had been promoted to the new position from within the team that he was to manage. The office was small with about six people working in it. The main activities within the office were the administration associated with sales planning and customer service on an international scale. As a result there was a considerable amount of information and paperwork flowing through the office at any one time. Customer records had to be kept up to date as had the information flow to other departments and sections within the organization. A considerable proportion of the time was spent in liaison with customers and dealing with their queries. This process was made the more difficult because of the different time zones involved.

During the interview it became clear that the quality of administrative systems were not of the highest order, in terms of records, accuracy and information content. The department had grown very quickly and the previous manager had not been thorough in ensuring that the systems introduced were adequate. Also staff had been recruited without any previous experience in that type of work, neither had they been trained adequately in customer care and the work of the department. Consequently, a 'slack' attitude to work existed and the unit creaked along rather than playing its full part in progressing the aims of the company. As might be expected, a crisis occurred and senior management had been forced to take action by replacing the previous manager. The new manager was judged to be capable of making the changes necessary to the operational frameworks of the department. Unfortunately, he was resented by the other staff, who saw him as a threat to their old, easy-going ways.

The new manager suggested that his boss considered that senior management would not wish him to take a hard line with the staff in order to implement change, that things would eventually calm down and that the other staff were good at their job (if they were given good procedures to work within and so on). Consequently, pressure was put on the new manager to make the situation work. Unfortunately, the staff became more entrenched in their views and openly hostile towards him. At one point saying to his face that he was the problem in the office and that they hated him. Repeated requests to his boss for help produced little action. By this time the new manager was of the view that even if the other staff were capable of doing the work, they were not acceptable to him. This inevitably made the situation even worse.

The more senior manager would not take action against the other staff, neither would he take action against the new manager. After a couple of months the staff went over the head of the more senior manager to the director responsible and complained that the new manager was no good and that the more senior manager was showing favouritism by supporting the new manager. They claimed to have no confidence in either manager. When the more senior manager found out that the other staff had gone to his boss (the director) without telling him first he was furious. At that time his view of them changed and they suddenly became less than acceptable for the work within the department. What was previously the result of inadequate staff training and system design, was now the fault of the staff themselves. He was attributing the behaviour of the staff to particular causes, they did not want to cooperate with management and were trying to hide incompetence. Previously, his view was that they felt threatened by the situation and needed help to provide the expected service.

Arriving at the attributions for particular behaviours is an important process as the subsequent responses depend upon how individuals interpret the original causes. In the instance described above when the manager returned a report marked up for correction it did not cause offence or a problem. The reaction would be different where demands for reworked reports were the exception.

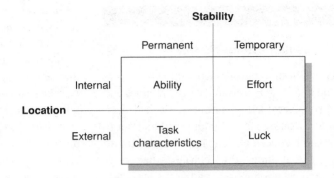

Figure 2.11   Attributions and response determinants (source: Weiner, B (1975) *Achievement Motivation and Attribution Theory*, General Learning Press, Morristown, NJ).

Weiner (1975) developed a framework for determining a classification for different types of attribution and therefore appropriate response behaviours (see Figure 2.11).

The diagram is designed assuming that the purpose is to identify the attributions of, and provide a response to, a subordinate's performance. The diagram is built up from two axes, *location* and *stability*. Location can be determined from the perceived source of the behaviour:

■   Internal. Based on the attributes of the individual in terms of ability, motivation, skill and effort for example.
■   External. Based on the factors outside the individual, such as family circumstances, company policies and the attitudes of managers.

Stability is determined on the basis of the perceived degree of permanence of the attribute:

■   Permanent. This reflects an enduring feature, something that is ongoing and which will remain a force in the future.
■   Temporary. A transient feature, something that is likely to change over time. An example would be someone who is late for work one morning as a result of their car breaking down.

Each of the four cells in the matrix has been given a title that represents the underlying characteristics of behaviour that fall into that area. Consequently, the response to the attributions implied by those concepts will also differ:

■   Ability. This implies that there is an underlying problem with the person themselves and their ability to do what is expected of them. If a subordinate were to make a serious mistake in a situation that implied this cell of the matrix, then retraining might be appropriate.
■   Effort. This implies that the subordinate is capable of doing what is expected of them, but did not apply themselves adequately to the job. Under these circumstances, a telling off or some other punishment might be considered.
■   Task characteristics. This implies that the subordinate had little direct control over what happened, therefore putting it right would also be beyond their control. Consequently, an appropriate response might be to seek ways of improving their ability to deal with the situation in future.

■ Luck. There are occasions when things do not go according to plan. The subordinate in question may have experienced difficulties in obtaining information from another department because they were busy or short staffed. Whatever the attribution, the appropriate approach will be to overcome the problem quickly. For the future, any lessons should be learned to try and prevent reoccurrence.

Attribution theory does not identify the actual cause of behaviour. What it does provide is the perceiver's view of the cause of the behaviour. This provides the essential foundation for what is called the fundamental attribution error (Harvey and Weary, 1984). This holds that there is a tendency to see others' behaviour as the result of stable, internal characteristics; whilst one's own behaviour is a function of temporary, environmental forces. In a work context this implies that managers tend to see employees behaviour as a reflection of the underlying characteristics of the person (good or bad). On the other hand, employees tend to interpret the same events as a feature of the circumstances at the time.

Response behaviour

Individuals react to the perceptual world depending upon needs at the time. In the usual course of events the decision as to which stimuli will gain attention is dependent upon the balance of forces at the time. These include:

■ Pressure to achieve a particular objective.
■ Interest in the task in hand.
■ Distraction opportunity.
■ Consequences of failure to achieve the end result.
■ Physiological state.

The actual behavioural responses to a perceived stimulus can fall into one of two main categories. They are:

■ Internal behaviour shapers. These response categories are not observable behaviours themselves. They are, however, the motivations, attitudes and feelings that help to determine much of the observable behaviour in people.
■ Observable behaviour. This refers to the actual behaviour that would be seen by other people. It is the tangible and physical expression of the underlying behaviour shapers. It is the reactions such as leaving a building when the fire alarm sounds, or work activity following job instructions from a supervisor.

The learning loop

The role of *learning* on the perceptual process itself is something that the model described in Figure 2.2 recognizes as *feedback*. This is intended to indicate that individuals learn from experience. The person involved will perceive the consequences of their behaviours and as a result adjust their subsequent behaviour and perceptual frameworks. An individual who is disciplined by their manager for being late for work will, hopefully, change their future behaviour and arrive punctually. Similarly, an employee praised for good work will continue to repeat it in the future.

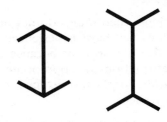

Figure 2.12 The Müller–Lyer illusion.

The effect of learning on the perceptual process can be demonstrated through a number of illusions. Figure 2.12 is the Müller–Lyer visual illusion (named after the originators) which it has been suggested has a basis in the prior learning of individuals. Which of the two vertical lines is the longer? They are both the same length. It can be suggested that this illusion of differing line length arises because of an association with rooms and buildings with corners based on these models. Individuals, therefore, attempt to place a perspective or context onto the shapes.

Person perception

Person perception is of particular interest in organization behaviour because of the significance of interpersonal interaction within a work setting. How individuals perceive managers, subordinates, fellow workers is the basis of the effectiveness of any organization. Much of the day-to-day activity in employee relations is concerned with the management of perceptions and subsequent attitudes relative to the work setting. Warr (1971) offers a schematic model of person perception (see Figure 2.13).

The model comprises five sets of components, all linked together in a complex array of information flow and interdependency. They are:

- The person and context information base. These provide the current and previously acquired information on the target person and the context within which the perception is set.
- Input selector. This refers to the process by which the vast array of current and previously obtained information is to be sifted. The assumption being that it is not possible to process all available information and that a filtering device is needed to weed out unnecessary information.
- The perceiver's state. This is intended to provide for the variable effect on perception of the perceiver. Their current physical, psychological and emotional state will influence their perceptions, as will their underlying personality characteristics.
- The processing centre. This is a series of decision rules built up from experience of interacting with people over time. It therefore allows a form of probability output from the available data. This is reminiscent of the mechanisms involved in the attribution theory discussed earlier.
- The response level. Having developed a profile of the target person in terms of the attributes and expectations, the perceiver will develop an appropriate response. This will not just be in terms of actual behaviour, but include liking, respect and interest for example. These judgmental facets to person perception all feed back to the other components as the process is

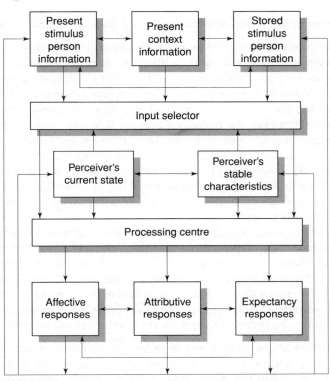

Figure 2.13 A schematic representation of person perception (taken from Warr, PB (1971) Judgements about people at work. In *Psychology at Work* (ed Warr, PB), Penguin, Harmondsworth, Fig. 10.1).

cumulative. The stored information is updated by current events and is interactive in real time.

A simplified form of person perception is to envisage it as a three-factor process. The characteristics of the perceiver, the characteristics of the perceived and the situational variables. Figure 2.14 illustrates the main features of this approach to person perception.

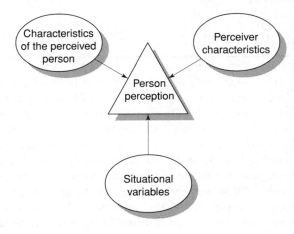

Figure 2.14 Person perception: a simplified model.

This has strong links with attribution theory. Taking each factor in turn:

- Perceiver characteristics. Those internal aspects of an individual that determine perceptual selection and attribution, personality, motivation, objectives, learning, past experience and the individual's value system for example. Working with someone from another culture is a useful way of experiencing the scope of a value system on person perception.
- The characteristics of the perceived person. When we meet someone, there are a wide variety of clues available. Their physical appearance, skin colour, gender, age, general appearance, voice, behaviour and apparent personality all provide information to the perceiver's sensory receptors (DePaulo *et al.*, 1987). Although the characteristics of the perceived person can make a positive contribution to the process of person perception, there is a danger that it leads to stereotyping.
- Situational variables. Meeting someone for the first time in the company of either a friend, or someone that you dislike, would be likely to influence the initial perception of the new individual. A social, business or general context with their differing degrees of formality are also likely to influence initial perceptions. The room decoration, its standard and the general atmosphere all produce stimuli which influence person perception. The impression of the surroundings are linked, or associated with the person in them.

Table 2.1 provides an illustration of person perception in action. It reflects the perceptions of supervisors and subordinates about each other. The perception that was being examined related to the views that each group held about the other in terms of recognition for good performance.

Table 2.1
Person perception in the context of recognition behaviour (adapted from Rensis Likert, New Patterns in Management (McGraw-Hill, New York, 1961), p 91)

Types of recognition	Frequency with which supervisors say they give various types of recognition for good performance (%)	Frequency with which subordinates say supervisors give various types of recognition for good performance (%)
Gives privileges	52	14
Gives more responsibility	48	10
Gives a pat on the back	82	13
Gives sincere and thorough praise	80	14
Trains for better jobs	64	9
Gives more interesting work	51	5

Table 2.1 indicates a clear difference in perceived behaviour between the two groups. Supervisors perceive that they provide a much more positive response to good performance than do their subordinates. The difference between the two groups is startling, not just marginal. The perceptions of the subordinates about the supervisors is clearly different to the supervisors perception of their own behaviour. One implication of this is that managers in general need to be much more aware of the signals that they give out if they are to avoid misunderstandings.

Hastorf and Cantril (1954) studied the reaction to an American rules football game between two university teams. The subjects of the research were students from the universities concerned, Princeton and Dartmouth. General reports about the game suggested that both teams had engaged in rough play, but that Dart-

| | Average fouls committed by: | | Table 2.2 |
	Princeton team	Dartmouth team	Observed fouls in the Princeton and Dartmouth football game
Dartmouth students (48)	4.4	4.3	
Princeton students (49)	4.2	9.8	

mouth had been the most aggressive. From a film of the game both sets of students were asked to score the number of fouls committed by each side (see Table 2.2).

The Princeton students saw a much larger number of fouls being committed by the Dartmouth team than the Dartmouth students did. They perceived the situation in a different light, based on their attitudes towards their own team. However, this would not explain why the Princeton students did not significantly under-report their own teams performance.

There are many possible explanations for this result, including the extreme behaviour of the Dartmouth team causing the need to *sanitize* their misdeeds by their supporters. This implies a group reaction to the result, the game being the same perceptual stimulus for each observer, the stimulus being interpreted in the light of the attitudinal model. It would also be possible to argue that the attitudinal frameworks influence the perception itself, making the game different for each observer. The observer would therefore *see* only that which had meaning and significance for that individual. It is in this form that the significance for organizations becomes apparent. Individual perceptions and attitudes are informed through group interaction and therefore managers need to function at both levels in shaping appropriate behaviours.

Attitude formation

The term *attitude* has entered everyday usage in that people are occasionally said to have an 'attitude problem'. At work managers frequently look for a 'good attitude' in potential recruits. So it clearly reflects a potent force in dealing with people. Management in Action 2.3 overleaf provides an illustration of how attitudes to work can change, even in Japan, where it has often been assumed that society actively seeks to retain its traditional values.

The basis of attitudes

Attitudes are linked with many other aspects of behaviour. They have traditionally been considered to be relatively stable dispositions to behave in particular ways towards objects, institutions, situations, ideas or other people. They are also usually considered to develop as a result of experience. In other words they influence an individual's response to something or someone. All people have attitudes towards things – school, university, parents, work, politics, sport, religion and other people. Some attitudes are deeply held and difficult to change, whilst others are more superficial and easy to drop or amend.

In one approach to the study of attitudes (Rosenberg, 1960) suggests that to change an attitude it is necessary to change either the underlying feelings or beliefs. This approach relies on a model of attitudes based on that shown as Figure 2.15.

More than the job's worth

In Japan it is the devotion to duty of the salaryman that is responsible for much of the economic growth that turned the country into an economic superpower since World War II. In return for their devotion to the interests of their employer the salaryman was guaranteed both a career and a job for life.

However, there was a high price to pay for the life-time job protection and it is increasingly being called into question by the very people who were thought to be most benefiting from it. There are an estimated 10,000 deaths each year from karoshi, literally meaning sudden death from overwork. There is a growing willingness to take employers to court over infringements of employee treatment and human dignity. There exists a recognition of the lack of appropriate values in managing people by large employers. For example Mr Haruo Kawaguchi sued his employer (Teikoku Hormone Manufacturing) for compensation for a six-year separation from his family as a result of a job transfer to another location.

Employees are slowly beginning to rethink their perceptions about the nature of work and its role in their lives. In a poll of 1600 executives the values that made Japan successful such as efficiency, growth and competition were thought to be least important to the future of society. Creativity, fairness and symbiosis were identified as the most important qualities for the future development of society. Individuals are also beginning to shun the pursuit of career progression in favour of performing an interesting or worthwhile job. For example, Mr Tetsuro Handa moved from being a high-flying section manager in the export department with Mitsubishi to their environmental affairs department because he felt that it would be more important and rewarding in his life irrespective of promotion opportunity.

This shift in perception is being fuelled by the worst recession in Japan for 20 years and by the early retirement or semi-redundancy among salarymen. During the recession in the early 1990s Japanese companies had to make strenuous efforts to cut back on labour costs, putting the notion of lifetime employment for salarymen under threat. To get round the difficulties that would have resulted from dismissing many thousands of such employees a number of measures were introduced by companies. These included, unpaid (or reduced pay) leave, enforced holidays, early retirement and compulsory transfers to remote satellite operations. It has been estimated that there are about 1 million surplus workers on the books of Japanese companies as a result of this recession. One of the consequences to emerge is an adverse impact on the health of individuals. Increased incidence of mental health problems (such as depression and loss of confidence) and being afraid to tell their families of their true position are common examples. Under these conditions, it is hardly surprising that traditional loyalties are being questioned and a new perception of the way that life and work interact is being formed.

Adapted from: Dawkins, W (1993) More than the job's worth. Financial Times, 16/17 October, p 9.

Looking at each of the three components in turn:

■ Cognitive component. This refers to the beliefs and values that the individual holds. Looked at in terms of support for a football club, say Sunderland AFC. One belief related to support for the club is that it is the best around. A related value to support of the club would perhaps be that it is important to the individual supporter to have something from their home town that provides a source of pride. The important points to note from this analogy are that beliefs are evaluative in nature, for example the 'best' football team. Values on the other hand tend to be the judgmental criteria against which beliefs are measured. For example, an individual may *need*

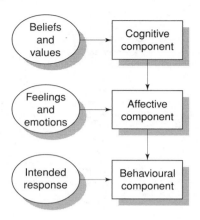

Figure 2.15   Construction of an attitude.

something from their roots to hang onto. The football team may or may not serve these purposes, depending upon its success.

■ Affective component. The feelings and emotions that make up the affective component arise from the evaluation between the two elements within the cognitive component. A supporter of the football club mentioned above could be expected to develop feelings and attitudes according to the relative success of their team. The affective component of an attitude tends to be socially learned. We acquire the ability to express our reaction to the balance between the cognitive elements in ways that align with our social environment.

■ Behavioural component. This reflects the outcome of the process. It is the actual, or intended behaviour. In the case of support for a football team, an individual could continue support, change their allegiance to another club, or give notice that if losses continue they will stop supporting them. The behaviour resulting from the affective component would also be influenced by the attitude and the degree of intensity with which it was displayed. For example:

– a supporter could say that they might leave in the future whilst hoping for better results
– simply change allegiance to another football club
– become annoyed and complain loudly at their performance
– completely switch to a hostile view and indicate that the individual could not understand why anyone would want to support such a club.

The description of attitudes provided so far assumes a dispositional perspective. This approach assumes that an attitude is a relatively stable disposition to act in particular ways towards objects or people, and that it is based on experience. Another approach from Salancik and Pfeffer (1977) suggests that attitudes develop from the encountered social frameworks and experiences. In diagrammatic form this process would be as shown in Figure 2.16.

By means of the socially derived cues and markers the individual is sensitized to the prevailing attitudes and behaviours in particular contexts. The pressure is then on the individual to reach an accommodation between their previously held attitudes and behaviour norms and those expected in the current context. From this perspective attitudes are suggested to be situation specific rather than reflecting underlying frameworks within the individual.

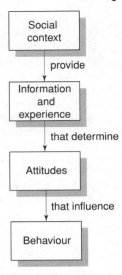

Figure 2.16 Situational construction of attitudes.

Of course, the two approaches are not mutually exclusive. In some contexts it is necessary to suppress one's own feelings and values if continued acceptance by the group is to be maintained. For example, in a work context employees are primarily employed to undertake the tasks demanded by management. From that point of view the personal beliefs and values of the individual need to be subjugated to those of management.

Attitudes and behaviour

Attitudes have an influence on behaviour, but it is a complex relationship. Katz (1960) suggests that attitudes serve four main functions:

- **Adjustment.** This allows the individual to adapt to the environmental circumstances that they encounter. It contains elements of rationalization and justification for the behaviours displayed by the individual.
- **Ego-defensive.** This allows the individual to protect their self-esteem from potentially threatening situations or knowledge.
- **Value-expressive.** This allows the individual to externalize the important values that they hold.
- **Knowledge.** This allows the individual to provide a structure to the world around them. It allows the individual to group together facets of the world into a common category for ease of working.

Festinger *et al.* (1957, 1958) developed the concept of *cognitive dissonance* to explain behaviour in situations where conflicts existed between attitude components. It contains three main elements:

1 There may exist dissonant or 'non-fitting' relations among cognitive elements.
2 The existence of dissonance gives rise to pressures to avoid any further increases in it and to actively seek reductions in the level experienced.
3 Manifestations of the operation of these pressures include behaviour changes, changes of cognition, and circumspect exposure to new information and new opinions.

Essentially, Festinger describes a mechanism which provides consistency between perceptions, attitudes and actions. A feeling of anxiety is produced when there is a contradiction or incongruity between the components of the attitude and behaviour. An employee may hold an opinion that they are a good worker and indispensable to the organization. The manager of that same individual may perceive that the person is a poor employee and barely acceptable. If the manager tells the employee of their opinion then the employee will be in possession of two sets of contradictory information. In order to deal with the dissonance created and rationalize the discrepancy the individual may adopt a number of strategies. These could include working as the manager expected, or, suggesting that the manager does not have the knowledge to form a correct judgement and is biased and unreasonable.

Management in Action 2.4 illustrates the concept of dissonance. Japanese graduates find that employment with foreign companies does not provide the same benefits as a Japanese company. Consequently, the dissonance is reduced by *labelling* the foreign organizations and by not seeking to join them.

Management in Action 2.4

Foreign company jobs lose allure

Working for a foreign company creates additional perceptual consequences compared to working for one that originates in the same national environment as the employee. There are the very obvious differences in loyalty that might be expected to exist. For example an American company operating in Britain could be expected to have a higher level of commitment to its American operations than those in Britain. If problems were to emerge it could reasonably be expected that the British operations would be cut back first. Equally there are cultural differences to be considered. Would an American company operating in the UK be expected to treat (in all respects) its employees in ways identical to British companies?

There are problems and perceptions that have had an impact on the perception of employment in foreign companies by Japanese employees. Students leaving university in Japan tend to be channelled into careers and companies by several factors, just as they would be in any country. These include the preferences of professors, networks of contacts and the 'play-safe' views of parents. Considering foreign employers in Japan as a source of employment for jobs creates particular difficulties for the potential recruits. There have been considerable public

reporting and comment on the actions of several large US companies in Japan as they attempt to cope with recession. Large companies such as Eastman Kodak, Northwest Airlines, NCR and IBM have undertaken a range of measures as they cut back recruitment levels and cancel agreements to hire fresh graduates. Even though a number of Japanese companies adopted similar strategies the adverse media coverage created a climate of hostility for the foreign (predominantly American) companies.

Western companies are perceived as having a much more aggressive attitude towards employees and to be much more likely to dismiss them than are Japanese employers. For many potential employees the security of lifetime employment and the flexible career patterns adopted by Japanese companies are much more attractive than the benefits offered by overseas employers. Working life in a foreign-owned company is perceived as likely to be brief and unpredictable. Mr Thomas Lynch, a partner at KPMG Peat Marwick advises foreign companies in Japan to face up to the problem and emphasize the benefits available to Japanese employees in order to offset the negative perceptions created by the negative publicity.

Adapted from: Thomson, R (1993) Foreign company jobs lose allure. Financial Times, *19 March, p 3.*

Impression management

So far in the discussion, perception has been described as a phenomenon in which the individual learns to make sense of the world in which they live. This is a uni-directional view of the topic. Recognizing that humans undertake a judgmental and categorized evaluation of people and events around them provides an opportunity for individuals to present a particular image to the world around them and so encourage a desired response.

Impression management is something that all actors and politicians become very familiar with in the course of their work. An actor has to be credible in the part they are playing and they use a variety of techniques, make-up, lighting, costume and set design to create the illusion that they are *in reality* the character that they are playing. Politicians similarly must present themselves as credible, honest and trustworthy if they are to be elected or hold one of the offices of state. The use of public relations experts and media consultants can assist with the development of particular images and impressions of the individuals concerned. Marketing specialists use many of the same techniques in attempting to position the goods or services of an organization in the perceptions of potential customers.

Within an organization there are several aspects associated with impression management in addition to the marketing perspective indicated above, including:

- Career strategies. In order to enhance prospects of promotion and limit the likelihood of demotion it is necessary to create particular impressions. Giacalone (1989) identifies a number of what he describes as *demotion-preventing* and *promotion-enhancing* strategies. These include being associated with the right people at the right time and providing plausible excuses for particular courses of action.
- Public image. The use of corporate identity symbols can include a badge or logo of some description, but it can also be taken further through the design of company premises and staff dress codes. Many fast food chains have a house style for their restaurants that allows instant recognition anywhere in the world. Rafaeli and Pratt (1993) developed a basis for the comparison of organizations based on requirements for dress codes among employees.
- Managerial. In industrial relations situations it is necessary for the management team to present a unified front and to create an *impression* of the organization that supports the public stance adopted. Attempts to hold down pay increases by suggesting that bankruptcy is a danger, whilst at the same time allowing managers unlimited access to perks is unlikely to be believed.

Perception within organizations

Perception, attitudes and organizations

Organizations have many aspects of perception and attitudes to contend with:

A **The attitudes and perceptions of actual customers.** A considerable proportion of company marketing effort goes towards encouraging particular attitudes and perceptions in their customers. The effort of organizations to

Figure 2.17 Attitudes and perception.

achieve this are not restricted to an advertising or marketing approach. The results that a school achieves in examinations taken by its pupils will do much to encourage parents to send their children to it. The cartoon included as Figure 2.17 provides an illustration of the negative attitudes and perceptions of customer care which organizations attempt to prevent.

B **The attitudes and perceptions of potential customers.** This category within the environment are the people who do not currently buy the product or service offered by the organization. Much organizational effort goes into attempting to understand the characteristics of these people and how to influence them.

C **The attitudes and perceptions of the wider community.** This is where public relations emerges as the discipline involved with the presentation of the organization's perspective. This can be in response to either a negative situation (bad publicity) or it can be an attempt to optimize the positive value from an organization's activities.

D **The attitudes and behaviours of employees.** Management in Action 2.5 illustrates the management reactions to an employee who developed what could be described as deviant behaviour patterns. Deviant, that is, in terms of the norms expected by managers and delivered by most employees in that situation.

E **Supplier attitudes and perceptions.** The purpose for seeking to influence the attitudes and behaviours of suppliers is to provide the organization with a favourable basis for trading. This could involve obtaining extended credit terms, rapid and frequent delivery patterns or improved quality at a reduced price.

F **The organization's competitors.** These must also be encouraged to consider the organization as a 'solid' market player. If the organization is to be taken seriously in an industry it is necessary to generate an image that encourages that view. Competitors will ignore, or even worse attempt to destroy a competitor considered weak or a threat.

Management in Action 2.5

Have long holiday, will travel nowhere in job.

The perception and attitude towards work in Japan is noticeably different to that in the West. Employees are expected to place the interests of the employer above personal interest. This is taken to such a level that it is not uncommon to find that individuals introduce themselves in terms of their company first. For example, (and using a British illustration) a typical greeting might be 'Hello, I'm Hull University's Mr John Martin'. The same level of dedication applies to the time spent at work and the taking of holiday. The director of one government ministry retired after 35 years service and proudly announced that he had never asked for any time off work other than for public holidays and that he had accumulated two years of time off, which he could not now take as he was retiring.

One employee of the Ministry of Health dared to break this unofficial code of honour and his story became a best-seller as a popular book. However, it did nothing for his career prospects. Mr Masao Miyamoto lived and worked in America for 11 years after he had initially studied medicine in Japan. On moving to America he undertook postgraduate work at Yale University and subsequently practised psychiatry. Upon his return home he was appointed to a position in the Ministry of Health. He found the work culture and attitude of long hours spent at the office difficult to accept after living in America for so long. It was common for staff to not leave before 7 pm, even if there was no work to do, they would not seek more than about four days holiday and would work for seven days each week.

Each year a holiday request chart was circulated and junior staff were expected to apply for holidays for that year by filling in the desired spaces on the form. No one ever applied for their full allowance and people always applied for less holiday than their superior. Mr Miyamoto applied for two weeks holiday and began a controversy that sabotaged his career and resulted in him being exiled to a menial job checking sailors for cholera in Yokohama. Mr Miyamoto's immediate boss attempted to persuade him to withdraw his application but after much long debate (and sake drinking) agreed with his holiday request. However, the director of the section was less amenable and although the holiday was eventually agreed, Mr Miyamoto was accused of selfishness, causing disruption and of dishonouring his position. It was also suggested that he might like to resign rather than remain in such a difficult position.

However, it was only after Mr Miyamoto applied for a holiday the next year to visit Tahiti that he was transferred to Yokohama. It was at that point that he wrote his book poking fun at the bureaucratic nonsense that he perceived around him. This further infuriated his superiors and some of his colleagues, but others quietly began to voice some measure of support for his personal stand. His bosses still find ways of undermining his confidence and of pointing out that he does not fit in, even in his choice of clothes. Even in a suit and tie, just like his colleagues it is pointed out to him that he does not dress in a way which conforms to the dress code usually adopted within the Ministry. A high price for taking a holiday, to which by law he was entitled.

Adapted from: McCarthy, T (1993) Have long holiday, will travel nowhere in job. The Independent, *12 August, p 11.*

G   **Regulators.** The power of regulators to control organizational activity through legislation and other rules tends to make them subject to the attempts of many pressure groups. This is done in an attempt to influence the future direction of legislation and policy. This is usually an area shrouded in mystery and behind-the-scenes activity, rather than direct intervention. Study tours, lectures, seminars, reports and fact-finding visits are just some of the 'tools' adopted by the professional lobbyist.

H   **Shareholders.** These are technically the owners on whose behalf managers run the organization. In the public sector it is the general public, through parliament that are the *owners*. There is a need for organizations to develop approaches to the presentation of shareholder information in such a way that the individuals and institutions involved are encouraged to maintain their investments. In the financial markets a considerable number of analysts are employed to get behind the public output from organizations and identify the true position. It is, therefore, a game of cat and mouse with the stock market value of the organization being the prize.

Perception, attitudes and control

Whatever the ownership structure of the organization, managers find themselves having to achieve objectives through other people. Therefore, managers need to shape the behaviour of other people in order to direct them towards the goals sought. In order to control behaviour within the organization, managers have to either:

■ order others to carry out management wishes, or
■ persuade individuals to willingly undertake what is required of them.

The first option implies force and coercion by managers whilst the second implies rationality linked to the exercise of free will on the part of the employee. In practice managers utilize a mixture of both approaches. The use of excessive force and direct orders is unlikely to produce a willing response among those subject to them. Neither is it likely to produce the high levels of productivity required of organizations these days. Perception and attitudes provide the concepts through which managers can control the behaviour of employees. If successful, this should encourage employees to be more compliant in doing management's bidding. Also, employees would be encouraged to see themselves as stakeholders in the organization, thereby, through association and commitment, encouraged to invest in positively helping management to further its objectives.

Garrahan and Stewart (1992) provide a review of Japanese management practices in a new car assembly plant, in which the whole question of participative management practice as a control process is explored. From that discussion it becomes apparent that careful initial selection of employees to join the company is reinforced through subsequent training and management practice. The effect being that employees have their perceptions and attitudes towards work and the organization *shaped* to a management preferred model.

Information (or perceptual stimuli) is influenced through the attitudinal frameworks held. Reinforcing the view that managers and employees do not register or respond to the 'facts out there'. It is a more complex process and potentially leads to errors in the assessment of a situation that can be wrong and damaging to any of the stakeholders or the organization.

Perception and attitude formation: a management perspective

The world is constantly changing and managers must manage in that dynamic situation. Perceptions are a constant source of information to each individual as they attempt to make sense of the world in which they live. As a continuous process perception is potentially amenable to adjustment in the light of new information on attitude formation. Part of the purpose of the perceptual and attitudinal mechanisms is to introduce the familiar into an uncertain world. It allows the individual to filter out the unnecessary and concentrate on significant aspects.

Perception is a truly personal experience. Employees and managers are not likely to interpret the *facts* in the same way, or even in a consistent way across time. It is these aspects of uniqueness and interpretation through the familiar that create the difficulties for managers. Managers attempt to operate in a three-dimensional world in this context (Figure 2.18):

- ■ Time. Managers are constrained by events of the past. The size, culture and organization of the company were all determined in the past. Managers are working in the present time in attempting to ensure that the organization is able to meet its present commitments. They are also working in the future in order to provide for an ability to survive.
- ■ Locus. Managers deal with internal and external events. The locus of emphasis can either be internal or external (or both) depending upon the circumstances. For example, a hostile take-over in the City will force an external perspective as managers attempt to fight off the raiders. Of course, much of the impact of the action will be felt within the organization as costs are cut in an attempt to win the support of existing shareholders through improved returns on their investment, forcing up the cost of the take-over.
- ■ Direction. This dimension in the model attempts to reflect the degree of introspection in the process. Managers will be forced to consider either their own perspective or that of others, not necessarily within the organization. Managers can either operate according to their own agenda, or can find it necessary to function according to the dictates of others.

Managers attempt to extract the maximum utility from these concepts in *manipulating* the perceptions and attitudes of others. Many managers might find the use of the word *manipulation* in this context difficult to accept. It is a word with connotations that imply an unacceptable approach to making people do things against their will. However, efficiency can only be achieved if employees and managers work in unison towards the same objectives and with the same vigour. It is in achieving that particular synergy that Japanese organizations have been particularly successful (Oliver and Wilkinson, 1992). The needs of the organization are determined by managers, largely as a result of their interpretation (or perception) of the situation (see Figure 2.19).

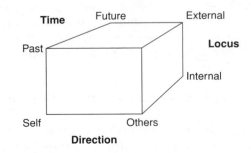

Figure 2.18 Three-dimensional view of management activity.

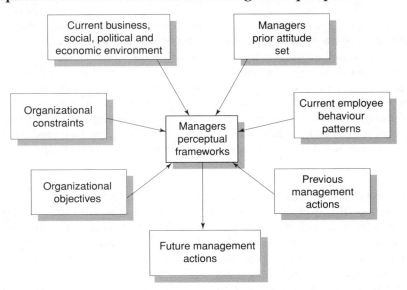

Figure 2.19 Managers perceptions and the impact on subsequent actions.

From Figure 2.19 it can be seen that managers receive a great many stimuli from a variety of sources, all of which are interpreted through the process within the managers' psychological makeup. The result is a response set that directs subsequent action in the running of the organization. If a manager interprets the business environment as hostile, they may well use the situation to exert additional pressure to force changes or concessions from an otherwise unwilling labour force.

It is the formal role that managers play within an organization that make their perceptions of particular importance. Managers are charged with the responsibility of running companies, therefore their perceptions and attitudes, linked to their subsequent behaviours, influence the direction of the organization and the manner through which it is achieved. That is not to suggest that employees have no influence on the process, simply to state that the ultimate influence rests with managers.

Part of the perceptual selectivity process directs individuals to give credence to information provided from sources that are regarded as authoritative. This helps to explain why employees in some organizations do not believe management when they attempt to communicate. Previous management messages may not have been reliable therefore employees come to rely on more credible sources. This demonstrates the concept of *perceptual set*, or the predisposition to perceive what we expect to perceive. Employees expect to see a management that is consistent with previous experience. They respond accordingly. They may receive the signals telling them how desperate the situation is, but simply read the signals as more of the same, and therefore safe to ignore.

This phenomenon also influences how men perceive women. Deaux and Emswiller (1974) demonstrated that men interpreted competence in women as the result of luck rather than skill. Given that most managers are male, this approach provides a mechanism to inhibit the progress of females by attributing any success to chance factors. It also provides an opportunity for men to reinforce the solidarity of their male identity by maintaining a perceived superiority over women. Ragins and Sundstrom (1990) studied the perceived power of male and female managers by their subordinates. They found that generally there were no differences between the sexes in this context, although women managers were suggested to display higher levels of expert power than men.

Direct attempts to influence attitudes and perceptions are not usual. Clearly, any obvious attempt to influence either would run a high risk of failure. The process of influence is usually much more subtle. It can be detected indirectly through many activities associated with management control and authority, including:

- ■ Conflict determination and resolution. Many behaviours that are considered deviant or the subject of conflict have their roots in attitudes and perception. What is perceived as acceptable behaviour is based on the attitudes and perceptions of managers. By taking disciplinary action on particular behaviours a signal is given indicating those that should not be repeated.

  Employee problems with regard to management's attitudes and behaviours can usually be referred to a grievance procedure for resolution. The purpose of these procedural mechanisms is to provide an institutionalized process for exploring the immediate problem and arriving at a mutually agreeable solution. Another way of describing this process would be as arriving at a better perception of the other person's point of view. Management in Action 2.6 reflects this approach through the provision of mechanisms dealing with sexual harassment.

- ■ Culture is another area where attitudes are strongly associated. If culture is defined as broadly 'the way that we do things around here' then it should be apparent how perceptions and attitudes support it.

- ■ Communications. The communications frameworks of the organization can educate and so influence attitudes and subsequent perceptions. It is for this reason that organizations can find themselves at odds with trade unions over who has a right to communicate directly with employees. A message is much more than the actual words used to convey it.

- ■ Management style. The way that managers go about their tasks gives clear signals to all around them as to what is seen as important. This provides clear insights or clues to employees on what management is seeking so that they can react accordingly. A workforce that perceives that the management style is to push for higher worker productivity, whilst at the same time enjoying long lunch breaks itself will encourage a cynical attitude base.

- ■ Work organization, job design and satisfaction. The way that work is organized, planned and jobs designed also provides a clear signal to employees about the professionalism of managers and the degree to which they are serious about the business. Job satisfaction is an important attitude indicator, employees who perceive that their work is boring, menial and of little worth are likely to react accordingly.

- ■ Participative management practices provide for the perceptions of employees to be taken into account in the decision-making process of the organization. This not only provides a clear signal on what is seen as important within the organization, but it allows the differing perceptions to be taken account of, along with providing the opportunity to influence attitudes through discussion.

Management in Action 2.6

American sailors see red over sex

The issue of sexual harassment creates many difficulties for managers attempting to identify and deal with issues of unwelcome or unacceptable behaviour. This is particularly true in the armed forces. Until recently men and women had separate categories of activity within the military environment, which kept the opportunity for offensive conduct between the sexes to specific environments and of manageable proportion. However, over recent years with a growth in the combat role of women along with other opportunities for mixed-sex work activity, harassment has been forced high on the military agenda.

There have been a number of high profile instances over recent years where military personnel have been held accountable for their actions in this area. One such case was the 1991 Tailhook scandal, when American navy pilots went on the rampage at their annual party. This involved what has been described as a drunken sexual rampage and created a situation which the navy could not ignore. One consequence of this was the development of a code of conduct intended to provide guidance on acceptable and unacceptable behaviour between the sexes. Although generally welcomed it raised a number of comments and issues about how the military manages its personnel.

The code provides for three levels of behaviour between the sexes, each colour coded. Green light behaviour could include putting a hand on someone's elbow or making reference to appearance, provided it refers to their uniform. It reflects behaviour that would be acceptable. The amber light is intended to indicate behaviour which could be interpreted as sexual harassment, even if this was not intended. It includes whistling, lewd jokes, staring and violating personal space. The red light level indicates those behaviours that would always be interpreted as sexual harassment and which would result in punitive action if continued. This category includes offensive letters, grabbing, forced kissing, fondling, sexual assault and rape.

The problem for military authorities is that it is not possible to categorize social behaviour in the neat and precise way necessary for most military purposes. Most military commands and training are based around short, precise instructions that are not capable of misinterpretation. However, in the field of sexual harassment this is not possible. There are examples in behaviour in the green light category of the naval code of conduct that would, in a particular context, place it in the red light area. For example, the phrase, 'My, what a nice set of epaulettes you have', said in a particular tone of voice and with the emphasis on part of the phrase could be directly intended as harassment. Equally, there are examples of amber category behaviour that could be either green or red in nature depending upon the context. There is also a view that suggests that it is worrying that someone in the navy might hold the view that rape would not automatically be classed as unacceptable behaviour.

The US Navy stands by its approach on the basis that it represents a step in the right direction and provides clear guidance on acceptable behaviour. Rear Admiral Kendell Pease supported its use saying that in an age of sound-bite communications and bumper-sticker mentality the code was a means of grabbing people's attention and forcing them to take account of the issues. It was aimed at the young people in the navy who are very familiar with motor cars and traffic signals as a way of controlling behaviour. Therefore it was hoped that the same approach to behaviour between the sexes would improve standards.

Adapted from: Macintyre, B. (1993) American sailors see red over sex. South China Morning Post, 22 June, p 16.

■ Power and control. Managers assume the right to manage and therefore to control the activities of others. This task is made much easier if the individuals to be controlled are compliant and amenable to the process. This requires that their perceptions and attitudes are shaped accordingly.

Management in Action 2.7

On the shelf at 45

There has been a debate over recent years about the perceived value of older workers. It has become apparent during recent recessions and productivity-enhancing initiatives such as delayering, downsizing, rightsizing or whatever it might be called that is has been the older, longer serving employee that has been cast aside in favour of younger people. There are many reasons for this trend including the relative cost advantage of younger employees and a perception that they are easier to train, more adaptable and willing to change. The older worker has, however, begun to fight back.

In a letter to the *Financial Times*, one researcher from the Institute of Manpower Studies indicated that the perception of employers about age-related performance was based on inaccurate stereotypes. The correspondent goes on to quote research findings that older people tend to have lower turnover rates, less frequent absence for sickness, better commitment and time-keeping habits than younger people. Even with this type of research finding employers still tend to discriminate against older people with research from Industrial Relations Services showing that almost one-third of all job adverts contained an age bar. This represented an increase from the level of one-quarter of adverts four years earlier. In addition to those specifying an age bar, four out of five wanted someone under the age of 45.

Examples exist in a wide range of industries of the application of the perception that younger people are better. For example, Simone Kesseler from Cornhill Publications expressed views that their kind of business (telesales) attracted younger people (between mid-20s and early 30s) for management positions, although it was not a formal company policy. Roger Steare, a director of

Jonathan Wren, a City recruitment consultancy, explained that in the dealing rooms it was de rigueur that new entrants to the derivatives markets were under 35. In the computer industry age can be closely aligned with experience. Russell Clements, director of the IT recruitment consultancy Computer Futures, suggested that with seniority comes a limitation in being able to demonstrate practical experience with the most recent computer systems. This creates difficulties for older managers in seeking jobs at a lower level following redundancy.

Reed employment agencies attempted to influence the attitudes of employers by offering a discount of 50% on their fee to employers taking on workers over 50 years of age. Some employers are beginning to recognize that with age comes experience and that this forms an important asset to the organization in many situations, according to Chris Trott from Chusid Lander, a career consultancy. Subsequent to an article in the *Financial Times* there was a small flurry of letters in support of the older worker and in praise of their qualities. However, it was also pointed out that the same newspaper frequently printed job adverts and articles generally supportive of the ageist stance. Another letter pointed out that certain pension schemes made it prohibitively expensive for employers to take on older workers. So the issue of being too old to work is far from being resolved and is largely based on the perceptions and attitudes of employers.

Adapted from: Summers, D and Milton, C (1993) On the shelf at 45. Financial Times, 19 March, p 12. In addition, extracts from the letters pages of the same newspaper as follows: Older people often make better workers than the young, 17 March 1993, p 16; The over 45s: possessed of wisdom but rejected in advertising, 24 March 1993, p 20; No ignoring the actuarial facts of age, 26 March 1993, p 18.

■ Reward structures. Pay is the most obvious reward. Basic wages or salary are often supplemented with bonus payments for extra output or performance. In addition, promotion, access to development opportunities and praise or punishment are all elements of the reward structures available for managers to use in encouraging appropriate behaviour. It can, however, be argued that reward structures do not produce fundamental shifts in attitudes or perceptions. It is possible to achieve the desired reward through compliance behaviour, an instrumental approach. In other words, employees deliver what is expected without changing the underlying attitudes or perceptions. Rambo and Pinto (1989) demonstrate the complex interactions between variables in the creation of a perception of a pay increase. In reaching this perception, it is not just the scale of money that is being taken into account, many other variables influence the decision. Future promotion opportunities and size of the current salary being just two.

Perceptions are not directly observable and are usually inferred through the behaviour or attitudes of individuals. One form that these links take is in the discriminatory behaviour adopted by managers towards categories of employee. Sex and race discrimination are the main forms that have a legislative basis to their intended elimination and control. Management in Action 2.7 is about age discrimination. It is clear from the discussion that a number of facts, attitudes and opinions are used to support or oppose the practice of using age as a job selection criteria.

Conclusions

The subjects of perception and attitude formation are key aspects of management. They raises issues of ethics as a result of the potential for managers to seek to influence others in an attempt to manipulate events. They are processes that involve every individual all of the time. They are dynamic processes and are of value in helping to simplify the complexity of the world. Unfortunately, by so doing they also make people vulnerable to mistakes in classification by grouping stimuli together when this should not be done.

The challenge facing managers is to make positive use of these concepts whilst not becoming so cynical and manipulative that individuals simply become pawns in the game of life, there to be manipulated at the whim of the master. Perception is one of the fundamental ways in which attitudes are formed and it provides the basis of creating the perceptions of the self by others.

Discussion questions

1 Provide definitions for the following key concepts from this chapter:

Perception	Halo effect	Figure ground principle
Attitude	Covariation	Projection
Attribution	Perceptual set	Person perception
Contrast effect	Stereotyping	Stimuli

2 Describe the perception process.
3 Are the attributions that we make about the consequences of our behaviour more important than the consequences of that behaviour?
4 Do attitudes depend on perceptions, or the other way around?
5 Provide an explanation for the phrase, 'Beauty is in the eye of the beholder'.

6 Why is perception described as an active process rather than a passive one?

7 Why might different people interpret the same situation differently? Provide examples from your own experience.

8 Can managers influence the attitudes and perceptions of their subordinates? How could they set about doing so?

9 Why is it that attitudes cannot be directly measured?

10 What is perceptual selection and how does it link with the other stages in the perceptual process?

Research activities

1 Arrange to speak to a manager and a shop floor worker about a situation that they have experienced. Perhaps they have just completed the annual pay negotiations, or are undertaking some form of change. If it is not possible to speak to two people from the same organization then make whatever arrangements you can. Discussion issues should centre around how each person perceives a management issue of the day that they have both experienced. What conclusions can you draw from this exercise about perception and attitudes?

2 In the library search out 10 research papers from different journals on the subject of perception and 10 more on attitudes. Summarize the information obtained and identify in what ways the material supports or refutes the material presented in this chapter. Develop an argument to justify the different viewpoints identified.

3 Along with a friend identify a third person known to you both. Provide independent descriptions of the third person. Use the simplified model of person perception included as Figure 2.14 in this chapter and attempt to account for the different descriptions obtained.

Key readings

Taken from: Clark, H, Chandler, J and Barry, J (1994) *Organization and Identity: Text and Readings in Organizational Behaviour*, International Thomson Business Press, London:

- Eysenck, HJ: The rat or the couch? p 82. This identifies the basis of psychological inquiry, how it developed together with its contribution to understanding phenomena such as perception.
- Mead, GH: The self, p 99. Of historical interest. As such it illustrates some of the value gained by individuals from perceiving the world around them in the creation of the self.
- Milgram, S: Conformity and independence, p 132. Considers the effects of social pressure on the perceptions and behaviour of people.
- Friedan, B: The forfeited self, p 124. This reflects on the gender aspects of theory development.
- Labov, W: The logic of nonstandard English, p 178. Language as a basis of group identity and as a means of communication is part of the creation of the perceptual world.
- Mackenzie, G: Class, p 189. The perception of social differences between individuals and groups within society is the basis of control and power within that context.

Further readings

Ajzen, I and Fishbein, M (1980) *Understanding Attitudes and Predicting Social Behaviour*, Prentice-Hall, Englewood Cliffs, NJ. A thorough review of the attitude literature and its implication for social behaviour.

Bromley, DB (1993) *Reputation, Image and Impression Management*, John Wiley, Chichester. A social psychological review of the subject of impression management in a variety of forms.

Cialdini, RB (1985) *Influence: Science and Practice*, Harper Collins, London. An interesting and readable text covering the psychology of influence and related behaviours. As such it covers many of the issues relevant to the behavioural consequences of attitudes and perception.

Pease, A (1981) *Body Language: How to Read Others' Thoughts by Their Gestures*, Sheldon Press, London. A practical guide on the interpretation of body language. Not an academic book but it does offer a wide-ranging review of areas that form a significant stimulus input to the perceptual system.

Segall, MH, Dasen, PR, Berry, JW and Poortinga, YH (1990) *Human Behaviour in Global Perspective: An Introduction to Cross-cultural Psychology*, Allyn & Bacon, Needham Heights. Offers a broad review of the subject matter. There are a number of references to attitudes and perception, but Chapter 4 is of particular relevance.

References

Deaux, K and Emswiller, T (1974) Explanations of successful performance on sex-linked tasks: what is skill for the male is luck for the female. *Journal of Personality and Social Psychology*, **24**, 30–85.

DePaulo, BM, Kenny, DA, Hoover, CW, Webb, W and Oliver, PV (1987) Accuracy of person perception: do people know what kinds of impression they convey? *Journal of Personality and Social Psychology*, **52**, 303–15.

Festinger, L (1957) *A Theory of Cognitive Dissonance*, Harper & Row, New York.

Festinger, L, Riecken, HW and Schacter, S (1958) When prophecy fails. In *Readings in Social Psychology* (eds Maccoby, E, Newcombe, T and Hartley, EL), Methuen, London.

Garrahan, P and Stewart, P (1992) *The Nissan Enigma; Flexibility at Work in a Local Economy*, Mansell, London.

Giacalone, RA (1989) Image control: the strategies of impression management. *Personnel*, May, 52–5.

Gibson, EJ and Walk, RD (1960) The visual cliff. *Scientific American*, 202, 64–71.

Harvey, JH and Weary, G (1984) Current issues in attribution theory and research. *Annual Review of Psychology*, 35, 431–2.

Hastorf, AH and Cantril, H (1954) They saw a game: a case study. *Journal of Abnormal and Social Psychology*, **49**, 129–34.

Katz, D (1960) Determinants of attitude arousal and attitude change. *Journal of Personality*, **24**, p 81.

Kelley, HH (1973) The process of causal attribution. *American Psychologist*, February, pp 107–28.

Likert, R (1961) *New Patterns in Management*. McGraw-Hill, New York.

Oliver, N and Wilkinson, B (1992) *The Japanization of British Industry: New Developments in the 1990s*, 2nd edn, Blackwell, Oxford.

Rafaeli, A and Pratt, MG (1993) Tailored meanings: on the meaning and impact of organizational dress. *Academy of Management Review*, January, 32–55.

Ragins, BR and Sundstrom, E (1990) Gender and perceived power in manager–subordinate relations. *Journal of Occupational Psychology*, **63**, 273–88.

Rambo, WW and Pinto, JN (1989) Employees' perception of pay increases. *Journal of Occupational Psychology*, **62**, 135–46.

Rosenberg, MJ (1960) A structural theory of attitudes. *Public Opinion Quarterly*, Summer, 319–40.

Salancik, G and Pfeffer, J (1977) An examination of need-satisfaction models of job attitudes. *Administrative Science Quarterly*, **22**, 427–56.

Warr, PB (1971) Judgements about people at work. In *Psychology at Work* (ed Warr, PB), Penguin, Harmondsworth.

Witkin, HA, Lewis, HB, Hertzman, M, Machover, K, Meissner, PP and Wapner SS (1954) *Personality Through Perception*, Harper & Row, New York.

3

Personality

▤▤ browse this web site ▤▢

www.itbp.com

Chapter summary

This chapter introduces the concept of personality. We begin with a description of what personality is and how it is defined. This leads into a consideration of how personality has been measured, along with a review of the major theories. The development and application of psychometric tests is also integrated into the discussion. The use of personality is then analysed in the context of an organization, followed by a review of the management perspectives.

Learning objectives

After studying this chapter and working through the associated Management in Action panels, discussion questions and research activites, you should be able to:

■ Outline the concept of personality.
■ Describe the major theoretical approaches to the study of personality.
■ Appreciate the links between personality and other aspects of individual difference.
■ Understand the strengths and weaknesses of each of the major theories of personality.
■ Detail the relevance of personality for other levels of analysis within an organizational setting.
■ Discuss the basic process involved in the development of a psychometric test.
■ Explain the distinction between psychometric tests and the projective approach to personality measurement.
■ Assess the significance of personality as a basis for taking decisions relating to people within organizations.

Introduction

The concept of personality has a long tradition within psychology and can be traced back to the early Greeks. Theophrastus was a philosopher, who 2000 years ago asked why it was that with a common culture and education system people displayed different characteristics (Eysenck, 1982). Personality is about *individual difference*. Each human being has the potential to behave in similar ways, yet they do not. Individuals find themselves attracted to some people and repelled by others. Some of the reasons are based on the perception and attitude factors discussed in chapter 2. However, friendship (or enmity) can be based upon personality. The sayings that particular individuals are too much alike to be friends or that opposites attract imply that there are characteristics that make it more or less likely that two people will 'get along'.

Personality eludes precise definition. Allport (1937) identified about 50 different interpretations of the concept. Since then many writers have attempted to define personality through areas of study implied by the term. Hall and Lindzey (1970) suggest that the definition preferred by writers reflects the theoretical perspective adopted, rather than conceptual insights. In other words the definition of personality becomes apparent through the description and justification of a particular theory.

The problem underlying this arises because it is not possible to observe a psychological phenomena. Consequently, inferences must be drawn from what can be seen. The construct of the personality is a convenient way of grouping together a number of characteristics relevant to describing the ways that people differ from each other. Consider for a moment two friends and how they differ from each other? Perhaps a description would include some of the following:

- Physical description. Height, weight, build, hair length and colour.
- Emotional description. Gushing, withdrawn, nervous or manipulative.
- Sociability description. Friendly, generous, giving, likeable and 'nice'.

All of these and more reflect ways that people can be differentiated. However, they are not all aspects of personality. Some are aspects of ability, or physical characteristics, others are probably a reflection of transient emotional states.

Management in Action 3.1 describes how a number of famous people behave and discusses how (as employees) they might be dealt with by their managers. The question is, however, does ego as described in the article form part of personality?

The study of personality

There is no single definition of personality that would be accepted by all theorists. Essentially, personality is considered to represent those personal characteristics that result in consistent patterns of behaviour (Burger, 1986). This rather loose definition provides some insight into the concept, but leaves many issues undecided. For example, an individual's abilities (say driving a motor car) provide a basis for many behaviour activities, yet they would not usually be regarded as personality characteristics. Also ignored in this definition is any reference to the source of personality. Is personality something that each individual is born with, or does it develop over time with experience? The answer is, probably both. The relationship between these variables can be shown as a diagram (see Figure 3.1).

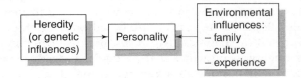

Figure 3.1 Relationship between the determinants of personality.

Management in Action 3.1

Down with super egos

There are many examples of individuals with very large egos. They exist in the acting profession and the arts as well as the media and other areas of public life. They are the larger than life individuals who frequently make the headlines and demand everything just as they prefer it irrespective of other considerations. In the entertainment business, sport and other forms of public life such super egos can be a positive asset in creating publicity, filling theatres and attracting attention for fashion designers. Examples are frequently said to include Dustin Hofman, John McEnroe, Naomi Campbell and Armand Hammer.

Super egos are also to be found in business and commercial life and can make life very difficult for the smooth running of a company. Robert Maxwell was a famous example of a super ego in this category. It is when such individuals reach the top of the organization that they find most opportunity to express the ego that they possess.

At the lower levels of an organization the super ego manager might be able to make life difficult, if not impossible for a subordinate or even a group of people, but they would be unlikely to impact on the whole organization. Manfred Kets de Vries (from Insead, a business school in France) argues that individuals need a degree of narcissism to become a business leader, but that when such an individual gets to the top strange things begin to happen. Because of seniority it is frequently necessary for subordinates and colleagues to find ways of containing the effects of the ego and of co-existing with it. Only rarely does a super ego find themselves in a position of subordinates engaging in open revolt and of attempting to oust the individual before they bring the whole organization down. The situation is made worse if the super ego is the owner of the company as they are able to exercise a greater degree of control over direction and their own activities in relation to it.

Based on child-rearing practice it has been suggested that two basic options exist for dealing with super egos within an organization. The first involves the practice of kow-tow, going along with the super ego for a quiet life. This according to Peter Honey (a management consultant) involves bowing, scraping, following orders and tugging the forelock. As an approach it can work in situations where contact is irregular. For example one literary agent who deals with difficult authors accepts their little quirks and attempts to anticipate the issues that each will pick on and deal with them before they become problems.

The second approach is to directly take the super ego on. However, according to Honey this needs to be done carefully if it is to have any effect on the situation. Facing up to a superior with a super ego could simply result in dismissal and so it becomes essential to pick the times, places and issues over which to stand fast. Manfred Kets de Vries suggests that in large public companies the only option in many situations is for the subordinate to seek alternative work if they find it impossible to cope with a boss with a super ego. The option to approach another executive with the problem might appear attractive, but might also create problems for the whistleblower.

Gerrard Egan from Loyola University in Chicago suggests that organizations need to allow managers to develop appropriate skills in managing others and in being able to capture the benefits of mentoring and the use of confidantes who will tell an individual when they are going too far. The inclusion of subordinate and peer appraisal assessment should also provide an opportunity to contain the effects of the super ego within an organization. According to Manfred Kets de Vries the successful leaders are those who are able to put their narcissism to good use rather than simply allow it free reign.

Adapted from: Kellaway, L (1993) Down with super egos. Financial Times, *Monday 11 October, p* 12.

Taking each element in turn:

A   **Genetic influences**. It is not absolutely clear how much of the personality is determined by the genetic inheritance of the individual. In common expression there are many examples of heredity being used to justify behaviour. For example, 'That (particular behaviour) is just like your father (or mother)'. However, an equally strong case has been put forward for the lack of genetic determination of personality, suggesting that it develops through interaction with people and events. This is the so-called nature–nurture controversy.

More recently, it has been suggested that both nature (genetics) and nurture (environment) play a part to varying degrees in the determination of personality. For example, that genetics determine the range of possible development for a particular characteristic, but that environmental influences determine the actual extent achieved (Pervin, 1984). There is also some recent evidence from studies on twins by Holden (1987) that the genetic determinants of personality are more significant than previously thought.

B   **Environmental influences** include:

■   Family. When we are born we become part of a family. In our early years we are socialized into and by that family group. Parents and siblings all have parts to play in introducing the individual to the behaviour patterns accepted within that culture. Family in this context also includes grandparents, aunts, cousins and so on as all have a part to play in establishing behaviour patterns in the child.

There are many ways in which the family influence the development of the individual's personality. They include:

– The process of interaction with children which will encourage particular behaviour patterns.
– Older members serving as role models for the younger members to imitate.
– The circumstances surrounding the family, including family size, economic status, religion and geographic location.

■   Culture. The culture that an individual is born into has a considerable influence on the behaviour norms to which they are exposed. For example, Western cultures tend to emphasize individual characteristics whilst Asian cultures tend to emphasize collective values. Consequently, appropriate personality characteristics will be encouraged in the individuals within each culture. One of the difficulties with the concept of culture is that it can lead to the assumption that all individuals within it will display the same characteristics. The concept of culture is an ideal type. That is, it will be found to a greater or lesser extent in each individual.

■   Experience. The friendship and other groups to which individuals belong and the general experiences of life all have an effect on behaviour. For example, the experience of being shunned by other children in the infant school playground can have a significant influence on the personality and self-esteem of a child (Bradshaw, 1981).

Nomothetic theories offer an approach to the study of personality based upon the identification and measurement of characteristics. This is achieved through the application of personality tests and tends to assume that the genetic determinants of personality are the most significant.

Idiographic approaches, on the other hand, claim that it is necessary to take into account the uniqueness of each individual in describing personality, also that tests are limited in measuring personality when it is defined in terms of the self-concept of the individual. As such personality is a function of the dynamic interaction between the individual and the environment in which they live.

As with many areas of psychological research, the above classification scheme does not account for all of the theories developed. There is a third approach to the understanding of personality that combines elements of both idiographic and nomothetic approaches. The approaches from this perspective are not easy to integrate into a single classification scheme because they are essentially individual contributions to the field.

One challenge in the organizational application of personality refers to the need to identify which of its many dimensions are the relevant ones. It is assumed, for example, that intelligence is necessary for success, but is it? Management in Action 3.2 (overleaf) would imply that common sense is a far more important issue from an organizational point of view.

Nomothetic perspectives

The nomothetic approach concentrates on the identification and measurement of the common characteristics of personality. This is based on the analysis of data obtained from large numbers of individuals. The purpose being to develop measurement scales reflecting the characteristics of personality. This allows the measurement and comparison of personality profiles for individuals. There are many personality tests of this type, but the best known were developed by Eysenck and Cattell

Eysenck and the study of personality types

As far back as Galen, the so-called classical temperaments of sanguine, phlegmatic, melancholic and choleric were being used to describe personality types (Eysenck, 1965). Quoting a source first published in 1798, Eysenck described the four temperaments as follows:

- Sanguine. A person 'carefree and full of hope; attributes great importance to whatever he may be dealing with at the moment, but may have forgotten about it the next. ... He is easily fatigued and bored by work but is constantly engaged in mere games – these carry with them constant change, and persistence is not his forte'.
- Phlegmatic. A person who displays a 'lack of emotion, not laziness; it implies a tendency to be moved neither quickly nor easily but persistently. ... He is reasonable in his dealing with other people and usually gets his way by persisting in his objectives while appearing to give way to others'.
- Melancholic. A person who will 'attribute great importance to everything that concerns them. They discover everywhere cause for anxiety and notice first of all the difficulties in a situation, in contradistinction to the sanguine person. ... All this is not so because of moral considerations but because interaction with others makes him worried, suspicious, and thoughtful. It is for this that happiness escapes him.'

How do you rate on the common sense scale?

Common sense is an illusive quality that is popularly claimed to be widespread and yet is difficult to identify, particularly in management activities. It is something that recruiters look for in aspiring applicants, particularly potential managers. Einstein defined common sense as the collection of prejudices that people have accrued by the age of 18. Victor Hugo claimed that it was acquired in spite of, rather than because of, education.

However, as Furnham points out there are three major problems with the notion of common sense as a management characteristic. Firstly, the tenets of common sense are frequently contradictory. Consider for example, 'Clothes make the man' and 'You can't make a silk purse out of a sow's ear'. They both can't be right in every situation. Secondly, if successful management is the application of common sense then no failure can be attributed to faulty reasoning by the individuals concerned. Thirdly, if successful management reflects common sense, and most people have (supposedly) this characteristic, why is there so much disagreement on the issues, processes and procedures associated with the practice of management?

Furnham provides the following true/false quiz to allow you to test yourself on how much common sense you possess. Perhaps you would like to try it for yourself? Remember, however, that it is just for fun!

1   If you pay someone for doing something they enjoy, they will come to like the task even more. True/False.
2   Most people prefer challenging jobs with a great deal of freedom and autonomy? True/False.
3   Most people are more concerned with the size of their own salary than with the salary of others? True/False.
4   In most cases, workers act in ways that are consistent with their attitudes? True/False.
5   In bargaining with others, it is usually best to start with a moderate offer – near to the one you desire? True/False.
6   In most cases, leaders should stick to their decisions once they have made them, even if it appears they are wrong? True/False.
7   When people work together in groups and know their individual contributions cannot be observed, each tends to put in less effort than when they work on the same task alone? True/False.
8   Even skilled interviewers are sometimes unable to avoid being influenced in their judgement by factors other than an applicant's qualifications? True/False.
9   Most managers are highly democratic in the way that they supervise their people? True/False.
10 Most people who work for the government are low risk takers? True/False.
11 The best way to stop a malicious rumour at work is to present convincing evidence against it? True/False.
12 As morale or satisfaction among employees increases in any organization, overall performance almost always rises? True/False.
13 Providing employees with specific goals often interferes with their performance: they resist being told what to do? True/False.
14 In most organizations, the struggle for limited resources is a far more important cause of conflict than other factors such as interpersonal relations? True/False.
15 In bargaining, the best strategy for maximizing long-term gains is seeking to defeat one's opponent? True/False.
16 In general, groups make more accurate and less extreme decisions than individuals? True/False.
17 Most individuals do their best work under conditions of high stress? True/False.
18 Smokers take more days sick leave than do non-smokers? True/False.
19 If you have to reprimand a worker for a misdeed, it is better to do so immediately after the mistake occurs? True/False.
20 Highly cohesive groups are also highly productive? True/False.

Answers

True = questions 6, 7, 8, 9, 10, 18, 19.
False = questions 1, 2, 3, 4, 5, 11, 12, 13, 14, 15, 16, 17, 20.

Furnham offers the following advice for interpreting the results:

- Score 5 or less right answers - try early retirement.
- Score between 6 and 12 right answers - consider taking an MBA degree.
- Score between 13 and 15 right answers - pretty average, but no room for gloating.
- Score 16 or over – you do appear to have that most elusive of qualities: managerial common sense.

Taken from: Furnham, A (1993) How do you rate on the common sense scale? Financial Times, 5 May, p 14.

- Choleric. A person 'said to be hot-headed, is quickly roused, but easily calmed down if his opponent gives in; he is annoyed without lasting hatred. Activity is quick but not persistent. ... He loves appearances, pomp and formality; he is full of pride and self-love. He is miserly; polite but with ceremony; he suffers most through the refusal of others to fall in with his pretensions. In one word the choleric temperament is the least happy because it is most likely to call forth opposition to itself'.

Eysenck was a prolific writer and produced many books and papers over the years. His 1967 and 1971 texts provide a good overview of the development of his work. His research involved both the rating of individuals and the completion of questionnaires by subjects in the UK, USA and Europe. The results of this research were subjected to factor analysis to identify the underlying dimensions of personality. The outcome was the identification of two dimensions along which personality could be said to vary:

- Extroversion. Measured on a scale of *extroversion* and *introversion*. The extrovert likes excitement, is sociable and lively. The introvert is quiet and retiring.
- Neuroticism. This implies a scale from *neurotic* to *stable*. The neurotic tends to worry, is anxious, moody and unstable. The stable person tends to be calm, even-tempered, carefree and reliable.

The relationship between Eysenck's personality dimensions and the older temperaments is reflected in Figure 3.2. It is possible to identify the main characteristics of each of the 'types' in the words around the perimeter of the outer

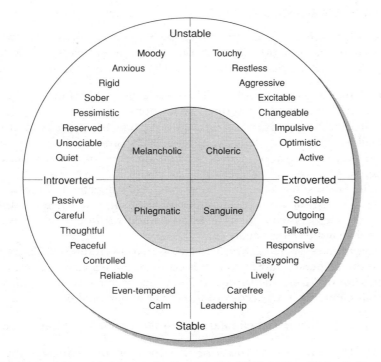

Figure 3.2 Eysenck's model of personality (Eysenck, HJ (1965) *Fact and Fiction in Psychology*, Penguin, Harmondsworth, Fig. 8).

circle. The angle between the characteristics is a reflection of the relationship between them. For example, there are about 90 degrees between the characteristics of 'sober and rigid' and 'aggressive and excitable', implying that there is no correlation between them. On the other hand, between the characteristics of 'sober and rigid' and 'lively and easygoing', there are 180 degrees and a negative correlation. More of one means less of the opposite characteristic.

Assessment of the theory

Eysenck claims that the personality dimensions are linked to physiological functioning of the human body. For example, neuroticism is positively linked with those aspects of the autonomic nervous system that control body temperature, heartbeat, etc. He has attempted to use his theory to explain criminal behaviour and mental illness. For example, criminals are said to be highly extroverted, which he claims means that they are slow to condition and any conditioned behaviour is quickly extinguished.

There have been many criticisms of the work of Eysenck, including the role that nature and genetics is said to play in the development of personality. Also, that having a theory based on just two dimensions is overly simplistic when considering the complexity of human behaviour. However, his work has been based on a considerable amount of detailed research and so has strength. Eysenck himself does not claim that there are only two dimensions associated with personality, simply that they account for most of the published research. By implication, therefore, they are the most significant in the description and understanding of personality and individual difference.

Cattell and personality characteristics

Cattell (1965) developed a test known as the Sixteen Personality Factor Questionnaire, or *16PF*, for short. Using factor analysis he sampled the variables in what he refers to as the *personality sphere*. His research process is, in outline:

1   Trait elements were identified. This was achieved through a dictionary search for all words that described behaviour.
2   Initial research. Synonyms were taken out from the initial pool of words. A small sample of students was intensively studied over a six-month period and rated (by trained observers) on each of the remaining trait elements.
3   Analysis. The results of the initial research were subjected to a cluster analysis. This statistical process identifies relationships (clusters) within the data. Fifty clusters were identified and named *surface traits*. These were then subjected to factor analysis.
4   Identification of *source traits*. The factor analysis of the surface traits produced the 16 personality factors. It is claimed that because the source traits are determined from the surface traits, which in turn were identified from the trait elements, they account for the whole personality.

In developing the theory Cattell made use of three sources of information:

■   **L-Data.** This refers to information, or ratings, obtained through the use of trained observers. The 'L' stands for Life. For example the initial research programme described above.

■ **Q-Data.** This refers to questionnaire responses. An example, of these would be the 16PF. He also developed tests of personality for other groups, including:
  - Child's Personality Quiz (CPQ), for children aged from 6 to 11 years
  - High School Personality Questionnaire (HSPQ), for young people aged between 12 and 15 years.

■ **T-Data.** This refers to data obtained through test applications. The results are obtained from the performance on tasks specifically designed to measure personality. These objective tests, as Cattell referred to them, were carried out when the subject had no knowledge of their true purpose. Cattell and Warburton (1967) describe over 200 such devices, including:
  - A chair that recorded the movement of anyone sitting in it. The purpose being to record the 'fidget' score for each person.
  - As part of a paper and pencil test the inclusion of two sets of identical questions, separated by a few pages. Included in the second presentation was some visually distracting material (say cartoons). The difference in time to complete the two sets of questions measuring the person's distractibility score.

The 16 factors used by Cattell in the 16PF questionnaire (the source traits) are as shown in Figure 3.3.

The first 12 factors have been identified in L-data as well as Q-data. The last four items have only been found in Q-data. That is why they have been given a reference designation beginning 'Q', rather than following on from the previous alphabetical designation. The scale for each bipolar factor ranges from one to 10, thus allowing each individual completing the questionnaire to have their results plotted onto the score sheet. The actual questionnaire contains a number of questions appropriate to each of the factors. After completion by the individual the results for each question are converted to a score on the scale of one to 10 by comparison with published norms for the population to which the subject

Scale		Scale of measurement	
A	Reserved, detached, critical, aloof	1 ←——→ 10	Outgoing, warm-hearted, easygoing
B	Less intelligent, concrete thinking	1 ←——→ 10	More intelligent, abstract thinking
C	Affected by feelings, easily upset	1 ←——→ 10	Emotionally stable, calm, mature
E	Humble, mild, conforming	1 ←——→ 10	Assertive, competitive
F	Sober, prudent, taciturn	1 ←——→ 10	Happy-go-lucky, enthusiastic
G	Expedient, disregards rules	1 ←——→ 10	Conscientious, moralistic
H	Shy, timid	1 ←——→ 10	Socially bold
I	Tough-minded, realistic	1 ←——→ 10	Tender-minded, sensitive
L	Trusting, adaptable	1 ←——→ 10	Suspicious, hard to fool
M	Practical, careful	1 ←——→ 10	Imaginative, careless
N	Forthright, natural	1 ←——→ 10	Shrewd, calculating
O	Self-assured, confident	1 ←——→ 10	Apprehensive, troubled
Q1	Conservative, respects established ideas	1 ←——→ 10	Experimenting, radical
Q2	Group dependent, good 'follower'	1 ←——→ 10	Self-sufficient, resourceful
Q3	Undisciplined, self-conflict	1 ←——→ 10	Controlled, socially precise
Q4	Relaxed, tranquil	1 ←——→ 10	Tense, frustrated

Figure 3.3 Cattell's 16 PF factors (adapted from Cattell, RB, Eber, HW and Tasnoka, MM (1970) *Handbook for the Sixteen Personality Factor Questionnaire (16PF)*, Institute for Personality and Ability Testing, Champaign, IL).

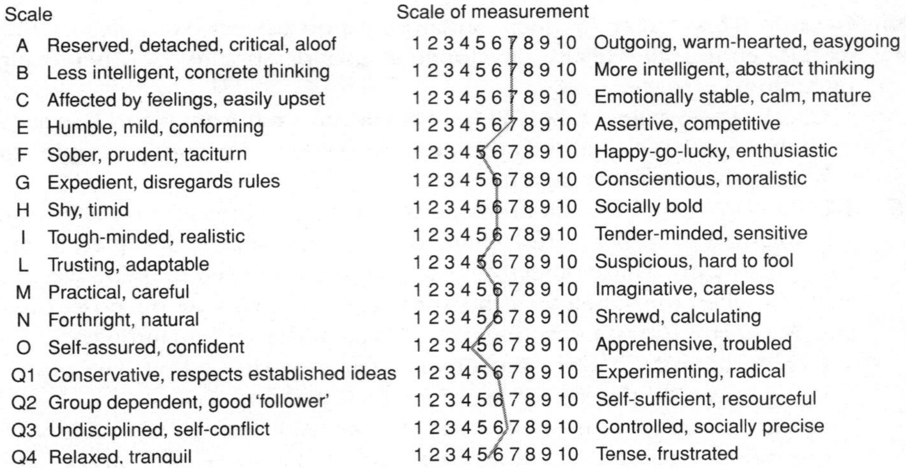

Scale		Scale of measurement	
A	Reserved, detached, critical, aloof	1 2 3 4 5 6 7 8 9 10	Outgoing, warm-hearted, easygoing
B	Less intelligent, concrete thinking	1 2 3 4 5 6 7 8 9 10	More intelligent, abstract thinking
C	Affected by feelings, easily upset	1 2 3 4 5 6 7 8 9 10	Emotionally stable, calm, mature
E	Humble, mild, conforming	1 2 3 4 5 6 7 8 9 10	Assertive, competitive
F	Sober, prudent, taciturn	1 2 3 4 5 6 7 8 9 10	Happy-go-lucky, enthusiastic
G	Expedient, disregards rules	1 2 3 4 5 6 7 8 9 10	Conscientious, moralistic
H	Shy, timid	1 2 3 4 5 6 7 8 9 10	Socially bold
I	Tough-minded, realistic	1 2 3 4 5 6 7 8 9 10	Tender-minded, sensitive
L	Trusting, adaptable	1 2 3 4 5 6 7 8 9 10	Suspicious, hard to fool
M	Practical, careful	1 2 3 4 5 6 7 8 9 10	Imaginative, careless
N	Forthright, natural	1 2 3 4 5 6 7 8 9 10	Shrewd, calculating
O	Self-assured, confident	1 2 3 4 5 6 7 8 9 10	Apprehensive, troubled
Q1	Conservative, respects established ideas	1 2 3 4 5 6 7 8 9 10	Experimenting, radical
Q2	Group dependent, good 'follower'	1 2 3 4 5 6 7 8 9 10	Self-sufficient, resourceful
Q3	Undisciplined, self-conflict	1 2 3 4 5 6 7 8 9 10	Controlled, socially precise
Q4	Relaxed, tranquil	1 2 3 4 5 6 7 8 9 10	Tense, frustrated

Figure 3.4 16 PF profile of managing directors (after Cox, CJ and Cooper, CL (1988) *High Flyers*, Basil Blackwell, Oxford).

belongs. The individual scores for each factor can be plotted on the scale to provide a profile of the individual's personality. To illustrate this point, Figure 3.4 shows the 'average' profile of managing directors obtained by Cox and Cooper (1988). The test result for a specific managing director could be calculated in comparison with the average for that population and shown on the chart.

Cattell subjected his 16 source traits to another round of factor analysis. From that he identified eight second-order factors. Of these there are only four that are of major concern. Two of the others are not clearly defined and the other two are very close to the existing source traits of intelligence (B) and conscientiousness (G). The four factors were called:

- Anxiety. Defined in terms of worry over problems and difficulties, feelings of guilt and tenseness.
- Exvia. Defined at one extreme as outgoing, uninhibited and a good mixer. At the other extreme a shy, self-contained person.
- Radicalism. Measures the degree of aggression, independence and self-direction within the individual.
- Tendermindedness. Defined in terms of sensitivity, liability to frustration and emotionally controlled conduct.

Exvia is a neologism, not found in an ordinary dictionary. It is an example of one of many words coined by Cattell in an attempt to define the dimensions used in his theory.

Assessment of the theory

The approach adopted by Cattell depends very much on the first step in his research process. If he has been able to identify all the possible trait elements in the personality sphere, then the rest must follow. The statistical tests carried out on his findings are such that the surface and source traits must account for the variation in behaviour. The basis of the claim is that because the behaviour exists, a verbal label is necessary to describe it. If no label exists then the behaviour cannot exist. This of course raises many questions relating to behaviour, language and the way that personality interacts with both. Words are used to describe ideas and feelings as well as needs and wants. There is a complex relationship between the observable behaviour of individuals and the underlying personality characteristics that help to shape that behaviour. The links between what is observable, the words used to describe it and the associated psychological structures are far from clear.

Idiographic perspectives

The idiographic perspective emphasizes the development of the self-concept rather than concentration on the measurement of characteristics. There are difficulties for the test-based approach of Ensenck and Cattell as a result of the imposition of the researcher's own frame of reference on data collection and analysis. Therefore, idiographic theorists argue that in order to understand unique personality characteristics it is first necessary to understand how the individual relates to the world in which they live and the individual qualities that make each person different from every other person.

Cooley, an American psychologist, introduced the concept of the *looking-glass self* to the debate on personality. He draws attention to the interactive nature of much behaviour and the development of self-image as a result. We begin to see ourselves as others see us through the responses that we generate from others. This is the *looking-glass*, or mirror, that reflects a perspective back to us. Through the interactions with the people around us we come to understand who we are and learn to adapt our personality to accommodate our environment.

Mead (1934) added to this approach through the concept of the *generalized other*. This concept is intended to reflect the existence of two components in the 'self', they are:

- I   Being the unique, spontaneous and conscious aspects of the individual.
- ME   Being the internalized norms and values learned through experience within society.

The *generalized other* refers to the understanding that the individual develops of the expectations that society have of them. It is in the *ME* element of the 'self' that this evaluation takes place. The *I* component is the aspect of personality that attempts to ensure that the individual meets their own expectations, rather than becoming a creature totally of the *ME* component. It also allows the opportunity to provide for evolution in society through the adaptation of social norms to meet the needs of the individuals within it.

Rogers (1947) proposed that the main objective of personality is a desire to fully realize one's potential. Like Mead, he also used the two components of *I* and *ME* in describing the self-concept. As a diagram, his view of the linkages between *I*, *Me* and the *self-concept* is illustrated in Figure 3.5.

One implication of this model of the self-concept is that the personality will be subject to change as the underlying personal self and social self change due to experience. This linkage is demonstrated in the model by the connections between the elements and the relationship implied by them. If this change did not occur then a tension would be created which could lead to the emergence of personality disorders within the individual.

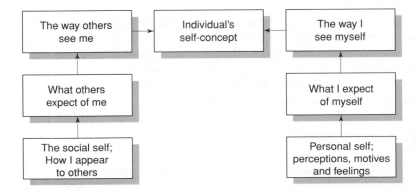

Figure 3.5 Rogers view of the 'I' and 'me'.

Other perspectives: Freud, Jung, Murray and Kelly

Freud and psychoanalysis

Sigmund Freud lived from 1856 until 1939. He trained as a physician and then specialized as a neurologist and most of his life was spent in Vienna. He began to work with Joseph Breuer, who was using hypnosis in the treatment of hysteria. In 1895 Freud and Breuer published a book, *Studies on Hysteria*. However, at the time of its publication Freud was beginning to move away from working with Breuer as a result of the former's substitution of hypnosis with free association for the treatment of hysteria. This was the critical step in the development of psychoanalysis.

Free association is a process that begins with an item of emotional significance for an individual. The individual then allows their ideas and thoughts to flow from that starting point, until for what ever reason they *break off* the chain of association. This is then repeated for other items of significance for the individual. The points at which the individual breaks off the thought chain are held to be the points of resistance, at which the individual's internal psychological processes attempt to protect them from bringing out into the open those things which the individual wishes to be protected from. It was these resistance points that became the focus for Freud's research and the development of psychotherapy. Freud identified dreams as a potent source of ideas with which to begin the process of free association.

Freud was a prodigious writer and his collected papers amount to some 24 volumes (Strachey, 1953–66). His theorizing was complex and covered many aspects of life, from cannibalism to the choice of career. According to Freud, there are three levels of mental activity:

■ Unconscious. This refers to mental activity that is inaccessible, hidden deeply and only accessible through the process of psychoanalysis. Although hidden from the conscious mind, these motivate much of our behaviour.
■ Pre-conscious. This refers to those ideas that are unconscious, but unlike the unconscious category, they can be recalled when necessary. People's names and telephone numbers often fall into this category.

- Conscious. This refers to the thoughts and ideas that we are aware of in the normal course of activity.

In addition, Freud classified the mind as consisting of three areas:

- Id. The *id* is the area of the mind that contains all the inherited information available to the individual. It is the cauldron of our very being, it is the part of our mind that follows the pleasure principle in seeking immediate gratification and satisfaction regardless of the consequences.
- Ego. The *ego* develops during childhood and serves to balance the demands of the id. In doing so it follows the reliability principle in assessing the consequences of behaviour originating in the demands of the id.
- Super-ego. This becomes the internalized version of parents. It becomes the observer of the ego and controls through the same devices as the parent. Freud claimed that the *super-ego* developed by about the age of five.

Behaviour is a balance between these three components of the mind. A well-adjusted individual will be controlled by their ego, a neurotic (driven by anxiety) through their super-ego, and the psychopath (driven by their own desires) through the id. The intention of psychotherapy is to restore, or provide the opportunity for, the *natural* balance between the three components to be restored.

In terms of personality, Freud described a process of development from birth through to early adult life. The development of personality was the outcome of internal struggles and involved passing through a number of stages:

- Oral. The initial stages of life from birth to about the age of two years. It reflects the importance of feeding, pleasure achievement and bonding with the mother.
- Anal. From about two years until four years of age. It reflects the focus of attention shifting from the 'input' to the 'output' aspects of life.
- Phallic. At about the age of four the child enters the final stage of development which ends with puberty. This reflects the development of the individual in the initial awareness of genital significance in subsequent sexual activity.

It is through the *id, ego and super-ego* that adults manage their interaction with the world around them. Freud described a number of defence mechanisms adopted by the ego in order to maintain the balance between the id and super-ego. Defence mechanisms protect the individual from the 'damage' that could result from unresolved internal conflict. The main forms of *ego defence mechanisms* are:

- Sublimation. This allows the id to be expressed in an acceptable manner. For example, pottery making and painting can be described as a sublimation for the anal drives to handle and smear faeces.
- Repression. This describes a process where the existence of something is deliberately kept hidden from the conscious thinking level.
- Denial. This is a defence mechanism similar to repression, except that the ego alters the perception of the situation in order to maintain the balance.
- Projection. The transmission of feelings and motives to other people. A manager might justify political activity on the basis that others began such behaviour first.

- Reaction-formation. This produces the opposite feelings and behaviour at the conscious level to the unconscious level, So, love becomes hate.
- Regression. The avoidance of problems between the id and super-ego through the adoption of earlier patterns of behaviour that once produced satisfaction. A child may suck its thumb when being scolded by its parents.
- Isolation. This results in a separation of feelings and emotions from the experiences that normally produce them.
- Undoing. This attempts to 'undo' something that is thought to have happened. The obsessional washing of hands, over and over again, could reflect a person attempting to cleanse themselves in a deeper way.

Assessment of the theory

Freud's approach to personality is not a single theory as such. It is a complex model, including aspects of intellectual and sexual development, training, education, mental structure, social process and the dynamics of interaction. As such it is difficult to offer specific criticisms and equally difficult to defend it against any that are raised. Eysenck (1953) sets out the major objections to the theory, essentially on the basis that it was not scientific:

- Lack of data and statistical analysis. The data was not subjected to the processes considered acceptable by psychologists trained in the 'scientific method'.
- Sample base. The sample for his theory were mostly private patients, middle class and female. Furthermore, they put themselves forward for his treatment of their neurosis. They are not a representative sample, and claims for a theory developed on such a population must be open to question.
- Inadequate definition of terms used. The terms used to define Freudian theory are ill-defined and consequently it is not possible to be absolutely certain of the meaning or even their existence.
- Lack of 'testability'. Because of the 'richness', and complexity of Freudian theory it is not possible to falsify it. The scientific method involves a reductionist approach. Freud adopted a holistic model and attempted to reflect the complexity of life in a complex model.

Other arguments against his work include that it offered circular arguments to support the ideas in it, and that by emphasizing early childhood it produces a model that is deterministic and ignores the possibility of subsequent development. However, the model offers a 'richness' in attempting to encompass the whole of personality in a grand theory. Parts of the theory have been subjected to a more rigorous form of testing with some success (Kline, 1972).

At a practical level much of Freud's work led on to other research and subsequent thinking on the complexity of personality. Freud was interested in understanding the whole person and the part that early development played in the formation of the adult personality. The theory can be seen in some behaviour at work, for example, employees' and managers' 'temper tantrums' when things do not go according to plan.

Jung and the cognitive approach

Jung was a close associate of Freud but the relationship was not destined to last for long and they parted company in 1913. Jung developed an approach to personality based on Freudian theory, but which provided for the future rather than emphasizing the past (Jung, 1968). It postulated three levels of personality:

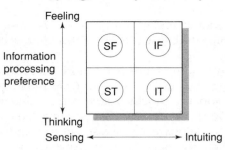

Figure 3.6 Jung's cognitive styles.

■ A conscious level. This allowed for reality in the everyday experience of the individual.
■ An unconscious level. This consists of the individuality of each person and is composed of the complexes and facets within each personality.
■ A collective unconscious. This is the pool of inherited and socially derived universal experience that each person carries with them inside their personality.

Personality differences were reflected by a number of dimensions within Jungian theory, including the use of the extroversion and introversion. Another was cognitive style, reflecting four approaches to information gathering and evaluation:

■ Sensing. People who prefer to deal with hard information in a structured context.
■ Intuiting. People who dislike routine activities, but who prefer to deal with possibilities rather than certainty.
■ Thinking. People who prefer the use of logic and rationality as the basis of problem solving, without the feelings of others entering into the process.
■ Feeling. People who prefer to have social harmony around them, get along with others and have sympathy for those around them.

From the above description it might be apparent that there are two dimensions involved in this framework; *sensing* and *intuiting* are at opposing ends of a continuum; as are *thinking* and *feeling*. This is reflected in Figure 3.6. The main personality characteristics for each cell in the matrix are shown in

	Jung's Cognitive Style			
	Sensing/Thinking (ST)	Intuiting/Thinking (IT)	Sensing/Feeling (SF)	Intuiting/Feeling (IF)
Prefers	Facts	Possibilities	Facts	Possibilities
Personality	Pragmatic, down-to-earth	Logical, but ingenious	Sympathetic, sociable	Energetic, insightful
Work preferences	Technical skills	Theoretical solving problem	Providing help and services to others	Understanding and communicating with others
	Physician, accountant, computer programmer	Scientist, corporate planner, mathematician	Salesperson, social worker, psychologist	Artist, writer, entertainer

Table 3.1
Differences between Jung's cognitive styles (adapted from Vecchio, RP (1991) *Organizational Behavior*, 2nd edn, The Dryden Press, Hinsdale, Table 3.2)

Table 3.1. This indicates the application of Jung's theory in differentiating personality and in describing the consequences of that approach for job preferences.

Assessment of the theory

The theory developed by Jung lends itself more easily to testing than that of Freud. The Myers-Briggs Personality Indicator (referred to as the MBTI) is based on Jung's view of personality, to which was added a dimension reflecting lifestyle (Myers-Briggs, 1987). This is now a well-established psychological test and is widely used by organizations as an assessment tool and by researchers interested in occupational choice, personality and management style.

However, the work of Jung has not gone without criticism. Eysenck (1965) claims that the concepts of extroversion and introversion were already in existence. However, it must be remembered that Eysenck offers a theory of personality based on the scientific method and that he is dismissive of approaches based on a holistic perspective.

Murray and personology

Murray was another writer who attempted to reflect the whole individual in the theoretical model. Indeed, he preferred the term personology to psychology as a description of his work. He emphasized the study of personology as a 'science of men taken as gross units' (1938). Murray worked intensively with a small number of subjects. The potential advantage being a fuller understanding of the individual case, with generalizable theory resulting.

Murray identified a total of 44 variables in his approach including:

- Needs. These form the main motivating factor in behaviour. He identified *20 manifest and eight latent needs*. Manifest needs he described in familiar terms, for example, play, achievement, understanding and autonomy. Latent needs he described as being inhibited and usually expressed in fantasy rather than overt behaviour.
- Presses. These are the external determinants of behaviour. *Presses* operate on the needs of the individual, depending upon the circumstances. Successful organizations are able to create environments which encourage achievement oriented cultures among employees.
- Internal states. Murray identified *four internal states* that are capable of influencing behaviour. For example the ego ideal. This refers to an aspect of personality that reflects unrealized achievement drive based on a high level of, as yet unmet, aspiration.
- General traits. Murray listed 12 of these, including anxiety, emotionality and creativity. They are intended to embrace the broad characteristics that influence much behaviour. They can be seen as qualifiers to the other variables. For example, a person with a high level of anxiety will respond differently to the need for play than will a highly creative person.

Murray developed his theory over a number of years and through the application of a range of measurement devices. He tested his subjects on 24 different test applications in a single 36-hour period. This inevitably placed his subjects under considerable strain. Among the tests were:

- Autobiographies. Subjects wrote about their lives and this was analysed to identify any of the 44 variables described above. Particular emphasis was placed on childhood events.

Figure 3.7   Ambiguous picture.

- Interviews. Murray and his team interviewed each subject about such issues as their memories of childhood, family relationships and problems currently being experienced.
- Experiments. A number of tests were used to measure specific aspects of the theory. For example, one test required subjects to print words quickly using a hand-printing set.
- Projective tests. A projective test is an ambiguous stimulus and subjects are asked to describe what is happening. The interpretation of the picture is considered to reflect something about the individual's life and inner thinking processes. Figure 3.7 is similar to those used by Murray in that the events in the picture could be interpreted in many different ways. The description provided by the subject is therefore based on their elaboration of the limited (and ambiguous) information provided.

Assessment of the theory

Murray drew heavily on the work of Freud and Jung as his inspiration, but he provided a broad range of measurement to support his work. Eysenck (1959) claimed that there is almost no validity for the projective technique and that testers do not agree with each other on the interpretation of test protocols. He goes on to claim that projective tests are the vehicles for the riotous imagination of clinicians.

Murray was not the first person to use the projective test as a means of gaining insight. Leonardo Da Vinci was the first person to record that paint smudges tended to be interpreted differently depending upon occupation and experience (Rabin, 1958). In more recent times, the Rorschach test was named after the Swiss psychiatrist who developed the approach. They are also frequently referred to as the 'inkblot' test, as they are created from a series of shapes formed from inkblots (see Figure 3.8 overleaf).

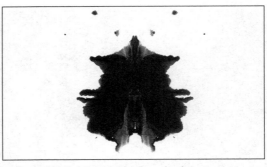

Figure 3.8   An 'inkblot' figure like that used in the Rorschach test.

The type of projective test used by Murray differed from the Rorschach test in that he required subjects to create a story from an ambiguous drawing, rather than responding to a shape such as Figure 3.8. He went further than many of his contemporaries in providing a scientific basis for his work. However, it is still susceptible to the claim that it is weak in this respect.

Kelly's personal construct theory

Kelly suggested that everyone was a scientist in developing the ability to interact with the environment. This implies that human beings are essentially predictive in their approach to behaviour within the environment, reflecting a process of reformulating hypotheses about the world in the light of new information and seeking to adjust the behavioural repertoire accordingly.

Human beings develop a series of constructs through which to view the world around them. These form the basis of the ability to categorize the similarities and differences in events as they occur in the environment. A construct in this context is a bi-polar continuum of extremes. For example, happy–sad; I am now–I would like to be; friendly–hostile; and work I enjoy–work I hate, are illustrations of constructs defined by Kelly. These constructs are arranged into a complex framework as the individual's *personal construct system*. It is described as a hierarchical network as they interlink in a web of expectation and relationship. For example, an individual classified as trustworthy will be expected to display many other related behaviours: honesty, reliability, friendliness, and so on. For Kelly, the personality is the way that the individual develops a framework for, and experiments with, their world.

There are a number of characteristics relating to the way that individuals utilize their network of constructs and the dynamics associated with the process, including:

- Individuals develop a personal prediction model for future events based on the identification of a replication of patterns in past events.
- Individuals differ in the networks of constructs that they develop. One of the consequences of this is that it produces a relatively unique interpretation basis within each person.
- The constructs that people develop have a limited range of application. Every construct contains a field of relevance for its application. This is psychologically based and meaningful only for the individual concerned.
- Construct systems are dynamic. They are essentially a basis for effective functioning in the future. The frameworks are liable to modification in the light of the feedback provided by behaviour.

Significant people

	Self	Father	Mother	Brother	Friend A	Friend B	
Loving	1	1	1	0	0	1	Cold
Friendly	1	0	1	1	0	1	Unfriendly
Trustworthy	1	1	1	1	1	1	Untrustworthy
Helpful	1	0	1	0	1	0	Unhelpful
Like me	1	0	0	0	1	1	Not like me

Constructs

Figure 3.9 Simplified repertory grid.

This approach to the study of personality implies that the personal construct theory accounts for individual difference. It allows for two individuals respond differently to the same situation. The hierarchy and network of constructs is unique for each individual, therefore, the experience of a situation is different for each individual exposed to it.

Kelly developed the 'repertory grid' as a means of identifying and measuring the constructs utilized by an individual. The process for developing a repertory grid is as follows (Kelly, 1961):

■ The individual is asked to identify an important way in which two significant people (to the testee) are similar, but differ from a third. This is the construct dimension underlying the channel of thought used by the individual.
■ This process is repeated until between 20–30 separate distinguishing features are identified.
■ A matrix is formed with the significant names along the top and the constructs identified listed down the side.
■ A binary number (zero or one) would be entered in each cell of the matrix, based on the subject's assessment of whether each named person was more like one extreme of the construct or the other.
■ The completed matrix can then be factor analysed to identify the similarities and differences between the constructs identified. The cell entries can be examined to identify patterns among relationships. Figure 3.9 is an example of a repertory grid indicating the basic appearance of the matrix and constructs identified.

Assessment of the theory
The personal construct approach to personality allows the development of an understanding in terms that are meaningful for the individual. The repertory grid mechanism allows the identification of how the individual construes the world and how they set about interacting with it. From this perspective it is grounded in a broader interpretation of personality than many of the other theories. Kelly suggests that personal construct theory is relevant to an understanding of an individual's perceptual frameworks and attitudes as well as personality and its development. It is a theory concerning the way that an individual makes sense of their world and experiments with it.

This notion of experimenting with the world has lead to some criticism of the theory. It is often assumed by scientists that they are the people who experiment and that only they are in a position to utilize the scientific method effectively. But of course this need not be the only definition of experimentation. Young children experiment with the world around them when they are engaged in play activities. They are learning the skills needed to manipulate aspects of their environment and how to behave towards it. This approach continues in adult life according to Kelly, reflecting a form of experimentation.

The theory provides an explanation of personality that takes the whole person into account. It provides a means of developing an understanding of personality in a way that is relevant to the individual being studied. It does not force the person into a framework developed on other people. The theory provides an approach to the study of personality that does not pre-judge the form of personality; it is defined by the individuals being studied.

Personality measurement

Personality measurement is an area of considerable interest in psychology. Several ways in which personality characteristics can be measured have been introduced. For example, the 16PF personality inventory. This could be described as a *hard systems* approach to the measurement of personality. The use of the psychoanalytical method allows much more richness to be taken into account in developing an understanding of the whole person and their personality. This approach could be described as a *soft systems* approach to the study of personality. A combination of hard and soft systems are used in the work of Murray and Kelly as they attempt to utilize qualitative and quantitative approaches to the understanding of personality.

A psychological test is usually defined as a set of tasks presented in a standard form and which produce a numerical score as the output. This is called *psychometrics*, or the process of mental measurement.

There are two main reasons that psychometric tests are used. The first is to undertake scientific research into behaviour and an understanding of people. The second is in order to enable decisions relating to people to be made. For example, who to appoint to a particular job and for career counselling advice. In both there is a need for accurate information of those aspects of people that are of interest to the purpose. There are many tests available that can offer insights into aspects of people. They include tests of particular skills, abilities, intelligence, aptitudes, job preferences, psychological functioning and personality. This chapter concentrates on tests of personality.

There are three ways in which tests can measure personality:

1   Comparison of performance against a standard. Response times to undertake a particular task is an example.
2   Norm-referenced measurement. This compares an individual's performance on a test with that of a peer group.
3   Criterion-referenced measurement. This compares performance on a test with an 'ideal' result.

Usually the responses given by the testee are interpreted as an indication of an underlying characteristic. Therefore, a test is claimed to be 'valid' if it measures what it claims to measure. In addition a test needs to be 'reliable' in producing the same answer over time. There are different forms of validity and reliability, including:

- Face validity. This refers to the degree to which a test appears as if it ought to measure what it sets out to measure.
- Predictive validity. This form of validity reflects the ability of tests to predict future events. A test would have predictive validity if high scoring individuals were successful, whilst low scoring individuals performed badly in the job for which the test was being used as a selection aid.
- Construct validity. This refers to the extent that a test can be related back to a theory.
- Test/retest reliability. This reflects the ability of a test to produce the same score when it is administered on two different occasions.

Management in Action 3.3

How to cheat on personality tests

There are many organizations that make use of psychometric tests in the search for the perfect match between the organization, work and worker. This is nothing new and as early as 1956 one author was offering the following advice on how to make the best of having to take a personality test. The output from such tests being a comparison of the individual taking the test with the population of which they are part. They are premised on the view that while there are some tests in which a high score would be beneficial to the individual, many require the individual to demonstrate that they are broadly similar to everyone else. So for example if the test was intended to identify who would make a 'good chemist' then a high score in comparison with the population at large would be beneficial to the career prospects of the testee. On the other hand in a test of personality, it would be beneficial to find that the test results indicate that the individual displays 'normal' characteristics in common with the bulk of the population.

To specifically quote from the advice offered by the author when taking personality tests:

By and large, however, your safety lies in getting a score somewhere between the 40th and 60th percentiles, which is to say, you should try to answer as if you were like everyone else is supposed to be. This is not always easy to figure out, of course, [...] When in doubt, however, there are two general rules that you can follow: (1) when asked for word associations or comments about the world, give the most conventional, run-of-the-mill, pedestrian answer possible. (2) To settle on the most beneficial answer to any question, repeat to yourself:

(a) I loved my father and my mother, but my father a little bit more.
(b) I like things pretty well the way they are.
(c) I never worry much about anything.
(d) I don't care for books or music much.
(e) I love my wife and children.
(f) I don't let them get in the way of company work.

The rationale behind this advice is that psychometric tests are intended to identify the presence of those characteristics desired by organizations. The feeling emerging from the above quotation is that the individual so described would be an 'organization man' of the highest order. Someone who would not think much and would not be distracted from the task in hand. Performing the tasks identified by management in a way which would not question them or pose a threat to the position of management. The human equivalent of the computer – after all remember this was written before the computer was used within organizations. It was also offered at a time when the masculine choice of words would have not seemed out of place – because there were so few women in career positions within management. However, the main point that emerges from considering these words of advice are that tests are intended to identify those characteristics deemed important by the test creators. That is as true today as it was when they were first written.

Taken from: Whyte, WH (1960) The Organization Man, A Penguin Special. Penguin, Harmondsworth.

- Alternative form reliability. Some tests are developed in two or more different forms. All of the forms available should produce the same score.
- Split half reliability. This is the internal consistency within a particular test. Splitting the test up and comparing the results from the various combinations of activities is a means of measuring this consistency.

Tests go through a considerable development process before being accepted as useful for general application. The process of test development can be summarized as follows:

- **Step 1.** The initial ideas for a test often emerge from a practical need, for example, assisting personnel managers to identify the most appropriate job applicants. Tests can also originate from a theoretical need to measure some characteristic as part of theory development.
- **Step 2.** The development of appropriate test items is a creative process. Many items will be unsuitable for any number of reasons, chiefly that they do not contribute to measuring the characteristics. It takes a considerable amount of time and ingenuity to identify an appropriate range of test items for final use.
- **Step 3.** The final forms of the test are developed and the administration arrangements designed. Attempts to prevent 'faking' an answer are built into the test. As far back as 1956 William H Whyte was offering advice on 'How to cheat on personality tests', see Management in Action 3.3 on the previous page.
- **Step 4.** The 'standardization' and 'norming' process. The populations for whom the test is intended must be identified and statistically valid test scores collected for them. These are used to calculate the standard scores against which a particular individual will be compared. It provides the basis of comparison between an individual and others from that population.
- **Step 5.** At this stage, the data will be subjected to the various reliability and validity analyses described earlier. This is done in order to establish the credibility and value of the test.

At this point the test becomes available for use. However, it is not the end of the process. Norms for other populations may be developed if the test were found to be useful for other purposes or groups than those for which it was originally designed. Also the test could be subjected to criticism from other test designers, academics or users. Management in Action 3.4 illustrates the strength of the debate about the use and validity of psychometric tests for the measurement of personality.

Personality: the organizational perspective

The study of personality has tended to concentrate on providing mechanisms for describing the characteristics that separate individuals from each other. However, there is an interesting paradox involved in this process. The measurement process provides a basis of comparison for the individual against a group of others, a population. This very approach allows a subtle shift in emphasis in the organizational application of personality measurement away from the identification of individuality and towards the identification of appropriateness or suitability. The identification of individuals with characteristics that are acceptable to management.

Management in Action 3.4

Personality tests: the great debate

The debate about the value of personality tests has been going on for many years and is still far from being resolved. The basis for the use of such tests within organizations is quite simple. It is argued (by the supporters of tests) that there are in existence a number of personality characteristics that can be measured. Furthermore, certain personality characteristics are of value in the execution of particular jobs. Put simply, a sales job is assumed to require a high degree of extroversion. Therefore, if organizations can identify the personality requirements associated with particular jobs and then measure the existence of these same characteristics within job candidates a good match can be made. The result being higher individual and company performance. There are also indirect benefits possible in that training needs can be identified and individual work satisfaction could be improved through the analysis of test results.

The counter argument is that the results of test use do not match the predictions made in terms of increased organizational performance. In short they do not deliver high performance compared with organizations and individuals that do not use tests as the basis of decision making. It is argued that the normal experience of work for an individual is very complex and rich in terms of events and interaction with other people. Consequently, there are many other variables active in the dynamic achievement of performance than implied by a personality test.

Given that the value of tests is evaluated through the use of statistics the debate is frequently likened to the old saying about, 'lies, damned lies and statistics'. Without a sophisticated understanding of the use of statistical analysis and the implications of test design and evaluation an extreme view is likely to be taken towards test use. Most professional test designers would not claim to be providing the ultimate ability to understand individuals and make decisions about them. They would argue, as does D Mckenzie Davey, a chartered psychologist, that tests should be used in the same way that a physician would use data on blood counts. Temperature and pulse rate would be used along with observation in order to reach a diagnosis and before deciding on a treatment plan based on discussion with the patient.

The debate is perhaps a futile one in that not all aspects of work are personality based and intuitive methods of determining job opportunities are also limited in their ability to predict subsequent performance accurately. Perhaps both approaches are needed, but caution should be exercised in interpreting the results of tests, just as it should with the opinions of human beings about other human beings. Training in the use of tests and their interpretation is as necessary as it is in other areas of decision making and management.

Adapted from: Fletcher, C (1991) Personality tests: the great debate. Personnel Management, *September, pp 38–42.*

At one time personality tests were used for management positions and ability or aptitude tests were the preserve of manual jobs. This is now being questioned in some quarters. Some managers feel that the use of personality tests provides the opportunity to identify individuals who will 'fit' more effectively into the organization. In effect, these managers are arguing that they can achieve organizational objectives more easily if they can identify individuals with the 'approved' characteristics. Management in Action 3.5 overleaf provides a review of the appropriateness of personality and other tests for manual jobs.

The concept of personality can be utilized as part of the management process aimed at more effectively controlling the organization. Personality tests can be used for recruitment purposes, but they can also be used to provide a profile of the people already in the organization. This can be used in providing a basis

Management in Action 3.5

Put to the test down the line

Most tests are developed for white-collar, professional and managerial level jobs. Even if computerized, they tend to be of the paper and pencil type, requiring high levels of literacy and numeracy. However, for blue-collar jobs this approach might be inappropriate and not tap into appropriate characteristics and abilities. A worker on an assembly line needs a different range of skills to an office worker or manager. They are manipulators of tangible things rather than data, information or records. They make the goods that are sold by the company and so require the physical and mental characteristics that are appropriate to those activities rather than the personality and aptitude skills of the professional engineer or manager. The language barrier can be a major hurdle for ethnic minority groups and those people with a lower education level than required for most professional jobs.

Companies faced with recruitment decisions in the blue-collar areas are faced with a potential problem. They can either seek out the most appropriate existing test and hope for the best or they can commission the design of an appropriate test for their own circumstances. The first option carries with it the possibility of inappropriateness and the second the high development cost as well as the time delay in developing the test. However, with the high levels of unemployment over recent years the recruitment process has become difficult for many companies. It is not uncommon to find many thousands of applications for just a few jobs. A major sifting process which is effective becomes essential not just desirable. For example, when Toyota opened a new production unit in Derbyshire some

19,000 applications were received for about 950 jobs; when Motorola built a two-way radio and pager factory in Dublin it tested about 2000 people for about 150 jobs; Nissan opened a car factory in Sunderland and received about 11,500 applications for about 300 jobs, a later expansion involving a rolling programme of 1500 vacancies attracted some 32,000 applications.

Toyota commissioned the development of a specific test to identify the ability of potential recruits to work in the flexible assembly environment that they were creating. The test involved the individual going through a 90-minute procedure based on a video approach to learning a range of spurious tasks and then being tested on the ability to do the work described. By concentrating on practical skills this approach removed any possible bias in the results based on ability to understand the language used or from inappropriate characteristic identification.

Other companies such as Motorola in Dublin were more cautious about the use of tests but envisaged that there could be a role for them. Nissan used a variety of aptitude tests for mechanical, verbal and numerical comprehension and a practical skills test aimed at dexterity and hand–eye co-ordination. This was in addition to the usual interview and site visits as part of the selection process.

It has been suggested that the costs and time involved in developing new tests for blue-collar jobs is so high that there are many existing tests that might be applied as an alternative. However, the fairness and objectivity of the test for the particular circumstances should be the prime concern in taking such decisions.

Adapted from: Ring, T. (1992) Put to the test down the line. Personnel Today, 30 June, pp 21–4.

of control through access to promotion, development and related organizational 'rewards'. People with 'approved' characteristics, or prepared to develop them (assuming that is possible) will be the ones who find advancement within the organization. Thus management is able to achieve its objectives more easily as employees align themselves with the preferred behaviours.

Finding the child inside the manager

Trainers frequently claim that much of the training that they provide for managers is wasted because the classroom activity is not effectively transferred back to the workplace. They are constantly seeking ways to increase the level of impact of the training message and of improving the transfer of learning to the workplace. Abe Wagner, a psychologist from the USA, has attempted to find new ways of getting managers to improve their ability to communicate effectively by adapting the principles of transactional analysis.

Wagner claims that every adult is made up of six personality states:

(a) The natural child.
(b) The adult.
(c) The nurturing parent.
(d) The rebellious child.
(e) The compliant child.
(f) The critical parent.

He argues that the first three of these personality states are helpful in communicating and managing effectively. The second three are unhelpful in these respects and should be resisted personally and in others. He provides training for managers in how to make use of these ideas in their work.

The personality mode can be identified from the behaviour and verbal expressions of the individual. For example, an autopsy following the failure to clinch an important sale can often be a reflection of the critical parent mode. It concentrates on identifying the inadequacies in others involved in the process. Wagner suggests that the best way to deal with these situations is to articulate the thoughts about the situation and recognize which mode is dominant from them and then allow the adult mode to take over through a pep talk with oneself.

He also suggests that recognizing the dominant personality state in others allows effective response strategies to be developed. For example, imagine a subordinate in a rebellious child mode, with negative attitudes, being generally obstructive and working badly being the observed behaviour patterns. The worst approach to attempting to improve the behaviour and performance of that person would be to adopt the critical parent mode. The criticism of the behaviour and attitudes in the subordinate would be likely to reinforce their rebellious child personality state. Wagner recommends that the best way of encouraging appropriate personality modes in others is to adopt the adult or nurturing parent behaviour patterns oneself.

On occasions it could be more effective to adopt the same personality mode as another person in order to influence their behaviour. Wagner quotes the example of an employee playing a child by refusing to work on a Saturday. If the manager adopts a child perspective in response they might be able to appeal to emotions within the employee and persuade them to work. Being an adult and appealing to their sense of responsibility would not be likely to work.

Managers have a natural tendency to function, look and talk like parents, reinforced and encouraged by employees who perform in the child mode. This situation Wagner describes as leading to a co-dependency of personality modes between managers and workers. The training of managers usually emphasizes how to make changes involving others, ignoring the need to change the manager first. For this reason most training courses fail to deliver their intended objectives. Wagner argues that to be successful, managers should allow the natural child within them to come out and his training courses are designed to allow that to happen.

Adapted from: Kellaway, L (1993) Finding the child inside the manager. Financial Times, 7 April, p 12.

Another organizational effect of personality is the growth of an industry around the measurement of it. There are a considerable number of psychologists and consultancies that offer services to organizations based on the existence of personality and the measurement of it. Naturally, it is in the business interests of those practitioners to ensure that the opportunities for the application of personality is brought to management's attention. This includes the training of company staff to use and interpret particular instruments, the development of new tests and the application of the techniques in organizational activity. The difficulties that can arise from poorly trained individuals applying psycho-metric tests has long been recognized and has lead the British Psychological Society to introduce formal accreditation training. In addition the Institute of Personnel Management have introduced a Code Of Practice on Psychological Testing.

Personality: a management perspective

Managers are supposed to have particular personality characteristics in order to be successful; intelligence and initiative are often quoted as examples. In Management in Action 3.6 (on the previous page), one management trainer using ideas from *Gestalt psychology*, explains an attempt to influence how managers function. This includes the utilization of personality concepts.

Managers can also be affected by the application of personality testing through the development and promotion opportunities that they provide. Within an organizational setting the concept of personality is inseparable from the opportunities that it provides. It is not that the identification of personality is an interesting activity in its own right, but that it allows managers to take decisions about other people. However, it also allows managers to take decisions about other managers. It is a concept that serves a *gatekeeper* function. The idea that personality can be defined in terms of certain characteristics and that some of these characteristics are helpful to managers leads naturally to the conclusion that if the *right* characteristics can be identified then the *best* candidates can be selected. Consequently, who is selected as management material in the first place and how far they progress in the management hierarchy can be strongly tied to personality testing.

The process of testing allows managers to specify the characteristics that they consider as important in employees of the organization. It is therefore a process of *social engineering*. A model employee is identified and individual candidates measured against that particular standard. This could relegate into second place the ability to perform the job by the individual as the managers seek personality *fit* with their ideal employee. In an extreme situation this would allow managers to systematically manipulate the shape and form of the organization in terms of the people characteristics. This approach is taken to its logical conclusion in the view that recruitment should be based on 'organizational fit' not just the job requirements (Bowen *et al.*, 1996).

Change is a natural part of organizational life. This can include personnel changes, product changes, market changes, economic changes and legal changes. Among the consequences of change are the influences on the people employed. As the organization changes so do the jobs within it and the people performing those jobs. Part of this process influences the personality characteristics actually present (assuming that it is the people that are changing), and the characteristics valued and therefore sought by the organization.

There are a number of situations where the application of personality concepts could be of value within an organization. For example, there are obvious links between extroversion and jobs which require a high level of interpersonal activity, such as sales, hospitality and public relations. There are also links between aspects of personality and organizational objectives. For example, as managers seek to improve effectiveness through initiatives such as employee empowerment, there is a need to tap into different human attributes than if employees are simply regarded as a 'pair of hands'.

The selection and development of technical specialists and managers is another area where testing has been used as the basis of reflecting personality characteristics. Tests such as the Occupational Personality Questionnaire (the OPQ) have been developed by Saville and Holdsworth (a firm of occupational psychology consultants). It utilizes a series of 30 dimensions, or scales, to reflect the profile of an individual's personality. Examples from the OPQ questionnaire are shown as Table 3.2.

This particular test can be used in a number of ways including management selection and/or development. In selection terms it could be used as a means of providing a profile of an individual, which could then be used as the basis of a decision. The profile, or score of the individual on each of the 30 scales, would be compared against the *ideal* profile for the job for which they were being considered. The OPQ can also be used for determining a development programme for individuals. Based on the results of the test the individual would be offered advice and support in undertaking any training or development to change their work performance and/or career options. The test could also be used where jobs were expected to change significantly. The intention being to identify appropriate training needs for the individuals concerned or identify appropriate job moves.

As with all instruments that measure personality, the OPQ does not imply that it should be the only basis of a decision in relation to selection and development. Indeed, research by Blinkhorn and Johnson (1990) using three of the most widely used psychometric tests (including the OPQ) found little evidence of a long-term relationship between test results and performance at work. There are other factors to be taken into account, and there is no substitute for seeking a variety of information inputs to a decision.

Persuasive:	negotiates, enjoys selling, convincing with arguments	**Table 3.2**
Controlling:	takes charge, directs, manages, organizes	Examples from the Saville and
Competitive:	plays to win, determined to beat others, poor loser	Holdsworth Occupational
Decisive:	quick at conclusions, may be hasty, takes risks	Personality Questionnaire (OPQ)
Traditional:	prefers proven orthodox methods, conventional	
Practical:	down to earth, likes repairing and mending things	
Artistic:	appreciates culture, shows artistic flair	
Critical:	good at probing facts, sees disadvantages, challenges	

Management in Action 3.7

How to plan an assessment centre

Assessment centres are widely used as the basis of selection, promotion and career development decisions within organizations. They offer improved decision making as a result of the incorporation of a wider range of test and evaluation opportunities into the process, compared with reliance on a single measure such as an interview.

The basis of an assessment centre is that a small group of participants undertake a series of tests and exercises in order to allow the evaluation of their skills, competencies and general suitability for specific roles within the organization. They can also be used as the basis of career development planning through the possibility of identifying training needs and particular preferences for types of work. The evaluations of participants are made during the assessment centre by a number of specially trained staff. An assessment centre replicates a number of features of the organization and work, which allows informed judgements about the strengths and weaknesses of the participants to be made.

There are three main types of assessment centre used by organizations. They are graduate recruitment, job selection (usually managerial or technical specialist) and for internal or development purposes. Each is different and requires a specific design of assessment centre. For example, graduate recruitment would need to assume much lower levels of company knowledge and work experience than a centre designed for internal promotion purposes.

The key features in the design of an assessment centre are:

- Skills and competencies. It is necessary to begin with a clear idea of the important skills and competencies being sought. For example one organization assumed that sociability was a key quality required among sales personnel. Only later was it discovered that this was irrelevant and that independence and persistence were much more significant qualities in relation to success.
- Tests and techniques. Given that most assessments last about two days a variety of techniques and tests is common. They might include structured interviews, self-assessment questionnaires, psychometric tests, in-tray exercises, group discussion, group problem solving exercises, job simulation exercises and job-related role play.

- The assessment process. In designing an assessment centre there are three main elements to consider. Firstly, the qualities and competencies being sought and how they are to be measured. Secondly, the weighting to be applied to each element of the process. For example, should the psychometric tests be more highly rated in the overall result than the group discussion? Thirdly, the form of assessment used in order to ensure consistency of judgement between raters and the avoidance of discrimination or stereotyping of participants.
- Assessors. The selection of assessors can be difficult in that a mix of specific training and experience is often needed. Specialist training is required in the application and scoring of psychometric tests, for example. Line managers have the experience in work practicalities but might not have the ability to consistently rate individuals on group discussions. Generally a mix of assessors is used in a centre and training provided for them as necessary.
- Feedback. Decisions need to be made about the level and form of any feedback to participants. Clearly, the more participants the more difficult and costly in time and money it is to provide detailed feedback. However, delegates frequently appreciate some indication of their strengths and weaknesses. Clearly, if a development centre is being run then its whole purpose is to provide feedback to individuals on their future needs. There is always a difficult area in relation to the creation of management reports from assessment centres. Participants frequently feel uneasy at the thought of managers being provided with information about them, particularly if this is not released to the participant.
- Validation. Any assessment centre is only as good as its ability to contribute to the effectiveness of the people working within the organization. There is little point in undertaking lengthy and costly procedures if they add little to the quality and performance of staff. Consequently a process of monitoring and evaluating the assessment centre needs to be developed so that the impact on the business can be reviewed and corrective action taken as necessary.

Adapted from: Fowler, A (1992) How to plan an assessment centre. PM Plus, December, pp 21–4.

Assessment Centres were first used during World War II as a means of selecting officers for the military. Since then they have evolved to the point where many organizations use them for selection and development purposes. Centres are events that are made up of a range of different activities, requiring solo and group performance. Individuals are observed by assessors and scored on their performance on each activity. At the end of the process the scorers pool all the information gained from the activities and decide on the outcome. The justification for this assessment being that the tasks can be designed to reflect real work activity, performance is assessed in a live situation, multiple measures of personality and performance are obtained and the results are the combined effort of a number of trained assessors. Management in Action 3.7 provides an indication of assessment centres and how they could be designed.

Conclusions

The concept of personality is a difficult one for managers to deal with. It operates at many different levels within the organization and has a number of different theoretical roots along with many different measurement mechanisms (over 5000 are available). At a common-sense level personality is something that most people, including managers, would claim to recognize. It reflects how we get on with each other and features such as sociability, intelligence and so on. It is only when an attempt is made to be more precise in the definition of personality and its measurement, followed by establishing specific links with work activities, that the real difficulties emerge. The links between personality and particular jobs are an area where managers might be expected to show interest, but there is little by way of agreement about the precise nature of that relationship.

Discussion questions

1 Provide definitions for the following key concepts from this chapter:

Personality	Nature/nurture debate	Repertory grid
Psychoanalysis	Psychometrics	Ambiguous figure
Idiographic	Personality dimension	Rorschach test
Nomographic	Construct	Assessment centre

2 To what extent does personality explain individual differences between people?
3 Describe the genetic and environmental origins of personality. Which do you consider the most important to the development of adult personality? Why?
4 Would it be desirable for all the employees within an organization to have the same personality? Why, or why not?
5 Is it possible for two people to have the same personality? Justify your answer from the theories presented in this chapter.
6 In what ways might personality and perception be linked?
7 Can personality be measured accurately by any form of psychometric test? Why or why not?

8   It has often been suggested the Freudian theory tells us more about Freud than personality. Discuss.
9   Kelly's Personal Construct Theory provides a useful theory of personality. However, it is not practical to use the repertory grid technique in an organization as it is too complicated. Discuss.
10 'Any organization needs "different" people within it in order to optimize performance and effectiveness through the unique contribution of each individual.' Discuss.

Research activities

1   In the library, seek out 10 books and journal articles that discuss personality theory and/or its application to organizational activity. Include at least one article that reviews personality test results as a means of providing 'norms' against which to compare individual results. What do these views of personality contribute to your understanding of personality and its organizational value?
2   In a group of three people, each person write down a description of the personality of the other two. After you have done this compare notes. Are the two descriptions of the third person similar or different? Why? Each person should use an ambiguous drawing, to create a story. Are there any points of similarity between the way that an individual described the picture and the personality description provided by the two other people? Why, or why not?
3   Obtain a piece of A4 paper and fold it in half, lengthways. With a fountain pen, poster paint or something similar put five random 'blots' on one side of the paper. Fold the paper to create a mirror image of the 'blots'. Let it dry and then looking at it let your imagination create meaningful pictures from what you see. What might this tell you about your personality?

It is important to understand that you are not a trained psychologist, nor an expert in the field of personality. Therefore, the exercises described above are not to be taken seriously. They are intended to provide you with some experience of working with personality concepts. You are not able to offer professional or meaningful advice from them, neither should any information obtained be interpreted as providing a meaningful or accurate picture of any individual's personality.

Key reading

From Clark, H, Chandler, J and Barry, J (1994) *Organization and Identities: Text and Readings in Organizational Behaviour*, International Thomson Business Press, London:

■ Freud, S: The dissection of the psychical personality, p 71. This introduces the basis of Freud's approach to psychoanalysis.
■ Eysenck, HJ: The rat or the couch, p 82. Introduces the debate between behaviourism and psychology.
■ Mead, GH: The self, p 99. Introduces another perspective into the development of the human personality.
■ Merton, RK: Bureaucratic structure and personality, p 144. This examines the relationship between personality development and the need to work within an organizational framework.

References

- Whyte, WH: The organization man, p 149. This considers the implications for individuals of having to work within commercial organizations.
- Kanter, RM: Men and women of the corporation, p 152. This considers the process organizations use in 'moulding' individuals into a form which meets the requirements of management.

Further reading

Bartram, D (1992) The personality of UK managers: 16PF norms for short-listed applicants. *Journal of Occupational and Organizational Psychology*, 65, 159–72. This is a study which examines the 16PF test results of 1796 managers applying for jobs. From the analysis the 'norms' are developed, against which to compare individual manager's test results. As such it provides the basis for interpretation of the results for UK managers.

Cook, M (1988) *Personnel Selection And Productivity*, Wiley, Chichester. In concentrating on selection it has several chapters that are relevant to the subject of personality and psychometric tests.

Deary, IJ and Matthews, G (1993) Personality traits are alive and well. *The Psychologist*, July, 299–311. This review provides strong support for the view that traits provide a basis for predicting and explaining behaviour.

Heriot, P (ed) (1989) *Assessment and Selection In Organizations: Methods and Practice for Recruitment and Appraisal*, Wiley, Chichester. This text covers many aspects of the application of personality, tests and assessment centres.

Robertson, IT and Kinder, A (1993) Personality and job competencies: the criterion-related validity of some personality variables. *Journal of Occupational and Organizational Psychology*, 66, 225–44. This is a classic example of a research paper which examines the issue of the validity of psychometric tests.

Toplis, J, Dulewicz, V and Fletcher, C (1987) *Psychological Testing: A Practical Guide for Employers*, Institute of Personnel Management, London. As the title implies this is intended to provide guidance to employers on the nature and use of various forms of test.

Woodruff, (1992) *Assessment Centres; Identifying and Developing Competence*, Institute of Personnel Management, London. This is intended for the practitioner market, but does provide an excellent insight into the assessment centre process, as used in selection and development.

References

Allport, G (1937) *Personality: A Psychological Interpretation*, Holt, Rinehart and Winston, New York.

Blinkhorn, S and Johnson, C (1990) The insignificance of personality testing. *Nature*, 348, 671–2.

Bowen, DE, Ledford, GE and Nathan, BR (1996) Hiring for the organization, not the job. In *The Effective Manager: Perspectives and Illustrations* (ed Billsberry, J), Sage, London.

Bradshaw, P (1981) *The Management of Self-esteem*, Prentice-Hall, Englewood Cliffs, NJ.

Briggs-Myers, I (1987) *Introduction To Type*, Oxford Psychologists Press, Oxford.

Burger, JM (1986) *Personality: Theory and Research*, Wadsworth, Belmont, CA.

Cattell, RB (1965) *The Scientific Analysis of Personality*, Penguin, Harmondsworth.

Cattell, RB and Warburton, FW (1967) *Objective Personality and Motivation Tests*. University of Illinois Press, Urbana, IL.

Cox, CJ and Cooper, CL (1988) *High Flyers*, Basil Blackwell, Oxford.

Eysenck, HJ (1953) *Uses and Abuses of Psychology*, Penguin, Harmondsworth.

Eysenck, HJ (1959) *The Rorschach Test*, In *Fifth Mental Measurements Yearbook* (ed Buros, OK), Gryphon Press, New Jersey.

Eysenck, HJ (1965) *Fact and Fiction in Psychology*, Penguin, Harmondsworth.

Eysenck, HJ (1967) *The Biological Basis of Personality*, Thomas, Springfield, CT.

Eysenck, HJ (1971) *Readings in Extraversion and Intraversion*, Vols 1, 2 and 3. Staples Press, London.

Eysenck, HJ (1982) *Personality, Genetics and Behaviour*, Prager, New York.

Hall, CS and Lindzey, G (1970) *Theories of Personality*, Wiley, New York.

Holden, C (1987) Genes and behaviour: a twin legacy. *Psychology Today*. September, 18–19.

Jung, CG (1968) *Analytical Psychology: Its Theory and Practice*, Routledge and Kegan Paul, New York.

Kelly, G (1961) *The Abstraction of Human Processes. Proceedings of the 14th International Cognitive Psychological Conference*, Copenhagen, pp 220–9

Kline, P (1972) *Fact and Fantasy in Freudian Theory*, Methuen, London.

Mead, GH (1934) *Mind, Self and Society*, University of Chicago Press, Chicago, IL.

Murray, HA (1938) *Explorations in Personality*, Oxford University Press, New York.

Murray, HA (1943) *Thematic Apperception Test*, Harvard University Press.

Pervin, LA (1984) *Current Controversies and Issues in Personality*, 2nd edn, Wiley, New York.

Rabin, AI (1958) *Projective Methods: An Historical Introduction*, In *Projective Techniques in Personality Assessment* (ed Rabin, AI), Springer, New York.

Rogers, CR (1947) Some observations on the organization of personality. *American Psychologist*, **2**, 358–68.

Strachey, J (1953–66) *The Standard Edition of the Complete Psychological Works of Sigmund Freud*, Volumes 1–24, Hogarth Press/Institute of Psycho-analysis, London.

Whyte, WH (1956) *The Organization Man*, Simon & Schuster, New York.

4

Training and development

Chapter summary

This chapter begins with an introduction to the concepts of training and development. This is followed by a review of a number of learning theories that underpin much of the training activity within organizations. This leads naturally into a review of training and development from an organizational perspective. Following this will be a consideration of the application of the concepts within organizations from a management perspective.

browse this web site

www.itbp.com

Learning objectives

After studying this chapter and working through the associated Management in Action panels, discussion questions and research activites, you should be able to:

■ Outline and differentiate between the concepts of training, development and education.
■ Describe the major theoretical approaches to the study of learning.
■ Understand the concept of a learning organization.
■ Appreciate the links between training and development and individual difference.
■ Discuss the strategic perspective on training and development.
■ Detail the relevance of training and development for the management and other groups within an organization.
■ Assess the organizational implications of training and development.
■ Explain the benefits that can be obtained from the use of technology in training.

Introduction

Training and development are major activities within society as a whole, not just organizations. Children spend a considerable number of years in the formal school system and many go on to advanced academic or vocational training. Organizations are faced with trading and economic situations that require flexibility from existing workers and so find themselves in a position of having to constantly train and retrain employees in order to retain organizational viability. In some locations skill imbalances exist, with unfilled vacancies co-existing alongside high unemployment. In some countries or job sectors skill shortage and high employment levels co-exist and create high labour turnover as employees 'job-hop'. In this context training and development has an important role to play in helping employers retain staff who might otherwise leave. The opportunity for personal and professional development are important 'weapons' in management's attempt to attract and retain good staff, as well as the means of enhancing organizational performance.

Training and development

The terms training and development are often used as if they were inter-changeable. Education is another term that has a strong association with train-ing and development. *The Oxford Dictionary* defines these three concepts in the following way:

■ Develop. To unfold more fully, to bring out all that is potentially contained within.
■ Educate. To bring up so as to form habits, manners, intellectual and physi-cal aptitudes.
■ Train. To instruct and discipline in or for some particular art, profession, occupation or practice; to make proficient by such instruction and practice.

From these definitions the obvious similarities and differences between the concepts and their application to an organizational setting become apparent. The concept of *education* would seem to be a general process representing the basic preparation for adult life in a specific environment. In an organizational setting, this would equate with the *socialization* or *induction* process for new employees to a company. Examples of which would include meeting appropri-ate managers and colleagues, and learning about the basic rules, procedures and product range of the company.

Training is a job-specific form of education. It can either be organization-specific or general. For example, a company would train its staff for the particular word processing package that it used. This training would be specif-ic to that particular organization, but could also be transferable to other com-panies if they use the same package. In December 1993 a national initiative by the then UK government attempted to place work-based training on a par with academic qualifications in order to enhance its value, transferability and perceived significance (Wood, 1993).

Development is a less specific activity which relates to potential. Development is about the future. It does not necessarily relate to the job that an individual presently undertakes. It could be a set of experiences that provide the individual with a basis for future career moves. It could also be used to enhance the skill lev-els of an individual in anticipation of future change in the nature of work or prod-ucts. For example, the planned introduction of high technology equipment is frequently preceded by introductory courses for those affected. The content might deal with computers in general and specifically the equipment being considered, together with applications and familiarization with keyboards and screens. Devel-opment as an activity has traditionally been reserved for managers. However, it is being increasingly used to describe the full range of training and development activity. The argument being that it is a less restrictive term than training, does not preclude the use of training activities within its sphere of influence and is more easily associated with the concepts of individual and organizational growth. This approach is often associated with the notion of Human Resource Development, in which individual, career and organizational development are brought together as an integrated approach to mutual benefit (Beardwell and Holden, 1997).

Training and learning

Each of the terms education, training and development assume that some form of *learning* takes place within the individual. In other words, the individual is affected in some way or other as a result of the process. Learning can be defined as the relatively permanent change in behaviour or potential behaviour that results from direct or indirect experience (Hulse *et al.*, 1980). The major elements in this definition are:

- Learning implies change. The acquisition of a new skill suggests that the individual will be different by comparison with 'before'. For example, if an employee learns a new skill, that person can undertake a different range of tasks. The difference becomes more difficult to detect, however, when the learning is cognitive in nature. For example, how will you be changed as a result of reading this chapter? You will have increased your level of understanding in the organizational behaviour field. In that sense *you* will have changed. But such *changes* might not be detectable as behaviour.
- Learning implies sustained change. The definition of learning suggested above implies a long-lasting change consequence. Conversely, anything that produces a short-term effect is not true learning. So, for example, a student that *learns* the appropriate material for an exam and then puts it from memory has not *learned* anything.
- Learning influences behaviour. In some instances this is comparatively easy to see. For example, acquiring the skill of being able to drive a car. In other cases, the individual is learning to influence future behaviour. Your course in organizational behaviour is partly intended to introduce you to the behavioural aspect of management and consequently to influence your future management style and decision-making abilities.
- Learning results from experience. Some form of direct experience is necessary in order to produce learning. In the case of learning to drive a car, it is necessary at some point to actually get behind the steering wheel and drive on public roads. Indirect experience leads to vicarious learning. For example, an employee cheating on their time sheet and so earning more bonus will frequently be following the example of other employees.

The learning process is outlined in Figure 4.1. This indicates the relationship between the learning event itself and the purpose to which it is being put.

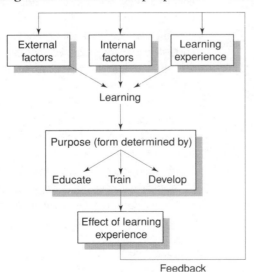

Figure 4.1 The learning process.

Also indicated in the model are those elements that precede learning, but which influence it:

■ External factors. For example, the pressure placed on individuals to undergo *learning*. Children must by law be educated in an approved manner.
■ Internal factors. For example, mood, intelligence, ability, personality and motivation all influence the *learning* process.
■ Learning experience. A poorly designed learning event may result in the trainees not *learning* that which they were intended to learn.

Management in Action 4.1 provides an insight into some of the links between success and how to acquire (or learn) it.

The process by which people learn has long been an area of interest in psychology. There are three main approaches that have emerged over time, each one adding to the understanding of the process by building on top of the earlier approaches and accounting for different learning experiences. The three approaches are:

■ Behaviourist theories.
■ Cognitive theories.
■ Social-learning theories.

Management in Action 4.1

Take it from the top

The Performance Group, a Norwegian management consultancy, spent two years talking to 40 'world class performers' in order to tease out the secrets of success at the top. They included a Brazilian archbishop, a French chef, an Australian marathon runner, a Russian conductor, the manager of the Los Angeles Dodgers and the chief of an American Indian tribe. The researchers claim that the results identified that all high performers have a number of characteristics in common and that how to succeed can be learned by anyone.

The common characteristics among the top performers interviewed included:

■ A sense of compelling purpose.
■ A greed for knowledge.
■ The ability to learn from their mistakes.
■ The ability to learn from others.
■ Strong powers of concentration.
■ Strong personal discipline.
■ A high level of intensity in what they were doing.

■ Most had integrity.
■ A recognition of the need to motivate others.
■ A recognition of the value of relaxation.
■ A recognition of delegation.
■ A competitive streak.

The Performance Group argue that each one of these characteristics can be learned and used to enhance the performance of both the individual and the organization that they work for. However, some of the interviewees suggested that they believed that some of their success was due to inborn gifts. For example, Valery Gergiev suggested that the key feature was the abilities that each individual was born with, that could subsequently be developed by training and experience. Many of the interviewees indicated that their fathers were the most important influence in their lives, mothers were hardly mentioned. Some even inherited their position from their fathers. So perhaps success at the top is not just a question of learning the key qualities after all.

Adapted from: Kellaway, L (1993) Take it from the top. Financial Times Weekend, *23/24 October, p 9.*

Later in this chapter the concepts of a *learning organization* and *strategic training and development* will be briefly introduced as relevant to how people (and organizations) learn through the experience of training.

Behaviourist theories of learning

The behaviourist school of psychology has enjoyed a long and illustrious tradition. The two best-known names from this field of psychology are Pavlov, who developed the theory of classical conditioning, and Skinner, who developed the theory of instrumental conditioning.

Pavlov and classical conditioning

Pavlov worked in Russia and his research was concerned with the learning experienced by dogs in relation to their natural reflexes. Pavlov noticed that whenever his laboratory dogs were given food they salivated (1927). This was a natural reaction in the dogs, to which he gave the term an *unconditioned response*. This became the first step in the process. The second step was to link the *unconditioned stimulus* (the food) with a *conditioned stimulus* (Pavlov used a bell). This was done by ringing the bell when the food was presented. Eventually, the dogs would salivate when the bell was rung. This was the third step, the *conditioned response*. A direct link between the stimulus and the response had been made. This series of steps can be shown as a diagram (see Figure 4.2). In the *classical conditioning* model, the salivation was conditioned to occur as a result of the previously established link between the bell and the food.

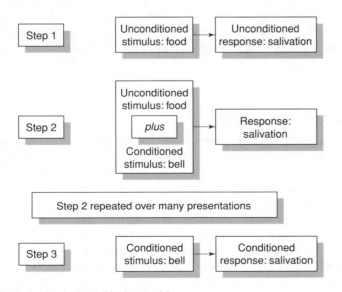

Figure 4.2   Pavlov's classical conditioning model.

This conditioned response is a relatively simple reaction when compared with the behaviour of humans, particularly in a social setting. The theory was able to explain some of the simpler forms of learning but the conditioned response quickly died away if it was not frequently reinforced. This feature was referred to as an *extinction response*. Pavlov was able to make his experimental dogs respond to a wide range of bell related variables.

Assessment of the theory

The work of Pavlov was running in parallel, although independently, with a number of American theorists. They included Watson, who coined the term *behaviourism* to describe the emphasis on observable behaviour rather than the introspective analytical approaches common in psychology at that time. Watson believed that learning in the environment was responsible for almost all development, ability and personality in the growing child. He introduced into the field of behaviourism the concept of stimulus–response associations (*conditioning*) as the basis of human behaviour (Watson, 1924).

Thorndike built on the stimulus–response model through his studies of the ability of cats to escape from puzzle boxes (1932). From these observations he concluded that the cats could learn by *trial and error* (slow learning). Thorndike suggested that what was happening was a slow strengthening of the stimulus–response connection through a number of repetitions of the cat being placed in the puzzle box, being allowed to escape and receiving a food reward immediately afterwards. The reinforcement offered by the food made it more likely that the cat would repeat the same behaviour next time it was placed in the puzzle box.

With the linking of the early behaviourists and Pavlov's classical conditioning the groundwork had been established to allow the introduction of this approach to more complex forms of learned behaviour. The behaviour so far described was at the unlearned reflex level, rather than the conscious purposeful forms seen in much human activity. It is good at explaining the simple cause and effect relationship in some activities. However, it is difficult to explain the wide variety of observed behaviour, particularly when it involves complex learning. Pavlov showed that there was the likelihood of some behaviours being repeated if the stimulus–response connection was adequately reinforced. But the classical model does not allow for choice in response options.

Skinner and instrumental conditioning

Skinner is associated with the *instrumental* approach, but he was not the first person to be associated with it. Instrumental in this context refers to behaviour being 'instrumental' in producing an effect. For example, a hungry rat can be conditioned to press a lever to obtain food. Pressing the lever (behaviour) releases the food and allows feeding (the effect).

Skinner put forward a distinction between two types of behaviour, *respondent* and *operant* (1953). *Respondent* behaviour was said to be under the direct control of a stimulus. This was the stimulus–response relationship in classical conditioning. For example, salivation in response to food presentation. *Operant* behaviour was seen in terms of spontaneity, with no direct or obvious cause. A stimulus controlling operant behaviour is referred to as a

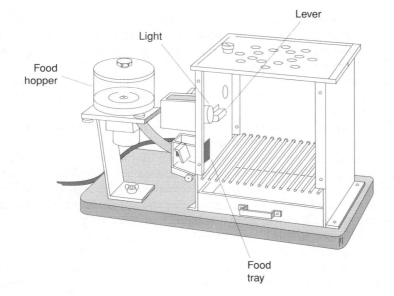

Figure 4.3 A skinner box.

discriminative stimulus. An example would be the knocking on your front door, which tells you that someone is trying to see you for some purpose, but does not force you to answer the door. It might be hard to ignore the knocking, but you can choose to do so. In this way the concept is synonymous with the term instrumental in that the behaviour is instrumental in producing an effect. It is for the same reason that the term *instrumental conditioning* is used.

The best-known experiments in this area involve laboratory rats being placed in a *Skinner box*, named after the designer. There are many variations of this type of experiment and so only a simple generalized account will be provided here. Imagine a small cage, bare except for a feeding tray, a lever and a light source. Figure 4.3 is a schematic diagram of such a Skinner box.

A hungry rat is placed in the box and left to explore its new surroundings under the watchful eye of the experimenter. As the rat approaches the lever in the box a pellet of food will be made available in the food tray. After a few repetitions of this, the rat may touch the lever and again food will be made available. From then on, only touching the lever will produce a food pellet. Eventually this is replaced and the actual pressing of the lever is required in order to obtain food. The lever pressing is being reinforced by the presentation of food. There are an enormous range of variations that can be introduced to this basic process, and it has been used on a wide range of animals. Pigeons have been taught to 'recognize' colours and play table tennis, whales and dolphins trained for wildlife shows and dolphins trained to plant mines on enemy ships in a military context.

The process of reinforcement is used to *shape* the behaviour pattern desired. Once established, it is not necessary to reinforce every occurrence of the behaviour in order to maintain it. There are four variations to reinforcement schedules that can influence repetition of the desired behaviour. They are:

■ Fixed ratio. Reinforcement takes place after a fixed number of repetitions of a particular activity. For example, one pellet of food every 20 lever presses. This tends to produce a rapid and consistent rate of response in order to maximize the reward.

■ Variable ratio. This provides reinforcement after a number of repetitions of the desired behaviour. However, unlike the fixed ratio, this time the number of repetitions required to produce the reward is randomly varied. This produces a rapid rate of response as the animal has no way of predicting which produces the pellet of food.

■ Fixed interval. This approach produces a reinforcement after the first appropriate behaviour following a set time interval. The behaviour pattern under this regime almost stops after a reward until the next time interval is due, when it starts again. This suggests that the animal is able to judge time and work out the schedule that it is being conditioned to.

■ Variable interval. In this approach the time interval is randomly varied between upper and lower parameters. Under these conditions, the animal responds with a steady rate of lever pressing. This would be expected as there is no way for the animal to know which lever press will activate the food delivery.

It is the partial reinforcement schedules that produce the most sustained and rapid response rates and are therefore the most effective in maintaining the desired behaviour. In one experiment a pigeon was reinforced on average once every five minutes. That equates 12 times in every hour. Yet it sustained a pecking rate of approximately 6000 per hour.

So far in the discussion we have described only *positive reinforcement*. That is, the subject being rewarded for doing something. There are also:

■ Negative reinforcers. This refer to an unpleasant event that precedes behaviour and which is removed when the subject produces appropriate behaviour.

■ Omission. This refers to the stopping of reinforcement. Naturally, it leads to a reduction and eventually the extinction of the particular behaviour.

■ Punishment. This relates to an unpleasant reward for particular behaviours. The slap on the leg of a child who does something wrong would be an example. Negative reinforcement and punishment decrease the occurrence of the behaviour in question.

The relationship between these four forms of reinforcement can be shown in a diagram (see Figure 4.4).

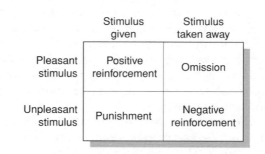

Figure 4.4   Reinforcement framework.

Many experiments have been carried out on human conditioning. For example, Verplanck (1955) carried out a reinforcement exercise during an informal conversation with a student. The student was not aware of the reinforcement process being carried out. It is worth noting that in this form such experimentation would not meet the ethical standards required today. The reinforcement schedule required the experimenter to reward all statements of opinion made by the student. These included phrases such as, 'I believe', 'It is my opinion', 'I think', when used by the student within the conversation. The reinforcement was in the form of positive feedback to the student through the experimenter using phrases such as, 'I agree', 'You are right', 'That is so'. The use of verbal reinforcement increased the number of statements of opinion used by the student. In another part of the same experiment, extinction was also demonstrated. This was achieved by the experimenter failing to reinforce any statement of opinion by remaining silent when one occurred. Not surprisingly, the use of these statements by the student reduced under this regime.

Assessment of the theory

The process of instrumental conditioning has a wider application than the classical approach. It provides for the shaping of behaviour into particular patterns. It has also been used to account for many of the beliefs and superstitions that pervade human life. Examples include blowing on the dice to make them lucky; putting on a particular item of clothing before an exam in order to guarantee success; and never watching a favourite football team live on television to improve their chance of success. That instrumental conditioning can explain much of human behaviour has been established over many years. The difficulty arises in being able to explain how reinforcement operates in the every day exposure of multiple and random experience. The experiment described above might explain how one lecturer can influence the behaviour of one student. But is it enough to explain how a teacher can shape the behaviour of a large class?

If reinforcement is delayed then it may become associated with other behaviour by default. For example, a profit-share scheme that rewards employees with a bonus for higher company profits would be paid after the financial year end of the company. However, the 'behaviour' of the employees in increasing productivity would have covered a full year, beginning perhaps 15 months before the payment is received. Such indirect links between behaviour and reward stretch the conditioning principle beyond credibility. Under such circumstances it is more likely that employees will interpret such payments as a random event by an arbitrary management selecting a level of payment that under-represents their true effort over the year.

The *conditioning* approach to learning cannot explain all the thought and behaviour patterns observed in people. Individuals have objectives and purpose behind many of their behaviours which do not easily fit into a conditioned model. However, *instrumental conditioning* does have a place in the management of people as Management in Action 4.2 implies. This case illustrates the complexity in the real world and how instrumental conditioning can be used to influence behaviour.

In this particular case, it is apparent that the reinforcement process was mixed in with many other aspects of the job. The management issues, the need to work within set procedures and guidelines and the opportunity for

Management in Action 4.2

The domestic supervisor and conditioning

The Domestic Supervisor in a university hall of residence had been appointed to the job following the retirement of the previous incumbent. The previous job holder had held the job for approximately 10 years. With the change in personnel, management had decided to restructure the duties of the post and take the opportunity to increase the level of direct supervision of the domestic staff working in the hall. At the same time the job title was changed from Housekeeper to Domestic Supervisor. Previously, direct supervision of the domestic staff had fallen under the responsibilities of a Supervisor who looked after two halls specifically for these activities.

The new Domestic Supervisor described how she was initially concerned about how to approach the job to ensure that she obtained a positive response from the staff. It was necessary to increase the level of direct supervision of the staff, which inevitably meant increased levels of work inspection. Given that the staff had all been in the same jobs for many years and worked under a different regime, this could become a problem.

The new Domestic Supervisor had held supervisory jobs previously and at one time ran her own business. Calling on this wealth of experience she decided on the following course of action. The first stage was to let the existing staff get to know her and that 'things' would inevitably change. This involved several actions, including the provision of a bag of sweets on the desk from which all could help themselves, 'for a bit of energy to start the day'; frequent visits to each worksite to get to know the job and meet the staff on their own territory; only gradually over the period of a couple of weeks to begin to offer advice and suggestions on what needed to be done. This was usually done in terms of, 'Would it not be easier to try it this way?' or 'Why not do this job when you

have finished that one?' The 'suggestion' would only become more like an instruction if the individual would not enter into the spirit of the process and 'did not take the hint'.

This approach began to create a team in which the individual employee did not feel threatened. This was important as a number of them had applied for the Domestic Supervisor's job when it was advertised and felt some resentment at being rejected. They began by resisting the approach. Not in a serious way, but by finding excuses for not doing things that the Domestic Supervisor wanted doing, or doing them in the old way. This required the most tact on the part of the Domestic Supervisor as she attempted to change the behaviour patterns of the staff. The approach adopted was to keep a 'light touch' in the way that issues were raised. Making a joke or a light-hearted comment about something. For example, it was pointed out to the staff, whilst laughing, that they should clean the light fittings on their way to their longer than strictly allowed tea break as they had said that they did not have time to do this job. The point was made in such a way that could not be seen as a direct order, given in an offensive manner. But it was a clear signal of what was expected and the possible next step and penalty if it was not implemented. This was followed by frequent and obvious checks on that particular job, with comment on the result. Praise if it had been done, a jocular, 'Not had time to do these yet?' if they had not.

This reflects the application of instrumental conditioning in shaping the behaviour of the employees. This was not done deliberately by the Domestic Supervisor, It was, however, described as common sense in achieving the objectives necessary without causing problems. The staff are apparently unaware that their behaviour had been shaped. They considered that they have gone through a period of 'getting used to working with a new boss'.

managers to use some discretion when interpreting the policies in an operational setting are all incorporated. The approach adopted in Management in Action 4.2 is an informal version of what has become known as *behavioural modification*. The basis of the approach being that managers should seek ways of maximizing appropriate behaviours among employees. Figure 4.5 is a representation of the behavioural modification process.

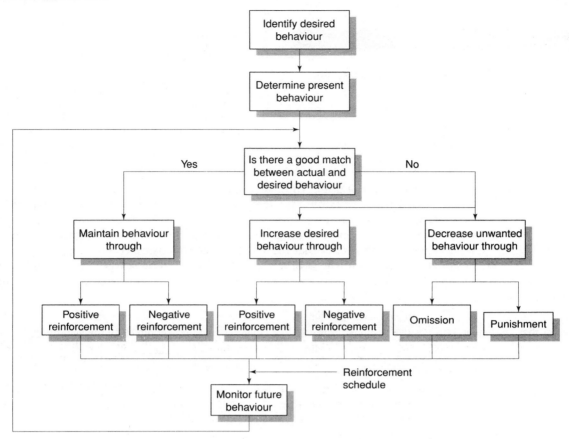

Figure 4.5 Behavioural modification (adapted with permission from: Lunthans, F (1985) *Organizational behaviour*, 4th edn, McGraw-Hill, New York).

The model is self-explanatory in that it begins with a systematic review of the requirements and actuality of behaviour in the situation. This is then followed by a selection process which results in the identification of the appropriate reinforcement approach. Once selected and operational, the results should be monitored and any remedial or follow-up action taken.

Cognitive approaches

The basis of cognitive theories of learning are that an individual develops internal frameworks that allow them to more effectively interact with the environment around them. This approach creates the need to study the internal working of the mental processes involved in learning.

The early work in this field was carried out on animals and was based on the behavioural model. Kohler describes an experiment in which a chimpanzee demonstrated insight as a learning process (1925). Sultan (the name of the chimpanzee) was placed in a cage and given a short stick. A piece of fruit was placed outside the cage and beyond the range of the short stick. A longer stick was also placed outside the cage, but within range of the short stick. After a few

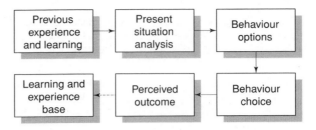

Figure 4.6   A cognitive model of learning.

attempts at obtaining the fruit by using the short stick, Sultan began to seek other ways of obtaining the fruit. After a number of false starts, he paused for a lengthy period and just looked around him. Suddenly, he jumped up, used the short stick to pull the long stick into range and thereby obtain the fruit. This suggested to Kohler that the chimpanzee was using cognitive processes to create insights into the problem and how it could be solved. This would seem to differ from trial and error learning in that a sudden insight is apparent in the achievement of a solution.

This led to a number of other approaches to the development of cognitive learning. Essentially, this approach assumes that people are actively involved in the process of learning. They are not simply at the mercy of outside forces and internal drives. A simplified way of thinking about this cognitive approach is shown in Figure 4.6.

A more recent approach to the cognitive perspective on learning is based on information processing as a psychological process. According to Fitts and Posner (1967) the three primary characteristics of skilled performance are:

- Organization.
- Goal directedness.
- Utilization of feedback.

The process of providing feedback enables the individual to more effectively achieve the goal being sought. There are many obvious examples of feedback in action. Central heating systems function through feedback, based on the thermostat. The most easily understood form is negative feedback. Negative feedback allows the system being controlled to remain on target (see Figure 4.7).

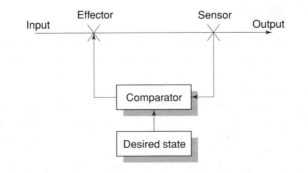

Figure 4.7   Negative feedback.

Essentially, negative feedback reduces the gap between the current and intended situations. So, in a central heating system, the feedback process measures the actual room temperature, compares it with the desired temperature and switches the boiler on if the room is too cold. In an organizational setting a manager will usually receive monthly financial reports setting out expenditure against budget (feedback). If the manager is spending more money than is allowed for under the budget, they are then able to seek ways of reducing future expenditure in order to ensure that the costs match those planned.

Feedback can originate either from within the individual, or from the environment around the individual. Feedback can also arrive at the same time as the originating event, for example, the room thermostat constantly responding to the temperature. It can also be delayed, as in the case of the financial information that is published after the end of the reporting period. Delayed feedback is of no value in maintaining current performance, but can be of value in influencing future behaviour. By the time the financial reports reach a manager the money is spent, nothing can change that situation. However, the manager can adjust spending in future financial periods.

Feedback, as described, is a useful means of controlling activity in the dynamic world in which we live. However, it is rare in behaviour that a simple chain of events is the major determinant of activity. Take, for example, driving a car. This involves a co-ordinated set of feedback loops (steering, accelerating, changing gear, visually searching the road around the car, and so on) arranged into a framework which allows a priority to be given to particular behaviours. For example, braking at one moment, accelerating at another. This reflects the hierarchical notion of response habits within the stimulus–response model. One way that the concept of feedback has been combined with the hierarchical notion of response habits is in the application of a *TOTE* unit.

TOTE refers to a Test, Operate, Test, Exit sequence and was first described by Miller *et al*. (1960). The *TOTE* model is shown as Figure 4.8. In essence the test phase of the model reflects the feedback loop in that if a mismatch between plan and goal is detected then the operate phase is activated. This sequence is repeated until a match between actual and goal is identified, when the cycle ends and that particular behaviour ends.

The benefit of the *TOTE* unit is that it can be used to describe a series of hierarchically organized behaviour sequences. The example used by Miller is hammering a nail into a piece of wood. One phase is the identification of the position of the nail, the goal being to have it flush with the surface of the wood.

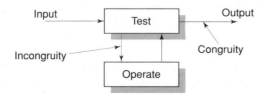

Figure 4.8 Tote unit (after Miller, GA, Galanter, E and Pribram, KH (1960) *Plans and the Structure of Behaviour*. Holt, Rinehart & Winston, New York, Fig. 1).

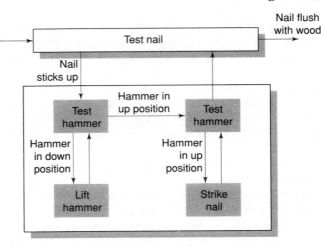

Nail flush
with wood

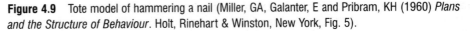

Figure 4.9   Tote model of hammering a nail (Miller, GA, Galanter, E and Pribram, KH (1960) *Plans and the Structure of Behaviour*. Holt, Rinehart & Winston, New York, Fig. 5).

The second phase is the hammer position (lifting or striking). The process of hammering the nail then, consists of a *TOTE* model that looks like Figure 4.9.

In describing this process Miller *et al*. (1960) say, 'If this description of hammering is correct, we should expect to see the sequence of events to run off in this order: test nail. (Head sticks up) test hammer. (Hammer is down) lift hammer. Test hammer. (Hammer is up) test hammer. (Hammer is up) strike nail. Test hammer. (Hammer is down) test nail. (Head sticks up) test hammer. And so on, until the test of the nail reveals that its head is flush. Thus the compound of TOTE units unravels itself simply enough into a co-ordinated sequence of tests and actions, although the underlying structure that organizes and co-ordinates the behaviour is itself hierarchical, not sequential.'

The TOTE unit so described is made up of sub-units. But the hammering of a nail into a piece of wood may in itself be part of a much larger set of goals. For example, the particular nail might be part of a tree house for a child, or it may be part of the construction of a house for a family. As such the person doing the hammering may be an employee and have as a goal the need to earn bonus in order to pay for a summer holiday, or it may be a manager checking that the employees have done their job correctly.

Assessment of the theory

The notion of cognitive learning based on *feedback* is central to learning. Take, for example, attempting to learn all the subject matter from your course without any *feedback* from lecturers before your final exams. The process of linking feedback into a dynamic hierarchical framework provides an important framework for understanding how learning fits into a cognitive based model. It is also vital for the practice of human resource management within organizations. For example, appraisal systems rely on the provision of feedback on individual performance as a means of identifying training needs, development and career opportunities, as well as salary or bonus levels. Handled well, feedback can be of significant mutual benefit to the individual and organization. Handled badly, or not undertaken at all, it can lead to people not doing those things which need to be done, personal under-achievement and organizational failure.

Social learning approach

The social environment within which learning takes place is a major influence on the process. Infants are *socialized* into a family unit, young people are *socialized* into various social groups. Often the first lecture in a course is designed as an introduction, the purpose being to 'get you onto the same wavelength' as the lecturer. The process of *socialization* becomes apparent when we encounter a different culture and become aware of the differences compared with our own experiences. In organizations, the process of *socialization* is frequently referred to as an induction process, the main intention being to ensure that new employees rapidly become more effective.

This process of *socialization* can also be regarded as a programmed period of experience. Social learning attempts to embrace this idea and deveop a theoretical base from it. Perhaps the best known exponent of this approach is Kolb (1985). He proposed a *learning cycle* as the basis of learning.

Kolb views the learning process as a circular and perpetual in that the output of one cycle (experimentation) creates the experience that begins the cycle over again. Looking briefly at each stage of the model:

- Concrete experience. This can either be of a planned or unplanned nature. This refers to an experience of some description. In organizational terms this could be experiencing praise from a manager for a job well done.
- Reflective observation. This stage relates to the cognitive process of thinking about the experience, the cause of the experience along with the implications of it.
- Abstract conceptualization and generalization. This stage is about the conclusions that emerge from the review process. Issues including the identification of when it may happen again and under what circumstances, and so on.
- Experimentation in new situations. For example, transferring the experience to other job situations. In effect, this becomes the basis of new experiences to begin the cycle all over again.

This model has many implications for training and development activities within organizations. For example, for the learning process is to be fully effective each of the four stages needs to be provided in the programme. Individuals need to have the opportunity to reflect and generalize about the experience if they are to be able to make full use of the learning points. If this is not done adequately then the transfer of learning to the real world of work will not happen and much of the potential is lost. For example, learning to drive only on one street would not prepare an individual for regular city and motorway driving. This model also paves the way for structured 'on-the-job' learning. Through discussion, coaching and mentoring based on the model individuals can be encouraged to identify learning and development opportunities in everyday work activity.

Assessment of the theory

Social learning is a process which emphasizes the individual in the learning process. In this model, learning is not possible without the active involvement of the individual in reflecting and concluding about the experiences encountered. It places the responsibility for learning on the ability of the individual to establish links between behaviour and experience through evaluation. External forces can only facilitate and encourage the process through provision of experience and encouragement of reflection. This implies that those individuals who are more willing or able to develop this strategy will actively seek out developmental opportunities and therefore become the more highly skilled employees. The differential access to self-development opportunities provided by some jobs also influences the process.

The concept of *continuous development* implied by social learning has been utilized as a major theme within individual and organizational development. For example, the need to foster an organizational culture which values continuous development has been identified as significant to its success. Wood *et al*. (1990) suggest a five-stage process of continuous development:

■ Integration of learning and work. The use of continuous development as a mechanism of incremental work improvement.
■ Self-directed learning. The identification by the individual of their own development needs.
■ Emphasis on process rather than techniques. The acquisition of what can be referred to as generalized skills rather than specific task oriented skills. In other words, to develop understanding and commitment.
■ Continuous development as an attitude. This reflects the approach to learning through the development of appropriate attitudes to reflection and experience rather than technique acquisition.
■ Continuous development for organizations as well as individuals. The objective of continuous development is to achieve organizational objectives through the recognition of the links between learning and performance. As individuals develop, so do the organizations.

These approaches tend to provide a model of learning that, although strongly tied to the social setting within which the individual functions, are isolationist in practice. Learning as a process is a very personal affair. It is the individual that reflects and develops as a consequence of the experience. However, individuals are invariably in an interactive relationship with other people and their environment and learning is also influenced by those variables, a point made by Stuart (1986).

Training

Most training is based around the notion of the *learning curve*. It reflects the idea that performance is a function of time and experience, in other words, practice makes perfect. The curve in Figure 4.10 is a very much simplified one and should be considered as an *ideal type*. In practice, the effectiveness of the training will influence the rate of increase, as will the ability of the trainees along with situational and emotional factors. Some skills require substantial periods of reinforce-

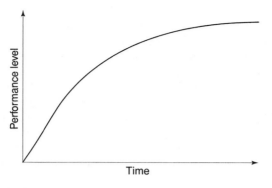

Figure 4.10 The learning curve.

ment or practice before any increase in performance can be made. In other cases, performance improvement is categorized by a series of jumps and plateaux.

The training process

There are many forms of training used within organizations. They should be used on the basis of meeting an identified need. *Training needs* can be identified from a number of sources. For example, a performance appraisal, the existence of low productivity or quality, the introduction of new products or technology, the carrying out of a formal skills audit. What these all have in common is a gap or difference between what is expected and what currently exists. Once the gap has been identified, then appropriate mechanisms can be designed to meet the need. Training programmes should be planned around the following issues:

- Training objectives. The objectives should provide a target for measuring performance. An example might be, 'On completion of the course the trainee will be able to type at 75 words per minute, with no more than 1% error rate'.
- Training content. The content will have been determined by previous analysis.
- Duration. The length of the training programme will be determined by the range of material to be covered and the amount of practice required.

Training methods

These include:

A Demonstration. This refers to being shown how to do something and then allowed to get on with it. It is a commonly used approach, but relatively inefficient as it does not provide structure or feedback to effectively improve performance.

B Coaching. This provides an interactive, encouragement based approach to training. Consider the coaching process for a sports team as an example. It includes practice, feedback, reflection, structure and motivational perspectives.

C Discovery training. This assumes that people learn more effectively if they discover 'it' for themselves. Consequently, it aims to provide this through an experiential environment. It needs very careful planning so that the 'right' learning is acquired. Managers are frequently exposed to discovery learning.

They are put into situations and expected to sink-or-swim, developing solutions to problems as they go.

D   Job rotation, secondments and special assignments. These provide for training by systematically moving people between jobs, activities or projects in order to give them experience. These may be permanent changes or of limited duration. Whilst this may provide employees with additional skills, together with a broader experience of the context around the work, it can lower productivity as extensive learning occurs. Also, if employees do not then get the opportunity to practice the full range of skills acquired, there is little practical benefit to either the organization or the individual.

E   Action learning. Typically a team would be established and expected to solve a specific problem perhaps with the help of an external facilitator. Several masters degrees are based upon these principles. Students are expected to work in groups on research topics and problem solving issues (often within their own organizations) and then submit a dissertation on the process and the learning achieved through it.

F   Job instruction. This is the systematic application of learning theory to skill acquisition. It involves setting objectives and by demonstration, coaching, practice and feedback allowing trainees to become skilful in the task.

G   Lecture. The process of delivering information with little or no direct involvement from the audience.

H   Talks and discussion. Informal lectures with higher participation levels and for smaller groups.

I   Case studies. The use of predetermined situations to provide opportunities for analysis and presentation of solutions without the risk of failure inherent in 'live' situations.

J   Role play and simulation. These allow the participants to act out situations as if they were real. Much of the basic training for police officers is based on role play, reflecting situations that they will encounter. Pilots spend a considerable amount of time in flight simulators in order to gain flying experience in a safe environment.

K   Computer-based and programmed learning. For example, learning to type on a computer with a typing programme built into it. The computer provides the instruction and tests ability before moving on to more difficult skills. Interactive video can also be used to provide film quality graphics approach to the training programme. An example would be a bank training its staff in customer care and dealing with customer queries. Filmed sections of information and examples can be interspersed with computer-based questions and scoring of understanding. The ability to provide experience in this way allows individuals to pick their own route through the learning package at their own pace. A recent review of the use of this approach is included in the Management in Action 4.3.

L   Distance learning. This is a varied form of activity. It now embraces a wide range of programmes from basic skills acquisition to higher degrees. The process of distance learning includes a variety of instructional approaches, the written word, television, video, audio, electronic, and residential periods offering face-to-face contact. In addition to academic courses, many organizations adopt this approach for in-house programmes as do the professional institutes for membership qualifications.

Management in Action 4.3

On the right lines

The use of technology in training first appeared in the early 1980s and has since developed rapidly. The ability of staff to make use of computer-based technology at or near to their place of work introduces many benefits not available through other training methods. For example, it allows the employee to work at their own pace and to concentrate on those aspects of a programme that are of interest and value to themselves. It also allows training to be done at a time appropriate to both the local line manager and the trainee, rather then at a time chosen by the training department. Neil Walker, senior technology-based training designer for the TSB Retail Banking and Insurance Division suggests that:

> Historically, the role of trainers has been to run training courses ... now it is to discuss with the line manager what the training needs of the individual are and then make suggestions, which could be anything from technology based training to short, off-the-job courses.

At Abbey National, a leading finance organization, CD technology has been added to desktop computers within the branch network. This makes it easier for branch managers to keep track of student training and performance as well as improving the administration of distance learning activities. John Buttriss, manager of the distance learning unit within the bank, describes the system as follows:

> There is rather a shopping list approach with 70 courses on the CD that is out at the moment. Theoretically, what we would like to do is keep the shopping list but make the computer come up with a suggested training log for each individual. That way, you are empowering the student to provide the line manager with the necessary information.

British Airways have used self-directed courses for use by 10,000 cabin staff in preparation for the annual safety equipment examination. Staff who fail the test are prevented from working and this causes individuals severe stress before the exam and difficulties for managers should they fail. Tim Dyer, BA's training services manager, indicated that:

> A multi-media training application was developed with the AimTech Corporation which enables employees to study for the test at their own pace. ... The possibility of using the application with a video information system which connects into the back of a television is being researched. If we deliver this application on the visual information system, it can be installed in each cabin crew hotel room in major cities like New York, Johannesburg and Tokyo, allowing crew members to prepare for the test during their down-time.

Adapted from: Sheppard, G (1993) On the right lines. Personnel Today, *9 November, pp 22–4.*

Training evaluation

Evaluating the benefits of any training is a difficult process. Ultimately it is an attempt to measure the transfer of training to the organizational context but there are many complications involved. For example, trainees can enjoy the training event, yet gain little practical job-related benefit from it. Conversely, trainees may not enjoy the experience and yet subsequently find the job relevance high. There may be other change initiatives active at the same time which restrict the ability to claim training as the only source of improvement.

However training is provided, it has a specific purpose and as such needs to be evaluated in order to ensure that it is effective in meeting its objectives.

According to Hamblin (1974) evaluation takes place at a number of levels:

- Reaction. The immediate responses of the trainees on issues such as the perceived benefits, feelings towards the experience and content.
- Learning. This reflects the actual benefit taken away from the training event. It is the degree to which the training has been internalized by the trainees in the form of new skills, etc.
- Job behaviour. In an organizational context, the training is usually designed to impact on the job that the individual is expected to perform.
- Organization. At the organizational level training is intended to improve the effectiveness in terms of productivity, quality, output, customer relations, and so on. Consequently, the need to justify training in terms of a positive effect at the organizational level is crucial.
- Ultimate value. This refers to the intangible benefits that the organization gains from any training activity. This could be its ability to survive in a hostile market, profitability, or even its contribution to society as a whole.

Three features are apparent in these evaluation levels:

- Measurement. This becomes increasingly less certain and vague as one moves from the immediate reaction to the ultimate value level. It is relatively easy to assess individual reactions to a particular training event. It is difficult to quantify the extent to which a particular event impacts on the whole organization.
- Time. This is another variable in the list. Reactions from trainees tends to be determined immediately after the event. Assessment of the impact on the organization as a whole can only be determined after some considerable time has elapsed. By the time organizational value can be determined, other variables will have invariably 'contaminated' any cause and effect links that existed.
- Hindsight. The initial assessment of trainees reaction to a particular event is an important evaluation measure, but would the reaction be the same say six months later when the opportunity to take a broader perspective has evolved, or when other factors change in the context?

The evaluation of training is not a precise science and this results in difficulties for both managers and trainers in identifying the justification for such interventions. Management in Action 4.4 indicates one approach to this issue.

Development

Development can be applied to any category of employee and the term *employee development* is increasingly finding favour over that of training. It is a process that allows potential to be realized. As such, it places a higher level of responsibility on the individual. The individual must want to be developed and must be prepared to co-operate in development activities. Because of the longer time frames implicit in development the return is not likely to become apparent for many years. For these reasons organizations are tending to make use of the concept of *development centres*, which broadly consist of the same type of activity as an assessment centre (Rodger and Mabey, 1987).

Management in Action 4.4

Measuring the gains from training

Many companies and training specialists have struggled with the attempt to justify training activity. To misquote a well-known saying, '... many employers suspect that half the money they spend on training is wasted – the problem is, they don't know which half'. In some cases the evaluation of training benefit is relatively easy to measure. For example, consider the provision of a training course intended to increase the proficiency of typing within the organization. It would be possible to measure the cost of typing both before and after the training course and to demonstrate the savings made.

The level of difficulty in measuring any gain increases dramatically when considering the area of management development. The fruits of such training activity may not become apparent for many years, by which time other things will have changed dramatically. As Bickerstaffe suggests:

> Most human resource specialists are forced to rely on more or less unscientific methods of evaluating training. Usually this involves visiting programmes and providers, debriefing participants and tracking the career development and promotions of managers and employees after they have attended training courses.

Sundridge Park Management Centre have developed a Performance Improvement Process (Pip) in an attempt to measure the effectiveness of the training that it provided on behalf of clients. Bickerstaffe describes the system:

Pip is based on a system of questionnaires, designed to elicit an indication of a person's knowledge on key areas, their attitudes and styles of work and to trace how these change over the duration of the course and in the longer term.

To an extent the system is competency-based, but each questionnaire is tailored to the particular course being evaluated and to the needs of the organization.

The first questionnaire is completed by both the delegate and their boss before the course. After the course each delegate completes another questionnaire. This should demonstrate an increase in the knowledge acquired as a result of the course. After three months both delegate and boss complete another questionnaire which is intended to reflect the retention of knowledge and the application of skills in the workplace. There have been several conclusions that have emerged from early applications of the Pip approach. The Prudential financial services group were among the first to use the system and identified a number of interesting results. These include an increased understanding of the importance of self-development among managerial employees and the need to regard change as a bottom-up process rather than top-down. Also, training should involve whole departments, not just individuals or groups.

Plans are already in hand to create a database of results from Pip findings in order to allow organizations to profile themselves and form comparative judgements about their training effectiveness.

Adapted from: Bickerstaffe, G (1993) Measuring the gains from training. Personnel Management, November, pp 48–51.

The emphasis being to identify strengths and weaknesses as the basis of individual and organizational development activity.

In the context of development, Pedler *et al.* (1989) identify the notion of a *learning organization*. They describe it in terms of the facilitation of learning for all employees and the constant transformation of the organization in response to the new knowledge and ability. Mumford (1989) suggests that the main characteristics of a *learning organization* include:

- Encouragement for managers to accept responsibility for the identification of their own training needs.
- Encouragement for managers to set challenging learning goals for themselves.
- The provision for all employees of regular performance reviews and feedback on learning achieved.
- Encouragement for managers to identify learning opportunities in jobs and to provide new experiences from which employees and managers can learn.
- Encouragement of a questioning attitude to the accepted ways of doing things within the organization.
- The acceptance that, when learning, some mistakes are inevitable, but that individuals should learn from them.
- Encouragement of on the job training and other learning activities.

The notion of the learning organization with its constant renewal and adaptation to employees as they continually develop themselves is of fundamental importance in creating a modern, flexible and adaptable organization. It reflects an approach that allows the organization to more effectively meet the needs of all of the stakeholder groups associated with it and is important in the strategic human resource management perspective adopted by many organizations today (Mabey and Salaman, 1995).

Training and development: an organizational perspective

Training and development are important aspects of organizational activity. They impact on all aspects of the employment of people, from the induction of new employees to the development of future generations of directors. Unless individuals are effectively trained they cannot be expected to undertake the duties that are expected of them, even if they know what they are. The workforce is male dominated at a senior level and there have been a number of initiatives to broaden the access of women to these positions. Management in Action 4.5 introduces the debate about the value of separate training for women in this context.

Individuals are not totally responsible for achieving organizational goals. It is the various groups and teams within the organization that achieve objectives. Therefore, it is a necessary part of organizational life to be able to work as part of a team. Within organizations trainers spend a considerable amount of time on team building exercises and courses to enhance employee and management ability in this area. Because organizations rely heavily on groups to perform much of the activity, they form a significant focus of attention for managers. Training in group formation and dynamics can provide a basis for shaping the behaviour of groups and so influence the level of effectiveness achieved.

Training and development are usually regarded as internal activities. However, most organizations are in a position to need to influence the external environment as well. Customers need to be persuaded to buy products and services from the organization. Suppliers need to be persuaded that the organization is a good credit risk. Government needs to be convinced to follow one set of policies rather than another. All of these activities involve the organization attempting to influence (train) people in these other organiza-

Management in Action 4.5

Trial separation

Given that the workforce in most organizations is male dominated it has been argued by many that special training courses for women provides the kick-start necessary to both meet their needs and boost confidence. However, it has also been argued that women-only training can be counter-productive in advancing their position in the workplace.

Opportunity 2000, an employer-led campaign to boost the status of women, has prompted many large employers to establish action plans to achieve this objective. Companies such as Barclays, Midland, the BBC, Lucas and BP have incorporated women-only training into their equal opportunity programmes. Others such as United Biscuits, British Airways and Rank Xerox have not given this type of approach such a high priority within their equal opportunity development.

Among those organizations that provide women-only training it is claimed that such courses provide benefits both to the individual and the organization. For example, Ashridge Management College has provided for many years a one-week intensive programme called Business Leadership for Women. From a survey of former students approximately half had subsequently been promoted and more than 90% thought such training was essential. It is not just the career and professional categories of women that have benefited

from the provision of such training. Springboard, as a training organization, has developed courses for women at the lower levels of the organization. It reports that individuals perform better after attending their programme and that they frequently take on more responsibility, even if they do not seek promotion.

Among those organizations that have not specifically provided single-sex courses it is suggested that women themselves do not want to be segregated. For example, United Biscuits conducted a survey in one of its divisions that produced a 70% response rate. One of the findings was that if women wanted training it was more general training, not special single-sex courses. However, a similar survey within another division found that women wanted special courses. This suggests that people and circumstances do vary and perhaps change over time. As a special-needs category it is not appropriate to assume that women will automatically want such provision. Other companies have found that attempting to tackle issues such as organization culture and individual training need determination for both men and women is a more effective route to influence the role and position of women in the workplace. As the Campaign Director for Opportunity 2000 said when interviewed, the best time to provide women-only training is when women themselves want it.

Adapted from: Tchiprout, G (1993) Trial separation. Personnel Today, 9 February, pp 32–3.

tions, or groups of consumers. Much of the purchasing, marketing and lobbying activity within organizations utilizes approaches that are based on the underlying concepts and principles discussed in this chapter.

The challenge facing managers and organizations is how to make cost effective use of training and development concepts within the organization. There are limitless opportunities for the utilization of these activities. If that were the only variable involved, then there would be no decision to take. Unfortunately there is always a cost associated with these activities and the benefits are not always easy to identify, or quick to materialize. Therefore managers are required to exercise judgement in determining the best application of training, just as with any other resource.

Human beings are naturally adaptive and creative in the ways that they approach events around them. Consequently, if no training or development were to take place in the formal sense of the term, individuals would simply

Management in Action 4.6

Quick on the uptake

Motorola, the giant electronics company, has begun to reach future generations of employees and customers through a number of innovative training programmes. It became concerned that in the USA the education system was developing children who lacked the sophistication to use its products. It viewed the US education system as teaching children that to collaborate with others was to cheat and that success was a function of being able to memorize facts and to be able to recite them at will. Consequently, it ran a series of week-long summer camps for the 12–15-year-old children of employees to explore the world of science and technology.

The company also provided classes for parents intended to show them how to manage their children's education and compare it with similar provision in China and Taiwan. The argument being that future competition for jobs will be from those countries and that to retain job opportunities in the USA it is necessary to ensure that US children are able to perform at a high level.

In the UK and many other countries local Motorola companies have begun similar initiatives to get close to education. In Scotland, for example, a drive is on to encourage girls to take an interest in engineering subjects and to see it as a career option.

In the USA retired employees are invited back to tell stories about the history of the company. This is intended to provide a depth of understanding among current employees about current activity in the context of company history as well as indicating how things have been dealt with in the past. It is a form of developing a continuity of culture, tradition and life pattern, thereby enabling current employees to regard themselves as part of an ongoing, dynamic process and as guardians of the future.

Adapted from: Williams, M (1993) Quick on the uptake. Personnel Today, *12 October, p 31.*

'muddle through'. This is frequently relied upon in times of financial hardship, when organizations cut back on training and development in order to save money in the short term. People are the most flexible, adaptable resource available to an organization and can cope in the short term without clear direction, unlike most computers.

It is easy to imagine that more training and development activity would solve all management's problems and produce an optimally effective organization. As with many organizational activities, that is too simplistic to be credible. The challenge is, therefore, one of finding the appropriate level of activity commensurate with organizational requirements in the short, medium and long term. Management in Action 4.6 describes how one organization sees its role in this context.

Training and development: a management perspective

Organizations are subjected to change in many forms. People join and leave the organization for many reasons. The nature of activity within the organization is subject to change as technology impacts different aspects of operations and products or services are subject to development. Consequently, there is a permanent background of training activity to ensure present and anticipated needs are met. There is also the natural career progression movement for individuals, necessary to meet the future need for senior specialists and managers. The failure of many organizations to meet these basic requirements has been a source of criticism in many reports and investigations into the subject. In the determination of an appropriate level of training and development, management face a dilemma in the need to balance the costs and benefits. Too often in the past the benefits have been undervalued by managers. Over recent years in many countries there have been a number of major initiatives attempting to improve the impact and level of training and development at all levels within organizations.

For the training specialist in the real world of organizations, these are not just interesting issues for debate. Managers under pressure for cost-effective output in the short term and being asked to divert employee time to training activities need to be convinced of the value. Organizations also need to be convinced of the value of the activity, particularly in times of economic stringency. Yet, as has already been indicated, there is no one right theory or approach that will guarantee success. Managers must work things out for themselves, taking into account the variables active in the particular situation.

It is an unfortunate fact of commercial life that when economic stringency is necessary, training activity is often the first to suffer cutbacks. There is still a considerable amount of persuasion to be done in convincing senior managers of the commercial necessity of training and development. The potential of training and development to contribute significantly to the control and shaping of behaviour, together with its motivational properties, has already been suggested in this chapter. Therefore managers ignore the value of it at their peril. Management in Action 4.7 (overleaf) provides a review of how training specialists are coming to grips with the political as well as the technical dimensions of their work.

Within organizations training and development have many applications. They include:

- Induction of new employees. The purpose being to enable new employees to become effectively integrated into the organization in the shortest possible time.
- Initial job training. Not all new employees will possess the necessary skills to perform the tasks expected of them.
- Subsequent job training. Over the course of employment the jobs that individuals perform will change. New equipment, new products, etc., all produce a need to acquire new skills.
- Training on transfer or promotion. When moving to another job within the same organization different skills will be required. This is particularly true in the case of a first appointment to supervisory or management positions.
- Training for special groups. There are a variety of special groups for whom particular training provision needs to be made. They include disabled people, women returners, ethnic minorities, employee representatives and employees with responsibility for dealing with customers.
- Development. It can be argued that as a distinct activity development has little relevance for most employees, as their responsibilities are tied to the present time. Management has the responsibility for the future, and so requires development. Conversely, it can be argued that the commitment of employees is enhanced through development and that they are therefore more likely to adopt a positive attitude to work, to the benefit of the individual, management and the organization.

Management in Action 4.7

Coming in from the cold: a new role for trainers

The context in which training is carried out within organizations has changed over recent years for two reasons. Firstly, organizations contain more complex training needs. Secondly, the nature of personnel activity within the organization is also changing. With the evolution of the human resource approach to the function and the downsizing and delayering of structures has come an empowerment of line managers. One of the consequences of this is a need to see the training specialist as a facilitator of the process, rather than a provider of training activity.

Sloman argues that the new role for trainers is reflected in a model which comprises two linked propositions:

A   The training function
  ■ Modern training practice requires the articulation of a clear training strategy with clear targets, clear control and accountability.
  ■ The training resource thus makes a significant and distinctive contribution to the process of skills enhancement to allow the organization to function at the strategic, tactical and operational levels. It should also assist in the capture of wider human resource benefits through the development of people.
  ■ This is achieved in part by developing an appropriate training culture for the organization in which all play an active part in achieving business plans.

B   The trainer's role
  ■ The role of the training professional is to develop and articulate the training strategy and promote a training culture.
  ■ This is achieved by defining appropriate relationships with all managers to achieve the maximum leverage for the training resource. It requires the adoption of a proactive role in presenting options and alternatives to line managers. It also requires the development of appropriate information and appraisal systems that can meet the perceived needs of managers and employees as they perform their duties.

In order to achieve this role, Sloman argues that trainers need to become strategic facilitators and to develop a number of new skills including:

  ■ Strategic awareness. The ability to acquire and translate business strategy information into action plans and options for managers as well as providing an assessment of the training implications.
  ■ Diagnostic capacity. The ability to offer appropriate expertise in skill analysis, training needs analysis and of methods of skill enhancement.
  ■ Influencing skills. The ability to influence the organization in seeking to capture the value potential of training and achieve a training culture. This is likely to require the individual to achieve influence beyond their formal status within the organization.

Adapted from: Sloman, M (1994) Coming in from the cold: a new role for trainers. Personnel Management, January, pp 24–7.

  ■ Professional development. Many employees undertake work in which job training is related to professional development. For example, accountants are trained by following a course of study leading to membership of one of the accounting bodies.
  ■ Specialist career development. Within many of the specialist areas of an organization there are occupational hierarchies. Examples are common among engineers, computer specialists and accountants. Progression with-

in these jobs often depends upon technical competence rather than managerial responsibility. However, their development can be of critical importance to the success of their organizations.

■ Managers' career development. Managers need to be developed in terms of their own specialism, in order to ensure that they keep up-to-date. They also need development in the management areas of their responsibilities, the intention being to develop individuals for more senior responsibility as well as for improved performance in their present job.

■ Development for directors and senior managers. The nature of senior management work is dramatically different to that of more junior managers. It is not unusual to find separate senior management programmes within large organizations, intended to meet these needs.

■ Job termination training. Every person recruited leaves the organization at some point in time. It could be that they find alternative work; or that they retire; or that they die whilst in service; they may be dismissed by the company; or they may be made redundant if their job disappears. In some of these cases the organization will provide counselling or training to help the individual adjust to the new circumstances.

■ Special initiative training and development. Frequently organizations engage in a particular activity that generates a training or development need. Examples include the development of a new product, the need to improve productivity or quality and the introduction of new equipment.

The importance of training and development gains increasing significance from the inclusion of a more obvious strategic perspective to the management of the human resource within organizations. Figure 4.11 overleaf illustrates the stakeholder approach to strategic training and development (Mabey and Salaman, 1995). It attempts to link together the main elements of the process whilst reflecting its fluid nature. This model also recognizes that business direction is determined through the stakeholder process and forms part of the generally negotiated balancing between agendas and priorities for the groups involved.

Conclusions

Training and development is an activity that continues for much of the life of every individual. Human behaviour is influenced in many ways by the experiences that are encountered in daily life. Psychologists have attempted to understand and explain the processes involved in this phenomena and in doing so have developed a number of models. Organizations need trained people in order to achieve objectives and they need to develop the talents of individuals in order to make provision for the future. The strategic human resource approach practised by many organizations today places a high priority on the development of employees in order to capture the benefits of the learning organization.

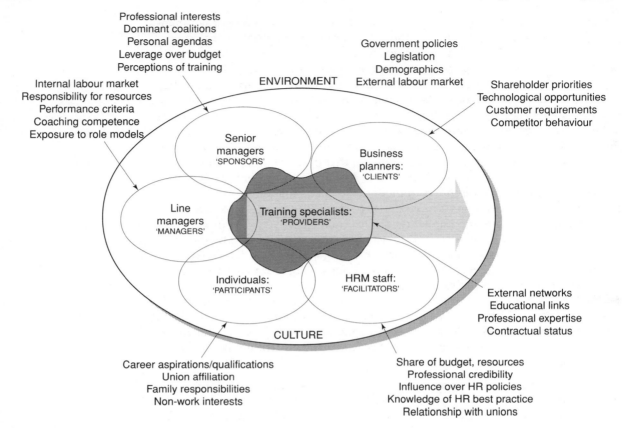

Professional interests
Dominant coalitions
Personal agendas
Leverage over budget
Perceptions of training

Government policies
Legislation
Demographics
External labour market

Shareholder priorities
Technological opportunities
Customer requirements
Competitor behaviour

Internal labour market
Responsibility for resources
Performance criteria
Coaching competence
Exposure to role models

ENVIRONMENT

Senior managers 'SPONSORS'

Business planners: 'CLIENTS'

Line managers 'MANAGERS'

Training specialists: 'PROVIDERS'

Individuals: 'PARTICIPANTS'

HRM staff: 'FACILITATORS'

External networks
Educational links
Professional expertise
Contractual status

CULTURE

Career aspirations/qualifications
Union affiliation
Family responsibilities
Non-work interests

Share of budget, resources
Professional credibility
Influence over HR policies
Knowledge of HR best practice
Relationship with unions

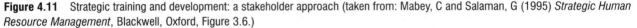

Figure 4.11 Strategic training and development: a stakeholder approach (taken from: Mabey, C and Salaman, G (1995) *Strategic Human Resource Management*, Blackwell, Oxford, Figure 3.6.)

Discussion questions

1 Provide definitions for the following key concepts from this chapter:

Training	TOTE system
Operant conditioning	Education
Behaviour modification	Feedback
Reinforcement	Technology-based training
Learning organization	Development
Social learning	Strategic training and development

2 Kolb describes learning as a circular process (Figure 4.10). Identify an occasion when you learned something and explain the process using Kolb's model. What conclusions about training can you draw from the process?
3 'Each individual should accept responsibility for their own training and development. It is not up to organizations to provide more than essential job related training.' Discuss.
4 'Training and development are nothing more than elaborate mechanisms for ensuring worker compliance with management's wishes.' Discuss.

5 How can the effectiveness of management training be evaluated? Justify your answer.
6 How would you recommend to your lecturers that they keep attendance at lectures high and ensure that work is handed in on time? Justify your views.
7 'Successful management requires considerable experience, it cannot be taught in a classroom.' Discuss this statement and identify the implications for management training and development.
8 Can the notion of the learning organization and strategic training and development provide an effective basis for the profitable employment of individuals within an organization? Justify your answer.
9 What should a manager do if a training programme designed to improve employee performance fails to have any effect?
10 'Technology can never replace the value of human interaction in training and development.' Discuss this statement and identify under what circumstances technology might have an advantage over traditional forms of training.

Research activities

1 Find a company that claims to use strategic human resource management as the basis of its activities in this area. Arrange to interview some of the training staff and seek to identify how they differentiate between strategic training and development and other forms of approach. What do they see as the benefits and problems for their work under the strategic perspective? Do they consider the strategic approach to be beneficial to the trainees, managers and organization, and if so why, or why not?
2 In the library, seek out 10 books and journal articles that discuss training and development theory and its application within organizations. What do these views tell you about either theory or practice of training and development?
3 In groups of three, each person identify a simple task that could be taught to the others in the team. This could be any practical task, such as repairing a puncture in a bicycle tyre, or making home brewed beer. However, it must be something relatively simple and completely safe, you must not put the person in any risk of danger or hurting either themselves or others. Using one of the theories described in this chapter, develop a training programme to enable one of the other team members to undertake the task. Train that person how to do the job. Discuss with the trainee and the third member (an observer) the effectiveness of the programme along with the relevance of the theory used. What general conclusions emerge?

Key reading

From Clark, H, Chandler, J and Barry, J (1994) *Organization and Identities: Text and Readings in Organizational Behaviour*, International Thomson Business Press, London:

■ Eysenck, HJ: The rat or the couch, p 82. This considers some of the behavioural aspects of training in the context of a review of psychology and psychoanalysis.
■ Vroom, V: Motivation: a cognitive approach, p 125. This piece previews the next chapter but in a way which has relevance to training as a cognitive process.

- Labov, W: The logic of nonstandard English, p 178. This introduces the distinction between formal education and an ability to function effectively in a particular social context.
- Bowles, S and Gintis, H: Schooling in capitalist America, p 185. This material addresses the purpose and results of education and suggests a bias in the process towards a particular end result.
- Fiedler, FE: Leadership – a contingency model, p 272. By introducing the Least Preferred Co-worker scale, the material provides an insight into the training of managers.

Further reading

Clark, FA (1992) *Total Career Management*, McGraw-Hill, Maidenhead. Although this text concentrates on career issues, there are many links with training and development.

Gilley, JW and Eggland, SA (1989) *Principles of Human Resource Development*, Addison-Wesley, Reading, MA. This work reviews many aspects associated with the development of individuals within an organizational setting. It is intended to meet the needs of a wide variety of readers and is not specifically an 'academic' text.

Harrison, R (1992) *Employee Development*, Institute of Personnel Management, London. A textbook on the subject of training and development intended for personnel practitioners. It is a comprehensive review of the practice and theory of the subject. This book also includes numerous examples and case studies.

Institute of Personnel Management/Incomes Data Services European Management Guides (1993) *Training and Development*, Institute of Personnel Management, London. This is a practical book that reviews the training and development practices in member states of the European Union.

Nilsson, WP (1987) *Achieving Strategic Goals Through Executive Development*, Addison-Wesley, Reading, MA. This text sets out to provide a justification for a link between strategic management and development.

Patrick, J (1992) *Training; Research and Practice*, Academic Press, London. A comprehensive review of the training debate. It takes a psychologist's perspective and concentrates on an in-depth review of the topic.

References

Beardwell, I and Holden, L (eds) (1997) *Human Resource Management: A Contemporary Perspective*, 2nd edn, Pitman Publishing, London.

Fitts, PM and Posner, MI (1967) *Human Performance*, Brooks-Cole/Prentice-Hall, Belmont, CA.

Hamblin, AC (1974) *Evaluation and Control of Training*. McGraw-Hill, Maidenhead.

Hulse, SH, Deese, J and Egeth, H (1980) *The Psychology of Learning*, 5th edn, McGraw-Hill, New York.

Kohler, W (1925) *The Mentality of Apes*, Harcourt Brace Jovanovich, New York.

Kolb, DA (1985) *Experiential Learning: Experiences as the Source of Learning and Development*, Prentice-Hall, New York.

Mabey, C and Salaman, G (1995) *Strategic Human Resource Management*, Blackwell, Oxford.

Miller, GA, Galanter, E and Pribram, KH (1960) *Plans and the Structure of Behaviour*. Holt, Rinehart and Winston, New York.

Mumford, A (1989) *Management Development: Strategies for Action*, Institute of Personnel Management, London.

Pavlov, IP (1927) *Conditional reflexes*. Oxford University Press, New York.

Pedler, M, Boydell, T and Burgoyne, J (1989) Towards the learning company. *Management Education and Development*, **20,** part 1.

References

Rodger, D and Mabey, C (1987) BT's leap forward from assessment centres. *Personnel Management*, July, 32–5.

Skinner, BF (1953) *Science and Human Behaviour*, Macmillan, New York.

Stuart, D (1986) Performance appraisal. In *Handbook of Management Development* (ed. A Mumford), Gower, Aldershot.

Thorndike, EL (1932) *The Fundamentals of Learning*, Teachers College, New York.

Verplanck, WS (1955) The control of the content of conversation: reinforcement of statements of opinion. *Journal of Abnormal and Social Psychology*, **51**, 668–76.

Watson, JB (1924) *Behaviourism*, University of Chicago Press, Chicago, IL.

Wood, L (1993) TECS hail work training scheme. *Financial Times*, 1 December, 26.

Wood, S, Barrington, H and Johnson, R (1990) An introduction to continuous development. In *Continuous Development* (ed S Wood), Institute of Personnel Management, London.

5

Motivation

▓▓ browse this web site ▓▓

www.itbp.com

Chapter summary

In this chapter we consider the topics of motivation and reward. We begin the discussion with a description of the major theories in this field. This is followed by an organizational review along with an introduction to the management perspectives relevant to the topic. The social context within which work is carried out means that there is a continual reappraisal of the role of work in people's lives. It is against this backdrop that managers must achieve objectives by motivating and rewarding employees.

Learning objectives

After studying this chapter and working through the associated Management in Action panels, discussion questions and research activities, you should be able to:

- Describe the major motivation theories.
- Outline the relationship between motivation and employee reward.
- Explain why motivation is a concept of considerable significance to managers.
- Understand what makes the study of motivation difficult.
- Discuss the dilemmas facing managers in applying motivation theory to a work setting.
- Appreciate the links between motivation and activities such as pay determination, employee participation and job design.
- Detail the various ways in which motivation theories can be classified.
- Assess the significance of classifying motivation theories.

Introduction

The term *motivation* is a familiar concept. Reflect on any team sport; the players spend considerable time and effort on the field in attempting to exhort the other players to perform more effectively. In other words, to *motivate* individuals to produce better results. Within organizations, managers are constantly seeking ways to improve *performance* at every level of the business, in order to raise *productivity* and reduce cost.

The *Pocket English Dictionary* defines motive as 'What impels a person to action, e.g. fear, ambition, or love'. This, however, is only part of the richness of the concept as it would be used in organizational behaviour terms. Psychologists have long recognized the distinction between *drives* and *motives*, reflecting the distinction between unconscious physiological reactions and the social process reflecting controllable behaviour in people.

Drives reflect those behaviour forces that are based on the physiological/biological needs of the body. For example, if we are hungry, the smell of food will tend to *push* our behaviour in the direction of eating. On the other hand, a motive reflects *learned patterns of behaviour*. For example, we actively seek out situations involving interactions with other people in an attempt to socialize with them rather than spend time on our own. Baldamus (1961) developed the concept of *traction*, to indicate the feeling among some workers of being pulled along by the rhythm of a particular activity. This could be taken to infer that a highly repetitive job is not automatically boring and could contain some motivational properties. However it is defined, motivation clearly relates to the willingness or energy with which individuals address their work activities.

Management in Action 5.1 overleaf illustrates a number of recent attempts to improve the motivation of senior managers by directly linking reward to the performance of the company. When you read these examples consider the assumptions underlying the plans described. For example, what are the underlying views of motivation; the views about managers and the basis on which they work; can financial reward ensure motivation?

It is known that many managers quickly sell off shares allocated to them as a reward through share option schemes. Therefore, it is argued, they must be thinking (and acting) only in the short-term interests of themselves and their organizations. Senior managers seeking to ensure that other managers think and act in the long-term interests of the organization developed the reward strategy indicated in Management in Action 5.1 in an attempt to ensure a long-term perspective. There are a number of assumptions behind this process that are worth considering, including:

1 That 'owners' (the city) have a longer time horizon than managers when it comes to measuring results.
2 That managers will be motivated and feel themselves rewarded through the acquisition of shares.
3 That requiring managers to purchase and hold shares will not demotivate them.
4 That increasing the ownership among managers will not (in time) create different, and perhaps less desirable, problems.
5 That the proposals will not create hostility and resentment among non-participating employees.
6 That managers will accept the new policy.

It is interesting to note in Management in Action 5.1 that the attempt to motivate is being applied to senior managers by even more senior, senior managers. The implication being that it is not just factory workers who need to be motivated. The organizations mentioned in that case clearly believe that the best results can only be achieved if the people at the top are rewarded for the achievement of results in the long term. This is an interesting approach, particularly as the stock and financial markets are frequently criticized for forcing organizations to adopt short-term policies.

Early approaches to motivation

In the pre-industrial era, communities and individuals were motivated by the drive to survive and the perishable nature of much of the means of doing so.

Management in Action 5.1

Executives forced to buy slice of pie

It is generally accepted that managers with a significant part of their personal wealth tied to a business will be more concerned about its performance than managers without such a stake. In the search for optimal returns a number of large multinational organizations have begun to insist that senior managers purchase nominated levels of stock in their organizations.

Union Carbide, Kodak and Xerox are among the large companies to go down this route. Organizations that have not gone as far as to require executives to buy shares, but 'encourage' them to do so include CSX, a US-based transport group. It offered loans to 160 of its top executives to buy shares at the prevailing market price.

Attempts to link the financial interests of managers to those of the shareholders is not new. Profit-share and share option schemes have existed for many years. Profit-share schemes pay a bonus to each executive, usually expressed as a percentage of salary, and dependent upon the profit level achieved by the company. Executive share option schemes allow individual managers to buy shares at today's price but at some point in time in the future. Both forms of linking reward to profit have limitations. Profit share tends to emphasize a one-year time frame in thinking and action planning. Executive share options allow the manager to judge the 'value' between the price to be paid and current market price. If the market price has gone down the executive can refuse the option to buy. If the price has risen, then the temptation to cash the shares in and take the 'profit' is high.

Brian Dunn, who specializes in executive compensation with Towers Perrin in New York, suggests that managers tend to hold less than 25% of the shares acquired under a share option scheme. The rest are sold quickly to take the profit as cash. This supports the views expressed by Washington-based Institutional Shareholder Services who have been campaigning for a change in share option scheme rules to limit executive freedom to sell shares.

The Kodak scheme requires Kay Whitmore, the Chairman, to purchase and hold shares to the value of four times his annual base salary. The more junior of the top 40 executives within Kodak will have to acquire shares over a five-year period to the value of one year's salary. Xerox requires its top 50 managers to acquire only one year's salary worth of shares, but this has to be achieved over 18 months.

The requirement to force executives to buy a specified amount of shares creates a number of dilemmas for both organization and individual alike. To resist buying shares is tantamount to arguing that a stake in the business is either undesirable or will not influence the decision making of the individual. To acquiesce is tantamount to accepting that the company has the right to determine how an executive spends their money. It can also be argued that executives are paid a salary to take decisions in the best interests of the shareholders. Any shortcoming in that area should be dealt with through the normal company procedures and management control processes. Just how insistent can a company be and what are the rights of intrusion into an executive's financial planning if these plans become popular is the key area of debate?

Adapted from: Dickson, M (1993) Executives forced to buy slice of pie. Financial Times, *1 February, p 11.*

Much of the available food could not be stored for long periods and so the *need* was to adopt behaviour patterns that maintained the flow. In addition, the political and social structures were such that individuals had less freedom of choice in their lives. Slavery, bonded or enforced labour meant that individuals could be required or forced to perform tasks on behalf of others, frequently for a subsistence living in return.

The issue of how much work management should expect from employees began to emerge in the middle ages. There are examples of the pace of work

---

Management in Action 5.2

Printing in early Korea

In sixteenth- and seventeenth-century Korea methods of printing had developed from the carving of pages of individual text to the use of a movable type. As there were literally thousands of characters in the language and the workforce were illiterate, good quality and accurate printing proved to be a difficult task to achieve.

In order to circulate official documents it was necessary to first have them printed and published. Under these circumstances the composing of the printing blocks and the subsequent printing process itself was a very skilled job. In order to ensure the accurate reproduction of documents a motivation scheme was introduced for the printers and supervisors.

The scheme was based on a negative incentive principle, in other words punishment for mistakes rather than reward for accuracy. The punishment was that for every mistake or unclear printed character the supervisor, compositor and printer would be flogged 30 times. The consequence, not surprisingly, was very high quality printing, but difficulty in the recruiting and training of people as compositors, printers or supervisors. As with most incentive schemes some benefits were achieved, but other problems were created.

Adapted from: Boorstin, DJ (1983) The Discoverers, *Random House, New York, pp 505–8.*

---

being set by management at the arsenal of Venice in the 1400s (George, 1972; Wren, 1987), and of monks estimating the time to build churches and cathedrals at about the same time, (Currie, 1963). Management in Action 5.2 describes one early approach to this subject.

At the beginning of the twentieth century FW Taylor was attempting to develop and introduce *scientific management* to the companies in which he was working, initially Midvale Steel (1878–98) followed by Bethlehem Iron Company (1898–1901). It involved identifying the *one best way* to carry out a job and then motivating employees to follow the work method specified through linking the payment of wages (reward) to the output achieved. His initial attempts were successful, the workers earnings increased, productivity increased and costs reduced, as Table 5.1 (based on Taylor, 1947) indicates.

The level of production increased considerably, but the wages of employees changed very little by comparison. Table 5.2 reflects the changes resulting from the use of Taylor's scientific methods.

Looked at in this way the figures provide a clear picture of benefit for both employer and employee, but the employer gains far outweigh those of the employee. However, Taylor's success was short lived and he was dismissed from the company in 1901 as the result of the growing hostility towards his methods from managers and workers alike.

Chester Barnard described what he saw as the major activities associated with being a senior executive in the 1930s. As a practising manager (the president

	Prescientific management	Using scientific management
Earnings per employee per day (average)	$1.15	$1.88
Tons per employee per day (average)	16	59
Labour cost per ton (average)	$0.072	$0.033
Number of yard labourers	500	140

Table 5.1
The effect of scientific management

Table 5.2
The benefits of scientific management

	Change as a result of scientific management	Percentage change
Earnings per employee	+$0.73	+63.5%
Tons per employee	+43	+268.8%
Labour cost per ton	−$0.039	−54.2%
Number of yard labourers	−360	−72%

of a large telephone company) he was writing from experience rather than theory. In terms of motivation he suggests that it was a balancing process:

> The net satisfactions which induce a man to contribute his efforts to an organization result from the positive advantages as against the disadvantages which are entailed. (Barnard, 1938, p 140)

He suggests in a footnote on the same page that the individual did not usually invoke a logical process in this decision-making process. In these views he was adopting a human relations approach, but also anticipating some of the later theoretical approaches to the subject.

The theories of motivation

There is no one theory of motivation that can be claimed to embrace the entire range of organizational and personal circumstances. Things that motivate an individual today may not work tomorrow, yet may become viable again the day after.

In this chapter we will use the convention of classifying theories into *content* or *process* theories wherever possible. Content theories concentrate on identifying the motives that produce behaviour. Process theories emphasize those mechanisms that encourage (or reward) behaviour in the dynamic context. Figure 5.1 provides an overview of the way that these approaches emerged from the earlier work in this area.

An *intrinsic motivator* is one that originates inside the individual. For example, an architect will be motivated to produce exciting buildings because of the satisfaction gained from having the opportunity to realize their design ideas. An *extrinsic motivator* is one that originates outside of the individual and which influences their behaviour. For example, Taylor was prepared to reward employees with higher wages providing they worked to his methods. Both of these ideas can be used with some effect in designing motivational practice within organizations.

Content theories

Content theories emphasize particular aspects of an individual's needs, or the goals that they attempt to achieve. The major theories falling into this classification, include:

- Maslow's hierarchy of needs theory.
- Alderfer's existence, relatedness and growth (ERG) theory.
- McClelland's acquired needs theory.
- Herzberg's two-factor theory.

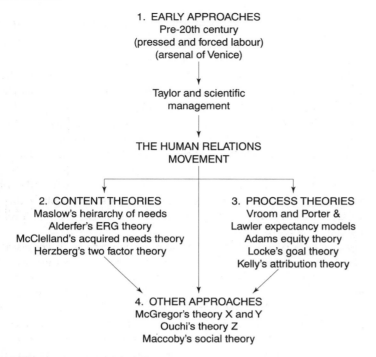

Figure 5.1 Evolution of motivation theory.

Maslow's hierarchy of needs

Maslow was an American psychologist who produced the idea that a hierarchy of needs could explain purposeful behaviour (Maslow, 1943, 1987). The basis of the model is that all individuals have *innate needs or wants* which they will seek to satisfy. In addition, these needs have an inbuilt prioritizing system. Figure 5.2 shows the model, indicating the hierarchical nature of the innate needs.

Figure 5.2 Maslow's hierarchy of needs.

The five levels included in the above hierarchy can be defined in the following way:

- Physiological needs. These include the wide range of basic needs that every human body requires in order to stay alive and function normally. Examples would include the need for food, air to breathe water to drink and sleep. In an organizational context this would include the need for wages.
- Safety needs. This category incorporates needs that provide for the security of the individual in their normal environment. Examples would include the need to be free from harm and to have shelter from the elements. In an organizational context this would include the need for job security.
- Social needs. From this category individuals would look to draw on social support necessary to life. Examples would include friendship and a sense of belonging. In an organizational context this might include the need to work as part of a team.
- Esteem needs. This would include having self-respect. Incorporated into this definition are concepts of achievement, adequacy, recognition and reputation. In an organizational context this could include recognition by management of useful ideas relating to the running of the business.
- Self-actualization needs. This is related to the opportunity to realize one's full potential. That is, the ability to have a significant influence over one's own life. In an organizational context this could include the freedom to organize one's job to suit personal preferences and to be managed on the basis of ends not means.

Maslow suggests that the above elements in the hierarchy are not to be considered as a rigid framework, within which individuals move in a totally fixed and predictable way. He suggests that the hierarchy displays the following properties:

- A need once satisfied is no longer a motivator. For example, once employees become accustomed to being consulted by the employer on matters of company policy, it becomes the norm.
- A need cannot be effective as a motivator until those before it in the hierarchy have been satisfied. It would be of little value to offer employees who are currently very poorly paid the opportunity to work in teams in an attempt to increase productivity.
- If deprived of the source of satisfaction from a lower order need it will again become a motivator. If a self-actualizing employee is given notice of redundancy, their natural reaction would be to start looking for another job (reversion to a lower level need for security).
- There is a innate desire to work up the hierarchy. Employees working in a team may in addition seek to plan and organize their work without management involvement.
- Self-actualization is not like the other needs; the opportunities presented by it cannot be exhausted. A marketing manager who has just enjoyed a successful sales campaign may also have a number of similar campaigns at earlier stages of development.

Assessment of the theory.
Maslow did not specifically describe his theory as applicable to the work situa-

tion, although that is where it has gained most exposure. There are a number of difficulties in applying his theory to all humans in an organizational context:

■ Not everyone is motivated only by things that go on inside the organization. For example, a young employee saving up to buy a motor car will be motivated by different factors to an employee five years away from retirement.

■ The amount of satisfaction needed at a specific level before a higher level need is activated is unknown.

■ The theory cannot explain all behaviour. For example, how can it explain that many actors are prepared to endure personal hardship in order to pursue their art?

■ It is a theory based upon the USA in the 1940s and reflects the values of that time along with the culture base of US behaviour.

■ Organizational events can reflect or be aimed at satisfaction at more than one level in the hierarchy. Money can be used to satisfy needs at every level in the hierarchy.

■ Individuals will place different values on each need. For example, some people prefer to work in relative security but with lower pay.

Having said that, Maslow's theory has been very influential over the years in assisting managers to prioritize elements in their attempts to motivate employees. It is an approach which encourages managers to 'get the basics' right before they attempt to undertake complex motivational initiatives. It forces managers to examine motivation from the employee perspective and to seek out how they perceive the situation. It also provides the opportunity for managers to reinforce what they already provide through benefit and support programmes as part of the employee reward package. For example, reminding employees of the existence and value of counselling and pension schemes.

Alderfer's ERG theory

Alderfer (1972) describes a three-level hierarchy, compared to the five levels proposed by Maslow. They are:

■ Existence needs. This category is grounded in the survival, or continued existence, of the person. As such it would include many of the issues covered by the physiological and safety needs identified by Maslow.

■ Relatedness needs. This category is grounded in the need for people to live and function in a social environment. It would include the need to be part of a group and belonging to a valued organization. It would include many of the issues covered by the safety, belonging and esteem needs described by Maslow.

■ Growth needs. This category is grounded in the need for people to develop their potential. As such it would cover the self-actualization and much of the esteem needs described by Maslow.

Assessment of the theory

Having described the Alderfer model as being strongly related to the Maslow framework, that does not imply that Alderfer merely simplified the original material. He does suggest that individuals move through the hierarchy, from *existence needs* to *relatedness needs* to *growth needs*, as each become satisfied. However, he does make more of the variability inherent in all motivational situations. For example, more than one need could be functioning at the same time, individuals may also regress back down the hierarchy. Alderfer also postulated a *frustration–regression* mechanism that would, in effect, substitute growth needs as the ultimate aim of the individual if they were continually frustrated in achieving it.

Maslow's theory was not specifically work related. Alderfer, on the other hand, contains a more direct organizational basis in grouping together categories of need into a more usable framework (at least for most managers). It is also a stronger or more robust theory than Maslow's. It postulates that managers should seek to motivate by addressing all three levels of need, but that if one (say growth) cannot be met then additional effort will need to be put into providing for the others as they will increase in significance for the individual.

McClelland's acquired needs theory

This theory develops a different set of needs as the basis of motivation, McClelland (1961):

- Achievement. He abbreviates this to nAch.
- Affiliation. He abbreviates this to nAff.
- Power. He abbreviates this to nPow.

To some extent these can be seen as elements within the higher order needs described by Maslow. His ideas were developed by using projective psychological techniques. He also suggests that needs are acquired through the social process of interacting with the environment. McClelland suggests that all people have these three needs to some extent although there is a tendency for only one to be dominant at any point in time. Questionnaires similar to that included as Figure 5.3 are suggested to be able to identify individual needs.

Assessment of the theory

Questionnaires can be of use to managers in attempting to motivate their employees by sensitizing managers to individual needs and the job implications. Table 5.3 is one such attempt. It provides a work preference and job example for each category of need. One difficulty associated with such tables is the generalized nature of the preferences and examples. Also, if needs provide

Table 5.3

Work preferences based on McClelland's needs theory (*source*: Schermerhorn, JR, Hunt, JG and Osborn, RN (1982) *Managing Organizational Behavior*, John Wiley, New York, p 113)

Individual Need	Work preferences	Example
High nAch	Individual responsibility Challenging but achievable goals Feedback on performance	Field sales person with challenging quota and opportunity to earn individual bonus
High nAff	Interpersonal relationships Opportunities to communicate	Customer service representative; member of work unit subject to group wage bonus plan
High nPow	Control over other persons Attention Recognition	Formal position of supervisory responsibility; appointment as head of special task force or committee

1.   Do you like situations where you personally must find solutions to problems?

2.   Do you tend to set moderate goals and take moderate, thought-out risks?

3.   Do you want specific feedback about how well you are doing?

4.   Do you spend time considering how to advance your career, how to do your job better, or how to accomplish something important?

If you responded yes to questions 1–4, then you probably have a high need for achievement

5.   Do you look for jobs or seek situations that provide an opportunity for social relationships?

6.   Do you often think about the personal relationships you have?

7.   Do you consider the feelings of others very important?

8.   Do you try to restore disrupted relationships when they occur?

If you responded yes to questions 5–8, then you probably have a high need for affiliation.

9.   Do you try to influence and control others?

10. Do you seek leadership positions in groups?

11. Do you enjoy persuading others?

12. Are you perceived by others as outspoken, forceful, and demanding?

If you responded yes to questions 9–12, then you probably have a high need for power.

Figure 5.3   How to identify McClelland's needs. *Source*: based on Steers, RM and Porter, LW (1979) *Motivation and Work Behavior*, McGraw-Hill, New York, pp 57–64.

a basis for job suitability, how can this be linked with the fluid nature of the needs themselves? For example, nAch tends to emphasize the individual aspects associated with work, typified by a sales representative. If the person then moves towards nAff as the dominant need, there may be no suitable job opportunities available.

Herzberg's two-factor theory

The original research carried out by Herzberg involved interviews with 203 accountants and engineers from organizations around Pittsburgh in the USA (Herzberg *et al.*, 1959; Herzberg, 1974). He used the *critical incidents* approach by asking questions about what had made the individual feel good or bad about their work. The answers were then subjected to a *content analysis* which identified that those factors which led to satisfaction were fundamentally different to those issues that lead to dissatisfaction. This he labelled the *two-factor theory of motivation* and named the categories *motivators* and *hygiene* factors. The theory offers some insight into the relationship between motivation and job satisfaction.

The hygiene factors were those that, if absent, caused dissatisfaction. They are predominantly concerned with the context within which the job is carried out and other extrinsic issues. The presence of these factors will not motivate individuals as such, but their absence will serve to create dissatisfaction with the job and organization. They included:

- Salary.
- Working conditions.
- Job security.
- Level and quality of supervision.
- Company policies and administrative procedures.
- Interpersonal relationships at work.

The motivating factors were those that could motivate the individual to improve their work performance. They were primarily concerned with the content of the work, together with the way that it formed a meaningful whole. They included:

- Recognition.
- Sense of achievement.
- Responsibility.
- Nature of the work itself.
- Growth.
- Advancement.

Although Herzberg did not claim a hierarchical relationship for the two factors, it is possible to compare this theory and those of Maslow, Alderfer and McClelland. This is most easily illustrated with a diagram (see Figure 5.4).

The significance of Herzberg's model is that the two factors are not opposite ends of a continuum. Lack of positive levels in the hygiene factors does not lead to demotivation, but to dissatisfaction. High levels in the hygiene factors does not lead to motivation, but to non-dissatisfaction. High levels among the motivation factors will, as might be inferred, lead to positive motivation. However, low levels of motivating influences will reduce the overall level of motivation, but not create dissatisfaction. It would, however, create feelings of non-satisfaction. So in effect there is a non-overlapping middle ground between these two factors which can be shown in a diagram (Figure 5.5).

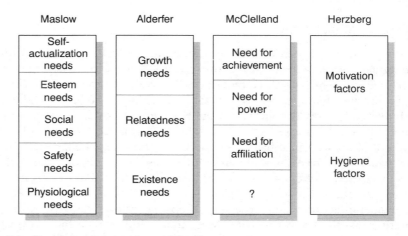

Figure 5.4 Comparison between the need theories.

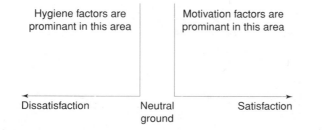

Figure 5.5 Satisfaction and Herzberg's two factors.

The consequence of this theory for managers is that they need to concentrate on two sets of factors at the same time if motivation and job satisfaction are to be maintained.

Assessment of the theory

There have been a number of criticisms of Herzberg's work. They include:

■ The results are research method dependent. Studies which use the same research methodology as Herzberg tend to arrive at broadly similar conclusions. Research using different methods is less supportive of the conclusions.

■ The results are capable of different interpretations. This is the line developed by Vroom (1964). Also the theory is not clearly set out which has resulted in different interpretations when replicating his work (King, 1970).

■ It does not provide for individual difference. For example, close supervision may be resented by some and yet welcomed by others.

■ It is restricted to manual or unskilled workers. This is surprising, given that it was developed from a research base drawn from accountants and engineers. It is often claimed that manual workers adopt an instrumental approach, concentrating on pay and security rather than the intrinsic aspects of the work. Work by Blackburn and Mann (1979) suggests that people in low-skilled jobs rely on a wide range of work approaches, not just economic factors, a result that reinforces the traction concept referred to earlier.

Process theories

Process theories attempt to provide a model of the interactions in the motivation process. The major process theories include:

■ Vroom, Porter and Lawler expectancy models.
■ Adams' equity theory.
■ Locke's goal theory.
■ Kelly's attribution theory.

The Vroom/Porter and Lawler expectancy models

Vroom's expectancy model

The basis of expectancy models is that motivation is a function of the desirability of the outcome of behaviour. In other words, if an individual believes

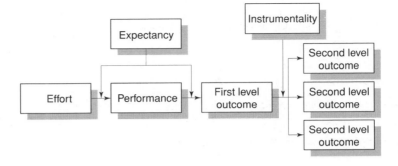

Figure 5.6 Vroom's expectancy model.

that behaving in a particular way will generate rewards that the individual values and seeks, they will be motivated to produce those behaviours. This is also referred to as a *path–goal* theory, because it is possible to identify a distinct path leading to particular goals (Figure 5.6).

This implies that individual behaviour will be moulded by what they see as the available rewards on offer and their importance to the individual. For example, offered the opportunity to attend training courses leading to a professional qualification in return for higher performance, an employee seeking such an opportunity will be motivated. If on the other hand an employee was not interested in becoming professionally qualified, it would have no effect on their behaviour. Such an offer would not motivate if the employee was interested in becoming qualified but did not believe that the manager could or would deliver the opportunity.

Vroom (1964) was the first person to link expectancy theory to work motivation. The model contains three key elements:

■ Valance. This refers to the importance of the outcome for the individual. Valance can either be positive or negative. It is positive if the individual wants to acquire or achieve the outcome. Negative valance refers to the opposite effect. Valance should be distinguished from value. Valance is based on anticipation, value implies the satisfaction from actually possessing something. In deciding whether to work overtime, an individual may take into account the family wish to go to the cinema that night. If the individual does not want to see the film, working late will allow them to achieve that objective (the valance). Subsequently, if the individual finds that the family could not get seats and so went to a restaurant instead, the value gained (realized valance) through working overtime may be altered.

■ Instrumentality. This concept links together the ideas of *first and second level* outcomes. It is necessary to become familiar with the notions of first and second level outcomes before *instrumentality* can be fully understood.

First level outcomes are those things that emerge directly from behaviour and are related to the work. Examples include productivity, labour turnover, absenteeism, quality and 'doing a good job'. Whilst these results may hold valance for the individual, the opportunities that these first level outcomes provide contain the highest levels of it. For example, higher levels of productivity (first level outcome) may generate a financial bonus. The bonus is a second level outcome and as such tends to be need related. The importance of second level outcomes is that they are dependent on the first level outcomes, not on the original effort. For example, working harder may increase productivity (first level outcome), but if the company did not have an incentive scheme then no financial bonus would be paid (no second level outcome). Equally, individuals are usually rewarded for actual achievements not for the amount of effort expended.

■ Expectancy. This is about the probability that a particular first level outcome will be achieved. Machines are liable to break down, parts may not arrive when required and other workers may not work hard. The result of these and other sources of variability is that a first level outcome may not be certain.

The model can be described in an equation. The use of an equation has the advantage of reflecting the motivational process in the way that it would be experienced by an individual. The equation allows the forces acting on the behaviour to be identified and the positive and negative influences taken into account, and the cumulative effect determined:

$$M = \Sigma \, (E \times V)$$

where M refers to the motivational force resulting from the sum of all the expectancy and valance elements in the equation, E refers to the expectancy measure reflecting the probability that effort will result in a particular first level outcome, and V refers to the valance (or attractiveness) of a particular outcome for the individual.

The Porter and Lawler extension

Porter and Lawler (1968) develop the model by attempting to link motivation and performance. In their model they draw attention to the fact that it is not just motivation that produces performance, but a range of variables such as the individuals view of work. Figure 5.7 gives a diagrammatic view of the extended model.

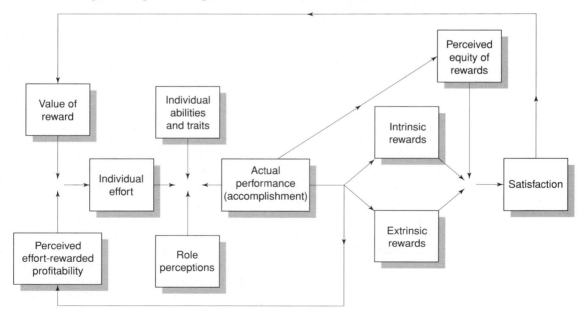

Figure 5.7 Porter and Lawler expectancy model.

Assessment of the theory

According to the expectancy model, individuals always seek to optimize the return on their investment of effort. One illustration of this concept is to consider a manager faced with a crisis needing the staff to work late one night. Individuals will have completed their basic work commitments for the day and will have plans for the evening. If the manager is to achieve the objective it will be necessary to work through the path-goal for each person involved. For some it might be the extra money, for others it could be the thought of helping the boss out of a difficult position, for others it could be ensuring that the department maintains a high reputation with customers. The point being that it will vary for every person, and every person will evaluate for themselves the balance of rewards, effort and probability of receipt.

One of the implications of this theory is that managers must seek ways of strengthening the links between effort, performance and reward. Rewards should be linked to employee values. In order to apply this approach managers need to be able to identify the employee calculus in order to be able to design appropriate arrangements. Because of the many and varied components in the equation, together with the changeable nature of it, this would become an almost impossible task to achieve with any accuracy. The complexity in attempting to apply the theory is reflected in Hollenback (1979) in which matrix algebra was needed to deal with the number and combination of variables.

Adams' equity theory

People develop strong feelings about the *relative fairness* in the treatment that they receive at work. When reaching a conclusion on fairness, individuals need a point of reference against which to judge what is happening. The main source of such information being the perceived treatment of other people. This formed the basis of the *equity* approach to motivation (Adams, 1965), based on social exchange theory. This suggests that individuals operate social interactions as a form of trading. A balance sheet in which individuals invest in relationships to the extent that they anticipate a return.

Equity theory in motivation is part of an evaluation and investment process. The most obvious application of these ideas is in the field of financial reward. Every employee is paid a wage and it provides many opportunities for comparison. Examples include other employees performing the same job, the same job in other companies, friends, neighbours and professional colleagues. Industrial relations specialists are well aware of the difficulties of equity in pay comparisons. Management in Action 5.3 reviews the concept of fairness, including equity.

For Adams, the process of comparing can produce two possible outcomes, equity or inequity. Equity is achieved when a perceived balance between the individual and the target is achieved. Inequity arises when the balance is disturbed in either a positive or negative direction. The individual would feel that an inequitable situation existed if, for example, they were paid more than the comparator, not just if they were paid less. Figure 5.8 reflects the operation of equity theory. Which option is chosen to restore equity will depend on a number of factors within the situation and the individual.

Management in Action 5.3

Moving tale of a fair day's work

Furnham reports the experience of a group of underwriters in the USA who were forced to move offices during a refurbishment programme. Among the group of underwriters were varying degrees of seniority, yet all performed at approximately the same level before the move. As a result of the move the reassigned work places meant that some staff moved into an office normally allocated to someone of a higher grade. Some moved into offices normally inhabited by staff of a lower grade, and others were allocated offices appropriate to their grade of seniority. The productivity of staff allocated lower status offices dropped dramatically. Conversely, staff allocated offices of a higher status dramatically increased their productivity. Staff allocated to appropriate office accommodation stayed at the pre-move levels of productivity.

Furnham provides one explanation for this phenomenon through the concept of 'equity'. It is suggested that there are three possible approaches to the determination of what it is 'right' to expect in relation to exchanging 'work' and 'reward'. The options are:

- Equality. Imagine a group of friends who go out for a meal and order what they wish from the menu and drink as they see fit. The bill at the end of the meal could be split equally between all the friends irrespective of what each individual actually 'spent'. Those who choose modestly subsidize those who have expensive inclinations.
- Taxation. This would suggest that food and drink consumption should be separated from payment responsibilities. The greediest (or hungriest) should order as they wish. The bill on the other hand would be split according to ability to pay. The wealthiest having to bear the heaviest responsibility for their contribution.
- Equity. This approach requires each individual to show restraint in ordering both food and drink to comply with the desires of the group to fund the evening. It is not unusual to find an individual seeking to retain an expensive option, compared to group desires, being told to pay for themselves under this approach. Equity requires that no individual is markedly out of line compared to the others in both consumption of food and drink and payment of an equal share.

Of the three approaches the equity view tends to be the most commonly found. The taxation option is the least popular – apart from those individuals that deliberately seek advantage from a situation. In the case of the underwriters moving offices it is suggested that they each reviewed the 'rewards' received (the office allocated) for the 'input' of work expected and adjusted their work activity to match the perceived 'value' of the offices provided.

These same principles apply in many other aspects of organizational life. It is not unusual to find people who feel unfairly dealt with taking more time off work, going slow or generally being unhelpful to the work of the organization. The problem for managers is that it is for each employee to undertake the evaluation of what 'equity' means to them. Managers are not in a position to judge on behalf of employees what is an 'equitable' situation, they cannot know against whom or what the comparison is being made.

Adapted from: Furnham, A (1993) Moving tale of a fair day's work. Financial Times, 24 March, p 14.

Assessment of the theory

Much of the research on equity theory has concentrated on its application to pay and rewards. Dornstein (1989) examined the basis of comparison in people's judgements about the fairness of received pay and found that it changed depending upon a number of factors. Consequently, it is not clear how individuals apply the principles of equity theory, neither would managers find it easy to be sure that equity was being achieved for each individual.

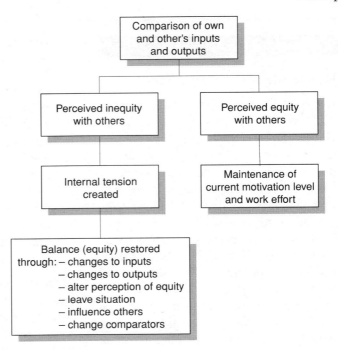

Figure 5.8 Adams' equity theory.

Working relationships are much less personal than those based on friendship and it is less likely that the same level of commitment to them exists (Campbell and Pritchard, 1974). Consequently, it is argued that the perception of inequity will be less in a work context when overpayment is involved. It is more likely that individuals will change the basis of their view of what forms an equitable payment (Locke, 1976).

Even with the possible limitations described, the model provides a useful mechanism for considering the issue of equity between employees. This is particularly relevant to the subject of pay and other rewards. The theory implies that organizations should give close attention to the comparison process when designing pay structures, incentive schemes, merit awards and even the basis of promotion.

Locke's goal theory

Locke (1968) suggested that the intentions that people have play a significant part in formulating their behavioural patterns. In a work context, this can be used as a mechanism to motivate behaviour. It is from this perspective that many performance appraisal systems attempt to shape behaviour. An individual needs feedback in order to gauge the extent to which their goal is being achieved. Performance appraisal systems are a formal feedback mechanism to direct employee behaviour towards the achievement of management objectives. A generalized model of goal theory is shown as Figure 5.9.

Within the model there are a number of issues surrounding the notion of goal setting and feedback that can significantly influence the outcome. They include:

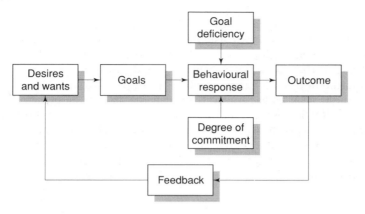

Figure 5.9 Goal theory.

- The more specific the goal the more likely it is to be achieved.
- The completion requirement (finish date) should be specific.
- Difficult to achieve goals are more likely to be achieved than easy to achieve goals.

Assessment of the theory

There have been a number of studies of goal setting approaches to motivation (for example Early *et al.*, 1990; Erez *et al.*, 1985 and Shalley *et al.*, 1987). Generally the results have been supportive of the approach, but raise questions that remain unanswered. For example, what degree of subordinate involvement is required in setting goals to achieve optimal results? Another problem is the need to understand how to maintain impetus once the goals have been agreed.

Issues such as individual difference, personality, previous education and training and career path are among the factors that could be assumed to have an effect on the validity of the goal setting model. These aspects remain to be researched in any depth. The approach is widely used as the basis of performance appraisal systems, particularly where projects, tangible results or change is a feature of the job. However, it does have limitations. Some jobs are not amenable to goal setting (for example, assembly line tasks). With an increasingly turbulent operating environment being common for many organizations, goals will be subject to frequent change. This makes it increasingly difficult for individuals to maintain performance targeted at specific goals.

Attribution theory and motivation

Attribution theory suggests that motivation is a response by the individual to a self-perception of their behaviour. Individuals decide (through perception) whether their behaviour is responding to internal or external influences. On the basis of this decision, the individual will decide whether or not they prefer to be intrinsically or extrinsically motivated. The result of this decision affects the form of motivation that will be effective for that individual (Kelly, 1971).

The effects of an intrinsically motivated individual being managed in a regime that was based on extrinsic motivation was studied by Deci (1971). He found that such individuals became extrinsically motivated. Wiersma (1992) also concluded that the links between extrinsic and intrinsic motivation were complex and could work against each other in particular situations.

It is argued that intrinsic motivation provides the 'best' approach to obtaining a totally effective employee, one who will perform well and take a pride in producing good quality work. However, many motivation strategies rely on incentive schemes or other extrinsic principles to motivate employees through tangible rewards. The criticism of such approaches being that they *purchase* output, generating at best an instrumental or compliance response.

Additional perspectives on motivation

McGregor's theory X and theory Y

McGregor (1960) explicitly introduced the underlying assumptions concerning human nature into motivation when he proposed the notion of theory X and theory Y. His claim was that managers tend to hold beliefs that would classify employees into either a theory X or theory Y category. Consequently, managers operate policies and practices (including motivation) that are based on one or other of these sets of assumption (see Figure 5.10).

Ouchi's theory Z

Ouchi investigated the ways that Japanese and US managers managed their subordinates. In doing so he identified a number of cultural differences between the two:

- American organizations
  - short-term employment
  - explicit control processes
  - individual decision making
  - individual responsibility
  - segmented concern
  - quick promotion
  - specialized careers
- Japanese organizations
  - lifetime employment
  - implicit control processes
  - collective decision making
  - collective responsibility
  - holistic concern
  - slow promotion
  - generalist careers

From these profiles it is possible to identify a number of implications for motivational practice. Ouchi developed his theory Z on motivation from the work of McGregor on theory X and Y, suggesting that it would tend towards the Japanese profile. For example, adopting longer term employment contracts, but not as long as the Japanese.

> **Theory X**
>
> 1   The average man is by nature indolent – he works as little as possible.
>
> 2   He lacks ambition, dislikes responsibility, prefers to be led.
>
> 3   He is inherently self-centred, indifferent to organizational needs.
>
> 4   He is by nature resistant to change.
>
> 5   He is gullible, not very bright, the ready dupe of the charlatan and the demagogue.
>
> The implications for management are:
>
> 1   Management is responsible for organizing the elements of productive enterprise – money, materials, equipment, people – in the interest of economic ends.
>
> 2   With respect to people, this is a process of directing their efforts, motivating them, controlling their actions. modifying their behaviour to fit the needs of the organization.
>
> 3   People must be persuaded, rewarded, punished, controlled, their activities must be directed.
>
> **Theory Y**
>
> 1   People are not by nature passive or resistant to organizational needs. They have become so as a result of experience in organizations.
>
> 2   The motivation. The potential for development, the capacity to assume responsibility, the readiness to direct behaviour towards organizational goals, are all present in people. It is a responsibility of management to make it possible for people to reorganize and develop the human characteristics for themselves.
>
> 3   Management is responsible for organizing the elements of productive enterprise in the interest of economic ends. Their essential task is to arrange the conditions and methods of operation so that people can achieve their own goals best by directing their own efforts towards organizational objectives.

Figure 5.10   McGregor's theory X and theory Y (*source*: McGregor, D (1960) *The Human Side of Enterprise*, McGraw-Hill with permission).

Hofstede and cultural influences on motivation

Hofstede (1980) introduced the impact of national culture into the debate about motivation. In his research he used the following framework to study the differences between 40 countries:

- Power distance. Reflects the degree to which a society accepts that organizational power is distributed unequally.
- Uncertainty avoidance. Reflects the extent to which a society feels threatened by uncertainty and ambiguity and actively seeks to minimize these situations.
- Individualism – collectivism. This reflects the underlying arrangement of society into a loose (everyone is responsible for themselves) framework; or an integrated, tight social arrangement involving collective responsibility.
- Masculinity. This reflects the degree of domination of society's values by 'masculine' characteristics.

In his research he put forward the idea that each of the theories of motivation reflected a particular set of cultural norms. As such they could be expected to be most effective in situations reflecting that particular cultural orientation. This introduces into the debate on motivation the notion that motivation theories may not be mutually exclusive. A more recent cultural perspective is offered by Trompenaars (1993) in which he offers seven different dimensions of national culture which could impact on organizational behaviour, including motivation. For example, some societies rely on achievement as a measure of success, whereas others favour ascription or favour based on age, experience, etc.

Maccoby's social theory

A more recent approach to the concept of motivation is that of Maccoby (1988). He argues that the social and work environments have changed over recent years, particularly as a result of the growth of new technology. The effect has invalidated the underlying value of traditional approaches to motivation. He argues that a new motivation theory is needed, based not upon the *partial man* assumptions of Maslow, but specifically including concepts of trust, caring, meaning, self-knowledge and dignity. Emerging is a new type of worker, interested in self-development and motivated by opportunities for self-expression and career development, combined with a fair share of profit.

Motivation, reward and productivity

The management of performance is a major issue for managers in the search for stable and high levels of productivity. One way of achieving this is through the achievement of a *controlled performance* from individuals. To see this in context, imagine a team sport where each member of the team played at their own speed and not giving a consistent effort. The result would be a team that did not win many games. It is the same within organizations; managers continually seek to achieve operational *consistency* . Looked at as a model this can be seen as a process of managing a number of variables concerned with motivation and rewards (see Figure 5.11). The model also reflects the cyclical process between motivation, reward, productivity and objectives.

Taking each of the elements in turn:

■ Work environment. This refers to the physical circumstances in which the activities take place. The level of technology, methods of work used and equipment provided are examples.
■ Ability. The skills and abilities that individual employees possess. It is also a reflection of the organization's recruitment and selection processes along with training and development provision.
■ Clarity of objectives. If individuals are to be expected to achieve high levels of job performance they need to be provided with clear objectives. If the employee does not know what they are trying to achieve then anything will seem acceptable.
■ Motivation to perform. This refers to the behavioural influences known as motivation. The precise content of which depends upon the particular drivers at the time.

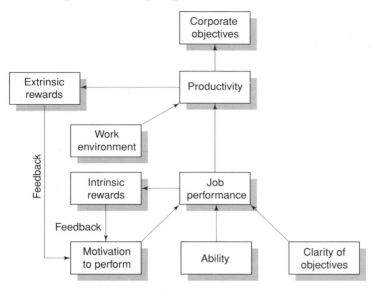

Figure 5.11 The links between motivation performing and rewards.

- Job performance. This relates to the observable activity level from the individual. It would encompass not only the pace of work but also the quality produced. Job performance is a function of individual level activity, it has to be linked with environmental elements in order to produce productivity.
- Intrinsic rewards. Intrinsic rewards are those that accrue to the individual as a direct result of the job itself. Rewards obtained in this way act as internal reinforcement. Consequently, there is a feedback loop to motivation from intrinsic rewards.
- Productivity. Productivity has been described as a relative term, a measure of conversion. Relative effectiveness in producing more goods for the same input of labour.
- Extrinsic rewards. Such rewards are generated from outside the job itself. The most obvious example being bonus schemes in which pay is based on output. These rewards are also intended to influence motivation and objectives. For an extrinsic reward system to be effective the individual must have a good knowledge of the basis of any reward, and hence clear objectives (see Management in Action 5.4).
- Corporate objectives. The level of productivity achieved will determine to a significant extent the degree to which corporate objectives are achieved. This last element also refers to the guiding principles within the model. Consequently, motivational practices should be designed to encourage the delivery of things that are of value to the organization, based on corporate goals.

Motivation: an organizational perspective

Motivation is an individual level phenomena. People as individuals are motivated to a particular degree on a scale running from not motivated to completely motivated (see Figure 5.12).

Management in Action 5.4

Extrinsic reward and service standards

The following quotation was taken from an insurance company report to policy holders.

Staff Developments

We believe that our staff are our most important resource and it is through their efforts that our service standards have been recognized with a plethora of awards. Using human resources effectively means recognizing and rewarding performance and we have, with this in view, introduced a performance-related pay system. Our system will reward achievement rather than awarding 'across-the-board' cost of living rises regardless of individual merit.

Taken from the Scottish Amicable policyholders report, 1992.

Not motivated   Highly motivated

Figure 5.12   The motivation scale.

All motivation theories allow for the existence of cognitive processes. Content theories adopt the needs and wants perspective and process theories concentrate on the decision making that guides behaviour. The common factor with both categories is that individual behaviour is motivated towards the achievement of goals.

Motivation is based on internal cognitive processes that are not available for direct inspection. Consequently, in order to assess motivation inferences must be drawn from observable activity. Human beings are employed to undertake those things that the organization seeks, irrespective of personal wants or desires. This adds additional complexity to the use of the concept of motivation for a number of reasons:

■ Managerial assumptions. Managers cannot be aware of why individuals are behaving as they are, so wrong assumptions may be made. For example, work behaviour will be subject to motivational forces from outside the organizational setting.

■ Situational context. Employees who have never been given any degree of involvement in the organizational decision making may find participative management styles motivating. However, when memories begin to fade the basis of comparison will change. Employees will see participation as the norm and as a *frame of reference* against which to measure future events.

■ Personal preference. Not all individuals actively seek increased levels of motivation at work. Some employees will see work as instrumental to support other aspects of their life. Lee and Lawrence (1985) suggest a four-factor model of decision-based motivation based on the goals sought, strategies adopted, coalitions formed and the power available with which to achieve the goals.

■ Instrumentality. Managers can mistake instrumental behaviour for motivated behaviour. One recent survey showed that more than 40% of workers were worried about losing their jobs during the following 12 months (Summers, 1993). This might imply a compliant workforce adopting an instrumental approach to work.

■ Bio-social basis of behaviour. The needs and wants held to underpin motivation are not themselves constructs that are problem free. In order to function biologically humans need certain things such as food and sleep. However beyond these basic requirements, many needs are socially determined. For example, what type of food, how much and how should it be prepared, cooked and served?

Society determines many aspects of life that are classified as a basic need. For example, television sets are now 'essential' to life compared with 30 years ago. A Marxist analysis would bring into question the basis of motivation grounded on 'needs' that are socially constructed and which are used as the basis of 'forcing' individuals to increase their effort within the capitalist system. This, it would be argued, is a circular process in which the individual is trapped into meeting the ever-increasing *needs* of the capital owners. This results in the manipulation of both consumption and of work practice. It has been argued that motivation only became an issue when meaning was lost from work: 'In consequence, motivation theories have become surrogates for the search for meaning' (Seivers, 1986).

It is reasonable to suggest that a motivated individual will feel a higher level of commitment to work. There is, however, a problem for managers in this proposition in that individuals might claim ownership of the activity and attempt to divest management of its presumed right of control. Garrahan and Stewart (1992) provide a review of more recent motivational practices, such as teamworking, quality circles and company culture. These are practices frequently associated with Japanese organizations or European and US organizations attempting to emulate them. In their description, the negative impact on the individuals can clearly be identified through increased stress reported by some individuals and a take it or leave it approach by management.

Motivation: a management perspective

Increased productivity is the major management objective being sought in an attempt to achieve corporate goals. Motivation is a mechanism through which this is achieved and rewards are the device through which motivation can be triggered. In this way motivation can be seen as a manipulation to achieve management's goals. Management in Action 5.5 reflects the way in which many organizations see the links between corporate objectives and reward.

For managers there are a wide range of motivational options available. It could be argued that every aspect of the experience (real or perceived) in the workplace influences the motivation level of the people within it. Indeed this could be expanded to encompass events and situations outside the immediate working environment including:

■ Family relationships and events. Crises at home can divert the energies of individuals.

■ The local community. A win by the local football team can have beneficial effects, although the effect is far from certain, as Moreton (1993) suggests.

Management in Action 5.5

Nice little earner

Profit sharing has been in existence for many years in one form or another. In the UK the government provided tax breaks for such schemes when it allowed up to £4000 of salary to be tax-free, provided it was earned under an approved profit-related pay scheme. In the late 1980s very few schemes had been registered by the Inland Revenue, covering only about 100,000 employees. However, the popularity of such schemes grew rapidly and by 1993 approximately 1.2 million workers were covered by almost 5000 registered schemes. In the 1996 budget the government announced the phasing out over a number of years of the tax breaks associated with such schemes and so it is for the future to decide what the effect will be.

There is little doubt in the minds of many managers that an approach linking the commitment of employees to the financial interests of the company is an attractive option. Kellaway reports that in one accounting practice (Stoy Hayward) all but five of the 1000 employees indicated that they would like to participate in a profit-related pay scheme. Many other large organizations have opted to participate in these type of schemes, including Boots The Chemist, The Halifax Building Society and Asda Property.

The original intention behind the introduction of profit-related pay schemes was that by linking pay to profit it effectively becomes a variable cost. Consequently, employees would be encouraged to work more effectively in pursuit of higher profit levels. In good times they would benefit from the additional reward. In bad times their pay would naturally fall in line with the lower profit (or even losses) achieved.

Some employers have designed schemes that pay a variable bonus (depending upon the level of profit achieved) in addition to the basic salary. In this approach the worst that can happen is that employees only receive their basic salary. No profit (or a loss) equates with no additional bonus. The other alternative, favoured by some as the way to achieve maximum impact from such schemes, is to transfer a proportion of existing pay to a profit-related basis. It is this last possibility, of allowing pay to actually fall, that has proved to be the controversial aspect of some profit-related pay schemes.

In a scheme which transfers a proportion of existing salary to a profit basis there can be attractive aspects for both parties. Assuming the scheme is designed to produce the same level of gross pay at current levels of profit then the employee will gain as a result of the tax free nature of the profit-based pay. If profit levels rise then the employee will gain even more as the total level of pay will increase. However, should profit levels slip then the employee will find that their usual level of pay actually falls and they will take home less pay.

There are problems with the notion of profit-related pay from a number of directions. Those on low pay and with little or no tax liability would not benefit, for example. Some industries are notoriously volatile and would find it difficult to engage in the level of financial or profit planning necessary. Profit-based schemes are inevitably group in nature and in motivation terms the link between individual effort and profit level is remote in the extreme. Equally, employees can work much more efficiently, yet profits can fall due to market pressure, leading to a negative association being recognized between effort and pay.

Adapted from: Kellaway, L (1993) Nice little earner. Financial Times, 23 April, p 14.

■ Commercial environment. The closure of a competitor can help to secure the jobs in other organizations, as can economic effects such as changes in the exchange rate.

Most of these would only be expected to have an indirect effect on motivation within an organization, and then only for a relatively brief period. This illustrates the dynamic nature of much human behaviour, an issue not always apparent from particular motivation theories. Motivation is not something that is achieved and then fixed at that level, it is fluid, subject to variation in the forces acting on the individual. This makes managing motivation difficult for managers, as they must be permanently sensitive in relation to employees and adjust their own behaviour accordingly.

Managers face major difficulties in attempting to motivate employees. To begin with, the construct of motivation is an abstract one. There are a number of theories offering a view on the nature and process of motivation but not all offer a realistic option for being able to motivate employees. Imagine attempting to apply the expectancy model calculation for each employee on a regular basis! Finally, managers individually do not have complete freedom to change company policy to a significant extent in order to personalize motivational opportunities. Although motivation is an individual level response, managers must maintain consistency in the treatment of employees across groups. It was to address this issue that the so-called cafeteria or flexible approach to employee benefits was developed. The idea being that individuals are able to *pick and mix* a personal benefits package, up to a set limit, from the total range available (Stock, 1992). In effect a personalized pay package, intended to optimize the motivational effect from collective arrangements.

Another difficulty facing managers is deciding which theory to follow. Each has something to offer and brings a slightly different perspective to bear on the subject. The theories discussed predominantly originate from a Western (US) culture and may not be valid in other cultural settings. The meaning of work, acceptance of ambiguity and power distance all could be expected to play a part in determining a cultural perspective to motivation, according to Hodgetts and Luthans (1990).

The options (or levers) available to managers with which to influence levels of motivation include:

- Pay levels and structures. Also the other terms and conditions of employment.
- Incentive schemes. Including monetary, gift and prizes; Hilton (1992) reviews the use of non-financial incentives as a motivation facilitator.
- Organizational factors. The structure, job design and the way that employees are integrated into the business processes (for example, decision making) can be adjusted to influence motivation levels.
- Performance appraisal. There are many of these systems, including management by objectives – MBO techniques.
- Management style.
- Feedback, praise and punishment.
- Management by example. The letter in Management in Action 5.6 is an example of how one person feels about the example set by senior people.
- Company policies. Including issues such as compassionate leave, equal opportunities, study and further education possibilities can all affect employee motivation.

The range of these motivation levers is another set of issues that makes it difficult for managers to optimize motivational strategies. This complexity is increased further when interaction between the elements is accounted for.

Top managers should show the way in radical rethink on pay

The following letter is quoted from a national newspaper. It is clear that the writer feels strongly about the symbolism of pay levels at board and senior manager levels.

Sir, Shares can go down as well as up, circulars from my bank and insurance company have warned me since the collapse of the 1987 financial 'bubble'. Can executive salaries do the same?

I have followed the debate in your columns on the troubles of the financial sector; ... Entirely missing has been the question of whether the disproportionate increase in top salaries of the early 1980s, justified on grounds of the quality of judgement of senior executives, should be reversed.

I appreciate that a cut in remuneration for board members and general managers would contribute only a little to redressing the balance of bank reserves and profits. But such a signal that top management recognizes its share of the responsibility for the evident errors of the last decade, and is prepared to share in the cuts and added burdens of the 1990s as fully as it shared in the added profits of the 1980s would do much to rebuild the battered confidence of staff and customers. No such signal has yet been given.

There is a wider point at issue. If the British economy is to hold low inflation – as bank economists exhort – attitudes to salaries throughout the economy have got to change radically.

No stronger signal could be given of the acceptance of radical change than a reversal of the continuing trend for top salaries to increase.

The Quaker families who laid the foundations for more than one of England's clearing banks understood the importance of gestures and symbols, and of demonstrating by the way they behaved the responsibilities they shouldered towards their fellow men. I fear that their descendants have lost sight of that sense of shared responsibility to the wider community. The impact on bank profits of a 10–20 per cent cut in board remuneration would be minimal. But think of the potential impact on the economy and on British society!

William Wallace
London

Taken from the Letters page in the Financial Times, *19 February, p 14.*

Managers do not have the opportunity to adjust all of the levers potentially available, for the following reasons:

- **Availability.** Not all organizations employ every option. Not every organization uses incentive schemes to reward higher output, for example.
- **Freedom of action.** Some levers are centrally determined and so individual managers do not have the freedom to alter the application. Company policies are not usually open to variation in application.
- **Personal preference.** Not every employee is equally amenable to the rewards on offer. For example, a young employee may be more interested in higher wages or career opportunities, whereas an older employee may be interested in pension benefits.
- **Variability.** Employees vary each day in what will motivate them. These personal factors can be as simple as feeling unwell, or perhaps feeling hostile to the organization as a result of a 'telling off' from the boss.
- **Group norms.** This and peer pressure can significantly influence the behaviour patterns of employees, irrespective of management's hopes and desires.

Management in Action 5.7

An encouraging start to employee motivation

There are many different approaches to the motivation of employees. Some companies attempt to achieve high levels of motivation through the use of payment systems and bonuses; others attempt to achieve it by encouraging staff to become involved in decision making activities. One such company is Appor Ltd. This organization makes plastic soap dispensers, predominantly for its parent company, the Deb group.

The managing director, Martin Williamson, was himself motivated to attempt to involve and empower employees through a leadership course run by Heslegrave Gill, a firm of business consultants. The course was facilitated by the consultants who encouraged the use of discussion, business games and other activities to help groups of participants solve problems.

Back in Appor, Williamson had experienced the failure of quality circles as a result of their degeneration into 'dumping grounds' for problems. He began to develop a new approach to the way that people worked by increasing the level of employee contribution and teamwork in pursuit of clearly understood common goals. A training strategy was developed which involved weekend residential training sessions run by Heslegrave Gill and which were open to all managers and employees who cared to attend. The intention was to demonstrate in a non-work environment that every individual had the ability to solve problems. A second weekend course was arranged which was intended to encourage the transfer of the confidence achieved at the first session into dealing with work-related issues.

Back in the factory, the progress made in the training weekends was not translated into positive action.

Consequently, a specific event was organized in which the factory was stopped for one half-day and people encouraged to identify problems that needed solving. Small teams were set up and sent away to work on the problem. Teams were allowed one hour each week to work on the problems that they were attempting to solve. The teams disbanded once the problems had been solved. If the expenditure of money was required to implement a solution approval from a line manager was necessary as they retained control of budgets.

Several other initiatives were also introduced in the company, including the circulation of company accounts and a profit-share scheme. Successful implementation of solutions by a team was rewarded by the opportunity to present their work to the whole company. All employees vote for the most innovative or successful solution and the winning team wins a small cash prize.

However, all has not been good news in the programme. The momentum generated by the scheme began to slow and managers would not always co-operate fully with the teams. Some managers felt threatened by the scheme and found it difficult to deal with empowered employees. All managers have been given training in leadership and motivation in order to encourage them to adapt to their new roles and adopt an open style of management. Some of the employees are also reluctant to participate fully as they find talking openly in teams or in public difficult. However, these problems, once identified, can be tackled through ongoing programmes intended to maintain involvement and motivation at a high level.

Adapted from: Arkin, A. (1991) An encouraging start to employee motivation. PM Plus, April, pp 18–19.

Management in Action 5.7 describes how one organization has attempted to link together several issues into a motivating process.

Conclusion

Motivation is essentially an individual level response and yet managers must operate most of the time at a group level. Company policies and procedures have to be applied consistently if claims of inequity or injustice are to be avoided. This places a heavy burden on most managers as they attempt to increase the levels of motivation among their employees by adopting both personal, collective and personalized collective methods.

The general conclusion, therefore, seems to be that motivation is a concept that may be intuitively attractive in explanatory terms and offer some opportunity for managers to enhance the nature of work for individuals. However, it is not possible to offer a definitive definition of the concept or how it is and should be used by managers. It is a social and a political concept as well as being a psychological one.

Discussion questions

1   Provide definitions for the following key concepts from this chapter:

Motivation	Maslow's theory
Drive	Alderfer's theory
Extrinsic motivation	McClelland's theory
Intrinsic motivation	Herzberg's theory
Content theories of motivation	Vroom's theory
Process theories of motivation	Locke's theory
Adams' equity theory	Porter and Lawler's theory
Attribution theory	

2   Content theories of motivation offer a more realistic view of the concept in an organizational setting. Discuss.
3   If you were a manager, would you prefer to have a team extrinsically or intrinsically motivated? Why?
4   Motivation is best achieved through offering employees a monetary reward for working harder. Discuss this statement.
5   Are needs socially, physiologically or psychologically determined? What are the implications for motivation?
6   What are the similarities and differences between the approach to motivation adopted by the scientific management theorists and those following the human relations tradition?
7   What is motivation? Describe two theories of motivation and suggest where you think they might be most useful. Justify your answer.
8   The most effective way to motivate employees is through participative management practices. Discuss.
9   It would be impossible for an organization to fully motivate all employees all of the time. Discuss.
10   Compare and contrast one content theory of motivation and one process theory of motivation.

Research activities

1 Make arrangements to speak to a manager. This may be someone at your college or university, or a friend of the family, perhaps even someone where you have worked during vacations. Find out from them what they understand about motivation and how they seek to motivate the people that work for them. Compare your findings with others in your class.

2 This is similar to assignment 1, but this time based on the perceptions of a manual worker or someone who works in an office. Ask them what they understand by the term motivation. Also ask how they are motivated at work and how they would prefer to be motivated. Discuss your findings with others in your class.

3 Return to Management in Action 5.1, 'Executives forced to buy a slice of the pie'. Imagine that you are the human resource manager of a large company and your managing director has just read this article. He has asked you to prepare a management report for him setting out a case for or against the adoption of this type of policy for your organization. Prepare a report that offers a conclusion and justify your views.

Key reading

From Clark, H, Chandler, J and Barry, J (1994) *Organization and Identities: Text and Readings in Organizational Behaviour*, International Thomson Business Press, London.

- Bell, D: Work and its discontents, p 44. It is against the backdrop of control that motivation forms a means of control of human activity.
- Maslow, AH: A theory of motivation, p 106. An introduction to one of the major motivation theories.
- Vroom V: Motivation: a cognitive approach, p 125. An introduction to motivation by one of the leading researchers of his day.
- Thompson, EP: Time and work – discipline, p 216. This also provides a perspective on the organizational context within which motivation takes place.
- Taylor FW: Scientific management, p 231. An introduction to the ideas from the pen of the original writer.
- Mayo E: The work group and 'positive mental attitudes', p 237. This extract considers the influences within group activity that impact on output.
- Roethlisberger FJ and Dickson WJ: Group restriction of output, p 247. This provides another perspective on the Hawthorne research.
- Herzberg F: Motivation through job enrichment, p 300. This provides another insight into aspects of motivation from the work of the original researcher.

Further reading

Anderson, GC (1993) *Managing Performance Appraisal*, Blackwell, Oxford. This text provides a practitioner's handbook on the subject of performance appraisal together with its links with pay, reward and development.

DeCenzo, DA and Holoviak, SJ (1990). *Employee Benefits*, Prentice-Hall, Englewood Cliffs, NJ. Although the book is of American origin (and therefore many of the legislative and tax implications of the work will be different to the UK and Europe) it does suggest the links between motivation, productivity and reward.

Garrahan, P and Stewart, P (1992) *The Nissan Enigma: Flexibility at Work in a Local Economy*. Mansell, London. This text reviews the establishment of a Japanese car assembly plant in the north-east of England. In doing so it also provides an alternative insight into the group working activities operating within the plant. Also it describes the nature of motivation, productivity and reward in that context.

Sargent, A (1990). *Turning People on: The Motivation Challenge*. Institute of Personnel Management. Intended to be a practitioner's review of the main points associated with motivation. The book is designed to review the subject for managers and to prompt them into accepting the 'motivation challenge'. As such it is rather simplistic in its coverage of the material, but can serve as a useful summary and managers' guide.

Weiner, B. (1992) *Human Motivation: Metaphors, Theories and Research*. Sage, Thousand Oaks. This text is described as a source book in the sphere of motivation theory. In that sense it incorporates a much greater level of detail than is possible in a single chapter. It offers an approach to motivation that places it in a social context.

References

Adams, JS (1965) Injustice in social exchange. In *Advances in Experimental Social Psychology* (ed L Berkowitz), Academic Press.

Alderfer, CP (1972) *Existence, Relatedness and Growth*, Free Press, New York.

Baldamus, W (1961) Tedium and traction in industrial work. In *Men and Work in Modern Britain* (ed D Weir), Fontana, London.

Barnard, CI (1938) *The Functions of the Executive*, Harvard University Press, Cambridge, MA.

Blackburn, RM and Mann, M (1979) *The Working Class in the Labour Market*, Macmillan, London.

Campbell, JP and Pritchard, RD (1974) Motivation theory in industrial and organizational psychology. In *Handbook of Industrial and Organizational Psychology* (ed M Dunnette), Rand McNally, Chicago, IL.

Currie, R (1963) *Work Study*, Pitman, London.

Deci, EL (1971) The efforts of externally mediated rewards on intrinsic motivation, *Journal of Applied Psychology*, **18**, 105–15.

Dornstein, M (1989) The fairness judgements of received pay and their determinants. *Journal of Occupational Psychology*, **64**, 287–99.

Early, PC, Northcraft, CL, Lee, C and Lituchy, TR (1990) Impact of process and outcome feedback on the relation of goal setting to task performance. *Academy of Management Journal*, March, 87–105.

Erez, M, Early, PC and Hulin, C (1985) The impact of participation on goal acceptance and performance: a two-step model. *Academy of Management Journal*, March, 50–66.

Garrahan, P and Stewart, P (1992) *The Nissan Enigma: Flexibility at Work in a Local Economy*, Mansell, London.

George, CS (1972). *The History of Management Thought*, 2nd edn, Prentice-Hall, Englewood Cliffs, NJ.

Herzberg, F, Mousener, B and Synderman, BB (1959) *The Motivation to Work*, 2nd edn, Chapman & Hall, London.

Herzberg, F. (1974). *Work and the Nature of Man*, Granada Publishing, London.

Hilton, P (1992) Using incentives to reward and motivate employees, *Personnel Management*, September, 49–52.

Hodgetts, RM and Luthans, F (1990) International human resource management: motivation and leadership dimensions. In *International Human Resource Management Review*, Vol. 1 (ed A Nedd).

Hofstede, G (1980) Motivation, leadership and organization: do American theories apply abroad? *Organizational Dynamics*, Summer, 42–63.

Hollenback, J (1979) A matrix method for expectancy research. *Academy of Management Review*, **4**, 579–87.

Kelly, HH (1971) *Attribution in Social Interaction*, General Learning Press, Morristown.

King, N (1970) A clarification and evaluation of the two-factor theory of job satisfaction. *Psychological Bulletin*, **64**, 18–31.

Lee, R and Lawrence, P (1985) *Organizational Behaviour: Psychology at Work*, Hutchinson, London.

Locke, EA (1968) Towards a theory of task motivation and incentives. *Organizational Behaviour and Human Performance*, **3**, 157–89.

Locke, EA (1976) The nature and causes of job satisfaction. In *Handbook of Industrial and Organizational Psychology* (ed M Dunnette), Rand McNally, Chicago, IL.

Maccoby, M (1988) *Why Work: Motivating and Leading in the New Generation*, Simon & Schuster, New York.

Maslow, AH (1943) A theory of human motivation. *Psychological Review*, **50**, 370–96.

Maslow, AH (1987). *Motivation and Personality*, 3rd edn, Harper & Row, New York.

McClelland, DC (1961) *The Achieving Society*, Free Press, New York.

McGregor, D (1960) *The Human Side of Enterprise*, McGraw-Hill, New York.

Moreton, A (1993) Linking sport with productivity. *Financial Times*, 19 February, 12.

Porter, LW and Lawler, EE (1968) *Managerial Attitudes and Performance*. Richard D Irwin, Homewood, IL.

Schermerhorn, JR, Hunt, JG and Osborn, RN (1982) *Managing Organizational Behaviour*, John Wiley, New York.

Seivers, B (1986) Beyond the surrogate of motivation. *Organization Studies*, **7**, No. 4.

Shalley, C, Oldham, G and Porac, J (1987) Effects of goal difficulty, goal setting method, and expected external evaluation on intrinsic motivation, *Academy of Management Journal*, September, 553–63.

Stock, J (1992) Introducing flexible benefits, *Institute of Manpower Studies*, Report No. 231.

Summers, D (1993) Fear of unemployment still high. *Financial Times*, 4 May, 18.

Taylor, FW (1947) *Scientific Management*, Harper & Row, New York.

Trompenaars, F (1993) *Riding the Waves of Culture*, Nicholas Brealey, London.

Vroom, VH (1964) *Work and Motivation*, John Wiley, New York.

Wiersma, UJ (1992) The effects of extrinsic rewards in intrinsic motivation: a meta analysis. *Journal of Occupational and Organizational Psychology*, **65**, 101–14.

Wren, D (1987) *The Evolution of Management Theory*, 3rd edn, John Wiley, New York.

Part III

Groups within organizations

6
Group formation and structure

Chapter summary

This chapter begins with a consideration of the concept of a group. It then goes on to review the ways that groups are used within an organization and the distinctions between formal and informal groups. A short review of research into group working will be introduced before outlining a number of approaches to the study of how groups are formed and structured. This will be set into a critical review of the ideas discussed along with some indication of their relevance to management and organizations.

▓█▓ browse this web site ▓█▓

www.itbp.com

Learning objectives

After studying this chapter and working through the associated Management in Action panels, discussion questions and research activities, you should be able to:

■ Outline the concept of a group as distinct from a collection of individuals.
■ Understand the differences between formal and informal groups.
■ Describe the Hawthorne studies and their significance in understanding the nature of groups.
■ Discuss the different approaches to the study of how groups form and are structured.
■ Appreciate the links between the group level of analysis within organizational behaviour and the individual and organizational levels.
■ Detail some of the links between group formation and structure and job design, organization design and motivation.
■ Explain the difficulties facing managers in attempting to manage both formal and informal groups.
■ Assess the organizational implications of group activity.

Introduction

Groups form a significant part of the everyday experience of people. There are many different types of group categorized under three distinct headings:

■ Organizational. These groups are established by an organization in order to meet its own needs. Examples would include the production and finance departments.
■ Self-interest. People form a number of groups as a means of protection, or to further their plans and objectives. Examples would include trade union groups and pressure groups.
■ Affinity. These groups offer members the opportunity to meet the basic

human need to 'belong'. Examples would include sports teams, social groups and family groups.

This approach provides for the classification of a group according to the purpose that it serves. But, what is a group? Would every collection of human beings constitute a group? Superficially the answer is yes. How else could a collection of people standing on a railway platform waiting for a train be described? But are they a group in any deeper meaning of the term? Is there any reason or purpose behind their *togetherness* other than a need (or desire) to travel on the same train? Perhaps some of the individuals will be travelling together as a group, for example, a school outing. Others will be travelling to work as individuals and may not know the other people.

Shaw (1981) suggests that a group consists of two or more people who interact with each other in such a way that each influences and is influenced by the others. Schein (1988) suggests that a group can be any number of people who interact with each other, are *psychologically aware* of each other and think of themselves as a group. Although different in emphasis, both of these definitions have a number of features in common, including:

- More than one person involved. It is not possible to have a one person group.
- Interaction must take place. The people waiting on the platform are not a group unless they interact with each other. This may occur in some situations, for example if the train is late in arriving then the individuals may begin to talk to each other and collectively protest to the railway staff.
- Purpose, or intention. Schein suggests that the individuals must perceive themselves to be a group. This implies a purpose or intention behind the *collection* of people.
- Awareness. It implies that the individuals take cognisance of each other in their psychological processes. It is part of the interaction and influence process as described by Shaw.

Groups and organizations

Organizations are made up of many groups. It would not be possible to achieve the objectives of the organization without the existence of groups. The scale and complexity of activity requires that it be broken down into manageable chunks. For example, sales activities form a convenient grouping of activity and one which can usefully be separated from manufacturing. However, as a result of such segmentation it is necessary to provide integration arrangements in order to ensure that the organization is able to function effectively. An example would be the need for production planning to ensure that sales intentions can be realized by the production department.

In addition, there are many other forms of group that function within an organization. Some of the more obvious are indicated below:

- Hierarchical differentiation. The split of an organization into management, staff and manual worker categories. This can be further sub-divided into senior, middle and junior management levels.
- Specialism groupings. The collection of people into the work teams within

a function. An example would be the recruitment team within the personnel department, or the electricians within the maintenance department.

- Activity groupings. These are the means through which much organizational activity is co-ordinated. The most common examples being committees and working parties. It could be the remuneration committee of the
board of directors, or the regular meeting of a quality circle within one of
the departments.

- Boundary spanning. In this category, groups are formed to span the boundary between one organization and another. One example would be a customer liaison group, intended to provide an interface between customers
and the organization. Another would be the regular meetings between
senior managers and the bankers to review aspects of company finances.

- Professional. This could involve the grouping of professionals within the
organization into an institute or similar association.

Likert (1961) developed the idea that organizations should be considered as a
collection of groups, rather than individuals. Individuals would inevitably
belong to more than one group and consequently the groups would overlap.
This he described as a 'linking-pin' process and is shown as Figure 6.1.

Whilst Figure 6.1 is a simplistic representation of the nature of groups within an organization, it is useful as a means of describing the overlapping mem-
berships as part of the formal structure. Likert recognized that this basic model
underestimated the true level and complexity of group activity within an organization. It also ignores the instrumental value of groups to individual members. For example, Handy (1985) argues that individuals use groups for a
number of purposes, including meeting social and affiliation needs and gaining
support for their objectives.

In an organizational setting groups are frequently described as teams and
Management in Action 6.1 reflects the importance of these to Reuters, the
financial and information services company.

Looked at from a top-down perspective, groups are designated by the hierarchy within the organization. Senior managers decide on the form that the
organization will take. In terms of the formation of groups this represents a
given for most people within the organization. Thereafter the formation of formal groups is a process of *selection* and *socialization*. New recruits are chosen
to join the existing organization and part of this process is an assessment of the

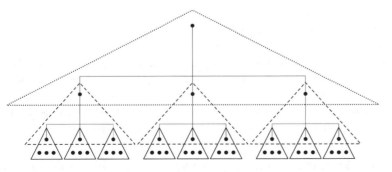

Figure 6.1 Likert's linking PIN model of organizational groups (Likert, R (1961) *New Patterns of Management*, McGraw-Hill, New York, p 105).

Management in Action 6.1

Restoring order from chaos

In the words of John Parcell, from Reuters:

> By the late 1980s it [Reuters] had acquired a reputation for poor service and arrogance. Many orders were handled wrongly, late or not at all. So customers got angry and often refused to pay their bills.

John Parcell and Geoffrey Sanderson were brought into the UK operations of Reuters as managing director and deputy to apply re-engineering principles. What they found was that customers would have to wait between three and six months for new hardware and services, and even two weeks if only services were involved. Once the order had been met it took another two months to send the bill and another three or more to collect payment. Even simple orders would go through a dozen departments and five computer systems. The sales staff and engineers who formed the direct interface with customers did not know each other.

Parcell and Sanderson identified, with the assistance of management consultants, a process which included:

- The creation of four geographic divisions. This focused the company on customer location.
- These divisions were organized into multifunctional account teams of about six people. Each team was responsible for the business of about 50 customers.
- The customer order, delivery, installation, billing and follow-up system (the order life-cycle) was totally re-designed. The number of "hand-offs" between people was reduced from about 24 to four.
- Performance criteria were identified indicating when the order stages had to be completed.
- Training and change management assisted the transition and ensured that everyone knew what was expected of them and possessed the necessary skills.

Two years after the initial change it has been reported that the multifunctional teams are working well and are beginning to press for more autonomy in dealing with customers. It is reported that employees find the working atmosphere one of mutual help and covering for each other. In excess of 95% of all orders are now installed on time. Those involving hardware and services are operational between three and four weeks after orders are placed, and less than one day for services. Bills are also more than 98% accurate. Surveys have shown that customer dissatisfaction has dropped to less than 10%.

Adapted from: Lorenz, C (1993) Restoring order from chaos. Financial Times, 2 June, p 11.

---

fit between the existing people and the applicant. Once inside the organization the individual is subjected to an extended process of socialization into the organization and the groups to which they will become affiliated.

Formal and informal groups

The emphasis so far has been on those groups that exist as part of the formal activities within an organization. They are established by management and function according to management's rules and standards. It is possible to differentiate formal from other groups on the basis of purpose. Based on the work of Argyle (1989) it is possible to identify formal groups involved in the following activities:

- Teams. Frequently project or activity groups. Usually given a high degree of freedom in terms of deciding on the processes to be used to achieve the objectives set.

- Tasks. The nature of the objectives to be achieved are more clearly set out and so there is little discretion in terms of activity and method. Most work groups would fall under this heading.
- Technology. The nature of this classification is that the *technology*, or process dictates the *activities* and *methods* involved. There exists little opportunity for the group to exercise discretion in either of these areas.
- Decisions. Much management time is taken up with meetings associated with decision making. Of course this form of group activity is not restricted to managers. Many specialist and administrative staff would also be involved.
- Management. In addition to decision making, management must collectively plan, guide and monitor organizational activity.

Informal groups exist within all organizations. It is also true that within most formal groups there exist a number of informal ones. Informal groups serve a number of functions both positive and negative. It is usual to describe informal groups in either friendship or interest terms. Membership of an informal group is voluntary and the significance of their existence is frequently understated. In most organizations *things get done* on the basis of the informal groups and networks that exist.

The role of informal relations and networks in excluding women from management positions was demonstrated by Cooper and Davidson (1982). There have been moves towards the formation of women only groups or networks, the purpose being to enhance the ability of women to progress in the male dominated professions and management. Management in Action 6.2 illustrates some of the difficulties facing women in attempting to progress into senior positions.

Friendship groups form on the basis of relationships within an organization. They are not restricted to level or functional area within the company and frequently act as information channels. In practice much friendship group activity has a social basis and becomes a mutual *looking out for each other*. If friendship groups become too strong, they may attempt to influence events in their favour, perhaps through clandestine means. Consequently, there is a danger of friendship groups working against the interests of management. It is also possible for such groups to form the basis of resistance to change. It is at this point that friendship groups become interest groups. Interest groups could also form as a response to a perceived threat. For example, comments from senior managers that a delayering exercise was being considered might encourage junior managers to form a group (or join a trade union) in order to protect their jobs by seeking to influence or frustrate management's intentions.

The existence of informal groups is something that is frequently seen as a matter of concern by managers. However, as has been implied, there is a degree of inevitability about their existence and they can be of value to management. The grapevine can be a useful means though which to communicate with individuals in the organization according to Dalton (1959). Katz (1973) also suggests that informal groups can assist the integration of employees into the organization by blurring the distinction between work and non-work activities.

Informal groups form the lifeblood of an organization in that they depend on

Management in Action 6.2

Men's room only

The first women's colleges were opened in Oxford a century ago yet the representation of females among the higher levels of academic staff is still relatively small.

In 1993 when this material first appeared in print it was reported that only six out of 178 professors and four out of 69 readers at Oxford were women. It was argued that this couldn't be due to a shortage of potential applicants as women represent about 13% of university lecturers, 27% of college lecturers and 42% of undergraduates. Nationally, the Association of University Teachers, the trade union representing academic staff in universities, claimed that the position of women was not much better with only about 5% of professors in the 'old' universities being women. Two-thirds of female professors have been appointed since the late 1980s.

It has been suggested that universities suffer from the existence of a 'glass ceiling', a phenomenon evident in many organizations and professions. It represents an invisible barrier to promotion. Women in an organization or profession reach a certain level within the hierarchy, to find that they can see the senior levels above them but they are unable to reach these positions.

At Oxford University a group of academic staff were determined to challenge the decision to allocate money available for promotion to fund additional professorships rather readerships. The argument being that this approach reinforced the position of men as professors because few women had the status allowing them to be successful in seeking promotion to that rank. On the other hand if the promotions were to be concentrated at the level of readerships then more women would be likely to be successful because of the greater number that would be eligible for promotion. The justification for the decision, put forward by Oxford University, was that in terms of international status and recognition of its work, the title professor would be of greater benefit to both the individuals and institution.

Oxford claim that they are making good progress from what was a very low base in the promotion of women. Until 1979 only one-third of colleges accepted women. Those seeking to enhance the position of women claim that the predominantly male culture of British universities is generally intimidating to women and that this needs to be addressed. As one student explained:

> The problem is that the system has been built around men for 750 years. Are we prepared to change ourselves to reflect the diversity we now have?

Adapted from: Authers, J (1993) Men's room only. Financial Times, *18 May, p 17.*

a level of mutual need among the members for their existence. Informal groups form because the individuals wish to *band together*, perhaps for protection against a management decision; perhaps because they enjoy similar leisure interests; or perhaps because there is a work-related dependency. Whatever the reason for the existence of an informal group many of them contribute to the effective running of the organization. It is the ability of one employee to speak directly with another and discuss work related events and problems that is mutually beneficial and keeps things running smoothly. Standard operating procedures provide guidance on what should be done, people in their working relationships actually make this happen.

Many of the recent attempts to increase levels of employee commitment can be interpreted as attempts to tap into already existing informal processes. Management in Action 6.3 provides an indication of the processes involved in reorganizing people into teams and the associated training required.

Sense of involvement

Du Pont's printing and publishing business introduced an annual hours work system in 1992 and as a result moved from four- to six-shift working. The 750 workers were organized into 30 self-managed teams. Within the teams employees are trained in all tasks performed by the group, some retaining a core skill function. Each team is responsible for every aspect of the process, including production, costing, productivity, quality, safety and work allocation. This is achieved through a weekly pre-shift meeting supported by a training day each six weeks. The gains achieved are tangible and Pat Tunney, the personnel manager at Du Pont, indicated that productivity rose by 36% in the first year of operation and he predicted a 25% rise the following year.

Team building can be achieved in many different ways. Sue Bradshaw, the dealer development manager with Peugeot, described their approach. In pursuit of accreditation to the BS5750 quality standard an improvement cycle was identified thorough which continuous change could be made within the dealer network. The company introduced a 'team builder' programme which began with a PC-based questionnaire to generate information for the individual's team profile. This was used to discuss role preferences and team communication style with each individual before a two-day team development workshop. This led naturally into ongoing discussions by the team about how to improve the performance of the business.

Other companies opt for outdoor training as the means to encourage understanding and develop the trust and confidence between individual members. Rank Xerox CSD manger for human resources, Christine Hands, indicated that:

> Group members need mutual trust and respect for each other's skills, knowledge, opinions and commitment. They need to communicate freely and easily with each other.

The team training provided by Rank Xerox was provided by a US company and was described by Hands as a mini-Olympics in the following way:

> It went down as a lot of fun. Their style was very un-English – it took some people a while to come to terms with it. But by the end of the week no-one wanted to leave.

Adapted from: Haughton, E (1993) Sense of involvement. Personnel Today, *29 June, pp 26–30.*

In an organizational context there are two major reasons why groups are a significant factor for both employers and employees. Firstly, it is necessary to use groups or teams of individuals to achieve the organization's objectives. Secondly, most humans prefer to associate with other people. The main reasons that groups form include:

- The need to have more than one person to undertake the work. In organizations of more than one person it is necessary to separate the activities to be done and to allocate people into teams.
- The need to incorporate the expertise of a number of people in order to achieve the end result. For example, a project team set up to design a new product may need the skills of designers, engineers, accountants, production and marketing specialists.
- The need for organizations to match complexity in the environment through the provision of internal operating methods and arrangements. Ashby (1964) termed this as the *law of requisite variety*. He suggested only variety could destroy variety. Among the implications of this is that the

creation of teams can encourage synergy, creativity and innovation through group membership.

■ The opportunity to allow employees to minimize the worst aspects of their work by sharing it out, or rotating it among the group. This should enhance satisfaction, or minimize dissatisfaction.

■ Groups provide for the social needs of individuals. Friendships provide a form of social significance for the individual within the work setting. It allows the individual to be more than just a number, or a means of production. Such networks and relationships allow for the support of the individual in the work setting by other workers.

■ The groups to which an individual belong provide a basis for socialization into the *norms* of behaviour within the organization. This includes the extent to which official rules are followed and the way that employees maintain the balance between management demands and employee preference.

Management in Action 6.4

Construction on a united front

MW Kellogg is an international construction company employing some 4000 skilled workers. The UK operation specializes in petrochemical design and construction projects, lasting anything from a few weeks to several years. Each project requires a dedicated team of anything up to 100 people from a range of professions and disciplines. Project teams can also involve individuals and groups that are not directly employed by MW Kellogg. This situation can create many difficulties as people have to work effectively together and at the same time look after the interests of the organization that they represent. Add to this the cultural, language and professional differences that exist when operating internationally and it surprising that any project is completed.

Angela Freddi, senior personnel officer for MW Kellogg, attempted to find ways of encouraging the creation of effective teams in this context. Purpose-designed courses were introduced with the help of an outside training company, Arete. The process for each project group follows a similar pattern:

■ Once the project group is selected Arete visit each member in order to identify potential problem areas.

■ This information is discussed with the personnel department and a three-day course is designed to address the issues identified and create a team.

■ Courses have a common theme to them. The first two days are intended to break down barriers and to build team spirit. The third day focuses on issues relevant to the project that the team is to undertake.

■ Non-company people who will be part of the project team are encouraged to attend the course.

■ Members of the project group will be taken off their current job in groups to go through the course. Participants on each course are from a range of the disciplines and professions represented on the project.

Another aspect of these courses worthy of note is the use of either indoor or outdoor activity, depending upon the background and experience of the participants. These activities involve the solving of problems, where every member of the team has to experience being a team leader and operating at the lowest level. This is intended to provide individuals with the experience of what it is like to allow someone else to have the lead role as well as to reflect on their own strengths and weaknesses.

Adapted from: Simons, C (1992) Construction on a united front. Personnel Today, 30 June, pp 33–4.

- Group membership also provides the individual with a measure of protection from outside threat. It has been argued that employment conditions and protection have been improved across Europe as a result of the high levels of trade union membership.
- Groups also emerge as a result of the nature of the work to be undertaken within an organization. This can be to acquire information; seek clarification of that already obtained; pass work on (or obtain it); cross-reference something; or elicit help in undertaking something. The result is that mutual dependency is formed with people either helping (or hindering) each other.

The discussion on groups reflects the complexity in organizational activity. The concept of *variety* has already been introduced as a useful means of reflecting this state of affairs. Management in Action 6.4 on the previous page reflects how one organization attempted to deal with this notion of variety.

Research approaches

One of the earliest research activities into group activity was reported by Triplett (1897). Triplett observed that racing cyclists performed better when accompanied by a pacemaker than when alone. Table 6.1 below indicates the results that he observed for two leading racing cyclists to cover a one mile training 'race'.

The gain from having a pacemaker was an improvement in performance of approximately 20%. This in itself was an interesting result as the experiment was not a competitive situation. Triplett interpreted these findings in terms of the arousal of the competitive instinct from the presence of the other cyclist. This became known as *social facilitation*, the presence of others producing an enhanced performance in an individual.

These co-action effects (changes in behaviour through the presence of others) have been observed in a wide range of species. Table 6.2 has been developed from Zajonc (1965) and demonstrates this.

| | Time to cycle one mile | | |
	Paced	Unpaced	Gain from pacing
Person X	99.6 seconds	123.8 seconds	+19.5%
Person Y	102.0 seconds	130.0 seconds	+21.5%

Table 6.1
Racing times for one mile

Harlow (1932)	Laboratory rats ate more if fed together than when fed alone
Chen (1937)	A species of ant worked harder at nest building when working in groups than when alone
Rasmussen (1939)	Thirsty laboratory rats would drink more when in the presence of other rats than when alone
Tolman and Wilson (1956)	Repeated the Harlow (1932) findings but with chicks rather than rats

Table 6.2
Social facilitation in non-human species

Another form of social facilitation is referred to as an *audience effect*. The mere presence of others producing an enhancement in behavioural activity.

The British experience

During World War I the British government established a committee to study the relationship between working conditions, fatigue and output. After the end of the war this committee changed its focus and in 1918 came under the control of the Medical Research Council. It became the Industrial Fatigue Research Board. Initially the board concentrated on issues surrounding the nature of work and its effect on people. The board published 33 research studies relating to aspects of the employment of people.

Commissioned by the Board, Wyatt *et al.* (1928) reported a study carried out in a number of organizations involving women performing a number of jobs, including wrapping soap; folding handkerchiefs; making bicycle chains; weighing and wrapping tobacco; making cigarettes and rifle bullets. Among the conclusions drawn from their work was that the social conditions within which the work was done had significant consequences for the people. Also that boredom was less likely to arise when people worked in groups rather than on their own.

In the USA work was underway at the same time that, when linked with the ideas from the research activity already described, was to lead to the development of the human relations movement. The significance of the social aspects of work emerged as a major alternative to the task emphasis prevalent up to that point.

The Hawthorne studies

The Western Electric Company had begun a series of investigations at its Hawthorne works in 1924. The studies were initially carried out by staff within the company, as it was intended to identify improvements of practical value. In 1927 researchers from the Harvard Business School became involved in the research and those names of Mayo, Roethlisberger and Dickson are now the most closely associated with it.

It is Mayo who is credited with the leadership of the research team from Harvard. He was an Australian by birth and spent time during and after World War I working with disabled military personnel. It is hardly stretching credibility to imagine that such an experience would have a major impact on his thinking about people, work, organizations and life in general. The significance of people in a collective setting was a predominant theme of the Hawthorne research and the subsequent interpretation of the results.

The studies within the Hawthorne works can be separated into four stages:

■ The illumination experiments.
■ The relay assembly test room study.
■ The interview programme.
■ The bank wiring observation room study.

Looking briefly at each in turn.

The illumination experiments
The intention of these experiments was to identify the relationship between levels of light and output. The experiment was undertaken by splitting the

workers into experimental and control groups. The experimental group was subjected to situations in which the level of illumination was systematically varied and the output monitored. The control group continued in conditions of normal levels of light and the levels of output recorded.

The results of the experiments were inconclusive in that production levels did not appear to vary in relationship to the level of light. The level of output increased even when the level of light was very poor. Output also increased in the control group, with no change in lighting. The highest level of output recorded was when the experimental group returned to their normal working conditions.

This unexpected set of findings led to the conclusion that worker output was influenced by many factors and prompted the subsequent research in an attempt to identify them.

The relay assembly test room study

The work in this room involved female workers assembling a number of small components to make the relay switches used in telephone equipment. Because of the nature of the work it was highly repetitive and boring. To conduct the research, a group of six women were selected from among the regular workforce. Two of the women (who were friends) were selected by the research team. The two women then selected the other four workers. The six women to be studied were transferred to a special room designated for the research study.

Working conditions in the normal department were replicated in the experimental room. The experiment began with a period during which the work practices were identical to those in the normal department. For example, a 48-hour working week with no rest breaks, or provision of refreshment. The normal output on assembling relays was 50 per hour worked. This level of output allowed the research team to detect even relatively small changes. There followed a research period of almost two years, in which a number of variables associated with the work arrangements were systematically varied (see Table 6.3).

The researcher was located in the room with the women workers and created the records for later analysis by noting all that happened. The women were generally kept informed about the experiment and consulted about events that were to take place. The observer also tried to maintain a friendly atmosphere in the room through his general approach.

Output increased under each of the experimental manipulations during this phase of the research. Output even increased when the experiment was ended and the women went back to the normal working arrangements operated in the main department. The main reasons put forward as an explanation for the results obtained included:

- The special status accruing to the women as a result of having been selected for involvement in the experiment resulted in an increased motivation to co-operate and perform at their best.
- The influence of being consulted and kept informed by the experimenter enhanced output as a result of the increased level of participation.
- Morale improved as a result of the general friendliness of the observer and conditions of the experiment.
- The management approach to supervision during the experiment was different to that experienced normally. The increased freedom experienced by

Table 6.3

Examples of the experimental conditions used in the relay assembly test room

Duration of experiment (weeks)	Experimental condition
8	Incentive introduced to reward increased individual effort
5	A morning and afternoon rest period of five minutes allowed
4	Rest periods extended to 10 minutes each
4	Introduction of six five-minute rest periods
11	Introduction of 15-minute morning and 10-minute afternoon rest periods with the company providing refreshments
7	In addition to the two rest periods immediately above finish work at 4.30 pm (30 minutes early)
4	As previous rest periods but finish work at 4.00 pm (60 minutes early)
9	Saturday working eliminated, plus one 15-minute and one 10-minute rest period allowed each day
11	Introduction of 15-minute morning and 10-minute afternoon rest periods with the company providing refreshments
7	In addition to the two rest periods immediately above finish work at 4.30 pm (30 minutes early)
4	As previous rest periods but finish work at 4.00 pm (60 minutes early)
9	Saturday working eliminated, plus one 15 minute and one 10-minute rest period allowed each day

the women within the work setting reduced stress and encouraged higher output.

■ The group was self-selected, thereby allowing the better than normal relationships to create a climate of mutual dependence and support appropriate to group working.

The results of this stage of the experiment encouraged the researchers to seek out the social and other variables operating in the work setting through an extended interview programme.

The interview programme

More than 20,000 interviews were conducted in this phase of the research. Among the earlier findings was the suggestion that output and productivity were related to supervision and working conditions. The interview programme was designed to identify employee attitudes and feelings towards these issues using structured questions. However, it quickly became apparent that workers wanted to talk about other aspects of their work. As a response, the process was changed, involving open-ended and non-directive questions. This allowed interviewees to discuss things that they considered important.

There were a number of findings that emerged from the analysis of this vast amount of research data. Employee views about management in general, the company, even society as a whole were obtained. Indications were also obtained that there was a network of informal groups in existence within the organizationally based work teams. These groups were the primary means by which supervisors and leading employees controlled the productive activities and behaviour of other employees within departments. The techniques developed in this stage of the research programme played a significant part in the subsequent introduction of counselling and attitude surveys as part of human resource management practice.

The existence of informal groups within the formal, an organization within an organization, led to the final stage in the research programme. The Bank Wiring Observation Room study was intended to discover how these informal groups functioned and exercised control.

The bank wiring observation room study

This stage of the research consisted of the direct observation of 14 men employed in the department. The men were organized into three teams each consisting of three wirers and a supervisor. In addition, there were two inspectors checking the work of the department as a whole.

The observation of this department identified the existence of two informal groups. These groups did not coincide with the formal structures within the department. Figure 6.2 below reflects the composition of these groups, and is based on Roethlisberger and Dickson (1964, p 504).

From Figure 6.2 it can be seen that one supervisor, one wirer and one inspector were not affiliated to either informal group. In addition, two wirers were only partially integrated to the groups.

The two informal groups developed their own behaviour standards, or *group norms* as they became known. The norms covered a number of features of the work of the department, including output. Much of the activity of the informal groups was intended to control the behaviour of members with the aim of protecting the group from interference by management and maintaining group cohesion.

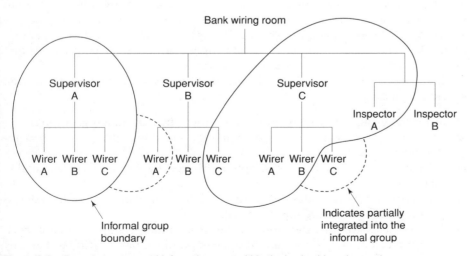

Figure 6.2 Formal structure and informal groups within the bank wiring observation room.

The groups became adept at being able to 'manage' management by providing a picture of activity within the department that met the expectations of managers. Output was reported as being constant over the week, even if it had varied on a daily basis. The overall level of output was correctly reported, but the pattern of production was smoothed. Managers had a tendency to expect consistency in work activity. Deviation from expectation would become a focus of attention and investigation. By 'meeting' that expectation, employees retained effective control over their day-to-day working environment.

The norms of behaviour under which the informal groups operated consisted of a number of rules in which individual workers would be named according to the following criteria:

- Chisler. A person who turned out too little work. Someone who was not doing their fair share of work.
- Rate-buster. A person who produced more than a reasonable volume of work.
- Squealer. A person who reported anything to a supervisor that could be to the detriment of a fellow worker.

One rule was that an inspector or supervisor should become part of the informal group structure and not act as part of management. This included an expectation of co-operation with the group in enforcing its norms and not acting in an officious manner.

The informal groups were reducing the opportunity for members to earn at their maximum level, or at their personally preferred level, in favour of the maintenance of group cohesion. In practice, the group looked after the collective interest of the members, but the price was a loss of individualism and earnings potential.

Within the bank wiring room the group norms were enforced through a number of sanctions. Control was enforced through a hierarchy of negative sanctions. These ranged from light-hearted comments about the individual's output level. If this was not successful, or a more serious breach of the norms occurred then the comments became more pointed and tapping on the upper arm (referred to as *binging*) occurred. The inspector who was not part of an informal group considered that he was superior to the wirers and generally acted in an officious manner. The workers played tricks on him with equipment, they ostracized him and generally applied so much social pressure that he asked to be transferred to another department.

There are a number of key findings that emerged from the Hawthorne studies, including:

- Informal groups inevitably form within formally designated groupings.
- Informal groups will not always match the groupings designated by management.
- Individuals at work are not simply motivated by pay and other tangible benefits.
- Informal groups will attempt a form of bottom-up management in order to influence their working environment.
- The rewards that an individual gains from membership of an informal group may be more significant and meaningful to that individual than any benefit that can be obtained from management.

- Informal groups may seek to frustrate management's intentions and objectives.
- The groups to which an individual belong will have a significant influence on their behaviour and attitudes towards work.
- First-line managers and supervisors are subjected to strong and competing pressures for their affiliations from those above and below.
- Management has little or no influence on the establishment and form or membership of informal groups within the organization.
- Informal groups can engage in competitive activities that are against the interests of the organization as a whole.

As society changes so to do the forms of control that can successfully be applied. Early approaches to managing relied heavily on coercion and force. This continued, with a small number of notable exceptions, until the time of the Hawthorne studies, which began a more concerted move towards the humanization of work. The Human Relations Movement, as it became known, was interested in how to adopt a social dimension to work organization and motivation.

Another way of thinking about this notion of humanization of work is to consider it as an attempt by managers to maintain control within a changing social environment. It had become apparent that social attitudes and structures were beginning to change and that existing methods of control were not producing the levels of output and quality required at an acceptable price. This, if nothing else, had been demonstrated by Taylor in his application of scientific management. However, given the adverse reaction that his approach generated alternative ways were needed to improve productivity and retain control. The human relations approach offered an opportunity to achieve these objectives in a different way.

The Hawthorne studies have been very influential in providing ideas and theory relating to groups within an organizational setting. Management in Action 6.5 provides an illustration of how one organization attempted to combine formality and informality into its teamwork activities.

Group formation and development

Formal groups are created by the organization of which they form part. However the informal groups that exist are created by the people within the host organization. They both feed off and interact with the formal groups around them. Informal groups come into existence for a number of reasons, including:

- The nature and form of the formal organization. The way that the formal organization operates can influence the way that individuals organize themselves and interact.
- The need for human beings to function in a social environment and to form relationships of their own choosing. Schein (1956) describes the manipulation of prisoners-of-war by the Chinese Communists during the Korean War. The use of rank was dispensed with and groups were re-organized when it became apparent that something approaching an effective structure was emerging.

Working as a team member

Sherwood Computer Services set about changing itself. Kevin Crane, the personnel director, explained the rationale:

> Every software house can provide the software and systems the client wants. It is the efficiency with which the client is handled that makes the difference and that comes down to the way we are organized.

Dramatic losses had shaken the company and many costs were cut, including the number of staff (to below 500). Having identified that changes in work organization were needed, Crane brought together two teams of 10 employees to work out how the company should be organized. Staff from Ashridge Management College facilitated progress. The results of these groups were circulated around the company and applications were invited for places on 10 task forces to review aspects of reorganization.

Six weeks later each task force reported its findings to the board. Not surprisingly the range of views covered all eventualities from do nothing to eliminate the structure completely. The new structure created managerless client teams of about 15 people, a business team of 14 senior managers reporting to the three members of the board of directors. Each team was to be responsible for all client activity. Potential internal competition for clients was controlled through the creation of market co-ordination groups covering the major areas of business.

Each client team was responsible for managing its own efforts and work activities. Each client team determined its business plan and agreed it with senior management, performance being monitored against that plan. The team assessed the performance of its members through peer assessment of the personal, professional and technical skills as identified by those with whom individuals most closely interacted. Sherwood introduced a pay system in which additional pay was obtained through the acquisition of additional skills of value to the client team.

In moving to the new structure it was the middle and junior managers that needed most convincing because their jobs were disappearing and they had most to lose. Senior managers spent considerable amounts of time talking to small groups of managers in order to convince them of the ultimate benefit to themselves as well as the company.

Adapted from: Carrington, L (1991) Working as a team member. Personnel Today, 22 January, pp 38–9.

- The voluntary nature of many informal groups offsets the involuntary nature of many formal, organizational groups.
- The approach adopted by managers to the running of the organization will also influence the formation of informal groups.
- The need to run the organization. Organization structures and procedures are the mechanisms that determine what should be done where and when. However, procedures cannot cater for the interpersonal and dynamic nature of organizational activity. Organizational functioning depends to a significant extent on individuals co-operating in a reciprocal network of activity. Inevitably, in such situations self-help networks of mutual dependency (informal groups) form.

Group formation

Homans (1950) proposed that any group (he used the term *social system*) existed within an environment consisting of three elements:

- Culture. The norms, values and goals that make up the shared understanding within which the group will function.
- Physical. The geographical context, involving the actual location and its tangible characteristics within which the group will operate.
- Technological. This relates to the facilities, etc. that the group will have access to in pursuing its activities.

Homans argued that this environment imposed a range of *activities* and *interactions* on the individuals and groups within the system. As a consequence of these impositions, a variety of *emotions* and *attitudes* are engendered among the members towards the environment and the other participants. This Homans called the *external system*. He also suggested that frequent interaction between people would lead to a more positive attitude and a better relationship between them. The converse was also true, that is, better attitudes lead to a higher frequency of interaction. This chain of events and reactions leads to the formation of a group (as shown in Figure 6.3).

With an increased level of interaction Homans observed a tendency for individuals to develop attitudes and emotions not dictated by the external system. This led to the development of new frames of reference and norms between the individuals concerned. In turn these embellishments produced new activities not specified by the external system. This Homans called the *Internal system*, in effect an informal group.

Homans suggested a number of features of these external and internal systems:

- The external and internal systems are mutually dependent. A change in one will produce a change in the other. For example, a change in work structure can change the patterns of interaction between individuals. Conversely, attitudes in the internal system can influence the way that work gets done.
- The two systems and the environment are mutually dependent. Individuals will mould and adapt work activities to suit themselves. Multidisciplinary project teams are an example of this process, incorporating the opportunity to tap into the internal system as well as the external.

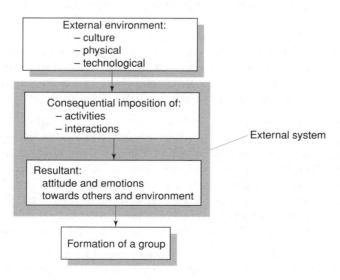

Figure 6.3 Homans explanation of group formation.

Homans' theory is an important view of how groups are formed for two reasons. Firstly, it stresses the mutual dependency between the many elements associated with the existence of groups. Secondly, it exposes the distinction between behaviour required by the environment and external system and the emergence of behaviour not required by the formal system, but equally as significant.

Group development

The existence of a group is no guarantee that it will be an effective or meaningful arrangement for either the organization or individual members. Groups do not automatically become effective at meeting their objectives and satisfying the needs of the individuals concerned.

Consider for a moment an organization that you have encountered. This could be your university, or a company that you have worked for. Reflect on the groups that you were part of. It should become quickly apparent that within an organization a number of different groups and collections of individuals exist. For example:

■ There exist a number of units within an organization that would not qualify as a group. Just because individuals work on similar activities and are classified as part of the same department does not qualify them as a group.
■ Within formal units in an organization there may exist a number of smaller, formal and informal groups. For example, a large department may contain a number of sub-sections.
■ Within organizations there will exist a number of informal groups. Friendship groupings and task dependent networks across formal boundaries are common examples.
■ Some groups (formal and informal) will be relatively permanent. For example, a project group may be formed to design a new product and see it through to the market; or a standing committee on remuneration policy might meet twice each year but change membership frequently as people leave the company or are promoted into other jobs.
■ Some groups (formal and informal) will be transient. Such formal groups are widely used within organizations as project teams, task forces or problem-solving groups. Informal groups of this type tend to form in response to particular events. For example, employees who feel threatened by a management proposal may form a pressure group.

Each of these situations present different behavioural situations. It is impossible to present a single comprehensive theory of how all groups develop. In some cases it is the existing members of a group who must adapt to new circumstances. In other cases it is individuals who must become part of an existing group. In other situations it is a new collection of individuals who must become a group to undertake a new situation. In this area there are two approaches that offer an insight as to how groups develop.

Bass and Ryterband (1979) identify a four stage model of group development:

■ Initial development of trust and membership. Individuals coming together for the first time need to learn to trust each other and to feel confident enough to contribute to the activities within the group.

■ Beginning of communication and decision making. Once trust begins to develop and the individuals are able to communicate more easily mutual dependence emerges. This allows decisions to be made and problems to be solved.

■ Performance improvement. In the previous stage conflicts can arise between individuals as the group norms are being developed. In this third stage, these teething problems have been largely overcome and the effectiveness of the group improves. Individuals focus on the work of the group and become collectively motivated to achieve the objectives.

■ Ongoing maintenance and control. At this stage individuals have become accustomed to working together on routine group activities. Consequently there is a degree of independence between members and flexibility in adapting to new situations.

This model has a number of similarities to the better known work of Tuckman, who in 1965 described a four-stage model of group formation. Tuckman and Jensen (1977) added a stage to the basic model. The five stages are as follows:

■ Stage 1. Forming. This stage occurs when the individuals first come together. It involves each individual getting to know the others, their attitudes, personalities and backgrounds. Individuals use this stage to make a personal impact within the group. It is also likely that anxiety is felt by the individuals as they attempt to define their position within the group. This process also begins to define the hierarchy and roles within the group.

■ Stage 2. Storming. As a formal structure begins to emerge and individuals begin to feel more confidence in their position within the group, conflict arises. Individuals begin to bring to the group their own agenda. Issues begin to emerge as the group *storms* its way towards the next stage. If successfully handled this stage leads to a more focused group in terms of relationships between the members and the ease with which it can achieve its goals. Not all groups successfully negotiate past this stage and lingering problems continue to inhibit progression. In extreme cases groups can collapse at this stage.

■ Stage 3. Norming. This stage reflects the process of establishing the norms to be operated within the group. This includes the behavioural standards among members, for example to allow (or prevent) jokes and other diversions. Also the procedural rules are developed that provide the group with its operating framework. Someone with a hidden agenda may seek to bring in items that allow them to achieve their objective. Norming is a process that goes on within a group and as such management has only limited opportunity to influence it.

■ Stage 4. Performing. Only when the group has successfully completed the three previous stages can it make significant progress in its work. In that sense the group is now mature and able to operate effectively.

■ Stage 5. Adjourning. This stage involves the leaving by individuals or the complete dissolution of a group having achieved its objectives. Frequently, at this stage a period of reflection and reorientation is undertaken as individuals consider past glories and anticipate future success.

In practice a group may not successfully negotiate itself through one of the stages described above. Unresolved difficulties will result in subsequent problems. For example, a lack of clarity on humour is likely to result in frustration as some people tell jokes whilst others resent the diversion. The ability of individuals to progress and achieve items from a hidden agenda can be another major source of difficulty for a group. The consequences of these factors being a reduction in the level of effectiveness or member satisfaction in the group.

Group norms are the means through which a group regulates the behaviour of its members. The norms of behaviour become internalized by the individuals and institutionalized in the accepted patterns of behaviour. They provide a powerful group mechanism through which to release time and energy in order to concentrate on important issues. Imagine if a group had to establish behaviour standards and codes of conduct every time it met. The goals would never be met. Conversely, the workings of a group can become overly concentrated on establishing norms and regulating the behaviour of its members. Some committees fall into this trap by concentrating on procedural matters and minutes, losing sight of the objectives to be achieved.

Feldman (1984) suggests that groups will adopt a satisficing approach to regulating individual behaviour, unless:

- Group survival is at risk. If the behaviour of an individual threatens the group, then they will be dealt with.
- Lack of clarity in the expected behaviour of group members is creating problems in group activity or performance.
- By taking action the group can avoid bringing into the open things that it would be embarrassing or difficult to resolve.
- The central values held by the group are being threatened. If by allowing something to continue the status of a group might be compromised then action would be taken.

In this section we have described how groups develop to the point that would allow them to function effectively. But that is only one aspect of a group that needs to be considered. All groups have a structure within them. Formal groups have formal structures, the Chair, the Secretary and so on. Informal groups have informal roles within them, dominant individuals that lead the activities, and direction of the group.

Group structure

In formal groups the structure of the group may be dictated by the situation. For example, a department (or project team) will often be appointed by management. The individuals have no direct say in who will be appointed and what role they will perform. In other situations, particularly informal groups, the membership is self-selected and members have a greater influence on both structure and roles. Many groups within an organization are comprised of representatives of other groups or departments or even from outside the organization itself. Consequently, these representatives are subject to report back requirements and direction from their sponsoring groups. This can often create conflict between personal and group loyalty for the individuals concerned.

There are a number of ways of considering group structure. For example, Huczynski and Buchanan (1991) identify a number of dimensions on which the structure of a group is dependent:

- **Status.** The reflection of the value placed upon particular positions within the group. It can also be seen as a reflection of the value of a particular person in the eyes of other people.
- **Power.** The ability to influence other people. This can either be a function of the position of a person, or a reflection of personal influence.
- **Liking.** The personal affiliations among members of a group. It is inevitable that individuals will prefer the company (and ideas) of people they like at a personal level, and distance themselves from people that they do not like. This affects the patterns of communication within the group.
- **Role.** This concept refers to the behaviours that accompany a particular function or position within a group. The roles that exist, or that people identify for themselves, determine to a significant extent the behaviour patterns that they engage in.
- **Leadership.** The style adopted by the leader of a group can also have a distinct influence on events within that group.

Roles and descriptions – team-role contribution	Allowable weaknesses
Plant: Creative, imaginative, unorthodox. Solves difficult problems.	Ignores details. Too preoccupied to communicate effectively.
Resource investigator: Extrovert, enthusiastic, communicative. Explores opportunities. Develops contacts.	Overoptimistic. Loses interest once initial enthusiasm has passed.
Co-ordinator: Mature, confident, a good chairperson. Clarifies goals, promotes decision-making, delegates well.	Can be seen as manipulative. Delegates personal work.
Shaper: Challenging, dynamic, thrives on pressure. Has the drive and courage to overcome obstacles.	Can provoke others. Hurts people's feelings.
Monitor/evaluator: Sober, strategic and discerning. Sees all options. Judges accurately.	Lacks drive and ability to inspire others. Overly critical.
Teamworker: Co-operative, mild, perceptive and diplomatic. Listens, builds, averts friction, calms the waters.	Indecisive in crunch situations. Can be easily influenced.
Implementer: Disciplined, reliable, conservative and efficient. Turns ideas into practical actions.	Somewhat inflexible. Slow to respond to new possibilities.
Completer: Painstaking, conscientious, anxious. Searches out errors and omissions. Delivers on time.	Inclined to worry unduly. Reluctant to delegate. Can be a nit-picker.
Specialist: Single-minded. self-starting, dedicated. Provides knowledge and skills in rare supply.	Contributes on only a narrow front. Dwells on technicalities. Overlooks the 'big picture'.

Table 6.4

The nine Belbin team roles (Belbin, M (1993) *Team Roles at Work*, Butterworth Heinemann, Oxford, p 23)

Belbin (1993) identifies nine team roles that it is suggested determine the performance of a group. Whilst detailed consideration of this will be held over until the next chapter, it is appropriate to introduce the ideas here because they contain a relevance to the structural aspects of group activity. The roles themselves (Table 6.4) cover the main requirements of group structure and also provide, according to Belbin, for the achievement of high performance.

It should be apparent that in addition to role definitions, structural issues as identified in the Huczynski and Buchanan framework can be detected. Also the Belbin roles identify the primary weaknesses common to each role. These he describes as allowable weakness that are inevitable but can be controlled or tolerated. The Belbin model also allows for the possibility of a mismatch between formal organizational status and group membership role. Management in Action 6.6 includes a review of the Belbin model and how it can be incorporated into a team development approach.

Management in Action 6.6

How to build teams

Based on the work of Belbin, Fowler suggests that 10 is a satisfactory number of members in a management or project team. For a complex topic involving intensive work on a clear issue, six members represents a good number. Over 12 members and groups tend to subdivide. With only three or four members any group is unlikely to have the range of team skills necessary and may be dominated by a single personality. Naturally there are many varied and practical reasons why a group may not adhere to these principles. For example, a management group will consist of as many members as report to the chief executive, irrespective of size. The role that specific members adopt in a group will also be determined to a significant extent by their purpose in that group. For example, in a negotiating group a trade union representative is there to represent the interests of members, not to help managers to find ways of meeting their objectives.

The work of Belbin on team roles offers one way of helping to ensure that there is a balance of skill within the group. Managers should be able to display some flexibility in team roles. In some team situations they will be expected to take a lead role, whereas in others they will be subordinate to more senior managers. This requires team training if team membership is to be effective. Fowler identifies two forms of team training:

- Team theory training. This involves the training of individuals in recognizing their own team style and that of others. It would also involve an understanding of team dynamics. This type of training is an individual approach and need not involve a particular team being trained at the same time.

- Team building training. This type of training should involve the entire team. It attempts to create a team from a group of individuals. It should also be specific to the project or purpose for which the group has been established. This approach frequently uses outdoor or simulation training as a means of putting teams into situations in which they must learn to depend, support and encourage each other.

Team training is not simply restricted to the start of a project, it is something that should be ongoing if the group is to avoid becoming stale. For example, a long-standing management group might take time out every few months to review how well it is performing as a group, perhaps with the support of a skilled consultant.

Adapted from: Fowler, A (1992) How to build teams. PM Plus, March, pp 25–7.

Group formation and structure: a management perspective

Groups are of particular significance to managers. There are a number of reasons for this, including:

- The process of management involves the management of groups. This could be a section, a team, a factory, or even a whole organization made up of many groups. Yet managers cannot directly manage all of the groups for which they are responsible. Delegated authority provides for subordinates to take responsibility for the management of some committees, for example.
- Managers must be part of some of the groups that they manage. Recall the Hawthorne studies. There were supervisors working in the sections in which the research was being conducted. The group pressure on them to conform to group norms placed the individuals in a difficult position because of the potential for divided loyalties.
- Managers are part of a management group in addition to any others to which they belong.
- There are moves towards managers empowering employees. This is usually described in terms of pushing decision making and responsibility down to the lowest level possible within the organization. One form of this process is the self-managed team. However, it is a movement that demands different approaches to control, and can lead to new difficulties between groups and managers.

It is not uncommon for individuals to seek out personal or career benefits from group membership. Such behaviour is political in that the individual is attempting to manipulate events to their advantage. Promotion opportunities can be enhanced by membership of the 'right' committees and being seen to be active on successful projects. It is perhaps cynical, but essentially true, that once it becomes apparent that a project is likely to be successful, people previously not involved suddenly want to be associated with it. Conversely, if there is a danger of the failure of a project, people actively begin to distance themselves from it.

Management is a political process. Managers are continually in competition with other managers for resources, influence and recognition. Promotion, and in times of recession (or delayering) continued employment frequently depends on being able to deliver objectives with reduced resources. The ability to squeeze additional productivity out of subordinates is a prized ability. It from this perspective that the ability to manipulate the use of groups (both formal and informal) to achieve objectives within an organizational setting gains significance.

The significance of formal groups is self evident, in that some form of compartmentalization of activity is necessary to carry out the work. Indications are that informal groups are also an inherent part of organizational life. They exist irrespective of management intentions on the subject. Managers need to develop an understanding of the importance of groups within an organization as well as an insight into issues such as how they form and function as well as how they can go wrong, a topic for the next chapter.

Within an organization the groups that exist are constantly subject to change. New people join a department; existing members leave or are transferred onto other duties; existing groups are reformulated as the tasks for which they were established change; and new groups are created as new tasks emerge. It is within this constantly changing milieu that managers must provide a framework of consistency and stability. Of course, not everything is changing all of the time. But there is a steady flow of people and task related change, sufficient to create instability and lack of security, particularly in large organizations.

It is in an attempt to provide stability within an otherwise changing environment that groups have a significant part to play. Rather like the individual strands of a spider's web the relationships formed within a group can help to provide strength in times of difficulty. If the individual strands in a spider's web become broken, then all is not lost, the damage can quickly be overcome and normality restored. Similarly, within an organization the groups that exist can provide task and personal support to individual members as well as continuity of operational activity.

Managers find themselves in a number of different groups as part of their work. They also manage many groups in order to meet the objectives of their position. It is not uncommon to find that managers ignore the formation and structural aspects of the teams that they create. It is often assumed that the roles within formal groups will naturally overcome any difficulties and deliver what is expected of them. Informal groups are frequently ignored as nothing to do with the organization, irrelevant, an inconvenience, or of little practical impact. Clearly most of these assumptions are questionable, or even false.

The challenge for managers is to provide the formal groupings within the organization that will allow the necessary activities to be undertaken whilst at the same time retaining some control or influence over the informal groups. Given the nature of informal groups as they have been described in this chapter, it should be apparent that their very nature makes this an impossible objective. Under these circumstances how can managers expect to control the activities and formation of these informal groups? It could be argued that the very existence of these informal groups is a function of management's attempt to maintain control. In other words an informal group is a response to ensure a degree of employee independence from the all pervading management domination in what can be described as a coercive employment relationship.

It can also be suggested that the informal group is a mechanism through which individuals seek to achieve some personal level of social meaning in a context where so much of the contact and activity is dictated by others. The individual has little opportunity to influence events in the working environment and the emergence of social arrangements that meet the needs of the individuals involved more effectively is hardly surprising. For example, the nature of the job to be done is prescribed by management; the colleagues with which one works are appointed by management; the physical working environment is designed and provided by management; and the standards of performance are set by management. Consequently, the formation of informal groups provides the opportunity for individuals to display a little of themselves in what is a largely prescribed situation.

Perhaps, therefore, the challenge facing managers is not one of how to control both the existence and formation of both formal and informal groups, but how to direct the energies of the groups that exist in the interests of the organization. In the formal groups that exist, management should consider the features of the group that might be expected to influence the outcome. In the context of this chapter, this could include the purpose, composition and other formation issues discussed. If the formal groups are to be effective in achieving their objectives then issues such as the Belbin roles and the Tuckman and Jensen stages in development need to be taken into account in order to ensure that the basis of success is provided.

In the case of informal groups, managers can utilize their existence to the benefit of the organization without appearing to exert covert control. For example, the provision of social facilities for employees can provide an opportunity for interaction among employees that can offset the *givens* within the organization. The use of group working as the basis of task achievement can also provide an appearance of lack of management control, which if linked with appropriate socialization and training can direct employees' behaviour in company preferred directions.

The difficulties facing many managements in terms of how to provide for control has lead to particular problems in some family organizations. Management in Action 6.7 illustrates these problems from a number of public disagreements in India over structure, control and related issues.

Management in Action 6.7

Portraits of families at war

With economic reform in India changing the way that business is run, a number of splits in large family run business groups have emerged. One of the added complexities in running family businesses in India is that the principle of primogeniture does not exist and potential heirs will squabble for years over what constitutes a fair share from an estate.

Wagstyl indicates:

Even after a family has launched companies on the stock market and diluted ownership to 20% or less, family members usually dominate management. Directorships, chairmanships and even whole companies are created to accommodate personal whims.

In the mid-1980s one group's interests in sugar, oil, chemicals, textiles, and engineering were divided between Mr Ram, his two sons and his brother. In the shareout Mr Ram had control of Jay Engineering, a maker of sewing machines. It performed badly and so Mr Ram turned to his son Mr Shriram for help, he agreed; providing he was given a free hand. Mr Ram promised to hand over the chairmanship to Mr Shriram, but failed to do so. It is suggested by people who know the company that the real problem is the favour that Mr Ram has shown to a senior manager within Jay Engineering, giving him substantial blocks of shares and suggesting publicly that Mr Shriram could learn from this 'favoured' individual. Naturally Mr Shriram would not take such advice easily and so a public dispute resulted.

Arguments around the cement, textiles and chemical businesses owned by the family of Mr Kedar Nath Modi are also interesting. Mr Modi divided his business interests between his three sons over a decade ago. In the late 1980s he insisted on a redistribution of these businesses and wealth as his middle son was making considerably more money than his two brothers. Having reluctantly agreed to the redistribution Mr Yogendra Modi subsequently repeated his success and proved better at making money than his two brothers. His father attempted to impose a second redistribution of the family businesses and wealth on Mr Yogendra Modi, but this was resisted. A former cabinet minister who was called upon to find a solution to this dispute was unable to do so.

Adapted from: Wagstyl, S (1993) Portraits of families at war. Financial Times, 25 October, p 18.

Conclusions

This chapter has considered the research into the significance of groups along with the effects of group membership on organizational activity. It is clear that groups both formal and informal are significant in terms of organizational activity, employee and management functioning. However, there are still many areas of research to be explored in defining how groups function across all the variables involved. The existence of groups within organizations is closely associated with the need for managers to exercise control over the processes for which they are responsible. It could be argued that informal groups are a natural reaction to that situation. That groups are formed and have structure has been established in this chapter. It is now appropriate to go on to consider issues such as group dynamics and performance in the next chapter.

Discussion questions

1   Define the following key terms from this chapter:

Formal group	Social facilitation	The Hawthorne studies
Informal group	Group norms	Homans' theory
Psychological group	Frame of reference	Group structure
Tuckman and Jensen's model		Bass and Ryterbrand's model

2   Groups within organizations are different to groups in other contexts. Discuss this statement.

3   Is the distinction between the concept of formal and informal groups a useful one?

4   Explain the results obtained by Triplett (when he studied the performance of racing cyclists) by reference to the concepts of a group introduced in this chapter.

5   The Bank Wiring Room observations demonstrate that employees can effectively manage managers without them being aware of it. Give and justify your own views on this statement.

6   Should management do everything it can to prevent informal groups from forming in the organization? Justify your answer.

7   Describe the group development stages identified in this chapter. Distinguish between the theoretical models offered as an explanation of this process.

8   Describe Feldman's ideas of when groups will attempt to regulate the behaviour of an individual. Do you agree with his views? Why or why not?

9   Are groups within an organization an attempt to provide managers with the means of social control?

10   The management team within an organization cannot be considered as a single group. Discuss this statement, justifying your answer.

11   Should individuals be trained in the theories of group formation and structure in order to ensure that they can become effective contributors to group activities? Why or why not?.

12   The Hawthorne studies show that it is important for managers to take an active interest in their subordinates if they are ever to be truly successful. Discuss.

Research activities

1 Search through the library stock available to you for about 10 journal or magazine articles relating to group formation and structure. Summarize the points made by the writers and compare and contrast those ideas with the material contained within this chapter.

2 In a group of which you are a member work with some of the other members and attempt to identify the individuals within that group that fall into the roles identified by the Belbin model of team roles. Do this individually at first and then compare your answer with the others in the group. Do you all agree with the roles allocated to each person? Explain any differences.

3 In this chapter it has been suggested that managers should attempt to ensure that informal groups within their organization are at the very least sympathetic to management's goals. Is this possible and how might this be achieved? In attempting to address these issues discuss the issues with a manager, trade union officer and an employee. Incorporate their thoughts and ideas into your work and reflect on the implications for both theory and practice.

Key reading

Clark, H, Chandler, J and Barry, J (1994) *Organization and Identities*, International Thomson Business Press, London.

■ Mayo, E: The work group and 'positive mental attitudes', p 237 and Roethlisberger FJ and Dickson WJ: Group restriction of output, p 247. Both of these extracts provide the opportunity to read original material from the researchers involved in the Hawthorne studies in which they reflect and conclude from the process.
   For material relevant to a consideration of the nature of the sexual division of work and the continuance of the male group dominance, see for example:
■ Kanter, RM: Men and women of the corporation, p 152.
■ Dex, S: The sexual division of work, p 177.

Further reading

Armstrong, P (1984) Competition between the organizational professions and the evolution of management control strategies. In *Work, Employment and Unemployment* (ed K Thompson), Open University Press, Milton Keynes. This text considers how professional groups attempt to 'engineer' access to decision making through restrictions on the interpretation of information and what can be described as hostile strategies towards other groups.

Belbin, M (1993) *Team Roles at Work*, Butterworth-Heinemann, Oxford. This is the latest edition of the text in which Belbin reviews his work on the subject of teams and the roles within them. It covers a wide range of issues relevant to both this chapter and the next one.

Bensman, J and Gerver, I (1973) Crime and punishment in the factory: the function of deviancy in maintaining the social system. In *Understanding Sociology Through Research* (ed DR McQueen), Addison-Wesley, Reading, MA. This text provides an insight into sociological research in general. However, the specific reading indicated describes the use of informal practices within the assembly operations of an aircraft factory. Essentially, 'illegal' practices were condoned by supervisors and inspectors as part of complex web of control and group behaviour. It is therefore worth reading from this perspective alone.

Gillespie, R (1991) *Manufacturing Knowledge: A History of the Hawthorne Experiments*, Cambridge University Press, Cambridge. As the title suggests, this work looks at the intellectual and political dynamics of this famous collection of research into work activity. In doing so this work examines the way that scientific knowledge itself is produced.

Leavitt, H (1972) *Managerial Psychology: An Introduction to Individuals, Pairs and Groups in Organizations*, 3rd edn, University of Chicago Press, Chicago, IL. Develops the theme of how groups control individual members. This point was initially discussed in relation to the Hawthorne studies. Leavitt develops a formal framework of escalating pressure points to be applied to 'deviant' members.

Markham, SE, Dansereau, F and Alutto, JA (1982) Group size and absenteeism rates: a longitudinal analysis, *Academy of Management Journal,* December, 921–27. This paper considers a number of features associated with the size of groups, particularly the absence rates of members.

Smith, KK and Berg, DN (1987) *Paradoxes of Group Life*, Jossey-Bass, San Francisco, CA. This text discusses the conflicts that exist for the individual as a result of group membership. Some cultures have a cultural orientation towards the group, others lean towards an emphasis on the individual. In either context, the individual must forgo certain freedoms once within the group. This text introduces the main issues surrounding this debate.

References

Argyle, M. (1989) *The Social Psychology of Work*, 2nd edn, Penguin, Hormondsworth.

Ashby, RW (1964) *An Introduction To Cybernetics*, Methuen, London.

Bass, BM and Ryterband, EC (1979) *Organizational Psychology*, 2nd edn, Allyn & Bacon, Boston, MA.

Belbin, M (1993) *Team Roles At Work*, Butterworth-Heinemann, Oxford.

Cooper, C and Davidson, M (1982) *High Pressure; Working Lives of Women Managers*. Fontana, London.

Dalton, M (1959) *Men Who Manage*, John Wiley, New York.

Feldman, DC (1984) The development and enforcement of group norms. *Academy of Management Review*, **9**, 47–53.

Handy, CB (1895) *Understanding Organizations*, 3rd edn, Penguin, Harmondsworth.

Homans, G (1950) *The Human Group*, Harcourt Brace, New York.

Huczynski, AA and Buchanan, DA (1991) *Organizational Behaviour: An Introductory Text*, 2nd edn, Prentice-Hall, Hemel Hempstead.

Katz, FE (1973) Integrative and adaptive uses of autonomy: worker autonomy in factories. In *People and Organizations* (eds G Salaman and K Thompson), Longman, London.

Likert, R (1961) *New Patterns of Management*, McGraw-Hill, New York.

Roethlisberger, FJ and Dickson, WJ (1964) *Management and the Worker*, John Wiley, New York.

Schein, EH (1956) The Chinese indoctrination programme for prisoners-of-war. *Psychiatry*, **19**, 149–72.

Schein, EH (1988) *Organizational Psychology*, 3rd edn. Prentice-Hall, Englewood Cliffs, NJ.

Shaw, ME (1981) *Group Dynamics: The Dynamics of Small Group Behaviour*, 3rd edn, McGraw-Hill, New York.

Triplett, N (1897) The dynamogenic factors in pacemaking and competition. *American Journal of Psychology,* **9**, 503–33.

Tuckman, B and Jensen, N (1977) Stages of small group development revisited. *Group and Organizational Studies*, **2**, 419–27.

Wyatt, S, Fraser, JA and Stock, FGL (1928) The comparative effects of variety and uniformity in work. Medical Research Council, Industrial Fatigue Research Board, Report No. 52. HMSO, London.

Zajonc, RB (1965) Social facilitation. *Science*, **149**, 269–74.

Group dynamics and effectiveness

Chapter summary

This chapter begins with a consideration of the behavioural and control issues surrounding group activity. We then move on to consider the dynamics of the interaction within and between groups. Organizational requirements for effectiveness in group activity and the associated decision making are the next areas for consideration. This is followed by a critical review of the material and an introduction to the managerial and organizational context.

Learning objectives

After studying this chapter and working through the associated Management in Action panels, discussion questions and research activities, you should be able to:

- Outline the nature of the dynamic processes that occur within and between groups.
- Describe the concept of effectiveness as applied to group activities.
- Explain how decisions are made in groups and the difficulties that can be encountered in reaching agreement.
- Understand how control can be operated within groups.
- Discuss the similarities and differences between models of how groups can be made more effective.
- Appreciate the complex relationships that exists between the groups to which individuals belong.
- Detail some of the links between groups and communications, negotiation, group formation and organizational design.
- Assess the management implications of groups.

Introduction

All groups, particularly those within organizations, function within a broader *environment*, containing other groups and individuals. This carries with it a number of implications, including:

- The need for communication and interaction between the members of a group.
- The need for communication and interaction with other groups both inside and outside the organization.
- The need to achieve the objectives set for the group.
- The need to control the activities within the group.

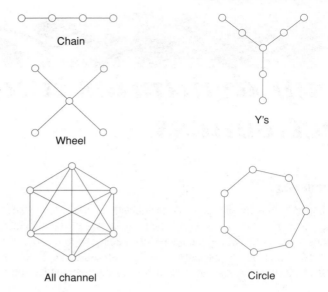

Figure 7.1 Communication patterns.

- The provision of a means through which to meet the social needs and aspirations of the group members.
- The need to take account of the social and political dimensions surrounding the group.

There are different patterns of communication that can be identified within a group, each of which has implications for the behaviour of individuals. Figure 7.1 indicates the major communication linkages based on the work of a number of writers, including Bavelas (1948), Leavitt (1978) and Shaw (1978).

Each of these communication networks have implications for a number of group features. For example, the style of leadership adopted and the ability of individuals to contribute to group decision making.

Moreno (1953) developed the *sociogram* as a means of charting preferences and interactions between group members. It is based on the positive and negative feelings of individuals towards other members of the group. To construct a *sociogram* each member of the group is required to express preferences (usually up to three) for other group members in specific situations. For example, who would you most (or least) prefer to work with? The results can be displayed in diagrammatic form, illustrating the *relationships* involved (Figure 7.2).

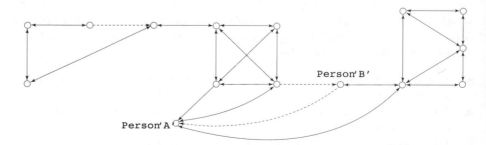

Figure 7.2 Example of a sociogram.

Introduction

A solid line between two individuals indicates that a two-way preference has been identified. A dotted line, that a one-way choice has been expressed – in the direction of the arrow. Examination of Figure 7.2 indicates that there are three sub-groups (or *cliques*) within the overall group. Person 'A' is a *star* in that they are a frequent preference, person 'B' is comparatively isolated, with few preferences.

Another approach to describing group activity was that of Bales (1958) who developed *interaction analysis*. He used small group activities such as committees to study how patterns of interaction developed during decision making. He identified 12 categories of activity clustered together under four headings. Table 7.1 reflects the Bales' categories.

Bales' work indicates that there are two significant aspects to group activity:

- The task and the solution being sought. This is referred to as the *task function*.
- The group atmosphere and member feelings. This is referred to as the *maintenance function*. It describes behaviour intended to preserve relationships, maintain cohesion and minimize the harmful effect of conflict.

In addition there is the *political dimension* to the behaviour of individuals within groups. Individuals may have many reasons for seeking to pursue their own objectives rather than those of the group. For example, a sponsor could have laid down 'things' to be achieved by an individual group member. Promotion opportunity could be enhanced by an individual seeking to be 'noticed' within the group – *self-interested* behaviour.

A well-balanced group will display the three functions (task, maintenance and political) in proportion appropriate to the purpose of the group, the individuals forming it and the context surrounding its existence. Management in Action 7.1 overleaf suggests that team activities are important to organizations but that there are problems facing managers as they attempt to gain the advantage available.

Table 7.1
Bales' categories of interaction

A. Socio-emotional: positive reactions
1. Shows solidarity, raises others' status, gives help, reward.
2. Shows tension release, jokes, laughs, shows satisfaction.
3. Agrees, shows passive acceptance, understands, concurs, complies.

B. Task: attempted answers
4. Gives suggestion, direction, implying autonomy for others.
5. Gives opinion, evaluation, analysis, expresses feeling, wish.
6. Gives orientation, information, repeats, clarifies, confirms.

C. Task: questions
7. Asks for orientation, information, repetition, confirmation.
8. Asks for opinion, evaluation, analysis, expression of feeling.
9. Asks for suggestion, direction, possible ways of action.

D. Socio-emotional: negative reactions
10. Disagrees, shows passive rejection, formality, withholds help.
11. Shows tension, asks for help, withdraws out of field.
12. Shows antagonism, deflates others' status, defends or asserts self.

Management in Action 7.1

Reaping the benefits of teamwork

No chief executive as an individual can produce all that the organization makes and administer the company as well. Other people are needed and so working in groups and teams is a necessity. The predominant culture in the West is based on the achievement of the individual and that of the East (Japan and other Asian countries) on the collective efforts of groups. It is argued, therefore, that if Western businesses are to emulate the success of those from the East then more effort to generate effective team working is needed.

As Furnham points out groups are a natural part of life experience in the West and that:

> We are, however, loyal to some groups: usually those we have been forced to join, or with whom we have endured hardship and difficulty. The family, school class-mates, fellow military conscripts do often command our loyalty. But, because we don't have jobs for life and find it easier to get promotion by moving between organizations, we rarely stay long enough in a team to be really part of it.

There are many implications that emerge from these words for the ways that teams are formed and function within organizations. For example, given the move for individuals to take more responsibility for their own career development how can teams be superimposed in the work setting? Equally, most performance management procedures and practice within companies place a heavy emphasis on individual effort and achievement, not contribution to team activities. In recruitment situations most of the emphasis is placed on the job-related skills of the individual. Only subsequently are the organizational and colleague 'fit' aspects considered.

So deciding that team working is a good thing for both the organization and the individual is one thing. But actually carrying through the implications that follow from that perspective would create many effects within the organization. Team working should not to be taken lightly, regarded as a fad or quick-fix solution to an organization's ills!

Adapted from: Furnham, A. (1993) Reaping the benefits of teamwork. Financial Times, 19 May, p 14.

Control within groups

Groups have the ability to influence the behaviour of the individuals within them. Sherif (1936) demonstrated that for two and three person groups, individuals could be influenced by the other person(s) present. Subjects were placed in a darkened room and given the task of tracking a light source. The light was stationary, but subjects perceive it to move. An illusion referred to as the *autokinetic phenomenon*. There was a wide variation in the movement reported by individuals 'seeing' this effect. Figure 7.3, shows the results obtained by Sherif.

There were four trials in the experiment. The first trial recorded the amount of movement reported by each subject independently. Successive trials were reported in the knowledge of the other subjects' responses. The results indicated that knowledge of the opinion of others influenced subject judgement. Once established the 'norm' became the basis of subsequent judgement for individuals. It was also noted that few subjects tested were aware of that their judgement was being influenced.

Socialization takes place when new people join an existing group and is a process of learning how 'things' are done. Many groups exist for long periods

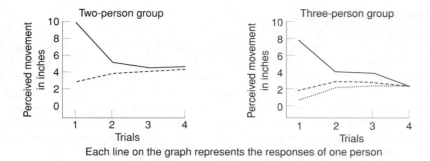

Each line on the graph represents the responses of one person

Figure 7.3 Results of a Sherif experiment.

and it is individuals who join and leave. An example would be an existing work group with a new employee replacing someone who has left the company. That person is joining an existing set of relationships and interactive networks. The group will ensure that the new member conforms to the established *task* and *maintenance* requirements. At the same time, any tendency for *self-interested* behaviour will elicit a negative response.

Management in Action 7.2 was found pinned to the wall in a personnel department and it is something that reflects both the positive and negative aspects of group formation and activity.

The Hawthorne studies identified several ways in which groups controlled their members. *Binging*, for example, referred to tapping on the arm. Other sanctions applied could involve a light-hearted joke or sarcastic comment and ridicule of the individual concerned. In effect a scale of 'punishment' existed.

So far the discussion ignores the opportunity for the 'deviant' to seek to change the attitudes of the rest of the group towards their position. This possibility introduces *political* and *negotiation* perspectives into group behaviour. Factional activity and conflict are possibilities when an individual decides to 'fight back'. Observation of this aspect of control mechanisms can most clearly be seen in politics and industrial relations when attempts are made to 'do a deal' involving groups compromising on previously held positions. Frequently, the positions adopted by groups (or individual members) become publicly stated positions and therefore more difficult to contradict or overcome.

Management in Action 7.2

Teams and progress

We trained hard but it seemed that every time we were beginning to form up into teams we would be reorganized.

I was to learn later in life that we tend to meet any new situation by reorganization, and a wonderful method it can be for creating the illusion of progress while producing confusion, inefficiency and demoralization.

Petronius Arbiter, 210 BC.
Source: Unknown.

Decisions within groups

Many groups within an organization have a major decision making aspect to their purpose. This applies whether the group is a manufacturing department seeking ways to assemble toasters, or a Board of Directors seeking to develop a business strategy. The *team roles* identified by Belbin, described in the previous chapter, are an attempt to provide an effective basis for decision making within the group. Kretch *et al.* (1962) describe a more comprehensive model of group effectiveness in which the decision-making component forms part of the process. An adaptation of their model is reflected in Figure 7.4.

In this model the *givens* provide the constraints that the group must work within. The people who will be in the group and the purpose are examples. The *intervening factors* reflect the *decision-making* process which includes motivation and the leaders' approach. Interaction in this context is the basis on which decisions will be taken.

That the quality of group output is of importance to organizations has long been recognized. In seeking to achieve this, it is often suggested that incentive schemes encourage groups to take 'more effective' decisions. Management in Action 7.3 indicates how senior managers can benefit from such arrangements. It also indicates the natural reactions of other groups who do not perceive that they receive the same benefit for their efforts.

Dynamics within groups

Groups must come to terms with their own internal functioning before they can effectively address the tasks facing them. Freud was among the first to address these issues (Strachey, 1953–6) and provided the basis for much of the later work on *group dynamics*. For Freud, group activity is based on the libidinal impulses of the individual which become transformed through group membership. It is the libidinal (or sexual) impulses that create the links between people and which help to maintain the group.

There are other aspects of the group dynamics that Freud seeks to explain. The competition between group members he explains as ambivalence towards

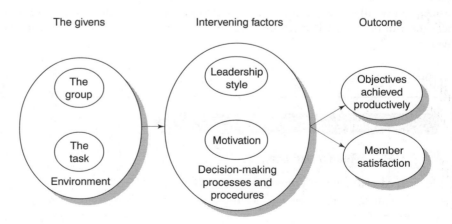

Figure 7.4   The determinants of group effectiveness (adapted from Kretch *et al.*, 1962). Kretch, D, Crutchfield, RS and Ballachey, EL (1962) *Individuals in Society*, McGraw-Hill, New York.

Management in Action 7.3

LWT managers likely to receive £55m payout

London Weekend Television introduced an executive share option scheme as part of a capital restructuring programme during 1989. Managers in post at that time were able to purchase unlisted management shares at 83.2p each. The management shares could be converted into ordinary shares over time according to a sliding scale based on the price of the quoted shares.

The maximum conversion rate for the management shares was 4.048 ordinary shares for each management share, providing the quoted share price was an average of 278p over the 20 business days following the announcement of the half year results in September 1993. On 6 May 1993 the quoted share price was 392p and predicted as a good prospect to rise further.

There was little doubt about the improvement in company performance since it had retained its ITV franchise. The share price on 6 May 1993 was a reflection of the market's view of that performance, together with an anticipation of continued growth in television advertising.

The board and senior management team of 44 people had been given the right to apply for the special management shares under the scheme. One of the key purposes of the scheme was to tie senior managers to the company during the period of the franchise. This was in addition to the desire to motivate them to enhance the market value of the company. Other employees did not receive special payments or share schemes as a consequence of the franchise deal. There was, however, a company profit-sharing scheme to which all employees belonged.

It was predicted by the trade union representing employees in the broadcasting industry that the special share scheme would pay out £55m to the management team. In sharing out the money it would create 15 millionaires. The chairman of the station stood to gain a gross profit from the deal of in excess of £7m, the chief executive, sales director and the former chairman were also set to receive more than £5.3m each. The lowest gross profit for an individual within the scheme was calculated as £73,750, by the trade union, which also described the scheme as obscene.

Adapted from: Snoddy, R (1993) LWT managers likely to receive £55m payout. Financial Times, 7 May, p 18.

the leader who, in effect, becomes a substitute parent. The members compete for supremacy in an attempt to become a new leader. Whatever the views about the value of Freud's work, it does draw attention to the *emotional power* present in group activity. The ability of a group to create powerful forces in favour of conformity, and indeed rebellion, is without question. Freud's work also points to the clear existence of both a conscious and unconscious level of behaviour in relation to group activities.

Bion (1961) developed a psychotherapy model that relied upon the dynamics of group activity to create changes in individual behaviour. He developed this approach whilst treating soldiers suffering breakdowns during World War II. As with Freud, Bion was part of the process which he was describing and so his results do not carry the 'weight' of experimentation. Bion concluded that much group experience was the result of conflict between three aspects of group life:

■ The individual and their needs. Each individual brought with them their needs and aspirations to the group. They would also have an expectation that their needs would be addressed by the group.

■ The group mentality. This related to the feelings and atmosphere within the group.
■ The group culture. This Bion described as the need for structure and leadership within the group.

The conflicts and tensions experienced between these three features produces a *second level* of grouping within the *primary* one. These second level groupings, or *basic assumption groups*, act to resolve the tensions for the individuals. It has been suggested that these mechanisms are particularly active when the group is under pressure to achieve results. These effects can be dealt with through:

■ Fight and flight responses. In this mode, individuals will switch between attack and retreat against the identified threat. The purpose being to protect the group from a threat that might cause it to break up.
■ Dependency. The group defends itself by increasingly turning inwards upon itself. Rather than face up to the issue at hand, a group will concentrate on the procedural aspects of what it is doing.
■ Pairing. It involves pairing through a ritualized approach to interaction between individuals. It would seem to serve the purpose of providing an alternative leader. It is a metaphorical change in leadership.

Tuckman and Jensen in describing the stages of group development provide a framework for understanding the process of forming and defining the purpose of the group. It should be apparent that there are points of similarity between the discussion of Freud and Bion and the material on group development. Another way of describing the dynamic processes within a group is shown in Figure 7.5. This attempts to bring together a number of the elements associated with the internal behaviour of groups.

Within Figure 7.5 there are multiple interactions between the elements in the Group Behaviour box. For example, the style of leadership will influence the process of decision making; and the characteristics of the individual members

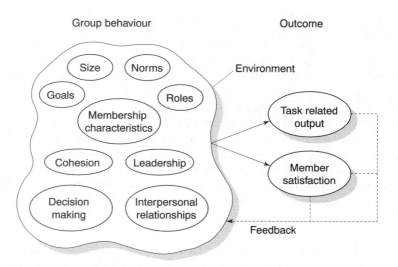

Figure 7.5   Determinants of dynamic activity within groups.

will influence the style of leadership that will be most effective. There is a feed-back loop between the output and the other elements within the model. This is because the group will receive feedback on its progress during its life. For example, if a group produces minutes of meetings, there is likely to be a response from the people that see them.

Taking each of the elements within Figure 7.5 in turn:

- Size. The larger the group the more complex the communication process. Within a group there is a trade-off in relation to the number of participants. The larger the number of participants the broader the range of experience that can be brought to bear on the task. On the other hand, the more people involved the smaller the contribution any individual can make. Other considerations associated with size include the need for rules and procedures, the potential domination of a group by a sub-group and the fact that the time to reach a decision increases and there is a tendency for factions to form.

- Norms. Sanctions can be imposed by the group on those individuals who do not abide by the norms operational in the group. Some groups can also have *anarchic* norms.

- Goals. Group output is made up of two components: the objectives set for the group and the satisfaction level of members. In most group activity both of these are necessary for success. Imagine a situation where a negotiating group is given the task of agreeing a new pay deal on behalf of workers. If the deal is presented by management as a 'take-it-or-leave-it' situation, the workers may accept it, but morale is likely to drop along with productivity.

- Member characteristics. Individuals differ along a wide range of dimensions, including problem solving style. A preponderance of one problem solving style within a group may make it more likely that a result is achieved rapidly, but there are dangers through such issues as *groupthink*.

- Roles. The Belbin model of group roles have already been introduced. Another model was developed by Margerison and McCann (1990) and is called the *team management wheel*. It is reproduced as Figure 7.6 and attempts, according to the authors, to go beyond the Belbin model by, '... show[ing] that people have particular work preferences that relate to the roles they play in a team'.

There are a number of other role frameworks that attempt to define what happens within a group. Hoffman (1979) provides the following framework clustered around three categories:

– Task roles. These roles encourage the achievement of the objectives of the group. Specific roles include initiator; information givers and seekers; co-ordination and evaluation.

– Relationship roles. These roles help to maintain the team whilst it is functioning. Examples include encouragement; gatekeeper; follower; standard setter and observer.

– Individual roles. These concentrate on the needs of the individuals within the group. Examples include blocker; dominator; recognition seeker and avoider.

The main difference between this last classification and those of Belbin and Margerison–McCann is that Hoffman is describing what *can* exist rather than what *should* exist in order to achieve an effective team.

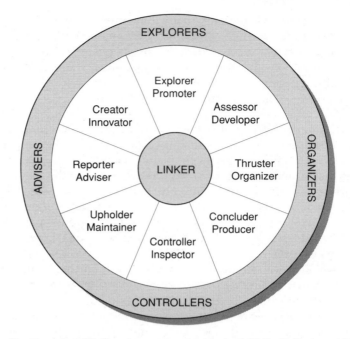

Figure 7.6   The Margerison–McCann team management wheel (© Prado Systems Ltd. Reproduced by kind permission of TMS Developments International Ltd. Tel 01904 641640).

■ Cohesion. This refers to the degree to which a group feels itself to be a group. At an individual level it is reflected in the desire to stay as part of the group. There is a relationship between *cohesion* and *conformity*. For example, a group with low conformity to group norms might be high in cohesion if the norms were only loosely structured and enforced.

■ Leadership. The approach of the leader is important in setting the pattern of behaviour within a group. Informal leaders emerge over time and tend to be influential in an indirect way.

■ Decision making. The way that a group goes about taking decisions can also have an effect on the outcome. Clearly, a group that spends its time talking and arguing without any real sense of purpose is unlikely to produce meaningful results.

■ Interpersonal relationships. The way that the individuals relate to each other within a group can also have a major impact on it. For example, members of a working party that do not like each other at a personal level are less likely to co-operate effectively. The art of sabotaging an 'enemy' within a committee can be carried off with some finesse and become a great source of personal pleasure, even if it is counter-productive in terms of the objectives being sought.

■ Environment. All of the above features are carried out within a particular organizational environment. Every organization has its own culture and ways of working. In some instances group activity is seen as very informal and a means of solving problems. In other cases it is seen as a formal process of communication and passing on decisions taken elsewhere.

Dynamics between groups

Groups invariably function in a world of groups. Take as an example a joint management trade union negotiating committee. Although this would be a group in itself, it must interact with a number of other groups, who in turn will interact with other groups. Figure 7.7 attempts to reflect this complex situation.

In Figure 7.7, the trade union negotiators have no choice other than to consult with the employee group. Similarly, management representatives must consult with the senior managers of the company. Other interactions will be less formal and some only evident as influencing forces. For example, all participants will interact with their family groups and some influence could be

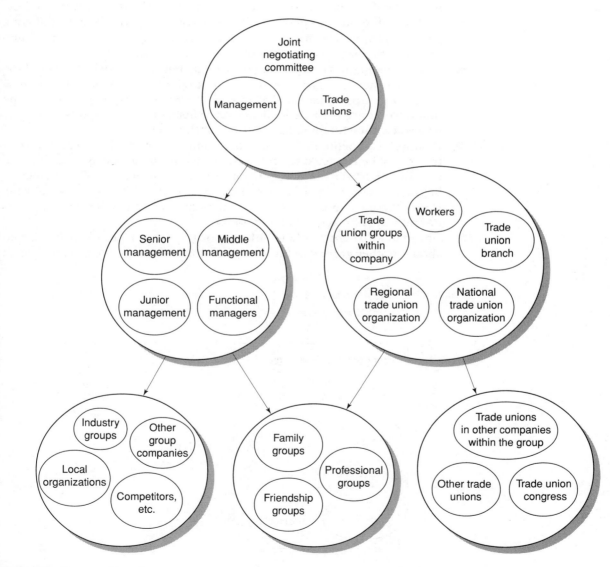

Figure 7.7 The group hierarchy.

expected as a consequence. Interaction with professional or occupational groups could also be expected to have some influence on the primary group's activity.

The influences that could be expected to operate between groups can be shown as a diagram (Figure 7.8). This model assumes that there are several intervening variables that interact on the relationships that exist between groups. Not all of these variables will function all of the time, neither will they have equal potency. The dynamic of the relationship between groups and the behaviours that result are, however, affected by them. Taking each of the factors identified in Figure 7.8:

- Objectives. The objectives that each group have may well differ. This affects the relationship between the groups depending how each group *perceives* its own and the others *objectives*. Within an organization it would be the ideal for all groups to perceive their objectives as part of the overall company objectives. The nature of conflict between groups is strongly influenced by the perception of the objectives that exist.
- Task competition. Groups that are strongly linked together because of the nature of the work are more likely to develop a *power* basis to the relationship. A typical example of this would be employees joining a trade union to reduce their dependency on management. At the other extreme groups can function independently of each other.
- Resource competition. Where groups must compete for resources then they could be expected to seek ways of gaining an advantage over the others. Two departments may put forward bids for additional resources to improve productivity, but there may be a limit to the finance available. Under these circumstances the two departments can either begin a 'war', or find ways of reaching a compromise.
- Uncertainty. There is often little opportunity for a group to be certain about another groups motives or intentions. Among the consequences of

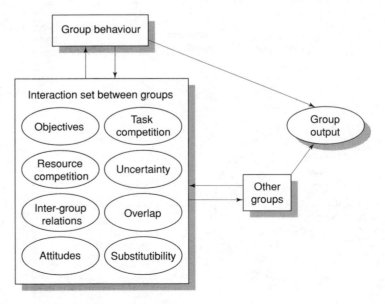

Figure 7.8   Influences on intergroup behaviour.

uncertainty are a lack of trust and an increase in political behaviour towards other groups.

- Inter-group relations. Previous experience of interaction with other groups can determine future behaviour. A management that is found to have lied to its workforce will find future interactions tainted by that experience.
- Attitudes. Frequently, inter-group relations are based on attitudes established over many years. McGregor's theory X and theory Y are examples of how the attitudes of individual managers can form the basis of stereotypical inter-group behaviour.
- Overlap. Over the past 200 years many trade unions came into existence in the UK, largely based on occupational groupings. As a consequence, overlap in their claims to represent particular groups of workers arose. Consequently, a set of rules were agreed between the trade unions as the basis of regulating competition for members.
- Substitutability. The opportunity to bypass or circumvent another group provides an opportunity to exercise a degree of control over that group. The threat of alternative suppliers is a classic way for one organization to pressure another into conceding lower prices.

A number of the issues raised above can be identified in Management in Action 7.4. This considers the frequently subtle ways that male dominance of organizations can be maintained accidentally, or is it deliberately?

Management in Action 7.4

Old boys' network

In October 1992 the Institute of Manpower Studies published a report into the merit pay systems used by four organizations. The work was funded by the Equal Opportunities Commission (EOC). In one case the report found that within a performance-based pay system bosses gave different targets to men and women. Men were expected to demonstrate intelligence, energy, dynamism and assertiveness. Women on the other hand were measured against organizational ability, honesty and dependability. It was also discovered that in comparing men and women of similar job level and performance ranking, the men were more likely to have been offered training and promotion. As deputy chairwoman of the EOC, June Bridgeman noted, 'Employees, especially women, need to be aware they may lose out in pay and promotion if appraisal and merit pay is adopted'.

In another report, the Institute of Management, supported by Bhs (the large retail organization) found that women were pessimistic about promotion oppor-

tunities, feeling that they were held back by their mainly male employers. Only 20% of women expected internal promotion as their next move, compared with 36% of men. Again, almost 50% of women managers felt that childcare responsibilities had adversely affected their careers, whereas only 16% of men in equivalent managerial jobs felt that children had held their careers back. Career breaks for women can also work against individuals. In this study, 29% of respondents had taken a career break, of which 39% had returned to work at a lower level. A level of 74% of women strongly agreed that women managers brought positive skills to the workplace, but only 33% of men expressed the same view.

One woman respondent indicated that, 'If you leave work to have a child, you effectively lose all skills in the employer's eyes and have to start again'. Another indicated that in her view, 'Old Boy's networks are alive and strong'. Yet another indicated that, 'There is a subtle way in which we are never given quite the full authority, never quite the full credit, never quite the full respect'.

Adapted from: Lowe, K (1992) Old boy's network. Personnel Today, 10 November, p 14.

Group effectiveness

What makes an effective group? Figure 7.4 suggests that there are two different outputs from group activity:

■ The achievement of objectives in a productive way.
■ Member satisfaction level with the experience.

This implies that effectiveness should be measured against both of these criteria. A group could be *productive* and achieve its objectives, but the members not enjoy the experience. Conversely, the individuals could have a good time, but fail to achieve anything. For example, a manager described that they worked in an organization where the management style was very autocratic and senior managers took very little notice of their subordinates. Morale among middle managers was very low and they felt 'driven' in their work. Labour turnover among this group was quite high, but the company paid high salaries and was very profitable. This falls quite clearly into the category of group success (management) measured by financial results, but with low personal satisfaction. Conversely, a community association set out with the aim of ensuring that a by-pass was built around a village. Most active in the association were the retired people who had most time to devote to the aims and objectives of the group. However, everything was done with such precision, elaboration and over such a long time that the by-pass is still not built. The individuals concerned continue to express commitment to the objectives and approach the task with considerable enthusiasm. It helps to provide a sense of social worth and value to the individuals concerned. This seems to provide a clear example of individual satisfaction but limited achievement of the *stated* objectives.

These illustrations raise the question of how effectiveness should be measured. Should it only be a reflection of the achievement of objectives, or should it reflect the individual perspective? It also raises the question of dependency between the two elements. Is it possible for a group to be effective in achieving its objectives if the individuals are not 'satisfied'? Results from the Hawthorne studies suggest that both factors interact and that satisfaction has a significant effect on output. However, for most groups it is impossible to know what the degree of relationship is because it is not possible to run experiments where the variables are systematically manipulated and results measured. It is not usually possible to know what might have been achieved.

McGregor (1960, p 228), describes the concept of *unity of purpose* to explain the way that some managerial groups perform effectively. By this term he draws attention to the commitment of individuals to the group and to the achievement of the objectives. He goes on to describe the features that differentiate *effective* from *ineffective* groups. The main features of his ideas are included as Table 7.2.

The ideas contained in Table 7.2 could be used to record the way that a particular group functions. This in turn would allow the members to review their own approach and improve the level of group effectiveness.

The two 'team systems' already introduced define the requirements for a balanced set of abilities and preferences among the members, if success is to be achieved. These ideas were the Belbin model and that of Margerison and McCann. It is now to a consideration of these two approaches that we turn.

Dimension	Effective group	Ineffective group
1 Atmosphere	Informal, comfortable, relaxed	Indifference, boredom, tension
2 Discussion	Participative, pertinent to task	Dominated by a few people, drifts of point
3 Objectives	Understood and accepted by all	Lack of clarity, not fully accepted by individuals
4 Active listening	Members listen to each other, contribution to debate and ideas	Pushing of own ideas, no evidence of building on others, talking for effect
5 Disagreement	Brought into the open and resolved or accepted	Not resolved, suppressed by leader, perhaps warfare domination is the aim
6 Decision making	By consensus	Premature decisions and actions before full examination. Simple majority voting
7 Criticism	Frank but not personal	Embarrassing, tension-producing. Involves personal hostility, destructive approach
8 Feelings	Expressed on group activity as well as ideas. Few hidden agendas	Hidden, not thought appropriate to group activity
9 Action	Clear allocation and acceptions	Unclear in allocation, lack of commitment to achieve result
10 Leadership	Not chair dominated, 'experts' lead depending upon circumstances, no power struggles	Chair dominated
11 Reviews	Self-consciousness about present operations, frequent reviews	No discussion of group maintenance issues

Table 7.2
Features of effective and ineffective groups (adapted from McGregor D (1960) *The Human Side of Enterprise*, McGraw-Hill, New York. With permission, pp 232–8)

Belbin's team roles

Belbin's team roles were included as Table 6.4 in Chapter 6, taken from Belbin (1993). These roles are:

- The plant.
- The resource investigator.
- The co-ordinator.
- The shaper.
- The monitor evaluator.
- The teamworker.
- The implementer.
- The completer.
- The specialist.

In his 1981 book, Belbin describes what he considers to be the attributes of successful and unsuccessful teams. These conclusions are based upon his work associated with the application of the *team roles model* in training and research contexts. Unsuccessful teams display the following characteristics:

- Morale. There was only a tenuous link between the level of morale among the individuals and degree of success in achieving group objectives.
- Mental ability. This proved to be a critical factor in that without someone of high ability in a creative or analytical sense, failure was relatively certain.
- Personality. Organization culture creates a tendency to create organization with a preponderance of particular personality traits. The consequence is a negative impact on group decision-making effectiveness.
- Team composition. Some groups will fail because of organizational deficiencies rather than anything specific to the group. However, unless a balance of team roles is achieved then the group is likely to be ineffective in operation.
- Individuals with no team role. Belbin identified about 30% of the managers tested as having no clearly defined team role profile. The consequences of the inclusion of such individuals into a team are in effect to destabilize what could otherwise be an effective group.
- Unknown factors. Between 10–15% of managers failed to take the tests that would determine their team role. This suggests that individuals that avoid being tested tend to associate with ineffective groups more frequently than would be expected.
- Corporate influences. Few groups operate in isolation. There are constraints and political influences active in all situations. There is also a lack of, and imperfect information, available. Among the consequences are that groups can be *channelled* in their outputs and suffer *interference* in their activities.
- Role reversal. Occasionally Belbin found that individuals who displayed a particular team role profile would switch and adopt another role, less suited to their abilities. This produced a negative effect on the group activity.

Successful or *winning teams*, as Belbin prefers to call them, display the following characteristics:

- An individual in the chair who could make use of the role to ensure an effective process. An ability to work with the talent in the group.
- A strong plant, essentially a creative and clever person, within the group. Someone able to make an effective contribution.
- A good range of mental ability spread across the individuals in a way that complemented the team roles.
- Wide team role coverage within the group. The key team roles within a group provides a basis for effective interaction and balanced decision making.
- A match between team roles and personal attributes. In many groups activity is allocated on the basis of past experience rather than team role profile. Successful teams were able to achieve a balance in these features.
- The ability of the team to compensate for role imbalances. This refers to the ability of a team to compensate for its own weaknesses.

The Margerison–McCann team management wheel

Margerison and McCann (1990) use the analogy of a wheel to describe their team management system (Figure 7.6). Their approach to effective teams is also based on research. The authors claim that they span the psychological and sociological traditions and go further than Belbin in providing an explanatory and practical model. Figure 7.9 reflects the relationship between the team management wheel and other approaches.

The model is based around the *team management profile questionnaire*, which is a forced-choice normative questionnaire. It measures individual work preferences on four dimensions:

- Relationships. Measured on an extroversion–introversion scale.
- Information. Measured in terms of the preferences in the way that information is used.
- Decisions. Measured in terms of the approach adopted to taking decisions.
- Organization. Measured in terms of structure or flexibility preferences.

The information collected provides a profile of the individual in terms that can be translated onto the 'Wheel'. The profile identified falls into the segments on the Wheel. The segments imply the following characteristics:

- Creator-Innovators. These individuals are independent and likely to challenge the present ways of doing things. They can develop new ideas.
- Explorer-Promoters. Individuals who generate new ideas and sell them to other people. They develop other people's ideas and push them towards implementation.
- Assessor-Developers. Individuals good at linking the creative and operational sides of a team. They are good at taking an idea in principle and making it work in practice.
- Thruster-Organizers. The people who can get things done. They can organize resources and people to achieve results.
- Concluder-Producers. These people can ensure that results are achieved and the output will be 'up to standard'.
- Controller-Inspectors. These individuals ensure that information is available to the group and that it is correct.

Psychological approach	Socio-psychological approach	Sociological approach
Individual differences	Individual role preferences	Role differences
Who am I?	What do I wish to do?	What role do I have?
Jungian and other theories	Psychological and sociological theories	Belbin and other theories
Myer-Briggs® type indicator and other measures	Margerison-McCann Team Management Wheel	Measures of role structure

Figure 7.9   Different approaches to understanding teams (© Prado Systems Ltd. Reproduced by kind permission of TMS Development International Ltd. Tel 01904 641640).

■ Upholder-Maintainers. Good at providing support and stability to a team. They support and advise rather than lead.
■ Reporter-Advisers. The data collection and interpretation specialists. They are the seekers out of 'truth' along with the collectors of information.
■ Linker. This activity is not seen as a preference as such, but as a skill that can be developed by any manager. This activity is central to team activity in that it performs a *connecting* role in ensuring that the team operates in an effective manner.

The concept of effectiveness in this model is defined in terms of a balance of individuals across the preferences in the wheel. Different situations and teams require different combinations of roles from the Wheel. What the authors term a 'high-performing team', should:

■ Accept that all team members have a responsibility to undertake Linking.
■ Have high expectations and set high targets.
■ Gain high levels of job satisfaction.
■ Experience high levels of co-operation.
■ Provide team managers who lead by example.
■ Develop teams that have a balance of roles matched to skills.
■ Experience high degrees of autonomy.
■ Learn quickly from mistakes.
■ Develop teams that are 'customer' oriented.
■ Display good problem-solving skills and review performance.
■ Be motivated to perform.

The reasons that teams fail, according to Margerison and McCann, include:

■ A lack of balance across the team roles.
■ A lack of effective linking between the roles.
■ A lack of effective relationship management within the team.
■ A lack of effective information management within the team.
■ The existence of impoverished decision-making processes.
■ The tendency to want to take decisions too early in the process.

That effectiveness in group activity is a key factor in organizational success is demonstrated in Management in Action 7.5. This extract not only demonstrates the need for work group effectiveness, but stresses the importance of the people/technology interface.

Decision making within groups

The work of both Belbin and Margerison–McCann includes an element of decision making. The team roles described in both models are couched in terms of the contribution that they make to the work of the team and this invariably involves decision making.

One feature of decision making within groups is the degree to which the group can ensure consistency in the views of the members. This can be achieved either through conforming to the norms of the group, or by following the lead of the authority figures within it. Asch (1951) describes an experiment in which

Management in Action 7.5

New plant puts GM in the fast lane

The Eisenach plant of General Motors (GM) is located in what was East Germany and originally built Wartburg cars. In those days the output statistics of the plant were about 100,000 cars built by 10,000 people. Following the reunification of Germany and the acquisition of the plant by GM it now produces 125,000 cars with only 2000 people. An increase in productivity of over 500%.

It takes 18.3 hours to manufacture a car in Eisenach compared to 30 hours in the GM factories elsewhere in Germany and Spain, and 25 hours in the UK. Quality is also better than other GM plants with only six faults per completed car in Eisenach, compared with 20 defects per car elsewhere in Germany and 14 in Britain.

To achieve this revolution in productivity and quality the company introduced so-called lean production processes and team working. Just-in-time working methods require minimal stocks of raw material and work-in-progress between processes as buffer protection to cover breakdowns. It is not uncommon in conventional manufacturing to find considerable levels of stock held between stages in the process to allow production to continue if a breakdown occurs. For example, Bochum (a

GM plant in Germany) would have 365 underbodies in stock to be able to keep the assembly lines running should production in the body shop be halted. In Eisenach the same figure is 10 underbodies. This level of buffer converts to 20 minutes of production time to fix a problem before the whole factory comes to a standstill, compared with six hours at Bochum.

Team and flexible working practices have also been introduced. For example, there are 10 skilled maintenance people per shift compared with 300 in Bochum. In Eisenach if a breakdown occurs the assembly line workers help the maintenance personnel to rectify the problem, rather than simply sit and wait for it to be fixed.

The plant at Eisenach is being used as a test bed for new managerial ideas in production and for the training of prospective senior managers for other locations, the intention being to export the advantages of lean production and team working to other parts of the company. However, a new factory is in a completely different position to one that has been part of GM for many years and which will have a history and tradition of particular working practices. Thus existing factories will require a different management of change approach.

Adapted from: Parkes, C (1993) New plant puts GM in the fast lane. Financial Times, 9 June, p 2.

subjects were asked to decide upon the relative length of a number of lines. To do this they were presented with a diagram similar to that in Figure 7.10.

The subjects were asked to judge which of the three lines (A, B or C) was the same length as line D. The experiment was carried out in groups of about seven people, only one of whom was a true subject. The order of giving the individual judgement was also fixed so that the real subject was near the end of the process and so would be aware of the judgement announced by the others. The 'plants' were instructed to select the wrong answer. Most subjects (about 80%) displayed agreement with the opinions of the rest of the group. Asch suggested three reasons why subjects would adjust their opinions:

- Perceptual movement. Subjects changed their judgements as the result of what they felt to be group pressure. They perceived the majority to be right.
- Judgement movement. Although this category knew that they were reporting incorrectly they believed that their judgement was wrong.

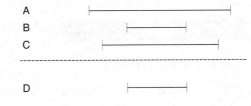

Figure 7.10 Diagram similar to that used by Asch.

■ Action movement. This category simply went along with the majority, but were aware of what they were doing.

Milgram (1974) considered response orientation based upon the influence of an authority figure. This experiment involved a simple memory test. A correct response by the subject resulted in the progression to another question in the test. Failure to give a correct response resulted in an electric shock being administered and the question was repeated. After each electric shock the voltage was increased for the next test. The equipment was clearly marked with a scale of electric shock, at the top end of which was a danger warning indicating that if it were used it would be fatal for the subject.

The experimenter in this process was in fact the subject for the experiment, although they were not aware of it at the time. The equipment for the experiment was not connected to the subject. The supposed subject was strapped into a chair and electrodes were fixed to their body (the experimenter helped to do this), but the electrodes were not wired up to the electric shock generator. The supposed subject for this experiment was 'in' on the subterfuge and responded to the questions incorrectly. The shock generator was wired up to an electric light and the 'subject' was instructed to respond with increasing cries of pain when it was illuminated and as the voltage increased. The 'subject' was in a separate room and could not be seen by the experimenter.

When the 'experimenter' began to show signs of resistance to the continuation of the process they were encouraged to go on by Milgram or other confederates. Most of the 'experimenters' continued with the experiment to the point where harm would have been done to the 'subject'. Milgram concluded that the power of an authority figure was able to pressure individuals to exhibit extreme behaviour. In the group variation of this experiment, it was noted that the reaction of the group tended to determine the reaction of the individual. If the group were rebellious the true subject would be as well, if compliant they tended to react in the same way.

During World War II, the US government was attempting to encourage the consumption of cheaper cuts of meat. Lewin argued that the decision on meat purchase was based on group norms, rather than a decision at the time of purchase. In 1943 a number of groups of housewives were exposed to either a lecture or engaged in a group discussion on the relative benefits of cheaper cuts of meat (Lewin; 1958). One week after the experiment 32% of those who engaged in the group discussion had tried a cheaper cut of meat, compared with only 3% who had attended the lecture. The group discussion was significant in influencing behaviour and setting the group norms.

Whyte (1956) argues that in most cases a group does not produce the best decision. Groups tend to *mediocrity*:

In your capacity as a group member you feel a strong impulse to seek common ground with the others. Not just out of timidity but out of respect for the sense of the meeting you tend to soft-pedal that which would go against the grain. And that, unfortunately, can include unorthodox ideas (p 53).

Stoner (1961) suggested that groups take decisions that involved greater risk than an individual would take. This became known as the *risky shift* phenomenon and has been identified in a number of different countries and among different groups of subjects. Essentially the experiment involved the administration of a choice dilemma questionnaire. There were 12 situations described in the questionnaire, all of which required a dilemma to be resolved and a decision to be made. A sample of one of the dilemmas to be addressed is included as Figure 7.11.

The research process involved three stages and two experimental conditions. This is most easily shown as a diagram (Figure 7.12).

Experiments of this type are known as *repeated measures* experiments and for the *risky shift* reveal that individuals tend to make more risky decisions after group discussion and that groups tend to make more risky decisions than individuals. A number of explanations have been put forward for this, including:

Mr E is president of a light metals corporation in the United States. The corporation is quite prosperous, and has strongly considered possibilities of business expansion by building an additional plant in a new location. The choice is between building a new plant in the United States where there would be a moderate return on the initial investment, or building a plant in a foreign country. Lower labour costs and easy access to raw materials in that country would mean a much higher return on the initial investment. On the other hand, there is a history of political instability and revolution in the foreign country under consideration. In fact, the leader of a small minority party is committed to nationalization, that is, taking over all foreign investments.

Imagine that you are advising Mr E. Listed below are several probabilities or odds of continued political stability in the foreign country under consideration. Please tick the lowest probability that you would consider acceptable for Mr E's corporation to build in that country.

❑   The chances are 1 in 10 that the foreign country will remain politically stable.

❑   3 in 10

❑   5 in 10

❑   7 in 10

❑   9 in 10

❑   Please tick here if you think Mr E's corporation should not build a plant in the foreign country, no matter what the probabilities.

Figure 7.11   Choice dilemma questionnaire, sample questions (taken from Kogann and Wallachma, 1967, pp 234–5) Risk Taking as a function of the situation, person and the group. In Newcombe TM (ed) *New Directions in Psychology*, Vol III. Holt Rinehart & Winston, New York.

Condition	Stages in the experiment		
	1st test (individual)	2nd test (group)	3rd test (individual)
Experimental group	Subjects complete questionnaire as individuals	Group completes same questionnaire (concencus decision)	Individual completes questionnaire (being told that it is a personal decision and to disregard previous group decision)
Control group	As above	No activity	Repeat individual completion of questionnaire

Figure 7.12   The research process for the risky shift experiment.

■ Responsibility diffusion. It is argued that within a group there is less individual responsibility. Consequently, individuals can avoid personal responsibility for any failure. Phrases such as, 'I knew that it would not work, but the others insisted on adopting that approach', are all too familiar in most groups. However, this does not seem to be the only possible explanation. Nordhoy (1962) re-examined the original data and found that some of the original questions included consistently produced group responses that were more cautious than individual ones. Perhaps the phenomenon produces an exaggeration effect, rather than a one-way shift in risk taking.

■ Cultural values. Perhaps the phenomenon can be explained in terms of the cultural values surrounding the group. If a group is composed of individuals for whom risk is a normal part of life, then perhaps they will tend to favour that approach in their joint decisions.

■ Rational decision making. It is possible that in attempting to reach a decision, any group is able to utilize the talents of the members in the discussion process. This increases the opportunity of the group to fully assess the arguments and make a more balanced and rational decision than an individual.

■ Majority decision making. If a group relies upon simple majority voting then it is possible for minority views to be overruled. This in turn minimizes the opportunity for full discussion of the points raised.

■ Polarization. Moscovici and Zavalloni (1969) suggest that groups function in a way which tends to move individual attitudes towards extreme positions. This they describe as a function of the values within the group and an increase in commitment to the decision brought about by discussion.

Janis (1982) reviewed a number of foreign policy decisions involving the US government and as a result coined the phrase *groupthink*. His research included studying the Bay of Pigs disaster (when the USA invaded Cuba, ignoring information that the Cuban military was able to defend that area) and the Vietnam war. As a result he concluded that such effects were the result of concentrating on harmony and morale to the exclusion of other points of view. Janis identified a number of symptoms that signalled that a group was likely to be suffering from *groupthink*:

- Invulnerability. The group becomes overly optimistic and convinced of its own invulnerability. In the Bay of Pigs fiasco, the US planners could not envisage that they could be beaten by Cuba.
- Rationalization. Such groups find ways to rationalize any evidence or opinion that might suggest an opposing point of view.
- Morality. A fundamental belief in the moral correctness of any proposed action. The USA was morally right to seek to overthrow the 'wicked' regime in Cuba – according to the planners.
- Values. Individuals with opposing points of view are frequently stereotyped as weak, stupid or evil. Any evidence or information from these sources is therefore automatically disregarded as irrelevant, contaminated or of no value.
- Pressure. Direct pressure can be used with great subtlety in order to provide an appearance of free speech whilst preventing active consideration of the views expressed.
- Self-censorship. Members of the group develop a means of self-censorship in order to hide any doubts and to protect the group cohesion.
- Unanimity. A carefully orchestrated unanimity with the careful exclusion of divergent views. Silence is taken as a clear signal that all members are in agreement with the decision.
- Mindguards. The creation of mindguards to filter information flows and to protect the group from adverse comment. Collective responsibility is invoked as a justification for supporting the decision and to marginalize any dissent.

Janis also suggested a number of mechanisms through which groups could guard against *groupthink*. They included encouragement for individuals to voice any doubts; the use of sub-groups to broaden the search for ideas and to serve as a cross check on ideas and analysis; encouraging self-criticism among the group and ensuring that junior members are allowed to speak first.

One of the ways of encouraging managers to recognize the benefits of teamwork and of adopting appropriate behaviour patterns is to expose them to situations where they are forced to take collective decisions in hostile environments. Outdoor training is one such environment and it is reviewed in Management in Action 7.6.

Group dynamics and effectiveness: a critical analysis

The Hawthorne studies are the basis of thinking about groups in an organization. However, it has been suggested that the studies were 'rigged'. Employees were required to participate in them and the researchers became counsellors in not only collecting information but seeking to direct employee dissatisfactions (Thompson and McHugh, 1990, p 78). The same authors draw attention to the views of Mayo on issues such as trade unions and conflict (p 80) (see also Gillespie (1991) for a review of context). The design of the research and interpretation of the evidence was a function of the individual researchers' attitudes, beliefs and values.

However, the same point could be made of many research endeavours. In analysing the data available, a researcher is looking for patterns, associations

Management in Action 7.6

Dispelling the macho myth

Outdoor training frequently has a macho image based on individual, generally unfit executives being forced to undertake silly exercises in the cold and damp. It has also been suggested that the people that provide such courses are either overgrown boy scouts, taking pleasure in the pain and discomfort of others, or they are professional trainers who have a particular set of development skills that can be useful to organizations.

The advocates of outdoor training suggest that it represents a vehicle for the learning process and has particular relevance in the areas of leadership, communication, team working and the management of change. Not all outdoor training is based on mountain climbing, white-water rafting or potholing. Some involve problem-solving such as rescue simulation and bridge building, linked to classroom discussion and analysis of the activity itself. Management supporters of this form of training claim that it takes individuals out of the usual company or classroom environment and therefore leaves many of the restrictions behind that might inhibit effective learning. It also allows individuals to fail in an environment which is safe in that it does not contain the status and 'baggage' associated with the normal organizational context.

A number of women on an appreciation course run by one such training provider considered that the approach offered a good opportunity for women. It was felt, however, that situations in which individuals (of either sex) were forced into situations causing excessive mental or physical stress should be avoided as they were likely to be counterproductive.

There are a wide range of outdoor training courses provided involving a wide range of approaches to the topic. Raleigh International (previously known as Operation Raleigh) have used this type of activity as part of their selection of young people for a long time. They have now broadened their scope and market their schemes to employers as management development tools. Employers can use the selection weekend scheme for junior personnel or graduate trainee level staff as a means of building leadership and confidence in the individual. It also encourages team working skills as part of the group activities involved.

Adapted from: Dickson, T and Milton, C (1993) Dispelling the macho myth. Financial Times, *30 June, p 19.*

and trends. It is inevitable that links will be identified that are not relevant, and perhaps do not stand up to subsequent critical scrutiny. This is all part of the process of creeping forward in the creation of new knowledge. In knowledge terms the Hawthorne studies are a comparatively recent event. It is hardly surprising that the results are still being questioned and re-examined in the light of modern researchers considering what the original research team actually did.

As the Hawthorne studies illustrate, groups can have a significant effect on the behaviour of members. The balance between output and effort by members of the group described in the Bank Wiring Room study illustrates the power to shape behaviour. Other studies, for example, those of Asch, illustrate the ability of groups to produce conformity. Yet conversely the same experiment, repeated in the UK by Perrin and Spencer (1981), did not produce a compliance effect. This suggests that such effects could be a function of culture and social conditions at the time.

In a study of the informal group practices in maintaining output and control, Bensman and Gerver (1973) studied assembly in an aircraft factory. Company policy stated that if wing parts were not in alignment disassembly and complete rebuilding should follow. This inevitably resulted in a long delay and a loss of production. The 'informal' practice was to use a hard steel screw to force the components together, thus saving time. The company did not allow employees to acquire such screws and anyone found in possession of one was liable to instant dismissal. However, all employees carried one 'for emergencies'. Supervisors and inspectors knew of the practice and would turn a 'blind eye' as long as it was not used too frequently. By allowing specific infringements of the rules, a balance of power was maintained through tolerance of this *focused deviancy*.

Many other groups are influential in the general milieu of organizational life. Interest groups such as trade unions and environmental groups have the potential to influence management. The gathering of information about these groups is an issue of concern to managers. In a recent television documentary (BBC 2, 1994) it was reported that during the 1985 British miners' strike the government and managers employed *agents* to collect information from the various trade union areas. This led to the encouragement of groups that were prepared to go through the picket lines and work normally.

The work of Belbin and Margerison and McCann provides managers with the techniques to *design* teams through the selection and training of individuals. Naturally, this process is not a precise enough guarantee that individuals will perform in totally predictable ways. However, it provides the opportunity to improve the probability of success, in terms defined by management. It is also likely (assuming that the underlying theory is valid) that such groups will produce a more satisfying experience for the individuals. In some ways this can be described as a form of *insidious control*. Control achieved through indirect and covert means. This should be compared with the random *natural selection* that would allow individuals to apply themselves naturally to the situations that they find themselves in. All management decision making is *manipulative* in that it seeks to influence events one way or another. So perhaps attempts to make groups more effective should be described as a form of subtle *manipulation*.

Training is an attempt by managers to *shape* the behaviour and attitudes of employees in appropriate ways. Appropriate, that is, as defined by managers. Such an approach attempts to *infuse* a management determined perspective and value-set throughout the organization. Group working as a means of continuing to reinforce that perspective is a useful means to provide follow-up and *reinforcement* to the original *socialization*. The institutionalization of inter-group and intra-group ways of working and interacting could provide a means by which corporate *standards* can be continually reinforced. The term *esprit de corps* takes on a new depth of meaning when considered in this light.

In order to achieve the objectives of the organization, two main conditions are necessary:

■ There must exist appropriate sub-groupings. This includes the use of groups designed to meet the operational needs of the business and the ways that these groups interact in pursuit of the common objective.
■ Within individual groups there needs to be appropriate mechanisms to meet the purposes set for them. This includes the composition of the group and the dynamics of how they operate in order to achieve their objectives.

The informal groups within the organization should not be hostile to the intentions of management if success is to be achieved. If there is hostility towards the objectives being sought by management, it is unlikely that they will be achieved. Even if they are achieved it will not be done effectively or efficiently. Consequently, the ability of a manager to put together a team of people who are likely to produce the best outcome for organization and individual is equally as important as ensuring that the interactive processes between groups functions in a positive way.

Group dynamics and effectiveness: a management perspective

In the previous chapter it was suggested that groups are in an almost constant state of flux as people leave and join; new groups are formed; and the objectives for existing groups are subject to change. This affects the way that groups operate as well as the processes through which they go in undertaking their allotted tasks. Because of the significance of groups within an organization managers need to develop the ability to make effective use of groups. This includes how groups function and the outcome from group activity. The failure to understand these issues or make effective use of them in managing group activity is likely to adversely influence the outcome.

The influences arising from the dynamic nature of the environment create a situation where *uncertainty* and *risk* are high. For example, employees may have accepted a wage rise below the rate of inflation for the past five years, on the basis that it helped to preserve jobs within the company. However, that is no guarantee that they will agree to do so in future. Circumstances change and the range of influences acting upon the totality of the situation and individuals involved may well create a change in collective attitude. Consider the links providing a basis for interaction between linked groups illustrated in Figure 7.7 in this context.

Because of the risk and uncertainty involved in group activity it is tempting to suggest that surplus capability is required within a group in order to be able to deal with crises. In other words, on average any group should be operating at a sub-optimal level. The surplus capability being used to absorb some of the variety from the environment. However, this runs counter to much of the work on organizational efficiency. In practice this issue depends very much on the purpose for which the group was established and the nature of its operations. In a formal organizational group (say a department) there is frequently a structural means of limiting the dangers from risk. For example, a manager may appoint a deputy to act in his/her absence, thereby minimizing the potential of the department grinding to a halt if the manager is away for any length of time. Groups will make different provision for the need to deal with uncertainty and risk, depending upon the perceived risk and its possible consequences.

Groups can be used by individuals towards their own ends. Management is a *political* process as well as being a decision-making one. The achievement of objectives through competitive forces is a necessary feature of organizational life. For example, no company has unlimited supplies of money for expansion and other projects. The allocation of funds to those activities that can provide the best return is more of an art than a science. There are a number of quantitative techniques that exist to make the decision easier, but the competitive

---

Management in Action 7.7

How incentives can drive team working

Having invested heavily in new technology during the 1980s senior management of AA Roadside Services wanted to retain the essential people focus of the business. For example, 10 layers of management were reduced to four and the 5500 staff (including patrol staff, emergency operators and fleet maintenance staff) were reorganized into 250 teams of between 20 and 30 staff, each led by a team leader. There was considerable emphasis on team-building activities at all levels in the new structure. Other initiatives introduced included a total quality action programme intended to empower the teams in changing the business and improving customer service.

There were a number of incentive schemes in existence prior to the introduction of teamwork. One paid a bonus to staff within a geographic area based upon the achievement of lower monthly expenditure compared to the budget. Whilst this type of scheme is comparatively easy to run, it encourages people not to do things (spend money), rather than actually doing something positive (provide good customer service). Clearly this form of incentive was not in sympathy with the ethos of the teamwork-based organization.

In seeking to identify a new approach more in keeping with the team concept a staff survey was undertaken, which indicated, among other things, that staff valued recognition as much as money. A specialist consultancy, Integra Business Solutions, was brought in to assist with the design of new incentive arrangements. The scheme designed was given the title 'Teamwork Pays'. There are two main components in the scheme. The first element is business-performance related. This produces a sliding scale of incentive payment depending upon improvement in business performance. The second element is related to the achievement of local operational performance by each team. To encourage effort at a local level the 350 teams are split into 18 leagues and so each team is effectively in competition with about 20 others. The rewards for this incentive element provide recognition for the achievement of the winning team, and involve prizes given out at award ceremonies.

For both of the incentive elements there are sub-factors that measure contribution. For example, business performance is measured by a combination of quality and financial targets. About 2500 pieces of information have to be supplied each month to the consultancy administering the scheme on behalf of AA Roadside Services. This is needed to provide feedback to the teams and management on performance achieved, and so on, as well as the calculation of bonus and league tables. The scheme is being supported by an expenditure of approximately £3m per year on direct rewards. The key factor in the design of the incentive scheme was to find a way of reinforcing the teamwork operating culture and AA Roadside Services feel that they have achieved that. Changes to the management performance-related pay scheme have also been introduced to reinforce at a senior level the 'Teamwork Pays' approach.

Adapted from: Pickard, J (1993) How incentives can drive teamwork. Personnel Management, September, pp 26–32.

---

nature of the process means that all participants have a vested interest in attempting to make their project the most attractive. This process can colour the way that groups function in decision making, presentational, interactive and political terms, whilst preparing such cases.

If groups are a key aspect of organizational life then management has a duty to ensure that they perform well. Just as there is a responsibility to ensure that other resources are effectively utilized. From that point of view, how groups take decisions, interact, and the roles that individuals adopt for themselves are all important issues.

That organizations perceive an operational advantage from the application of teamwork should be obvious. The difficulty facing managers is how to ensure that they can realize the potential. Within the complex web of organizational activity it is all too easy to create a situation where forces are acting in opposition to each other. One common example is the encouragement of teamwork in operational activity, but reward being determined by individual effort. The pressure on individuals being to maximize individual results in order to optimize their earnings levels. Management in Action 7.7 (on the previous page) is an example where this danger was recognized and management attempted to align the various components involved in support of the teamworking objectives.

Conclusions

In this and the previous chapters, we have considered how it is that groups set about structuring themselves; how they function and take decisions. The groups that are relevant to an organization are many and varied, both internally and externally. It is in making effective use of the ideas contained within these chapters that management can attempt to ensure that internal effectiveness is enhanced and external threats from even more effective groups minimized.

Groups, both formal and informal, are an important part of organizational life. As the pressure on managers to produce ever higher rates of return from ever fewer resources increases, the significance of achieving a form of self-management within the organization becomes apparent. In this chapter we have introduced some of the main issues surrounding the ways that groups operate and achieve success. As managers seek to improve the performance of their organizations the levels of effectiveness of the groups within them becomes a critical factor.

Discussion questions

1 Define the following key terms from this chapter:

Groupthink	Belbin's team roles	Team management wheel
Risky shift	Communication patterns	Hoffman's model
Group dynamics	Group cohesion	Milgram's experiment

2 What is a sociogram? How might you use it as a means of analysing group interactions and the dynamics between individual members?
3 Explain in your own words the team roles described by Belbin.
4 Describe the different patterns of communication that might be found in groups and suggest how each might influence subsequent decision making by the group.
5 Define in your own words the team management role preferences described by Margerison and McCann.
6 How might leadership style and motivation affect group decision making?
7 It has been suggested that experiments like those carried out by Milgram are unethical and should not have been carried out. Make a case for and against the Milgram experiments.
8 What is group cohesiveness? How does it relate to group conformity?

9 In your own words distinguish between the features of effective and ineffective groups as described by McGregor in Table 7.2.

10 What determines the dynamics within a group?

11 Figure 7.7 describes a hierarchy of group inter-relationships. Describe such a hierarchy for a tutorial group to which you belong.

12 Can Bales interaction analysis method be used to describe behaviour in all groups?

Research activities

1 Research activity 2 in the previous chapter asked you to attempt to apply the Belbin model to a group of which you are a member. Repeat that exercise, this time using the Margerison and McCann model. Compare the results obtained with those from Belbin. What conclusion do you draw from this?

2 In an earlier section, the ideas of McGregor in the area of group effectiveness were introduced to you. These were summarized in Table 7.2, and it was suggested that this could form the basis of profiling the operation of a group.

   This activity requires you to draw up a profiling chart from Table 7.2, using a scale of 1–5 between the extreme points. Identify a group of which you are a member and carry out an analysis using the sheet that you have designed. As this could be a sensitive topic, it would be best to carry this activity out on your tutorial group. Having drawn up the profile of the group in question, what are your conclusions regarding the level of effectiveness suggested by the profile as compared to your intuitions? What do other team members feel about your analysis, is it similar to theirs? What would you suggest as ways to improve the effectiveness of the group studied?

3 For a group that you are a member, draw a sociogram. What conclusions can you draw from this about how that group operates, the decision-making process and the general level of effectiveness? How would you recommend that the group improved its level of effectiveness?

Key reading

From Clark, H, Chandler, J and Barry, J (1994) *Organization and Identities: Text and Readings in Organizational Behaviour*, International Thomson Business Press, London:

■ Milgram S: Conformity and independence, p 132. An extract from the classic studies of group pressure on member decision making.

■ Kanter KM: Men and women of the corporation, p 152. Considers the ways in which male-dominated organizations function in attempting to maintain a consistent approach to dealing with women.

■ Oakley A: Myths of woman's place, p 169. Introduces a perspective on how men retain the dominant position within organizations.

■ Dex S: The sexual division of work, p 177. This article looks at the division of work and its ability to retain the dominant position of the male 'group'.

■ Cockburn C: Male dominance and technological change, p 197. Introducing an employee and trade union perspective on the gendered aspects of organization.

■ Perkin H: The rise of professional society: England since 1880, p 204. This extract introduces a class-based perspective on how the professions have been able to influence events over the past 100 years.

■ Illich I: Disabling professions, p 207. This piece describes some of the negative implications of allowing some groups to become overly dominant.
■ Mayo E: The work group and 'positive mental attitudes', p 237. An extract from the
  classical Hawthorne studies.
■ Roethlisberger FJ and Dickson WJ: Group restriction of output, p 247. Similarly an
  indication of what the researchers from the Hawthorne studies wrote about their
  work.
■ Coch L and French JRP: Overcoming resistance to change using group methods,
  p 260. This piece reviews how change can be achieved through an emphasis on
  group problem-solving approaches.
■ Janis IL: Groupthink and poor quality decision making, p 279. An extract from this
  classic review of group influence on decision making.
■ Needham P: The 'autonomous' work group, p 310. A perspective on group work in
  an organizational setting.
■ Hyman R: The power of collective action, p 322. The power of the various groups to
  influence events is crucial to an understanding of how industrial action achieves its
  purpose and Hyman reviews this.

Further reading

Adair, J. (1983) *Effective Leadership*, Pan Books, London. Reviews group activities from
  a leadership perspective. It clearly indicates the inter-relatedness of many aspects of
  group activity.
Cartwright, D and Zander, A (1968) *Group Dynamics: Theory and Research*, 3rd edn.
  Tavistock, London. Although quite old now, this text is a research-based text which
  gives an insight into how these issues can be studied.
Gregory, M (1994) *Dirty Tricks: British Airways' Secret War Against Virgin Atlantic*. Little, Brown, London. An interesting review of some of the main features of the campaign of BA against Virgin. It shows how the perception of the activities of groups can
  form a basis for future action. It also highlights how 'lobbying' can be used to influence decision making in groups.
Hackman, JR and Walton, RE (1986) Leading groups in organizations. In *Designing
  Effective Work Groups* (ed PS Goodman), Jossey-Bass, San Francisco, CA. Part of a larger text (all of which has something to offer) this work considers the group and contextual issues that influence activity.
Shaw, ME (1976) *Group Dynamics*, McGraw-Hill. Covers a number of issues relevant to
  how groups function and behave in the collective activities.
Zander, A (1983) *Making Groups Effective*, Jossey-Bass, San Francisco, CA. A good
  review of the subject and related topics.

References

Asch, SE (1951) Effects of group pressure upon the modification and distortion of judge-
  ments. In *Groups, Leadership and Men* (ed H Guetzkow), Carnegie Press, New York.
Bales, RF (1958) Task roles and social roles in problem solving groups. In *Readings in
  Social Psychology* (eds EE Maccoby, M Newcomb and EL Hartley), 3rd edn. Holt, Rine-
  hart & Winston, New York.
Bavelas, A (1948) A mathematical model for group structures. *Applied Anthropology*, 7,
  19–30.
BBC Television (BBC 2) (1994) Close up north, 10 March 1994.
Belbin, M (1981) *Management Teams: Why they Succeed or Fail*, Butterworth-Heine-
  mann, Oxford.
Belbin, M (1993) *Team Roles At Work*, Butterworth-Heinemann, Oxford.
Bensman, J and Gerver, I (1973) Crime and punishment in the factory: the function of
  deviancy in maintaining a social system. In *Understanding Sociology Through
  Research* (ed DR McQueen), Addison Wesley, Reading, MA.

Bion, WR (1961) *Experiences in Groups*, Tavistock, London.

Gillespie, R (1991) *Manufacturing Knowledge: A History of the Hawthorne Experiments*, Cambridge University Press, Cambridge.

Hoffman, LR (1979) Applying experimental research on group problem solving to organizations. *Journal of Applied Behavioural Science*, **15**, 375–91.

Janis, IL (1982) *Victims of Groupthink: A Psychological Study of Foreign Policy decisions and Fiascos*, 2nd edn, Houghton Mifflin, Boston, MA.

Kogan, N and Wallach, MA (1967) Risk taking as a function of the situation, person and the group. In *New Directions in Psychology* (ed TM Newcombe), Vol 111, Holt, Rinehart & Winston, New York, pp 111–278.

Kretch, D, Crutchfield, RS and Ballachey, EL (1962) *The Individual in Society*, McGraw-Hill, New York.

Leavitt, HJ (1978) *Managerial Psychology*, 4th edn, University of Chicago Press, Chicago, IL.

Lewin, K (1958) Group decision and social change. In *Readings in Social Psychology*, 3rd edn (eds EE Maccoby, M Newcombe and EL Hartley). Holt, Rinehart & Winston, New York.

Margerison, C and McCann, D (1990) *Team Management: Practical New Approaches*, Mercury Books, London.

McGregor, D (1960) *The Human Side of Enterprise*, McGraw-Hill, New York.

Milgram, S (1974) *Obedience to Authority*, Tavistock, London.

Moreno, JL (1953) *Who Shall Survive?* Beacon House.

Moscovici, S and Zavalloni, M (1969) The group as a polariser of attitudes. *Journal of Personality and Social Psychology*, **12**, 125–35.

Nordhoy, F (1962) Group interaction and decision making under risk. Unpublished Master's thesis, School of Industrial Management, MIT, Cambridge, MA.

Perrin, S and Spencer, C (1981) Independence or conformity in the Asch experiment as a reflection of cultural and situational factors, *British Journal of Social Psychology*, **20**, 205–9.

Shaw, ME (1978) Communication networks fourteen years later. In *Group Processes* (ed L Berkowitz), Academic Press, New York.

Sherif, M (1936) *The Psychology of Social Norms*, Harper, New York.

Strachey, J ed (1953–6) *The Complete Psychological Works of Sigmund Freud*, Vol I–XXIV, Hogarth Press, London.

Stoner, JAF (1961) A comparison of individual and group decisions involving risk. Quoted in Brown R (1965) *Social Psychology*, Free Press, New York.

Thompson, P and McHugh, D (1990) *Work Organization: A Critical Introduction*, Macmillan, Basingstoke.

Whyte, WH (1956) *The Organization Man*, Simon & Schuster, New York.

8

Communication, decision making and negotiation

Chapter summary

This chapter introduces the concepts of communication, decision making and negotiation. It begins with a review of the relationship between each of these concepts and organizations. The chapter then moves on to consider each concept in detail. The discussion examines the nature of each concept, its theoretical basis and its significance within an organizational setting. This is followed by a critical assessment of the implications of each and the management perspectives on them.

Learning objectives

After studying this chapter and working through the associated Management in Action panels, discussion questions and research activities, you should be able to:

■ Outline the concepts of communication, decision making and negotiation.
■ Describe communications, illustrating the process involved and the media options available.
■ Explain how decision making takes place, differentiating between programmed and non-programmed decisions.
■ Understand how communications, decision making and negotiation are linked together.
■ Appreciate the organizational significance of communication, decision making and negotiation.
■ Discuss how communication, decision making and negotiation link to other chapters in this book.
■ Detail how principled negotiation is intended to achieve a satisfactory and consistent result for all parties.
■ Assess the organizational significance of communications, decision making and negotiation.

Introduction

Communications, decision making and negotiation are fundamental aspects of everyday life for all managers and in all organizations. *Communications* is a process of information and influence. *Decision making* is a means of selecting a particular course of action from among the many options available. *Negotiation* is a process of difference reduction through agreement between individuals and groups.

There are strong links between these three activities in an organizational context. Not every act of communication involves decision making or negotiation. Decision making, however, requires a flow of information to make it effective. Also every negotiation requires communication and decision making as part of the process. For example a company may automatically communicate its annual results to employees without a specific decision being implied as a consequence. However, a production manager cannot make a decision on which orders to make without information on priority, capacity and raw material availability. During the annual wage negotiations between managers and trade unions communication between the parties on issues such as desires, expectations and ability to pay are the basis of exploring possible solutions and ultimately decisions on what will determine an acceptable agreement.

Communications and organizations

Communication differs from the passing of information from one person to another in that it implies the two-way process. Sitting in front of a television set watching a news programme is not a process of communication, it is *information transmission* because there is no direct interaction involved. Individuals may discuss some of the news items with other people, or even shout at the television screen, but the direct link with the presenters and producers does not exist. The nature of communications within organizations is reflected in Figure 8.1.

Figure 8.1 includes an element of external communications. Managers engage in a considerable degree of communication with organizations and groups outside of their own. For example, suppliers, government departments, customers, professional associations and competitors.

Organizations are complex entities, the larger ones exceedingly so. This is reflected in many aspects of organizational activity, including communications. Complexity in communication is an exponential function of the number of people involved. Consider the possible number of interaction combinations in an organization consisting of just five people (see Figure 8.2).

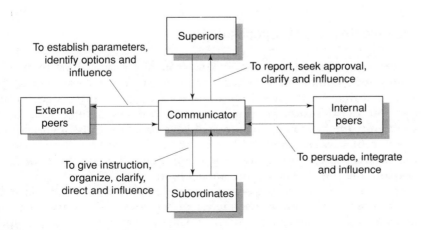

Figure 8.1 Organizational communications.

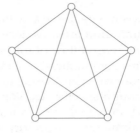

Figure 8.2 Communication channels.

There are 10 channels between the five people in Figure 8.2, reflecting the number of communication possibilities. Any particular episode could be initiated by either party which increases the number of directional channels to 20. Now consider the number of channels of communication possible in a company of 2000 people. Clearly, in large organizations the communication process needs to be managed carefully if total chaos is to be avoided. There are many ways in which this is achieved in practice, including:

- **Limitation.** Not every employee would be expected to interact with every other member of the company. This is achieved through a number of organizational *devices* including hierarchical and departmental structures.
- **Procedure.** The development of appropriate reporting arrangements sets out to ensure that only *appropriate* information is circulated to individuals.
- **Teamwork.** The use of teams and committees attempts to simplify communications through the use of *representatives* and by *concentrating* the communications on relevant issues at specific times.
- **Automation.** The use of *electronic media* for the transmission of information increases the opportunity for easier communications.
- **Separation.** The identification of activities that require communication and those which can be *designated* as information flow. For example, employee communications is often separated into categories such as newsletters (one way) and formal meetings between employee representatives and human resource managers (two way).

Decision making within organizations

There are many areas of decision making from the minor short term to the major long term commitment of capital resources. Decisions are taken by all levels of employee within the organization. For example, word processor operators have to decide upon the sequence for processing allotted tasks. At the other extreme, the board of directors will have to consider issues such as the construction of new factories and launching of new products. The major distinction between these two types of decision making being the *scale* of the decision and the *time frame* for the impact of it.

At the lower levels within the organization, decisions tend to be focused on immediate events involving the sequence of activities and the use of current resources in order to achieve the desired daily/weekly output. For example, a supervisor in a factory will constantly monitor the flow of work in order to divert people to bottlenecks, or to adjust production to achieve the best output every day. At a senior level, the directors may only review the financial results of the company every quarter. The rest of the time they may consider issues such as the implications of industry news about trends, etc. on the *strategic development* of the company.

At senior levels business decision making can involve many facets and take considerable time. It is reported that Margaret Thatcher began to *court* Japanese business leaders in the mid-1970s, well before she became British prime minister. Her approach to them being that when (in the future) she was elected prime minister she could be trusted to create an appropriate business climate for them in Britain. It was approximately 10 years after this level of approach that Nissan became one of the early Japanese companies to invest in large-scale production facilities in the north-east of England (Garrahan and Stewart; 1992).

The foregoing discussion illustrates the third property associated with decision making within organizations, that of *risk*. Generally speaking the larger the decision and the longer timescale involved the greater the degree of risk associated with it. For example, consider the options facing a medium-sized bank if it wants to become a large organization. Although there are many options available, the main ones are to either open a large number of new branches, or to take over a competitor and gain size through the additional resources acquired. There are considerable dangers in either approach. The cost and refurbishment of new outlets will be high and training of new staff will take time. The level of additional business gained may not justify the additional expenditure, but this may not become apparent for some considerable time. With a take-over (or merger) there are also many difficulties to be resolved. For example, overlap in customers and retail outlets, duplication in management and incompatible computer systems are just some of the issues to be addressed. The end result may be that the growth achieved will not equal the business levels of the two separate organizations.

The three elements associated with decision making can be reflected in a diagram (see Figure 8.3).

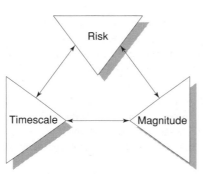

Figure 8.3 Dimensions of decision making.

Negotiating and organizations

Managers are involved in negotiations in one form or another for much of their time. Negotiations are frequently considered to be restricted to circumstances when industrial relations problems are to be solved, or formal contracts and money are exchanged. However, if *negotiation* is defined in terms of the *resolution of difference* and the *making of agreements*, then it assumes a much broader significance in managerial activity.

Negotiations can take place either formally or informally. The annual negotiations between managers and trade unions over rates of pay and negotiations over the terms to be included in a sales contract are typical *formal negotiations*. Informal negotiations take place every day between people at all levels within the organization. For example, the sales director might seek to *persuade* the production director to change the priority on a particular order. To do so an *informal negotiation* might take place in which mutually acceptable compromises would be explored and agreed over a cup of coffee. Equally, two colleagues may *negotiate* informally every day over who should collect the post from the main office. Other tasks to be done over the day might be *traded* as part of the process.

Management in Action 8.1 provides an example of the scope of formal negotiations and the links with other business decisions.

Management in Action 8.1

Unions agree to staff cuts at Aer Lingus

Decision making between senior managers and trade union officials frequently involves some tough negotiating. Events in Aer Lingus late in 1993 demonstrate this complexity very clearly. Aer Lingus is the state-run airline in the Irish Republic and had been suffering financial difficulties in the increasingly competitive and deregulated airline business. In the financial year ending March 1993 the company posted pre-tax losses of I£190.7m on a turnover of I£817m. Some progress in dealing with these problems was made and later in 1993 losses had been reduced to about I£1.2m per week.

Clearly this situation could not be allowed to continue and steps were taken to mount a rescue plan. This involved cutting costs within the company and an injection of equity from the government. The savings within the company were to include a reduction of I£21m in the airline's payroll costs and I£15m in non-labour overheads. The equity injection of I£175m from the government was conditional on the airline achieving a total cost saving of I£50m.

In people terms this plan required the airline to reduce its headcount by 800 from a total of 5500 people. The management argued during negotiations with the trade unions that of the 800 people who had volunteered for redundancy only 300 could be released unless radical changes in working arrangements were also agreed. Mr Paul O'Sullivan, the trade union officer representing staff in the company, indicated that the negotiations were the most difficult and tough that he had been engaged in. He said that it was, 'heartbreaking' to negotiate over job losses on such a scale. He also indicated that the changes to working arrangements being asked of the workforce were vast, but that they were necessary to the survival of the company. The deal struck between the company and trade union needed to be agreed by staff through a secret ballot before it could be implemented.

To make the negotiation process even more complex there was an outstanding pay claim to be determined. As part of the proposals over job losses and work reorganization an agreement to go to arbitration was included to examine the management's claim that it could not afford pay increases.

Adapted from Coone, T (1993) Unions agree to staff cuts at Aer Lingus. Financial Times, *2 November, p 27.*

Communications

Figure 8.4 reflects the main interaction networks which form the basis of communication for managers. In addition to the work related internal and external network reflected in Figure 8.4, managers will (in common with other employees) be part of friendship and family-based frameworks.

Communication serves three general functions within an organization:

■ Information processing. Communication is more than the simple transmission of information. Data will be collected and turned into information that has meaning and purpose. The ability of individuals to create and share information is what generates effective activity. It is on the basis of information that decisions and planning can be undertaken.

■ Co-ordination. Communication also allows the integration of activity within the organization. For example, if a sudden drop in sales is identified all departments can be alerted to take action. This could include reducing expenditure, cutting output, product review, speaking to customers and bankers, etc.

■ Visioning. Communication expresses thoughts and ideas. It is a process that can convey vision, mission and strategies to employees throughout the organization. It can also help in shaping the organizational culture of the organization by creating shared understandings.

■ Personal expression. Everyone in an organization will have their own views and opinions about work and non-work issues. These include opinions about the products and services offered, the individuals that manage the organization and how it compares with other employers. Individuals at all levels will also have opinions on the way that the company is run. Understanding these *feelings* is an important aspect of management activity.

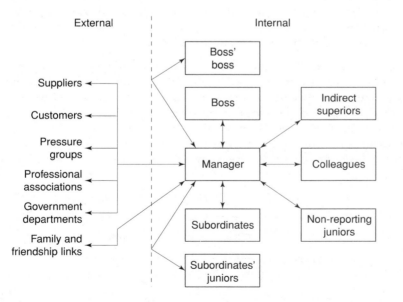

Figure 8.4 The manager's communication network (adapted from: Hellriegel, D, Slocum, JW and Woodman, RW (1989) *Organizational Behaviour*, 5th edn, West, St Paul, MN, Figure 7.3).

The methods of communication that occur within organizations include:

- **Written.** The use of memos, letters and reports are the chief means of communicating through this medium. In addition, there are the company procedures, the majority of which will be committed to writing.
- **Oral.** Individuals interact with each other in a variety of ways within organizations. Meetings to discuss important items involve considerable oral communication. Less formal interactions also take place frequently. For example, an administration assistant may telephone the accounts department to query a particular entry in the weekly budget report.
- **Non-verbal.** There are a host of non-verbal communication signals that accompany interaction and which provide interpretative information between the individuals involved. Examples include tone of voice, body posture and spatial positioning. For example, the seating arrangements can set the tone for a meeting. Sitting across the corner of the desk (Figure 8.5A) provides a less *threatening* layout than sitting across the desk (Figure 8.5B). The physical environment in which an individual works can also provide powerful clues to the authority of that particular person
- **Electronic.** With an increase in the availability of electronic devices the opportunity to communicate in new and novel ways has emerged. The ability to use electronic mail instead of written memos, teleconferencing in place of face-to-face meetings and the use of the fax machine to send written information have all changed the nature of much communication. Management in Action 8.2 provides a review of the uses for electronic mail.

The communication process

The process of communication is a social activity involving two or more people across time. Figure 8.6 reflects the essential nature of this process and it should be noted that it is circular. The process involves the sender initiating a communication sequence with the receiver responding and providing feedback to the originator.

Taking each element described in the model:

- **Source/receiver.** This part of the communication process represents the originator (or group of people) who initiate an exchange. For example, in a discussion between a manager and subordinate it would be the manager's opening remarks about its purpose.
- **Encoding.** This stage is about the conversion of ideas into a form for transmission. In sending a letter to customers ideas must be encoded into the words on paper before they can be sent. In converting an idea

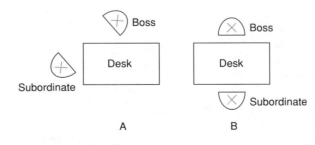

A   B

Figure 8.5 Seating arrangements for effect.

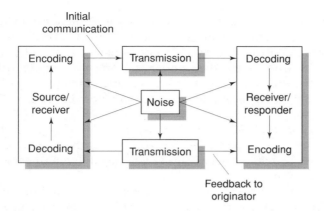

Figure 8.6   The communication loop (adapted from: Moorhead, G and Griffin, RW (1992) *Organization Behaviour*, 3rd edn, Houghton Mifflin, Boston, MA, Figure 11.2).

Management in Action 8.2

Secret messages

Electronic mail (e-mail) is now a very common means of communication between individuals and organizations. It is not uncommon to find 'state-of-the nation' messages from the chief executive being circulated to all employees via the e-mail system. It has also been known for individual managers to inform individual employees of their annual pay increase by e-mail, rather than through a face-to-face meeting.

There are many positive benefits obtainable through the application of an e-mail system. Companies can ensure that suppliers and customers have all the information necessary to ensure an instantaneous and smooth operation with a satisfactory exchange of product. The rate of increase in e-mail traffic is estimated to be approximately 19% per year, based on the number of new users.

However, there are also many potential problems with the e-mail systems. For example, one executive was caught spreading false information that had been deliberately placed in another executive's mail box. He was moved to another job as a result of the 'illegal' access to another's mail. Disciplinary action against the abusers of access to e-mail files is growing in response to this type of situation.

Information overload is another real danger. The rapid and easy circulation of information makes it easier to allow everyone to have access to it, rather than attempt to channel or direct it. Many people receive information that they do not need or want in order to be able to do their work effectively. Some companies have introduced bulletin boards for less essential and general circulation information. Others have attempted to 'manage' the flow, route and timing of data in the system.

The possibilities for subordinates to communicate directly with senior managers through the e-mail represents just one of the culture differences that has resulted from the introduction of this form of technology. Before its introduction the existence of a secretary could protect a boss from being disturbed by subordinates. With e-mail they are able to by-pass these gate-keeping functions easily. Some organizations seek to restrict the use of e-mail and electronic data interchange (EDI) on the grounds that they restrict the contact between people. The true interaction possibilities between human beings is missing from any form of electronic communication and it is suggested that ultimately the organization is impoverished if it does not encourage communication between people.

Adapted from: Simon, B (1994) Secret messages. Financial Times, 28 February, p 13.

into words (expressing them in symbolic form) there is inevitably a loss of precision and richness from the original thought. Words also have shades of meaning and can convey different things to different people. This is particularly true when the sender and receiver come from different cultures and therefore have a different frame of reference against which to judge meaning. Figure 8.7 is a letter from a newspaper that illustrates this point.

Spoken words also take on meaning from the context in which they are used and the non-verbal cues that accompany them. For example, 'can I help you?' said with a sneer conveys a totally different meaning to when it is said with a smile.

■ Transmission channel. This reflects the actual channel of communication chosen to convey the message from sender to receiver. In speaking it is sound waves, in written communication it is words on paper and electronically it is radio waves or electrical impulses. The choice of medium may involve more than one conversion of form. The use of the telephone involves the transmission of speech into the mouthpiece, a conversion into electrical impulses, then the conversion into sound energy in the ear piece at the other end.

Aussies did not 'run away'

AS AN AUSTRALIAN WRITER living in Malaysia, I am well aware of the sensitivities of language and language translation.

Take the Malaysian-English expression, to "run away" for example. Here in Malaysia I find it a rather quaint expression meaning to leave a place in a hurry.

In Australian-English it is taken far more literally, and it is rarely applied to adult behaviour. There, it means to drop everything and run. If used in a military context, it would mean desertion of duty and absolute cowardice.

Unfortunately this expression has found its way into the nightly English-language Sound and Light performance in Malacca. It is used to describe the withdrawal of British and Australian troops from Malaya to Singapore during World War II.

While that very military manoeuvre (withdraw, recall, regrouping, etc.) is indeed a very sensitive issue in British-Australian-Malaysian historical relations it cannot be described as "running away". To call it that is deeply offensive to the dozens of Australian and British tourists who come to watch this show each night.

There is every chance that the older tourists that this show attracts may even have been here during the war. Almost every elderly Australian knows people who were in Changi Prison, on the Burma Railway or who died in Borneo.

On behalf of the disgruntled group that I happened to join last week, I'd like to ask the organizers to change those two words, so as not to offend the very people for whom the show is designed

Pauline Bruce
Kuantan

Figure 8.7   Words are a different form of communication (adapted from: Letters page, *New Straits Times*, Malaysia, 13 May 1994, p 11)

■ Decoding. This involves the receipt of signals and the application of prior experience and knowledge to their interpretation. This can be an automatic process, as when speaking to someone in a language understood by both sender and receiver; or it can require interpretation, as with the need to refer to a phrase book if translation between languages is necessary. The meaning attached to a signal by the receiver may not be that intended by the sender. For example, managers may intend that a message reassures employees by signifying that although orders are down and that costs will have to be cut, job cuts are not planned. Employees may interpret the message in terms of costs needing to be cut now and jobs being at risk in the future. Prior experience and expectation influences the interpretation of messages.

■ Feedback. The receiver may become a sender and provide a signal to the originator that conveys a response on how the first signal was interpreted. For example, an employee about to step off a walkway into the path of a truck may stop walking in response to a shouted warning. It is possible that a response is conveyed though body language, an expression of boredom for example. Communication without feedback does not allow the sender to know if the recipient has received or understood the message. Imagine a manager issuing instructions for the days production activities without having any idea if they are being actioned.

■ Noise. This refers to the contamination of the signal as a result of interference surrounding the process. In an organizational setting it could be the background noise in a busy office that makes it difficult to hear a telephone conversation.

Interpersonal communication

At its most basic level, interpersonal communication involves two people in a dyadic interaction utilizing all of the elements of the process described in Figure 8.6. Of the communication channels open to individuals non-verbal signals are the least obvious and yet carry much information. Table 8.1 provides a summary of the main non-verbal communication categories used to support other forms of communication.

Taking each category in turn:

■ Body language. An individual can stop speaking but their body keeps on sending signals. The following example illustrates this process, 'In 20 minutes Mr. Roosevelt's features had expressed amazement, curiosity, mock alarm, genuine interest, worry, rhetorical playing for suspense, sympathy, decision, playfulness, dignity and surpassing charm. Yet he said almost nothing' (Gunther, 1950, p 22). There are a number of features of body language that provide meaning or interpretative clues to other

Body language	touching, eye contact, gestures, dress, etc.	**Table 8.1**
Paralanguage	voice tone, speed, pitch, etc.	Non-verbal communications
Proxemics	seating arrangements and personal distance, etc.	
Environment	room design and facilities, etc.	
Temporal	the use of time to create effect and influence	

communication activities. They include gestures, touch, posture, facial expression and eye contact. There are also cultural differences in the meaning of many of the signals given (Pease, 1981).

- Paralanguage. This aspect of verbal communication conveys a number of clues and can be split into four separate areas, Trager (1958). Voice quality (pitch, range, resonance, etc.), vocal characteristics (whispering, groaning, coughing, etc.), vocal qualifiers (momentary variations in volume or pitch) and vocal segregates (pauses, interruptions such as 'ah', 'um', etc.).
- Proxemics. This refers to the spatial needs of people and their environment. This links together communication distance and the type of message. Seeing two people physically very close, heads almost touching would tend to suggest that a secret was being shared, whereas the same individuals separated by several feet could be discussing the weather.
- Environment. The layout of a room can have a powerful effect on the communication process. A meeting between a boss and a subordinate over a pay rise will be more likely to take place in the boss's office (or territory), a home base to give support to the boss's views. The following describes the feelings of a lawyer summoned to appear before the US Justice Department to explain why criminal proceedings should not be instituted. 'They were immediately shown to the criminal division's coldly utilitarian conference room. "It's the most perfect government room you ever saw," Trott says. "It's nothing but a table, some chairs, a picture of the president and the attorney general on the walls." "It was," he adds, "an icebox, a meat locker" ' (Carpenter and Feloni, 1989, p 74).
- Temporal. The use of time to create an impression is well understood by most managers. Calling all employees together for a meeting at a time which requires them to interrupt their normal work will give the message greater impact. A manager making someone wait outside their office a few minutes before a meeting creates pressure and can destabilize the person kept waiting. Management in Action 8.3 is a true story of how one manager used time to control an industrial relations situation.

Electronic communications

In today's organization the use of computer-based technology to communicate is widespread and becoming increasingly commonplace. The facsimile (fax) machine is now a key piece of equipment for sending messages and documents between locations. The use of copier and electronic mail systems allow information to be circulated more widely and more rapidly than ever before.

In manufacturing companies, the ability to design products on computer systems that produce parts lists and production schedules makes the task of ordering and invoicing that much easier. In service organizations the ability to call up a client file on computer allows the transaction to be more effectively tailored to client needs.

Organizations can design computer systems that allow designated individuals access to appropriate information from a database. For example, a computerized personnel system can hold information on each employee's career history, references, performance markings, pay progression, attendance record, disciplinary warnings and so forth. Access to the available information can be

Management in Action 8.3

The power of time

The industrial relations manager of a large privately owned manufacturing company told the following story, which he claimed was true. Industrial relations within the company was difficult at the best of times. For example, whenever management attempted to introduce a new machine into the factory a dispute with one or more of the trade unions would result. From a management point of view everything was an uphill battle. It was not uncommon for the senior shop stewards to refuse to accept a piece of equipment unless manning levels and outputs were agreed before it was commissioned. Not infrequently threats of strike action were also used to force management into conceding to employee demands.

In one instance (on a Friday), the shop stewards had threatened that unless a particular manning level could be agreed immediately a strike would be called. The factory finished work at 12.30 lunch time each Friday and so any strike would mean an early finish and Monday off work (effectively a long weekend). The managing director (who had decided to deal with the matter) said to the shop stewards that he had been called to a meeting with the group chief executive, but that he would be back as soon as possible. The shop stewards were asked to wait in the managing director's office and they were given coffee.

The managing director had a short meeting with his boss and sent for the industrial relations manager to meet him in the head office complex. The two managers then had lunch together at the instigation of the managing director. Protestations by the industrial relations manager that a strike was imminent drew little reaction and a leisurely lunch resulted. By this time the factory employees had gone home, having finished work, but the shop stewards were still waiting in the managing director's office. A strike could not be called as management had not refused a meeting, so all the shop stewards could do was wait. Clearly they became frustrated and made several attempts to contact the managing director to press for the meeting, as they could see their original advantage slipping away. Responses from the managing director were that the senior managers were still meeting and would be back in the factory as soon as possible.

After a very leisurely lunch, that lasted until about 4.30 in the afternoon, the managing director decided that it was time to return to the factory. Not surprisingly the shop stewards had left by then, refusing to wait any longer. Consequently, the two managers also went home for the weekend. First thing on the following Monday morning the shop stewards stormed into the managing director's office to demand an explanation of the events from Friday. The response of the managing director was calm and he asked if they would have preferred him to have left the group chief executive and a discussion that could influence the future of the factory? He had the long-term interest of the factory and its employees at heart, even if they could not see beyond today. In any case, he had returned as early as he could, only to find that the shop stewards had gone home. Clearly, the problem that they wished to discuss was not important enough to make them want to give up some of their free time to solve it. There was no response from the shop stewards and the dispute ended. Management had 'won' this time, through the effect of using time to their advantage. However, this was not a tactic that could be used often as the shop stewards would find ways to counteract it. In this particular company it was a continual battle of wits between management and employees.

restricted in various ways. For example, job history, references and previous performance markings could be available to the department head but not the immediate supervisor of the person. The same principles can be applied to any of the company information systems including finance, budgets and marketing data.

As with all areas of management activity the potential of electronic communication needs to be balanced with the other forms of communication available in order to produce an effective process at a cost that the organization can afford. For example, there is little to be gained from introducing teleconferencing between two locations only five miles apart and when the usual communication between them is twice each year. However, with more frequent need to visit and/or seek assistance it may be justified.

Communications and the law

In the management of organizations it has long been realized that information is a source of power and that there is unequal access to it between managers and employees. In an attempt to redress the balance slightly British employment legislation requires managers to communicate certain information to trade unions in specific industrial relations circumstances. This includes areas of collective bargaining and proposals to declare redundancies. Where trade unions have a need for particular types of information they can reasonably expect employers to disclose these so that they can undertake their responsibilities more effectively.

Additionally, limited liability organizations with more than 250 employees have to include a statement in their annual reports identifying any actions taken over the year to introduce, maintain or develop communication with employees.

Within the European Union there are expectations that employee participation will go further than simply being entitled to information and regular communication. The introduction of works councils is now built into the European Union's employment legislation, see Management in Action 8.4.

Decision making

Decision making is a major part of organizational life. It is the basis of action and of choosing between alternatives. Decisions affect every person at all levels in an organization. Directors must decide on policies and strategies aimed at long-term success, manual employees must take decisions within a much narrower set of variables and over a much shorter time frame.

Approaches to decision making

Decisions are about choice. If there were no choices then decisions would not be necessary. For example, a production manager may have had a machine out of service for two days and as a consequence be late in deliveries. The choices facing the manager are to cancel some of the orders; increase the speed of the machine; work overtime; subcontract some of the orders; or continue to deliver late on existing work and reschedule future orders. The problem facing the manager is identifying which option provides the most appropriate course of action. Each possibility has advantages and disadvantages. Customers would seek to encourage a decision which delivers the product on time. The maintenance team would prefer a decision which is less likely to result

Management in Action 8.4

Talking shop soon open for ideas

The Commission of the European Union proposed a form of works council to be established for companies operating on a European scale. These would be Europe-wide committees of about 30 management and employee representatives drawn from across the operations in member countries. Meetings would be at least once each year, although sub-committees could meet more frequently if necessary.

The trade union movement across Europe has been supportive of the works council requirement. For example, John Monks, General secretary of the British Trades Union Congress, indicated that his movement had long been in favour of the stakeholder approach to running a business. One consequence of this perspective was that employees have the right to be consulted over matters of significance to their interests. However, there exists a more sceptical view where some unions have experienced employers using the consultative process as a delaying tactic for difficult decisions. Also, by making the unions part of the decision-making process it can provide a way of embracing and therefore limiting their freedom of action over industrial relations issues. Equally, some unions point to the fact that the agenda of any works council is largely determined by a management perspective. Counter to that view Mr Brian Revell, a trade union official on the Nestlé works council, indicated that the company had been receptive to ideas that emerged, covering issues such as the promotion of more women to senior positions.

From a management perspective there were a number of companies that experienced difficulty in conforming to the requirement to have a works council at a European level. For example, British companies were generally exempt from these requirements until the Social Chapter was signed by the Blair government in 1997. However, about 100 UK-owned companies have operations in Europe that would have qualified for works councils anyway and so they faced a dilemma on whether to include representatives from their British operations or not. Most decided to include the UK operations in order to create a unified system and in anticipation of being required to do so.

There are, however, companies that do not have a 'European' level in their hierarchy. Guinness, for example, anticipated having to establish a new tier of management in order to comply as it did not currently organize at that level. Burger King faced a difficulty as it included the Middle East and Africa within its European business group.

The possibility of including an employee perspective in the decision-making processes of any organization remains an attractive option for many managers and trade unionists. However, the means by which to achieve that relatively simple objective remains as elusive as ever. Many employers argue that the approach proposed is too bureaucratic and does not match the dynamic reality of most organizational functioning. As suggested by one executive at Philips, the Dutch electronics group, 'The directive is the wrong, static approach. It will certainly slow down decision making'.

Adapted from: Goodhart, D (1994) Talking shop soon open for ideas. Financial Times, *20 April, p 22.*

in future damage to the equipment. The quality specialists and designers within the company would be keen to maintain product standard and the finance people would not wish to see costs exceed revenue. In addition employees and other managers will have views that could influence the solution adopted. The difficulty facing the manager is that many of these viewpoints and expectations are in conflict. For example, if employees work overtime and get paid extra for doing so, unit cost will inevitably increase. However, the customer will be happy and may provide further orders as a result of the service provided. It is finding ways to balance these competing pressures that forms the basis of decision making.

Decision making takes time, is resource demanding and carries with it a degree of risk. In situations where the *problem* has not occurred before it is necessary to work out the options and relative benefits for each before deciding which to follow. If the problem is new then there is no experience on which to judge the likely success of any course of action. The decision is taken before the result is known. The actual chain of events that will follow from any decision cannot be fully anticipated and there are frequently extraneous factors that emerge as time passes. The D-day landings of the allied forces in France in June 1944 was the culmination of considerable planning and training activity. However, by chance a crack German armoured regiment was on exercise in the area of one of the landing zones and so was able to reinforce the defence of the area more effectively than had been anticipated. In that situation, there was no opportunity for the military commanders to take another decision in the light of the new information. It simply had to be dealt with as the landings progressed. In other words, only subsequent decisions could take account of the new situation. This perspective has led commentators to describe a *stream* of decisions rather than a single activity.

Simon (1960) describes decisions as falling along a continuum from *programmed* to *non-programmed*. Programmed in this context refers to the existence of decision rules that lead from problem to the solution. If a photocopier stops reproducing copies part way through a run a code number on a control panel indicates the type of problem and the machine manual indicates how to clear the blockage or repair the machine. The programmed aspects of this process are created through the design of the machine, the inclusion of sensors to detect certain malfunctions and the development of an operator's manual. Similar effects can be seen in the training of airline pilots using flight simulators. The purpose is to expose the pilot to a wide variety of flying experiences and train them how to respond effectively without putting lives and expensive aeroplanes at risk.

Non-programmed decisions on the other hand are novel, new, cannot be anticipated, or do not have pre-existing methods of resolving them. A recent example of this is the situation facing the cross-channel ferry companies on the opening of the Channel Tunnel rail links between the UK and France. Although not a rapid emergence of a new product (the tunnel took several years to design and build) the effect on the ferry companies is dramatic. The ferry companies have never experienced this situation before (at least not across the English Channel) and so they are forced to rely on their internal ability to solve problems intelligently. Only time will tell how successful they are in this.

Comparing these two approaches to problem solving a number of conclusions should be apparent, including:

■ Risk. There is less risk of failure in a decision which is based on the programmed approach. Decisions based on this approach are familiar, there is considerable experience of the 'behaviour' of variables and the outcome has a higher predictability as a result. In a situation requiring a non-programmed response the relationships between the variables must be worked out each time. The distinction between these approaches can be compared to the difference between a sporting event and a theatrical performance. In both of these situations careful planning, training and practice occurs. However, in the case of a sporting event, the intention is to beat the opposing side and that introduces the non-programmed dimension to the process. Each side will attempt to create new situations and actions in order to gain an advantage. In a theatrical performance the rehearsal is intended to produce replication for each performance. The aim is to ensure that each individual knows what they must do at every stage in the show. The risk of getting it wrong is thereby greatly reduced.

■ Cost. Reliance on non-programmed decision making incurs a higher cost for the organization. In a company producing designer clothing each item must be different, and tailored for the client. The cost of producing each item is therefore much greater because there is no opportunity for economies of scale. Conversely, in situations where considerable effort has been applied to the development of programmed decision approaches, the cost of operations can be reduced. For example, air travel safety has been greatly increased as a result of the efforts of pilot trainers, aircraft designers, maintenance planners and air traffic control specialists to *routinize* much of the process, learn from experience and *programme* into the decision-making activities as much of this as is possible.

■ Performance. Measured in units of output per person, the performance of an organization using a high proportion of programmed decisions will be greater. Programmed decisions need less processing time and therefore individuals can take more of them. Consider, for example, the lending policies of banks and financial institutions. If a programmed decision approach is adopted the 'formula' is applied and an answer produced quickly. The process can be speeded up to the extent that it becomes a marketing advantage and is used as such by a number of banks.

■ Variety. Unique situations cannot be dealt with in a programmed mode of operation, they must be channelled out and dealt with separately. In a pure form, organizations would be faced with an 'either-or' situation, emphasizing a programmed, or non-programmed approach because of the different requirements. However, as a result of technology developments it is less significant today. Motor car design and manufacture is an excellent example of the ability to combine programmed and non-programmed aspects. The designers of a motor car will begin with a small number of variations for a particular model, engine size, number of doors and basic style. However, from the basic model there are a wide range of optional extras available that produce a vast number of end product variations. The use of technology allows the appropriate components to be made available to the factory at the correct time to provide cost effective assembly, with the illusion of relative uniqueness built into the product.

■ Employee skill. Where non-programmed decisions are the norm, the skill level of employees must be of a higher order than required for programmed decisions. Programmed decisions are a process of situation recognition, identification of the appropriate decision rules and applying them to the situation. For non-programmed decisions, the employees involved must be capable of high level analysis and trained in a wide range of techniques to cope with the process. Imagine the level of knowledge and skill required to deal with a computer crash if there were no handbooks available.

■ Organization design. The structure of the organization in terms of the number of departments and their function will be affected by the approach to decision making. The lower skill levels implied by the programmed approach produces a large number of people at the bottom of the organization. The design of a company specializing in designer clothing will be very different to one specializing in ready to wear apparel.

The approach described by Simon is one based upon the need to apply differing levels of pre-planning into the process. Programmed decisions require careful thought and anticipation, but this can be separated from the events themselves. So, an airline can train pilots to deal with anticipated emergencies before they actually occur. As the decision sciences evolve and develop the opportunity to include ever more complex problems in the programmed category emerges. Complex, non-programmed decisions can be broken down into a network of sub-problems, many of them programmable, therefore a *simplification* process becomes available.

Problem-solving preferences

Another way to think about decision making is to consider the preferences that individuals have for approaching the process. In Chapter 3 the views of Jung in describing information gathering and evaluation approaches were outlined. The *information gathering* approach is defined in terms of either *sensing* (preference for facts) or *intuition* (preference for possibilities). The *information evaluation* approach is defined in terms of *thinking* (preference for logic) or *feeling* (preference for values) in analysing available information. This view of the individual preferences in problem solving can be reflected in a diagram (see Figure 8.8). Each cell in the matrix reflecting a different approach to solving problems.

Another approach to individual problem solving is that described by Thompson and Tuden (1959). Their model is based upon two dimensions:

■ Preferences for outcomes. This is about the goals that are being sought. It is measured along a continuum from clear to unclear. So if the end result is known (fix the photocopier) then it would fall at the clear end of the spectrum. If on the other hand the end result is not clear (design a new product) then a different set of choices emerge.

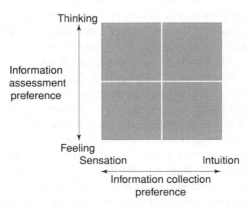

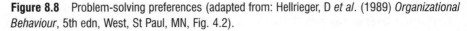

Figure 8.8   Problem-solving preferences (adapted from: Hellrieger, D *et al*. (1989) *Organizational Behaviour*, 5th edn, West, St Paul, MN, Fig. 4.2).

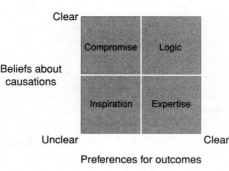

Figure 8.9 Two dimensions of decision making (from: Thompson, TE and Tuden, A (1959) *Comparative Studies in Administration*, University of Pittsburgh Press, Pittsburgh).

■ Beliefs about causation. This is also measured along a clear/unclear continuum. It refers to the understanding that the individual has about the relationship between cause and effect in that specific situation. For example, in original research there can be little clarity as to how the variables will interact. On the other hand a knowledge that clearing a paper jam will allow the copier to function properly would fall at the 'clear' end of the spectrum.

This model goes further by providing an indication of the problem solving approaches that arise from these dimensions. Each of the four cells in Figure 8.9 implies a different approach to the problem solving process. For example, where the outcome and the relationship between the variables is clearly understood, then a logical approach will achieve the best result. On the other hand, where neither variable is clear, then inspiration is the best guide to dealing with the problem.

Decision-making models

There are a number of models that attempt to describe how decisions are made within organizations, including:

■ Rational model. This assumes that decision makers always follow a rational approach. Their actions are based on data collection and analysis, along with evaluation of alternatives. Appropriateness of the decision is measured against the benefit to the organization as a whole, rather than any specific group or individual (Harrison, 1987).
■ Restricted rationality model. Although the rational model may be the ideal for many organizations, it ignores the 'humanness' in the process. Individuals may lack the intellectual capacity or technical competence to rationally evaluate every option. Perceptual bias group dynamics and politics can play a part in the decision-making process. There are many aspects of behaviour within an organization that influence how decisions are taken (March and Simon, 1958).
■ Pragmatic model. Pragmatism is a means of combining both rationality and the reality of human behaviour into a systematic approach aimed at achieving the best decision in the circumstances. Figure 8.10 reflects the main elements of this approach.

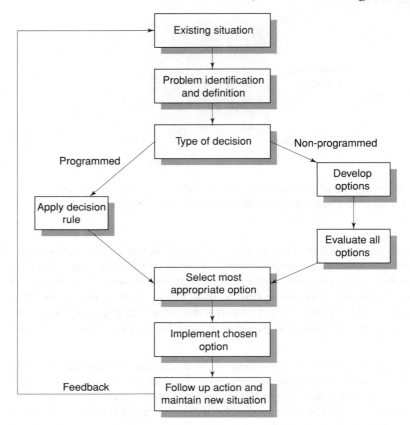

Figure 8.10 Pragmatic decision making model.

■ Political model. In this model, decision making becomes a process intended to achieve personal objectives through organizational activity. As such, information becomes part of the political process, as does its interpretation. One form of this was described as a *garbage can* model by Cohen *et al*. (1972). This is based on the idea that organizations consist of solutions looking for problems. A company may purchase a number of components. The production managers may wish to bring under their direct control this sub-contracted work. They are likely to continually seek ways to demonstrate that the company would be 'better off' producing the items in house. Quality problems will be highlighted, as will late delivery and so on. In effect, the solution already exists (expand the production department) all that is necessary is for the 'problem' to occur. Cohen *et al*. see the *garbage can* as a receptacle for solutions and situations, both waiting to be matched up.

■ Conflict model. Janis and Mann (1977) describe a model based on five assumptions. Firstly, it is applicable to important life decisions only. Secondly, procrastination and rationalization are part of difficult decisions as they allow individuals to deal with stress. Third, some decisions will be wrong and that this can effect future decisions. Fourth, that alternative options will be compared against personal moral standards. Finally, individuals will be ambivalent towards the alternative decision options, making it difficult to choose between them. Figure 8.11 describes the algorithmic nature of this approach.

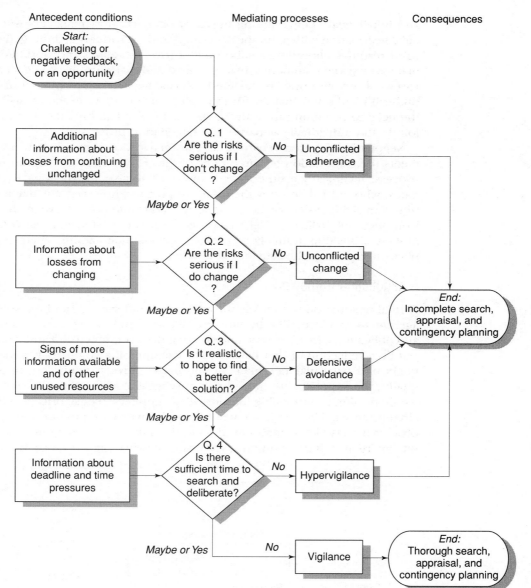

Figure 8.11 Conflict model of decision making. (Janis, IL, Mann, L. (1977) *Decision Making: a Psychological Analysis of Conflict, Choice and Commitment*. The Free Press, New York.)

Negotiation

One of the key areas in which managers engage in communication and decision making is in the field of negotiation. Negotiation is frequently thought of as involving personnel managers and trade unions, but it is a much more broadly based activity than that. For example, applicants for jobs invariably negotiate some aspect of their appointment with the prospective employer, starting date and initial salary being among the most obvious. Most managers will experience negotiation with a number of groups and individuals including, their boss (over resource allocations); subordinates (over deadlines and workrate); other managers (over common activities and decisions); suppliers and customers (over delivery and price issues) and external agencies (government inspectors on health and safety matters for example). Each of these examples will involve the need to communicate with the parties involved and to take decisions both jointly and individually as part of the negotiation process.

Negotiation is often regarded as a formal process, as when management meets the trade union to agree rates of pay. However, it is often an informal process. Technically, a superior is empowered to give 'instructions' to subordinates, who must then carry them out. In practice, however, any manager who relied on giving orders as the only way to lead would not achieve the best result from their subordinates. Negotiation is, therefore, best seen as an *interactive process* of making mutually agreeable bargains in situations where one party needs to *influence* the activities of another.

A negotiating framework

Formal negotiation is a means through which differences can be resolved and agreement specified, thereby allowing all parties to have a record of their rights and obligations. In all relationships there is a power dimension and negotiation can be a reflection of that balance. For example, if a company has many suppliers of a particular raw material and each source is equivalent in terms of quality, the suppliers are individually very weak compared to the customer. It would be almost impossible for individual suppliers to raise prices under these circumstances. The customer would simply switch to another supplier. This process has also been apparent historically in the employment field and led to the emergence of trade unions as a means of providing a balance in the power

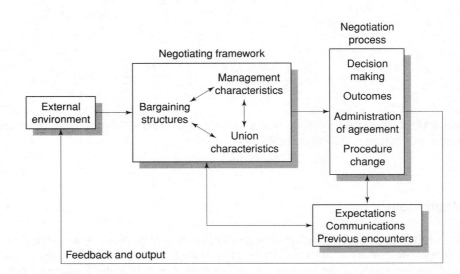

Figure 8.12   A negotiating framework (adapted from: Kochan, TA (1980) *Collective Bargaining and Industrial Relations*, Irwin, Homewood IL, Figure 2.1).

between employers and employees. Figure 8.12 provides a framework for understanding the formal negotiation process within employee relations.

It is clear from Figure 8.12 that negotiations are a process dependent to a significant extent upon previous encounters, expectations and external forces. It should also be apparent how communications and decision making fit into this model of the process.

Negotiating tactics

There are a number of approaches to dealing with conflict which are relevant to negotiations. They include *avoidance* (simply ignoring the problem), *smoothing* (seeking to 'patch up' a rift through calming actions), *forcing* (one's own point of view onto others), *compromise* (seeking an acceptable middle ground) and *confrontation* (facing up to the differences and seeking accommodation) (Torrington and Hall, 1987).

The tactics that negotiators encounter depend on a number of features of the process itself. They include the preferred style of the individuals involved; the relative power balance between the parties; the degree of change involved; the willingness of the parties to accept change; previous encounters; environmental influences; training and experience in negotiation along with the dynamics of the process itself. It is naive to suggest that all negotiations are a means by which both parties can discuss differences and reach mutually acceptable compromise. Many negotiations are undertaken from a *win–lose* perspective. In other words, one side must 'win', so the other must of necessity 'lose'. This is based upon the notion that the issues are *fixed* and can only be shared out like cutting a cake into pieces. In this analogy, a piece once cut and allocated is no longer available for the other party. In extreme cases the tactics employed by individuals using this approach can become very aggressive. Typically, a *deep diving* approach is taken on each item to be covered until a win is recorded and then moving on to the next issue. Similar tactics include (Scott, 1981):

- Probing. From the outset seeking information of value, without giving anything away that may help the other side.
- Get/give. Seeking to gain something before conceding anything. Matching what is given to what was gained.
- Emotion. The use of voice tone and other body language signals to create emotion in the process. The use of anger would be a typical example.
- Good guy/bad guy. The 'reasonable' member follows the 'aggressive' and 'unreasonable' one and builds on the advantage gained by the threat of more to follow.
- Poker face. The ability to manage the body language and verbal cues allows the fighter to cloak their feelings and intentions.
- Managing the minutes. The person producing the minutes is in a strong position to slant the official record. The careful choice of words and phrasing can be used to great effect, as can the selective inclusion (or exclusion) of items discussed.
- Understanding not agreement. One side may *understand* the other's position without *agreeing* with it. A customer may understand the need for the supplier to raise prices, but may not agree to pay it. Fighters can be very clever at seeming to reach *agreement*, only to return to the discussions claiming that only *understanding* was reached and further negotiations are

necessary. This destabilizes the other party and frequently allows change to be achieved. This tactic can be used to great effect at the close of a negotiation. To think that agreement has been reached and to relax, only to have a crucial point threaten the whole process is a difficult position to find oneself in.

- ■ Getting upstairs. Going over the head of the negotiating team to the boss is a threat that can be used to effect. It can encourage the team to lean towards a settlement rather than bring in the boss to the process.
- ■ Forcing. There are various forms of force that can be used. Threats of withdrawing from the relationship (strikes or stopping of supplies) is one form, but bribes, blackmail and dirty tricks are other options that have been used.

The fighting tactics described above are intended to gain and retain control of the process. There are various ways in which these tactics can be dealt with, but essentially it comes down to remaining in control of temper, emotions, content and process.

There are few occasions where the power balance is completely one-sided and therefore negotiation should be regarded as a joint process. Often this comes down to understanding what the best alternative to a negotiated agreement is. In other words, what will happen if no agreement is reached? This is a point made by Fisher and Ury (1981) in their description of *principled negotiations*. This requires negotiators to concentrate on four aspects:

- ■ Separate the people from the problem. It is the issues that are important, not the people conducting them. By forcing attention onto the issues, the people involved become focused on finding mutually acceptable solutions.
- ■ Focus on interests, not positions. The purpose of a negotiation is to reach agreement. All parties to the process have an interest in the final solution rather than the position from which they begin. Again, this should force an emphasis on finding mutually acceptable solutions.
- ■ Invent options for mutual gain. This is the major difference from the win–lose approach. There is no single cake to be split into a fixed number of pieces. For example, in negotiations over price increases, the discussions need not be about profit, loss and cost alone. It is possible that an increase in price may be acceptable if conditions regarding delivery, quality and packaging can be met. It is up to the negotiators to seek out ways by which they can both win from the process. It is a *win–win* process.
- ■ Insist on objective criteria. The means by which success and failure should be judged need to be objective and sound in the circumstances. Often a negotiation can degenerate into a horse trading event in which issues are traded so that each party wins some and loses some. Objective criteria means a decision basis that is independent of either side. This approach should ensure that it is the merits of the case that decide the outcome, not pressure or trading tactics.

The authors recognized that not every negotiator operates by these principles and they include in their work a number of tactics for dealing with such situations, including knowing what the alternatives to agreement are. After all, it may be in the best interests of one party to walk away from a particular negotiation, rather than reach an unacceptable agreement.

Communication, decision making and negotiation: a management perspective

There are many applications of communications, decision making and negotiating in the field of management. Managers must develop appropriate policies and practices with regard to these issues. For example, some organizations adopt a high profile and consequently court publicity at every opportunity. Other organizations adopt the opposite approach, preferring to stay out of the public eye and seeking to operate in private. There is, however, a fine line between simply avoiding publicity and actively seeking to divert attention from something that should be brought into the open. The first case is an example of not using communication to its fullest potential, the second is a sinister and manipulative approach in order to hide something. However, this is the road to corruption and is not in the long-term interest of any individual, company or society. Corruption in all its forms has a long history and has affected managerial behaviour in every continent, its effect being to wear down the fabric of society (Alatas, 1991). The challenge facing managers is how to achieve operational effectiveness without abusing the resources available to them through the unethical and inappropriate use of communication, decision making or negotiation.

Most communication within an organizational context takes place between individuals and groups. The more formal external contact tends to be restricted to specialist departments and senior managers acting on behalf of the organization. However, word of mouth and accidental communication should not be underestimated as active sources of information and influence. Employees and managers invariably talk to other people as part of their social life outside work. The views and opinions expressed can have a significant impact on public perception of an organization, sales and its standing in the local community. Rumours originating from such interaction can easily build pictures that form the basis of investigative journalism and city speculation, both of which can have adverse impacts. Not everyone is a good communicator and not all channels offer equal effectiveness in getting the message across (see Table 8.2).

Many of the situations relating to communication will also involve decision making and negotiation. Communications can form part of a negotiation process with the trade unions, a government department, customers or the banks for example. It is a management responsibility to establish who can negotiate what with whom. Also who can take what level and type of decision. Not to establish these frameworks can result in major difficulties for the organization. It is reported (Carpenter and Feloni, 1989) that a respected Wall Street financial institution had little by way of formal financial accountability at the top of the organization and so was unable to control and monitor the level of 'check-kiting' (a complex

Team briefing	57%
Roadshows/staff meetings	11%
Newsletters	7%
Noticeboards	6%
House journal/newsletter	6%
Other	5%
E-mail	4%
Video	1%

Table 8.2
Effectiveness of employee communication channels.
Source: *Personnel Today*.
3 May 1994, p 3

process of moving cheques around various bank accounts to obtain loans). The organization eventually collapsed and was absorbed into another Wall Street firm. This example shows the complex interactions between communication, decision making, negotiation (local managers were free to negotiate deals with local banks), management structure, accountability and operational activity.

Poor communications (along with poor judgement and decision making) can also impact on an organization in ways that were not intended. The chief executive of a large and successful chain of discount jewellery shops found that sales dropped to nil overnight after a careless comment in an after-dinner speech in which he cast doubts on the quality of his company's products was widely reported. As a consequence, most of the shops closed down and he lost his job along with many of the staff!

There is a world of difference between a manager communicating the technical features of the organization's products to customers and the same manager attempting to convince employees to work harder because of the reduction in numbers employed as a result of a delayering exercise. The intended audiences are different, as is the purpose of the message, but so is the relative power relationships that will influence events. The political nature of decision making was described well by Pettigrew (1973) in linking a hierarchy of power to control of resources.

In decision-making terms the *groupthink* phenomenon is of particular importance (Janis, 1982). The decision to establish a group to take a decision could itself be flawed. It is often assumed that a group will take a better decision than an individual, the justification being the inclusion of a range of expertise and opinions. Unfortunately, this view assumes that such a group will undertake its tasks without *interference* factors *corrupting* the process. There are many other pressures acting on the members of a group, even when it is made up of senior people. In decision making there are number of creative approaches to the process, of which those developed by Edward De Bono are perhaps the best known. Management in Action 8.5 indicates his latest views on how to improve decision making.

Managers are collectively and individually responsible for the actions carried out within the organization. They may not personally take a decision but they have a responsibility to ensure that those who undertake these activities in the name of the organization do so to the highest levels of professionalism. That is not to say that perfection should be expected on every occasion, that would be unrealistic. What it does imply is that managers have a responsibility to ensure that it is done to the highest standard *in the circumstances*. In taking decisions managers have access to a variety of sources of information as shown in Table 8.3.

The notion of programmed decisions should allow organizations to channel many of the decision-making areas towards the routine (and controlled) end of

Table 8.3
Source of information available to managers. Source: *Personnel Today*, 3 May 1994, p 36

Newspapers journals and magazines	98%
Word of mouth	95%
Market reports	85%
Company reports	83%
TV/radio	75%
On-line information sources	59%
Microfiche	34%
CD-ROM	19%

Management in Action 8.5

Put on your thinking caps

In an interview with Lucy Kellaway, Edward De Bono, the person who developed 'lateral thinking', talked about his latest approach to creative thinking – the six thinking hats. He argues that approaches to thinking adopted in the west are too rigid and lock creative process into patterns that are no longer appropriate to the fast changing world of today. In making this claim he refers to Socrates, Plato and Aristotle as the 'Gang of Three', who developed the approach to thought still dominating today.

His latest approach to making people more effective in their lives and work is to adopt the perspectives and processes of the six thinking hats. Each hat is a different colour and represents a different thought process. The colours are:

- White. This hat is used to denominate the information gathering stage of thought.
- Red. This hat represents the feelings and emotions towards the thought object.
- Black. This hat incorporates the evaluation of risk, critical appraisal and the adopting of a cautious approach to the focus issue.
- Yellow. This hat requires the wearer to concentrate on issues associated with the feasibility of solutions and the benefits to be gained from them.
- Green. This hat is the one that emphasizes the development of new ideas, options and possibilities.
- Blue. This hat is described as the 'meta' one. It is intended to concentrate on the total process, ensuring that the end result takes all hats into account.

In a meeting context, everyone would wear the same colour hat at the same time and would examine the issue or problem from that perspective. The meeting would work through each of the hats in sequence, considering the issue or problem from every angle.

Companies in the USA which have already used his 'six hats' approach include IBM, Rothmans, Du Pont, Federal Express and the Mormon Church. The approach has spread to other parts of the world, including Canada, Japan, South Africa, Italy and the UK.

De Bono argues that by adopting the logical and concentrated approach to creative thinking implied by the six hat approach, the chemical actions in the brain are different in comparison to when an undifferentiated approach is being used. The result is a more efficient thinking process in which each person concentrates on the same perspective at the same time thereby eliminating the political and ego-based 'contaminants' that otherwise disrupt effective thought and decision making. By everyone emphasizing the same aspect at the same time he suggests that a much more effective inclusion of each perspective occurs. He claims that meeting times can be reduced by approximately 50%, saving some executives the equivalent of about one day each week in wasted time.

Adapted from: Kellaway, L (1994) Put on your thinking caps. Financial Times, *17 June, p 17.*

the spectrum, thereby allowing managers time to concentrate on strategic and non-programmed decision areas. However, as Child (1973) points out, this further differentiates the organization on the basis of technical expertise as a prerequisite for access to and interpretation of information relevant to non-programmed decisions.

The view of limited rationality introduced in the context of decision-making models leads to a notion of *satisficing* rather than a selection between optimal choices. This leads to a short-term approach to control, based on frequent reviews of performance against target, rather than a strategic approach based on the longer term achievement of goals. Lindblom (1959) describes this as the *science of muddling through*. In other words, a continuous process of readjustment of actions in line with perceived deviation from a short-term objective in an attempt to achieve what Cyert and March (1963) call *uncertainty absorption*. Decision making can be a career limiting event if the decision turns out

Management in Action 8.6

On the road to procrastination

There are many light-hearted observations found on company notice boards and office walls about the benefits or otherwise of meetings. The following is not uncommon:

> Are you lonely? Work on your own? Hate making decisions? ... Hold a meeting! You can see other people, draw flowcharts, feel important, and impress your colleagues. All in work time. **Meetings** – the practical alternative to work.

It has been long established that making decisions is stressful. The well-known 'executive monkey' studies from the 1960s demonstrated that by forcing the animals to decide between options, the results of which determined if an electric shock would be applied, caused the animals to become ill. There are many parallels between these experiments and the work experience of modern managers. Under pressure from many quarters to cut costs and at the same time enhance customer service it is hardly surprising that many attempt to slow down the rate of change and decision making. In his light-hearted review, Furnham draws attention to the decision avoidance possibilities of committees and individuals.

Committees, claims Furnham, represent the most popular decision avoidance technique. He goes on to explain that the best committees at this process are those that include individuals that prefer to do nothing who can then legitimately meet and decide that nothing can be done. At an individual level, the more popular decision avoidance techniques are claimed to be:

- The temper tantrum. Adopting the behaviour typical of a spoilt two-year-old child can frequently manipulate the reactions of others to the extent that any decision becomes unnecessary, or at least favourable.

- The hush-hush approach. Pointing out to a colleague that information exists that they could not possible be party to can effectively halt any work. It effectively means that any progress on the problem would result in severe embarrassment or even worse at a personal or professional level.

- The clarification method. This approach can also be classed as elaboration. It adopts the approach that continually referring back an issue for further information or clarification; or for the delineation of decision boundaries can simply exhaust the person being targeted and so halt a project.

- The double-talk method. This approach is much beloved of those individuals with the ability to use long words and complex sentences. It is a jargon-based approach intended to confuse others and to make them look inadequate as the basis of controlling their behaviour.

- The denial approach. Simply stating over and over again that no decision is necessary can frequently be used to avoid having to take one.

- The 'that's your problem' response. Simply handing the problem back to the originator can be an effective way of avoiding a decision. It can involve trying to make them feel that they should be adapting to a situation, or be capable of taking the decision themselves without the need to refer it to other people.

Furnham finishes with two quotes demonstrating opposite perspectives on procrastination. Victor Kiam is reputed to have said that, 'Procrastination is opportunity's natural assassin'. James Thurber on the other hand suggested that, 'He who hesitates is often saved'. A view which perhaps explains the popularity of decision avoidance techniques.

Adapted from: Furnham, A (1994) On the road to procrastination. Financial Times, *4 May, p 17. Plus an unknown original source for the meetings quotation, but this version taken from the* Australian Family Physician *(1992), 21, p 904.*

to be wrong and costly or embarrassing for the organization. There are many ways that individuals attempt to deal with this aspect of life, including the holding of meetings. Management in Action 8.6 illustrates how meetings and decisions are frequently seen by individuals.

Decisions can be categorized into one of three categories: operational, tactical and strategic. The time frames and consequences of each varies. For example, operational decisions represent the day-to-day activities involved in meeting the immediate needs of the organization. As such they tend to be the low cost, small impact and low risk decisions. At the other extreme, strategic decisions involving issues such as acquisitions, divestments, new products and new facilities tend to be in the high cost, high risk areas. The decision to build a new factory may take five years from first idea to post commissioning handover, by which time the market and product may have changed considerably. Strategic decisions are expensive to correct if they turn out to be wrong.

Managers can experience the theories that underpin communications, decision making and negotiation through training courses and degree programmes. Experience within organizations adds to this by providing practice opportunity in live situations. The hierarchical structure of organizations can be seen as allowing experience in these skills to be gained by individuals in a structured and relatively risk free environment. Junior staff and managers are allowed to take comparatively small decisions and are usually monitored by more senior managers. Promotion brings with it the opportunity to become experienced in dealing with ever larger issues. One of the consequences of delayering organizations over recent years has been to reduce the amount of practice opportunity particularly in *graded* decision making and negotiating, with a possible increase in the level of risk and failure for both individuals and organizations. Management in Action 8.7 provides an illustration of how communications and decision-making link with negotiation to provide the basis of an effective result.

There is a unique relationship between the three concepts of communication, decision making and negotiation that is not often found in management theory. There is a cumulative relationship between them. Communication can take place isolated from the other two. The simple exchange of information and interaction does not imply either decision making or negotiation. Decision making, however, cannot take place without communication, but can take place without negotiation. The chief executive reviewing the financial performance of the company can decide on an appropriate course of action based upon the financial reports available and other information communicated by and discussed with senior managers. This does not necessarily require that the chief executive must negotiate with anyone over the intended course of action. Negotiation, however, can only take place in conjunction with the other two. In order to negotiate the parties must communicate and take decisions.

Conclusions

Communications, decision making and negotiation are three of the most important aspects of managerial activity. They are interlinked in a way that makes them difficult to separate and consider in isolation. From a manager's point of view they are all about the process of influencing others in some way or other. For example, communication has as one of its main features the

Management in Action 8.7

How clever negotiators get their way

Lunn, quoting the work of the Huthwaite Research Group, who have studied negotiating behaviours for over 20 years, identifies a number of ways in which successful negotiators distinguish themselves:

■ Seeking information. Skilled negotiators spend about 20% of their time in negotiations asking questions, compared to only 10% by average negotiators. This is thought to give a degree of control over the discussion and avoid direct disagreement.

■ Testing understanding. Skilled negotiators spend twice as much time as average ones in testing that they understand what the other party is saying. This aspect is about the clarity of the issues under discussion and how each party understands the other's point of view. It is about statements such as, 'Let me see if I have understood what you are saying ...?'.

■ Summarizing. The same can be said of summarizing the arguments as it goes along as about testing understanding. Summarizing flows naturally from testing understanding. It is about statements such as, 'Can I just take a few minutes to review where we have got to?'.

■ Behaviour labelling. This aspect of effective negotiation is about providing advance indication of what is to be said next. For example, rather than simply saying, 'What is your best discount for bulk orders?'. The skilled negotiator would say first, 'Can I ask you a question? What is your best discount for bulk orders?' It is suggested that labelling the following behaviour in this way takes some of the surprise out of the process, slows the whole process down, focuses attention on the second sentence rather than the label and so is more likely to gain a response.

Lunn also identifies behaviours that successful negotiators tend to avoid:

■ Irritators. By avoiding saying unpleasant and offensive things about opponents arguments can obviously be avoided. However, average negotiators are more likely to offer favourable comments about themselves and their case. For example, 'This represents a very favourable offer'.

■ Defend/attack spirals. By directly avoiding the use of attack or defend behaviours a spiral of deteriorating quality of discussion can be avoided.

■ Counter-proposals. Simply using counter-proposals avoids the opportunity to explore the merits in the other case or to find ways for mutual benefit. Skilled negotiators make significantly fewer counter-proposals.

■ Argument dilution. Skilled negotiators use many fewer justification claims to back up their case. This runs counter to the argument that the more reasons to back up a case the stronger it becomes. However, more reasons provide more potential points of disagreement if the other party hold a different perspective. This can dilute the strength of the underlying argument.

Adapted from: Lunn, T (1990) How clever negotiators get their way. Sunday Times, Appointments section. 21 January, p 1.

persuasion of others to a particular point of view. Decision making has as one of its main objectives the selection of a course of action that will inevitably impact on others. Negotiation has as one of its main features the persuasion of others to reach agreement on a mutually acceptable basis.

Discussion questions

1 Define the following terms:

Communication	Non-programmed decision	Tactics
Decision	Non-verbal communication	Groupthink
Principled negotiation	Negotiate	Feedback
Decoding	Programmed decision	Encoding

2 Compare and contrast programmed and non-programmed decision making giving examples of each.
3 Describe some of the tactics used in negotiation. How would you counter some of the aggressive tactics described?
4 Describe how communications can be thought of as a perceptual process?
5 Is rationality the only basis on which decisions are taken? Illustrate your answer from your own experience.
6 Is negotiation group dynamics in a particular situation? Justify your answer.
7 Why is decision making important for an organization?
8 'Negotiation is nothing more than a power struggle between two unequal parties.' Discuss this statement.
9 Would it be possible for managers to operate in such a way that negotiation with trade unions could be avoided?
10 'Communication, decision making and negotiation skills are so closely linked to the personality of the individuals that they cannot be learned.' Discuss this statement.

Research assignments

1 Obtain the annual reports for a range of large and small companies from the manufacturing and service industries. What can you infer about their approach to communications from the literature that you have obtained? Obtain the annual reports for a single company from a number of years. What can you infer about changes to the communication strategy adopted over time?
2 Attempt to make contact with a trade union officer and a manager and ask them to describe how they take decisions before going into an industrial relations negotiation and how they take decisions once the negotiation has begun? Ask the manager if they consider that industrial relations decisions differ from other areas of decision making, and if so why?
3 Make contact with a manager in a local organization and identify the groups with which they negotiate. In the discussion see if you can identify whether the manager uses different tactics and approaches for any of the different groups. Also identify how the planning and preparation for specific negotiations differ. How does the manager deal with difficult negotiations?

Key reading

From Clark, H, Chandler, J and Barry, J (1994) *Organization and Identities: Text and Readings in Organizational Behaviour*, International Thomson Business Press, London.

- Janis IL: Groupthink and poor quality decision making, p 279. A review of the potential problems in an institutionalized environment forms the basis of this extract.
- Brunsson N: The virtue of irrationality – decision making, action and commitment, p 294. This argues for an irrational perspective in decision making in order to improve effectiveness.
- Hyman R: The power of collective action, p 322. This extract introduces some of the distinctions between organized and unorganized conflict in the industrial relations field.
- Bradley K and Hill S: What quality circles are, p 364. Quality circles were introduced to improve the work experience of employees and productivity. As such employees are trained in communication and problem-solving skills.
- Hill S: Quality circles in Britain, p 366. This article indicates the development of quality circles in Britain and outlines some of the emerging issues.

Further reading

Checkland, P (1981) *Systems Thinking, Systems Practice*, John Wiley, Chichester. This is quite a difficult text for anyone new to systems thinking, but it offers a useful review of the hard and soft approaches to problem solving.

Cialdini, RB (1988) *Influence: Science and Practice*, Harper Collins. A highly readable text on the general topic of persuasion in all its forms. It includes consideration of all three topics covered in this chapter, but from a different perspective.

Fisher, D (1993) *Communications in Organizations*, 2nd edn, West Publishing, St Paul, MN. This text considers communication from many perspectives relevant to material within the organizational behaviour field.

Fisher, R and Ury, W (1981) *Getting To Yes*, Hutchinson Business, London. This book describes the principled negotiation approach developed by the authors. The subtitle for the book is 'negotiating without giving in', and this effectively describes the approach adopted by the authors. It was followed by a second text (*Getting Past No*, W Ury, 1991, Business Books, London) which outlines how to deal with difficult people in a negotiation context.

Hickson, DJ, Butler, RJ, Cray, D, Malory, GR and Wilson, DC (1986) *Top Decisions: Strategic Decision Making in Organizations*, Basil Blackwell, Oxford. This book describes the decision-making activities across organizations ranging in size from very small to very large. Among its strengths is that it shows how the political dimension of organizations manifests itself in the decision-making process.

Scott, W (1981) *The Skills of Negotiating*, Gower, Aldershot. This is a practical 'how to' type of book which covers many of the facets of negotiating in a range of situations. It is readable and sets out to improve the capability to carry out negotiations as well as describing the process itself.

References

Alatas, SH (1991) *Corruption: Its Nature, Causes and Functions*, S Abdul Majeed, Kuala Lumpur.

Carpenter, DS and Feloni, J (1989) *The Fall of the House of Hutton*, Henry Holt, New York.

Child, J. ed (1973) *Man and Organization*, Allen & Unwin, London.

Cohen, MD, March, JG and Olsen, JP (1972) A garbage can model of organizational choice. *Administrative Science Quarterly*, **17**, 1–25.

Cyert, RM. and March, JG (1963) *A Behavioural Theory of the Firm*, Prentice-Hall, Englewood Cliffs, NJ.

Fisher, R and Ury, W (1981) *Getting To Yes*, Hutchinson Business, London.

Garrahan, P and Stewart, P (1992) *The Nissan Enigma: Flexibility at Work in a Local Economy*, Mansell, London.

Gunther, J (1950) *Roosevelt in Retrospect*, Harper, New York.

Harrison, EF (1987) *The Managerial Decision Making Process*, 3rd edn. Houghton Mifflin, Boston, MA.

Janis, IL and Mann, L (1977) *Decision Making: A Psychological Analysis of Conflict, Choice and Commitment*, Free Press, New York.

Janis, IL (1982) *Victims of Groupthink: A Psychological Study of Foreign Policy Decisions and Fiascos*, 2nd edn, Houghton Mifflin, Boston, MA.

Lindblom, CE (1959) The science of muddling through. *Public Administration Review*, **19**, 79–88.

March, JG and Simon, HA (1958) *Organizations*, John Wiley, New York.

Pease, A (1981) *Body Language*, Sheldon Press, London.

Pettigrew, A (1973) *The Politics of Organisational Decision Making*, Tavistock, London.

Scott, W (1981) *The Skills of Negotiating*, Gower, Aldershot.

Simon, HA (1960) *The New Science of Management Decision*, Harper & Row, New York.

Thompson, TE and Tuden, A (1959) *Comparative Studies in Administration*, University of Pittsburgh Press, Pittsburgh, PA.

Torrington, D and Hall, L (1987) *Personnel Management: A New Approach*, Prentice-Hall, Englewood Cliffs, NJ.

Trager, GL (1958) Paralanguage: a first approximation. *Studies in Linguistics*, **13**, 1–12.

Part IV

The structure and design of organizations

Part IV

The structure and
design of organizations

9 Organizational frameworks

Chapter summary

This chapter begins with the consideration of the significance of an organization's structure and introduces some of the factors that determine the choices made. This is followed by the introduction of the major structural variations adopted by organizations and a brief review of the work of Mintzberg in describing the process. The organizational life cycle is also introduced as a factor in the decision-making approach to design. The chapter concludes with a consideration of the management perspectives on organizational design issues.

Learning objectives

After studying this chapter and working through the associated Management in Action panels, discussion questions and research activities, you should be able to:

- Outline the main structural choices available to organizations.
- Explain why organizations operating internationally have more variables to take into account when deciding structural arrangements.
- Describe the differences in design and control implicit in the product, process and matrix structural forms.
- Understand how Mintzberg approaches the topic of structure together with the differences and similarities with other perspectives.
- Discuss the limitations inherent in any organizational design.
- Appreciate how the work of Fayol and Weber has informed the approaches described in this chapter.
- Detail how the need to compartmentalize the work of an organization is at variance with the need to integrate activities.
- Assess the managerial significance of the structural choices made by organizations.

browse this web site

www.itbp.com

Introduction

There has always existed a need to arrange the resources of an organization in such a way that will achieve the objectives in the most effective manner possible. Imagine the organization structure necessary to build the great pyramid of Cheops in Egypt. It covers an area of 13 acres and was constructed from approximately 2.5 million blocks of stone, each weighing an average of 2.5 tons. Construction is estimated to have lasted some 20 years and the total labour force at 100,000 men (George, 1972, p 4). Obviously there are many differences between the ways that work was organized in ancient Egypt and modern Europe, but organizational design decisions had to be made even then.

The significance of structure

Traditional approaches to organizing emphasized the task aspects of work and hence the structure of the organization reinforced hierarchical control and segmented responsibilities. This is the essence of bureaucracy with its hierarchy of control, rule frameworks and task specialization (Weber, 1947). These ideas were developed at a time when organizations generally were becoming much larger but did not have the benefits of technology. The consequence was a need to develop the human equivalent of the computer in administering large bureaucracies efficiently.

Fayol was a practising manager who wrote about his experiences and thoughts based on running companies. He adopted a managerial perspective to the determination of what structural arrangements were necessary. In his 1916 book he identified the operations necessary to run a company as:

- Technical. The production and manufacturing activities.
- Commercial. Purchasing and sales activities.
- Financial. Funding and control of capital.
- Security. Protection of goods, people and the organization.
- Accounting. Stockholding, costing and statistical information.
- Managerial. The management process of organizing, co-ordinating, commanding, controlling, forecasting and planning.

Fayol also identified a number of principles of management which impacted on the structure of the organization. They included the division of work into compartments, a unity of command, centralization and decentralization issues, principles evident in many organizations today

The size of an organization and the complexity of operational activity creates the need for the work to be compartmentalized in order to ensure that it can be done. Kanter (1983) described this as individuals restricting themselves to the 'boxes' implicit within bureaucratic frameworks and referred to it as *segmentalism*. This she contrasted with the entrepreneurial spirit found in successful organizations. In addition to this distinction in approach she describes differences in problem solving between bureaucracies and innovative companies, leading to an *integrative* approach to structure and culture. This highlights the dilemma facing managers when they contemplate the design and structure of an organization. On the one hand structure creates differentiation. It separates out the 'different' and 'separate' tasks. For example, the production department is separated from the personnel and marketing departments on the basis of task specialization. This represents the classic structural configuration of an organization (Figure 9.1).

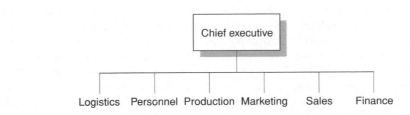

Figure 9.1 Functional organization structure.

On the other hand, there is a need for integration of activity and effort in order to complete the whole product or service. The different skills required to build a car can be grouped into various departments but there must be an integration between them or the end product will not be fit for sale.

The main advantage of this type of structure is that a high degree of expertise and efficiency can be achieved as a result of the opportunity for individuals to concentrate on a relatively small range of duties. The main problem with such structural arrangements is that they encourage the achievement of functional objectives as opposed the overall objectives of the organization. This view can be identified in the research interviews carried out by Watson (1994) in which one manager reported

> They are far more interested in steam-rollering in these new things [changes to work practices] so that they can move on in their careers than they are in trying to understand people and show them how these new ideas will advantage everybody. (p 155)

'They' in this context refers to managers who, it is suggested, function on the basis of benefit to their own careers rather than the benefit of the whole organization.

This illustrates the second need within an organization when it segments itself, namely the need to form integrative mechanisms to allow the 'segments' to work together in seeking to achieve the common objective. Not infrequently, this leads to the development of systems and procedures to ensure that all interested parties have the opportunity to contribute to the process. Watson's research demonstrates the extensive processes used to balance the forces of segmentation and integration when one of his interviewees reports that an order passed through 14 different pairs of hands before arriving in the manufacturing department (p 149). The relative slowness of the decision making within this type of framework, together with the potential for inter-functional conflict, is easy to envisage. Management in Action 9.1 describes how Electrolux attempted to deal with these conflicts.

The significance of structure lies in its ability to achieve organizational objectives and efficiency. Business process re-engineering is a modern approach to this which requires an organization to *organize* around customer needs and continually improve productivity. It assumes that the use of 'scientific method' can prescribe how to achieve organizational objectives. In other words, the structure of an organization should be a function of its objectives, technology and environmental forces. There is a wealth of research data that would support this view (for example Lawrence and Lorsch, 1967; Woodward, 1970; and Perrow, 1979). A summary of the business process re-engineering concept is included as Management in Action 9.2.

Figure 9.2 (on page 268) illustrates a strategic management perspective, intended to produce alignment between the organization and its identified objectives. Decisions resulting from this process have a significant impact on organizational design considerations. Structure in this context is the means by which effort is co-ordinated and through which results are achieved. Indeed, Porter (1985, p 23) argues that, 'Each generic [competitive] strategy implies different skills and requirements for success, which commonly translate into differences in organizational structure and culture'.

Management in Action 9.1

How to bridge functional gaps

For a considerable number of years Electrolux has pursued a strategy of growth by acquisition. Over the past decade it acquired Zanussi (Italian), Frigidaire (American) and AEG's appliances division (German). This phase has now ended and the company has begun a process of finding ways of integrating its diverse brands into cohesive operations that combine factory, sales, marketing and finance activities. In addition, there is a need to integrate the human side of the business, creating a shared set of goals and a willingness to co-operate among people, irrespective of formal reporting lines. The matrix approach to organizing did not provide the richness required from the complexity found within Electrolux and so alternative processes have been instigated to generate the 'competitive speed' sought by management.

Many multinational companies have moved over recent years towards structures based upon international product divisions or lines of business. This can provide some benefits but does ignore the other two dimensions of the matrix organization – functional and geographic management perspectives. The danger in moving too far in the international product division direction is that power begins to be concentrated at that level and also the motivation of local country managers drops. Both of these potential problems ignore the needs of local managers on whom so much depends.

Electrolux has essentially three product groups: 'hot' products, 'cold' products and 'wet' products. In late 1992 it set up pan-European industrial divisions for each of these three groups, which control product design and manufacture. A central marketing group was established for all product groups, with activity on the ground controlled through brand 'portfolio managers' in each sales area. It was not the intention to combine these two sides of the business as the complexity would be too great. For example, there are four different brands in most countries. To attempt to integrate manufacturing with marketing under these complex conditions would create financial reporting problems and functional difficulties. Customers also expect the marketing people to be capable of dealing with the full range of products from each brand, they do not want to deal with different personnel.

The company engaged in a wide range of initiatives intended to capture the benefits of the current structure whilst enabling better management information to be provided. Examples included the development of a comprehensive order-to-payment system which covered the entire product cycle from manufacture to delivery to customer payment across the whole of Europe for all products and brands. Another related to the attempt to develop financial information by brand and product division. This involved the collation of much cross border information and the production of product-based end-to-end cash models. These initiatives have been supported by other measures such as management information systems and reward systems to encourage local managers to release information to allow the debate to move beyond haggling over transfer prices.

Adapted from: Lorenz, C (1994) How to bridge functional gaps. Financial Times, 25 November, p 14.

The strategic approach to structure begins with an intention to create understanding of the environment within which the organization is functioning. Once in an understandable form this 'data' then becomes amenable to manipulation through a decision-making process. Management in Action 9.3 (on page 269) illustrates the strategic links with structure in attempts by Volkswagen to improve its position. This involves not only reorganizing the activities within the company but replacing individuals and relationships with suppliers.

Business process re-engineering

There have been many attempts over the years to find the most effective way to improve the productivity and customer service levels within organizations. It has been suggested that business process re-engineering (BPR) is either the key to achieving that in the modern organization or it is little more than a reworking of the ideas of FW Taylor and scientific management.

The term BPR emerged around 1990 following the work of two distinct sets of authors. Management consultant Mike Hammer wrote an article in the *Harvard Business Review* titled, 'Reengineering work: don't automate, obliterate'. This article talked about the need to re-engineer at both the business and process level. At about the same time an article appeared in the *Sloan Management Review* with the title 'The new industrial engineering: information technology and business process redesign'. Written by Thomas Davenport and James Short it talked of business process redesign, but not of re-engineering as such. The Hammer approach tended to suggest a fundamental review and change process whereas Davenport and Short adopted a more cautious and structured approach through the application of technology and industrial engineering principles. In practice the term Business Process Re-engineering was not used by either sets of writers and appeared only after the publication of both articles.

There are number of definitions of BPR but that offered by Hammer and Champey in a 1993 publication is a useful starting point:

> The fundamental rethinking and radical redesign of business processes to achieve dramatic improvements in critical contemporary measures of performance, such as cost, quality, service and speed.

Some organizations claim to have made considerable savings and improvements through the application of BPR. For example:

- Ford Motor Company reduced the number of people in the accounts payable department by 75%, with no reduction in service level.
- The Bank of America and Italy reduced cashier closing time by 91%, opened 50 new branches and doubled revenue without any increase in staff.
- Kodak reduced new product development time by 50% and reduced tool and manufacturing costs by 25%.

However, not all companies that attempt BPR achieve the success intended. Hammer estimates that 70% of organizations that attempt BPR do not achieve any benefits. BPR is about every aspect of the business, not just the manufacturing processes. It involves changing the structures, attitudes, culture, management style and values. It implies a fundamental re-evaluation of the purpose of the business and of developing the 'best way' of achieving that objective, taking nothing that currently exists for granted. Hammer uses the analogy of a 'paved cowpath' to describe the process that normally exists in an organization. Just as cows will tread familiar paths around the fields and to the milking parlours, organizations tend to accept the familiar as necessary and so change becomes a process of adaptation. Hammer argues that the only givens are the inputs and outputs, and that between the two lies the possibility to completely redesign new ways of doing things.

The usual organization structure gets in the way of effective working as it compartmentalizes activity and creates the need to hand over work and split responsibility. Hammer and Champey illustrate this notion through the example of IBM Credit Corporation. In arranging finance on behalf of customers five steps were necessary (each in a different department) and the processing time for each application was about six days, although it could take two weeks. After 'walking the process' it became apparent that the actual work time for each application was about 1.5 hours. The whole operation was re-engineered with a new job of 'deal structurer' being created to process each application from beginning to end. Supported by new technology and database systems the turnaround time fell to four hours with a small reduction in staff numbers and the capability to handle many more transactions.

Adapted from: Patching, D (1994) Business process re-engineering: getting to the heart of the matter. Management Services, *June, pp 10–13. and Patching, D (1994) Business process re-engineering: what's in a name?.* Management Services, *November, pp 8–11.*

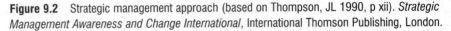

Figure 9.2 Strategic management approach (based on Thompson, JL 1990, p xii). *Strategic Management Awareness and Change International*, International Thomson Publishing, London.

From a philosophical perspective Michel Foucault considers many issues associated with the need for co-ordination and differentiation within an organization. He does this through a number of reviews not specifically associated with commercial organizations, but in ways that permit appropriate themes to be identified. Townley (1994) provides an insightful analysis of his work. Among the relevant features are:

■ Enclosure. In enclosing, boundaries are created and distinctions can be drawn between the distinct entities. This compartmentalization helps to create control through pattern and order in an otherwise chaotic milieu. Examples include the enclosure that creates particular organizations (IBM is a separate 'enclosure' to ICL), or the distinctions between paid labour (at work) to unpaid work (carried out at home).

■ Partitioning. This refers to a vertical and horizontal differentiation of people within an enclosure. It refers to the classification of people into occupational groups and hierarchies. In recent times the distinction between core and peripheral employees is an example of partitioning.

■ Ranking. This relates to differentiation on the basis of a hierarchy, perhaps determined by technical skill, or experience. So for example, it reflects the relative seniority within a sub-grouping – personnel manager, senior personnel officer, personnel officer and trainee personnel officer being examples.

These concepts provide the basis for interpreting how an organization is defined and how it creates a means of being able to control its own activities. This is achieved through differentiation and the creation of a web of meaning and externalization of activity. The key implication being that organization and structure are means of creating understanding as a precondition of the exercise of power and control. For example, worker participation in Polaroid was ended because, although successful, it was feared that it undermined the need for supervisory and managerial positions (Jenkins, 1973). However, in creating understanding people impose frameworks that make sense to them. Understanding is created in the minds of individuals in terms of the cognitive structures that already exist. In other words organizations are a creation of management's imagination, designed in such a way as to meet the requirements

Management in Action 9.3

Bitter pill from company doctors

The role of the company doctor is frequently a difficult one. Brought in to deal with a crisis hard decisions have to be made and there is a direct and inevitable impact on people and jobs. Volkswagen (VW) found itself in need of a company doctor in attempting to get itself out of its financial crisis in 1993. Pre-tax profits had been on the slide for a number of years, dropping from about DM3bn in 1989 to a loss of DM1.25bn for the first three months of 1993. The scale of the losses was very significant for both the group and country as the turnover of the company accounted for about 3% of the economic output of the reunified Germany.

Mr Ferdinand Piëch was appointed chairman of the Volkswagen group and within a few days had developed an emergency strategy. The range of measures proposed by Mr Piëch and his emergency team included:

- A reduction of 20,000 jobs by the end of 1993 and a further 16,000 by the end of 1997.
- Capital investment to be reduced by about 50% to DM6bn in 1993.
- A new factory in Mosel to be delayed or scrapped.
- Productivity and output improvements to be achieved in existing factory locations.
- Reduced the 1992 dividend from DM11 to DM2.
- Removed three of the management board directors, including the finance director.
- Appointed a new group purchasing director, Mr José Lopez, headhunted from General Motors (GM). He in turn recruited several senior purchasing specialists from his former team at GM.
- Proposed the number of suppliers to VW be cut from around 1500 to about 200.
- Design changes to cars in order to simplify the logistics, stock and cost aspects. For example, reduc-

ed the 16 rear-axle variations in the VW Golf to four.
- Change the nature of the supply chain so the VW could concentrate on core operations and source complete sub-units from outside. For example, buying complete brake systems from pedals to brake pads as a single sub-assembly, so that they could be fitted in one go, at the lowest cost and in the fastest time.
- Proposed the reduction in the number of management levels from nine to three.
- Building on the existing performance of satellite factories, overseas investments and other marques within the group. For example, the plant in Mexico supplied volume to keep the share of the market at 32% and Skoda (also part of VW, along with Audi and Seat) in the Czech Republic increased its deliveries by about 18% in the first two months of 1993.

Every aspect of the business had been identified for 'treatment' by Mr Piëch in his role as company doctor. He intended that no stone would be left unturned in the drive for lower costs and higher profits. He Indicated that suppliers would have to be more competitive and that costs would have to fall to the lowest level possible without driving either the supplier of VW out or business. He promised to help suppliers identify ways to reduce their production costs in order to create a symbiosis in joint survival. Anyone not in a direct operations jobs at VW such as central administration would have to justify their existence on the basis of contribution and earning their keep. It was also apparent from his actions that the traditional softly-softly approach of German management to change was being rejected in favour of a more direct and vigorous approach, led by individuals from other countries.

Adapted from: Parkes, C (1993) Bitter pill from company doctors. Financial Times*, 1 April, p 21.*

of the creator. Organization structure derives significance from its purpose as a mechanism of control and power. This contrasts sharply with the earlier view that the significance of structure is in its intention to achieve organizational objectives.

Another view of organization suggests a stage design as used in the theatre. Bolman and Deal (1994, p 95), claim that it is possible to interpret structure as, '... an arrangement of space, lighting, props, and costumes to make the organizational drama vivid and credible to its audience'. In making this claim the authors cite a number of studies that suggest, at least in the field of educational organizations, structure and activity are not strongly related. It is also suggested that a *symbolic logic* applies in the determination of levels of support through the perception of symbols, rather than any deeper measurement of performance. In effect, the authors argue that the structure of an organization creates a ceremonial stage for particular performances to be carried out for particular audiences. The symbol of structure provides the script and other props that allow the actors within the play (organization) to act out their parts in a controlled way and within a defined framework. The significance of structure from this perspective is that it has little direct link with commercial objectives. It is relevant to the way that the organization is perceived by those that come into contact with it and the way that it defines the roles and actions of those within it.

From this brief review of the significance of structure it is apparent that it is management that defines the boundaries and content of organizations. They also construct the reality which confines what other people must adapt to. This provides management with a range of benefits other than an ability to meet operational objectives.

Organizational structures

The decision areas that can influence the design of an organization include:

- Formalization. This relates to the notion of the formality and degree of prescription involved with the way that the organization undertakes its activities.
- Job design. The way that individual tasks are combined together to create specific jobs influences the structure of the organization. For example, a car manufacturing plant built around the concept of assembly lines, with each employee undertaking only a very limited number of tasks, will have a different structure than if assembly were done by teams of employees building a whole car.
- Height. A tall structure will have different structural frameworks to one that is relatively flat.
- Orientation. An organization that is designed around the functional activities (personnel, finance, marketing, etc.) will have different structural arrangements than one organized along product lines (all activities involved with a specific product grouped together).
- Centralization. The degree to which an organization operates in a centralized or decentralized manner in terms of decision making and delegated authority will also influence the structural design.

■ Co-ordination. The mechanisms for ensuring that whatever the form of segmentation within the organization the various sub-units are integrated in a way which provides a capability of contribution towards the objectives sought. The relationship between line and staff activities within an organization is also relevant to this process. Line activities are those with a direct impact on the main purpose of the business (manufacturing, sales). Staff functions are the support activities (accounting, personnel) to the main purpose operations.

Entrepreneurial structures

The entrepreneurial structure is typically found in small organizations where the owner also plays an active and dominant role in running them. In the early years there may not be enough work to justify employing staff. The most simple form of an entrepreneurial structure is shown in Figure 9.3.

In running an entrepreneurial organization all decisions of any significance are taken by the owner/manager, with employees being the resource to implement them. In this form of organization the management activities are largely inseparable from the personalities and personal preferences of the owners. Decision making is very often based upon personal feelings and needs, rather than those of the business. Personal relationships feature very heavily as an important feature of the activities within this type of organization. The relative lack of size together with the direct involvement of the owner creates a scenario where everyone needs to be able to work together effectively if major problems are to be avoided. Individuals typically become involved with a wide range of tasks in order to deliver the service or complete the order on time. It is not uncommon to find the owner 'rolling up their sleeves' and undertaking the most menial tasks when necessary. In a very real sense power and authority within the organization lie with the owner/manager.

There are a considerable number of entrepreneurial organizations in both the manufacturing and service sectors. In the service sector many small partnerships exist in the field of personal services. For example, legal firms, accountancy practices, travel agencies, retail shops and restaurants. Indeed, it was part of the job creation strategy of the UK government during the 1980s to encourage the establishment of many small enterprises. The intention being to encourage unemployed people to create their own jobs and in addition to create a number of jobs for other people. The failure rate of new businesses is very high, with something like 30% going into liquidation within two years. Figures

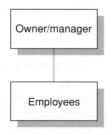

Figure 9.3 Entrepreneurial organization structure.

for 1994 indicate that for the UK 127,482 new businesses were formed, the highest number since 1989 (*Financial Times*, 1995).

Having survived the early difficulties associated with the start-up of a small organization, the entrepreneur is faced with the problems associated with success. Success brings with it the opportunity for growth. Increases in the volume of orders, demand for the product or service all carry with them the need for change in the organization. Growth in the volume of work in a business can be absorbed to a certain degree. Existing employees can work overtime or they can work more efficiently, new production methods can be introduced or the work can be allocated differently. However, at some point in time additional staff, new premises and equipment will be required. This poses a number of problems for the entrepreneur, but the main area for concern is often the reduced opportunity for day-to-day involvement in organizational activity. With a growth in size there is a need to manage other people who in turn do the work. It is not unusual to find entrepreneurs deliberately limiting growth in an attempt to retain personal involvement and levels of control.

The difficulties and choices facing the entrepreneurial manager and their successors were described in the work of Greiner (1972). He describes a process of having to address issues of centralization and decentralization along with differentiation and uniformity on a regular basis. Centralization creates an environment which encourages uniformity in all aspects of organizational activity. Decentralization on the other hand often originates out of a recognition that differentiation in organizational activity is necessary. Small organizations are by definition centralized. As they grow in size the opportunity emerges to differentiate activities through the introduction of different products and services and to open up new markets. In the early years these changes in direction can be absorbed by the existing structure and procedures, but eventually more radical and fundamental change is forced upon the organization. This forces management to deal with a series of crisis. This process Greiner demonstrates through a diagram, included as Figure 9.4.

It is clear that there are a number of growth strategies adopted by organizations, perhaps beginning with the creative enlargement or development of the product range. The next phase needs effective leadership to achieve growth through the integration of the volume provided by the creativity. But before that can happen, there will be a crises of leadership, requiring the previous leader to adapt their approach to the new circumstances. Failure to do so may lead to stagnation, failure of the organization, or a change in leader. It is to avoid facing up to the crises identified in Figure 9.4 that many owner/managers deliberately restrict the size of their organizations at the point at which they feel that they can retain effective control.

Product-based structures

Organization structures based on product require that the activities within the organization are categorized according to the use to which they will be put. In this approach the product or service becomes the focus for the efforts of the people and resources. Typically, each product group would be the responsibility of one manager, in effect the chief executive of a business unit within a business. The key features of this type of structure are:

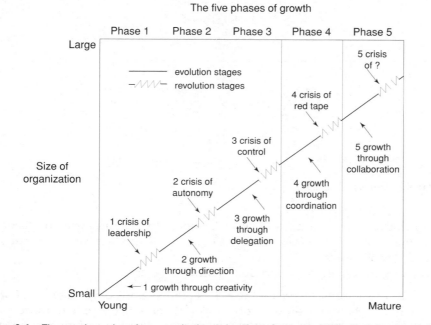

The five phases of growth

Figure 9.4 The growing pains of an organization (taken from Greiner, L 1972). Evolution, revolution as organizations grow, *Harvard Business Review*, July/August, p 41.

- **Product focus.** The focus for the structure is the range of products or services that the organization intends to provide. In the true product structure there would be no overlap between divisions supplying the service or product, each would be dedicated to its own specific range.
- **Single head.** This type of structure creates a number of businesses in their own right. Each concentrates on its own product or service range and deals with its own customers. In that sense each unit is a separate company. In practice there is invariably a single manager responsible for each business unit. This type of post often carries the title of divisional director or general manager to signify the importance within the company.
- **Limited autonomy.** However the organization designs its structure within this product-based approach the divisional manager will be accountable to the head office for the running of the business unit. It does not make operational sense to have a product-based structure with a manager responsible for its activities if that person is not given the authority to undertake their duties. However, there is a need to retain an overall consistency across the whole company. Consequently, each division will enjoy only limited autonomy. There has to be some restriction on the degree of freedom of action allowed to each division or anarchy and financial disaster could result as each attempted to become totally independent.

Product-based structures are advantageous when there is a need to get close to customers and the company offers a range of products, each serving specific markets. It is an option when there is instability in the various markets, requiring the organization to be proactive across a broad front. Splitting the product range into groups, each the responsibility of a separate business unit, provides the opportunity to concentrate on part of the overall problem.

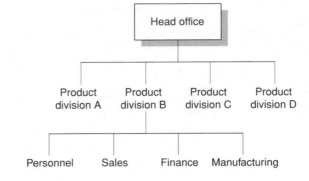

Figure 9.5 Product structure.

This achieves the advantages of specialization, but without losing the benefits of being a large organization. An example of a product-based structure is included as Figure 9.5.

The main advantages of a product structure include:

■ Risk. This approach spreads the risk of particular products failing and dragging the whole organization down with them. It is possible to more effectively control the overall operation because decision making can be split into the operational levels within the business unit and strategic decision making can be focused at head office.

■ Evaluation. The decision-making process becomes clearer as a result of the compartmentalization of the business. Those products and business units that are successful will be more visible through the cost and profit evaluation processes used within the organization. Equally, problem operations are more easily detected and remedial action taken.

■ Motivation and development. Being responsible for a specific business unit with well-defined goals and responsibilities should increase the levels of motivation among the managers and employees. Because of the responsibility given to business unit managers they should develop 'general manager' skills at an earlier stage of their careers.

■ Support. Depending upon the size of the organization there may be a range of support services available within the head office, or other business units. These could be utilized to support and enhance the resources available in business units that experience difficulties, or need particular skills. For example, a small division may not have its own training and development specialists, but can call on the group specialist to design an appropriate course if an identified need is detected.

■ Acquisition and divestment. The integration of acquired companies should be effected more easily if they are to be absorbed into an existing specialized structure. Even if the acquired company itself has a number of products which are to be split among separate business units, this should produce a more satisfactory result more quickly. Divestment can also be more easily achieved as the closure or sale of one complete division should have minimal impact on the others within the company.

■ Change. It is assumed that because each business unit will be closer to its customers and the market for its products that it will be more adaptable and responsive to the need for change. It would be more obviously in the interests of employees at every level to adapt and develop products, services and working practices to meet the ever changing needs of customers.

The disadvantages of a product-based structure include:

- Responsibility. There may be confusion or lack of clarity between the responsibilities and rights of head office to interfere with business unit activity, or to instruct a unit in what it must do in particular situations.
- Conflict. It is likely that there will be conflict between business units as a result of competition for resources. No company can support every request for additional resources. Every manager could make use of additional resources if they became available. An organization must find some way of prioritizing requests.
- Short-term perspective. Depending upon the career development patterns together with budgetary and incentive arrangements, it is possible that business unit managers will concentrate on short-term results. A manager faced with the option of taking decisions which will benefit the unit in (say) five years, but who knows that he will have moved jobs by then, will be tempted to take decisions that reflect on his or her immediate performance.
- Relative size. Not all business units will be the same size and co-ordination between them can become difficult as a consequence, particularly if there are commercial linkages between them. Smaller units often feel forgotten and dominated by the larger ones, which can lead to frustration, under performance and missed business opportunities.
- Customer confusion. It is possible that a single customer may have contact with more than one business unit. It leads to duplication and frustration for both parties.

Management in Action 9.4 on the next page shows the involvement of the Chinese military in business activities, reflecting elements of a product-based approach to organizing on a massive scale.

Process-based structures

Process-based structures split the organization according to the manufacturing or service activities involved. Another way of describing this type of structure is as a functional approach. For example, the typical process-based structure of a manufacturing company would group together the resources under production activities, personnel, marketing, finance and engineering (see Figure 9.6).

Typically process would be the structural form that an entrepreneurial organization would first evolve into when growth required change. It is also likely that the business units within a product-based structure would adopt a process orientation as the basis of grouping together the sub-tasks.

The advantages of the process-based structure are:

- Specialization. Categorizing in functional groupings allows individuals to develop a high level of expertise in that particular discipline. It also means that support is readily available to people in that function from the other specialists around them. The benefits of this approach should be apparent in the levels of productivity achieved and the ability of the organization to deal with crises that arise.
- Stability. Such structures are able to deal more effectively with circumstances in which there is a continuity across time. However, with specialization

Management in Action 9.4

The generals' big business offensive

The military in China is branching out into the running of commercial enterprises. This is the claim of a number of observers who specialize in the role and functioning of the military in China. China Poly Group is one such company and is on its way to being one of the country's largest conglomerates. For example, it is working on a number of commercial ventures including the development of a freeport complex and infrastructure on the island of Hainan off the coast of Vietnam in partnership with a Japanese construction company.

There are two main categories of military/commercial link developing within China. The first category are a cluster of manufacturing, investment and trading companies under the direct control of parts of the People's Liberation Army (PLA). The second category involve the application of state-owned defence industries to the development and sale of civilian equipment and products. This category falls under the direct control of the government. John Frankenstein, from the University of Hong Kong Business School and who specializes in the topic, refers to this military involvement in private enterprise as, 'Chinese bureaucratic entrepreneurialism'.

Among the major corporations set up as part of the military and government establishments are:

- China Poly Group. Founded in 1984 and part of the general staff structure within the military. It was set up partly to compete with Norinco and is involved in shipping, finance, property, trading, electronics, telecommunications and construction. It also controls two companies listed on the Hong Kong Stock Exchange.

- Norinco. Founded before 1984 by the government and with over 157 factories under its control. It is involved with arms sales, trading, construction, real-state, finance and car manufacture.

- Xinxing Corporation. Is heavily associated with the logistics branch of the military and represented at most of the major military depots. It is involved with pharmaceuticals, clothing, food, construction, fuel and vehicles.

In addition to these corporations there are about 20 other companies operating within the military/state commercial enterprise framework. This also includes the police who have a company specializing in security equipment. To some extent the military is able to cover its own costs as a result of the revenue generated from these organizations. For example, the estimated cost of running the military in China is put at about two or three times the Yn52 bn official budget provided by the government.

There is however a degree of unease about the situation within China; the Central Military Commission established an audit commission to control possible abuses through fraud and corruption. In addition there have been some attempts to control the further proliferation of these organizations through tighter control from the centre.

Adapted from: Holberton, S and Walker, T (1994) The generals' big business offensive. Financial Times, *28 November, p 19.*

comes loyalty to the functional group rather than business objectives. With markets that are unstable and which require frequent changes in product or service comes the need to respond quickly and effectively. This is not easy to achieve through a process structure.

- Centralization. At the lower levels of process-based organizations there is little integration of activity across the functions. Consequently, it is only at the higher levels that any form of holistic picture of the organization, its objectives and strategies is possible. This inevitably leads to a centralized approach to running the organization. It is the centre of the organization that directs, controls and regulates everything that goes on.

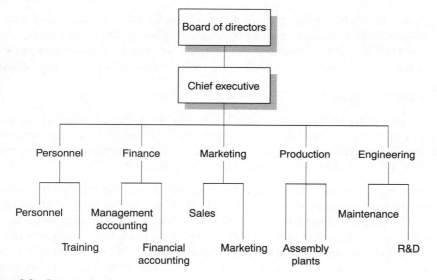

Figure 9.6 Process structure.

■ Clarity. Because of the compartmentalized nature of this form of structure individuals within it are able to concentrate on just part of the overall operation. This provides a clarity of purpose. It is argued that the encouragement of this single-mindedness allows both a clarity in operational terms but also a greater degree of specialization and efficiency among the operational level of employees.

The disadvantages of the process-based structure are:

■ Co-ordination. Specialization is also a disadvantage in that the very act of separation requires co-ordination between the functions. If co-ordination does not take place, or if it is ineffective, then the benefits of functional specialism will not be realized.

■ Budget orientation. As a direct consequence of breaking the organization into functional units, no one group is responsible for the profitability of the organization. That responsibility lies at the level of the chief executive. Within the specialist functions responsibility is for the achievement of a budget. However, the achievement (or otherwise) of a budgeted level of expenditure does not guarantee that the profit achieved will be the best that could have been achieved.

■ Succession. Because of the nature of the functional approach, individuals do not obtain the experience of general management until they are very senior within the organization. Functional managers are not responsible for the activities beyond their expertise. Without this experience problems can be created for career development, learning and succession planning activities for senior managers.

■ Growth. The growth of the organization can become a problem for the process structure. As the size of the organization and the product range grows it can create problems of co-ordination and thereby restrict the performance of the organization.

■ Political. It is likely that the emphasis on the function as the main focus of activity within the organization creates a primary loyalty to that group. This can lead to empire building and political behaviour as managers seek to enhance their importance, influence and careers within the organization.

International organizations

One of the difficulties in attempting to identify the types of structure used by international organizations is the range of size and type of such organizations. The type of involvement in international activity also creates an effect. The most commonly found forms of international activity include:

■ Exporting. Telephone, post or the faxing of orders being the simplest means of actually initiating this form of trade. The use of the post or an international freight company is the most common means of shipping orders to the customer. Larger organizations may employ overseas representatives to sell the products made in the home country. The essence of exporting is that a company based in one country sells its products or services in other countries though sales offices or directly in response to customer orders. In the case of the service industries this could involve sending a management consultant to another country to undertake an assignment.

■ Agents. A variation of the exporting approach is to sell through a number of agents in other countries. Typically the agent would be self employed, perhaps dealing with a number of suppliers across a broad range of similar products. The main advantage is that they have a better knowledge of foreign markets than the company itself. Among the disadvantages are a lack of direct control over the agent. Sales are in the hands of someone who may not be fully committed to selling the company products, particularly if they carry a portfolio of similar offerings. In addition, the organization does not build up any direct expertise in the foreign markets covered by the agent, as it is the interests of the agent to keep the company at arm's length.

■ Licensing. This involves a company granting a licence to another company to produce and sell something the first company has exclusive rights over. In return a fee would be paid to the original company. This can be an effective means of generating money for the original company without the risks and costs of setting up in other counties. However, it is also creating an opportunity for other organizations to obtain production technologies, design specifications and market information in a way that could be damaging to the original company.

■ Franchising. This is a process whereby the franchisee is granted a right to use a trademark in return for a payment to the franchisor. The franchisee is required to find a sum of money to start the franchise and is given help with the process. The franchisor would continue to support the franchisee in the running of the business in return for a fee. There are many franchise operations, hotel chains, fast food restaurants, business and domestic services being among the most common.

■ Management contracts. Essentially this form of foreign involvement is about managing an operation on behalf of another in return for a fee. In that sense it does not involve the parent company in any overseas sales of its own products or services. It is foreign involvement through the sale of its management expertise.

- Turnkey operations. This type of activity involves the construction of a new facility and its subsequent operation until the commissioning phase is completed. Then a fully operational facility would be handed over to the owners. This type of foreign involvement is again based upon the sale of expertise rather than the sale of products to a market.

- Contract arrangements. This could involve a range of activities in which one organization contracts with another to exchange goods and services. For example, the sale of military equipment to a specific country might also include the training over a number of years of local staff.

- Direct investment. This approach incorporates the various forms of ownership that could be found in foreign investment. This could embrace the total ownership of a company in another country or the part ownership through a joint venture or partnership. The essence being that a measure of direct control of the process is achieved through this type of involvement.

- Portfolio investment. This approach to international activity involves the financial involvement in operations in other countries, but not necessarily based on control of resources. It is an organizational form of investment. The parent company might hold a portfolio of investments in overseas organizations and would move its resources from location to location based upon objectives and returns. In that sense it does not reflect a business relationship in the normal sense of the term.

- Multinational enterprise. Often referred to as an MNE for short, such organizations engage in a truly international scale and type of operation. They engage in an integrated approach to the manufacture and marketing of products and services across a number of countries. In organizational design terms they can vary considerably in structure depending upon the nature of the business and the strategies adopted.

There are a number of ways that international activities can be incorporated into the organization. Following is a description of the main options for dealing with international activities, at least of those organizations that have a physical presence in more than one country:

- International division. The creation of an international division as a separate business unit within the company is a way of coping with relatively small international activities. A simple example of an international division is shown in Figure 9.7.

    The advantages of this type of structure include a basis for concentrating the international activities and expertise within one unit which allows the development of appropriate specialisms (export credit, customs documentation, etc.) within that grouping. It also allows the overseas company to be relatively small by comparison and for it not to be swamped by the larger operations.

- Product-based business units. This type of structure groups together international activities by product type, thus allowing for the development of appropriate expertise within each location. Product-based expertise is also spread across the spectrum of international activity for each product group (Figure 9.8).

    The main disadvantage of this approach to organizational structure is the potential overlap and duplication in particular locations. This can be inefficient, confusing and frustrating for the customers and staff.

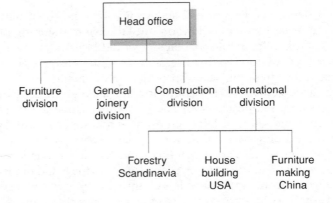

Figure 9.7   International operations as separate division.

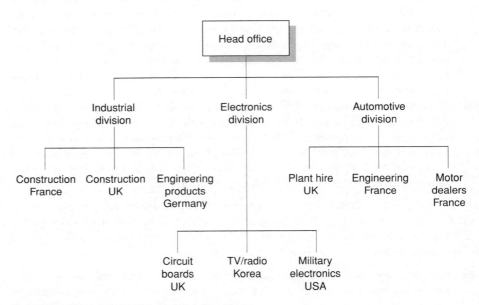

Figure 9.8   Product-based international operations.

- Geographic business units. This approach compartmentalizes operational activity by location (Figure 9.9).

  The advantages of this type of structure include an opportunity to group together specialists in particular parts of the world. It also provides an opportunity to provide a single company in a specific country or region. The difficulties include the potential for duplication of resource availability within the company. For example, each country will have its own production, marketing, finance and personnel specialists. This can lead to duplication of effort and additional cost within the group as a whole.

- Functional orientation. The functional approach to international operations differentiates activity by purpose and location. For example, the personnel people wherever they are based report through their line managers to head office rather than to any specific country general manager (see Figure 9.10).

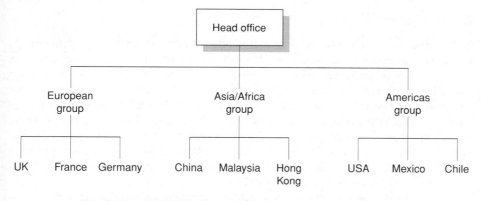

Note: There would be a differing range of business units within each country.

Figure 9.9 Geographic-based international operations.

Figure 9.10 Functional basis for international operations.

Because of the functional nature of the grouping of resources in this structural form there should be the opportunity to generate high levels of productivity and technical/professional support for the operations. The advantages allow for variability in functional presence in particular countries. For example, a marketing presence in a location without production facilities. However, the difficulties lie with the separation and functional loyalty engendered in each of the specialist groups. Because each group reports to head office through its own chain of command disputes can become a major hindrance to efficient operations. Integration among the specialists within each country is a major challenge for management.

■ Matrix organization. The concept of a matrix approach to organizational design is that there are dual reporting relationships in existence. In an international context that would be the equivalent of a combination of a product and geographic approaches. The dual reporting relationships being to both a product group for technical issues and the geographic group for national and locational responsibilities.

■ Holding company. Operating as a holding company results in the organization of the company into legally separate entities. Each then becomes responsible as a profit centre for its own activities.

Matrix structures

The matrix approach is based on the notion that vertical reporting relationships limit involvement in the overall activity of the organization. The matrix emerges as an attempt to integrate both functional and product responsibilities into the activities of individual managers and employees. It is not a new concept. For example, management consultants frequently work in multifunctional teams to undertake specific projects. Members retain a working relationship within their individual disciplines at the same time as reporting to a project leader for the specific project in hand. The same is true of large scale construction projects where the civil engineers and other specialists will report professionally to someone other than the manager in charge of a specific project.

Matrix ideas have been implemented in manufacturing and service organizations in an attempt to enhance the integration of functional specialization with more effective design, manufacturing and marketing of products and services (see Figure 9.11). The manager product A shown in Figure 9.11 would be specifically responsible for that product and bringing together a team drawn from the appropriate functions that would have an influence and impact on the product. That team is then responsible for optimizing the capability of the product to contribute to the company's profit, etc.

The level of success for the matrix organization has been less than would have been hoped for, partly as a consequence of the existence of the split responsibilities of the people concerned. These dual reporting relationships introduce additional levels of complexity into the organization of work.

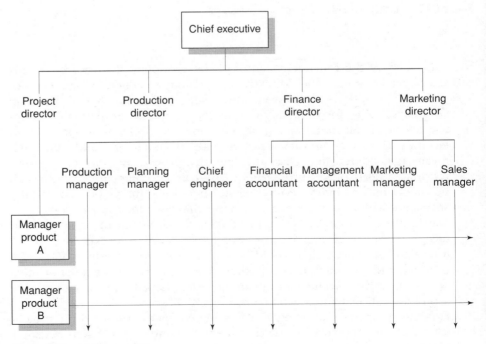

Figure 9.11   Matrix structure.

Horizontal structures

Horizontal organizations are an attempt to overcome the complexity generated by the matrix organization. In the previous discussion it was suggested that dual reporting relationships created a complexity in operational activity. One way to resolve this problem would be to remove one of the reporting relationships. Rationality would suggest that the one to be sacrificed should be the one contributing least to the overall success of the organization. The specific purpose of the horizontal links are to integrate effort across functions in support of the end product or service. This implies that the vertical reporting relationships should be of a lower significance to the organization and should be dispensed with. This is the basis of a horizontal structural form.

This structural form is organized around a number of key features, including:

- Flat hierarchy. The trend over the past few years has been to delayer organizations. This approach is a euphemism for cutting out layers of management, usually in the middle of an organization. It is also referred to as 'downsizing' or 'rightsizing', the effect being the same – fewer managers and organizational levels.
- Process organization. Customers usually experience an organization horizontally, not vertically. Consider, for example, shopping at a supermarket. In the supermarket you directly 'experience' the work of the shelf stackers, the delicatessen servers and the checkout staff, etc. Your experience of the supermarket is a direct function of how well those activities integrate into a complete package of services. So, the argument goes, if the customer is the driving force for the organization the structural basis for activities should be the units or processes experienced by the customer – horizontal, not hierarchical.
- Team activity. There are very few if any jobs within an organization that can be said to be individual in nature. It is almost inevitable that everyone depends upon other people for some part of their job. The cleaner requires someone to order the cleaning materials. The chief executive needs people to do the work of the organization. The sales staff require administrative support to process orders and a factory to make the products. So if group activity is inherently part of organizational life, then work groups should become the norm for organizing activity within it.

Bringing these ideas together should enable an organization to operate horizontally. Activities would be organized around the customer experience of the company and work teams ensure that all aspects of the delivery of the product or service are integrated effectively towards meeting those needs. An example of one horizontal organization is shown in Management in Action 9.5.

The holding company

The holding company framework is one in which the head office is a company in its own right and owns (fully or partly) a number of separate businesses. These in turn are legally constituted companies in their own right (Figure 9.12).

Within each of the subsidiary companies, the structure adopted could be any one of the frameworks described above. Some holding companies keep a very

What a way to run a company!

Orticon is a Danish company that makes hearing aids; it employs about 1200 people. Lars Kolind has been the president of the company since 1988. The company was very traditional in its approach to the ways that it went about its business, having been in existence for about 90 years. It had, however, lost touch with developments in technology and changes in the market. Having realized that the situation could not continue, Kolind set about changing how it functioned in order to be able to compete with its larger rivals such as Siemens and Philips. He suggested that, 'We did not have the same resources as our big competitors so we were forced to look for a different way to get ahead. We set out to create a company that doesn't work like a machine but functions like a brain'.

Out went the traditional organizational hierarchy and specific job titles. Office walls were removed and so was the right to work at a specific desk. Desks were provided for people to work at, but they were available on a first-come, first-served basis. If a junior was at a desk normally used by the boss then it would be the boss who would have to find somewhere else to work. Each person has a mobile phone and a personal trolley for their files and they tow it around with them as they go from task to task. People do whatever tasks are necessary without pre-allocation or thought of structure or status. There is also a high degree of freedom to come and go as the individual pleases, with no set hours or time-off constraints. The same degree of flexibility does not exist within the factory operations of the company, because of the higher need for control and in order to be able to produce efficiently.

The effect on the business has been dramatic. New product development has improved as a result of the greater degree of interaction between staff. Lounges, coffee bars and meeting rooms are provided to function as places for staff to mix and talk freely with each other away from the workplace. For example, the company was able to introduce a new product which was years ahead of the competition very quickly because of the recognition that the technology already existed. The technology had been available within the company since the late 1970s but the potential had not been recognized until people began to interact in different ways following the restructuring.

Profits also increased dramatically as a result of the changes. In 1990 profit before tax was 13.1m Danish Kroner, the forecast for 1994 was 124.8m Danish Kroner. People have not let the team down since the introduction of the much more relaxed approach to work. People do not appear to have taken advantage of the situation. Each employee is allocated a mentor within the company who would help to guide the work and behaviour of the individual. The mentor would also be involved with salary discussions about the employee with project leaders. Salary proposals are then put to the management committee for final approval.

It is a matter of debate whether the success of Orticon could be replicated in other countries and social settings, or whether it is situation specific. It is also necessary to consider the role of Lars Kolind in achieving success. He holds strong beliefs about human nature and how people function best together. Equally, the same structural and organizational flexibility is not possible in the manufacturing parts of the company. So it is not a universal panacea for achieving higher staff contribution. It does nevertheless represent a significant innovation and many large businesses and consultancies have shown interest in attempting to understand it by making visits to the company.

Adapted from: Piper, A (1994) What a way to run a company! The Mail On Sunday, *11 September, pp 76–7.*

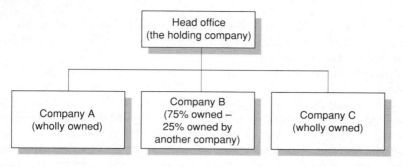

Figure 9.12 Holding company framework.

tight control on the way that each of the subsidiary organizations operate. In its pure form the holding company acts as a banker to the group. It brings together organizations that create a synergy within the group as a whole, and divests those companies that do not fit with the plan, or otherwise fail to live up to profit potential and forecast. In that sense the parent company is acting as an investment house on behalf of its shareholders.

One response to the desire for size in a commercial organization is to create a structure where integration and diversification exist at the same time. The holding company concept can help to achieve that requirement. The existence of separate companies within the holding company provides the potential to manage according to profit (or contribution) to the parent company. This should result in the individual company's displaying the following characteristics:

- Objectives. Being relatively free to pursue their own objectives.
- Market. Being able to get closer to the markets that they operate in.
- Motivation. The management have the benefit of being responsible for a company with its own profit targets, without the risks associated with the stock market.
- Funding. It should be possible to fund growth and development from within the group as there will be a greater level of knowledge about the risk and benefits from specific projects.

In practice this approach to organizational design is one step further than the divisional structure referred to earlier. It attempts to provide greater opportunities for the benefits of federalism to be realized, without the constraint of too much control. Some of the problems with the holding company approach are:

- Support. There may not be technical or other support available from within the group when subsidiaries need it.
- Risk. Subsidiaries are always vulnerable to the next deal. Subsidiaries are liable to be sold in order to raise capital to acquire a more attractive prospect.
- Part owned. When two or more parents own a subsidiary (company is in Fig. 9.12 for example) there is always the risk of a disagreement and a parting of the ways, an organizational equivalent of divorce. In this context the subsidiary can face uncertainty until one or other parent can buy out the others, a third party comes to the rescue, or a management buy out takes place.

- Cohesion. There may be a distinct lack of cohesion between the subsidiaries and only a limited perceived benefit or purpose behind membership in a holding company.
- Restrictions. It may be that competition for capital from inside the group restricts the opportunity for growth in some of the subsidiaries. It is never possible to support every request for more resources. It is also possible that there may be head office restriction on some of the commercial activities that might otherwise be attractive to a truly separate company. For example, transfer pricing between companies may be determined by group policy rather than market levels and trading in some markets may be prevented if it competes with another group company.

Design frameworks

In attempting to design an organization there are a number of components to be fitted together within a framework. Whatever the purpose or size of the organization it is necessary to integrate these components effectively so that the objectives can be achieved. The structure of the organization is only one part of this integration process. Other important elements are the systems and procedures that the organization utilizes in support of its activities. For example, the use of financial reporting can help to ensure that each operational unit within the organization knows how it is contributing to the overall financial well-being of the organization. The role of the corporate head office in running organizations is explored in Management in Action 9.6.

Other integration processes include the communication, consultative and reporting mechanisms adopted. The purpose being to ensure that separate parts of the organization keep each other informed about their activities, problems and requirements so that effective integration of effort takes place. Company policies on issues such as secondment and career development can also influence the degree of unanimity within the structure as a whole. The general conclusion emerging is that structure alone will not guarantee success (or failure) in seeking organizational goals. The weaknesses and deficiencies of a particular structural configuration can be offset to a significant degree by the support mechanisms introduced by management. Naturally, the converse is also applicable, that an effective structure can be weakened through poor support infrastructure.

It was Mintzberg (1979, 1981) who provided a simple view of the structural components that needed to be fitted together in the design of any organization. Figure 9.13 on page 288 is adapted from his work.

Each of the components has a different set of functions to perform:

- Senior management. Responsible for the direction of the organization and ensuring that appropriate objectives are set for the other people within the organization.
- Middle management. Responsible for ensuring that the resources of the organization are effectively utilized in pursuit of the objectives set by senior management.
- Technical support staff. The professional staff provide expertise across a number of necessary disciplines. For example, designers, engineers, lawyers and computer specialists.

Management in Action 9.6

The central question

The relationship between company head office functions, the divisions and outstationed operational activities can frequently be a strained one. One well-known reference to the style of management involved has been referred to as 'seagull' management. This refers to senior people who fly in from head office, make a lot of noise and consume as much food and hospitality as they can squeeze out of their hosts and then fly off again, invariably leaving a considerable volume of 'droppings' on their hosts as they do so! However, over the past few years, 0in seeking to cut costs, the role and size of head office activity has increasingly been under scrutiny.

Foster reports a study of 100 major UK companies carried out by Michael Goold and David Young, both from the Ashridge Strategic Management Centre, in which a number of the relevant issues were identified. From the results of the survey the following information has been extracted:

■ The largest number of staff in a head office was 2500.
■ The smallest number of staff in a head office was 10.
■ Thirteen companies with a total payroll size of between 10,000 and 50,000 people had head office sizes of 100 people or less.
■ Five companies with a total payroll size of between 10,000 and 50,000 people had head office sizes of over 1000 people.

A number of influences impact on the size of a head office, but it is not possible to offer definitive rules that would indicate a likely number of people involved. For example, the size of an organization might be expected to have some bearing on the size of head office. However, organizational life is never that simple. Other influences on the size of head office include the industry, company history, level of diversification within a company, the level of international operational activity and the strategic approach of the company.

One of the distinctions identified in the Ashridge study is between the obligatory functions such as financial reporting, taxation, legal and secretarial and those functions over which scope for managerial choice exists. It is in the areas over which choice exists that companies can adopt dramatically different policies towards the purpose and role of head office. In single business companies it is possible that the head office might be seen differently than in a widely diversified conglomerate. The links between head office and individual units in a single business company would be more likely to be regarded as a mixture of central services and direct support and control for the business as a whole. This would be less likely to be the case in a diversified company.

Zeneca was separated out from ICI as a fully functioning company with a solid reputation, but which had no head office as such. Previous to its separation from ICI it had been part of that set of structures. At separation Zeneca had the opportunity to create its own head office. The result was the creation of the possibility for separate business units to function with the maximum freedom and so a relatively small head office was created. This consisted of about 100 people.

One of the authors of the Ashridge report concludes by stressing that the size of a head office is not overriding. Companies should not simply strive for a minimal scale in numbers of people at head office. He believes that some companies have gone too far in this respect, driven by a desire to follow the current fashion for downsizing and delayering.

Adapted from: Foster, G (1994) The central question. Management Today, *April, pp 56–61.*

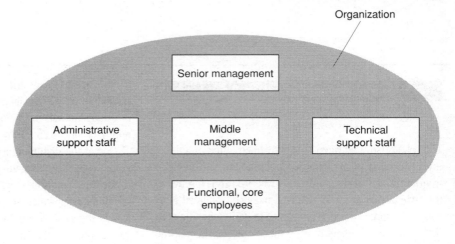

Figure 9.13 Organizational components (adapted from Mintzberg, H 1979). *The Structures of Organizations*. Simon & Schuster, NJ, pp 215–97.

- **Administrative support staff.** These are the staff who provide the indirect support in the form of clerical and administrative activities, maintenance of the production equipment and post room duties.
- **Functional core employees.** This category of employees actually work on the products and services offered by the organization. Production workers, teachers, management consultants and counter staff in a shop are clear examples.

A slightly different view of how to categorize organizational activity was described by Handy (1993). He adopted a classification based upon the type of activity undertaken by different parts of the organization:

- **Policy.** This is the guiding policy and direction of the organization. In addition, the allocation of resources and setting of priorities are important features in this category.
- **Innovation.** This aspect is about the development of new products and services, changing the organization itself and finding new ways to meet the needs of customers.
- **Steady state.** This category describes those parts of the business that function best in a programmed mode. For example, production facilities are most efficient when they are able to plan ahead and organize their resources effectively.
- **Crisis.** This deals with unexpected events that arise in every organization at some point of time. The repair of machines that breakdown is a clear example. However, responding to the needs of a customer who in turn is experiencing a sudden upsurge in demand for their products is also an example of a crisis.

Handy stresses in his work that the 'activity types' are not the same as functional groupings. Many of the functional groups will incorporate a number of the four types of activity described above. For example, a personnel department could be described in the following terms:

- Policy. The senior personnel team who have the responsibility for the determination of personnel policy and the integration of the personnel activities.
- Innovation. The development of new personnel initiatives such as the design of a new pay deal intended to encourage teamwork and flexibility.
- Steady state. This would be the routine processing of personnel data and statistical information. Monthly wage processing would be an example.
- Crisis. This could be the industrial relations section having to respond to a walkout by factory employees.

These examples indicate the complex nature of organizational activity and the difficulty in prescribing brief, although intuitively attractive descriptions of how organizations function. Handy does recognize this constraint but suggests that functions will tend towards one or the other 'activity types' as a dominant orientation.

Organizational life cycle

It is well understood that products go through a life cycle. A new product is designed and introduced to the market place. If it is successful then sales will begin to grow rapidly. Eventually the level of sales will stabilize as the product becomes mature. Thereafter sales will decline as the market changes and newer products emerge. Eventually the product will be withdrawn as it no longer meets the need for which it was intended. Occasionally a new lease of life will be generated for old products based on fashion or changes in taste.

The Greiner model of organizational growth (Figure 9.4) reflects one aspect of this life cycle perspective. But is growth always followed by death, or even contraction in size? The creation of large numbers of new companies each year is inevitably followed by the failure of a large number early in their existence. In that sense there is a life cycle. However, a number of companies will change form and many will be taken over and absorbed into other organizations. Have such companies died or ceased to exist in any meaningful way? Equally, companies that go into receivership and have their assets sold, only to reappear in another guise or under new ownership could be said to have died or survived, depending upon the definition of 'death'.

Quinn and Cameron (1983) describe four organizational life cycles:

- Entrepreneurial phase. This stage is typified by the presence of an owner/manager, little formal control and an emphasis on survival.
- Collectivity phase. During this phase the concerns are to increase the involvement of employees in running the business as it becomes less easy for the owner/manager to control every aspect of it. Delegation becomes a key part of the process during this phase.
- Formalization phase. During this phase an organization is mature and oriented towards stability and predictability. This includes the development of rules and procedures, together with structured meetings and communication between people in the company.
- Elaboration phase. The next phase introduces a process of differentiation into the organization as it attempts to fight the ravages of stagnation. It could include the introduction of a holding company concept or of a

divisionalized structure in an attempt to allow innovation, increase motivation and performance.

To the above stages a fifth phase can be added based on the work of writers such as Cameron *et al.* (1988):

- Organizational decline. There are two distinct forms of decline. The first is a decline in absolute terms, in other words reductions in the physical size of the organization. The second relates to what could be described as relative decline. In other words decline through stagnation. The lethargy brought on as a result of age, size, bureaucracy, and a passivity towards the competitive environment results in an inability to stay in close contact with the environment, and hence competitors begin to dominate the market.

Whetten (1980) identified four response options to decline:

- Generating. This response is about anticipation and continual adjustment. It begins with the identification of the need for constant adjustment of the organization to retain its relationship with the markets, etc.
- Reacting. By reacting to the decline organizations often take the view that 'it' is a temporary change and that the basic approach should be to follow existing procedures more precisely. Unfortunately, by the time the decline is recognized as a long-term threat it is often too late to take effective action.
- Defending. In adopting this approach management usually attempts to match the organization to the perceived situation. This inevitably leads to cutbacks across a broad spectrum of cost. As a consequence there is a real danger of sending the company into a downward spiral of continuous cutbacks which eventually leads to total closure.
- Preventing. By adopting this approach an organization attempts to influence the environment. This can be done through mergers and acquisitions, marketing initiatives and by lobbying politicians in an attempt to influence trading conditions.

Clearly, the generating approach should be the most effective way for any organization to remain in an integrated relationship with its environment over a long period of time. The major difficulty of achieving such a flexible organizational framework is in managing the process. Being adaptive implies being close to the numerous different elements within the overall environment. There is simply not the time, opportunity or knowledge at the higher levels of most organizations to effectively control and manage such complexity. It must rely less on the vertical hierarchy for decisions, communication and co-operation must occur at the lowest levels possible within the organization (Toffler, 1985).

Organizational frameworks: a management perspective

The relevance of the foregoing discussion for organizational design lies in the decision-making process around the options available. It is managers that make the decisions about the organization, its size and structure. It is therefore a process that is based upon the same perceptual, political and self interest factors that exist in every other area of managerial work. That is not to suggest that there are no rational or business related reasons for the choices that are made. It is simply to suggest that in making a choice, factors other than the 'facts' can influence decisions. This is not the place to begin to consider just how many things that are taken as 'facts' stand up to scrutiny. In this context it is relevant to point out that the reasons that justify the choice of a particular design configuration are just as vulnerable to perceptual 'interpretation' as any other stimuli. However, make choices with regard to organizational design managers are required to do.

In the discussion so far the different frameworks have been introduced as discrete types. The impression is easily gained that organizations consider at frequent intervals the structure that is best suited to their circumstances and then implement that form. Rarely does the process operate in that way. It has been suggested earlier in this chapter that organizations evolve and change over time in response to the success achieved and the desires of the owners. This process is reflected in the Greiner model included as Figure 9.4. However, the process is less well defined and less certain than is implied by that model. For example, a company may be taken over by another and integrated into an existing operation and structure. An owner/manager may decide to deliberately restrict the size of the organization in order to retain effective control. The original partners may decide to break up the company if they find that they can no longer work together. A sudden expansion opportunity may present itself as a result of a large order. All of these situations will force some rethinking of the organizational design, but they are far from the simple model implied in Figure 9.4.

Organizations evolve and in moving from one 'stage' to another in the life cycle the structure tends to adjust. It is frequently only when a major crisis occurs that a fundamental rethink of major activity, including structure, is undertaken. To radically change the way that work is undertaken within an organization requires time and additional resources. It also carries with it the risk of failure; lowers performance until employees become accustomed to the new patterns, practices and reporting arrangements; it may also disrupt the service to the customer as mistakes inevitably occur. Consequently, it is hardly surprising that evolutionary change is preferred to revolutionary change. However, *evolution* also carries a risk, lack of clarity in responsibilities during the gestation period, for example. The effect of evolutionary change in organization design produces a degree of mismatch between the structure in existence and that desired.

The Bank of England has been in existence for over 300 years. It has changed its structure a number of times over that period in response to the changing economic and political needs of the day. Management in Action 9.7 is an indication of a recent review of its latest evolution.

The technology utilized within an organization is an influencing factor in the structure. Technology is not a neutral factor in management activity. Management pays for the development of technology through the willingness to purchase it. The decision to use technology can be based on the desire to control activity within the organization as much as through a need to increase efficiency and reduce cost. In that context it influences both the design of jobs within the organization and the configuration of the units that make up the organization itself.

Management in Action 9.7

On a wing and a prayer

After over 300 years of existence even the Bank of England needs to review its organization structures from time to time. The world of high finance changes ever more rapidly and it is subject to increasing global influences. The requirement for the Bank of England to be able to meet its twin objectives of monetary and financial stability remains and so it must change to match the new circumstances in which it finds itself.

The project for identifying a new structure had been the responsibility of the Deputy Governor with the specific proposals developed by three working groups from inside the bank. Considerable consultation took place within the bank over a five-month period in drawing up the proposals. The resulting 'organogram' or diagram of the organization, reflected the two most important functions of the bank. The first wing containing those activities necessary to secure monetary stability. The second wing embracing activities relevant to financial system security. These clear distinctions were intended to replace a more fragmented set of departments and functions covering areas such as international activity, economics and banking supervision.

The proposed management structure of the Bank would retain the position of Governor and Deputy Governor as the two senior positions within the bank. Reporting to these positions would be four Executive Directors, two for each of the two wings of the bank's activities. The functions of monetary operations and monetary analysis would be allocated to the directors within the monetary stability wing. Within the financial stability wing one of the executive directors would be responsible for regulation, supervision and surveillance with the other taking responsibility for financial infrastructure, such as financial markets, stock exchange settlement, etc.

One of the concerns expressed about the proposed structure was that international aspects would no longer warrant a separate division. With some 500 foreign banks in the City and the huge financial flows passing through London, this could expose a potential weakness. The counter argument being that international issues touch every aspect of the Bank's work and so there existed a need to involve every aspect of its operations, not just as a separate unit. In addition, a wing liaison unit was intended to be included to improve co-ordination in such areas between the various parts of the new structure.

In addition to the two wings covering the main objectives for the bank, there would be a small number of central service units reporting directly to the Governor and Deputy Governor. These include legal, audit and central services as well as a special investigations unit. These functions either embraced all aspects of bank activity, or implied a statutory role, or even a special function arising from which a direct link to the top would be necessary. The overall purpose of the restructuring was intended to make the bank more flexible in achieving its objects of playing an effective part in running the financial matters of the country.

Adapted from: Norman, P (1994) On a wing and a prayer. Financial Times, 29 April, p 19

The design of an organization is the macro level arrangement of activities and responsibilities. It is also the basis of defining the jobs done within the company. For example, the existence of a personnel department implies that there will be personnel specialists working within that function. This defines the nature of jobs undertaken within the structure. It is difficult to sustain integrated, broad job content in a highly functional structure.

Conclusions

This chapter attempts to bring together the main options for the configuration of activity within organizations. It demonstrated that there are a considerable number of options available with regard to the design of an organization and that each has advantages and disadvantages.

The structural form of an organization shapes to a considerable degree the behaviour of the individuals within it. It determines the jobs that people do as well as the nature of interaction within and outside of the organization. It also determines the nature of any reporting and control relationships. At several points in the discussion in this chapter the notion of an interactive relationship with the environment has also been introduced.

Discussion questions

1 Define the following key terms used in this chapter:

Entrepreneurial structure	Product structure
Process structure	International structural options
Matrix structure	Horizontal structure
Holding company structures	Organizational life cycle
Line and staff activities	Mintzberg's organizational components
Fayol's management process	Bureaucracy

2 Compare and contrast the concepts of segmentalism and integrative as described by Kanter and the concepts of centralization and decentralization in relation to organizational design.

3 Organizational design is the same as organizational structure. Discuss.

4 Is it possible for an organization to ever be truly horizontal in structure? Why or why not?

5 'The ultimate demise of an organization is as inevitable as the demise of the people who work in it.' Discuss this statement.

6 Is the concept of a horizontal organization the same as the matrix organization? Identify and differences and similarities. Which would you prefer to work in and why?

7 Why might it be difficult to change the design of an organization that has been in existence for some years?

8 'Organizations with fewer layers of management will face significant problems in the future as their managers will not have the opportunity to gain experience in major decision making before they have that responsibility.' Discuss this statement.

9 To what extent can co-ordination reduce the conflict within a functional organization?

10 To what extent is effectiveness in operational activity dependent upon the organizational structure?

Research assignments

1 Obtain a number of annual reports (or organization charts) for six different types and size of organization. Include some small organizations from the service and manufacturing sectors as well as some that operate internationally. Identify the different structural frameworks that they employ. How are they similar and in what ways do they differ?

2 Repeat assignment 1 but this time compare two organizations across a number of years. Can you find evidence that the organizations have changed their structural form? If so why, and is there any evidence to indicate the level of success achieved as a result?

3 Seek an interview with a practising manager and ask them to consider the concept of the horizontal structural framework described in in an earlier section. Ascertain their views about the advantages, disadvantages and appropriateness of this type of structure to their organization. What does this tell you about what may be described as a novel structure? Compare the results with other students and put together a general view based upon a variety of industries and organizations.

Key reading

From Clark, H, Chandler, J and Barry J (1994) *Organization and Identities: Text and Readings in Organizational Behaviour*, International Thomson Business Press, London.

■ Kumar K: Specialization and the division of labour, p 13. Considers the topic from a historical and sociological perspective.

■ Kumar K: Secularization, rationalization, bureaucratization, p 17. Considers the relationships between church, state and organization as the basis of bureaucracy.

■ Friedman AL: Marx's framework, p 25. Introduces a Marxist point of view of organizations.

■ Merton RK: Bureaucratic structure and personality, p 144. Considers the relationships between bureaucracy and individual behaviour.

■ Whyte WH: The organization man, p 149. Offers some reflections on people in large organizations.

■ Kanter RM: Men and women of the corporation, p 152. Considers among other issues the gendered nature of work within organizations and the social basis of role and activity.

■ Perkin H: The rise of professional society: England since 1880, p 204. Describes the emergence of the professional as a dominant form of control in society, and hence organizations.

■ Weber M: Bureaucracy, p 225. An extract form the original work on this topic.

Further reading

Child, JA (1984) *Organization: A Guide To Problems and Practice*, 2nd edn, Harper & Row. Reviews a number of themes covered in this chapter in a very readable form.

Daniels, JD and Radebaugh, LH (1989) *International Business: Environments and Operations*, 5th edn, Addison Wesley, Reading, MA. This text covers a considerable amount or material relevant to international operations, their finance and management. It also incorporates a broad review of the structural and design choices facing organizations.

Drucker, PF (1988) The coming of the new organization, *Harvard Business Review*, January–February. This is an article that takes a futuristic look at what is around the corner in organizational design terms.

Handy, CB (1989) *The Age of Unreason*, Arrow Books, London. This text takes a view of organizations and their relationship with the environment as its core. It explores how this relationship has changed and the potential for future design frameworks.

Mintzberg, H (1979) *The Structure of Organizations*, Prentice-Hall, Englewood Cliffs, NJ. This text provides a broad review of the issues surrounding the topic of organizational design.

Toffler, A (1985) *The Adaptive Corporation*, Pan Books, London. A readable and futuristic view of how organizations need to develop in the future.

References

Bolman, LG and Deal, TE (1994) The organization as theater. In *New Thinking in Organizational Behaviour: From Social Engineering to Reflective Action*. (ed H Tsoukas), Butterworth Heinemann, Oxford.

Cameron, KS, Sutton, RI and Whetten, DA (1988) *Readings in Organizational Decline: Frameworks, Research and Prescriptions*, Ballinger, Cambridge, Mass.

Fayol, H (1916) *General and Industrial Administration*, translated by C Storrs (1949), Pitman, London.

Financial Times (1995) Jump in number of new companies, 18 January, 6.

George, CS (1972) *The History of Management Thought*, 2nd edn, Prentice-Hall, Englewood Cliffs, NJ.

Greiner, L (1972) Evolution and revolution as organizations grow. *Harvard Business Review*, **50**, 37–46.

Handy, CB (1993) *Understanding Organizations*, 4th edn, Penguin, Harmondsworth.

Jenkins, D (1973) *Job Power: Blue and White Collar Democracy*, Doubleday, Garden City, NY.

Kanter, RM (1983) *The Change Masters*, Allen & Unwin, London.

Lawrence, P and Lorsch, J (1967) *Organization and Environment*, Harvard University Press , Boston, MA.

Mintzberg, H (1979) *The Structuring of Organizations*, Prentice-Hall, Englewood Cliffs, NJ.

Mintzberg, H (1981) Organization design: fashion or fit. *Harvard Business Review*, **59**, 103–16.

Perrow, C (1979) *Complex Organizations: A Critical Essay*, 2nd edn, Scott Foresman, Glenview.

Porter, ME (1985) *Competitive Advantage: Creating and Sustaining Superior Performance*, The Free Press, New York.

Quinn, RE and Cameron, K (1983) Organizational life cycles and some shifting criteria of effectiveness: some preliminary evidence. *Management Science*, **29**, 33–51.

Toffler, A (1985) *The Adaptive Corporation*, Pan Books, London.

Townley, B (1994) *Reframing Human Resource Management: Power, Ethics and the Subject at Work*, Sage, London.

Watson, TJ (1994) *In Search of Management: Culture, Chaos and Control In Managerial Work*, Routledge, London.

Weber, M (1947) *The Theory of Social and Economic Organization* (trans AM Henderson and T Parsons), Oxford University Press, New York.

Whetten, DA (1980) Sources, responses and effects of organizational decline. In *The Organizational Life Cycle* (eds J Kimberly and R Miles), Jossey Bass, San Francisco, CA.

Woodward, J (1970) *Industrial Organizations: Behaviour and Control*, Oxford University Press, Oxford.

10

Contingency theory and beyond

browse this web site
www.itbp.com

Chapter summary

This chapter introduces the contingency approach to organizational design. It begins by introducing the background to contingency theory, followed by a review of a number of the perspectives on how organizations have operationalized these ideas over recent years. A number of alternative organizational forms are also introduced. The chapter concludes with a review of the management perspective on the topic.

Learning objectives

After studying this chapter and working through the associated Management in Action panels, discussion questions and research activities, you should be able to:

- Describe the origins of the contingency approach to organizational design.
- Explain the limitations of the standard organization chart in explaining activity within an organization.
- Understand the concept of determinism and how it relates to organization structure.
- Outline the socio-technical perspective on the structuring of organizations.
- Appreciate how matrix structures and the flexible firm reflect some of the attributes of the contingency model.
- Assess the contribution to organization design by the viable systems model.
- Discuss the contingency model and its relationship to structure and environment.
- Detail a number of alternative organizational forms and assess the degree to which they reflect a contingency approach.

Introduction

Over the past 25 years competition from the developing economies and Japan fundamentally changed the business environment. The consequential shock waves forced a massive rethink among business leaders on a wide range of issues, including organizational design. It lead to the seeking of more effective ways of organizing in order to meet the new competitive circumstances. Management in Action 10.1 illustrates the dangers associated with a failure to change together with the difficulties of doing so.

The contingency approach

The contingency approach arose out of a realization that the earlier perspectives were inherently limited. Scientific management produced a tendency for

Management in Action 10.1

The gospel according to Schonberger

Making changes in a company is a difficult process, and not always completely successful. BP, the international oil company, found this out in 1992. 'Project 1990' had been instigated by the new chairman, Robert Horton, to restructure the 'civil-service' style head office of the company and to introduce a new culture based on empowerment and teamwork. Among the results was a 40% reduction in the number of people working at the head office. One estimate suggested that the number of staff could reduce by as many as 10,000 by the end of the exercise. 'Project 1990' had been running for some time and rumours of morale problems had surfaced. This together with poor financial results in 1991 resulted in the share price dropping by one-third against the FT index, to its lowest level since 1989. This situation produced a new set of problems for the company to deal with.

It often takes a crisis to force a management team to seek radical change, by which time it is frequently too late. It is easier from many points of view for a company to keep going in familiar ways than to actively seek to do things differently. This approach, however, effectively ties a company up in chains of inertia and makes achieving the change necessary more difficult, even when it becomes essential to survival. Richard Schonberger, who first brought total quality management (TQM) and just-in-time (JIT) to the attention of British managers in the early 1980s, helps companies to improve themselves. He argues that it is often not the change itself that is difficult to achieve, what is lacking is the will to see things through – to deal with the vested interests that stand in the way of making the changes happen. To be effective, any change programme needs to decisively win the battle for the hearts and minds of all employees.

One company that used Schonberger's expertise to change themselves was Amtico, a flooring company and part of the Courtaulds group. As a starting point for the restructuring and change programme they arranged a two-day seminar by Schonberger for all 300 people employed by the company. Only a few people stayed at work to take phone messages and deal with customer enquiries. Everyone was to hear the same message at the same time not, as is more usual, a tiered and 'target group designed' version of the message.

The purpose of the two-day session was twofold. Firstly, to educate the audience on the basic concepts of TQM and JIT. Secondly, to send clear signals of company intent and to attempt to win the commitment to the process of those attending. After the two-day seminar, the management consultants working with Schonberger then assisted Amtico to make the transformation. The process achieved considerable success over the following few months. Manufacturing time was reduced from three weeks to three days. The product flow through the factory was reduced from four miles and five departments to a few hundred yards and one manufacturing cell. Inventory levels reduced by 65% and quality improved. Further plans were put in hand to improve things even more by increasing the use of cell manufacturing techniques and improving quality.

According to Schonberger the process must be driven by the people at the top, who must 'get religion before the troops will'. The drive and commitment must then be built lower down the organization. The intention being to kick-start the change process and provide it with enough momentum to keep it from getting bogged down and grinding to a halt.

Adapted from: Wheatley, M (1992) The gospel according to Schonberger. Management Today, *June, pp 74–6.*

organizations to become broadly similar in terms of the approach to structure and the tasks to be done. If there was *one best way* then every organization would eventually discover and follow it. This approach also underestimated the ability of individual employees to manage their own working environment by structuring activity in a way that best suited themselves. It assumed a managerial superiority.

The human relations movement recognized the significance of people in organizations. In performing the tasks designated to them, individuals are still people, they are not machines that can and will follow precise instructions over and over again without question. Human beings have free will and an ability to think. Based on the work of Elton Mayo and the Hawthorne Studies, it began where scientific management ended. Unfortunately, to concentrate on the people issues of an organization is to omit the commercial imperative of operating within acceptable cost levels.

The result was an equally limited perspective on what created an effective organization. As a consequence it was proposed that a broader range of factors influenced effectiveness, including the structural arrangement of an organization. There are two ways that the relationship between people, task and structure can be explained:

■ Separated. The relationship between the people, task elements and structure depend upon the impact of a range of factors from the environment surrounding that situation.

■ Integrated. Task and people aspects are themselves part of the environmental forces acting upon the situation. It is the perception and interpretation of these various forces by management that creates the basis of structural design.

Using the second approach, the design of an organization is said to be contingent or dependent upon the forces acting upon the situation. This is the basis of the contingency approach to organization design.

Organizational metaphors

So far in this discussion the notion of an organization has been taken for granted. In practice the way that an *organization* finds expression in the world is limitless. The variation covers differences in size, location, product or service orientation, culture, management style, level of profit, public or private sector, number of locations, etc. Therefore the umbrella term *organization* is intended to conjure up a generalized picture from which more specific meaning can be gleaned. This is a simple expression of a metaphor: 'Thus, metaphor proceeds through implicit or explicit assertions that A is (or is like) B. When we say 'the man is a lion,' we use the image of a lion to draw attention to the lion-like aspects of the man. The metaphor frames our understanding of the man in a distinctive yet partial way' (Morgan, 1986, p 13).

In this definition Morgan indicates that there are many aspects to the man that will not be like a lion. What the metaphor does do is to provide an insight through an efficient form of communication: the lion conjures up a picture that needs few words to express its meaning – provided that the receiver has the same understanding. To *know* that the man is like a lion provides a basis for action towards that person without having to have a detailed knowledge of him.

In the same way, we use *organization* as a metaphor to describe individual units, to disguise difference and simplify complexity arising from the existence of individual variation. This perspective adds another dimension to the contingency approach to organization design. If humans understand through the use of metaphor then perhaps the ways that managers relate to organizations determines how they subsequently structure them. Morgan identifies a number of metaphors that illustrates the perspectives implicit in them (Table 10.1).

Machine	A network of parts: functional departments …, which are further specified as networks of precisely defined jobs (p 27).	**Table 10.1** Organizational metaphors (based on Morgan, G (1986) *Images of Organization*, Sage, Newbury Park, CA)
Organisms	Living systems, existing in a wider environment on which they depend for the satisfaction of various needs (p 39).	
Brains	Utilizes the concepts of intelligence, feedback and information processing to model organizational functioning.	
Culture	Directs attention to the symbolic or even 'magical' significance of even the most rational aspects of organizational life (p 135).	
Political	Managers frequently talk about authority, power and superior–subordinate relations. … Organizations as systems of the government that vary according to the political principles employed (p 142).	

Metaphor become the basis of beliefs about how organizations *should* function. The 'facts' encountered are 'fitted' into the metaphorical image. The importance of metaphor in contingency thinking is that it provides a means through which humans understand organizations and how they function in a specific context. That understanding can provide a basis for deciding how the organization could be structured.

The significance of questioning the existing view of an organization and its purpose is demonstrated in Management in Action 10.2 on the next page. This describes how a Japanese company made several false starts before it identified its future direction. Its original perception of itself was limited by the assumptions made about its core technologies.

Limitations of the organization chart

The organization chart is a means by which organizations describe the structure and reporting relationships that exist. The organization chart can also be an effective means of tracking formal lines of communication, levels of responsibility and audit trails. Reproduced as Figure 10.1 is an example of the organization chart for a hypothetical medium-sized company in the fast food industry.

There are, however, severe limitations in the ability of the organization chart to reflect what actually happens within an organization. Not included are the cross-functional relationships that are necessary to ensure that information flows around the organization in an appropriate way. Neither does it reflect the decision-making processes that exist. Frequently organization charts do not reflect the levels of responsibility held by the individual posts indicated in them. For example, in Figure 10.1 the senior managers are all shown at the same level, reporting to the chief executive. But there are four directors and one manager in the job titles at that level. Does this imply that the business planning manager has less responsibility than the others, or does it simply reflect that the post holder does not have a seat on the board of directors? There have been attempts to reflect the relative seniority of people within an organization chart by scaling the vertical dimension of it (see Figure 10.2).

There are other ways of reflecting how an organization functions. For example, the concept of a *rich picture* provides a mechanism through which a dynamic situation can be reflected in a manner meaningful to the participants. Figure 10.3 is an example that illustrates the problems and influences acting upon a particular situation. The picture is reasonably self-explanatory in that the swords represent conflict and the joined hands areas of agreement.

Steelmaker that reinvented itself

The sharply rising yen following the 1985 Plaza accord together with the decline in world shipbuilding created a number of problems for Japanese companies. Not the least of which was the potentially terminal decline in profits for NKK, Japan's second largest steelmaker. Two lessons have been learned from the NKK experience of attempting to diversify. Firstly, the parent company was prepared to let the steelmaker take startling risks in the search for new business. Secondly, the financial support for the process was never in doubt. The aim, according to Mr Seigo Abe, manager of the leisure specialities department of NKK, was to simply find ways of surviving.

Mr Abe was appointed to the marine engineering department of NKK from its new business department in 1985, just after the need to diversify was identified. It took several years to identify new business that profitably makes use of the considerable skill and expertise available within the company. Initial thinking found that the key areas of skill within the company were associated with high performance welding, the design and testing of ice-breakers and the manufacture of wave pools for testing ship models.

Early attempts to diversify were into fish farming and making stretch limousines. The making of fish farms and limousines required welding technology and it was assumed that the other necessary aspects associated with those operations would fall into place. Not so. The fish farms were unproductive and the stretch limousines did not handle well on roads. This caused a review of what the core skill areas actually were within NKK. The definition of these was refined down to making ice and snow for ice-breaking test equipment and producing accurate wave formations for model wave machines. The possibility of making artificial beaches and ski-slopes therefore became the focus of attention.

A prototype pool in a water park in Osaka demonstrated that NKK could make very regular surfing waves, more consistent than could be found in nature. The company also learned how to design and build water parks as a consequence of contracts for laying pipes around water-slide complexes. The closure of a baseball ground as part of a cost-cutting exercise by the steel division of NKK presented the opportunity for the marine engineering unit to propose and, having been given the go-ahead, to build its own tropical beach complex. The facility is known as Wild Blue and is located in Yokohama. It lost money during its first three years of operation but Mr Abe claims that these difficulties have been addressed and that it was currently close to break-even, with 800,000 visitors each year.

NKK also built an indoor ski-resort as a contractor to the company that wanted to develop the facility. This was less of a financial risk for NKK as it was not faced with running the facility once opened. It also opened up opportunities for acting as advisers and contractors on similar projects throughout the Asian region. Another of the success stories for NKK was in making ice cubes for high-class Tokyo clubs. Using the company expertise in making ice to test ice-breaking equipment, NKK have been able to make ice cubes under high pressure from pure water. This produces an ice cube with many similarities to an iceberg, including many air bubbles trapped inside. When the ice begins to melt in the drink it makes a crackling noise which customers like and provides a profitable opportunity for the company!

Adapted from: Dawkins, W. (1995) Steelmaker that reinvented itself. Financial Times, *29 March, p 5.*

Another means of reflecting activity within an organization is through an influence diagram. This can illustrate the relationships and influences that exist between individuals and groups within and outside the organization. Figure 10.4 is a simple influence diagram based around a Village Playing Fields Committee (the organization). The type of arrow used between elements in the diagram reflects the form and/or frequency that interaction takes.

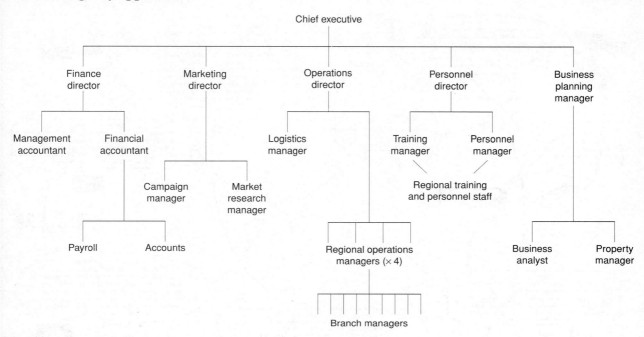

Figure 10.1 Organization chart for a fast-food chain.

Organizations are continually subjected to change. This can include individuals leaving or joining; jobs being declared redundant or new jobs created; promotions and changes in reporting relationships; acquisitions and divestments. Consequently the organization chart would need to be frequently updated in order to maintain its currency. Townsend (1985) goes so far as to

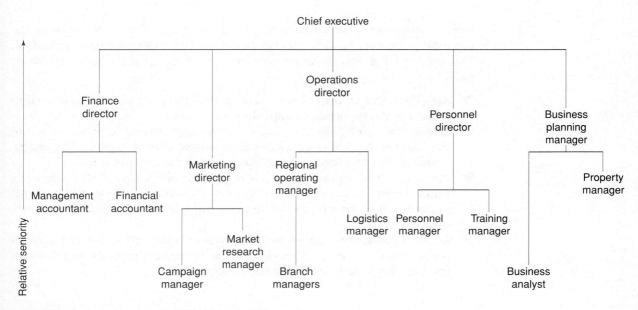

Figure 10.2 Organization chart scaled to show relative seniority.

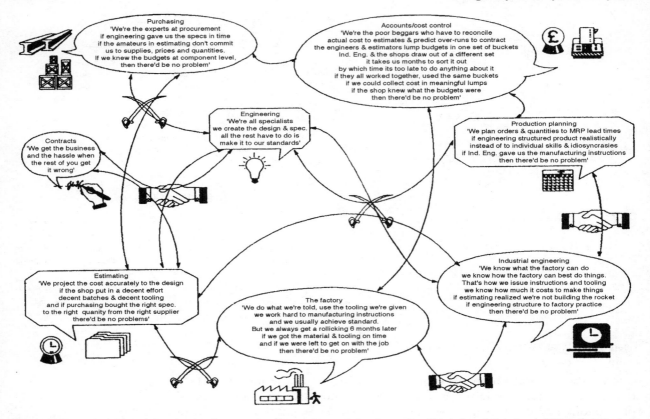

Figure 10.3 A rich picture of a situation in an engineering company (taken from: Checkland, P and Scholes J (1990) *Soft Systems Methodology in Action*, John Wiley, Chichester, p 46).

suggest that charts can demoralize people as they reflect how far from the top most people are and the number of bosses that exist above each individual. The validity of an organization chart is a function of a number of factors, including:

- Age. The older an organization chart is the less likely it is to reflect current structure and reporting relationships.
- Detail. The level of detail included in a chart reflects its value. It is not unusual to find that larger organizations have several organization charts, covering different levels and divisions within the organization.
- Purpose. The purpose for which the chart was designed also affects its value. A chart drawn up to reflect the main functional splits within the organization would be of little value in identifying who deals with customer queries.
- Need. Organization charts have limitations in being able to describe how an organization functions. This need might be more effectively met through the use of rich pictures and influence diagrams.

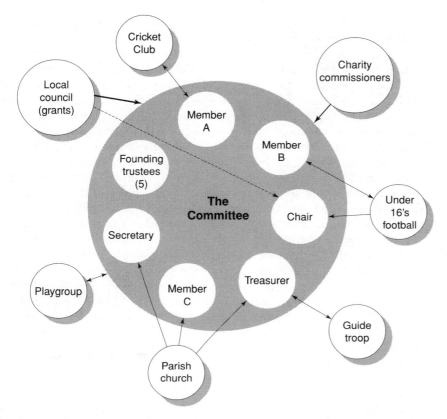

Figure 10.4 Influence diagram (taken from: Giles, K and Hedge, N (1994) *The Manager's Good Study Guide*, Open University, Milton Keynes, Figure 7.26).

Two perspectives on determinism

There are two basic approaches to the issue of determinism. One view (the deterministic approach) holds that structure is a function of the technology or other situational factors. The other perspective holds that organization structure is a function of managerial choice.

From the determinism point of view there are two main schools of thought:

■ Technological determinism. This holds that the production technology of an organization determines the structural frameworks that are adopted (Woodward, 1965). Woodward identified a number of tendencies among firms utilizing similar production technologies. There was a definite relationship between the technology used and a number of structural measures, including managerial span of control; length of the chain of command; relative proportion of indirect labour (support staff) and managers. Her conclusion was that those organizations that were structured in ways typical of their technological norms tended to be the most profitable. Perrow (1967) proposed a slightly different view of the influence of technology. His view was that the technology utilized within an organization could vary from the routine to the non-routine.

It is important to recognize that both Perrow and Woodward are using the term technology to refer to the production technology used rather than the use of computers. In a low technology environment the process would require highly skilled employees to produce small batches of product for the customer. At the other extreme, machines dominate with individuals undertaking a range of comparatively small tasks in support of mass production processes. Technology provides the opportunity for managers to make work predictable and the opportunity to tightly specify the jobs that people undertake. Also there is a greater need to introduce standard procedures to routinize the response to crises in situations where technology was more sophisticated. It was Perrow's contention that the form of structure adopted by the organization was a function of the tightness of job specification, which originated from the technology and predictability of the work. This differed from the view of Woodward in that it was her view that the technological complexity directly influenced the structural form.

■ Environmental Determinism. This view holds that it is forces in the environment that determine how an organization structures itself. This is similar to the ideas on mechanistic and organizmic organizations identified by Burns and Stalker (1961). They studied organizations in the electronics and traditional industries in Scotland and concluded that mechanistic organizations were best suited to stable environments and that organizmic organizations (fluid, flexible and responsive) were best suited to turbulent environments. They also concluded that to attempt to adopt the 'wrong' framework, or to fail to adopt the correct one, would in all probability lead to failure.

Environmental determinism is based upon the view of an organization as an interactive part of its own environment. Figure 10.5 reflects this relationship.

Figure 10.5 Organizational environments.

It is through the interaction between the organization and each of the groups identified in Figure 10.5 that the environment influences the structural frameworks adopted. Lawrence and Lorsch (1967) reported a study of three totally different industries and the associated environments. They concluded that the most successful organizations in each of the three industries were well integrated in the way that they organized their activities relative to the environment, but that each of the industries required different forms of internal segmentation. In other words, the environment required different structural frameworks, but success came from the individual organization's ability to integrate its activities effectively in pursuit of its goals.

Managerial choice is the other view of determinism. This perspective holds that it is managers who choose the way to respond to the situations that they encounter. This could either be reactive, simply responding to events as they impact on the organization; or it could be proactive in attempting to anticipate the future and organize in anticipation of circumstances. This latter approach is the essence of strategic thinking that is now such a dominant feature of managerial activity.

It is possible to reconcile these approaches to organizational structure in that managerial choice does not totally negate the influence of determinism. For example, it was pointed out in the discussion about the work of Woodward that there was a *tendency* for organizations to be more successful if they followed the norms for their industry and technology. This implies a variability in structural form, a point also evident in the work of Lawrence and Lorsch. So even in the deterministic approach managers can be seen to be exercising decision making by adopting slightly different structures. However, the commercial results achieved by the organizations were found to vary with the closeness of following the norms. Perhaps, therefore, managerial choice is an intervening variable between environment and structure, with the consequences being apparent in the level of success achieved by the organization.

Socio-technical systems theory

The notion of a *system* originated in the physical sciences as a means of reflecting how a number of elements or sub-systems interact within a cohesive whole. It has since been integrated into the social sciences and with particular success in the explanation of how organizations function. Some of the earlier ideas in this context were identified by Kast and Rosenzwieg (1972). Figure 10.6 represents an *open systems* view of an organization.

As an open system the organization is in an interactive relationship with its environment. It draws its raw materials, etc. from the environment, converts them into goods and services which are fed back into the environment. It is very much a cyclical and interactive process. For example, the Ford Motor Company makes motor vehicles which it sells to its customers for money. The money thus obtained is recycled in the form of wages, tax payments and the purchase of more raw materials. Information is also part of this process. For example, if a particular model is not selling, or is selling very quickly, the manufacturing process (or pricing policy) can be adjusted very quickly to respond to the new situation.

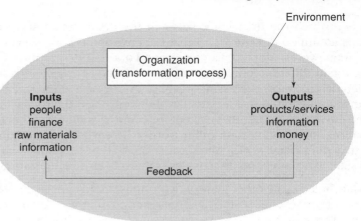

Figure 10.6   An open systems model of an organization.

Within an organization there are a number of sub-systems, each of which will have its own inputs, transformation processes and outputs, within an environmental context. For example, the transformation process of the Ford Motor Company consists of a number of separate, but integrated sub-systems, including manufacturing, design, finance, marketing and personnel. Each of these functional areas will have their own links to the environment and will become involved with the other sub-systems in contributing to the overall output of the organization. Management in Action 10.3 illustrates the effects of the cyclical nature of feedback between the organization and its environment as the organization grows through success.

The socio-technical approach to an organization recognizes that it is necessary to incorporate both the social and technical aspects of work if an effective system is to be created. The first work in socio-technical systems originated in studies of coal mining in the north-east of England in the late 1940s and early 1950s. The technology of coal extraction was changing as mechanical equipment became available. Previously, teams of men had worked as groups in driving tunnels through coal seams, removing the coal and sending it to the surface for sorting and sale. The members of each team were highly dependent upon each other in order to work effectively and earn a decent wage. With the introduction of machines the teams were broken up and people became machine minders, working in much larger groups. There was a marked deterioration in a number of aspects of work, including the number of accidents, industrial disputes, the level of absence and labour turnover. The Tavistock Institute, based in London, began a series of studies to try to solve the problems. Their suggestion was to change the ways of working with the new equipment, to build teams back into the work to encourage interdependence among the workers.

This work, described by Trist and Bamforth (1951) began a series of further studies into the design of organizations and the work done within them. The need being to design jobs and organizational structures that could meet the needs of both technology and people. For example, Emery and Thorsrud (1976) and Herbst (1976) reviewed the manning, operation and hierarchical organization structure of bulk carriers used by the Norwegian merchant navy. This approach is the beginning of the contingency model.

Management in Action 10.3

Excess of success

Small companies who achieve rapid success can be faced with very real problems. The demands of success on the business can lead to the company's resources being so stretched that it breaks. Success is every entrepreneur's dream, but it needs to be controlled and planned for, if it is not to become a nightmare.

Femcare, a Nottingham-based surgical instruments making and marketing company has been in business since 1982. One of its main products is the Filshie Clip, developed by Marcus Filshie, a consultant gynaecologist based at the Queen's Medical Centre in Nottingham. It is a device that can provide women with a potentially reversible sterilization and represents most of Femcare's sales of £3m per year.

In 1989 the company bought a new product that could assist women with incontinence difficulties following childbirth. The company acquired the rights to the product and began to both make and market Contrelle, as it is called. Unlike the other products handled by Femcare, which were sold to clinicians, Contrelle was available to women through pharmacies and could be bought as frequently as decided by the women herself. Femcare recognized that they needed to introduce Contrelle into as many markets as possible during its protected patent

life and so an extensive advertising campaign began. Sales took off rapidly, much faster than expected, and the company quickly recognized that it was getting out of its depth.

The demands on manufacturing were greater than Femcare could cope with, even if they could get the raw materials in large enough quantity, which in itself represented a problem. The option of raising money in order to expand the company quickly was considered. However, it was rejected in the belief that such a move could have threatened sales of the core medical instruments and placed the entire business at risk. Instead they searched for a global partner who could handle the anticipated level of business. Eventually most of the rights to Contrelle were sold to Coloplast, a Danish company specializing in medical equipment. A phased handover of the product was introduced, with Coloplast developing a new version of the original product and beginning production with that design.

Femcare would have preferred to have retained control of Contrelle. However, they recognized both that it had grown beyond their capability to handle it and the risk to the business. Instead the company is now concentrating on the potential of the Filshie Clip and seeking partners to work in the US market.

Adapted from: Gourlay, R (1995) Excess of success. Financial Times, *28 March, p 16.*

The contingency model

The contingency model postulates that the design of the organization is contingent upon a number of forces acting upon the situation. Previous approaches attempted to identify universal truths or prescriptions that would provide a simple answer to the need to be able to organize. Figure 10.7 differentiates the traditional and contingency approaches in this respect.

It is clear from Figure 10.7 that the contingency approach links together the circumstances and the structure, but in a different way to the traditional view. The traditional view seeks to impose a definitive cause and effect relationship between circumstances and structure. The contingency model takes a more holistic view and suggests that structure is a function of a range of forces impacting upon the situation, management's interpretation of them and their objectives. Figure 10.8 illustrates the contingency model.

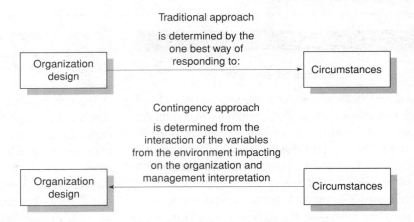

Figure 10.7 Traditional and contingency approaches to organizational design.

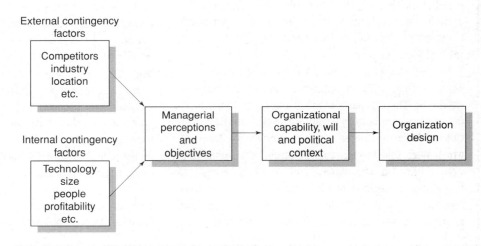

Figure 10.8 Contingency model of organization design.

Taking each element in the model (Figure 10.8) in turn:

■ External contingency factors. There are a wide range of factors that impact on the situation. For example, the activities of competitors can influence what is done. Clearly the industry in which the organization operates will have an impact on the structural arrangements adopted. The location in which the organization is based will also impact on the structural arrange-ments through the cultural norms, etc. operating. Burns and Stalker (1961) developed the concepts of *mechanistic* and *organismic* to describe the way that an organization organized relative to its environment.

■ Internal contingency factors. There are a wide range of internal forces that influences its design. The production technology identified through the work of Woodward for example. Clearly the size of the organization will have an impact on its design. Child (1988) argues that in very large organizations those adopting a bureaucratic approach to organizing were likely to be more profitable and grow faster than less bureaucratic organizations.

- Managerial perceptions and objectives. There is a few situations where a manager is given the opportunity to create an organization from first principles. It usually involves changing an existing organization. This can involve adapting to circumstances such as a new product introduction or competitive threat. Personal preference and preconceptions about how things should be organized influence the *metaphors* used as the basis of responding to circumstances. Culturally determined perspectives and preferences also influence the way that managers exercise their roles (Child and Kieser, 1979). This has implications for how they might respond to perceived forces. Management in Action 10.4 reflects how one organization *interpreted* its situation.
- Organizational capability, will and politics. The organization needs to have the capability to achieve its desired objectives. If an organization does not possess the expertise to do something or the will to make changes then it is likely to fail to match the needs of its situation. To succeed in adapting or changing an organization the political realities must be taken into account and appropriate strategies developed.

The contingency model is very useful for explaining the diversity in organizational design that is found to exist. It provides for the forces external to the organization to be mixed with forces internal to the company. These are interpreted by managers and filtered through capability, etc. to produce a structure that will be specific to that organization at a particular point in time.

It was during the 1960s that the Industrial Administration Research Unit emerged at Aston University as a leading multidisciplinary research group. They developed a research approach which examined three elements (Pugh and Hickson, 1989; pp 9–15):

- Change and complexity. Because of the degree of change that organizations are subjected to it is necessary to develop theories that are incremental rather than discrete. The structure of an organization is the result of a number of forces acting upon (and interacting with) the situation.
- Institutional arrangements. These include the control, hierarchical and work arrangements that exist. In many organizations these arrangements exist before employees join and will be there after they leave. Consequently, individuals are slightly detached from total ownership as they are in practice custodians of these features during their employment.
- Multiple perspectives. In order to create a full understanding it is necessary to consider more than one point of view. One way of illustrating this necessity is to consider the notion of perspective illustrated in Figure 10.9.

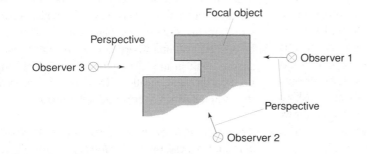

Figure 10.9 Multiple perspectives of an object.

Management in Action 10.4

Struggle to save the soul of IKEA

The international furniture retailer IKEA began over 50 years ago in the small railway town of Smaland in Sweden. Since then its founder, Ingvar Kamprad, has seen it grow into an international company with over 125 stores in 26 countries and with sales in 1994 of $4.7bn. As it has grown in size and complexity the company has vigorously attempted to retain the company principles set out by Ingvar Kamprad and enshrined in the 'testament of a furniture dealer' written by him in 1976.

The company headquarters in Smaland remains the hub of the business, although for tax reasons they long ago moved the legal base. The IKEA retail business is owned by a foundation established in the Netherlands and the legal headquarters is in Denmark. The family interests of the founder incorporate Inter IKEA, which owns the brand name and controls the franchise operations (a minority of the stores); and Ikano, a separate company with banking and finance industry interests. The company remains a privately owned business and retains a high level of secrecy about its trading position and profitability. As a policy they prefer to avoid having to raise public money or borrow from the banks in order to retain control of the business.

The style of management within the company attempts to retain the informal approach adopted from its early beginnings. Employees are referred to as co-workers, offices in headquarters are open plan, suits are non-existent as a sign of status and even ties are only rarely worn. Everyone in the company travelling on business is required to follow the example set by the chief executive of travelling economy class and using public transport rather than taxis. The trading policy of the company (from the testament) is to sell a basic high-quality product range that is typically Swedish and at a price that the majority of people could afford, wherever it operates in the world. Remarkably as a company it has achieved success without formal market research and adapting to local differences in taste. As indicated by Jan Kjellman, head of the Swedish division which incorporates the design team, 'We don't ask so many questions before we start up new things. Last year we launched the "Swedish Cottage" range without any market research – but the customer liked it very much'.

However things are having to change within IKEA in response to the consequences of market pressure for the financial performance of the company. Some of the forces acting upon the company include:

- Over recent years recession in some of its main markets have hit turnover hard.
- In the USA the company began operations in 1985, but found profit very difficult to achieve. For example, sales of beds and bedding were very poor in the USA and it was only following market research that it was discovered that larger beds and bedding were the norm in that country. Consequently when larger sizes were introduced sales improved considerably.
- With rapid expansion the structure and operation of the company had become more cosmopolitan and its original values and 'Swedishness' was under threat.
- The cost of operations had risen from around 30% of sales to around 37% over 10 years. This placed financial strain on a company whose margins were already tight.
- The distribution system required almost 90% of goods to be funnelled through the 12 distribution centres, causing delay and customer frustration. Already some 30% has been moved to direct store delivery from suppliers and plans are in hand to raise that to 50%.
- The inability to adapt products to local tastes restricts sales opportunities and some concessions are having to be made. For example, leather sofas in Belgium and corner sofas in Austria have been introduced.

The company is facing the twin pressure of attempting to retain the essential basis of success along with its Swedish origins whilst at the same time maximizing the turnover and revenue from its international operations. Many of the international markets have dramatically different requirements. For example plans exist for a new store to be opened in China where house sizes are considerably smaller than in the West and so the product range will need further modification. The battle is engaged, only time will tell which 'side' of IKEA dominates!

Adapted from: Carnegy, H (1995) Struggle to save the soul of IKEA. Financial Times, *27 March, p 12.*

Each one of the individual observers sees only part of the shape, and each view is different. Consequently, each can only be considered a partial reflection of the whole. For a realistic description of the object it would be necessary to integrate the three individual reports into a cohesive framework. The approach of identifying multiple perspectives is much more complex for social entities such as organizations.

The use of the concept of a contingency model does not imply that there is only one approach to explaining the links between organization and environment. For example, Burns and Stalker attempted to reflect the degree of fit between organization and the industrial environment; Perrow considered aspects of technology, as did Woodward; Lawrence and Lorsch considered the influences of internal factors such as degree of differentiation and integration. The Aston studies brought together a number of these approaches in attempting to reflect the dynamics of the process.

The contingency model has been the subject of a number of criticisms. These include that it assumes a relationship between organization and performance. The achievement of organizational performance is assumed to be a function of the structure and degree of fit with the environmental forces acting upon the situation. This ignores the ability and performance of managers at a personal level together with a range of other factors independent of structure. For example, an incompetent sales person is unlikely to win many orders irrespective of the structure of the sales department.

To suggest that it is necessary to incorporate social as well as technical aspects into organizational design is not to take into account the possible effects of this. The contingency model does not take account of the exercise of power or control in dynamic work relationships. Technology, for example, is not a neutral force within an organization. Managers decide that they will utilize a particular form of technology, they decide upon its actual use and application in order to achieve particular objectives, including control over operational processes.

Matrix structures and the flexible firm

Essentially, a matrix organization utilizes a twin reporting framework in an attempt to provide a more complex application of resource. It is two dimensional in that the vertical reporting relationships based on function are integrated with horizontal linkages based on the project group concept. The matrix organization reflects the principles of the contingency approach in that it allows a duality of emphasis. This should enable the organization to capture and use a greater amount of environmental detail in its operational activity.

It was Ashby (1956) who first suggested the law of requisite variety. In order to ensure that the variability (variety) experienced by any system is effectively controlled, it is necessary for the controller to match the complexity of it. The example often used to illustrate the notion of variety is a motor vehicle. Imagine there are 5000 possible causes for a motor vehicle not starting. If a repair technician has knowledge of only 4999 of these causes and the unknown one is the actual cause of the failure on a specific occasion, then they will not be able to repair the vehicle. In that sense the matrix structure is an attempt to improve the level of requisite variety by providing a higher level of internal complexity to more effectively match that found in the environment.

If it were that simple the matrix option would provide the most effective means of adding complexity to the organization in order to match that of the environment. However, there are a number of difficulties inherent with the matrix structure, including:

- **Complexity of operation.** The introduction of a matrix structure can add complexity to what may be an already complex situation. Imagine a very large manufacturing organization employing many thousands of people across a number of locations and perhaps countries. To add a matrix dimension to such an organization would increase the complexity of operation by a considerable order of magnitude. In communication terms alone the need to involve other people in the activities associated with product groups could create havoc.
- **Split responsibilities.** In the matrix structure managers (and others) will have split responsibilities. For example, in the construction industry it is common to find that professional staff (surveyors, engineers, etc.) are accountable to a site manager for the duration of a project, but to a senior professional in head office as their line manager. Responsibility for the activity of the organization is diffused across a number of people.
- **Split accountabilities.** Employees find that they have more than one superior. In the example used above, the professional engineers and surveyors would be responsible to the site manager for the actual day to day work that they were engaged in, but to the line manager for professional standards, career development, etc. This provides an opportunity for employees to take advantage of the situation leading to operational inefficiency.
- **Increased political opportunity.** The ambiguity that emerges as a result of the complexity created through the matrix approach can provide opportunities for individuals to engage in this form of behaviour. For example, it would be possible for a line manager to blame mistakes on a project team and thus avoid responsibility.
- **Lack of clear focus.** Because of the split responsibilities it is possible that a lack of focus creeps into organizational activities. Unless great care is taken in setting out individual responsibilities, it is possible that things of importance may be missed, everyone assuming that they are someone else's responsibility.
- **Requires specific skills.** Because of the need for people to work with two bosses there is a requirement for particular social skills and abilities. It is not easy to work effectively to two different people, each with different priorities and demands, particularly when accustomed to the unity of command espoused by the traditional organizations. The potential pressure on individuals is much greater in a matrix structure and they need the resilience, personality characteristics and training to be able to cope effectively.
- **Conversion.** Most organizations seeking to employ a matrix structure will already be in existence and hence find themselves needing to convert to that model. Change is very difficult to achieve when it involves a radical shift in operational activity. The process of being able to move from one framework to another, together with the time and resources involved, should not be underestimated.

One of the largest moves away from the matrix concept is described in Management in Action 10.5. Shell employed a three-dimensional matrix representing

Barons swept out of fiefdoms

The chill wind caused by flat oil prices, growing global competition and unrelenting shareholder pressure for improved financial returns has hit many of the major oil companies. Shell is no exception to those pressures. Large multinational companies must be capable of achieving several objectives at the same time. The difficulty is that these objectives contradict and conflict with each other and so a delicate balancing act is required if the organization is to survive in an ever more hostile environment. Mr Cor Herkströter, the Dutch chairman of Shell, elaborated these points by pointing out that the competing objectives included:

■ Marshalling their resources across the globe more effectively, rapidly and flexibly.
■ Slashing the costs of head office or the corporate centre.
■ Retaining an ability to respond to differing market situations around the world.
■ Retaining an ability to respond to differing competitive circumstances around the world.

These represent difficult aspects of international operations to balance. Companies have attempted to deal with these circumstances in different ways, but most involve adapting or changing the matrix approach to organizing that many international companies have adopted in the past. The major difference now is that the three-dimensional matrix of the past, in which national interest, business sectors and functions produced several layers of decision making with overlapping responsibilities, is being replaced by a simpler two-dimensional matrix structure. This was clearly the form recently proposed by the top management at Shell for a massive shake-up in its own structures.

Shell produced some impressive financial results over recent years. For example in 1994, earnings rose by 24% and the return on capital employed was 10.4%, in double figures for the first time since 1990. A shake-out among the operating companies had seen the workforce fall by over 10,000 people, representing a reduction of about 10%. Still the company felt the need to engage in a major restructuring which would inevitably further improve performance. The justification for the change was described by Mr John Jennings, the chairman of the UK part of the group, as being a need to improve the rate of return to enable the long-term future of the company to be secured. In other words the company, although profitable in the short term, would eventually run out of the momentum necessary to enable it to be viable in the long term.

The matrix structure of Shell had been organized around the operating companies at each location. For example, Shell Australia contained within it businesses in exploration, oil products, chemicals, gas and coal. However, above that level of organization there were the three matrix groupings associated with function,

region and business sectors. In addition, there were the professional services (legal, financial, etc.) provided by head office to the rest of the group. To be able to operate such a structure effectively required considerable numbers of co-ordination activities to be carried out as well as many levels of committee to make decisions. Mr Ernst van Mourik-Broekman, the head of human resource management, indicated that the company had a committee culture and that it needed to be changed.

The proposed structure was based upon the five business sectors covering the main activities of the group. They are exploration and production, oil products, chemicals, gas and coal. The operating companies will report to whichever of these business sector groups is appropriate to their activities. Each business sector will be headed by a committee made up of a small number of the heads of the operating companies. They will act in an investment co-ordinating and strategic capacity for the sector, leaving individual operating companies with the executive authority necessary for adapting to local conditions. Each committee will act in a collegial manner, with no formal hierarchy and members free to challenge each other on performance issues. The meetings will be chaired by a non-executive group managing director who will also report to the committee of managing directors, the most senior executive group.

The main aims of the restructuring are to focus decision making at appropriate levels within the company. For example, the operating companies need to be strongly focused on the needs of local customers and other front line issues. The executives of these businesses need to be personally responsible for operating performance. At the business-sector level decisions are about directing resources between units in the best interests of the sector as a whole. Above that level is the group, with its need to make decisions in relation to the whole company and taking account of the interests of shareholders and other stakeholders. The proposed structure should ensure that it retains a global cohesion, whilst at the same time being responsive to local conditions. This should be achieved by:

■ The retention of a dotted-line relationship between corporate headquarters and the individual operating companies, running parallel with the business reporting structures.
■ The retention of strong country management focused on local issues.
■ The retention of a professional service input to top management in an advisory capacity.
■ The reinforcement of the changes through changes to management processes and mechanisms.
■ The reinforcement of the mechanical, structural and cultural changes through training aimed at developing new skills and attitudes such as teamwork and mutual support.

Adapted from: Lascelles, D (1995) Barons swept out of fiefdoms. Financial Times*, 30 March, p 19, and Lorenz, C (1995) End of a corporate era. Financial Times, 30 March, p 19.*

national, business divisions and functions which will be streamlined as a means of simplifying the demands on central services and co-ordination.

The flexible firm is an idea based around the premise that employees can be trusted to do what is necessary to make the organization function effectively. It postulates that it is the horizontal perspective of an organization experienced by a customer which should determine structure. In that sense it further develops the matrix concept. Another approach to the notion of the flexible organization is that described by Atkinson (1984). In this approach the flexible firm could be created through:

- Numerical flexibility. The variability in physical size that could be achieved through a range of strategies related to security of employment. Only a small proportion of employees would be regarded as *core*. The variation in number being achieved through successive *layers* of *peripheral* employees on a short term, part-time or sub-contracted basis.
- Functional flexibility. This involves the ability of the organization to achieve multiskilling and non-demarcated working practices. Thus ensuring that core employees could be used across a range of jobs, reducing non-working time and the need for additional staff.
- Financial flexibility. This provides for expenditure variability through pay systems, etc. aligned with company performance, reducing the amount of fixed cost carried by the organization.

The viable systems model

Another approach to the notion of how an organization should be structured is the *viable systems model*. It is based upon cybernetic and systems principles and adopts a radical view of organizational design. Cybernetics is a term that originated from the study of control and communications in system functioning (Wiener, 1948).

The viable systems model takes a totally different view of an organization compared with that reflected in the traditional organization chart. The viable systems model begins with the notion of an organization as being an open system (Figure 10.6), made up of a number of sub-systems. Each sub-system has a part to play in ensuring that the organization is optimally organized to interact with its environments. Beer (1979) defines an organizational viable systems model as containing the following systems:

- System 1. The purpose of the activities that fall within this system are the achievement of organizational goals. For example, in a large international airline business the system one elements would be the operational divisions within the group. This could include a passenger division, cargo division and perhaps a travel agency division. Within a large manufacturing group it would be the manufacturing units. There would be as many System 1 elements as there are separate operational activities present in the system as a whole.
- System 2. The purpose of this system is to co-ordinate the activities of the System 1 elements. In the viable systems model each system 1 element is a separate entity and therefore capable of pursuing its own interests. Whilst this may be of benefit, it needs to be co-ordinated if such actions are

not to be detrimental to the whole organisation. This is the purpose of System 2. System 2 is a link between the operational parts of the organization and the control parts of the organization.

- System 3. This system is concerned with the control aspects of company policy. Policy for the system as a whole is determined by the systems yet to be discussed and it is the purpose of System 3 to ensure that the operational components (System 1 elements) are adhering to the established policies. To achieve this System 3 would act as a focal point for information from the other systems. The head office-based accounting function in a large multinational company would be a typical example of a System 3 activity.

- System 3*. This is designated System 3 star and refers to the audit activities within the system as a whole. Its function is to enable System 3 to find out directly what is going on in the System 1 elements. The most obvious example of System 3* is the internal audit activities of the organization. However, it could incorporate a broad range of special initiatives intended to monitor a broad range of activity, for example an employee attitude survey.

- System 4. This system is oriented towards the development of the organization. It has direct links with the environment and is in a position to be able to capture for the organization as a whole the environmental information necessary for designing future policy and operational activity. It acts as the switch for information passing from Systems 1–3 to System 5 and from System 5 to the other systems. Typical examples of System 4 activity would be market research and corporate planning.

- System 5. This system is intended to be responsible for the policy formulation for the whole organization. It has the responsibility for ensuring that the other systems are integrated into a cohesive whole and that the organization is effectively represented in the systems of which the organization is a part.

The viable systems model can be represented as a diagram, Figure 10.10. There are a number of conventions used in charting in this approach to describing organizations and these will be introduced following the diagram.

The first point to note is that the diagram should not be seen in the same terms as an organization chart. It is not hierarchical for example. System 5 is not senior to System 4, which in turn is not superior to System 3 and so on. Each system has its own responsibilities and functions that need to be integrated into an effective whole if success is to be achieved. Indeed, Beer has suggested that the most senior managers within the organization should be in charge of the System 1 elements, because that is where the ultimate responsibility for the achievement of operational objectives rests.

The second point concerns the identification of activity to be classified into the appropriate system. It is important in the application of the model to avoid the assumption that system equates with function. It is tempting to categorize functions as the systems, indeed in the earlier descriptions of each of the systems a functional example was given to illustrate the activity involved. This approach works as long as it is a very large, multidivisional organization that is being modelled. It becomes increasingly difficult to sustain this approach in smaller organizations.

Beer refers to one common problem for organizations as *autopiesis*, a tendency to over-elaborate and for support systems to seek to become viable

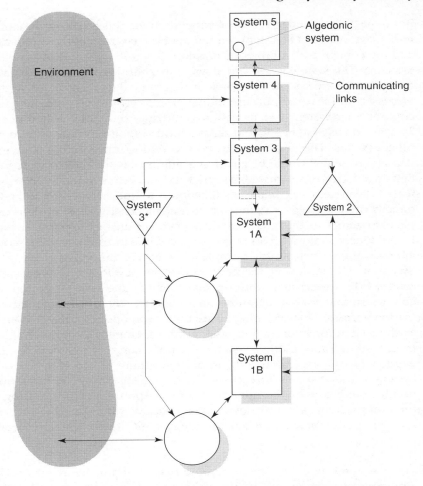

Figure 10.10   Viable systems model (adapted from Beer, S (1985) *Diagnosing the System for Organizations*. John Wiley, Chichester, Chart One).

systems in their own right. Clearly this is not possible. An accounting depart-ment cannot become an organization in its own right unless it fundamentally changes its purpose and becomes an accounting organization.

The channels of communication are shown as passing from one system to another. This is acceptable as long as a crisis does not develop. For example, imagine that there is a major fire at one of the company manufacturing units. There would clearly be a number of significant events and consequences that followed. The model recognizes this through the inclusion of communication channels that can in special circumstances circumvent the normal routes. This Beer referred to as an *algedonic* system.

Consideration of the model should suggest that System 3 is about stability and order as prerequisites for control. The view of the organization held with-in System 3 is that of a rational entity. System 4 on the other hand is interested in change, adaptation to market demands and therefore would tend to see con-trol as a hindrance. The conflict between these two perspectives needs to be balanced if the organization is not to become dangerously oriented one way or the other. This is a key function of System 5. If an organization is lead by

System 4, it will tend to be very fluid in approach to its business, frequently change its products and never gain the benefits possible through consolidation of its position. An organization that is lead by System 3 will tend to be overly conservative, resistant to change and may not see that the world and its markets are changing. In other words, it will become introverted.

The model as described so far relates to a single organization. In terms of the viable systems model this would be called the *system in focus*. The notion of *recursion* was introduced to describe the idea that every system was made up of sub-systems and was also part of a larger system. To illustrate the notion of being part of a larger system, imagine that the system in focus (organization under study) was an international airline. In turn it would be part of the larger airline industry, which in turn would be part of the transport industry. This is recursion on a larger scale. Within the system in focus, there would be a number of operating divisions (for example passenger, cargo, travel agents, caterers, maintenance, pilot training) all of which could operate as separate companies if they were to be broken away from the parent group. This is the notion of recursion at a lower level. It is possible to reflect this idea of recursion in a more elaborate form of the viable systems diagram (see Figure 10.11 on the next page).

The approach to describing an organization and how it functions within the viable systems approach is radically different to that reflected in the traditional organization chart. There is a considerable degree of additional detail in the viable systems model and it is based on a theoretical framework (cybernetics). It captures a considerable amount of information and is a useful means of reviewing the rationale associated with operational decision making. It has also been used to contribute to the introduction of initiatives such as total quality management (Flood, 1993).

Alternative organizations

So far the application of the ideas within this chapter has been in terms of conventional organizations, commercial companies and public sector organizations. These are not the only types of organization that exist. Organizations are social creations and there are as many variations as human ingenuity can create. Below is a brief introduction to some of the major alternatives that exist.

The human service organization

This type of organization has been in existence for many years. They include schools, hospitals, social work/welfare departments and public assistance providers. Notionally they are often organized along bureaucratic lines, usually because they are part of a larger public sector organization. However, there are differences in these organizations that make them a useful starting point for consideration of non-standard organizations. Hasenfeld (1992) suggests that it is the common experience of the recipients of these services that they evoke a mixture of 'hope and fear, caring and victimization, dignity and abuse' (p 4). He goes on to propose that employees of these organizations inevitably suffer a conflict between a personal need to provide the standards of service that professional standards and norms would require and the constraints and restrictions imposed by the managers of the organization. He identifies a number of reasons that could account for this pattern of contradiction (pp 4–9):

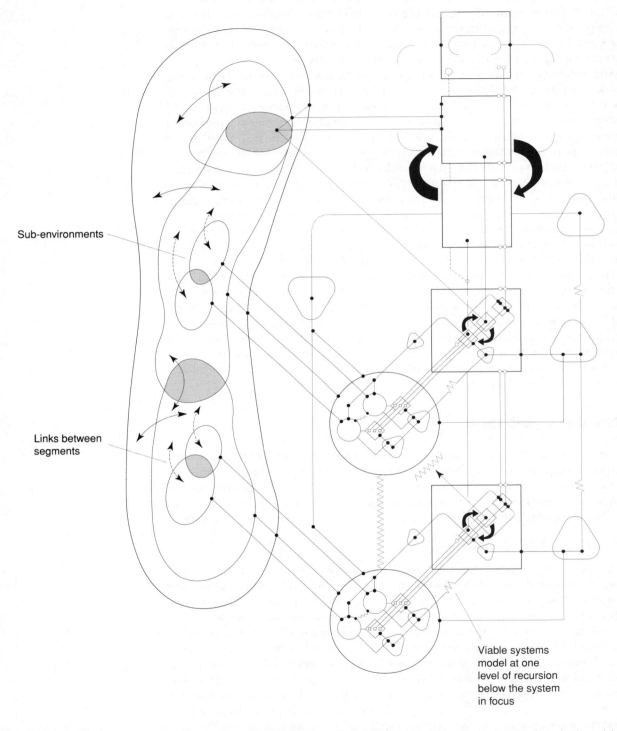

Sub-environments

Links between
segments

Viable systems
model at one
level of recursion
below the system
in focus

Figure 10.11 Viable systems model indicating recursion (adapted from Beer, S (1985) *Diagnosing the System for Organizations*. John Wiley, Chichester, Figure 13.10).

■ People as 'raw material'. Such organizations do not produce goods or services in the conventional sense. They do act in a very direct way upon the people that come to them for whatever purpose. This makes these organizations uniquely different to most others in achieving the transformations implicit in being an organization.

■ Human services as moral work. Because of the nature of human services there is a moral perspective involved in the activities. It conveys messages about the 'social worth' and 'self-identity' of the people on whose behalf the service is being performed. The definition of the processing of clients as being either *objects* or *subjects* also reflects the moral dilemma facing the providers of human services. If they are objects then the professional know best. If they are subjects then the individual should be involved in determining their own *processing*.

■ Human services as gendered work. It is historically indisputable that the caring and nurturing activities within society have been regarded as the domain of females. It has been argued (Hasenfeld, p 7) that this *fact* creates organizations that have a tendency to reflect feminine qualities when compared to the typically male qualities that dominate commercially oriented bureaucracies. He indicates that feminist oriented organization structures would emphasize collectivism rather than bureaucracy, together with participation rather than authority and control.

Hyde (1992) describes the functioning of a number of feminist health centres. Placing her analysis in an ideological framework, it is apparent that such organizations approach many aspects of organization differently to that of the traditional form. The analysis begins with a review of the way that ideology influences organizational activity (Figure 10.12). Many of the elements of the

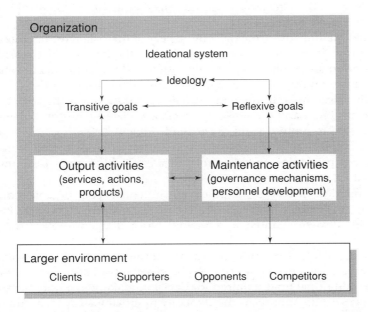

Figure 10.12   The interaction patterns of an organization and its environment (taken from Hyde, C (1992) The ideational system of social movement agencies. In *Human Services as Complex Organizations* (ed Y Hasenfeld), Sage, Newbury Park, CA, p 124).

analysis support the earlier comments about the distinctive qualities of human service organizations.

The co-operative and the kibbutz

The co-operative and the kibbutz are both examples of consensual organizations (Iannello, 1992, p 27). The writer quotes a definition from Rothschild and Whitt (1986) as, 'any enterprise in which control rests ultimately and overwhelmingly with the member-employees-owners, regardless of the particular legal framework through which this is achieved'. This work identifies the that the following aspects differentiate consensual organizations:

- Authority. Authority in a consensual organization is retained by the collective body and is not a function of position. Authority may be temporarily vested in a particular individual but is subject to recall and control by the whole group.
- Rules. Within a consensual organization rules emerge from the norms and ethical values associated with the founders and members of the group. Within a bureaucratic organization the rules are designed by management to control activity in support of their objectives. Rules are therefore a 'given' in that context in that employees have less impact on, and ownership of them.
- Social control. Unlike managerial organizations, social control in the consensual organization is based upon group dynamics and the value frameworks of the individuals involved. Social control in managerial organizations is based upon supervision, disciplinary sanction and the socialization of individuals.
- Social relations. These are also based on the values and ideals espoused by the collective. In managerial organizations they are more likely to be impersonal and professional.
- Recruitment and advancement. This aspect of the collective organization is based upon friendship networks rather than the formalized assessment of qualification and skill. Compatibility with the ideals of the organization is a significant requirement for employment in such organizations.
- Incentive structures. In the consensual organization it is the social, collective involvement and ideological aspects associated with the activities that is suggested to motivate and reward individuals.
- Social stratification. Consensual organizations attempt to function under egalitarian principles and therefore avoid the differences resulting from hierarchical stratification.
- Differentiation of labour. Emphasis in the consensual organization is on integration, flexibility and contribution. Consequently, differences between jobs and between 'manual' and 'mental' work is less pronounced.

Rothschild and Whitt also imply that in attempting to achieve a non-hierarchical structure, a number of issues restrict the possibility of its achievement. They include the additional time required for decision making in a non-hierarchically structured setting. Another is the difficulty in moving away from non-democratic habits, values and work practices. The environmental constraints arising from the conventionally organized world around the consensual organization also constrains structure and design.

Iannello indicates that the primary goal of consensual organizations is the humanization of the workplace in an attempt to re-establish the relationship between workers and society. The means of achieving this is to minimize the effect of hierarchy on the organization. In discussing research into this type of organization studies of the kibbutz, Yugoslavian worker organizations and the Mondragon operations in Spain are frequently quoted. Summarizing the work of Greenberg (1986), Iannello identifies the characteristic of a number of consensual organizations as:

- Kibbutz. Originating in Israel, the kibbutz is an attempt to combine work, social and family life into an integrated whole. Decisions are agreed at a weekly meeting of the whole organization. The leadership positions are elected and carry no special privileges or reward. Formal hierarchy is actively discouraged and control is achieved through a system of committees and the weekly meeting. Of the three types of organization described, only the kibbutz achieves any significant degree of employee influence over their sub-society. This is because the workers enjoy a high measure of control over all aspects of the productive process and social context. In the two following examples, workers set broad policy but then willingly subjugate themselves on a daily basis to a more conventional form of management control and work design.

- The former Yugoslavia. A national system of employee governed organizations evolved. Legislation required organizations of more than 10 people to establish a works council, the function of the council being to determine the main company policies. The council also elected (and could remove) the management board and the plant director. It was the job of the management board to run the company on a day-to-day basis under the general direction of the works council. Given the recent major political and social upheavals in this part of the world it can only be assumed that this organizational approach has largely ceased to function and that it did not engender any depth of harmony between the peoples involved.

- Mondragon. This type of consensual organization originated in Spain and consists of some 80–90 individual co-operatives, employing approximately 19,000 people. Responsibility in each of the separate co-operative organizations lies with the general meeting of all members, which meets once each year. Its function is to elect the board of directors and senior managers. Managers below this level are appointed in the conventional way. The organization seeks to function on the basis of shared ownership and egalitarian principles of operation.

The virtual organization

The term virtual organization appeared towards the end of the 1980s and described a number of organizational innovations. The term originates from the computer world and the concept of virtual memory. Virtual memory is a term that reflects the appearance of more memory within a computer than actually exists. Translated into an organizational context, it is a metaphor for an organization that appears to be larger and capable of producing more than its resources would allow.

Such organizations have been in existence in some industries for many years. For example, small consultancies have operated a network, using associates to expand their ability to accept large contracts by pooling resources as a tempo-rary measure. What makes the term more significant today is that it is being introduced into manufacturing organizations.

The basis of the virtual organization is that it is a temporary network of oth-erwise independent organizations for a specific purpose. It could include sup-pliers, customers, competitors and specialists such as designers, engineers and finance experts. The purpose being to take advantage of the particular strengths of each member of the alliance in achieving a specific objective, from which each member would benefit.

Clearly the main advantages of the virtual organization include the opportu-nity to provide a response to opportunities that would otherwise be beyond the capability of the individual members. There are potential dangers with this type of approach including the risk of providing potential competitors with commercially sensitive information and expertise. Also a failure to manage the dynamics of the relationship effectively could lead to a collapse of the venture.

In terms of the structure and design issues, there should be opportunities to reduce hierarchical frameworks to a minimum as each member of the alliance concentrates on only part of the process. However, there is a need for the integration of activity across the member organizations which would not exist in other forms of structure. Byrne *et al*. (1993) quote a number of key lessons (based on data supplied by Booz Allen & Hamilton Inc – a large consultancy prac-tice) for organizations attempting to develop virtual relationships, including:

- Marry well. It is necessary to identify and select the right members of the network for the right reasons. Success depends upon a high degree of trust and dependability among each of the members.
- Play fair. Each member needs to gain from their membership, or at least find that membership is in their interests. If the members cannot trust each other then important information and contributions will be held back and result in failure.
- Offer the best. To commit the best employees to collaborative activities provides a clear signal of commitment to the project and also increases the probability of success.
- Define objectives. It should be clear to each member of the network what the ultimate objective is and their part in it. To fail to identify the objectives will result in a lack of direction and targets against which to measure progress.
- Common Infrastructure. There needs to be an ability for each of the mem-bers to communicate with each other in a meaningful way. This requires some commonality in procedures and perhaps computer systems. Without the formality of hierarchy and clear lines of responsibility, it would be easy for communications to become confused, leading to failure.

Contingency theory: a management perspective

From a manager's point of view contingency theory offers a *richer* vehicle for considering the issues surrounding organization design. The earlier views about the determinants of structure assume a restricted metaphor on the nature of organizations and how they operate. The appeal of contingency ideas is the

potential to determine the relationships acting on their situations. This emphasis on a normative perspective delivers high levels of usability benefit to managers but perhaps offers little by way of fundamental explanation of what it is
that creates structure (Legge, 1978). Organizations are composed of a number
of smaller groups or departments and these can have very different perspectives and interactions with the environmental around them. For example, the
personnel department will interact with a number of the same groups and individuals as the production department, but a largely different set to those appropriate to the research and development function. This view of an organization
is reflected in the overlapping shapes in Figure 10.13.

The implication of Figure 10.13 is that an organization does not just have a
single environment, but many internal and external environments. This is a
complexity that the viable systems model (Figure 10.11) is capable of reflecting.
The discussion so far has concentrated on what can be described as organizational adaptation to environmental forces. The need for managers to integrate
both the formal and informal elements within the organization is a point made
in Management in Action 10.6 overleaf.

Another way of considering how organizations evolve over time has been the
use of population ecology approaches to the process. Using what can be
described as Darwinian theories this approach emerged in the late 1970s, but
it has not yet produced a significant alternative explanation. It attempts to
utilize the notion of *selection* to the way that structure evolves over time.
The most appropriate organizations are 'selected' for survival based on environmental fit and adaptation to the environment (Thompson and McHugh,
1990, p 98).

Whilst it may be an interesting academic debate to consider the nature of
structure, its determinants and evolutionary forces, managers function in
real-time in a dynamic context. Consequently, the advantages of models such as
displayed in Figures 10.8 and 10.10 can provide them with an improved opportunity to influence design and perhaps increase the probability of survival. The
notion of *selection* would imply that the environments are in some way choosing the most effectively adapted *specimens* for continued existence.

Structure is the means of organizing within the enterprise. It is the vehicle
for ensuring that the necessary work can be done without overloading individuals. It allows specialization to be introduced in order to reduce the skill
and training required within the organization. However, it also provides the

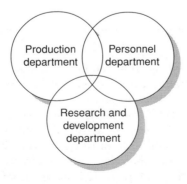

Figure 10.13 Overlapping interactions between organizational activity.

A mesh of the formal and the flexible

That every organization consists of a formal set of frameworks, systems, procedures and policies would not be denied. It is the existence of such architecture that provides the skeleton that holds the organization together and provides the outline shape. However, that is only part of the 'beast'. Also within every organization are the informal aspects that ensure that the formal frameworks actually do what they are supposed to do. Continuing the metaphor, it could be argued that the informal aspects of the organization represent the flesh and muscle of the 'beast' which creates the three-dimensional manifestation of it, as well as allowing movement and thought.

Now most practising managers are only too well aware of the existence of the informal organization. They must live and work with it and through it every day. It provides the networking, power and political dimensions within any organization. The informal is primarily about relationships not structures. That is why it is the informal that makes an organization work (or not as the case may be). The structure and systems can only provide the potential for future action to happen. It is among the academic and book-writing community that this reality of organizational life is somewhat ignored when the latest fashion or fad is promulgated as the best way to design an organization.

Lorenz discusses this in relation to the work of Nitin Nohria and James Berkley, who argue that the formal aspect of organization has been underplayed in the search for 'better' formal models. Nohria and Berkley go as far as to reject the notion of the concept of a new paradigm, arguing instead for a shifting action perspective as a more helpful metaphor. This view of an organization is as an organism, where many different things are happening at once and which are constantly in flux. This can often be as a result of low-level action within the organization.

To illustrate the need for informal aspects of an organization to be included in design change, Nohria and Berkley draw attention to the experiences of three divisions within Allen-Bradley. The company, which makes high-tech industrial control devices, opted to introduce a flat, team-based 'concentric' structure in 1990. However, within months the old hierarchy had reasserted itself. Business teams were formed to oversee the operational teams, and an executive council was formed to oversee the work of the business teams. Within a year the work of the teams was severely restricted and by 1992 much of the concentric structure was disbanded. A multidivisional structure was reintroduced.

Some of the benefits of the attempts to restructure were retained within Allen-Bradley. The two major benefits retained and which were necessary for a changed informal structure were IT systems that spanned the whole organization together with broader performance measures. In essence it is as necessary to change the informal structure within an organization as it is to change the formal if 'doing things differently' is to have any real meaning and to stand any chance of long-term success.

Adapted from: Lorenz, C (1994) A mesh of the formal and the flexible. Financial Times, 4 November, p 11.

simplified and repetitive tasks that can create alienation and a lack of commitment to the objectives being sought. It is a double-edged sword, providing benefits and disadvantages. It is in an attempt to offset some of the disadvantages arising from structural forms that alternative organizations introduced earlier are important. It is tempting to assume that the only structural forms that exist are the large private and public sector organizations that are the most apparent examples. This is simply not the case. There are many different forms of organization that exist and they can provide lessons for anyone who is prepared to study them.

Management in Action 10.7

Ford's global matrix gamble

Ford, the second largest vehicle maker in the world, unveiled a radical world-wide shake-up to be implemented with effect from January 1995. It was given the title 'Ford 2000' and was intended to take the company from a multinational organized on a geographical basis with regional profit centres, to a global company, organized along product lines. The annual turnover of the company is about £80bn and there is a total workforce of about 320,000 world-wide. The target of Ford 2000 is to produce a truly global company, able to meet its goal of becoming, 'the world's leading automotive company ... ultimately in every aspect of competitive comparison'. The essence of Ford 2000 is to provide a base for re-engineering the company to allow it to deliver more products at lower cost, and with better quality.

At the beginning of January 1995 Ford merged the North American operations with the European Automotive Operations into a single organization, called Ford Automotive Operations. The next step will be to integrate the Ford operations from the Asia-Pacific, South American and African regions into the same organization. That change is scheduled to take place by the end of 1995. The aim of these changes being to capture economies of scale, the elimination of duplication, encourage the spread of best practice and increase efficiency. As an example of the duplication that exists within the company the Ford Escort is available in both Europe and North America. However, although very similar in design the only common components are the oval name badge and the name of the car. In future the company will develop 'families' of cars that will be made to a single design and available across global markets.

To achieve this level of integration Ford has created five 'vehicle centres', four in America and one in Europe. Each centre has total responsibility for the development and profitability for specific vehicle ranges on a world-wide basis. For example, the European 'vehicle centre' which is physically based in the UK and Germany has responsibility for all Ford small and medium front wheel drive cars such as the Fiesta, Aspire, Escort, Mondeo ranges. The development of the Mondeo was expensive at around $6bn, but it did provide a valuable learning experience for the company in anticipation of the Ford 2000 initiative. Alex Trotman, chairman and chief executive of Ford believes that even with a global strategy it should still be possible to incorporate a local 'feel' into the vehicles produced. Some vehicles will be purely regional in market, such as the Ford Transit van sold in Europe. For sale across a number of markets interior design options can be built onto a common vehicle body providing a localization of the model.

Bob Transou, Ford group vice-president of manufacturing, and the man who led the reorganization team early in 1994, suggests that Ford 2000 is designed to eliminate all of the 'barriers, geographic or bureaucratic that have complicated our lives for generations'. Whilst many organizations are moving out of matrix structures, Ford considers that the introduction of this form of organization has much to offer.

Most employees will have at least two bosses. For example, the 'vehicle centre' is the control level for vehicle activity and so it reflects one 'level' of management within the system. However, people will still have their functional bosses as well, for example manufacturing, personnel, finance, purchasing, etc. Because responsibility is split within the matrix there is a danger of a lack of accountability. In the Ford model career development will be the responsibility of the functional manager, whilst performance evaluation is the responsibility of the vehicle programme team leader. Primary responsibility for each individual within the matrix is not to the 'function' but to the car team. By leveraging the balance between the two dimensions of the matrix in this way Ford have avoided the 'balanced conflict' problem by stating that the product focus takes precedence.

The number of levels of management has also been reduced in an attempt to prevent managers from 'micro managing'. The previous number of 14 levels has been reduced to seven. This has not been the only aspect of the restructuring to gain widespread attention. Other aspects include:

- The speed of the changes. Ford has achieved in one year what other companies have taken about a decade to do.
- The degree of re-engineering involved. The introduction of world-wide processes and systems within and linking product development, production, supply and sales.
- The scale of the behavioural and cultural change involved in achieving the new globalized operational structure.
- The training and development of staff before the introduction of the new structures as well as the introduction of appropriate personnel practices in reward and appraisal systems.
- The intention to only appoint senior executives in the future who have demonstrated an ability to work collaboratively in the new structure.

Adapted from: Lorenz, C (1994) Ford's global matrix gamble. Financial Times, *16 December, p 13 and Done, K (1995) Ford maps out a global ambition.* Financial Times, *3 April, p 11.*

Conclusions

The design and structure of an organization is an area in which managers make choices. The form of the organization is not something that occurs by chance, or as a result of some dictat from the government. It is appropriate to view an organization as something over which people have stewardship for a period of time. They are therefore constrained by a number of forces in moulding the organization. These constraints include the industry, size, history, technology, markets, legal constraints, profitability, the will and ability of individuals within the organization. Management in Action 10.7 provides an overview of the process that Ford is undergoing in order to position itself more effectively in its global markets.

The notion of a direct cause and effect link between a number of environmental forces and the structure of an organization is overly simplistic. It ignores the interactive nature of external and internal forces and managerial responses. The use of metaphor was introduced as a means of accounting for the understanding that managers have of what an organization is and how it should function relative to its circumstances. It is not the intention to suggest that contingency or systems approaches offer a perfect explanation and applied options for understanding organization design. They do, however, offer a richer means of attempting to understand the processes involved and a basis for future research.

Discussion questions

1 Define the following key terms used in this chapter:

Recursion	Variety	Metaphor
System in focus	Core/peripheral employees	System
Autopiesis	Kibbutz	Mechanistic/organismic
Algedonic system	Contingency	Alternative organization
Rich picture	Influence diagram	

2 Describe how the contingency approach to organizational design emerged.
3 What is the viable systems model? Explain each of the systems within the model and describe the significance of the algedonic system.
4 In what ways might a virtual organization differ from a conventional one? Would you like to work in a virtual organization, explain why or why not?
5 In what ways does the concept of a metaphor as described by Morgan (1986) contribute to understanding of how organizations are structured?
6 Describe the contingency approach to designing an organization. How does it differ from the traditional views on structure?
7 Assess the contribution of the Aston studies to the understanding of the contingency view of organizations.
8 In what ways do human service organizations differ from conventional ones?
9 Describe the approaches to determinism described in this chapter. Why do they offer a restricted view of organizational design?
10 What is a flexible firm and how does it reflect the contingency ideas described in this chapter?

Research questions

1 Identify an organization with which you are familiar. Find out as much as you can about the organization, its size, products or services, etc. Attempt to redesign the organization using the principles of the contingency model. In undertaking this exercise you should make whatever assumption you find necessary about the organization, its environments and the people within it. You will not be able to collect enough information to make this a real exercise, but it should allow you to consider the implications of the model.

2 Consider the viable systems model. Using the organization identified in Question 1 above undertake a review of the organization using the viable systems model. What conclusions do you draw about this model compared to the contingency approach?

3 In a group of four fellow students, seek out a number of unusual organizations. If you find real examples near to where you are based make an attempt to speak to some of the members or senior representatives. For all examples that you find, describe the structure of the organization together with some of the objectives that the designers were attempting achieve. Make an assessment of how successful they have been, together with the differences in structure compared with conventional organizations.

Key reading

From Clark, H, Chandler, J and Barry, J (1994) *Organization and Identities: Text and Readings in Organizational Behaviour*, International Thomson Business Press, London.

■ Burns T and Stalker GM: Mechanistic and organic systems of management, p 331. The original of this seminal work on the subject.
■ Baron RD and Norris GM: The dual labour market, p 335. An introduction to the emergence of differentiated labour markets.
■ Atkinson J: The flexible firm, p 337. The original article referred to earlier.
■ Pollert A: The flexible firm: a model in search of reality, p 343. An extract which considers some of the issues associated with the flexible firm.
■ Hirst P and Zeitlin J: Knowing the buzz word is not enough, p 345. This reviews the experience of flexibility in the UK as compared with experience elsewhere.

Further reading

Beer, S (1985) *Diagnosing the system for organizations*, John Wiley, Chichester. This book is intended as a workbook introduction for managers intending to find out more about the viable systems model and to attempt to redesign their organizations accordingly.

Brown, H (1992) *Women Organizing*, Routledge, London. Chapter 3 is worth reading in the context of the contingency and systems approaches as it provides a detailed review of social context within which organizations function and the basis of women creating organizations for their own needs.

Espejo, R and Harnden, R. eds (1989) *The Viable System Model: Interpretations and Applications*, John Wiley, Chichester. Provides a broad review of the viable systems model and reports several studies of its application.

Roberts, KH (1994) Functional and dysfunctional organizational linkages. In *Trends in Organizational Behaviour*, Vol 1 (eds CL Cooper and DM Rousseau), John Wiley, Chichester. This chapter considers the notion of linkages within organizations and how they contribute to (or reduce) the risk of disaster in an environmental context.

References

Ashby, WR (1956) *An Introduction to Cybernetics*, Methuen, London.

Atkinson, J. (1984) Manpower strategies for flexible organizations, *Personnel Management*, August, 28–31.

Beer, S (1979) *The Heart of Enterprise*, John Wiley, Chichester.

Burns, T and Stalker, GM (1961) *The Management of Innovation*, Tavistock. London.

Byrne, J, Brandt, R and Port, O (1993) The virtual corporation, *Business Week*, 8 February, 98–103.

Child, J and Kieser, A (1979) Organization and managerial roles in Britain and West German companies: an examination of the culture-free thesis. In *Organizations Alike and Unlike* (eds C Lammers and D Hickson), Routledge & Kegan Paul, London.

Child, J (1988) *Organization: A Guide to Problems and Practice*, 2nd edn, Paul Chapman, London.

Emery, FE and Thorsrud, E (1976) *Democracy at Work*, Martinus Nijhoff, Leiden.

Flood, RL (1993) *Beyond TQM*, John Wiley, Chichester.

Greenberg, ES (1986) *Workplace Democracy*, Cornell University Press, Ithaca, NY.

Hasenfeld, Y (1992) The nature of human service organizations. In *Human Services as Complex Organizations* (ed Y Hasenfeld), Sage, Newbury Park, CA.

Hyde, C (1992) The ideational system of social movement agencies: an examination of feminist health centers. In *Human Services as Complex Organizations* (ed Y Hasenfeld), Sage, Newbury Park, CA.

Iannello, KP (1992) *Decisions Without Hierarchy*, Routledge, London.

Kast, F and Rosenzweig, J (1972) General systems theory: applications for organization and management, *Academy of Management Journal*, December, 447–65.

Lawrence, PR and Lorsch, JW (1967) *Organization and Environment*, Harvard University Press, Boston, MA.

Legge, K (1978) *Power, Innovation and Problem Solving in Management*, McGraw-Hill, London.

Morgan, G (1986) *Images of Organization*, Sage, Newbury Park, CA.

Perrow, C (1967) *Organizational Analysis: A Sociological View*, Tavistock, London.

Pugh, DS and Hickson, DJ (1989) *Writers on Organizations*, 4th edn, Penguin, London.

Rothschild, J and Whitt, JA (1986) *The Cooperative Workplace*, Cambridge University Press.

Thompson, P and McHugh, D (1990) *Work Organizations*, Macmillan, Basingstoke.

Townsend, R (1985) *Further up the Organization*, Coronet Books, London.

Trist, EL and Bamforth, KW (1951) Some social and psychological consequences of the longwall method of goal-getting, *Human Relations*, February, 3–38.

Wiener, N (1948) *Cybernetics*, John Wiley, New York.

Woodward, J (1965) *Industrial Organizations: Theory and Practice*, Oxford University Press, London.

11

Organizational culture

Chapter summary

This chapter considers the concept of organizational culture. The chapter begins with a review of what culture means within an organization and the forms that it can take. The determinants of culture are then explored, followed by a consideration of the notion of national culture and its links with organizational culture. The relationship between culture and organizational design are discussed. The chapter concludes with a management review of organizational culture.

Learning objectives

After studying this chapter and working through the associated Management in Action panels, discussion questions and research activities, you should be able to:

■ Explain why the concept of culture is problematic as applied to organizations.
■ Describe the different levels of analysis used in cultural analysis.
■ Outline the forms through which organizational culture finds expression.
■ Understand the links between culture and organizational design.
■ Appreciate the relationship between culture as used within an organization and as used to describe national difference.
■ Discuss the significance of sub- and counter-cultures to an organization.
■ Assess the impact of the various determinants of culture on an organizational context.
■ Detail the management significance of the culture of an organization.

browse this web site

www.itbp.com

Introduction

The concept of culture began to make an impact on organizational thinking in the late 1970s and early 1980s. However, its existence is evident in a number of the ideas of earlier writers, for example, Barnard (1938) and Jaques (1952). It is a difficult concept to define in objective terms, being something that can be recognized but difficult to define. As a concept, culture emerges from the anthropological studies of ethnic groups and societies. Unfortunately there is no one dominant view of how culture should be conceptualized. According to Allaire and Firsirotu (1984) there are eight separate schools of thought on what the term 'culture' means.

It is comparatively easy to recognize that organizations 'do things different-ly', or that they 'feel' different. It is much more difficult to say with any degree of certainty in what ways these organizations differ. The phrase 'the way we do things around here' is frequently offered as an operational definition of culture

(Deal and Kennedy, 1982). However, whilst it may be a useful approach to understanding the parameters of the concept, it has little analytical power. Included in that definition is the procedural, work organization, job design and structural aspects of the organization as well as those regarded as cultural features. It may be that these issues are a reflection of the underlying culture of the organization, but the definition offered does not recognize the limits of the concept.

Definition of organizational culture

Kilman *et al*. (1985) suggest that culture reflects the ideologies, shared philosophies, values, beliefs, assumptions, attitudes, expectations and norms of an organization. It is also suggested to be something that emerges over time and is not specifically created. A much earlier definition offered by Jaques (1952), suggests that culture is the:

> ... customary and traditional way of thinking and doing things, which is shared to a greater or lesser degree by all members, and which the new members must learn and at least partially accept, in order to be accepted into the services of the firm (p 251).

Deal and Kennedy (1988) also offer a range of elements within culture, including the importance of symbolism and leadership as a means of achieving employee commitment. Thompson and McHugh (1990) provide an insightful review of this phenomena, pointing out the significance of personnel management in achieving and maintaining new and more appropriate (from a management perspective) cultures. They review a considerable body of evidence to demonstrate that, as far as the 'excellence' view of culture is concerned, it has little to offer by way of an explanation for the significance of culture in an organizational context.

The two definitions of culture provided above can be seen as supportive of each other. The Kilman *et al*. (1985) view of the 'things' that compose culture can be seen to provide the basis to the earlier definition provided by Jaques (1952) and through which the learning of it could be achieved. In other words, the later definition considers content and the earlier definition process. However, the process as described by Jaques is one of acquisition by individuals. It assumes that the individuals will either possess the same culture as the organization before joining it or that they will subsequently acquire it through the various forms of training and socialization. This implies it is something that it is management's interest to design or engineer. Particular cultures will be more supportive of management's objectives than others. Interest in the so called Japanese management phenomenon fuelled interest in this issue through the perceived need to build strong teams through what Thompson and McHugh call *compulsory sociability* (p 239). Management in Action 11.1 provides an insight into Japanese management practices.

Levels of analysis

From the foregoing discussion it might appear that the concept of culture is clear and easy to measure. This is not the case, particularly as the concept incorporates so many dimensions or variables (evident in the Kilman *et al*. (1985) definition). It is possible to identify three levels of analysis (see Figure 11.1).

Management in Action 11.1

East meets west

International operations are a fact of organizational life. Even very small companies find themselves in the position of having to trade or operate in countries other than their home base. Many large international companies have considerable experience in operating in other countries and with other cultures. However well established that experience might be it does not eliminate potential problems from the mixing of language, culture and business practice in overseas locations.

Over the past decade or so a number of Japanese companies have established manufacturing or other operational units in the UK. The need to be able to achieve operational objectives, inevitably determined by the Japanese head office, with a British workforce has provided some interesting examples of the effects of culture. For example, the Japan Travel Bureau (JTB) employs about 10,000 staff world-wide, about 400 of whom work within Europe, its European HQ is in London. Faced with rapid expansion of its market share (about 30% of Japanese travel business) the company was undergoing rapid change. In common with many international operations JTB was headed in Europe by a home country national, supported by a mixture of Japanese and European personnel. Company surveys during the late 1980s identified a number of problems. There was a lack of empathy between local staff and Japanese managers created by cultural and language differences. Also a lack of motivation and commitment among staff, together with a lack of understanding of the organization's goals and underpinning values. High labour turnover among local staff was also a problem. A lack of appropriate skill existed among many of the managers and local staff, partly as a result of the vicious circle created by the high labour turnover.

A number of initiatives were put in place to address these issues in conjunction with a carefully selected consultancy able to offer support across the language barrier as well as a flexible approach to the change programme. The result was an educational initiative given the title 'Issho-ni' or 'together'. It was to address the many issues identified through the survey, including cultural differences, customer first values, communications, relationships and managerial competencies. The programme was based around several monthly workshops, organized hierarchically as a precursor for a later integrated approach. Not surprisingly a number of problems emerged during the running of pilot programmes, including rejection, suspicion, and hostility. The programme attempted to deal with these issues and they did reduce, although not completely. Subsequently, customer service groups were established at each local office as an attempt to emphasize the local identification of issues and a local team-based resolution. The outcome of the process was positive in that labour turnover reduced and improvements in customer service occurred.

In the manufacturing sectors there has been much publicity for initiatives such as 'Kaizen' or the continuous improvement of an operation through small improvements to working practices. This approach was given considerable impetus through the arrival of large Japanese companies including Nissan and Toyota. Having identified the UK as an appropriate base for European operations the manufacturing units found it necessary to both compete with factory operations in Japan and ensure that the manufacturing infrastructure in the UK was compatible with their needs. A number of initiatives were introduced to achieve these objectives. For example, Toyota chose to refer to employees as 'members' in an attempt to generate a feeling of belonging. This went along with team working and employee involvement on a scale not usually seen in the UK (problem solving and daily briefings for example), even encouraging pre-work exercises.

Beyond that level of activity suppliers were encouraged to adopt the so-called Japanese manufacturing methods in order to ensure a continuity of supply in quantity, quality and price to whichever of the car manufacturers they supplied. Visits by company purchasing staff and other specialists take place in an attempt to assist the first and then second tier suppliers to improve their performance and to be able to meet the needs of what are increasingly important customers. However, some suppliers are sensitive to the competing pressures of better quality and productivity leading to job security on the one hand, but potentially the need for fewer worker to produce the output on the other. Not an easy tightrope to walk in any culture or location.

Adapted from: Fitzgerald, J (1991) A Japanese lesson in European togetherness. Personnel Management, September, pp 45–7, and Williams, M (1993) East meets west. Personnel Today, 26 January, pp 34–5.

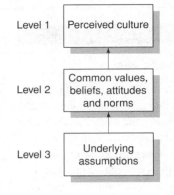

Figure 11.1 Levels of cultural analysis.

Taking each level in turn:

■ Perceived culture. This reflects the most apparent level of cultural analysis. It is based upon the 'way things get done around here' view of culture. Typically it would incorporate the rituals, stories and ceremonies that identify the group in action.
■ Common values, and so on. The second level of analysis attempts to get behind that which is observable and identify the factors that determine the perceived culture. Typically this level of analysis would incorporate the factors identified in the Kilman *et al.* definition.
■ Underlying assumptions. Behind the common values are the underlying assumptions that individuals hold about the world and how it functions. It is often very difficult to identify these hidden assumptions as they are not directly articulated in the behaviour and attitudes that people display.

The dimensions of culture

Schien (1985) identified six dimensions that reflected the composition of culture:

■ Behavioural regularities. This reflects observable patterns of behaviour. It might include induction ceremonies, the in-group language and the ritualized behaviour patterns that reflect membership of particular groups or organizations.
■ Dominant values. These are the specific beliefs expressed by groups and organizations. For example, an organization might attempt to create a 'quality' image through adopting a number of relevant initiatives and publishing its objective as a policy.
■ Norms. These are general patterns of behaviour that all members of a group are expected to follow. For example, many retail chains set specific behaviour standards for employees in terms of greeting customers and smiling.
■ Rules. Rules are specific instructions of what must be done, whereas norms are sometimes unwritten and informally accepted. They are the 'must do's'

of the organization. However, because they must be followed employees may simply *comply* with them. It represents the difference between doing something because it is necessary and doing it because of a belief that it is right.

■ Philosophy. These reflect the underlying beliefs about people and how they operate. Given that an organization is the managers who run it, this naturally reflects their values. In turn they determine the policies and practices that the company will create.

■ Climate. The physical layout of buildings, attitudes to open plan as opposed to enclosed offices, recreation facilities, management style and the design of public areas all help to create the atmosphere or climate within the company.

Each of the above dimensions of culture are complex ideas in their own right. They do, however, offer descriptive ability in beginning to tease out how culture influences organizations and how in turn organizations can influence culture. This circularity is reflected in Figure 11.2.

The circularity displayed in Figure 11.2 indicates that culture produces particular behaviour and associated belief patterns, which in turn influences what actually happens within the organization. Actual events are then measured against management objectives and the consequences feed back into culture. The implication being that if management perceive that a particular culture achieves the objectives being pursued it will be reinforced. If it does not contribute to the achievement of objectives then management will attempt to change it.

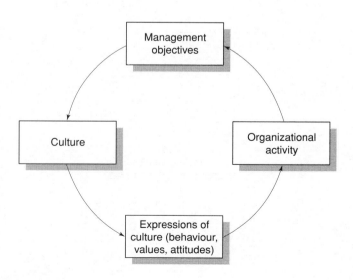

Figure 11.2   The cycle of culture.

Cultural forms

The previous discussion concentrated on the dimensions of culture evident at level two of the analysis model (Figure 11.1). It is now the intention to describe how culture manifests itself at level one. In other words, how is culture experienced in an organization? How is culture observed and detected? There are a number of different approaches to this question.

Handy's four types

Based on the earlier work of Harrison (1972), Handy (1993) describes four manifestations of culture:

■ Power culture. Typically found in small organizations, everything revolves around the focal person. All important decisions are made by them and they retain absolute authority in all matters. As a diagram Handy describes this culture as a web (Figure 11.3) and the *metaphor* of a spider's web very graphically illustrates this type of culture in operation.
  The main features of this type of culture are a single-mindedness in approach, dominated by the focal person and their personality, with a lack of bureaucracy in operations. The success of power culture depends on the capabilities of the focal person in technical, business and management terms.

■ Role culture. Based upon the existence of procedure and rule frameworks. It is typified by the form of a Greek temple (Figure 11.4) and the notion of bureaucracy.
  Within this type of culture everyone has a specified role to perform and is expected to restrict themselves to that function. Each of the specialist functions is co-ordinated in its duties and activities by the overarching functions

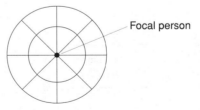

Figure 11.3   Power culture.

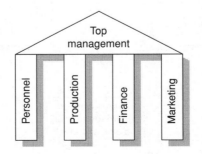

Figure 11.4   Role culture.

Figure 11.5 Task culture.

at the top of the organization. The two important attributes associated with the role culture are *predictability* and *stability*.

■ Task culture. Based upon the need to concentrate on the work of the organization. The expertise within the organization is vested in the individuals within it and it is they who must be organized in a way that meets the needs of the business. The description used by Handy to illustrate this culture is that of a net (Figure 11.5).

This type of culture is generally supportive of a team form of organization. It requires people to concentrate on the task to be achieved and nothing else. It is a flexible approach to the needs of the organization and would emphasize adaptability as a key requirement among its members. Decision making is frequently distributed throughout the 'net' and moves dependent upon the needs of the immediate task.

■ Person culture. This is based upon the individual. As such it should not be confused with the power culture described earlier. The power culture is based around a single focal point. The person culture allows each person to be a focal point depending upon the circumstances. A consultancy practice and barristers' chambers are used by Handy to illustrate this type of culture.

There are obvious links between the concept of culture as described here and the structural issues discussed in previous chapters. Some of the links have been made obvious, as in the case of bureaucracy, whilst others have only been hinted at. For example, the task culture has a number of associations with the matrix form of structure, with its emphasis on teams and dual reporting relationships.

Ouchi's type Z companies

Ouchi identified that Japanese firms operated from a different cultural base to that of Western organizations. He also introduced the notion that this originated from the societal culture in Japan and that it offered a likelihood of higher levels of productivity than cultures from the Western tradition. In his 1981 work he identified a number of key differences between Japanese and American organizations (see Table 11.1).

Ouchi gave his idea the title theory Z because it extended McGregor's theory 'X' and 'Y' (chapter 5) as a stereotypic organizational type. Ouchi suggested that some American organizations contained some of the features described in Table 11.1, but not to the extent found in Japanese organizations.

Table 11.1
Ouchi's cultural differences
(taken from: Pugh, DS and
Hickson, DJ (1989) *Writers on
Organizations*, 4th edn, Penguin,
London, p 110)

Japanese organizations	American organizations
Lifetime employment	Short-term employment
Slow evaluation and promotion	Rapid evaluation and promotion
Non-specialized career paths	Specialized career paths
Implicit control mechanisms	Explicit control mechanism
Collective decision making	Individual responsibility
Holistic concern	Segmented concern

A number of the claims made by Ouchi have been brought into question by later researchers. For example, the notion of lifetime employment in Japan applies to only a small proportion of employees in a few larger organizations. It is also suggested that far from being a more participative approach to organizing work activity, the Japanese approach produces a more tightly controlled approach to work. Little personal discretion exists and employees are pitted against each other in the relentless search for ever higher productivity and quality (Garrahan and Stewart, 1992).

The relationship between culture and company performance is demonstrated in Management in Action 11.2 which reviews the drastic action needed to enable one large company to survive.

Peters and Waterman's excellence and culture

Peters and Waterman (1982) attempted to identify what it was that made some American organizations 'excellent'. The research included reviews of the published data over a 25-year period on each of the 43 companies in the sample. This was supported by a range of interviews with senior executives. From this research (and in collaboration with Pascale and Athos) the McKinsey 7-S Framework was developed. It was so called because the four researchers worked for McKinsey and Company, one of the foremost management consultancy practices. The 7-S model identifies seven separate but interdependent features associated with running an organization. Each of the seven aspects begin with the letter 'S', and are shown in Table 11.2

The seventh item in the list relates specifically to organizational culture. From the 7-S Framework emerged a set of eight features that Peters and Waterman suggest are commonly found among excellent organizations. As such, these features prescribe the cultural dimensions of an organization from the perspective of 'the way things are done around here':

■ Bias for action. Based on the recognition that to delay can be fatal. This determines the need for managers to be action rather than analysis oriented.

Table 11.2
McKinsey 7-S framework

Structure	(organizational framework)
Strategy	(organizational direction)
Systems	(including procedures)
Style	(of management)
Skill	(company strengths)
Staff	(people issues)
Shared values	(culture)

Whessoe's culture change works wonders

Whessoe was a company with a long and proud tradition. Its roots were laid some 200 years ago at the start of the industrial revolution. The founder was one William Kitchin, who owned a corner ironmongery shop in Darlington in the North of England. The road outside the shop led to the tiny village of Whessoe, from where the company eventually took its name. Being located where Robert Stephenson built the first railway line, it was not surprising that Kitchin became involved in the project. Initially building steam engines for the railways, the company began to produce other forms of boiler and pressure vessels as the technology developed. For example it began to make the equipment that produced gas from coal at the turn of the century, then later equipment for the petro-chemical industry and more recently nuclear power station pressure vessels and instrumentation. The company built a world-class reputation for engineering excellence in pressure vessel technology.

Older technologies were replaced and changes in the nuclear industry to pressurized water reactors (PWR's) introduced new technologies which also undermined Whessoe's position. The Chernobyl disaster in the former Soviet Union created a downturn in the whole nuclear industry. This was bad news for Whessoe who found themselves in a difficult commercial position. The quality of its work was appropriate to the very high standards called for by the nuclear industry, but alternative markets were unwilling to pay for such high quality. Replacement business was therefore difficult to obtain. It was time for a fundamental rethink about the business and its future.

The relationship between Whessoe and the City was poor as a result of the unstable performance of the company, together with its ability to produce unpleasant surprises. The company had had no finance director for many years, believing that if the quality of its engineering was good, everything else would follow. Chris Fleetwood was appointed to that position in 1987. By 1989 when the crisis hit Whessoe, Chris Fleetwood had moved up from the position of finance director to chief executive and appointed a new senior management team charged with finding ways out of the crisis. The approach adopted contained a mixture of savage surgery and overseas acquisition.

The heavy engineering plant on a 36-acre site in Darlington was closed and flattened. Making modules for the offshore oil and gas industry was also dropped. The project engineering operation, for contracts in the petro-chemical and irrigation scheme businesses was sharpened up for future sale. The belief being that such an operation exposed the company to higher levels of risk than was acceptable for its size and that the business, although sound, would be better suited to a larger company. During this process the numbers employed reduced from a high of 5000 people world-wide to about 1100, with only about 450 in the UK. Although the surgery cut the group's turnover by about 50%, it opened up opportunities for acquisition as a result of the reduced costs and cash generated from the sale of businesses. The first acquisitions were in the USA and Norway in the instrumentation and control industry. It represented a clear shift in emphasis away from heavy engineering and towards the higher technology aspects of petro-chemical and related instrumentation products. One of the few parts of the Darlington-based operation to survive was the small instrumentation department, which was moved to Newton Aycliffe, a few miles away, to give it the opportunity for a new start. Out went the old ways of work and troublesome industrial relations with five unions representing 60 workers. Harmonized terms and conditions of employment between staff and manual workers were introduced in return for the elimination of demarcation restrictions.

Also retained was the group's pipework business, which specialized in the highly technical area of power station and petro-chemical operations. Pipework must be capable of coping with both very high pressures and temperatures in these areas and it represents a complex and specialized area of work for the company. The financial results of the dramatic business and cultural changes faced by Whessoe began almost immediately with healthy profit margins, the ability to raise capital through the City and the improved valuation placed on the company by the City.

The next phase for the company is to build on its established international base to expand into other countries and to capture the benefits of the integration of the different products across all markets. Companies in the group are encouraged to sell each others' products and to learn from each other in developing new applications and markets. The culture change achieved was from a heavy engineering company locked into the quality of its product, to an engineering company driven by profit and performance.

Adapted from: Levi, J (1993) Whessoe's culture change works wonders. Management Today, May, pp 36–42.

- Being close to the customer. Accepting that the market determines what will be successful drives a desire to get close to the customer in order to understand their needs. It also implies a depth of relationship within which it would be difficult to 'hurt each other', a necessary prerequisite for an effective future.

- Autonomy and entrepreneurship. The recognition that too much control from the centre stifles creative development. Employees should be encouraged to contribute and take risks in pursuit of products and services that effectively meet the needs of customers.

- Productivity through people. Acceptance that it is individual employees who deliver productivity in the dynamic, real-time world of organizations. Consequently, it is necessary for all employees to seek to perform better and all the management practices should support this ideal. It also recognizes that peer group pressure can be a major stimulant to the delivered performance.

- Hands-on, value driven. The philosophy of the organization needs to be seen by all employees as a clear set of values that all can subscribe to. The hands-on perspective allows managers to personally experience all aspects of the organization through their presence where the work is done. It also allows an opportunity to reinforce the organization's values to employees.

- Stick to the knitting. By staying close to those products and services that the organization already has experience of, the degree of risk is reduced. Management will have an understanding of the supply chain from beginning to final consumption, together with the problems and opportunities. Moves into unfamiliar territory reduce the depth of knowledge making the risk of failure that much higher.

- Simple form, lean staff. The temptation to elaborate organizational design and the accompanying systems and procedures should be resisted. Unless organizations are careful, they run the risk of creating situations where the level of bureaucracy stifles the creative and entrepreneurial spirit that generates growth.

- Simultaneous loose–tight control. The ability to achieve a balance between these two competing pressures creates effectiveness in operational terms. Peters and Waterman go further by suggesting that it is necessary to provide effective control without limiting the freedom of action necessary to take advantage of the circumstances pertaining at the time.

The ideas developed by Peters and Waterman have been subjected to considerable criticism. A number of the organizations that they identified as excellent very quickly ran into problems in the recessionary markets of the early to mid-1980s. Peters himself produced work which he claimed superseded the above ideas. For example, in *Thriving on Chaos* (1989) he describes even more radical approaches to dealing with the turbulence from market uncertainty.

Management in Action 11.3 provides an insight into the ideas of another writer who wants to encourage radical approaches to how culture can be used to influence corporate activity.

Management in Action 11.3

Secrets of the Semler effect

Semco is a company based in Brazil. Nothing special in that, it could be argued. However, the company is headed by someone very special. Ricardo Semler took over the company from his father at the beginning of the 1980s when he was just 21 years old. Since then he has taken the manufacturer of pumps, mixers and other industrial equipment to new heights, with sales growing by a factor of six and profits by 500%. In many ways the company is a vast test-bed for new and different ideas in managing and organizing.

The most startling impact of Semco from the outside is that employees are able to set their own working hours, some are even able to set their own salary levels and everyone from the highest to the lowest has open access to company financial information. The intention is to create a self-sustaining organization which can carry on without an obvious leader. For example, five people share the position of chief executive officer on a six-month rotating basis. Semler takes his turn along with the others.

Semler takes the view that, 'The main goal of a company should be to create an entity which everyone involved in feels is worthwhile. That will then manifest itself in good quality, good customer service'. He also considers that the company is an ongoing project and that change is not a once for all effect, 'Semco is an ongoing project and we think we are only half way there. We need another 10–15 years to finish the job'.

In setting the approach for Semco, Semler picked aspects from many other organizations and systems. Personal freedom, individualism and competition from capitalism. The control of greed and sharing of information and power from socialism. The flexibility of the Japanese was also added, although not the veneration of elders or strong ties to the company. The company was about to enter a consolidation phase in its evolution he suggested. For example, only about 25% of employees set their own salaries. Semler would like to see everyone undertaking that role as well as being involved with the financial analysis programmes. He would also like to see the level of working from home increased from the 20% of people who do so for between one and three days each week.

Clearly a sea-change is under way at Semco that influences the way work is organized and managed. Many other companies, researchers and students have sought Semler's advice on how to achieve the same level of success. This advice can now be acquired from his book on his approach at Semco, but Ricardo Semler claims not to be about to become a consultant, selling his vision to others!

Adapted from: Dickson, T. (1993) Secrets of the Semler effect. Financial Times, 25 June, p 13.

Deal and Kennedy's cultural profile

The work of Deal and Kennedy (1982) developed two particular aspects of organizational culture. Firstly, they describe four types of culture based on the effects of the degree of risk and the speed of feedback from the environment on decision making:

- Work and play hard culture. The people involved would tend to be a cohesive group that 'attacked' both work and play enthusiastically. This category would be typically found in organizations with low risk but rapid feedback loops.
- Process culture. The emphasis in this type of culture is on the systems and procedures associated with the organization. It is typified by a low-risk environment with a slow feedback response. Success comes from attention to detail.

■ Macho culture. This type of culture is associated with high risk and rapid feedback. It implies broadly similar features to the power and person cultures identified earlier. It is a culture based on the individual and the ability of the focal person to be able to achieve objectives.

■ Bet your company culture. The emphasis in this type of organization is on technical skill. The risks are very high but the feedback is slow in coming from the environment. This situation relies on the supremacy of the technical specialists to 'get it right' within the directional guidelines laid down.

The second perspective added by the work of Deal and Kennedy is that of the existence of strong and weak cultures. A strong culture would be evident if almost all members supported it, or if it were composed of deeply held value and belief sets. Table 11.3 indicates those features associated with a strong culture. A weak culture by comparison is one that is not strongly rooted in the activities or value systems of the group.

From the items included in Table 11.3 there are two of particular interest. The hero is a person who personifies the values and actions expected of the true believer in that particular culture. They are used as role models and exemplars for the population at large. The use of ritual and ceremony as the basis of reinforcement of the desired culture is also part of the mechanisms for ensuring that it is internalized by individuals. The importance of ritual and ceremony was demonstrated in a story told by Wright (1979). Retirement parties follow a predicable pattern. The purpose is to provide an opportunity to say good-bye to the 'old guard' and to demonstrate allegiance to the new team and the firm as a whole. As such the speeches and events are usually carefully scripted to meet these demands. At one such event a retiring GM executive broke the unwritten rules by openly criticizing a senior manager much to the visible embarrassment of the others in the room.

Managers frequently seek to inculcate a strong culture in order to achieve the simple form, lean staff type of organization (downsized, or rightsized) identified by Peters and Waterman. However, there is a conflict inherent in this situation in that strong cultures become difficult to change as a result of the depth of commitment and unity created by them.

Trice and Beyer's organization culture

Trice and Beyer (1984) describe culture in terms of a device for providing common meaning for a particular group. They describe eleven elements that go to make up an organizational culture, grouped together under four categories.

Company communications
The means through which culture is described, communicated to the group and continually reinforced across time.

Table 11.3
Deal and Kennedy's strong culture elements

■ Widely shared philosophy
■ Concern for individuals
■ Recognition of heroes
■ Belief in ritual and ceremony
■ Well understood informal rules and expectations
■ Importance of individual contribution to whole

- Stories. These reflect the past and are based on real events but elaborated in the retelling.
- Myths, sagas and legends. These include real and fictional events from the past and reinforce the 'greatness' of the group. They are often based upon activities involving its founders, heroes and other significant individuals.
- Folk tales. These tend to be fictional stories which carry meaning and reinforcement about the group and its culture to new and existing members.
- Symbols. These are the outward and visible signs that express the underlying values of the group. The use of slogans such as 'The Customer is King' reflect the approach to customers which individuals are expected to uphold.

Company practice
These are the activities that organizations engage in that demonstrate the culture in operation and reinforce its importance.

- Rites. An activity which demonstrates that the culture is beneficial to the members and that it espouses worthy goals. Typically it would involve the opportunity for the public reward for some noteworthy behaviour that reinforced the cultural norms.
- Ritual. Refers to behaviour that does not produce work related objectives, but helps to reinforce group cohesion. A gambler may blow on the dice before throwing them, in order to bring luck. Company outings and similar extra curricular activities can often serve the same purpose within organizations.
- Ceremonial. An official visit of a head of state to another country is accompanied by much ceremonial activity. This serves several functions including the importance of the visit for both countries and a reflection of the traditional forms of hospitality and culture in the countries concerned. Similar ceremonial practices are found in most organizations.

Common language
Every organization has its own terminology to describe events and activities. A major part of the socialization of new members into a new group involves them learning the common language for that group. The most obvious examples of this process come from professional occupational groups. For example, engineers must learn the technical terms for the area of engineering for which they are training. This serves to separate them from non-engineers as well as providing an effective form of communication. It also serves to reinforce group cohesion in that it helps to bind together the individuals through common forms of expression.

Physical culture
This reflects the physical nature of organizations and is the tangible reflections of the culture:

- Artefacts. The equipment and facilities provided are a strong signal about the culture. For example, the presence of director only car parking and dining rooms, as compared to single status facilities, provides a reflection of the underlying culture.

■ Layout. The physical layout of the buildings, open-plan offices and integrated work-teams, compared to functional and separate offices provides a reflection of the aims, intentions and operating preferences prevalent within the organization.

Sub- and counter-cultures

In the discussion so far the notion of culture has been used in what might be described as a unifying or integrating context. It binds together the individuals within the organization. However, that is not the only view of culture. It is possible to see culture as a differentiating feature of organizational life. The integration perspective tends to take the organization as a whole as the locus of attention. The differentiation view concentrates at the level of groups within that whole. At this level of analysis it becomes possible to identify differences and inconsistencies in culture (Meyerson and Martin, 1987).

The existence of informal groups within organizations has long been recognized. The existence of departments and functions within the formal organization is another categorization that operates on the behaviour of the people within it. It is hardly surprising that the existence of sub-units within the organization (both formal and informal) would create differences in the cultures operating across the organization. It would not be surprising to find that the organizational culture was a blend of sub-group cultures.

Counter-cultures exist where one or more groups are disaffected and have objectives that run counter to those of the dominant group. Within an organization counter-cultures can exist in parts of the company and can create hostility and anti-management feelings. For example, when one company is taken over by another the integration process can create situations where counter-cultures are created. Managers feel that their previous efforts are being undermined by the acquiring company and that their careers will be blighted in the future. Such resistance is often self-perpetuating in that it begins to isolate the individuals from the main groups and increases the value of the counter-culture to the deviants – as they become regarded.

It can also be argued that as the culture within society changes the dominant culture within an organization comes under pressure to change. This can be described as cultural diversity, or perhaps more accurately cultural fragmentation. One example of this type of cultural influence is indicated through the growing significance of women and ethnic groups in organizational life. Over the past few years there has been moves to more effectively integrate women and people from ethnic minority groups into mainstream organizational careers and jobs. Whilst reflecting changes in society as a whole, this requires changes in the white-male dominated organizational cultures of the past.

The usual description of culture being an integration process can be described as a limited perspective. The existence of sub- and counter-cultures forces consideration of disunity and even conflict as part of the cultural milieu. For example the UK record of industrial action has been very poor in the past, with an average of 3.2 million working days being lost each year between 1950 and 1967 due to strikes. This increased to 11.7 million days average each year between 1968 and 1980 (Salamon, 1992, p 388). This is a clear indicator of the power of counter-cultures as the trade union movement rejected the managerial perspective on how industry should function and the distribution of the rewards available to the workers for their contribution.

The role of human resource managers in attempting to achieve appropriate cultures is illustrated in Management in Action 11.4 overleaf. Part of this process is to ensure that improvements to industrial relations practice achieve higher levels of harmony and commitment to management's objectives. To achieve unity of culture in practise.

The determinants of culture

In the early days of an organization the culture is very much dependent upon the founders, their personalities and preferred ways of doing things. There are a number of parallels between this type of development of a culture and the Tuckman and Jensen (1977) stages in small group development. For example, employees must first get to know the boss and their way of doing things. This is followed by a period of adjustment as both parties become accustomed to working with each other, etc. Handy (1993) indicates a number of influences on the culture of an organization:

■ History and ownership. In a very real sense culture is something that is independent of most individuals within the organization. It existed before they joined it, and will exist after they leave it. The type of ownership will also have an impact on the culture of the organization. For example, a small company owned by an authoritarian figure will be managed in a totally different way to that owned by a humane bureaucrat. The corresponding cultures will also be different. Working for a US multinational company compared to a French equivalent will be different because the cultures and norms of the owners will be different. In these last examples the national cultures from the location in which the headquarters is based would tend to influence the norms, preferences, procedures and policies adopted throughout the organization.

■ Size. Size influences culture if for no other reason than the formality required in the operation of larger organizations. This does not automatically imply that large organizations have cultures that are 'better' or 'worse' than small organizations. They are simply different as a natural function of the scale of operations.

■ Technology. An organization that specializes in the use of high technology within its operations will emphasize the technical skills of employees in the values that govern its culture. Contrast that situation with a company in the service sector where the emphasis is on personal service in dealing with customers or clients.

■ Goals and objectives. What the organization sets out to achieve will also influence the culture. For example, the organization that seeks to become the best in customer service within its industry will seek to incorporate values inherent in that idea into the culture. The converse is also true, that culture influences the objectives being sought.

■ Environment. The organizational environment is made up of several independent and interdependent elements. There are the customer markets, the supplier markets, the financial markets, the governmental influences, competitor markets and the environmental lobby, to name just a few. The way that an organization chooses to interact with each of the elements in its environment will influence the way that it organizes itself and shapes its culture.

Management in Action 11.4

Winning ways with culture

Corporate culture has been variously described as the glue that holds an organization together, or the rock on which it founders. The role of the personnel function in relation to the corporate culture can also be somewhat difficult. As potential 'guardians of the corporate culture', personnel professionals can find themselves cast in the role of the guardians of an outdated culture and therefore vulnerable to be changed along with it. In a recent research project, the Institute of Personnel and Development sought to find out how personnel professionals could function in relation to the development and change of corporate cultures within international organizations. For international organizations there are two distinct types of culture active in any given context. They are the national culture and the organizational culture. There can be very real tensions and difficulties between these two cultural frameworks.

The study was based upon 15 case study organizations each at different stages of cultural 'management'. At one extreme there was a major bank undergoing a culture change programme and at the other a French retail company attempting to retain its 'family' culture built up over 40 years of history. As a working definition of culture the study recognized that corporate culture is largely determined by the environment in which it 'exists', including national values, national, business and customer characteristics as well as economic considerations. The four main determinants of corporate culture were identified as strategy, structure and technology, values and systems, and policies.

One of the key management skills in relation to the management of corporate culture or of any attempt to change it was identified as that of managing tension. Tension arises when the existing culture is being challenged during a change process, or when the components within an existing culture are incompatible. Given that all of the organizations studied had international elements in their operations it was on cross-border management that the study concentrated. It was argued that the approach to cross-border management determined the corporate culture and its management within the organization to a significant extent. A four-cell matrix was created, based on the dimensions of the closeness of the relationship between home base and local site, and an organization being either people or systems driven. The four cells in the matrix were:

- Value-driven. Being people driven and having a close relationship with the home base, this cell implied a common-values approach to culture within the organization. Some common policies and practices would be dictated by the centre, but considerable influence could be expected among individual locations to adapt to local circumstances.
- Centralist. Based on a close relationship with a home base and systems driven, this cell implied a desire to have a corporate culture that would be based on that of the parent company. Policies and procedures determined by the home country and issued to all locations with an implication that they would be followed closely, with little local discretion.
- Local autonomous. Being people driven and with a loose connection with the home base, this cell implied considerable freedom to allow separate cultures to co-exist within the company.
- Pioneer. Being systems driven and with a loose relationship with the home base, this cell implied a strong use of expatriate managers to 'take the message' out to local organizations and run them in line with centrally determined systems. In culture terms expatriates would be expected to epitomize the dominant corporate culture, but have some discretion to adapt to local conditions.

In terms of the role of personnel managers towards corporate culture the study identified several areas of initiative, including:

- Strategic development. The identification of appropriate cultural components and the associated personnel policies.
- Communication. The communication of policies and procedures in such a way that the cultural norms would be reinforced at every location and at all levels.
- Implementation. The encouragement of flexible personnel practices and appropriate training to encourage people to cope with change and to reinforce the desired culture.
- Review. To keep under constant review the people management strategies, policies and practices followed to ensure that they support the desired culture.

The research concluded with the view that diversity represented an important organizational strength not a weakness and that some organizations were making effective commercial use of this.

Adapted from: Baron, A (1994) Winning ways with culture. Personnel Management, *October, pp 64–8.*

- People. The preferred style of work among senior managers, the preferences among employees as to how they are managed both interact in the cultural dimension. If management attempt to enforce a culture that is unacceptable to employees there will be a reaction, examples being industrial action, sabotage, high labour turnover, low productivity, low quality and a need for tight supervision and control. Equally, employees who attempt to force management to accept their own culture are also courting danger, particularly if the preference is overtly anti-managerial. Management may decide that the cost of operations in such a volatile, hostile and confrontational environment outweigh the benefits and relocate.

Management in Action 11.5 outlines some of the strategies that may be necessary if a change in culture is desired, perhaps in difficult circumstances.

National culture

Organizations operate within a national setting. In that sense they are subject to the same cultural forces that act upon every other aspect of life in that situation. The employees of the organization will come from the national cultural setting into the organization. It would be natural to expect that the organizational culture would be based on the predominant local culture.

The *convergence* perspective on the relationship between national and organizational culture suggests that within an organization the national culture is subservient. This implies that organizations are able to separate culture out as consisting of two distinct forms (internal and external). Also that they are able to manage the internal form as necessary to support business objectives. The *divergence* view holds that national culture takes preference and that organizational culture will adapt to local cultural patterns (Lammers and Hickson, 1979). It is not difficult to envisage that both views could be correct in appropriate circumstances. For example, large international organizations that operate according to centralized styles could well display *convergence* characteristics. Whilst on the other hand organizations predominantly based in a specific country are more likely to demonstrate *divergence*. It is also possible that a middle line is likely. That organizational culture will frequently contain elements of national and company preference. In other words, adapting to meet the needs of both head office and local preferences.

Hofstede (1980, 1983) carried out an extensive series of studies over some 13 years into the subject of culture. He defines culture as mental programming on the basis that it predisposes individuals to particular ways of thinking, perceiving and behaving. That is not to say that everyone within a particular culture is identical in the way that they behave. It does imply, however, that there is a tendency to produce similar patterns of behaviour. He developed four dimensions of culture from a factor analysis of his questionnaire-based research data:

- Individualism–collectivism. This factor relates to the degree of integration between the individuals in a society. At one extreme, individuals concentrate on looking after their own interests and those of their family. At the other extreme there are societies that emphasize collective responsibility to the extended family and the community.

Management in Action 11.5

Cultivate your culture

Egan argues that there are often two levels of culture operational in any organizational setting. The 'culture-in-use' represents the dominant culture in any particular context. Organizations would hope that this would be the culture preferred by management and intended to support business objectives. Unfortunately this is sometimes not the case. There is often a 'culture-behind-the-culture' that represents the real beliefs, values and norms that underpin behaviour patterns within the company. These cultural norms frequently remain unnamed, undiscussed, undiscussable or even unmentionable. Egan points out that these covert cultures lie outside the normal managerial control processes. In either case, an espoused or covert culture adds cost or benefit to the organization. Cost is added if the dominant culture hinders the effective operation of the business or prevents it from changing in line with its environment. Benefit is added if the culture enables the business to function effectively.

Having audited the cultural scenario within the organization, Egan proposes a number of strategies for dealing with culture change:

1 Strategies based on business reality.
   ■ Use business strategy as a starting point. A change in business strategy can provide the necessary leverage for changing culture.
   ■ Use contemporary approaches. The approaches over recent years associated with total quality management and business process re-engineering are just two examples of approaches that can be used to lever culture change.
   ■ Use reorganizing as a basis. Restructuring and reorganizing work also provide opportunities for culture change.
   ■ Turn human resource systems into levers. Obvious areas in this category include the use of training and promotion to reinforce the message and move people into other jobs as part of a culture change process.
2 Change linked strategies.
   ■ Action-based approaches. Direct action in areas not apparently associated with culture can produce changes in culture as a consequence. For example a concentration on introducing 'lean production' into a

factory might take some time but in the process many things are likely to change, including culture.
   ■ Crisis approaches. Financial or other crisis situations are opportunities to change the culture. During a crisis, providing everyone accepts that one exists, people are more likely to adopt different behaviours and be willing to consider change across a broad front.
3 Frontal attacks.
   ■ The use of guerrilla tactics. During turnaround situations it is frequently possible to dislodge outdated cultural elements. The use of roving 'hit squads' (individuals with the power to turn up and ask difficult questions) can also be used to begin a culture change process.
   ■ Programme blitz. Simply flooding the organization with training courses and other programmes to promote the new values can also be an effective (if costly) way of 'forcing' the new culture into the system by 'swamping' the old one.
   ■ Symbolism. The use of symbols to convey powerful messages about both the demise of the old and emergence of the new can also assist in changing the culture. For example it is reported that Lee Iacocca, former chairman of Chrysler, having turned around the company was to be presented with a car by a grateful workforce. They duly made one ready to present to him, only to have him turn it down and ask for the next one off the assembly line. The symbolism being that every car produced should be capable of being presented to the chairman.
   ■ Cultural dissonance. Constant pointing out that the dominant culture does not serve the business can become so annoying that people change, just to stop the constant annoyance.
   ■ Critical mass. Form a critical mass of people who can champion the new culture and encourage them to work on the others in the organization who need to be convinced.
   ■ Imperial approach. Adopting a leadership stance and simply announcing 'what-will-be' might just achieve the change in culture. It is possible that others are simply waiting for positive direction.

Adapted from: Egan G (1994) Cultivate your culture. Management Today, *April, pp 39–42.*

■ Power distance. The degree of centralization of authority and autocratic leadership. The higher the levels of concentration of power in a few people at the top, the higher the power distance score. In those locations with a low power distance score there is a closer link between those with power and 'ordinary' people.

■ Uncertainty avoidance. This is described in terms of how the members of a society deal with uncertainty. Everyone lives in the present, the future remains uncertain and unpredictable. Consequently, ways must be found that limit the potentially negative effects of this. Societies in which individuals are relatively secure do not feel threatened by the views of others and tend to take risks in their stride. These Hofstede classified as weak in terms of uncertainty avoidance. In strong uncertainty avoidance societies there are policies, procedures and institutions that attempt to limit the effects of risk.

■ Masculinity–femininity. The division of activity within a society can be based on the sex of the individual, or it can be gender free. Those societies that Hofstede classified as 'masculine' displayed a high degree of social sex-role division. In other words activity tended to be gender based, stressing achievement, making money, generation of tangible outputs and largeness of scale. In those societies classified as feminine the dominant characteristics tended to be those of preferring people before money, seeking a high quality of life, helping others, preservation of the environment and smallness of scale.

Table 11.4 provides an indication of those countries that exhibit high and low levels of each of the four dimensions identified by Hofstede.

If the Hofstede classification is a valid reflection of the cultural basis of countries and as such a reflection of the major tendencies of most individuals, then organizations need to take these preferences into account. Organizations from particular cultures may be more easily accommodated into locations with similar characteristics.

It is also possible that the Hofstede framework could be used to describe organizations themselves. Hofstede himself considered that power distance and uncertainty avoidance were the 'decisive dimensions' of organizational culture (1990, p 403). This view clearly links organizational and national culture by implying that the preferred ways of managing and organizing in a

	Individualism	Power distance	Uncertainty avoidance	Masculinity
High	USA UK Australia Canada	Philippines Mexico India Brazil	Greece Portugal Japan France	Japan Australia Italy Mexico
Low	Mexico Greece Taiwan Colombia	Australia Israel Denmark Sweden	Denmark Sweden UK USA India	Sweden Denmark Thailand Finland

Table 11.4
Illustration of Hofstede's classification

specific context will be based upon the national tendencies. This assumption is not, however, directly tested. It is possible that organizational culture is composed of different dimensions to national culture.

The research itself can be criticized on the basis of its emphasis on description rather than analysis. Categorization of cultures is inevitably a simplification process based on frameworks and interpretation imposed by the researcher. Although there are statistical methods that can be used to identify clusters of related data (Hofstede used this approach) it is still left to the researcher to interpret the findings. By adopting this approach, Hofstede omits a more detailed consideration of how cultures form, change and are maintained (Furnham and Gunter, 1993). The categorization approach also underplays the variety found within culture. It has already been stated that culture as defined by Hofstede reflects tendencies rather than absolutes. However, as presented the dimensions give no clue as to the degree of difference that could be expected in any context (Tyson and Jackson, 1992).

Frans Trompenaars, who is Franco-Dutch, worked in nine countries for Shell before becoming a consultant to several major multinational companies. He built up a database of the cultural characteristics of 15,000 managers and staff from 30 companies in 50 different countries. In his book *Riding the Waves of Culture* (1993) he discusses several aspects of cultural difference and its relationship with organizational life.

His views contrast sharply with those that suggest that the world is becoming a 'global village', in that he argues firmly that what works in one culture will seldom do so in another. Included in his observations are the following examples:

■ Performance pay. He suggests that people in France, Germany, Italy and large parts of Asia tend not to accept that 'individual members of the group should excel in a way that reveals the shortcomings of other members'.
■ Two-way communications. Americans may be motivated by feedback sessions. Germans, however, find them, 'enforced admissions of failure'.
■ Decentralization and delegation. These approaches might work well in Anglo-Saxon cultures, Scandinavia, The Netherlands and Germany. They are likely to fail in Belgium, France and Spain.

Trompenaars identifies seven dimensions of culture. Five deal with the way people interact with each other. A sixth deals with people's perspective on time and the seventh concerns the approach to moulding the environment. These combine to create different corporate cultures including:

■ Family. Typically found in Japan, India, Belgium, Italy, Spain and among small French companies. Hierarchical in structure with the leader playing a 'father figure' within the organization. Praise can frequently be a better motivator than money in such cultures.
■ Eiffel Tower. Large French companies typify this culture, as might be expected from the title. It also embraces some German and Dutch companies. Hierarchical in structure, very impersonal, rule driven and slow to adapt to change are the dominant characteristics of such companies.
■ Guided missile. Typical of American companies, and to a lesser extent found in the UK. Egalitarian and strongly individualistic with a measure of impersonality for 'good measure'. Capable of adjusting course quickly, but not completely.

Management in Action 11.6

Bridging the divide

Japan frequently appears to outsiders to be very modern, high tech, and sophisticated. Yet just under the surface lies a culture that goes back many centuries with modern society retaining many of the ancient business practices and traditions. Walter Bruderer lived in Japan for 10 years and offers the following pointers to getting off to a good start when seeking to do business in that country:

■ Establish good relationships. The Japanese tend to be rather formal in the rituals associated with the start of a relationship. A slow start is regarded as a judicious way to begin a potentially long lasting relationship. A valuable business relationship requires careful cultivation, sales calls, courtesy visits, perhaps an occasional lunch or other social event.

■ Describe your organization. As well as getting to know the individual, Japanese business people expect to get to know the companies with whom they do business. Taking time to explain the company and its aims and intentions in relation to Japan are important.

■ Meetings. Arrange a first meeting through a mutual acquaintance by letter or telephone. Once a meeting is arranged do not change it as this would be considered disrespectful. Take time and do not rush between appointments. Be prepared to offer small gifts on a first meeting, perhaps a novelty item from the home country. Do not offer a gift made by your firm as this would be seen as a paltry give-away, not a gift.

■ Knowing how decisions are made. Decisions are frequently made by middle managers, not chief executives. Meeting the president of a company may only be for the purposes of exchanging greetings.

■ Waiting for a 'yes' or 'no'. Decisions are rarely made quickly in Japan. Having made a presentation on a business proposal it would be common to be told that the matter will be considered. This is because of a wish to avoid giving offence and also to allow a full review of the proposal, the company and the individuals. However, once an decision is taken it will be acted upon quickly.

■ Being patient, patient, patient. Traditions, customs and rituals are evident all around the business process within Japan. The most effective approach in this situation is to display patience.

■ Using the Japanese language. The use of Japanese in all literature and promotion material is essential. It creates a feeling of being serious and of wanting to belong. Make use of native Japanese speakers to ensure the accuracy of translations in order to avoid mistakes that might cause offence.

■ Speaking English. For all practical purposes the Japanese are not fluent English speakers. Equally, many people have some ability to speak English. If you have to speak English use simple words and speak slowly. Write down key words and numbers for meetings.

■ Adopting a moderate approach. The Japanese prefer foreign approaches to business to be similar to their own, moderate, low-key and deliberate. The hard driving and argumentative approach is regarded as self-centred, ostentatious, confrontational and the wrong way to nurture a relationship.

■ Dressing. In Japanese companies the conventional dress is plain and conservative. People rarely wish to stand out. The same applies to their perception of foreign business people.

Adapted from: Bruderer, W (1993) Bridging the divide. Financial Times, *3 April, p 16.*

Trompenaars advises companies to avoid a blanket approach to culture, based on the dominant head office variety. Instead he argues that a transnational approach should be adopted, in which the best elements from several cultures are brought together and applied differently in each country. Managers should also be trained in cross-cultural awareness and respect, and how to avoid seeing other people's cultural perspective as stubbornness.

Management in Action 11.6 provides a general insight into how the national culture of Japan translates into ways of doing business as experienced by someone from a Western tradition.

Changing organizational cultures

The discussion so far has painted a picture of organization culture in terms of something that evolves over time and reflects the needs of human beings to interact in pursuit of collective endeavour. Adopting the definitions of culture as 'mental programming' or 'the way we do things around here' implies that culture is a device that should allow higher levels of efficiency to be achieved.

This view of culture depicts it as the glue or cement that holds the organization together. Turner (1986) criticizes the view that culture can be managed, suggesting that it would not be possible to accurately manipulate it because it becomes such an integral part of the organization's fabric. In contrast Lundberg (1985) argues that it is possible to change culture and provides a six-stage programme for achieving this objective:

- **External.** Identify external conditions that may encourage a change to the existing culture.
- **Internal.** Identify internal circumstances and individuals that would support change.
- **Pressures.** Identify those forces pressing for change in the culture.
- **Visioning.** Identify key stakeholders and create in them a vision of the proposed changes, the need and benefits.
- **Strategy.** Develop a strategy for achieving the implementation of the new culture.
- **Action.** Develop and implement a range of action plans based on the strategy as a means of achieving movement to the desired culture.

There are a number of problems with both of the above views. They are equally rather simplistic in the view of culture and the nature of change. To suggest that there is only one culture within an organization is to deny the existence of sub and counter-cultures. Each non-dominant culture in a specific context is likely to seek to increase its own significance. Consequently there are political, power and control perspectives to take into account.

Perhaps, therefore *adaptation* over time is a more realistic perspective on culture. Equally, to suggest that culture is static understates the experience of organizational life. New products and production processes are developed; people move to other organizations and jobs; organizations change structures; competitive pressure results in take-overs and mergers. It is stability that is the exception. The definition of culture in terms that are relatively superficial, ensures that it is more amenable to change (Berg, 1985). For example, if culture were defined only in terms of the symbols used to reinforce it, changing the symbols would change the culture. A tendency to see culture as changeable would tend to push the definition of culture in the direction of concepts amenable to change.

Perhaps the 'problem' is not one of how to ensure that change happens, but one of ensuring that it moves in the right direction. Looked at from this point of view it is possible to reconcile the two apparently opposing perspectives concerning culture change. Perhaps culture can be described as very difficult to change in the short term, but viewed as a continually changing phenomenon, it can be manipulated in appropriate directions over time. It could also be amenable to rapid change in times of crisis.

The significance of culture for organizational design

Culture influences a number of aspects of organizational activity including how people interact in the course of their daily work. For example, the need for close supervision of activity should be reduced if the objectives to be achieved are internalized by the individuals. This is not the only type of organizational influence, there are also connections between culture and structure.

Choice is available to managers in how to compartmentalize activities in order to meet their objectives. This was reflected in the contingency approach to organizational design discussed in chapter 10. A definition of culture in terms of 'how things get done' would imply that structure is at least partly a function of culture. That is not to suggest that culture is a deciding feature in the design of an organization, but it is at least a silent partner in the process. It operates by colouring, influencing and shaping the perceptions and understanding of how things should be in pursuing objectives.

From that perspective culture is an intervening variable. This can be more easily shown as a diagram (see Figure 11.6). It is something that acts upon the forces that are in turn determining the design of the organization.

Figure 11.6 Culture as a design mediator.

Organizational culture: a management perspective

From a management point of view culture occurs naturally, it emerges out of the situation. It is not something that managers have to deliberately design and implement. However, that is not to say that managers should adopt a passive stance towards it. Neither does it imply that they should not, and do not attempt to create specific cultures. Managers have influence on the form of culture within their organizations. The discussion in this chapter has taken the view that there is an active relationship between managers and culture. This is

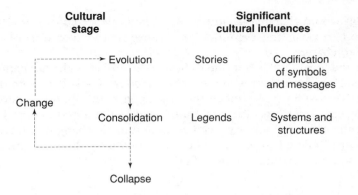

Figure 11.7   The development of culture (adapted from: Payne R (1991) Taking stock of corporate culture. *Personnel Management*, IPM, London).

also implied by Figure 11.7, based on a description by Payne (1991), which emphasizes the *managed* nature of the process.

The culture that emerges over time within an organization may not be an appropriate one for the achievement of the set objectives. For example, it could be that the dominant culture within an organization is hostile to management's intentions. This situation would make it very difficult for managers to achieve their goals. Of course this does assume that the goals being sought by managers are the 'right' ones and that they are the only ones worth pursuing.

It has already been established earlier in this chapter that the concept of culture provides managers with a number of opportunities. For example, a culture supportive of management's objectives should make it easier and cheaper to manage the organization as a result of the acceptance and internalization of the goals by employees. This opportunity manifests itself in three main ways:

■   Control. The existence of a strong managerially based culture should enable control mechanisms to be audit and record oriented. Such an approach would be evident in an organization that operates a *just-in-time* approach to its manufacturing. Just-in-time is an approach where suppliers and manufacturers are linked together in an extended process to ensure that work in progress stocks are minimized and that components are delivered to the user just-in-time for them to be used. Among the effects of this are a reduced need to check the quality and quality of components delivered. Reliance on getting everything 'right first time' is very high. Consequently, a higher level of trust in employees and suppliers 'to do what is necessary' is required. An appropriate culture helps to ensure that this can be achieved.

■   Norms. Culture provides the norms of behaviour which underpin how individuals go about the tasks that they are expected to do. Again, a management supportive culture should ensure that the norms in existence are favourable and automatically enforced through the dynamics among group members. An example of this would be the existence of a 'work until the job is complete' norm. The existence of such a norm among employees would allow managers to have confidence that customer orders would be despatched on time unless a real crisis occurred, as the employees would expect to stay behind until the order was complete.

■ Commitment. This last example also serves to demonstrate the third advantage of culture for managers. That of commitment. A strong management-based culture would produce a situation where employees were generally committed to and supportive of management's aims and objectives. This would be more than simple compliance by employees, it would be active agreement with and support for management objectives.

From a managerial perspective the main problem arises in attempting to create an appropriate culture. It is too simplistic to suggest that managers can decide, design, implement and maintain particular cultures. There are many other features and processes that need to be in place as well. For example, the decision to move towards a more participative culture in which employees are given greater autonomy and authority will fail if it is not supported by appropriate training, encouragement and tolerance of mistakes. Similarly, to attempt to change the culture of an organization without taking into account the structural and procedural dimensions is also likely to fail.

The maintenance of a culture once installed is also problematic. It has already been suggested that culture is subject to continuous adaptation. Consequently, the question of attempting to maintain a static position with regard to culture does not arise as it will change anyway. The problem is one of how to retain direction and alignment with organizational objectives. Assuming that a culture change has been made this process becomes one of preventing the new culture from slipping back towards the old or an undesired one. Assuming that the culture has been introduced effectively then it should not 'slip' as everyone would be convinced of the benefits to be gained from the new one. This is not always done fully or effectively however.

Watson (1994) studied one company in depth at a time when it was undergoing considerable change, including attempts to modify its culture. He describes a number of reactions to this process from people within the organization (pp 109–34):

■ Resistance from all levels.
■ A lack of confidence in the commitment, understanding and ability of senior managers.
■ Confusion about what culture was.
■ A cynical view of culture change being just another initiative designed by senior managers to further their own careers.

This reflects the political and situational reality within which culture exists and evolves. Indeed it could be argued that culture makes the management problem worse. The creation and reinforcement of groups through culture produces the very boundaries that differentiate them and creates separate but cohesive units. In the act of becoming a group an out-group is formed. Out-groups are generally considered as different and in extreme cases regarded as the enemy. In addition, anything that impinges on the way things are currently done is an infringement of the independence of the group and therefore something to be resisted. These are not conducive conditions to the useful application of culture as a managerially supportive concept.

Reference has been made to the existence of strong and weak cultures. A strong culture is one that is very noticeable and which would be actively supported by a high proportion of the members of the organization. A weak culture is one that is not as obvious and which would only be supported by a minority, or not actively supported by more than a few individuals. Strong cultures, if they are supportive of managers, have the advantage of being a positive benefit. A strong managerial based culture is the easiest situation to manage in that everyone has internalized the objectives sought by managers and will therefore function in the desired way. There is unity of purpose and intent. On the other hand strong cultures are less amenable to change, they develop a life of their own. Because of the internalization by individuals of the beliefs and values underpinning the group, ownership is dissipated throughout the population. Consequently the level of ownership (and hence control) in the hands of managers is that much less. Therefore the ability to attempt to direct such cultures is also reduced. It is for that reason that attempts to develop strong cultures (organizational or national) require that a figurehead dimension is also incorporated. In other words an attempt to incorporate a protection device into the culture which allows the retention of a measure of control and influence through common support for the leader.

In terms of organizational structure, culture is one of the internal contingency factors that influence the design (see Figure 11.6). This includes national as well as organizational culture elements. The cultural perspective on organization structure contains two main dimensions:

■ Managing internationally. In one aspect this describes the need to manage across cultures as part of international operations. Once engaged in operating internationally change in the requirements from a culture by the organization arise. Distances in both time and space produce a need to manage differently, as does the increase in scale of operations. This does not take into account the increased interaction between organization culture (which will have emerged within a compatible national culture) and different national cultures.

■ Accommodating cultural diversity. This aspect emerges as the result of the interaction of organizational and national culture. It is too simplistic to suggest that an effective mixing of different national and organizational culture can be achieved. Neither is it possible to suggest that such issues can be safely ignored. People's basic approach to work and organizational responsibilities are developed within a particular national culture. For an organization to superimpose its own cultural norms on that situation and expect that employees will adapt underestimates the strength of existing values and beliefs. This is evident from the work of both Hofstede and Trompenaars discussed earlier. It is likely that some form of accommodation will take place and that compliance will emerge on the surface with local preference being met in the *reality* of activity. For the managers of large international organizations the need to maintain some form of company consistency in culture whilst at the same time recognizing local differences is a major task. It is also one which requires particular sensitivity if problems are to be avoided. Expatriate managers find it particularly difficult to adjust to local conditions and can often fail in their assignments through not being able to balance these conflicting requirements.

Management in Action 11.7 provides an overview of a number of these issues as they were facing the managers of the Channel Tunnel as they began to create operational activity.

Management in Action 11.7

Breaking the executive mould

The opening of the Channel Tunnel presents a number of unique problems for the senior managers running the company. In many international companies there is a definite cultural, policy and procedural bias towards the home country. It is also likely that there will be a distinct cultural distinction between the home country and individual locations, for example the German employees of a US company would expect to be covered by German employment law and local traditions. However, with Eurotunnel this is not practical. With train services operating between a number of countries it is necessary to have a more definite combination of cultures and approaches within a single set of organization structures and arrangements.

Yves-Noel Derenne, the director of human resources for Eurotunnel, indicated that, 'The aim is not to recruit a particular nationality for a particular post, but to get the right person for the job, whether they be British, French, German or from some other country. There are some jobs which we would expect to be filled by one nationality rather than another. The servicing of rolling stock (because this is based in France) would naturally fall into this category. Headquarters for security, on the other hand, will be based in Britain.'

The holders of some jobs, however, will need to be capable of speaking both English and French as the nature of their jobs will require them to move between the two countries and deal regularly with customers and other staff from other countries. For example,

train drivers and traffic controllers are expected to be bilingual, as are customer service personnel, but to a lesser extent.

Alain Bertrand, Eurotunnel's chief executive responsible for transport operations said, 'We do not want a competitive culture to develop, Britain versus France. Unlike other national or multinational companies, which have separate management operations for different countries, we supply a single service irrespective of which country the customer comes from. It is important, therefore, that we establish a single management structure and corporate culture in which safety and customer service are the main driving force rather than nationalism.'

Considerable amounts of time and money have been put into language training for those staff who need it. Two weeks training for front-line customer service staff and four weeks for managers and engineers. The legal and cultural frameworks across countries has also had to be taken into account in designing employment policies. Generally speaking the approach adopted reflects a best of both worlds view of dealing with such difference. For example, French employees are covered by the legal requirement to have works councils and so this has been introduced for all workers. National cultural aspects involving such aspects as after work leisure activities might not be so easy to reconcile. Perhaps the exposure over time to different ways of mixing work and private life together with other aspects of cultural difference may be the only way to ensure that people get used to differences between groups of workers.

Adapted from: Taylor, A (1993) Breaking the executive mould. Financial Times, 4 June, p 14.

Conclusions

The subject of culture is one which influences a wide range of behaviour both within society as a whole and within organizations. It is not a precisely defined concept and is capable of being misinterpreted and manipulated by the managers who must attempt to make use of it in their work activities.

Taking into account the differences in definition referred to above, the concept of culture is generally recognized as being a valuable notion in describing a range of activities and features that are associated with organizational life. New employees must be effectively integrated into the organization if they are to become useful members of the team (as defined by management). It is not possible to manage every person all of the time that they are at work. Some internalization of responsibility and knowledge of requirements must be handed over if efficiency in management is to be achieved. This is where the concept of culture is able to deliver a meaningful way of accounting for these phenomena. However, the notion that culture, particularly strong culture, provides a conflict free way for managers to ensure harmony and the achievement of objectives is simplistic and does not reflect experience (Thompson and McHugh, 1990, p 236).

Discussion questions

1 Define the following key terms used in this chapter:

    Organizational culture   Power culture
    Sub-culture   Role culture
    Counter-culture   Task culture
    Dominant values   Ouchi's theory Z
    Norms   Ritual

2 Discuss the significance of 'culture' in the context of managing an organization.
3 To what extent does corporate culture depend upon national culture?
4 'The concept of culture is of little practical value to managers because it simply describes tendencies and ignores the variation between individuals.' Discuss this statement.
5 It has been suggested that strong organizational cultures are essential to the achievement of success. It has also been suggested that strong cultures could predispose an organization to failure. Can you find an argument that could reconcile these two positions?
6 How would you set about achieving a change in an organization's culture?
7 'The concept of culture is intended to provide managers with an opportunity to increase the level of control without increasing the level of management.' Discuss.
8 In what ways does culture influence the design and structure of an organization?
9 The section 'Cultural forms' describes a number of approaches to the 'form' that culture takes. Which approach most appeals to you and why is it superior to the others?
10 'Culture is such an imprecise term that it is not possible to measure it let alone change it within an organization.' Comment on this statement.

Research questions

1 Obtain about six annual reports from leading commercial organizations. Analyse the information contained in the reports and attempt to identify any connections between culture and structure. What conclusions can you draw about the relationship between culture and structure from the analysis?

2 Identify an organization, a long-standing group or club for example. Use one of the models in this chapter to describe the culture of that organization. In addition identify the major influences on the evolution of that culture and indicate its suitability for the future objectives of the organization or group.

3 For the same organization used in Research question 2, identify the stories, rituals, myths, legends and ceremonials that exist within it. Attempt to identify how these help to inculcate and sustain the culture of the organization.

Key reading

From Clark, H, Chandler, J and Barry, J (1994) *Organization and Identities: Text and Readings in Organizational Behaviour*, International Thomson Business Press, London.

- Bell D: Work and its discontents, p 44. Provides an insight into how organizations and society link together.
- Campbell B *et al*.: The manifesto for new times, p 49. Provides a basis for considering the context of culture and change.
- Pascale R and Athos A: Corporate cultures, p 351. Illustrates the notion of corporate culture and its consequences for the management of people.
- Axtell Ray C: Corporate culture as a control device, p 357. This considers culture as a control process within an organization.
- Höpfl H *et al*.: Excessive commitment and excessive resentment: issues of identity, p 373. Summarizes the notion of culture in an organizational context.

Further reading

Hampden-Turner, C (1990) *Corporate Cultures: From Vicious to Virtuous Circles*, Random Century, London. Provides a readable review of culture in an organizational context.

Kotter, JP and Heskett, JL (1992) *Corporate Culture and Performance*, Free Press, New York. Considers the general issue of culture and its relationship with organizational performance.

Martin, J (1992) *Cultures in Organizations*, Oxford University Press, New York. A well argued and comprehensive review of the subject.

Mohrman, SA and Cummings, TG (1989) *Self-designing Organizations*, Addison-Wesley, Reading, MA. This takes into account the relationship between culture and work organization as part of the design process.

Smith, PB and Peterson, MF (1988) *Leadership, Organizations and Culture*, Sage, Newbury Park, CA. Considers the relationship between the three major concepts.

References

Allaire, Y and Firsirotu, M (1984) Theories of organizational culture, *Organization Studies*, **5**, 193–226.

Barnard, C (1938) *The Functions of the Executive*, Harvard University Press, Cambridge, MA.

Berg, PO (1985) Organizational change as a symbolic transformation process. In *Organization Culture* (eds PJ Frost, LF Moore, MR Louis, CC Lundberg, and J Martin), Sage, Beverly Hills, CA.

Deal, T and Kennedy, A (1988) *Corporate Cultures: The Rights and Rituals of Corporate Life*, Penguin, Harmondsworth.

Furnham, A and Gunter, B (1993) Corporate culture: diagnosis and change. In *International Review of Industrial and Organizational Psychology* (eds CL Cooper and IT Robertson), John Wiley, Chichester.

Garrahan, P and Stewart, P (1992) *The Nissan Enigma; Flexibility at Work In a local Economy*, Mansell, London.

Handy, CB (1993) *Understanding Organizations*, 4th edn, Penguin, Harmondsworth.

Harrison, R (1972) How to describe your organization, *Harvard Business Review*, September/October.

Hofstede, G (1980) *Culture's Consequences: International Differences in Work Related Values*, Sage, London.

Hofstede, G (1983) Dimensions of national cultures in fifty countries and three regions. In *Expectations in Cross-cultural Psychology* (eds J Deregowski, S Dziurawiec and RC Annis), Swets & Zeitlinger, Lisse.

Hofstede, G (1990) The cultural relativity of organizational practices and theories. In *Managing Organizations: Text, Readings and Cases* (eds DC Wilson and RH Rosenfeld), McGraw-Hill, London.

Jaques, E (1952) *The Changing Culture of a Factory*, Tavistock, London.

Kilmann, RH, Saxton, MJ and Serpa, R (1985) Introduction: five key issues in understanding and changing culture. In *Gaining Control of The Corporate Culture*, Jossey Bass, San Francisco, CA.

Lammers, CJ and Hickson, DJ (1979) *Organizations Alike and Unlike*, Routledge, London.

Lundberg, CC (1985) On the feasibility of cultural intervention in organizations. In *Organization Culture* (eds PJ Frost, LF Moore, MR Louis, CC Lundberg and J Martin), Sage, Beverly Hills, CA.

Meyerson, D and Martin, J (1987) Cultural change: and integration of three different views, *Journal of Management Studies*, **24**, 623–47.

Ouchi, W (1981) *Theory Z: How American Business Can Meet the Japanese Challenge*, Addison-Wesley, Reading, MA.

Payne, R (1991) Taking stock of corporate culture, *Personnel Management*, July.

Peters, TJ and Waterman, RH (1982) *In Search of Excellence: Lessons from America's Best-run Companies*, Harper & Row, New York.

Peters, TJ (1989) *Thriving on Chaos*, Macmillan, London.

Salamon, M (1992) *Industrial Relations: Theory and Practice*, 2nd edn, Prentice-Hall, Hemel Hempstead.

Schein, EH (1985) *Organizational Culture and Leadership*, Jossey Bass, San Francisco, CA.

Thompson, P and McHugh, D (1990) *Work Organizations: A Critical Introduction*, Macmillan, Basingstoke.

Trice, HM and Byer, JM (1984) Studying organizational cultures through rites and rituals, *Academy of Management Review*, **9**, 653–69.

Trompenaars, F (1993) *Riding the Waves of Culture*, Nicholas Brealey, London.

Tuckman, B and Jensen, N (1977) Stages of small group development revisited, *Group and Organizational Studies*, **2**, 419–27.

Turner, BA (1986) Sociological aspects of organizational symbolism, *Organization Studies*, 7, 101–15.

Tyson, S and Jackson, T (1992) *The Essence of Organizational Behaviour*, Prentice-Hall, Hemel Hempstead.

Watson, TJ (1994) *In Search of Management: Culture, Chaos and Control in Managerial Work*, Routledge, London.

Wright, JP (1979) *On A Clear Day You Can See General Motors*, Wright Enterprises, Grosse Point, MI.

Part V

The influence of technology

12
Job design

Chapter summary

This chapter introduces the approaches to the design of jobs within an organization. The range of tasks to be performed as part of the organization's activities must be combined into jobs in such a way as to minimize cost. At the same time they should ensure that the individuals employed have something meaningful to contribute and feel committed to the objectives defined by management. The forces impacting on the design of jobs will be reviewed as will the ways that working patterns and practices can contribute to the value of work for employees and managers.

Chapter objectives

After studying this chapter and working through the associated Management in Action panels, discussion questions and research activities, you should be able to:

■ Understand the nature of job design as it impacts on organizational structure and employee perception of the value of work.
■ Describe the main approaches to job design.
■ Explain how work study attempts to influence job design activities.
■ Outline the interrelationship between technology and job design.
■ Assess the contribution of the quality of working life movement and the use of quality circles as an influence on job design.
■ Appreciate how issues such as flexibility and the pattern of work can influence the design of jobs.
■ Detail what is defined by the concept of a job.
■ Discuss how the socio-technical approach to job design attempted to incorporate the need to balance technical, economic and human aspects of operational activity.

browse this web site

www.itbp.com

Introduction

It is inevitable that the structural framework of an organization will significantly determine the type of jobs that exist. The configuration of activity into personnel, finance, marketing and production departments determines the broad area of specialism in the work to be performed. However, that in itself does not fully prescribe the nature of jobs in any given context. For example, within a personnel department it would be possible to arrange for the work to be undertaken by generalists (individuals being involved with all personnel activity) or to split activity into a range of specialist groups (a recruitment team, industrial relations team, etc.).

The design of jobs is frequently based on what has always existed – tradition. Increasingly, the formal design of jobs is being seen as a means of improving motivation, quality and commitment to the organization. This chapter brings together much of the work and thinking around this approach.

The nature of a job

It may seem obvious what a job is. People hold jobs, careers are made up of jobs and jobs form the basis of many stories on television, films and in books. It is widely understood what the job of a police officer or doctor is. However, not all police officers do the same job, some specialize in traffic duties, others in the detection of crime, whilst other patrol the streets, or manage the service. There are different police officer jobs.

Add to this the opportunity for individuals to adapt jobs to their own preferences and jobs can become unique even if they are performed by many people. For example, Roy (1960) identified the use of informal breaks and playing 'games' with fruit as a means of coping with monotony in a particular factory. Through these practices employees maintained some influence over their work activities. It has been suggested that the concept of work as we know it is a relatively new one. Management in Action 12.1 reflects the views of Professor Alain Cotta on this.

A job is a collection of tasks brought together as a practical *chunk* of activity for people to undertake. There is nothing sacrosanct about a job; it is a social construction created and adapted by people, for people. However, within an organization the beneficiary is management, not necessarily the job holder. Therefore the design of jobs serves particular interests. Whilst that is generally true, there are examples where jobs have been designed for the benefit of the job holder. Examples include professions such as the law and medicine. Traditionally it has been argued that entry should be carefully controlled to such jobs in order to ensure the perpetuation of the superior status (and often income levels) of these areas of work.

How do jobs vary? Jobs are usually described as varying in two dimensions, vertical and horizontal (see Figure 12.1).

Taking each dimension in turn:

■ Vertical. This dimension reflects the responsibility incorporated into a job. For example, an assembly line job with no responsibility for checking work,

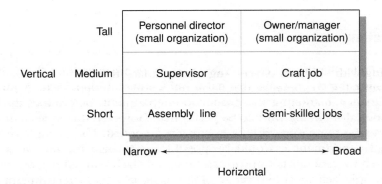

		Narrow ⟵—————————⟶ Broad
Vertical	Tall	Personnel director (small organization) / Owner/manager (small organization)
	Medium	Supervisor / Craft job
	Short	Assembly line / Semi-skilled jobs

Horizontal

Figure 12.1 Job dimensions.

Management in Action 12.1

Why not simply stop working?

Professor Alain Cotta from the Paris Dauphine University argues that the idea of work being an edifying pastime carrying social status is only about 200 years old. Before the Industrial Revolution only people with no other option worked. The more an individual worked, the lower their social status. The Industrial Revolution changed the social standing of work and introduced a meritocracy based upon work having moral value. The change in the perception of work created a situation in which people became part of a new type of 'machine state'. Order was achieved through the direction and control of the work process by the new hierarchy.

Cotta builds on the ideas of Elias Canetti, a Nobel Prize winner who predicted that the machine would replace muscle. Cotta refers to this as the 'neuron prosthesis'. It is based on the reality that, 'More than half of the people are now employed in sectors where they create, release, transfer, receive and utilize information. The crossing of the frontier between muscle and neuron may have as many consequences as the rise of industry.

'People are now looking forward to filling their time instead of producing. Man is trying to free himself from the original painful constraints of work.' Cotta points out that arguments against work today tend to focus not so much on the duration, but on the subordination of individuals to

orders. However as Donkin points out, delayering and empowerment over the past few years have in practice had a major impact on management in that the middle ranks see themselves as having been emasculated and the influence of the senior levels as having been challenged.

Cotta describes the emergence of three groups within society, differentiated by their relations with work:

- Middle class. Defined as those for whom work remains to be endured as their only way to make a living.
- Excluded from work. Excluded as a result of the ever-rising skills needed. Also includes those individuals who have retired, have a private income or voluntarily absent themselves.
- This group choose to work. They include the professions and other forms of work that the individual opts into without the need to.

Cotta does not have a category for the traditional working class. Equally he asks whether progress will create extremes in the approach to work, exclusion and predilection. The pressure on the middle class as their need to work is challenged by technology might well be to simply give up work and opt out. The alternatives being, 'The sentence to death of work or the assertion that it can be the reason for living'.

Adapted from: Donkin, R (1994) Why not simply stop working? Financial Times, *16 November, p 14.*

---

completing records and requisitions would contain very little vertical responsibility. On the other hand, the job of an owner-manager in a small company incorporates considerable vertical loading as the person concerned would be involved at every level of the organization all of the time. One moment they may be helping to pack an order, the next they may be dealing with the bank concerning overdraft facilities.

- Horizontal. This dimension reflects the breadth of activity in a job. Jobs with a narrow range of tasks included are limited in scope, highly routine and boring. Jobs with a broad range of tasks incorporated into them have task variety which can minimize levels of monotony and boredom. At the narrow end of the spectrum simple repetitive assembly line jobs would be found. At the other extreme would be a craft job, where a joiner may undertake the design and manufacture of a single piece of furniture.

A job is not something that is static and incapable of being manipulated by either management or the job holder. Jobs are *things* that can be consciously designed, providing managers with a vehicle through which they can control employees and harness *energy* in pursuit of their objectives. They are also something that provides employees with a basis for protecting a defined area of work, gaining power and an opportunity to relieve the boredom of control.

Management in Action 12.2 illustrates the benefits gained by both parties through multiskilling. Multiskilling involves providing employees with additional skills that would traditionally span a number of craft and semi-skilled areas.

Work study and job analysis

Work study is commonly thought to have emerged through the work of FW Taylor and scientific management in the early years of the twentieth century. The search by Taylor for the *One Best Way* produced techniques used to analyse and define the work methods and pace of work that should be expected from employees. The study of work has a long tradition, however, and there is some evidence that medieval monks used job times to determine the duration of monastery and cathedral building projects. Currie (1963, p 2) also describes an extract from a contract in which an individual undertook to secretly time jobs in a factory and report the outcome to the owner:

> I Thomas Mason, this 22nd day of December, 1792 solemnly pledge myself to use my utmost caution at all times to prevent the knowledge transpiring that I am employed to use a stop watch to make observation of work done in Mr. Duesbry's manufactory; and to take such observations with the utmost truth and accuracy in my power and to give the results thereof faithfully to Mr. Duesbry.

It was Adam Smith (1776) who was first credited with coining the phrase 'division of labour'. This described the increased output per person achieved in making pins by breaking up the overall task into specialized activities. Essentially, work study contains as its core activity two distinct elements: method study and work measurement. The contribution associated with each is reflected in Figure 12.2 on page 366.

Taking each aspect in turn:

■ Method study. There are a range of techniques that enable work methods to be described and analysed in great detail. Essentially the process requires the movement of both employee and material to be charted in such a way as to facilitate critical examination. In undertaking this systematic process a job is designed in terms of the tasks required of the employee being specified.

■ Work measurement. The measurement of work is essentially based upon the use of timing techniques to identify how long particular tasks should take to perform. Having identified the time to undertake the allotted tasks the determination of levels of output as well as of numbers employees and work/rest periods would also be identified.

The application of work study techniques to job design provides management with an opportunity to control not only the design of work but its delivery. This is part of what Torrington and Hall (1992) identify as the disciplinary aspect of

Management in Action 12.2

Clear benefits of multiskilling

Pilkington Glass employed some 1200 people in its two UK factories in 1991. The company specialized in making 'float glass', made by floating a ribbon of heated ingredients on a bed of molten tin to produce clear flat glass panels. Each week the two factories produced about 11,000 tonnes of glass on production lines half-a-mile long. The prospect looked bleak for the company due to a reduction in demand for its products and lower profit levels. The company determined to address its problems from three directions:

■ Creating one business out of two sites. One of the factories was over 100 years old, the other 10 years old. Each ran as a separate business with separate accounting, management and administrative functions. This was rationalized into one business with two sites and so duplication was largely eliminated.

■ Reducing the number of people employed. This was reduced from 1200 to about 900, with plans to further reduce to about 800 being in place.

■ Introducing multiskilling for the remaining employees. As a consequence of the first two changes the need for people to tackle more than one job became very important.

During the 1980s Pilkington had introduced two classes of craft job, either mechanical or electrical. In 1991 this was taken further by incorporating all maintenance within one job. Individuals concentrated on a few skill areas, but they were expected to demonstrate a reasonable ability to deal with any craft area. In the administrative areas these same principles have been introduced, with staff being expected to deal with all areas of clerical work from personnel to finance.

Clearly training was necessary to ensure that all employees had the necessary skills to be able to undertake their new responsibilities. A training programme was developed by Glyn Davies, Production Services Manager, and his training team that was linked to the NVQ national training structures. It was necessary to develop 1300 training modules in total to embrace all the needs of the staff. However, most staff needed only one module to provide them with the necessary skills. About 25% of employees needed two or three modules to equip them to do their new jobs.

The introduction of multiskilling was reinforced by a pay rise for accepting the new working practices. This was further reinforced by the payment of a higher wage when the full level of job flexibility was achieved. Employee reaction to the training process ranged from those that did not enjoy it, to those that found it beneficial and a contribution to improved job satisfaction. Supervisors were also trained as assessors and this improved the quality of supervision provided, according to Davies. The results of the multiskilling exercise also percolated into the output of the factories which doubled, with a higher yield of finished product from raw material.

Adapted from: Littlefield, D (1995) Clear benefits of multiskilling. People Management, 9 March, p 37.

management. Management ensuring they are satisfied that the employee is delivering what is expected under the contract of employment. One way of achieving that is the threat of sanction unless behaviour is appropriate. However, that relies upon negative reward – punishment for a failure to do that which is required. A more effective approach is to reward positive behaviours in which the delivery of appropriate behaviours gains the employee benefits – perhaps a bonus payment for increased output. This is what work study attempted to achieve. It failed to do so partly because of the negative reaction to being *spied* upon – as workers perceived it. This was often with some

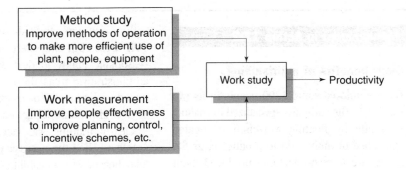

Figure 12.2 Work study (adapted from: Currie, RM (1963) *Work Study*, Pitman, London).

justification as such initiatives were frequently followed by job cuts, demands to work harder for less pay (or at least not a proportional increase) and a generally tighter control of work activity.

Discipline in the sense of control over behaviour is most effective if the underlying values are internalized by the individuals involved. If employees could adopt the same values, standards and norms as management then the job of management would become that much easier. Employees would require less supervision and would naturally function in ways that were supportive of management's objectives. Torrington and Hall identify three levels of discipline active within an organization that reflects this progressive internalization of discipline, as indicated by Figure 12.3.

The lowest level of discipline within an organization is that imposed by management. This equates with the imposition of a particular job design and rule framework by management. The highest level of discipline is associated with self-discipline. If the internalized standards and norms coincide with those of management then the result would be to their advantage. This encourages managers to seek to align employee *frames of reference* to their own. There are approaches to job design that attempt to encourage employee involvement to achieve higher levels of *appropriate* internalization – appropriate to management that is. It has been argued that these *softer* approaches are little more than attempts to achieve the same objectives as work study, but to disguise the objective in providing control with an acceptable appearance.

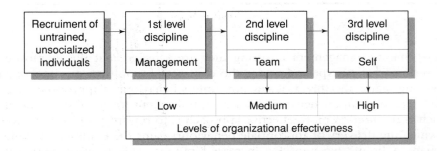

Figure 12.3 Organizational discipline (adapted from: Torrington, D and Hall, L (1993) *Personnel Management*, Prentice-Hall).

Job analysis is a systematic approach to the identification of the content of a job. It can be used to support a wide range of activities, including:

- Resourcing. A detailed knowledge of the jobs to be undertaken within the organization provides the basis for human resource planning in terms of the numbers employed, succession and career development. Knowing the skills being sought provides a means of being able to identify the most suitable candidates. In a downsizing exercise it is essential (to management) to retain the most competent employees; a job analysis would enable the skills required to be identified and matched against the profile of existing employees.
- Training. Knowing the content of jobs allows the skills required to be matched against employee capability. This allows training plans to be developed to ensure that employees are competent to deliver the tasks expected of them.
- Career development. Knowing the jobs that people have done allows career development paths to be identified. Career moves can be planned to provide additional experience and responsibility in order to ensure the appropriate development of senior staff.
- Payment. Job analysis provides the information required for the preparation of a job description. A job description is a document that sets out the duties and other requirements of a job. They are used to determine the relative magnitude of jobs through a job evaluation scheme. The rank order (or scale) of jobs produced forms the basis of the pay structure.
- Performance evaluation. Knowing the tasks that are to be performed by an employee provides a basis for understanding how much work should be produced by an *average* worker. Both of these pieces of information are necessary to determine the performance of an individual employee.
- Equality. The systematic analysis of a job provides a basis for decision making about jobs and people that is not dependent upon gender, race or any other irrelevant criteria. One definition of equality is inappropriate decision making and this is much easier to perpetuate and justify without clear information. Job analysis forces attention onto tasks and activity, rather than who undertakes the work.

There are two main approaches to job analysis, Ivancevich (1992):

- Functional job analysis. This approach requires consideration of four aspects of the work:
    - Employee activities relevant to data, people and other jobs.
    - The methods and techniques used by the worker.
    - The machines, tools and equipment used by the worker.
    - What outputs are produced by the worker.
  The first three of these categories require an assessment of the jobs undertaken and how they are achieved. The fourth involves the type and level of output expected from the employee.
- Position analysis questionnaire. This approach requires consideration of six aspects of the work:
    - Sources of information necessary to the job.
    - Decision-making aspects associated with job activity.
    - Physical aspects associated with the job.

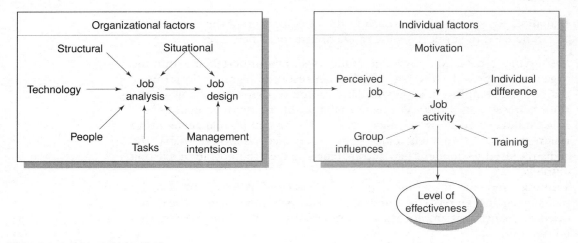

Figure 12.4 Job analysis and job effectiveness.

– Interpersonal and communication necessary to the job.
– Working conditions and their impact on the job.
– Impact of work schedules, responsibility, etc.
In addition to issues surrounding the work to be done, the position analysis questionnaire incorporates an assessment of the people dimension of the work.

Job analysis plays a significant part in the identification of what a job should be. It is, however, only one part of the process. Figure 12.4 reflects the nature of work as being a function of both organizational and individual factors. Two points are worth highlighting. Firstly, *management intentions* are indicated as an influence on both job analysis and job design. This is intended to reflect the decision-making aspects of management's involvement. Secondly, whatever the nature of a job as defined on paper, employees *perceive* and *interpret* the work expected of them and respond accordingly. This process is further *filtered* by such forces as motivation, training, etc.

Technology and job design

Technology influences job design through a number of routes. There is the technology used in the work itself. There are the administrative and procedural technologies that must be complied with. There are the social technologies that influence how people become integrated with the other technologies whilst undertaking the work. Management in Action 12.3 provides an insight into the relationship between people and the advanced manufacturing technology increasingly appearing in factory operations.

The three technologies combine to produce the form that jobs take. For example:

■ Equipment. This category includes the machines, tools and work methods required by the process itself. To extract ore from a deep mine requires tunnelling equipment, conveyor methods of removing the ore and crushing/filtering equipment to extract the minerals. It is not possible to operate a mine with the equipment required for building aircraft. There will

---

Management in Action 12.3

Matching AMT jobs to people

The starting point for considering the design of jobs involving Advanced Manufacturing Technology (AMT) is the level of human intervention necessary. Many system designers attempt to eliminate the use of human intervention in the running of systems, but this has not been completely successful. There are two forms of human intervention with AMT:

- Production intervention. This is a necessary part of the production process. It involves such tasks as changing tools, loading and unloading materials. These occur at predictable times and are necessary because it is not cost effective to fully automate a process.
- Corrective intervention. This is necessary because the system may make a mistake during the production process. These can be machine faults, human error, programming faults or material problems. This category of fault is impossible to predict and so the impact on human operators is difficult to define.

It is in the field of corrective interventions that most scope for job design exists. When a fault arises there are essentially two options available. Firstly call a specialist to diagnose and correct the fault. Secondly allow the operator to deal with some or all of the implications of the problem. Each option has its own advantages and disadvantages. For example, allowing operators to deal with problems may result in a lower downtime, but no operator could be expected to be expert in all aspects of the process and technology. Equally, the need to call out an expert wastes time and the problem may be easily rectified by the operator.

In one case where many corrective interventions were necessary a working party identified changes to the jobs which improved overall efficiency. Breakdowns reduced by about 40% and machine downtime reduced by about 28% after the changes to the job design. This demonstrated that allowing operators greater control over corrective interventions had a direct impact on performance.

In another case the process had a much higher level of reliability. In this instance, poor communications and low involvement in the planning of work caused problems for the workers. Regular communication meeting were introduced and workers were given responsibility for planning daily work priorities. Following some resistance from technical staff and supervisors the changes began to pay dividends in higher productivity and job satisfaction. Senior staff were freed from routine decisions and more able to think and plan ahead, whilst the workers concentrated on achieving the objectives for the current work period.

Adapted from: Martin, R and Jackson, P (1988) Matching AMT jobs to people. Personnel Management, December, pp 48–51.

---

however, be some common equipment: fork lift trucks exist in almost all organizations. In addition, the relative cost of labour is an influence on the technology used, as is the business that the organization is in.

- Administrative. Every organization needs procedures to identify and control the cost of operations. Although there are legal and professional standards to follow there is considerable freedom of choice in how these are implemented in practice. Developments such as just-in-time seek to eliminate much of this administrative process, substituting instead a needs-based *pull system* with flows activated according to a previous plan. Considerable savings in physical stock, time, space and money have been reported by such methods, see for example, Evans *et al*. (1990, pp 712–13, 715–19). They also influence the design of jobs for the workers who administer and manage organizations as well as manual employees.

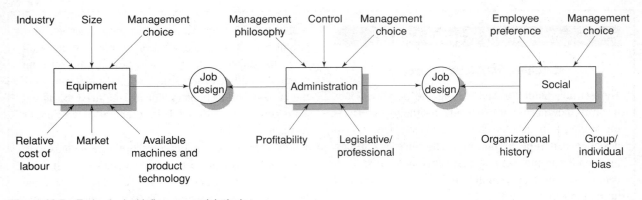

Figure 12.5 Technological influences on job design.

■ Social. With the influences of the two forces indicated above a considerable degree of the constraint in the design process is established. However, there are opportunities for influencing the actual design of jobs through the ways that people are *fitted-in* around these constraints. Examples include the use of teamwork and job sharing. The history of the organization and the way that it has used its employees in the past influences both the choices available for the future and employee preferences. For example, employees who perceive a history of employer exploitation are more likely to be suspicious of new initiatives.

The relationship between these technologies and job design can be shown as a diagram, see Figure 12.5.

Approaches to designing jobs

The tasks to be undertaken in an organization need to be combined into specific jobs. In most situations job design is about changing jobs that already exist. The design of totally new jobs, perhaps on the opening a new factory or department, does exist, but to a lesser extent than redesign. The reasons for job redesign can be many. For example, the adaptation of work to new equipment. It could also reflect an attempt to improve quality or productivity, or as the result of high labour turnover or other signs of employee dissatisfaction.

Simplification and job engineering

Historically jobs were based around whole activities and craft-based skill. Families would engage in the making of furniture, clothes, farming, etc. With the introduction of the factory system this process began to be eroded as opportunities emerged for increasing the output per worker through the division of labour. The notion of the division of labour was observed by Babbage (1832) to reduce training times, increase skill through constant repetition of a small range of tasks, which also reduced waste. Fewer tool changes and machine set-ups were also required as a result of the *batch* nature of production and the specialized nature of equipment to support it.

It was FW Taylor who introduced the scientific management approach to job simplification. Taylor considered that methods of work and equipment should be carefully designed before employees were *scientifically* selected. This approach to job design is referred to as job specialization, job engineering or job simplification. Job specialization because that was the work study aim. Job engineering introduced an engineering metaphor to the process – engineering the one best way of maximizing output and minimizing labour input. The application of scientific management to work produced considerably simplified jobs – hence the third title.

Job simplification involves combining a set of tasks into the smallest size to make an *efficient* contribution to the overall process. It is seen in many production jobs and assembly line processes. In assembly line approaches to production the workers stay in a fixed position and the item being made moves down the line until it is completed. The number of workstations and workers must be carefully balanced to provide an efficient assembly process with minimal idle time. The assembly of motor vehicles is the most obvious example of this process in action. Management in Action 12.4 provides an illustration of job simplification as applied to the slicing and packing of bacon.

Using work measurement techniques the number of operators (and tasks) at each workstation would be determined in order to produce the highest levels of output possible. In the example of the bacon slicing it has been suggested that a balanced line contains eight people. However, it could be that the slicer operator is only working for 50% of the time. Under these circumstances it would be common to recalculate the line speeds or redesign the jobs to keep worker utilization as high as possible.

The aim of job simplification is to maximize output and minimize labour input. Consequently, this approach lends itself to the application of technology in seeking to match human activity to the needs of production. The difficulties associated with job simplification were recognized very early. It can be argued that the founding of the human relations movement was a direct consequence of the de-humanizing effect of such work. As far back as 1952 Walker and Guest identified the dissatisfaction among car factory assembly workers, including:

- Lack of control over the pace of the assembly line.
- Repetitiveness (short cycles) of work.
- Low skill levels required to undertake the jobs.
- Limited social interaction with fellow workers.
- No control over the tools used or the methods of work.
- No involvement in a total product.

This approach to job design is not restricted to jobs in factories. It can also be found in administrative jobs. For example, in accounting departments, someone has to open the post, sort the invoices from the payments and enter the details into a computer system. Such jobs bear all the classic symptoms of job simplification, including monotony, boredom, high labour turnover, alienation and lack of commitment.

Job simplification on a slicing line.

The job involves the slicing and packing of bacon. It involves the following tasks:

■ A side of bacon needs to be cut into slices.
■ The slices need to be collected and stacked together in the pack quantity.
■ The individual stacks of bacon need to be placed into a packing machine.
■ The packing machine needs to be set up for the type of pack to be produced and needs to be operated during the packing process.
■ The packed bacon needs to be weighed, priced and labelled.
■ The packs need to be checked for presentation, label accuracy and quality.
■ Individual packs of bacon need to be put into cardboard boxes ready for cold storage and despatch to customers.
■ The cardboard boxes need to be labelled with the contents and customer details.

The layout below represents the work study approach to the work using a simplification approach.

The simplified tasks in this job involved:

1 Slicing. One person responsible for obtaining the bacon, setting and cleaning the slicing machine and pacing the slicing processes to keep the other workstations fully utilized.

2 Stacking. Four people working on either side of a conveyor belt splitting the cut bacon into stacks of the right quantity as it passes them by. The conveyor belt speed and rate of slicing paces the work for these operators.

3 Packing. One person responsible for setting the machine, placing individual stacks of bacon into it and generally ensuring a smooth operation. They would also monitor the quality of the packed product.

4 Pricing and boxing. One person responsible for setting the automatic weighing and pricing machine, boxing the packs of bacon, sealing and labelling the boxes, stacking the cartons on a pallet ready for transport to the cold store. This person would also monitor pack quality, rejecting faulty packs and stopping the line to reset the machine if necessary.

5 Transport. Someone else would remove loaded pallets and bring empty ones as part of a similar job for other packing stations.

In addition to these direct production activities there would be a need to keep records of output and quality. Also to ensure that the whole process worked smoothly with individuals working as a team.

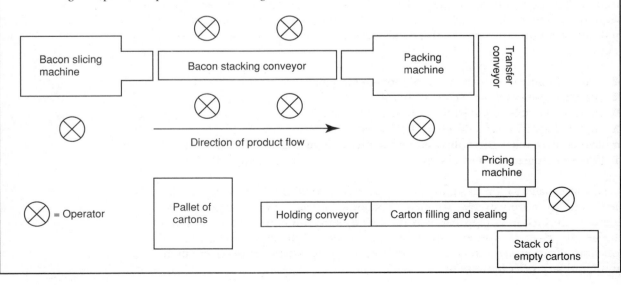

Job rotation

Job rotation as an approach accepts that simplified jobs provide the most efficient methods of work. However, it also recognizes shortcomings that limit the opportunity to achieve the full potential. The solution to this dilemma is for job designers to limit the adverse effects whilst retaining the benefits of specialization.

The simplest solution to this is to combine two (or more) simplified jobs into a pattern of work rotation. Taking as an example the jobs indicated in Management in Action 12.4, there are four different jobs identified in the bacon slicing team. Job rotation requires that each person be trained on each job and then spends a proportion of time on each. This provides some relief from the mind numbing effects of performing a narrow range of tasks all day, every day. The job rotation does not have to be based on a daily cycle, it could be weekly or monthly.

The rotation of jobs does not produce all the expected benefits and can reduce the efficiency gained through job simplification. The argument follows thus:

- Employees must learn a wider range of skills in order to undertake a broader range of tasks. This increases training time and the cost of labour. Also employees claim that their responsibilities and skills are higher and so claim more pay.
- With the reduced practice opportunity as a result of the rotation employees do not build up the same level of skill, speed or proficiency as in single simplified jobs.
- Rotation round a series of simplified jobs does not change the fact that the work is basically mundane, boring and monotonous.

Job rotation can provide a benefit through the ability of employees to take on a wider range of duties at short notice. This provides management with an increased degree of flexibility in labour utilization and an opportunity to cope with unforeseen situations.

Job enlargement

Job enlargement adopts a slightly different approach to job design in that it seeks to build up a job by adding more tasks into it to form a larger job. In effect it seeks to move a job along the *Horizontal* axis in Figure 12.1 towards the *Broad* end of the scale. It adds a wider *range* of similar duties to the job.

The potential advantages to be gained though job enlargement is that the perceived meaningfulness of the work is increased for the employee as a result of the broader range of tasks involved. It is argued that although productivity may not be as high on paper as for simplified jobs, overall it may be higher as employees are likely to be motivated and to have a higher interest in their work. In effect the utilization of labour is likely to be higher and consequently output could also be higher.

It is not always easy to introduce enlarged jobs into a factory as they require a different approach to the interaction between machines and people. It can conflict with the *purist* approach of work study to what should be happening at work. Work study attempts to eliminate or control activity considered to be irrelevant or unnecessary to the main purpose. In many situations this is unrealistic, but it can be difficult to change the control imperative in managing organizations. Imagine, for example, how you could enlarge the jobs described in Management in Action 12.4 without totally changing the layout of machines and processes.

Conant and Kilbridge (1965) provide an early description of the application of job enlargement to the assembly of water pumps in washing machines. The assembly of the pump had been done on a production line with each worker adding components as the pump body went past. The enlarged job allowed each worker to assemble the entire pump but still on an assembly line. The major problem with enlargement as a design option is that it is frequently restricted to simple assembly line jobs, which even when enlarged remain relatively small jobs. Consequently, the benefits to employees quickly dissipate and the job becomes monotonous once again.

Job enrichment

Job enrichment requires that activity and responsibility be added to a job in a *vertical* direction (as defined in Figure 12.1). It is a process intended to integrate responsibility and control over the tasks performed by the employee. Herzberg (1968, 1974) identified six forms of enrichment that designers should seek to include in jobs:

- Accountability. Provide a level of responsibility and support for employees that allows them to accept accountability for their actions and performance.
- Achievement. Provide employees with an understanding and belief in the significance of their work.
- Feedback. Superiors should provide feedback to employees on their performance and work activities.
- Work pace. Employees should be able to exercise discretion over the pace of work that they adopt, and be able to vary that pace.
- Control over resources. Employees should have high levels of control over the resources needed to perform their duties.
- Personal growth and development. Opportunities should be found to encourage employees to acquire and practice new skills and develop themselves through their work.

Another approach to job enrichment was developed by Hackman and Oldham (1980). They suggest that there are five core job dimensions which in turn combine and produce psychological responses, which in turn produce work and personal outcomes (Figure 12.6).

Taking each of the core job dimensions in turn:

- Skill variety. This element reflects the idea that a job should contain a wide range of different skill requirements. In addition the job should contain a wide range of activities and require a broad range of talents from the employee. The broader the range of skill required the more significant the job will be as it will have a longer training period and ensure that the individual is considered as a major contributor to the organization. Individuals vary in their need or ability to cope with variety and it is necessary to create balance in the degree provided and the employee's ability to cope. Too little variety will produce boring and monotonous work; too much will produce fragmented work activity with stress and uncertainty of output for the employee.

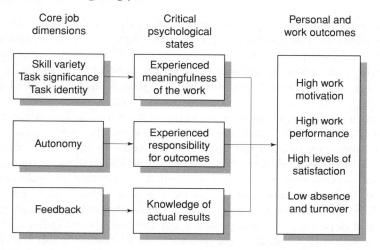

Core job dimensions

Critical psychological states

Personal and work outcomes

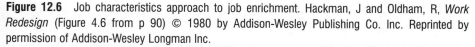

Figure 12.6 Job characteristics approach to job enrichment. Hackman, J and Oldham, R, *Work Redesign* (Figure 4.6 from p 90) © 1980 by Addison-Wesley Publishing Co. Inc. Reprinted by permission of Addison-Wesley Longman Inc.

- **Task identity.** This element is about the degree of *wholeness* in a job. It reflects the degree to which the employee undertakes a complete job. If the employee only undertakes a small number of tasks on part of a whole product then they are unlikely to think about the finished article. Neither are they likely to think that they are engaged in a meaningful part of the operation.
- **Task significance.** The importance of the job being done is of significance to the employee. This aspect is usually reflected through the degree of impact on the lives or work of other people. Very few people would be satisfied with their job if it was felt to be of no consequence to anyone.
- **Autonomy.** This is a reflection of the degree of freedom that the individual has to schedule and adapt their work methods. A closely prescribed job – working on an assembly line – has very little scope for autonomy compared with the job of a sculptor, who has considerable freedom to choose subject, tools and the artistic interpretation. Autonomy provides the individual with responsibility for their actions thus providing a sense of *ownership*.
- **Feedback.** This allows an employee to know how well they are doing in the eyes of others; it also provides an indication of how they fit into the organization effectively. This can be achieved through a number of routes from making employees responsible for whole jobs to formalized meetings with managers to discuss performance, etc. The purpose is to provide a learning opportunity for the individual in terms of performance, quality, integration and contribution.

The first three of the core job dimensions are linked together in Figure 12.6 because they lead to a feeling of relative *meaningfulness* in the job. Hackman and Oldham developed a means of being able to measure the level of job enrichment present in any job, the *motivating potential score* (MPS). The name recognizes the links between job enrichment and motivation indicated in the model.

The score produced through the application of the MPS is essentially a sub-jective response by the job holder, based upon their ability to compare with other jobs that they have experienced. It is a useful, although not altogether objective measure. There is evidence of general empirical support for the MPS, although not strong support for the causal linkages suggested (Wall *et al.*, 1978).

Based on a social information processing view of job design, Salancik and Pfeffer (1978) argue that the assumptions behind the job characteristics approach were open to question. Individuals have basic and stable needs that can be met through work and jobs display stable characteristics that people respond to in evaluating work. They argue that the process of evaluating the value of work for an individual is a more complex process than previously thought. It is a process based upon the social reality for the individual and as a consequence dependent upon a personal perspective of each individual. Man-agement in Action 12.5 reflects some of the debate surrounding job enrichment in car production.

Socio-technical job design and autonomous work groups

The work of the Tavistock Institute brought together the Taylorist tradition and the human relations movement into a single perspective on job design. Trist and Bamforth (1951) studied the impact of the mechanization of coal mining on the work of miners. Traditionally, cutting coal had been undertaken by small groups of skilled miners, supported by a number of labourers. Coal was extract-ed from short *faces* (a seam of coal being worked on) by teams of miners work-ing in groups. The introduction of machines and conveyor belts allowed much longer faces to be worked (referred to as the longwall method). Jobs had to be changed to allow the machines to be used efficiently. The small teams were combined into larger groups organized around the machinery and with a new hierarchical structure. As a consequence a number of other non-work behaviours changed as well. These included poor communications between workers across shifts and jobs; blaming other shifts for problems; increased absenteeism; increased number of accidents; increased stress; and generally deteriorating industrial relations.

Trist and his colleagues demonstrated that it was possible for a particular technology to support different types of work structure. The social and techni-cal aspects of the work needed to be integrated in an interactive socio-techni-cal system. In addition the work needed to be undertaken in an economically viable way. The Tavistock Institute has been involved in many similar studies and has reinforced the application of the *open systems* model of organization and job design in achieving effective operations.

Autonomous work groups are an extension of the socio-technical approach to job design. The job to be done is *contracted* to a work group who then decide for themselves how to undertake it. They effectively become responsible to man-agement for the output and cost of operations. This allows control to remain within the group for job design, work allocation, work rates and work sched-ules. There have been a number of variations of the basic autonomous work group concept. For example, the group can either have a leader appointed by management, or it can elect its own leader as a permanent or rotating job.

Management in Action 12.5

Steering the middle road to car production

The early approach of FW Taylor to the design of jobs was heavily criticized. Experiments by both Volvo and Saab in Sweden in the 1970s to introduce team working (called long-cycle dock assembly) into car production have now been largely abandoned. More recently the introduction of 'lean production' methods by Japanese car manufacturers are also being criticized. So what should managers do as they seek to achieve higher productivity and quality levels and prices that can compete with the lowest cost producers in the industry?

Wickens argues for a middle way involving a synthesis of teamwork, flexibility, continuous improvement and ownership of change as the basis of high efficiency, high quality work and jobs. All work contains two elements – prescribed and discretionary activities. The prescribed aspects of work are those over which the employee has no freedom of choice or action. They are activities that must be done in a specific way at a specific point in time and in a specific place. Discretionary aspects of work are those over which the employee has considerable freedom to choose how, when and where the jobs are done. A senior manager might have 95% of their time classified as discretionary, whereas an assembly line worker might only have 5% of the same category. Wickens argues that the challenge facing job design is to make the work experience as meaningful as possible for those that only have 5% of discretionary activities available to them.

The paradox of production described by Wickens is the need for top-down control of the production process at the same time as achieving commitment from the workforce. In his article he states:

The mistake is to believe that the production system itself gives the results. What counts is the relationship of people with the process. A controlled Taylorist process need not alienate if the workers are able to contribute, and long-cycle dock assembly will not satisfy if that is all there is (nor will it last if it cannot compete). What we must aim for is lean, people centred volume production.

The big challenge is the integration of new technology, new management practices and the people in the new flat organizations. No company has yet got it right. But if we are to have lean production, it must be managed by people who care about people. A synthesis between higher efficiency and higher quality of work and jobs is possible.

Adapted from: Wickens, P (1993) Steering the middle road to car production. Personnel Management, *June, pp 34–8.*

The most famous application of these ideas on job design have been in the Kalmar plant of Volvo, the Swedish car maker. It began operations in 1974 and used teams of between 15–20 people in car building activities. Socio-technical job design is also associated with concepts such as the quality of working life. Management in Action 12.5 reflects some of the more recent ideas on the integration of teamwork in the car industry.

Flexibility, empowerment and patterns of work

The notion of the flexible firm has already been introduced in relation to organization structure. However, it also contains an association with job design. Taking a broad view of an individual's perception of their job then it could be expected that many experiences at work would influence the evaluation process. For example:

- ■ Flexibility. There are a number of forms that flexibility can take. Flexibility could be job flexibility, location flexibility, or temporal flexibility. The opportunity to undertake a different job can help to develop the individual by introducing them to new skills, or old skills in a new setting, or it can simply introduce a fresh location to add variety to an otherwise predictable work routine. Temporal flexibility refers to changing the times of work. Management in Action 12.6 provides a survey indicating many forms of flexibility and some indication of their value.

- ■ Empowerment. Employee involvement in decision making is generally described as empowerment. It could incorporate at its lowest level consultation with a trade union over issues of common concern, or, at the other end of the spectrum, worker representatives on the board of directors. Whatever the particular form, the purpose is to involve employees in decisions relating to the direction of the organization and operational issues. If nothing else then empowerment should provide employees with a stronger view of the whole picture and their part in it, another of the core job characteristics identified by Hackman and Oldham (Figure 12.6).

- ■ Patterns of work. There are many different patterns of work. For example, shiftwork as compared to a daytime only pattern. Curson (1986) identifies a broad range of alternative patterns. Among the options are:
  - Annual hours. Based on variable hours worked each week, accumulated towards an annual total.
  - Compressed week. This provides for a smaller number of working days to be worked, but of longer duration. For example, four days at ten hours compared to five days at eight hours.
  - Overtime restrictions. This can be achieved by providing time off as an alternative to pay, flexing working hours, or simply restricting overtime working.
  - Temporary and part-time working. Allows individuals to choose the amount of time that they want to devote to a particular employer (or job). Of course there is an argument that employers gain an unfair advantage through pay and legislative limitations on protection for such workers.
  - Job sharing and home-working. Job sharing allows two (or more) people to share a specific job, by agreement taking a proportion each. Home-working allows individuals to work at home utilizing computer-based technology to communicate with clients or other employees. In both the employee is able to balance work with other commitments.
  - Sabbaticals and career breaks. This approach allows individuals to balance the various aspects of their life though compartmentalizing activity. For example, university lecturers may apply for a sabbatical in order to undertake some research that would otherwise be difficult to complete. Career breaks can provide a means of an employee with prime career responsibilities to retain a career whilst meeting their other obligations.

The links between each of these aspects of work experience and job design are not direct. Each could influence the ways that tasks are combined into jobs. More likely they are an influence on how the job is interpreted by the employee. For example, employees in a supportive environment in which they have

Management in Action 12.6

Juggling act

Personnel Today and Plantime conducted a survey to find out more about flexible working. Among the practices identified from the research were, part-time working, annualized hours, flexible hours, job sharing, telecommuting and home-working.

Earl's Court Olympia, an exhibitions and catering company, has a number of flexible practices and systems in order to be able to meet the needs of its clients. Jim Black, Group Personnel Director, points out that many exhibition facilities are used out of normal working hours and clients frequently make many last minute demands. So the company needs the maximum level of flexibility possible. For example, within the catering division of the company a database of all staff skill areas and work location and hours preferences is held to allow managers to match individuals to the tasks in hand. The maintenance department uses an annualized hours system (which allows for peaks and troughs in work demand within a total working time for the year) to allocate staff to particular projects.

Some of the findings from the survey include:

- 90% of organizations use part-time working
- 50% of organizations use flexitime
- 26% of organizations use job sharing
- 14% of organizations use annualized hours
- 11% of organizations use telecommuting.

The advantages of fle le working include:

- 40% of organizations report it helps to recruit and retain certain staff
- 39% of organizations report that it improves the ability to deal with peaks and troughs in demand
- 34% of organizations report that it improves flexibility from a management perspective
- 31% of organizations report that it reduces company costs
- 28% of organizations report that flexibility improves morale and it is popular among staff
- 16% of organizations report that it reduces overtime costs.

Some of the barriers to introducing flexibility include:

- 44% of organizations report management resistance
- 30% of organizations report administrative difficulties
- 24% of organizations report trade union resistance
- 24% of organizations report employee resistance because of fears over remuneration
- 18% of organizations report the costs of introducing flexibility
- 15% of organizations report practical problems such as fragmented workforce locations

The results of the survey show that organizations are using a wider range of flexible working practices in their attempts to provide a better match between customer, business and employee needs.

Adapted from: Hall, L (1994) Juggling act. Personnel Today, *8 February, pp 21–4.*

some opportunity to adapt their work and balance their commitments are more likely to see a boring job in a positive light. Management in Action 12.7 provides an insight into how one organization used *teleworking* and *flexiplace* working to the benefit of customers, employees and the organization.

Management in Action 12.7

Flexible work comes of age

Teleworking conjures up all sorts of images, most of them inaccurate. At the Basingstoke offices of Digital Equipment it was found that some employees only occupied their desks for about 40% of the day. Flexible working was seen as a way of retaining key employees and cutting some of the operational costs.

Ian Christie, deputy head of Digital's business design group, spends about half of his time at the Basingstoke office. The rest of the week he is either visiting clients, working from home or visiting other Digital locations. Telephone calls are automatically diverted to his home, his car phone or any other location that he specifies. Teleworkers frequently keep papers and other items normally found around an office at home or in the car. Some members of the 13 strong business design team spend more time in the Basingstoke office than others. The choice is theirs. Each has telephone, computer and e-mail systems provided by the company. When working at the company offices an individual would use one of the six desks allocated to the team. The only 'must attend' requirement is a monthly meeting for the whole group, which can last a full day and provides the only forum for the team to discuss plans, etc.

The team has a group secretary Barbara Prowse, who acts as a traditional secretary, but also undertakes a liaison and co-ordination role for the team. This is not always easy as the individuals can be at any one of a number of locations across the country. Staff are paid a basic salary with an individual performance element (dependent upon reaching targets). In this environment it is up to individuals to determine their own working hours as necessary for the jobs being done. Health and safety is an issue for staff working from home. For those with 'home working' contracts the company undertakes a safety inspection, provides a fire extinguisher and the individual is cautioned about the need for breaks when undertaking repetitive tasks such as sitting at a computer.

The result of the introduction of flexible working in the business design group at Digital has been a reduction in the operating costs of between 25–50% with a doubling of business handled in comparison with other groups.

Adapted from: Merrick, N (1993) Flexible work comes of age. Personnel Management Plus, October, pp 22–3.

Job design, productivity and satisfaction

Job design and productivity are both organizational imperatives, they both feature as management drivers. Job design is about grouping the tasks that need to be undertaken into convenient *chunks* of work. The basis of this decision can be subject to a number of forces including organization structure, historical job structure, employee or managerial preference. Productivity is a reflection of conversion efficiency and therefore cost. The continued existence of an organization is largely a function of its relative productivity within the competitive environment.

The search for productivity and control leads naturally to the job simplification approach to job design, based on the machine metaphor of organizational functioning. This view ignores the perhaps rather obvious truth that people are not machines. The realization of this *truth* led to the adoption of other job design approaches. In the service industries, for example, the contact between employees and customers is a particular feature of the design of both jobs and the service encounter.

A number of job design approaches attempt to incorporate satisfaction into work. This is based on the assumption that workers contribute more if they are happy and feel that they are contributing something of value to something of value. There are three possible links between performance and satisfaction (Petty *et al.*, 1984):

- Satisfaction generates performance. This would reflect the view that job design should aim to produce high levels of satisfaction as this in turn will optimize worker performance.
- Performance generates satisfaction. The converse view is that achievement generates satisfaction. Therefore every effort should be made to improve performance as this in turn will increase satisfaction.
- Satisfaction and performance link indirectly. This holds that the two are linked, but only under certain conditions. Intervening variables such as management style, pressure, personality factors, job design, equity and rewards are examples of the factors that could mediate between the two. Figure 12.7 illustrates this relationship.

In his book on motivation Vroom (1964) provides a clear indication that a satisfied worker is not necessarily a high performer. The relationship is less direct and a function of forces from a variety of sources acting upon the situation. These include, the individual, the job, working environment, management and the personal relationships involved.

Figure 12.7   Relationship between performance and satisfaction.

Quality of working life and quality circles

The quality of working life (QWL) movement emerged from a belief in the need to improve the experience of work for all employees. There is no single definition of QWL but one which captures the breadth of the approach is (Kopelman, 1985, p 239):

> A philosophy of management that enhances the dignity of all workers, introduces changes in an organization's culture, and improves the physical and emotional well-being of employees.

Implicit in this definition is a broad approach to work activity, including job design and the other factors identified in Figure 12.7. It attempts to integrate both organizational needs for a productive workforce and the late twentieth-century expectations that individuals have in relation to work. James (1991, p 16) describes QWL as being composed of:

- A goal. The creation of more involving, satisfying, effective jobs and work environments at all levels.
- A process. Achievement of the goal through employee involvement. Bringing together the needs and development of people with the needs and development of the organization.
- A philosophy. Viewing people as assets to be released and developed, rather than costs to be controlled.

QWL activity tends to be concentrated into eight areas of working life experience Walton (1973):

- Compensation. The rewards for work should be above a minimum standard for life and should also be equitable.
- Health and safety. The working environment should reduce the adverse effects of pollution that can adversely impact on the physical, mental and emotional state of employees.
- Job design. The design of jobs should be capable of meeting the needs of the organization for production and the individual for satisfying and interesting work.
- Job security. Employees should not have to work under a constant concern for their future stability of work and income.
- Social integration. The elimination of anything that could lead to individuals not identifying with the groups to which they belong. This includes the elimination of discrimination and individualism, whilst encouraging teams and social groups to form.
- Protection of individual rights. The introduction of specific procedures aimed at guaranteeing the rights of employees at work.
- Respect for non-work activities. Respect for the activities that people engage in outside of work. Recognize the impact of work activities on private life.
- Social relevance of work. Initiatives to increase the understanding among employees of the objectives of the organization and the importance of their part in them.

QWL initiatives have enjoyed mixed results, partly as a result of the complexity of the issues involved. There are external forces that influence how employees react to company initiatives. For example, the economic climate can either be hostile or favourable to the security of employment aspects of QWL. The activities of other organizations can also influence the perceptions of employees about the actions of their own employer. For example, being seen as following a trend. The wider social environment and attitudes can also influence events. For example, sex discrimination is a function of the prevailing social attitudes among predominantly male power holders.

From the perspective of QWL, job design is an important part of the overall experience of individuals at work. It should be undertaken to ensure that the other seven aspects are not compromised. The use of quality circles has been associated with attempts at continuous improvement. Whilst not part of job design as such, circles can play a significant part in shaping peoples experience of work. A quality circle is described as (Department of Trade and industry, 1985):

> ... a group of four to 12 people coming from the same work area, performing similar work, who voluntarily meet on a regular basis to identify, investigate, analyse

and solve their own work-related problems. The circle presents solutions to management and is usually involved in implementing and later monitoring them. The particular effectiveness of circles depends on these few key features which combine to give them a special character quite different from other proven forms of group working such as task forces. They are not always called circles but it is convenient to use this general term for descriptive purposes. The precise design too will vary from place to place but all circle-like groups follow an essentially standard pattern of approach to problems.

Quality circles originated in the USA but gained wide acceptance in Japan during the 1960s, since when they have been re-exported to the West as a result of their success in improving quality, commitment and productivity. For circles to be successful the members need to be trained in problem solving, communication and team working. They also need to be seen to be taken seriously by managers. There has been some hostility to the concept from trade unions, managers and employees for a number of reasons, including a perceived erosion of power, the need to give up free time and that it was a management attempt to reduce cost.

In introducing quality circles management need to demonstrate their commitment as well as recognizing that by allowing employees to solve problems a shift in control takes place. A quality circle approach to QWL can be suggested to impose a parallel set of structures onto the existing formal hierarchy (Goldstein, 1985; Bushe, 1988). These dual frameworks can become a problem if commitment to the quality circle begins to take precedence over commitment to the formal organization. Potentially becoming a struggle for power, circle members seek to increase their influence over their working life and managers to retain power over activity and agenda.

Job design: a management perspective

Not all jobs are in the gift of managers to design. The professions (law, medicine, etc.) ensure through training and so on that individuals are prepared in a nationally, or even internationally consistent way. This limits the ability of managers to fundamentally reconstruct some jobs. In addition, the more that a particular organization *personalizes* its jobs the more it is necessary to train employees to do the work. This increases the cost of labour which would need to be offset by productivity improvement if commercial disadvantage were to be avoided.

Boring and mundane aspects of work cannot be completely eliminated. They can be simplified, automated, incorporated into other activities or simply reduced in volume, but they are a certain aspect of organizational life. One difficulty with such activities is that personal preference plays a significant part in their definition. What is boring and mundane to one person is not so to another. Some people are able to cope with such jobs in a way which minimizes the negative impact of them. Every job becomes boring at some point in time. No matter how much an individual enjoys their work there are times when it is undertaken less than willingly and a change welcomed.

Managers also have multiple objectives to achieve which influences the design of the jobs for which they are responsible. Cost reduction, efficiency and 'City' expectation all tend to push managers towards job simplification in the

Cutting wages to preserve jobs

Arkin describes two very different organizations that used job sharing as a means of coping with a reduced volume of work. Sheffield City Council experienced a number of financial crises as a result of government spending limits and its own grandiose capital investment projects. Volkswagen found itself with a reducing demand for its cars and the resulting need to cut costs.

Employees at Sheffield City Council agreed to accept seven days extra paid leave in return for a pay cut of 3.25%. All employees including the chief executive were affected, apart from teachers and those earning less than £90 per week. This was one form of worksharing. Trade union officers were able to agree the arrangement with council managers as a one-off process, but were reluctant to attempt the same again. It was felt that employees would not be prepared to accept further reductions in pay or work. It is interesting to note that in the case of Sheffield City Council there was no diminution in the volume of work needing to be done, just the ability to raise enough money to pay for the level of services. The deal struck did allow £7m of savings to be made without creating more unemployment in the city.

Volkswagen had agreed with the engineering union IG Metall and a smaller staff association on the works council that in return for pay cuts of between 10 and 12% a reduction in the working week from 36 hours to 22.8 hours would be implemented. Some departments would work a four-day week whilst others might have found it necessary to work five days but fewer hours each day. Equally, it was not envisaged that the reduction in working hours would apply to managers. They would find it necessary to put in a full week. Equally, a company spokesman suggested that some people may be required to work longer hours to be able to ensure that the shorter hours worked smoothly. As with Sheffield City Council, the company were keen to find ways of avoiding large-scale layoff or redundancy of workers.

In the case of Sheffield, managers were able to avoid about 1400 redundancies through the effect of the longer holidays. Volkswagen were able to avoid about 30,000 people becoming unemployed through the reduced working week. Both organizations argue that this approach allowed individuals to remain economically active, they retained a degree of self-worth, kept the areas in which they lived alive and retained the skills needed within the organizations. So everyone gained from an otherwise difficult situation.

Adapted from: Arkin, A (1994) Cutting wages to preserve jobs. Personnel Management Plus, January, pp 18–19.

search for high work rates at minimal cost. Management in Action 12.8 provides an insight into how two organizations used worksharing linked to pay reductions thereby saving jobs.

To persuade managers to divert time from productive activity through quality circles as an aid to subsequent improvement is not always easy, particularly if the result is to be an erosion of managerial decision making, control and power. The Taylorist notion that managers *think and decide* and workers *labour* is still evident in many operational situations. Many managers are less than comfortable with the notion that employees can and should be empowered to organize themselves through such initiatives as self-managed teams. This can be seen to bring into question the very need for managerial existence. What it does introduce is an issue regarding the design of management jobs. There is an assumption that job design is about the work of people other than managers. In the language of metaphor, perhaps the job of management should be seen as conducting an orchestra, not policing a football crowd. This is about what defines management and leadership.

In deciding what combination of activities should define a job there are a number of factors to be taken into account:

- Operations. There are the operational objectives to be achieved, building domestic appliances or providing legal services for example.
- Philosophy. There are the guiding philosophies of the organization, approaches to empowerment and quality of working life for example.
- Technology. The level and type of technology available within the organization influences the form that the jobs required to support it take.
- Market. A service industry company will inevitably place significant store on the impact of employees on the customer experience. This influences the design of the jobs in question as well as the standards of behaviour expected. Equally, labour markets influence the skills and abilities that recruits can be expected to bring with them. Organizational deviation from *standard* jobs carries with it implications for training and cost.
- History. The evolution of the company and how it approached job design and generally managed its employee relations in the past will influence what is likely to be achieved in the future. This influences both management and employee perceptions and expectations.
- Creativity. The ability to create jobs that are interesting, stimulating, rewarding and enable high levels of productivity to be achieved is a function of the creativity of the people involved. It is too easy to adopt a *follower* approach to the design of jobs and seek to adapt other organizations ideas without thinking them through in the context. Equally, there is never a clean sheet on which to create something new and original on every occasion. Inevitably, therefore, job design becomes a balancing process between these two extremes.
- Political. Managers can use job design as a political tool in defining the control of employee activity. It can be used to reinforce the rights and status of managers, or it can be used to attempt to capture the commitment of employees. It can be argued that by empowering employees in ways defined by managers control is achieved through less directive means.
- Profitability. The level of profit within an organization determines the level of *slack* within the system. A highly profitable organization has the ability to direct resource towards experimentation and the development of alternative ways of working. An organization with little money available will have less freedom to concentrate on anything other than survival. There is an interesting paradox here because it is organizations with little spare money that actually need the best response from everyone to maximize the chance of survival. Situations of scarcity require the highest ability and creative responses from managers and employees in order to break the cycle of crisis.
- Work patterns. The patterns of work such as job sharing and shiftwork also have an influence on the design of jobs. It is not uncommon in factories to find shiftworkers being trained to undertake minor repairs to equipment in order to reduce the total number of engineers required during the working week.

Figure 12.8 Factors influencing job design.

- Preference. If the particular design of a job does not sit comfortably with either managers or workers then something will happen. Managers can initiate a redesign process. Employees can resign, seek alternative work, the level of quality could drop or there may be increased industrial relations problems.
- Risk. The level of risk aversion is also a factor in the job design process, just as it is in many other aspects of decision making. With any new idea there is a risk of failure. A new job design may deliver the anticipated benefits or it may not. It may even make some things worse. The attitude of the decision maker to risk determines how far away from the *tried and tested* they will move.

These influencing factors impact on the design of jobs in both direct and indirect ways. They also act upon the process in subtle ways that are not always recognized by the participants. Figure 12.8 summarizes the impact of these factors on job design.

Conclusions

Job design is something that influences a considerable range of aspects of work. Not just the physical carrying out of the necessary tasks. It can influence the way that the organization approaches the very nature of employment within it. Job design can reflect a belief about the rights of employees to high level involvement in the activities of the company, or it can reflect a basic view of workers being simply flexible (or necessary) alternatives to machines.

Job design is also something that can be used to draw out from employees additional commitment to the objectives of management without any reward other than job satisfaction. In other words, it is a facet of management that can be used to reflect the moral values and beliefs of the people involved, or it can be a form of cynical manipulation. The difficulty lies it being able to identify the proportion of each of these reasons at work in any given context. Anyone who is seeking to manipulate employee commitment for commercial or personal gain is unlikely to admit it.

Consequently a high level of trust is required if radical approaches to job design are to be adopted: trust that managers are not going to abuse employee commitment; trust that employees will not abuse the additional power that they would be given to self-determine work activities (if that were the option chosen). Trust is something that is hard to gain but easy to lose. Unfortunately managers generally do not have a good track record maintaining trust – at least as far as employees perceive it.

Discussion questions

1 Define the following key terms used in this chapter:

Job design	Autonomous work groups
Work study	Job simplification
Quality of working life	Job enlargement
Quality circle	Socio-technical job design
Job enrichment	Job satisfaction
Flexibility	Job rotation
Empowerment	Patterns of work

2 Why should managers be concerned with job design?

3 What is a job and why is job design such a complex concept?

4 If job design is a function of the many factors identified in Figure 12.8 how can work study techniques offer any real value in identifying the most effective design?

5 Compare and contrast the Hackman and Oldham job characteristics approach to job enrichment with the ideas associated with the socio-technical perspective.

6 Why would a satisfied employee not be the most productive?

7 Identify ways in which the job dimensions model (Figure 12.1) can be related to the organizational discipline model (Figure 12.3).

8 How does technology influence job design?

9 In the section 'Quality of working life and quality circles' it was suggested that the introduction of quality circles introduced a 'parallel organization' onto the existing hierarchy. Explain why this might be so, identify the consequences of this for management and suggest how the problems can be overcome.

10 Describe the main approaches to job design and justify circumstances in which each would be the most appropriate to adopt.

Research questions

1 Along with a group of about six or eight fellow students imagine that you are a quality circle within your university or college. Identify some aspect of your work as student that is causing you problems. Identify the causes

of the problems and develop ways of solving them. What implications do
your proposed solutions have for:

- Your 'job' as students.
- The 'job' of lecturers.
- The 'job' of tutorial or teaching assistants.
- The 'job' of university administration staff.
- The 'job of any other people that you identify as having an impact on
  your problems?

2 For the work that you identified in Research question 1 put together a plan
   of action for selling your ideas to the people that you identified as needing
   to change their jobs in order to help solve your problems. How would you
   seek to gain their agreement to help you change their jobs in order to help
   you? Discuss your ideas with some of the people involved and identify what
   factors may limit their ability to do what you would wish them to do. What
   lessons for job design do you draw from this?

3 Talk to about four people that you know that work in different organizations and at different levels. Find out how their jobs were designed. For
   managers, how do they review the design of those jobs for which they have
   responsibility. Compare what you find out with, and explain it in terms of,
   the material contained in this chapter.

Key reading

From Clark, H, Chandler, J and Barry, J (1994) *Organization and Identities: Text and
Readings in Organizational Behaviour*, International Thomson Business Press, London.

- Kumar K: Specialization and the division of labour, p 13. Reviews the way that work
  is structured within society.
- Bell D: Work and its discontents, p 44. Considers some of the parallels between the
  views of work and of religion.
- Dex S: The sexual division of work, p 177. Introduces the gendered nature of work
  and the reinforcement of male domination.
- Cockburn C: Male dominance and technological change, p 197. Reviews the gendered aspects of work and technology in the printing industry.
- Perkin H: The rise of professional society: England since 1880, p 204. Reviews the
  nature of the professions as they emerged as dominant forces in society.
- Illich I: Disabling professions, p 207. Examines the power of the professions and
  attempts to neutralize that effect.
- Herzberg F: Motivation through job enrichment, p 300. An extract from the classic text
  by Herzberg looking at the links between motivation and the enrichment of work.
- Needham P: The 'autonomous' work group, p 310. A case study-based review of the
  introduction of autonomous work groups in a factory setting.
- Atkinson J: The flexible firm, p 337. An introduction to the notion of flexibility at an
  organizational level, which has clear implications for job design.
- Pollert A: The flexible firm: a model in search of reality, p 343. This forms a response
  to the concept of the flexible firm described above.
- Hirst P and Zeitlin J: Knowing the buzz word is not enough, p 345. Reviews the application of flexibility practices in the UK.
- Bradley K and Hill S: What quality circles are, p 364. An introduction to the concept
  of quality circles.
- Hill S: Quality circles in Britain, p 366. As the title implies, this extract provides a brief
  review of the approach to quality circles in Britain.

Further reading

There are a number of occasional papers published by the ACAS Work Research Unit that have relevance to the ideas contained in this chapter. For example:

- No. 27 December 1983. Effective and satisfactory work systems, Geoff White.
- No. 29 February 1984. Employee involvement in work redesign, Geoff White.
- No. 43 May 1989. Quality circles – a broader perspective, Sean Russell and Barrie Dale.
- No. 46 July 1990. Self-regulating work groups, David Grayson.
- No. 50 November 1991. Quality of working life and total quality management, Graham James.

Handy, CB (1993) *Understanding Organizations*, 4th edn, Penguin, Harmondsworth, pp 318–34. Provides a concise review of the topic of job design in broad terms.

Barling, J (1994) Work and family: In search of more effective workplace interventions. In *Trends in Organizational Behaviour* (eds CL Cooper and DM Rousseau), considers the links between family and work roles and examines the assumptions surrounding the interrelationship between job design on family 'well-being'.

References

Babbage, C (1832) *On the Economy of Machinery and Manufactures*, Charles Knight, London.

Bushe, GR (1988) Developing co-operative labour–management relations in unionized factories: a multiple case study of quality circles and parallel organizations within joint quality of work life projects. *Journal of Applied Behavioural Science*, **24**, 129–50.

Conant, H and Kilbridge, M (1965) An interdisciplinary analysis of job enlargement: technology, cost, behavioural implications. *Industrial and Labor Relations Review*, **18**, 377–95.

Currie, RM (1963) *Work Study*, 2nd edn, Pitman, London.

Curson, C ed (1986) *Flexible Patterns of Work*, Institute of Personnel Management, London.

Department of Trade and Industry (1985) *Quality Circles*, National Quality Campaign, Department of Trade and Industry, London.

Evans, JR, Anderson, DR, Sweeney, DJ. and Williams, TA (1990) *Applied Production and Operations Management*, 3rd edn, West Publishing, St Paul, MN.

Goldstein, SG (1985) Organizational dualism and quality circles. *Academy of Management Review*, **10**, 504–17.

Hackman, JR and Oldham, GR (1980) *Work Redesign*, Addison-Wesley, Reading, MA.

Herzberg, F (1968) One more time: how do you motivate employees? *Harvard Business Review*, January–February, 53–62.

Herzberg, F (1974) The wise old Turk. *Harvard Business Review*, September–October, 70–80.

Ivancevich, JM (1992) *Human Resource Management*, 5th edn. Richard D Irwin, Homewood, IL.

James, G (1991) *Quality of Working Life and Total Quality Management*, ACAS Work Research Unit. Working Paper Number 50.

Kopelman, RE (1985) Job redesign and productivity: a review of the evidence. *National Productivity Review*, Summer.

Petty, MM, McGee, G and Cavender, J (1984) A meta-analysis of the relationship between individual job satisfaction and individual performance. *Academy of Management Review*, October, 712–21.

Roy, DF (1960) Banana time: job satisfaction and informal interaction. *Human Organization*, **18**, 158–68.

Salanick, GM and Pfeffer, J (1978) A social information processing approach to job attitudes and task design. *Administrative Science Quarterly*, **23**, 224–53.

Smith, A (1776) *An Inquiry into the Nature and Causes of the Wealth of Nations*.

Torrington, D and Hall, L (1992) *Personnel Management: A New Approach*, 2nd edn, Prentice-Hall, Hemel Hempstead.

Trist, EL and Bamforth, KW (1951) Some social and psychological consequences of the longwall method of coal getting. *Human Relations*, 4, 3–38.

Vroom, VH (1964) *Work and Motivation*, John Wiley, New York.

Walker, CR and Guest, R (1952) *The Man on The Assembly Line*, Harvard University Press, Cambridge, MA.

Wall, TD, Clegg, CW and Jackson, PR (1985) An evaluation of the job characteristics model. *Journal of Occupational Psychology*, **51**, 183–96.

Walton, RE (1973) Quality of working life: what is it? *Sloan Management Review*, **15**, 11–21.

13

New technology and work

▓▓▓ browse this web site ▓▓▓

www.itbp.com

Chapter summary

This chapter is based on the notion that technology inevitably influences both the nature of work undertaken by people within organizations and also the purpose of that work. Technology is not static, it evolves and changes all the time as new applications are found for existing technologies and new technologies are created. It is the intention of this chapter to identify some of the current and future issues that surround the use of technology in an organizational setting. It is not the intention to introduce a technological perspective, rather the behavioural and sociological points of view will be explored.

Learning objectives

After studying this chapter and working through the associated Management in Action Panels, discussion questions and research activities, you should be able to:

■ Understand what is meant by 'New Technology' and how it influences the context and jobs that people undertake.
■ Describe how new technology influences the operational and support activities within organizations.
■ Explain the relationship between new technology and the managerial perspective of organizational functioning.
■ Outline the technological determinism debate.
■ Assess the links between new technology and change.
■ Appreciate the relationship between new technology and rationality in managerial decision making.
■ Discuss the notion of diversity and the potential conflict between uniformity through technology and differentiation.
■ Detail the relationship between new technology and control.

Introduction

Technology is a broad term incorporating social and procedural issues as well as equipment aspects. From a historical perspective technology reflects a process in which human endeavour is oriented towards solving real problems, experimenting with new ways of doing familiar things or simply finding out new knowledge.

Technology is not static. The ability of the ancient Greeks to provide an automatically opening temple door when a particular altar fire was lit must have reflected pure magic to the people of the day (Klemm, 1959). It was certainly an example of new technology in its day. There would appear to be four major implications that emerge from a historical perspective on technology:

- Experience. All technology is *new technology* at some point in time. What we refer to as new technology today will not be so classified in the future.
- Loss. Political, military, religious and social events can conspire to *lose* a particular technology. The Roman occupiers of Britain (around 100 AD) had central heating for their houses. Because such systems would be operated by slaves some of the aboriginal inhabitants would have developed appropriate skills in utilizing that technology. However, when the Romans left Britain, the use of this form of heating died out, not to become widely available until the mid-1900s.
- Erratic. The development of technology does not follow a smooth or continuous pattern across time and location. Military need plays a significant role in technological advancement. One of the effects of the end of the Cold War – the peace dividend – has been a reduction in size of the defence industry as well as the military.
- Human. Decisions relating to technology are taken by people and it can support their objectives. The development of a machine-based factory technology could be used to replace human labour and reduce the power of trade unions. Conversely, the higher skills needed to operate and maintain sophisticated technology increases the power and value of the remaining employees.

This assumes that technology is not fundamentally distinguishable from new technology. New technology is simply new at a particular point in time. However, that is not the only interpretation of the term. Usage today implies that new technology incorporates computer-based technology. It is a term used in a specific sense reflecting the application of a particular technology. From a historical perspective this would seem to be a restricted use of the term.

Forester (1987) suggests that it is high (computer) technology that allows the development of new techniques that impact directly on work. Much of the computer-based technology is intended to provide improvements in the ability of organizations to process information in one form or another.

Information technology

Information technology argues Zuboff (1988) differs from the technology used in the nineteenth century in only one respect: it combines the replacement of people with machines *and* it provides a higher level of transparency through the ability of computer technology to process information. 'Activities, events, and objects are translated into and made visible by information when a technology *informates* as well as *automates*.' (p 10). It is the control potential from the transparency achieved via the technology that is the *new* dimension to the technology. It brings employee activity into the public domain. With knowledge comes the opportunity for control.

Buchanan and Boddy (1983) suggest four aspects of information handling capabilities that differentiate computer systems:

- Capture. Computer systems are able to passively or actively capture data in a number of ways. The collection of vehicle density through sensors placed on a road reflects an active collection of data.
- Storage. There are two types of storage in computer systems. Firstly, the program that governs the activities of the machine itself. Secondly, the information captured by the system as directed by the program.

- Manipulation. Computer systems are capable of manipulating the information captured and stored. A production line computer system could capture volume and dimension data on items passing across a sensor. It could then automatically calculate a range of quality control data for the production batch.
- Distribution. The information collated can be automatically distributed to anyone with access to the system and entitled to the information. In the case of a quality control analysis, the results could be displayed on a monitor at the worksite for all to see.

Management in Action 13.1 reflects the application of information technology to the computer needs of the Royal Navy, illustrating the Buchanan and Boddy framework.

Management in Action 13.1

Charting a course on high-tech seas

The Royal Navy has about 60,000 employees, all of whom must be paid each month. There exists a need for constant information flows from each of the Navy's ships and shore establishments on the status and movement of personnel. One key area of complexity is that of allowances. There are rules that cover entitlements such as lodging allowances (21 different categories covering London allowances, married personnel and even the use of a houseboat) and service at sea bonuses. It has been estimated that these rules are about 10 times more complex than in most commercial organizations.

Documents arrive daily at HMS Centurion (the central pay and personnel office) from 111 locations around the world. These locations include 42 ships, 12 mobile units, 19 reserve units and 38 shore establishments. Typically the operational personnel staff are a petty officer and a couple of ratings, known as writers. On board ship (or other establishment) this team looks after pay, allowances, leave, travel, foreign currency, cash, and provide advice on promotion, and so on. Each of these 'transactions' requires a record to be made and sent to HMS Centurion. This might be relatively infrequent if a ship is on an operational mission.

At HMS Centurion the data would be 'input' to the computer system and the accuracy of claims checked against the rule framework. About 90% of errors are identified at this point and the original form referred back to its source for checking and amendment, causing delay and additional expense. Frequent changes to the allowance rules caused the system to malfunction on a regular basis. To address the problems an 'expert system' was introduced via a task force headed by Commander Angus Ross. Writers at all locations were given PC terminals and enabled to input information to HMS Centurion directly via modem or satellite link. The system was able to check the accuracy of data before transmission and so improve the quality of information.

The system forces local units to ensure the accuracy of information before they send it, allowing staff at HMS Centurion to concentrate on exceptions and the overall management of the pay system. The benefits in financial terms are anticipated to be reductions in the cost of paying each employee from about £125 per year to around £55 per year, and an improved level of service. This figure is still high compared to an average of £25 per year per employee found in commercial organizations. However, given the complexity of the pay and allowances in the Navy and the nature of its operations, achievement of this level would be unlikely.

Adapted from: Ross, A (1995) Charting a course on high-tech seas. People Management, 9 March, pp 38–41.

It has been argued (Konsyski and Sviokla, 1994) that the failure by management to obtain the full value and potential from information technology is a consequence of the continued use of outdated paradigms of organizational functioning. They claim that *cognitive reapportionment* is necessary if managers are to obtain full advantage. The new paradigm sees organizations as *bundles* of decisions. Decision making being based on an appropriate allocation of *bundles* between humans, systems or a combination of the two.

Information technology is not restricted to computer applications. The portable telephone has made an impact on a number of job functions. Sales staff can be in constant contact with the office and can phone orders directly into a computer system or fax it directly from their car. Compact discs store vast quantities of data for subsequent retrieval and analysis. Electronic mail (e-mail) can eliminate the need for the traditional memo and provide immediate access for senior managers to all employees, by-passing the normal hierarchy. This last point has a number of connotations for open door management policies.

The development of neural networks, imitating human brain functioning, leads the way for the next generation of information processing. For example, the development of expert systems that solve problems in ways that reflect human activity can help to detect credit card fraud by scanning many thousands of transactions on a daily basis.

New technology: applications

The growth in new technology jobs in emerging countries is an aspect of the process that has major implications for jobs and organizations in the West, as illustrated by Management in Action 13.2.

The approach for the following discussion is to follow the major organizational classifications of manufacturing and service, with a section on administration. Few organizations are purely manufacturing or service, most contain elements of both. A theatre falls firmly within the service sector. However, within this sector groups of people will be engaged in *manufacturing* scenery, costumes and the preparation of food for the restaurant. Hill (1983) describes manufacturing being about the production of goods for purchase and *subsequent* consumption. Service by comparison involves the production of intangibles consumed at the time of provision, with the customer taking away the benefit of the service.

Manufacturing

Manufacturing is about making tangible items for subsequent sale. Motor cars, washing machines and toasters are obvious examples. New technology has impacted onto this type of operation in a number of ways. Machines can now process information and therefore demonstrate a relatively low level of thinking ability. This takes many forms and leads to more integration of activity as computers *talk* to each other.

It was the continuous process industries (oil refineries, etc.) that were the first to adopt automation as a means through which they could improve their operational activity. Without wishing to understate the complexity, or the skills of the people within those organizations, it was technically easier to incorporate the new technology of the 1950s and 1960s into such operations. The

Management in Action 13.2

Jobs for all in the global market?

Various predictions have been offered about the high-tech future. Sir James Goldsmith argued that some 4 billion people had recently entered the world labour markets from China, India, Indochina, Bangladesh and the countries that originally formed the Soviet Union. The labour cost being typically 90–95% less than that in Europe. Peter Jay suggested that high-tech development in India was not costing jobs in the UK, but that companies such as BA, BT, and IBM were using staff in developing countries to undertake technical jobs with the results being transmitted back to the UK via satellite.

Crabb reviewed developments in India to find out more about the possible impact on jobs within the UK. India has relaxed its closed economy, tariffs have fallen dramatically and returning graduates with experience of working in the USA have brought a new focus back with them. Salaries for highly skilled new graduates are very low by comparison with the West. For example, software engineers can start on as little as £1000 per year. At about five hours time difference there is sufficient overlap time to be able to engage in telephone communication with clients. There is also a sufficient period of non-overlap to allow uninterrupted access to computer systems on the client's premises. The level of business between the West and India has risen from about $39 million in 1986/87 to $14,200 million in 1993/4.

There are typically three routes for software developed in India to arrive in the West:

■ Outsourcing. Western companies outsourcing some or all of their IT operations to India. This route is the basis of the scenario which predicts the wholesale loss of IT jobs to India. Companies using this approach include Swissair and Lufthansa.
■ Joint venture. A variation of exporting with products developed by 'partners' being taken back to home locations. Examples include Mahindra–British Telecom, Tata–Unisys, IBM–Tata and Fujitsu–ICIM (ICL).
■ Exporting. The normal exporting of software products to the West by Indian companies. For example, London Underground commissioned CMC in India to develop a new train scheduling, signalling and timetabling system. Priced at around £200,000, the 18-month project cost was well below that proposed by European suppliers.

Perhaps Robert Reich in his 1991 book *The Work of Nations* sums up the situation and implications of high-tech development in countries such as India by suggesting that there are three types of worker in the modern world:

■ Routine production worker. The person whose job is moving to ever cheaper parts of the world.
■ In-person servers. Retail workers, domestic helpers, security guards, etc. This category of worker finds that they are being squeezed in wage terms due to competition for jobs and the application of technology to their work.
■ Symbolic analysers. In the UK these workers would be referred to as 'knowledge workers'. This category are the real winners according to Reich. 'If you are well educated, if you have skills, if you are a problem solver, you have a larger and larger market within which to sell your problem-solving skills. International trade is working to your advantage'.

Adapted from: Crabb, S (1995) Jobs for all in the global market? People Management, *26 January, pp 22–7.*

complexity in line and batch manufacturing operations, with the variability of raw material used, the number of discrete processes involved together with the nature of the end product creates a totally different context.

In traditional manufacturing activity the first machine tool was introduced just before 1800 with the development of the screw-cutting lathe. The technology did not change much until the numerically controlled (NC) machine appeared in the 1950s. NC machines were standard cutting or drilling machines adapted to be under the control of a punched tape rather than an operator. The punched tape contained instructions for the machine to drill a hole in a particular location or to cut a piece of metal to a particular shape. Machine centres were the next development of this technology though the addition of a broader range of functions, an ability to manipulate the piece being worked on and automatically changed tools.

Computer numerically controlled (CNC) machines appeared in the 1960s when advances in computing power resulted in paper tape being replaced by a computer. In practice this added back into the machinists' job a degree of choice and skill. Using punched paper tape required that the tape was produced away from the worksite, usually by a different category of worker to the machine operator. This deskilled the machinists' job as the decision making was removed from their work. They became machine minders, ensuring that the machine did what someone else decided it should do. The introduction of the computer allowed a wider range of design and specification data to be held at the worksite. The operator had a need for a different range of skills, based on the application of computer technology. They enjoyed more control of the machining process as a result of being able to adjust instructions via the computer.

Robots with the ability to pick up, move and position items began to appear in the 1960s. They were predominantly used for paint spraying, spot welding and stacking operations. Automatic trains could also follow a pre-determined path around a factory collecting and delivering pallets of components or finished goods. These driverless trains followed a magnetic strip buried in the floor and as computer technology developed were able to integrate a broader range of functions such as self-loading. From these early days there are many apocryphal stories of managers being pinned against walls or run over by runaway trains or robots. These stories, usually told by shop floor employees, often demonstrate that even the robots and computers have an *attitude* towards management. Management in Action 13.3 reflects the trend in the development and use of robots over recent years.

With the incorporation of vision and touch sensitive devices robots can be used for a wide range of tasks within the manufacturing process. For example, the quality and quantity of glass bottles can be determined as they travel down a conveyor belt and pass an electronic eye (sensor) linked to a computer. The dimensions of the bottles can be checked against a model held in the memory of the computer and the quality of the glass can be reflected in light patterns passing through the glass and checked against the norms anticipated. Pass/fail decisions can then be made by the computer about individual bottles and they can be channelled to either packing or recycling accordingly. In addition, records and analysis of quality data can be generated for subsequent interpretation by management.

Advanced manufacturing technologies (AMT) and flexible manufacturing systems (FMS) have also incorporated the computer to create more flexible

Management in Action 13.3

Reaching further into industry

Before 1980 the use of robot technology was considered by many to be expensive, the performance of machines fell short of both expectation and claims and the standard of service was frequently low. Countries with labour shortages and a relatively inflexible workforce tended to adopt robot technology much more rapidly than countries with low labour cost and plentiful labour. For example, by 1993 the USA had about 30 robots per 10,000 people employed in industry, compared to Japan with about 320 robots per 10,000 workers. Germany had about 62 robots per 10,000 workers compared to about 29 in France and 19 in the UK.

Poor robot programming and design frequently created collisions with surrounding buildings and equipment. Poor product design in relation to the use of robots also created difficulties. It is also possible to automate production processes without the involvement of robot technology. For example, the European 'white goods' industries (washing machines, refrigerators, etc.) have been able to achieve high levels of efficiency and automation without the extensive use of robots. Small production batches did not justify robot use according to Professor Arthur Collie from the University of Portsmouth. Very large batches tend to be moved to locations with cheap labour, in turn offsetting any potential advantage from the technology.

Changes within the robotics industry mean that the sphere of application for the technology is wider than at any time in its history. Low-cost robots for use in light assembly are being developed. The automotive industry (the highest user of robot technology) is sub-contracting more of its work and pressing suppliers for cost savings that encourage the application of robot technology. Robots are being improved in functionality and ease of programming. The range of functions that can be undertaken by a robot is being increased to allow faster movement, greater reach and heavier load carrying capacity. All of which should allow for a greater range of potential applications. Robot manufacturers consider that the small- and medium-sized enterprise (SME) market is the one with most potential growth for the new breed of robot.

Adapted from: Baxter, A (1995) Reaching further into industry. Financial Times, 6 June, p 13.

and consistent products. The purpose of such systems is to link together a number of machines so that items can be automatically transferred between them in successive stages of production. They also allow groups of machines to be linked together so that smaller batches of product can be made efficiently. These systems attempt to replicate the economy of large-scale production with small quantities. Small batch sizes with frequent deliveries is a function of what began as a very low technology approach to production, *just-in-time*.

Just-in-time originated in Japan as part of a philosophy of eliminating waste within operational systems. Stocks of raw materials and components are considered as a major source of waste. It is argued that they are only required by managers as a comfort blanket, providing reassurance of their ability to maintain production and to hide problems. Real efficiency comes, it is argued, by removing the stock and allowing the problems to surface. The problems can then be solved once, never to return. The levels of stock can then be reduced further and overall efficiency improved. This is seen as a never ending journey with the aim that components should be delivered instantaneously and only in quantities required for immediate use. This reflects a *pull* approach to manufacturing as components are drawn into the system on demand, not *pushed* into the system based on an intended demand. The methods for pulling components into the production system have frequently involved some very low technology devices including passing pieces of card, switching on lights and rolling a table tennis ball down a plastic tube. This indicates that not everything needs to be based on the computer in order to gain operational advantage, a point that is frequently overlooked.

The design of manufactured items has also been subjected to computer technology. Designs can be drawn directly onto a computer screen through a mouse, drawing palette, etc. These can be interpreted by the computer and converted into three-dimensional representations, parts lists, detailed drawings, etc. The combination of computer aided design (CAD) with computer aided manufacture (CAM) provides a very powerful approach for technology to automatically create and produce products. This can be totally integrated into computer integrated manufacture (CIM). However, this is very difficult and has yet to be achieved on a significant scale with any degree of success.

Evidence concerning the impact of new technology on work in manufacturing organizations is not consistent. Forester (1987, Chapter 6) reviews a number of texts and reports from Europe, USA and Japan that reflect this ambiguity. The major perspectives include:

- Take-up. The adoption of high technology has not been as dramatic has might be expected. In the USA in 1983 only 4.7% of machine tools were numerically controlled – remember these were the first generation new technology machines!
- Cost. Integrated systems are expensive to develop and install. Organizations that have opted for high levels of new technology have not generally enjoyed significant financial benefit over other organizations. However, there are some amazing results claimed: Normalair-Garrett in the UK achieved some very significant cost savings using FMS – labour down from £400,000 to £150,000; output per worker up from £70,000 to £210,000; work in progress held at any time reduced from £690,000 to £90,000.
- Reliability. Very high levels of reliability are required within integrated production systems, the failure of a single component can stop a whole assembly line or island of production. Production systems become more vulnerable than if they consist of individual machines not linked together.
- Japanization. At the end of World War II Japanese industry had to be rebuilt from scratch. Japanese managers were quick to learn from the American consultants helping in this task. In may cases the approaches that the consultants advocated had been ignored by American managers. Less than 30 years later the Japanese began to make significant inroads into American and European markets for cars, motor cycles, heavy construction machinery and machine tools. Western productivity and quality had stagnated and the Japanese were able to offer better products at a cheaper price. The Japanese penetration of Western markets grew rapidly during the 1970s and 1980s, but companies began to fight back – or go out of business. Productivity gains of up to 50% were reported in American motor manufactures during the early 1980s.
- Government policy. Governments in the major industrialized nations adopted different policies towards new technology. In the UK a form of passive facilitation is the best description of the approach adopted up to 1981,

---

Management in Action 13.4

Stretching an old machine

Sir John Harvey-Jones, former head of ICI, visited British manufacturing companies to see how they were coping (BBC1, 1995). He met the senior manufacturing manager of a company making motor cycles. One problem that he discovered was that they could not find component suppliers able to meet their needs for precisely made parts on a consistent basis. This led Sir John to visit suppliers to find out why. These small companies (jobbing shops) have always been the backbone of engineering, making the thousands of components that make up finished products. The company visited was typical of this type of organization with a wide range of machines available to produce the limitless range of components that might be required by customers.

The factory visited contained a number of skilled operators all operating old equipment, some of it 25 years old. The operators maintained the equipment well and applied their craft skills to meeting the product specifications. The owner of the company was very proud of his ability to acquire second-hand machines very cheaply, refurbish them and run them for many years with little cost. The business had also diversified into designing and making new products such as golf trolleys and bedframes without any real market research.

Sir John Harvey-Jones expressed the views that the company was spreading its energies too thinly and that the use of old, refurbished equipment could not meet the exacting needs of customers. Not surprisingly, the senior manager did not agree with this line of argument and suggested that it was the customers that were being unreasonable. He could not accept Sir John's view that the customer needed products made to an exact specification and delivered to a specific schedule. Customers could not operate in a world-class market unless these conditions were met.

Sir John was suggesting that the company did not understand the market that it was attempting to serve. The company operated on a push process – the supplier doing the best it could to meet the needs of the customer. Any deficiencies and faults were either sorted out 'on-the-run' or by the customer accommodating the variation in component supply.

Manufacturing on the basis of guaranteed quality, right first time every time with minimal work in progress was not understood by the company. It is a harsh fact of manufacturing life that there are no prizes for coming second – customers will not buy unreliable product. They will only work with suppliers who can operate according to their needs. They seek long-term, close trading relationships aimed at meeting their needs in the longer term.

Adapted from: BBC (1995) Troubleshooter Returns. Presented by Sir John Harvey-Jones. Number 4 – the series. Broadcast 21 June.

---

at which time the crisis in the machine tool industry as a consequence of Japanese penetration of the market became impossible to ignore. The result was a more positive encouragement of the adoption of high technology through conferences, grants and consultancy support.

■ Employee impact. There can be a considerable saving on labour with the adoption of new technology. Yamazaki (a Japanese machine tool manufacturer) claim that 12 day workers plus a night watchman using FMS can produce as much as 215 workers and four times as many machines using traditional methods. Also lead times (time to make the product) reduced from three months to three days. In the West the reduction of job opportunities as companies cut back in an attempt to slash costs concentrated the minds of both managers and employees on the need for high technology.

In the early years of the application of new technology it was claimed that humans would be replaced by automation. Whilst this has been true to a significant extent it does not reveal the complete picture. New jobs are created by technology – building computers and robots are examples. In addition, different types of jobs are created within organizations adopting high technology, for example computer programmers. Some jobs change as a result of the application of technology. For example, the job of production clerks changes from filling in forms to interpreting the implications of the data analysed by the computer.

- ■ Managerialism. Part of the lower take-up of high technology in the USA and Europe could be the result of low levels of technological expertise among managers. They fail to understand the complexity involved and resist adopting new systems. It is also suggested that where new technology is adopted the full benefit is not achieved because Western managers do not understand how to obtain maximum flexibility from it. An emphasis on short-term results also mitigates against the introduction of integrated technology which requires long time frames to become fully operational. More significantly, 34% of machine tools in the USA were found to be 20 years old. Newer tools are more accurate, consistent and cost effective. Management in Action 13.4 reflects a discussion between Sir John Harvey-Jones and a British manager on this.

- ■ Social factors. The social factors associated with high technology influence general attitudes towards it. For example, the management perspective on control. Braverman (1974) discussed *alienation* and the managerial imperative for control over workers. Shaiken (1985) introduces similar arguments in connection with work in a high technology factory and the demeaning effect on people's lives. The evidence is somewhat contradictory, some studies reporting employee satisfaction with CNC equipment.

Forester argues the negative arguments are not proved because of positive comments and engineers design systems to achieve tasks, not control desires. There are three weaknesses in this argument. Firstly, engineers design systems to a management agenda – they never have a completely free hand as management funds the process and demands influence over it. Secondly, opinion surveys can be unreliable – is an employee seeing many fellow workers made redundant likely to be critical of new technology provided by management? If so, they may be regarded as unreliable or uncommitted. There is no way of knowing if what interviewees say is what they actually believe. The third weakness is that technology can be neutral in principle, but be biased in practice. It is managers who decide how new technology will be used to meet their needs. The commercial justification of a particular technology may not be the only justification active in a particular context. The political, power and control justifications may never be articulated, but that does not mean that they do not exist.

Service

In the service industries a number of the applications are based on similar equipment to that described in the previous and subsequent sections. Among the major elements are:

- ■ Fax. The ability to transmit documents through telephone lines has created a number of opportunities for service enhancements. For example, legal practices can now rapidly send copies of documents to clients. It is also possible for surveyors to visit client properties, undertake an inspection, write a report and fax it to the office from their car immediately after the visit.

■ CD-ROM. Useful as a reference base to enable specialists to interrogate vast quantities of information quickly. In libraries the use of CD-ROM abstracts provides a means of being able to quickly scan publications for items of interest.

■ ATMs. Banks have made wide use of the aptly named 'hole-in-the-wall' as a means of allowing customers access to a wide range of services, without the need for human contact.

■ Laptop/personal computers. The ability of the worker to take computers wherever they go has produced a number of changes to working patterns. For example, some of this book was written on a laptop computer on an aircraft and in a hotel in Malaysia. The networked personal computer has provided opportunities for employees to undertake more activities than when reliant on central mainframes.

■ Medical equipment. The use of magnetic resonance imaging linked to computer-based memory and analysis allows improvements in diagnosis. Networked computer storage of X-ray photography plus associated notes eliminates the risk of loss of the physical records and makes the information available to any appropriate workstation. High-technology equipment in the operating theatre is now a common aspect of surgery.

■ EPOS. Electronic point-of-sale terminals in stores have replaced the traditional till. They can communicate with other computers in the store in order to calculate the day's takings and analyse sales for stock and pricing purposes. They also provide data on customer purchasing habits, volume and time of trade for logistics purposes. They provide a powerful tool in being able to provide information on sales, customer preferences and marketing strategies.

■ Multimedia. This represents the combination of a number of components including television, video, computer and CD-ROM facilities. Management in Action 13.5 describes some of the latest thinking on this particular topic.

The effect of new technology on employment in services has been noticeably different to that in manufacturing. The service sector was just beginning to develop when computer technologies arrived. There has always been a service sector in society, for example, doctors and markets traders. The growth of the service sector was enabled because of the release of labour from manufacturing as a result of technology. People also had money to spend on more than the essentials of life. Jobs have not been obviously lost in the service sector, growth having outstripped this tendency.

There is an unevenness in the effect of new technology on different categories and levels of job across the service sector (Reed, 1989). For example, the history and control of work within the medical profession gives practitioners a much greater say in the application and job impact of new technology than would be available to the staff in a bank. Some occupational groups are more able to control the impact on their jobs and working conditions than others.

Administrative

Prior to the introduction of the computer developments were adaptations of the typewriter and telephone. Forester (1987) indicates that a 1985 UK survey

Management in Action 13.5

Which way now for the multimedia revolution?

The term multimedia was coined in 1975 by Nicholas Negropoponte. The nature of multimedia involves the use of such products as video on demand, pay per view, interactive TV, CD-I and CD-ROM, synthesized databases and value added telecom services. These products can be delivered through a number of systems including cable TV, satellite TV, telephone networks, cellular networks and computer networks. The end users of such systems could include professional groups, corporate clients, educational users and general consumers.

Negropoponte established the Media Laboratory at the Massachusetts Institute of Technology in the mid-1980s. Paid for by 75 of the world's leading corporations it specialized in the development of 'visions of the future'. Each of the sponsoring companies has its own research and development departments with privileged access to the work of the laboratory. The resources available through the Media Laboratory provide the possibility to break free of individual organizational and technological constraints in seeking to identify what the future might hold. Some of the programmes at the Media Laboratory indicating the breadth of its work include:

- The television of tomorrow.
- School of the Future.
- Information and entertainment systems.
- Holography.

'The personal computer of the future knows about your job, the people you work with and what you need to do each day. The computer then helps you to achieve these goals. It takes care of tedious business and domestic chores without needing to be told, it filters out your junk (electronic) mail, telling you only what's important, it re-orders groceries before you have run out, it answers your phone and juggles your diary. It knows when you have a deadline to meet in the morning, so it filters out all but vital phone calls from your boss or customers.' This future sees the computer capable of seeing, hearing, talking and functioning intelligently on its own initiative in helping the owner achieve their goals.

The use of digital signals (rather than analogue) opens up the possibility of 'open' television and the opportunity for the consumer to adapt what is received to their needs and wishes. The consumer takes charge of what they receive, when they receive it and how they make use of it, using multimedia to its full potential.

Adapted from: Ellis, S (undated) Which way now for multimedia revolution? Open Enterprise Computing, *produced by Hewlett-Packard, pp 6–7.*

showed that less than 50% of office workers had direct access to any electronic equipment other than a phone or calculator. By the early 1960s most large companies had a mainframe computer undertaking routine processing of accounting and payroll information. Most computer departments began as data processing departments, often within the accounting section.

The original aim of administrative automation was a paperless office based around the mainframe computer. Administrative systems have been revolutionized through the adoption of information processing. The emergence of management information systems are the forefront of these developments, frequently bringing together expertise in computer hardware and software; centralized data processing; telecommunications management; management of network facilities and support to user departments.

The development of new technology in the office has concentrated on three main areas:

- Convergence. Much of the technology available began as separate pieces of equipment with different functions. This distinction is disappearing with the inclusion of microprocessors in such equipment. The multimedia workstation is rapidly making an entry as the major application of new technology.

- Visibility. The use of networks and data analysis packages allows greater visibility of information among managers. Once the raw data is entered into the system it can be analysed and reported on much more quickly. It is also possible for managers to *play* with the information available to them. Considering questions such as, 'If we reduced the expenditure on x, what would be the consequences?'
- Integration. Integration is not the same as convergence. Convergence is the bringing together of technological difference. Integration is about creating an office system as a single set of processes not a separate set of tasks. It is about being able to undertake several activities at the same time, accessing information sources as necessary to achieve the objective. It might be a budgetary control system as a single process, being able to access, analyse and extrapolate historical records, current information and future plans. All this carried out at a single electronic workstation, perhaps even remotely as a teleworking exercise.

The impact of new technology in the office has not been as rapid as originally envisaged. The computer industry has found it difficult to reach agreement on technology standards which has spawned many different systems that are incapable of interacting and fragmented the market. Many users have found that systems have not lived up to the initial expectations in terms of capability, ease of use, accessibility or speed of operation. Many users have found themselves *locked into* a particular supplier or system and being unable to take advantage of new opportunities. There is a level of cynicism among many managers who find themselves on the losing end (as they see it) of an industry not working in their interests. This inevitably creates a resistance to high technology solutions because of the commitment and risk involved.

The effects of new technology on work in the office can be summarized under four headings (Forester, 1987):

- Employment. Any reduction in the numbers of such jobs is difficult to separate out from the effects of economic downturns and cost cutting to improve productivity. There is also the need to take into account the creation of jobs in the computer and systems areas.
- Job quality. There is a common view that most jobs in high technology involve sitting at a computer screen, typing information into the system for hours. This view sees people being required only because the technology has not developed to the extent that they can be eliminated altogether. Whilst this view of technology is true to an extent, previously armies of clerical staff would have sat at rows of desks making entries in ledgers all day long. It is not clear which job would have the lowest *quality*. In job design terms data entry work can often be automated thus releasing time for analysis, interpretation and action at a lower level in the organization.
- Health and Safety. There have been fears expressed about the impact of prolonged use of computers on the health of workers. This has included the effects of radiation from the computer screen; the impact of constant

use of a keyboard on joints and muscles; and back problems from continually sitting in one position. Research into these issues is ongoing. The problems can be resolved to a significant extent by the use of correct seating and lighting, the introduction of regular breaks away from screens or through keyboard design and usage techniques, see Management in Action 13.6.

■ Social relations. Communication with or through a computer system inevitably reduces or eliminate the opportunity for people to interact with each other at work. There are however organizational benefits to be gained from human interaction, problem solving and innovation being among the obvious. A lack of human interaction can be used as a form of control – the divide and rule principle – leading to alienation and lack of commitment. The relationship between technology and the way that it is used is not automatic, managers determine how the technology will be integrated with employees.

New technology: impact

Structure

New technology can affect structure in a number of ways. The impact will depend upon management discretion and the ways in which the technology is

---

Management in Action 13.6

Piano gives a lesson for the workplace

The use of computer keyboards has dramatically changed the nature of much work within organizations. It has also increased the risk of injury for those using a keyboard inappropriately. Tenosynovitis, tendinitis and carpal tunnel syndrome are just some of the injuries that can be found in this context. Stephanie Brown, a New York-based professor of piano, noted similar injuries among those piano players who did not develop effective keyboard skills. She first noted these problems in relation to computers when she began to use a computer keyboard for the first time. She commented, 'It's well known that certain positions and motions can cause injury in practically every sport. Everyone has had the experience of watching someone swing a tennis racquet or golf club and think, "ouch!" It just looks wrong. Using a computer keyboard is no different. It's a vigorous micro-athletic workout for

the hands and fingers. Do it wrong and you're asking for trouble.'

Brown published a book, *The Hand Book*, to publicize 14 lessons in how to avoid some of the pitfalls to which she gave names such as the 'The cobra', 'The spider' and 'The Flying Pinky'. Athletes warm up before a race and so should computer users. There are also issues associated with injury, such as workstation adjustment, that are given recognition in her book. Some of the do's and don't's when using a computer keyboard identified in her book include:

■ Keep the natural wrist line.
■ Let the wrists float.
■ Let the elbows hang free.
■ Relax the ring and little finger.
■ Don't squeeze the mouse.
■ Rest the hands when not keying.

Adapted from: Boyling, J (1994) Piano gives a lesson for the workplace. Financial Times, *12 January, p 21.*

used within the organization. The impact influences three areas of structural design:

- Scale. New technology can impact on the number of jobs provided by an organization. The large-scale introduction of computers in an office or robots in a factory can be used to cut the numbers employed. Organization structure is a means of compartmentalization based upon the need to manage human activity. If the operation is automated a significant rationale for the structure also changes.
- Function. The introduction of new technology produces a need to accommodate new jobs or even functions within a structure. It is not unusual to find new jobs springing up within existing departments, for example, computer accountant, responsible for seeking ways of using new technology in accounting.
- Integration. The integration of new technology into existing jobs also influences the structure. For example, the use of CAD/CAM allows the integration of designers with production, logistics and marketing specialists. Under such operating circumstances it becomes increasingly difficult to justify the traditional separation of activity into functional compartments. This can be used as the justification for reviewing the structure of an organization.

Where new technology has been integrated into an organization to the extent that it dominates operational activity, Mintzberg (1983) describes the emerging structure as an *adhocracy*. This form of structure is typified by:

- Few levels of management.
- Little formal control.
- Decentralized decision making.
- Few rules, policies and procedures.
- Specialization of work function.

This form of structure can be particularly useful when the nature of the work facing the organization does not fall into regular patterns and the work itself is complex. Typical areas where this form of organization might be seen are in a hospital casualty area, or a consultancy organization where no two client problems are identical or amenable to the same solution. The introduction of expert systems is an attempt to harness some of the decision rules and diagnostic skill involved in such situations.

Job design

New jobs are created by technology; computer programmer is a job that did not exist 40 years ago for example. Some jobs have also disappeared from organizations. For example, punched card operator was an essential job with early data processing computers. It came into existence with a particular technology and existed only as long as direct keyboard entry was not possible. At that time the only way to enter information was to convert data into machine readable punched cards. Many thousands of these were required for every processing operation. A change in the technology eliminated the need for this job to be done and it disappeared virtually overnight.

Other jobs have been changed as a result of the application of technology to the work. For example, secretaries, '... as a group, have been affected by the introduction of word processing and their jobs look set to change further with the spread of computer systems offering electronic mail, diary management, graphics, spreadsheets and desk-top publishing' (Thompson, 1989, p 1). This source goes on to examine a number of options for the ways that the job of a secretary could be changed to make use of technology in becoming a personal assistant. In effect, receiving delegated authority to act on their own initiative on behalf of the superior.

Job performance has been changed through the application of new technology to the training of individuals. Management in Action 13.7 indicates the impact of simulation machines on the training of pilots, ships officers and power engineers.

Management in Action 13.7

Tournament of the skies and other simulations

In Japan, Ishikawajima-Harima Heavy Industry (IHI) developed a simulator to reflect a ship's bridge, but from the safety of a warehouse. To adapt the £6m simulator to any location all that is needed is a set of images and data about local tides and currents. The simulator screens stretch 225 degrees, providing realistic day or night visual imagery. Sound equipment reflects engine vibrations through the floor as well as noises such as metal tearing on impact. The performance of trainees is monitored for later feedback and analysis. In addition to its training use, the simulator can be used to recreate accidents, allowing an investigation team the opportunity to understand what happened.

In the UK electricity supply industry coping with emergency situations that disrupt power distribution is an important requirement. Staff controlling the system can work for many years without experiencing an emergency and so never develop the expertise in handling crises. They have to rely on general training, skill and manuals to assist in dealing with emergencies. With the introduction of a simulator realistic situations can be created that provide exposure to the more likely events. In the North this may be the effects of snow and in the South the effects of a power failure from France or high winds from the channel.

The Royal Air Force has introduced a simulator that can replicate battles. It is impossible to obtain and use the aircraft of possible enemies for practice work in the sky. The development of a combat simulator called 'Joust' was intended to be able to replicate many different flying situations and aircraft types. It is possible to train pilots how to fly in battle conditions and in different flying circumstances without the risk of losing planes or pilots. The increase in skill, reaction times and the ability to fly planes creatively in battle could make the difference between life and death for a pilot facing hostile action. Multiple aircraft can be simulated at the same time, pitting pilots against the machine or other pilots in group flying and bomber protection duties, etc.

Flight simulators are being used not just to train pilots but to examine how they interact with the technology. Monitoring the use of flight controls, reactions to equipment layouts and the medical consequences of flying are all possible with the new £15m simulator shared by Lufthansa and Berlin University's Institute of Aerospace.

Adapted from: Thomson, R and Fisher, A (1994) All at sea from the safety of a warehouse. The human factor. Collapsing the system without getting the sack. Financial Times, 3 February, p 12 and Boggis, D (1995) Tournament of the skies. Financial Times. 10 March, p 17.

Managerialism

Managerialism refers to the ability of managers to maintain control of the organization through the imposition of their perspective on every aspect of activity. It is management that determines the technology that will be used by the organization, and how it will be utilized. There are organizational differences in the degree to which new technology is utilized. Some organizations pride themselves on being at the forefront of technological applications, others prefer to be followers, allowing the cost and risk of development to be carried by others.

Management also decides the degree of employee involvement in determining the human interface with new technology. There are a range of options from full involvement in the design and selection of new technology to simply being told what employees will be expected to do. Terry Molloy, the Deputy General Secretary of the Banking, Insurance and Finance Union, writing on behalf of the trade union movement in a government report in 1984 is quoted (Thompson, 1985, p 5) as saying, 'To get the maximum benefit from IT, it is necessary to involve the workforce. This is not only right in principle, but right in practice, since the people who perform the tasks that will be changed by IT understand the practicalities better than any systems analyst or departmental manager. In our recommendations we lay great stress on the need for proper consultative mechanisms when introducing IT, and indeed, for consultation to start at the earliest planning stage'.

Thompson goes on to illustrate the problems for management if they do not take into consideration the employee point of view. Also demonstrated is the crucial effect of the attitudes of middle managers. A case study regarding the implementation of a new computer system to the freight operations of British Rail (undated but presumably during the early 1970s) illustrates the problems. A top-down approach was adopted, with middle managers and employees were given a new system to operate with very little involvement. All was well in the early stages until it became apparent that with implementation would come job loss and change. Resistance to implementing the system meant that only after 10 years was significant change beginning to happen.

This case clearly illustrates the exercise of negative power. Management have a controlling interest and can determine to a significant extent the form and direction of the agenda. They also have the resources to provide a higher than chance probability of success. However, they are vulnerable to the withdrawal of co-operation in achieving their intentions. That is one reason why the trade union movement is always sensitive to the removal of the right to strike or take industrial action. Ultimately, the withdrawal of labour or co-operation is the most powerful weapon in employee relations. This is the exercise of negative power – not doing something with the intent to influence.

New technology: determinism, rationality and control

There are compelling arguments that technology, particularly new technology, is independent of any particular organizational context and universally applied. However, Friedman and Cornford (1989) use the term *autogenerative* to suggest that computer innovations are as much a function of the user as they are the original designer. Taken in isolation, this view could support the deterministic perspective in that the development of technology is part of a cyclical relationship with the designer and user both developing the technology for each other's benefit. However, it can also be used to support the opposing point of view. If the user can influence the innovation process they are in a position to shape it and can control it to a significant extent. The economic imperative provides organizations with a basis for attempting to match (or better) competitor activity in the search for competitive advantage and so seek the maximum capability that technology can provide.

Management objectives play a significant part in the way that the environment is perceived and interpreted. The objectives that management seek also colour the way that the situation is interpreted and decisions taken. Decision making is a political process and can be used for reasons other than the benefit of the organization. For example, the director in charge of a computer department may seek to ensure that the company takes decisions that enhance the reputation and standing of the department. In that sense it is more effective to consider not a technological imperative as such, but to see things in terms of cause and effect, with technology being a major determinant of the options available. Figure 13.1 reflects this situation, and reflects the role of technology as a driver of options as well as being a feature of managerial interpretation.

This view is perhaps closer to the conclusion reached by McLoughlin and Clark (1988) in which they argue for a complex definition of determinism rather than the simple linear process suggested by many writers.

So far rationality has been assumed. This suggests that managers take decisions based upon a rational process in the best interests of the organization. That is a major assumption. Rationally might be implied in many decisions, but rational from whose point of view? Rationality is an illusive concept and is not necessarily obvious or apparent to everyone. It depends upon the point of view of the individual.

The justification of new technology is frequently based upon improvements in control in one form or another. Control of cost, control of a process, control of employees being among the most commonly used. Control can become a self-perpetuating process of management finding ways to improve control over employees, leading to adverse employee reaction, confirming the need for ever tighter control. Clegg and Dunkerley (1980) describe this as a vicious cycle of control (see Figure 13.2).

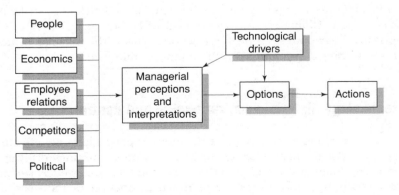

Figure 13.1 Technological choice and decision making.

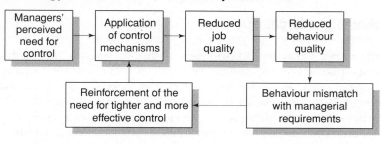

Figure 13.2 The vicious cycle of control (adapted from: Clegg, S and Dunkerley, D (1980) *Organization, Class and Control*. Routledge and Kegan Paul, London).

The application of high technology can be easily justified in control terms as it ensures a consistency of operation not possible through human beings. In addition, it is easier to fit people around the technology than adapt the technology to the people. Conversely, even sophisticated new technology is comparatively stupid by human standards. It is not very flexible in that it can only operate within program parameters, and certain narrow climatic conditions. It has been argued that the 'office of the future' is being significantly held back because of poor new building design and the limited availability of appropriate facilities in existing buildings (air conditioning and cable ducts, etc.). People on the other hand are flexible, they can adapt to changes in circumstances and are capable of solving problems for which they have not been *programmed* or trained. Even with the development of expert systems, computers are not as adaptable as people. It is this constriction in the way to that computers operate that provides the control possibilities through structuring the time, space and activities of the humans with whom they come into contact.

There is another form of people control achieved through the political use of events and activities that engage with their lives. It is this form of control to which Braverman (1974) refers when he began what became known as the labour process debate. Essentially, this debate turns on the use to which human labour is put in the transformation of raw material into commodities for capitalist markets, and the part played by managers in the organization of that work. It is management that determines the nature of any technology in any given context. Consequently, it is a management agenda that determines the use of technology and how human labour will be accommodated around it.

This debate revolves around the degree of *malice aforethought* that managers use in taking those decisions. Is it done to control labour and reinforce management's position, or is it done to further the commercial business objectives of the organization? One of the key problems in researching in this area is that of being able to find out the true causes of particular managerial actions. A manager who is attempting to manipulate workers is highly unlikely to admit it! Many writers prefer to limit consideration of decision making to a form of rationality. Schon (1994) for example talks of a *technical rationality* (p 243) in which the search for solutions to instrumental problems follows a logical pattern and competence can be measured in practice through the degree to which the intended effects are achieved.

New technology and change

Major differences between old and new technologies will inevitably create more change than if the differences are relatively small. Another aspect of the relationship between new technology and change is the nature of the cause and effect process. Does the process of change exist irrespective of a technological input, perhaps driven by the need to change the product or service, or reduce costs? If so then the development of technology is a function of change, rather than the other way round. If change already exists then the search for technological solutions to problems is what generates the process, not the development of a technology followed by a search for applications.

The relationship between technology and work is not just experienced at a work level. There are other levels of impact, for example:

- Employment. To build cars using manual labour obviously provides more jobs than would be the case if a fully automated process were employed. However, if cars made on an automated assembly line are of a higher quality and cheaper to purchase, then the organization may be able to employ more people as a result of increased sales. Equally, there will be employment opportunities that emerge as a result of the new technology itself. So some employment opportunities will disappear and others will emerge.

- Careers. Some careers change as technology changes the jobs within them. For example, to be a senior maintenance engineer today demands a working knowledge of computer-based equipment and electronics, as well as the traditional electrical and mechanical specialisms. Other career paths will disappear as the traditional types of work are replaced by computers. Careers will emerge out of the new work opportunities that are created by the adoption of a technology. For example, computer specialisms have emerged over the past thirty years as that form of technology has evolved.

- Products and services. New products and services emerge as technologies change and develop. For example, the building and selling of robot machines and computers. In the service sector the introduction of ATMs has provided a completely new range of service opportunities to banking customers. This provides for the creation of two distinct forms of new product and service. Firstly, those associated with the technology itself. Secondly, the products and services that can be developed as a consequence of the technology.

- Economic activity. Economic activity is both influenced by and influences technology. Companies not profitable enough to raise capital are in a difficult position when they need to invest in new technologies, which in turn may affect their chances of survival. The economic health of nations also influences the ability to be able to acquire new technologies.

- Risk. Every new venture carries with it an element of risk. With the introduction of new technology comes particular risk as so much of the processing is obscured from view. Earlier in this chapter it was argued that one of the benefits of information technology was the *visibility* that it provided. Managers are able to *see* in great detail (through reports and systems) what is going on. However, before that is possible much information processing takes place within the computer systems and is not therefore observable. It is the end result rather than the process that is visible.

Lengthy commissioning and de-bugging processes are necessary in order to ensure that the system delivers what is required. Apocryphal stories are legion about new computer systems that send the wrong products to customers, or keep sending an order over and over again.

- Internationalism. Companies of all sizes and types now compete for international markets for their products and services. New technology plays a significant part in this process. There is also the international trade in high technology itself. Companies and governments are constantly seeking ways to capture new developments for the benefit of their organizations or citizens. Companies buy competitors products and services and deconstruct them to learn about new manufacturing processes, etc. on a global scale.

- Fashion. Inevitably what significant organizations are doing becomes the norm for many others. This is one means by which risk can be reduced. The first adopters of a particular technology will encounter and solve most of the problems. Following also gives managers confidence (real and political) that something will work and produce benefits. Conversely, there is an element of avoiding thinking and of being less than creative as a result of simply following what others do. By simply following the trend and not working things out for themselves managers can be missing opportunities. The trick, if there is one, is to achieve an effective balance between following and innovating.

- Transition. It is never possible to move from one state to another instantaneously and without consequence. Change takes time to achieve. In implementing a new technology there is a series of time-lags between the initial idea and creation of the equipment and systems capable of meting the need. There is also a time-lag between installing equipment and being able to make full operational use of it. The transition period involved can be fraught with problems and difficulties. It is a time of running with two systems while a phased change-over takes place. Figure 13.3 reflects this transition period.

There are the cost, space and process-based implications associated with the need to keep old and new systems running in parallel. There are also people related problems associated with technology change. Frustration is a common experience as replacement technologies begin to encroach on the work of employees. Employees who consider that they have no future in the new order are less likely to willingly co-operate in solving the problems that emerge. They are more likely to engage in *Luddite* behaviour and further slow the change process.

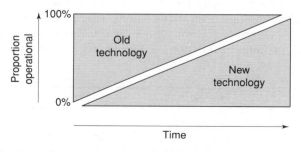

Figure 13.3 Technology transfer.

■ Limitations. New technology is not always capable of living up to its image or the claims of its designers and salespeople. Neither is it always the best solution to every operational need. An electric typewriter (or handwriting) can be a quicker way of producing a short letter than a word processor. Perhaps speaking directly to a colleague could be a more effective way of dealing with a problem than exchanging e-mail. Therefore a combination of old and new technologies integrated into a well thought out partnership can offer the most effective combination of options.

New technology: innovation and diversity

Innovation is about creating new things, or creating new ways of doing existing things. New technology is by definition an innovation. New technology can also help organizations to innovate in the design of new products and it can assist in improving existing operations. Betz (1987) describes innovation as falling into one of three categories (see Table 13.1):

■ Radical. This is the initial development of a technology. It represents the major breakthrough that allows the subsequent transformation of an industry, or the creation of a new one. The development of the first computer during the 1940s is an example. The highest level of risk is associated with this type of innovation as much cost and time is needed. Many ideas are developed but most do not achieve commercial realization.
■ System. This represents the commercialization of a technology. A computer by itself is simply a calculating and storage machine. However, linked to a typewriter it can develop into the multifunction workstation of today. The level of risk is lower than the radical level as it tends to involve the combination of existing technologies, rather than the creation of something completely new.
■ Incremental. This represents the least risk of the three levels and is a process of refinement. It represents the upgrading of a computer system through the miniaturization of components or improvements to a word processing package. It is the level of innovation that aims to extract the maximum capability and potential out of a particular technology.

There are many ways that innovation occurs. There are the research activities in universities that create many of the first radical versions of a particular technology. For example, my own university here at Hull played a pioneering role in the development of the liquid crystal, now an essential element of calculators and other forms of display screen. There are military laboratories specifically looking at technology from that context. There are science parks located near to universities intended to encourage the transfer and exploitation of pure research through commercial expertise. Within large organizations there is fre-

Table 13.1
Categories of innovation

Category	Example
Radical	Development of computer
System	Linking computer to typewriter technology
Incremental	Improvement in word processing package

quently research and development activity engaged on projects spanning the three categories above. Management in Action 13.8 overleaf provides an insight into how a number of organizations innovate as part of their survival activities.

Organizations require conformity. Products and services must consistently conform to the appropriate specification. One of the major benefits of technology is that it can produce conformity to a much higher level than human beings. The use of company uniforms, dress codes, rules and training are all part of the process of *engineering* (or socializing) the behaviour of people. Herriot and Pemberton (1995) argue uniformity is a weakness and through diversity comes strength.

They argue that uniformity leads to situations where inappropriate decisions are taken. The Bay of Pigs (Janis, 1972) is one of many decisions used to illustrate the point. This decision was about a group of people being so close in type and perspective that they could not entertain any different points of view. The result was military failure and embarrassment for the American government. By encouraging difference and establishing learning processes based on its incorporation into normal decision making higher levels of innovation are encouraged. In turn a higher success rate will be achieved. They link their argument to the Myers-Briggs indicator of personality to create balanced teams. You will recall that the Belbin and Margerison and McCann team roles were introduced in an earlier chapter. These provide a similar perspective on the need for a balance of personality and work preference if a team is to be successful.

New technology: a management perspective

New technology from a management perspective presents both problems and benefits. It can be used to improve products and services or to create new ones. It can be used to control employees, or to replace boring and monotonous jobs.

Risk of failure is one of the problems that technology brings. It is developing at such a rapid rate that no sooner has a particular technology been introduced than it has been superseded. The danger being that competitors adopt the next generation of new technology and steal an advantage. The cost of the adoption of a particular technology can be prohibitive and is not something that can be changed every year. Flexibility and keeping future options open is a key requirement of new technology. However, suppliers make this very difficult by seeking to *lock* customers into their own product range in order to protect future business. Variations in product and technology standards prevent the easy switching from one supplier to another. Consequently the successful adoption of new technology comes not so much from the technology itself but from its effective integration with other work activities and existing technology.

Very few managers have a depth of understanding of the technologies available. In progressing their careers managers progressively move away from the operational levels of activity. Increasingly technology becomes something that other people use regularly. Managers inevitably rise through a particular discipline, accounting, personnel or production for example. They will have some knowledge of new technology applications within their own areas of expertise but less in other areas. At some point in their careers, managers have to take responsibility for disciplines of which they have no direct experience. Inevitably when this happens technology continues to develop beyond that with which

Management in Action 13.8

Innovators keep on the ball

The Wellcome Cancer Research Campaign Institute in Cambridge believes that social interaction between researchers is one of the best ways of encouraging the flow of ideas. With a £3m annual research budget the institute undertakes innovative research. The building was purpose built in 1992 and has laboratories around the outside to maximize daylight in the workplace. Chemicals and research equipment are kept in communal areas to force staff to meet others. Journals are kept in individual's rooms so staff are encouraged to interact when they need information. People are free to come and go as they please. Dr John Gurdon, chairman of the institute, said that, 'There is an exceptional amount of movement here, people going around talking to others, sharing equipment. We believe time is saved by talking to people before doing something'.

Hewlett-Packard spends about £100m per year on long range research at its laboratories in Japan, California and Bristol. In Bristol the research staff dress informally and are encouraged to spend 10% of their time on any activity that interests them using laboratory facilities. Irreverence, humour and tolerance are encouraged. Every idea is regarded as having some merit until it is shown to be otherwise.

In non-research organizations which need creativity similar ideas are catching on. Hunt Thompson Associates, a London architects practice with 61 employees, uses lunch once each week as the time for swapping ideas. Each week one of the architects presents their work as either the basis of a discussion or simply to bring the others up to date on a project, the intention being to create an atmosphere of informality and encourage interaction and innovation through the involvement of as many people as possible.

Mitsubishi Heavy Industries sought some fresh ideas for its European marketing strategy by holding a series of brainstorming sessions with undergraduates from Pembroke College, Cambridge. Although many of the ideas were unrealistic they were thought provoking, radical and stimulating, according to Mr Henry Anderson, the European general manager of planning and development for the company.

In a recent survey, some 80% of American companies thought that innovation was important for their business, but only 4% thought that they were good at it. The job cuts, recruitment freezes and other downsizing/delayering exercises of recent years all sap the morale of existing employees as well as reduce the inflow of new people and ideas. The trend to decentralization can also see the break-up of central research departments and the lowering of morale among research staff, with a consequent loss of creativity and innovation.

The existence of an innovative capability does not guarantee success for the organization. Xerox failed to exploit some of the pioneering work from its own research laboratories on the personal computer during the 1970s. Senior management priorities at the time were in securing the future of its core business areas. Both creativity and the will to exploit the ideas must be present for the benefits to be realized.

Adapted from: MacKenzie, A (1995) Innovators keep on the ball. Financial Times, 1 May, p 11, and Houlder, V (1995) Caught in a brainstorm. Financial Times, 1 May, p 11.

they were familiar. The danger being that managers become reactionary and resist its application, or they become prey to the claims of vested interests. In most organizations senior managers have enough experience to be able to tread this line with some considerable skill, but it is a danger that exists. Effective measures are needed to ensure that senior managers are not left behind in understanding of new technology.

Another element of new technology for managers is the effect on jobs and employees within the organization. It is easy to see technology as an end in itself rather than a means to an end. Technology is not capable of running a company without input and support from that most capable and flexible of all technologies (an old technology at that) the human being. The true success of new technology comes from the effective integration of these two totally different expressions of creativity. After all it is technology that is intended to support people not the other way round!

Buchanan and McCalman (1988) studied the effects of computerized information systems in hotels and concluded that they offered a number of advantages, which they describe as a visibility theory:

- **Sharing.** Computer-based systems encouraged managers to share information more readily than with manual systems.
- **Confidence.** The more widely available information encouraged and motivated managers, thus increasing confidence levels.
- **Pressure.** The wider and timely availability of information as a result of computerization puts pressure on managers to react quickly and effectively in pursuing business objectives.
- **Visibility.** Improved information flows bring into the open the relative performance of individual managers.
- **Co-operation.** The four elements above combined produce a situation where managers find it easier to work together and levels of conflict generally reduce.

Conclusions

This chapter has reviewed a number of the new technology applications within organizations and the impact of these on how people operate. New technology was also considered in terms of decision making, rationality and as part of a change process.

It is inevitable that any discussion of new technology will quickly become dated as suppliers and innovators create new technologies and different applications for existing ones. The risk associated with new technology is that it begins to take a predominant position in organizational thinking and diverts attention away from human capabilities and diversity as an important element in survival.

Discussion questions

1   Define the following key terms used in this chapter:

Informates	Cognitive reapportionment	Visibility
New technology	Decision bundles	
Neural networks	Adhocracy	

2 What is new technology and how does it differ from previous technologies?
3 Identify the ways in which new technology has influenced the traditional ways of exercising control within organizations.
4 Describe the areas of impact of new technology on the manufacturing industries and make an assessment of its effect.
5 How are new technology, diversity and innovation linked together?
6 Describe the areas of impact of new technology on the service industries and make an assessment of its effect.
7 What is technological determinism and how does the nature of rationality in decision making influence it?
8 Describe the areas of impact of new technology on the administrative aspects of organizational activity and make an assessment of its effect,
9 Does new technology manage managers, or do managers manage new technology? Justify your answer.
10 What effect has new technology had on structure and job design within organizations?

Research questions

1 In the library seek out 10 journal articles that describe the impact of new technology on work. What similarities and differences are contained in that set of papers and this chapter? Why might that be so?
2 In small groups arrange to interview practising managers (preferably from a range of functional areas and levels of seniority). Attempt to find out how the technology in their organization is changing. Also ask about the impact of new technology on jobs. Make an assessment of the manager's view of new technology and how knowledgeable about it you think they are. Analyse your findings in terms of the material in this chapter.
3 Repeat exercise 2 above, but this time with a trade union officer. What differences exist between the views expressed by both sets of people? What conclusions do you draw about new technology and its impact on organizations and work from these interviews?

Key reading

From Clark, H, Chandler, J and Barry, J (1994) *Organization and Identities: Text and Readings in Organizational Behaviour*, International Thomson Business Press, London.

- Bell D: Work and its discontents, p 44. Considers the notions of efficiency and rationality in the context of work and technology.
- Campbell, B *et al*.: The manifesto for new times, p 49. This describes the evolution of Britain over the past 20 years or so. Its purpose is to provide one perspective of the context within which technology develops.
- Coyle, K: Post-modernism, p 58. This provides a critique of the post-modernist perspective on the evolution of the capitalist society.
- Dex, S: The sexual division of work, p 177. Reviews the gendered nature of work, including the role of technology in this process.
- Cockburn, C. Male dominance and technological change, p 197. Explores the gendered nature of work and the part played by technology in this process.

■ Brunsson, N. The virtue of irrationality – decision making, action and commitment, p 294. Considers the conflicting nature of decision rationality and action rationality and the inclusion of irrationality into the process.

■ Braverman H: The degradation of work, p 385. Considers one aspect of technology – the compartmentalization of work.

■ Mills, CW: The cheerful robot, p 396. This extract argues for individuality and a significant role for human beings as an response to alienation.

Further reading

Clark, J (ed) (1993) *Human Resource Management and Technical Change*, Sage. This text does not consider specifically the organizational behaviour issues associated with new technology, but it does reflect on the nature of technical change in its broadest sense and the human resource issues that emerge.

Forester, T (1987) *High-tech Society*, Basil Blackwell, Oxford. Provides a very readable review of the evolution and technicalities of technology. It also develops a number of themes associated with the application of technology in a work and social context.

Thompson, P (1989) *The Nature of Work: An Introduction to Debates on the Labour Process*, 2nd edn, Macmillan. As the title suggests, this text takes a detailed look at the labour process concept, its origins and implications. as such it elaborates the political and social context within which work exists.

References

BBC (1995) *Troubleshooter Returns*. Presented by Sir John Harvey-Jones. Number 4 – the series. Broadcast 21 June.

Betz, F (1987) *Managing Technology*, Prentice-Hall, Englewood Cliffs, NJ.

Braverman, H (1974) *Labour and Monopoly Capital: The Degradation of Work in the Twentieth Century*, Monthly Review Press, London.

Buchanan, DA and Boddy, D (1983) *Organizations in the Computer Age: Technological Imperatives and Strategic Choice*, Gower, Aldershot.

Buchanan, DA and McCalman, J (1988) Confidence, visibility and pressure: the effects of shared information in computer aided hotel management. *New Technology, Work and Employment*, **3**, 38–46.

Clegg, S, and Dunkerley, D (1980) *Organization, Class and Control*, Routledge & Kegan Paul, London.

Forester, T (1987) *High-tech Society*, Basil Blackwell, Oxford.

Friedman, AL, and Cornford, DS (1989) *Computer Systems Development: History, Organization and Implementation*, John Wiley, Chichester.

Herriot P and Pemberton C (1995) *Competitive Advantage Through Diversity: Organizational Learning Through Difference*, Sage, London.

Hill, T (1983) *Production and Operations Management*, Prentice-Hall, London.

Janis, IL (1972) *Victims of Groupthink: A Psychological Study of Foreign Policy Decisions*, Houghton Mifflin, Boston.

Klemm, F (1959) *A History of Western Technology*, George Allen & Unwin, London.

Konsynski, BR and Sviokla, JJ (1994) Cognitive reapportionment: rethinking the location of judgement in managerial decision making. In *The Post-bureaucratic Organization: New Perspectives on Organizational Change* (eds C Heckscher and A Donnellon), Sage, Thousand Oaks.

McLoughlin, I and Clark, J (1988) *Technological Change at Work*, Open University Press, Milton Keynes.

Mintzberg, H (1983) *Structure in Fives: Designing Effective Organizations*, Prentice-Hall, Englewood Cliffs, NJ.

Reed, M (1989) *The Sociology of Management*, Harvester Wheatsheaf, Hemel Hempstead.

Schon, DA (1994) Teaching artistry through reflection-in-action. In *New Thinking in Organizational Behaviour* (ed H Tsoukas), Butterworth Heinemann, Oxford.

Shaiken, H (1985) *Work Transformed: Automation and Labor in the Computer Age*, Holt, Rinehart & Winston, New York.

Thompson, L (1985) New office technology: people, work structures and the process of change. WRU Occasional Paper No. 34, April. ACAS Work Research Unit, London.

Thompson, L (1989) New office technology: the changing role of the secretary. WRU Occasional Paper No. 44, January. ACAS Work Research Unit, London.

Zuboff, S (1988) *In the Age of the Smart Machine: The Future of Work and Power*, Heinemann, Oxford.

Part VI

The management of organizations

14

Management and leadership

Chapter summary

This chapter sets out to introduce the nature of management and leadership. The main theoretical perspectives on the subject of leadership will be introduced. Trait, style and contingency perspectives will be discussed, followed by a brief review of a number of other views on the subject. International aspects of leadership will also be introduced as will consideration of the nature and impact of meetings and humour in leadership activities.

Learning objectives

After studying this chapter and working through the associated Management in Action panels, discussion questions and research activities, you should be able to:

■ Understand the distinction between leadership and management.
■ Describe what it is that managers actually do when carrying out their jobs.
■ Explain the roles that managers perform and the skills that they need.
■ Outline what leadership as a process involves.
■ Assess the significance of the trait, styles and contingency approaches to leadership.
■ Appreciate the significance of humour in leadership.
■ Discuss international aspects and the impact of meetings on management.
■ Detail the 'other' approaches to leadership identified.

```
▣■▯ browse this web site ▣■▯
      www.itbp.com
```

Introduction

The terms management and leadership are frequently used interchangeably. But are they the same? Is a manager automatically a leader and do leaders always manage? The study of management and leadership has covered many different aspects of the activity. Rothman (1987) light-heartedly concludes that birthdays are a key variable in selecting future leaders. This emerged because the senior managers of a number of large organizations shared the same birthday as their predecessors.

Leadership and management are two topics that between them generate a vast quantity of published material, training courses and seminars. This material frequently claims to provide a means of delivering increased performance to the organization through the more effective leadership of teams. Leadership characteristics can therefore be learned which ensure that *leaders* stand out from the ranks of *managers* who are not so successful. For the organization this effort can lead to enhanced commercial success in an increasingly hostile environment.

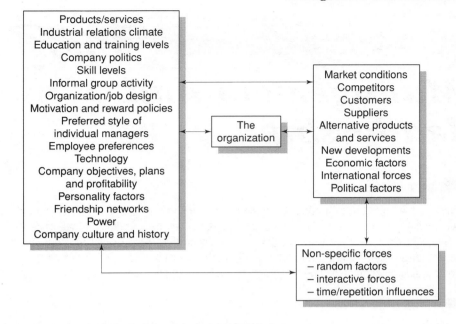

Figure 14.1 The complexity of the management environment.

However, there is little hard evidence for the success of any particular *formula*. The number and complexity of variables involved requires an equally complex set of responses in order to *manage* it. This is the basis of the law of requisite variety identified by Ashby (1956). Figure 14.1 attempts to provide an indication of the range of such variables impacting on the individuals and organization.

The non-specific forces identified in Figure 14.1 include:

■ Random factors. Things for which it is difficult to anticipate and plan. An employee being in a bad mood on a particular day or the failure of a supplier to deliver on time.

■ Time and repetitive influences. These reflect experiential influences that impact on activity. Over time behaviour patterns change and influence future actions. The simplest illustration is the story about the little boy who cried wolf once too often and as a result failed to protect the sheep for which he was responsible.

■ Interactive forces. The *action and reaction* nature of experience. An initiative to increase market share is likely to lead to a response from competitors seeking to protect their business. Subordinates are not passive and respond to their experience of being led, creating a dynamic between leader and led.

Leadership and management are complex processes. Simplistic attempts to explain them or train individuals to use a formula are doomed. This view is apparent in Management in Action 14.1.

There are groups that attempt to operate without a formal leader. For example, workers' co-operatives and autonomous work teams. A form of democracy would be likely to exist in such groups, replacing the traditional management role. These groups do not abolish the *functions* that would be carried out by a

Management in Action 14.1

The manager's dilemma

The key features of managing in the next millennium include, according to Heller:

- Managers will be concerned with unleashing the potential all around them.
- Managers will need to listen to the messages coming to them from below about what needs to be 'facilitated' to achieve objectives. Those that don't listen will find their basis of authority eliminated.
- Old style authority frameworks will crumble in an age when success and progress depend upon breaking the rules.
- The view of an organization as a 'system of inter-related parts' will grow and the complexity will be dealt with by outsourcing as much of the non-core activities as possible and networking more effectively.
- Success in management will be defined in terms of the ability to work effectively with colleagues from other companies to achieve results for the organization. The distinction between the management and consultancy modes of operation will become blurred.
- The tasks carried out by individual managers will be subject to frequent change in line with the changing perception of customer needs and how it should be met through the resources available. Predictable career paths and functional specialisms will erode significantly.
- With the emphasis on task groups and multidisciplinary team working, and as a consequence of the

delayering of recent years the opportunity for frequent promotion will largely disappear. Beyond the year 2000 managers will progress in status and reward terms by the successful achievement of assignments, rather than vertical progression and changing job titles.

- Theory 'Y' motivation perspectives will dominate the thinking and approaches of managers as they seek to involve as many people as possible in assignments.
- The effective integration of both 'hard' and 'soft' perspectives into their work will also be a characteristic of the next generation of successful manager.
- The ability to 'live the vision' as expressed in corporate values, rather than just pay 'lip service' to them, will also defining the new manager.
- Future commercial wars are going to be won with ideas, not whips and chains. As a consequence, managers will not plan, organize, control, etc. They will advise, facilitate, encourage self-management and ensure that adequate resources are available for the groups that actually achieve objectives for the organization.
- The comprehensive growth in various forms of strategic alliance will blur the boundaries between organizations. The consequences are vast for the management of ambiguity and boundary management in the job of the new manager. They become very aware of the true nature of the 'open' organization and job.

Adapted from: Heller, R (1994) The Manager's Dilemma. Management Today, January, pp 42–7.

leader. They redistribute the activities and functions in order to create greater involvement for every member.

The training and development of managers is often undervalued by organizations, particularly in Britain (Harrison, 1994). These days in-company training programmes for managers are sometimes validated by university management departments to improve content credibility and impact. Management in Action 14.2 provides an insight into the issues associated with the training and development of directors.

Management in Action 14.2

Business class

Invariably the staff who might be expected to identify training needs and provide training for senior managers and directors are lower in status than the managers targetted. There is also a degree of reluctance among directors to admit that they need training. To admit a training need might be seen to undermine their credibility. A survey by the Industrial Society found that one in six organizations provided no training for its directors. The personnel department determined training for board members in only 10% of cases and the board itself in 20%. Individual board members decided their own training needs in the majority of cases.

John Harper, Professional Development Director for the Institute of Directors, indicated that the situation was changing rapidly. The most obvious lack of training for directors was when they first took up a board-level appointment. Only 11% of organizations automatically review the training needs of new directors and one third of organizations rarely or never do so.

To meet the needs of board-level leaders of organizations a number of courses have been developed over recent years. Most involve the Institute of Directors and a university in some form of collaborative endeavour. The Institute developed a Diploma programme in company direction aimed at providing delegates with a solid basis in the duties and responsibilities of a director. There are also master's degree programmes that are becoming available and which aim to provide delegates with the skills necessary to perform at board level. The first one of these was offered by Leeds Metropolitan University in 1994.

One of the difficulties facing board members is the distinction between the responsibilities of directors and those of managers. For example, Judith Barras, course leader for the Masters course at Leeds Metropolitan University, suggested that directors who were appointed to the board after being managers within the same company sometimes had a limited vision of the needs of the firm as a whole. Work done in this area by Henley Management College produced a number of 'standards' such as organizing and running a board of directors, vision, strategy and responsibility to stakeholders. A number of personal competencies for directors have also been identified including, integrity, decisiveness, the ability to listen, and a willingness to adopt a 'helicopter' perspective. The provision of training for both newly appointed and more experienced directors is aimed at addressing these and similar issues.

Adapted from: Hall, L (1994) Business class. Personnel Today, *3 May, pp 31–2, and Merrick, N (1994) Taking training to the top.* Personnel Management, *December, pp 51–2.*

Leadership and management

The terms management and leadership tend to be used interchangeably. It would be unusual, however, to describe a group having a manager, unless in a specific context. That context is within an organization, and specifically a formal part of the structure. A department would have a manager as the formal leader of that group. The two terms are therefore synonymous, but only up to point.

What then distinguishes between management and leadership? The following provides some indication of the areas of distinction:

■ Role. Watson (1994) defines management as ensuring that the resources under control are appropriately directed. Torrington and Hall (1991) describe the '... role that members of the organization take on in order to exercise formal authority and leadership' (p 129). From this perspective leadership is to be understood as a sub-set of management. Something that managers do in order to be effective. Leadership as part of group activity may not be part of the formal structure. The leader of a group designing a new computer system may not be a manager but would be expected to *lead* the team. There are also informal groups within an organization which will have some form of leadership. Management can be suggested to be an outwardly focused activity. Leadership represents an inwardly focused activity intended to optimize performance and maintain group cohesion.

■ Situation. A manager is appointed and would hold that position irrespective of changes in the situation. Leaders are suggested to be much more situation specific. John Adair illustrates this with examples of shipwreck survivors appointing leaders depending upon the needs at the time: the soldier for defence, the farmer for food and the builder for shelter, (1983, p 15). Situational leadership makes best use of the specialized knowledge available to the group from among the members. The *company doctor* is frequently brought in to replace a senior manager not considered capable of saving a company. Such individuals usually stay for a very short period of time. Their leadership is invariably based upon the 'do it my way or out' philosophy. It is an approach which can achieve the desired results, albeit with much blood on the carpet.

■ Context. The military context is one in which considerable emphasis is laid on leadership rather than management. Constant training and drill leads to a highly capable military *machine*. There is an interesting contradiction in this situation involving such close and directive management with an emphasis on leadership as the dominant ideology. Much of this can be explained by reference to two unique circumstances peculiar to military activity. Firstly, the chaos and horror of war itself. Secondly, the need to motivate subordinates to undertake actions which are ultimately life threatening to the individual.

■ Purpose. Traditionally jobs and organizations were considered to have permanence into the foreseeable future. Therefore the role of management becomes routinized and symbolic. In times of turbulence and instability this changes. This is perhaps responsible for the shift in emphasis towards leadership as the dominant ideology in organizations as they attempt to manage temporary, insecure teams more effectively. Company trainers find themselves providing training for leadership more than for other aspects of management (Rowe, 1993, p 65). Scase and Goffee (1989) reported their survey of managers in which 69% of men and 82% of women indicated a need for more human relations and leadership training (p 68).

■ Scope. The usual differentiation is between senior, middle and junior management positions. This distinction is a very poor indicator of the type of job involved. For example, a junior manager in a very large organization may have a budgetary responsibility larger that a senior manager in a very small one. Stewart (1976) identified another basis for the classification of management jobs:

– Hub. Jobs that have much contact with subordinates, peers and superiors.
– Peer dependent. A high degree of persuading others to undertake specific actions. Frequently found on the boundary between groups.

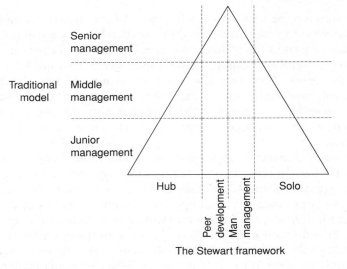

The Stewart framework

Figure 14.2 The management job matrix.

 - Man management. Such jobs emphasize the traditional boss–subordinate types of responsibilities.
 - Solo. Jobs that require the individual to work alone on assignments but which require a high level of seniority.

Although this framework provides a clear indication of the nature of different types of management job it does not provide any information about the level in the hierarchy. More than one dimension is required to describe management jobs. Figure 14.2 links together the traditional and Stewart views of management work in such a matrix.

What managers do

There is such a wide diversity of management work that it is not possible to specify what every manager will undertake. There have been a number of reports that consider management activity in the technological age. These are summarized in Management in Action 14.3.

Fayol (1949) identified the main activities for any organization, including administration, which would today be described as management. In this he included the following functions:

■ Forecast. The process of examining and foreseeing the future.
■ Plan. This followed from forecasting and involved preparing a plan of action.
■ Organize. The physical and human arrangement of resources in pursuit of the plan.
■ Command. The maintenance of appropriate activity among the people within the organization.
■ Co-ordinate. The integration of activity and effort in pursuit of objectives.
■ Control. This ensured that everything happened in accordance with the plan and proper procedures.

Management in Action 14.3

Whither management?

Collins reports two studies carried out during 1993 and 1994 on different aspects of the future of management. The first report by Cannon found that there were hopeful signs following the original Handy and Constable report. For example, the commitment to developing managers had not been as seriously hit in the recession during the early 1990s as had been feared by many. More people were studying for undergraduate business and management degrees than had been set as targets in the original report. More organizations claimed an awareness of the importance of developing people at work, and progress on the accreditation of in-company learning was growing. Perhaps more importantly the study also found that the majority of managers who could affect the performance of their organizations at the millennium were already in post.

The second report by Taylor identified a number of interesting features associated with management in the future including:

■ Managing the paradoxes between various competing pressures will remain an important aspect of organizational life. For example, long-term planning versus short-term performance.

■ Although fewer managers will be needed in manufacturing industry, new managerial activities will emerge in the health care industry and in non-traditional situations such as school management.

■ A recognition that people management is an important aspect of line management activity, not restricted to a specialist department.

■ A growth in generalist management and a decline in functional specialisms.

■ The development of teamworking in a variety of forms. This will by itself change the nature of management into a facilitation or indirect management activity.

■ The creation of many short-life teams with an increase in the short time allowed for the 'Forming', 'Storming', etc. process of acclimatization.

■ The development of new management techniques to manage the remote workforce. Homeworking and other forms of telecommuting require different forms of management to be exercised leading to changes in the 'command and control' aspects of management.

■ University education is intended to encourage individuals to enquire and challenge the *status quo*. Given the emphasis in much of the earlier organizational training on becoming 'good' employees this could lead to traditional authority being challenged, or even ignored. Respect and credibility being based much more upon the 'youth culture' views of situations, people and their capabilities.

■ More work still needed to be done to assist managers to make the jump from functional to general management levels within their organizations.

Adapted from: Collins, P (1995) Whither management? Management Services, July, pp 16–18.

A sociological perspective on management is provided by Reed (1989). He identifies four themes on what management is about, including:

■ Technical perspective. Management as, 'A rationally designed and operationalized tool for the realization of predominantly instrumental values ...' (p 2).
■ Political perspective. Management as, '... a social process geared to the regulation of interest group conflict in an environment characterized by considerable uncertainty over the criteria through which effective organizational performance is assessed' (p 6).

■ Critical perspective. Management as, '... a control mechanism that functions to fulfil the economic imperatives imposed by a capitalist mode of
   production and to disseminate the ideological frameworks through which
   these structural realities can be obscured' (p 10).
■ Practice perspective. Management as, '... a process or activity aimed at the
   continual recouping or smoothing over of diverse and complex practices
   always prone to disengagement and fragmentation' (p 21).

The practice view of management attempts to bring together elements from the
other three perspectives into a more holistic framework. What managers actually do is therefore a function of the dominant perspective.

These explanations offer very little of what it is that managers actually do
whilst at work. Most studies of management reflect a job not at all like that
implied by the Fayol model. They describe a fragmented, hectic job with
frequent switches in activity. Handy (1993) summarizes a number of studies
(chapter 11) into the job of managers, including:

■ Supervisors. Guest found that each one averaged 583 separate events in
   every working day.
■ Managers. Stewart found that on average each enjoyed only nine 30-minute
   periods without interruption over a four week period.
■ Chief executives. Mintzberg described many activities for this category fitted into 10-minute bursts of time. Meetings were also short, lasting one
   hour on average.
■ Organization size. Mintzberg reported differences in activity between chief
   executives of large and small organizations.

Mackenzie (1972) categorizes the time activity of managers as either *managing* or
operating and describes the changing balance between the two at different levels
of the hierarchy. Figure 14.3 illustrates this changing balance of activity type.

The specific nature, range and pattern of work undertaken by any manager
will depend upon a wide range of factors. Stewart (1985) identifies a number
of these, including:

■ Industry. The job of a personnel manager in a national retail chain employing 1000 people would be different to the same job carried out in a

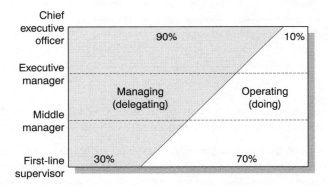

Figure 14.3 Managerial activity (taken from: MacKenzie, RA (1972) *The time trap: How to get more
done in less time*. McGraw-Hill, New York. Exhibit 10, based on an original study by Davis, RC (1951)
The fundamentals of top management).

heavy engineering company with the same number of employees on one site.

■ Role. The figurehead role carries with it a difference in activity compared to that of an entrepreneur.

■ Pattern of work. Most jobs contain a degree of cyclicality, perhaps weekly, monthly, quarterly or annually. Project-based jobs are different in activity to line management positions.

■ Level. The level within the hierarchy clearly influences the tasks performed by the manager.

■ Exposure. This reflects the degree of visibility in the performance of a manager's job. For example, a sales manager is highly exposed in that much of their time would be spent in contact with customers.

■ Contacts. The nature of interaction with other people is a key factor in work activity. The job of a public relations manager would be expected to be completely different in activity from that of a personnel manager.

■ Personal factors. Individual difference and preferences encourage variation in work activity to take place.

Luthans (1995) describes four general types of management activity as follows:

■ Traditional management. Planning, decision making and controlling. This accounts for 32% of management time.

■ Routine communication. Exchanging information and handling paperwork. This accounts for 29% of management time.

■ Networking. Interacting with outsiders, socializing and politicking. This accounts for 19% of management time.

■ Human resource management. Managing conflict, motivating, discipline, staffing and development. This accounts for 20% of management time.

There is a vast difference between activity and effectiveness. Simply *doing something* does not by itself result in achieving organizational objectives. Luthans also describes two attempts to link *success* and *effectiveness* (pp 384–5). Defining *success* as speed of promotion, networking activities correlated most strongly with it and traditional/human resource management the least. The implication being that promotion depends on socializing and politicking rather than task related activities. In terms of *effectiveness*, measured by quality, quantity, employee satisfaction and commitment, communication and human resource management activities were most strongly correlated. One implication being that achieving results does not advance careers! There are a number of other implications that arise from this work including how to measure effectiveness and success. These issues are illustrated in Management in Action 14.4 overleaf.

The leadership process

John Adair (1983) describes what a leader has to do in terms of a three circle model, Figure 14.4 overleaf. Each circle represents a major part of the process of leadership, principle responsibilities for which the leader will be held accountable.

Another approach to the management process is through the skills and abilities required of a leader. Hellriegal *et al.* (1989, pp 267–71) describe the leadership process in terms of:

Management in Action 14.4

Taking the lead in leadership

The distinction between leadership and management is explored in a book by Stuart Levine and Michael Crom, of Dale Carnegie & Associates, called The Leader in You. It identifies a number of distinctions between management and leadership. For example, 'A leader is a person who can communicate with and motivate people. A manager is someone who doesn't spend enough time recognizing people through a sincere appreciation of what they do. A leader understands that the way to motivate a person is not with a bullwhip and chair – the lion tamer's style of management – but with appreciation'.

Leadership is about listening to people, supporting and encouraging them and involving them in the decision-making and problem-solving processes, they say. Management involves telling people, what to do, and how, when and where to do it, and then closely supervising their performance. Levine and Crom suggest that no individual can assimilate all the information available to them, so leaders have to start building teams and relying on members of those teams to make the most of what is available and achieve the goals.

In their work they quote Sir Christopher Hogg, chairman of Reuters, as saying, 'Leadership is about getting the best out of people. It is about communicating a vision, and persuading, rather than compelling people. Management, on the other hand, is about an effective performance within an institutional framework, which secures the obedience of a lot of people'.

Robert Waterman in his book *The Frontiers of Excellence* argues that top performing companies are better able to meet the needs of their people. Looking after the needs of the people within the organization helps to attract better people in the first place and motivates them to place the needs of the organization and its customers above other interests. In meeting the needs of one's own people it is necessary to understand what motivates them and to have an effective alignment between culture, systems, procedures and leadership. This is far removed from the old idea of manager as one who tells people what to do.

Adapted from: Gretton, I (1995) Taking the lead in leadership. Professional Manager, January, pp 20–2.

Figure 14.4   What a leader has to do (taken from: Adair, J (1983) *Effective Leadership: A Self-development Manual*, Gower, Aldershot, Fig. 3.4).

- ■ Relationships. The quality of the relationship between the leader and sub-ordinates is a major determinant of the ability of the leader to function effectively.
- ■ Skills. The skills of self-understanding, visioning, effective communication and empowerment are necessary to achieve effectiveness in group activity.
- ■ Power. Power is what allows the leader to carry out the function. In the case of leadership situations these sources of power include:
  - – Legitimate. Subordinates accept that the leader has the right to be obeyed.
  - – Reward. The leader controls access and allocation of rewards valued by the subordinates.
  - – Coercive. The leader controls punishment including disciplinary action, withholding pay or demotion.
  - – Referent. The personal characteristics of the leader produce in subordinates the desire to follow directions.
  - – Expert. Subordinates believe that the leader has expertise over and above the others in the team.

To be effective the leader needs to take account of the preferences of the leader, the preferences of the group being lead, the task to be achieved and the context within which it is being carried out.

Trait theories of leadership

For much of history it was assumed that leadership was a set of qualities that someone was born with. Adair (1983) quotes from a lecture given to students of St Andrews University in 1934:

> It is a fact that some men possess an inbred superiority which gives them a domi-nating influence over their contemporaries, and marks them out unmistakably for leadership. This phenomenon is as certain as it is mysterious. It is apparent in every association of human beings in every variety of circumstances and on every plane of culture. In a school among boys, in a college among the students, in a factory, shipyard, or a mine among the workman, as certainly as in the church and in the Nation, there are those who, with an assured and unquestioned title, take the lead-ing place, and shape the general conduct. (p 7)

It is being argued that good leaders naturally display those characteristics that are required by the position that they hold. The significance of this approach is that leaders cannot be *trained* and therefore must be *selected*. It also implies that successful leaders will be situation specific. This originated from the aptly named *great-man* (as at that time they were mostly men) view of leadership which suggested that in every situation (particularly in times of crisis) the best leader would emerge from the crowd and overcome the difficulties.

Handy (1993) suggests that by 1950 there had been over 100 studies attempt-ing to identify appropriate traits. Unfortunately there was little commonality identified with only about 5% of the traits being common. Those associated with successful leadership include:

- ■ Intelligence. A high level of intelligence and good at solving abstract, com-plex problems.
- ■ Initiative. The ability to identify a need for action and to do something.

- ■ Self-assurance. Confidence in one's ability to do things and to be successful.
- ■ Overview. The ability to stand back and take a broader view of situations.
- ■ Health. To be of good health.
- ■ Physique. To be above average weight and height, or to be significantly below.
- ■ Social background. To be born into the higher socio-economic groups.

To find a leader with every characteristic (not just those above) would seem to be an impossible task. There are too many exceptions to imply that they are essential for success. Many successful leaders do not fit the profile implied by the characteristics. The terms themselves are imprecise. For example, socio-economic grouping is a relative term, peculiar to each generation and society.

Trait approaches to leadership are used in many assessment centres for the purposes of recruitment and career development. They are based on the view that there are personal characteristics that impact on effectiveness. Assessment centres involve a range of tasks with behaviour and performance being record-ed and evaluated by a team of assessors. Traits have not disappeared, they now appear as skill-based characteristics such as technical skill, conceptual skill and human skill, creativity, persuasiveness, tactfulness and ability to speak well.

Style theories of leadership

The basis of this approach to leadership is that subordinates will respond bet-ter to some *styles* than others. It is assumed that a positive subordinate response creates the success sought by the leader. There are many studies of this approach, each capable of classification on an autocratic–democratic scale. Leaders vary in the degree of involvement allowed to subordinates. At one extreme, leaders can direct activity, taking decisions themselves regarding sub-ordinates as a resource to be used – autocratic. At the other extreme, leaders can involve subordinates in planning and undertaking work, delegating some of their responsibility – democratic. It is appropriate to consider style theories in chronological sequence, providing an opportunity to reflect on the evolu-tion of knowledge

The University of Iowa studies

Carried out in boys' clubs during the late 1930s by Lippitt and White to study the consequences of leadership differences on aggressive behaviour among 10 year olds. They varied leadership style as follows:

- ■ Authoritarian. The leader was directive and did not allow participation among the boys. A friendly or impersonal style was adopted, hostile approaches were avoided.
- ■ Democratic. Discussion and group decision making was encouraged. The leader attempted to be objective but tried to avoid becoming 'one of them'.
- ■ *Laissez faire*. The leader gave complete freedom to the group of boys. This reflected a lack of leadership rather than a particular style.

It was the group of boys subjected to the democratic leadership style that contained the least levels of aggression and apathy, and should therefore have been the most successful. The management parallel being that a democratic style should produce similar beneficial results. However, there is a vast difference between clubs for boys and the management of complex formal organizations. It is unfortunate that the original studies did not report other measures of success such as productivity or achievement. The studies are criticized as not specifically organizational based and being experimentally weak. They were, however, the first serious examination of different styles of leadership.

The Ohio State University studies

The Ohio State University studies began in 1945 and used a questionnaire to examine leadership. Those questioned included officers, other ranks and civilian staff in the army and navy, manufacturing company supervisors, college administrators, teachers and student leaders.

The results were subjected to factor analysis and two factors emerged. They were called:

- Consideration. Indicating a concern by the leader for subordinate welfare, respect and rapport with them.
- Initiating structure. Reflects the degree to which the leader is task focused, emphasizes the achievement of objectives.

These studies are of prime importance in establishing the importance of the task and people dimensions of success. It has been argued that these studies don't necessarily identify actual leader behaviour but the perceptions of those completing the form. Leaders could answer on the basis of how they think they behave, or how they would like to behave. A subordinate might complete the questions on the basis of personal feelings towards their boss.

Likert's four systems of management

Likert developed this approach from the many years of work by a team at the University of Michigan. The four systems (or styles) of leadership are:

- System 1. Exploitative autocratic. The leader has no confidence or trust in subordinates and does not seek or get ideas from them on work problems.
- System 2. Benevolent autocratic. The leader has some confidence and trust in subordinates. Occasionally the leader will seek ideas and opinions on work problems from subordinates. Their style is paternalistic.
- System 3. Participative. There is significant confidence and trust in subordinates by the leader. However, the leader still seeks to control decision making by frequently seeking the opinions of subordinates and making use of them.
- System 4. Democratic. The leader completely trusts subordinates in all areas associated with the activity. The leader actively seeks the opinions of subordinates and always makes use of them.

Research into successful and unsuccessful teams was based on asking thousands of managers about the teams with which they had experience. The most successful departments were described in terms of systems 3 and 4 whilst the least successful were associated with systems 1 and 2 (Likert, 1967).

However, his work has not been without its critics. It was based on questionnaires and is subject to the criticisms common to such approaches. Also there may be circumstances where it is not appropriate to adopt democratic processes. For example, in a crisis there may not be the time to consult and seek opinion. Muczyk and Reimann (1987) argue that not every organization has the skill or quality of support to enable participation to be undertaken effectively.

The Tannenbaum and Schmidt continuum

Tannenbaum and Schmidt (1973) utilize concepts of *boss-centred leadership* and *subordinate-centred leadership* to describe the style continuum. In this they express the distinction between the exercise of managerial authority and freedom for subordinates. Figure 14.5 reflects this approach to leadership.

It should be noted that at no point in the continuum does the use of authority or access to freedom completely disappear. Even at the extremes of freedom for subordinates the boss has the power to say no. At the other extreme employees retain some freedom, even if only token resistance. Four main differences are identified:

- ■ Tells. The leader identifies appropriate solutions and actions and tells the subordinates what they are supposed to do.
- ■ Sells. The leader still decides upon the course of action but attempts to overcome disagreement and resistance selling the decision, justifying the actions required.
- ■ Consults. The leader allows time for subordinates to discuss the problem and present ideas and solutions. These are then used by the leader to make decisions which are actioned by subordinates.
- ■ Joins. The leader defines the nature of the issue to be decided along with any constraints and then becomes part of the group in finding acceptable solutions.

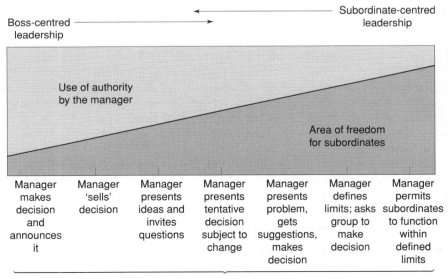

Figure 14.5 Continuum of leadership behaviour (taken from: Luthans, F (1995) *Organization Behaviour*, 7th edn, McGraw-Hill, New York, Figure 14.1).

The form of leadership that would be appropriate in a particular context depends upon leader preferences, subordinate preferences and situational variables. This model leans towards the contingency approach in recognizing that success depends upon a range of factors creating an appropriate match between need, expectation and style.

Blake and Mouton's grid

This approach emerged during the late 1960s and is based upon the idea that leadership is a function of:

- Concern for people.
- Concern for production.

These ideas were not new being similar to work from the Ohio State University studies discussed above. However, Blake and Mouton produced a more systematic approach to the identification of generic styles. A grid is the usual way to represent the relationship between the two factors in the model. Since it was originally published in 1964, the work has been revised several times, most recently as The Leadership Grid® (Blake and McCanse, 1991). Figure 14.6

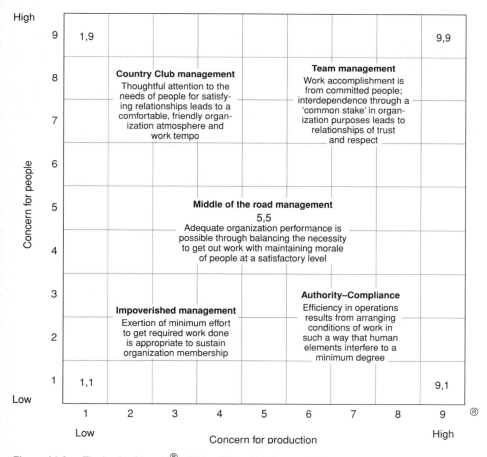

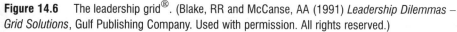

Figure 14.6 The leadership grid®. (Blake, RR and McCanse, AA (1991) *Leadership Dilemmas – Grid Solutions*, Gulf Publishing Company. Used with permission. All rights reserved.)

illustrates this latest version of the model with the five main leadership styles indicated within it.

The term *concern* is used in this context as *emphasis-in* rather than a welfare-based perspective. The score for individuals along each scale would be identified through a questionnaire. Looking at the five stereotypes in the model:

- Impoverished management. A low concern for both people and production. They would be considered as remote from subordinates with little interest in achieving their business goals.
- Authority-compliance management. A very high concern for production but very low concern for people. Relying on the standard procedures and policies to determine action. They would be considered *drivers* of staff in the search for the achievement of objectives.
- Country club management. A very high concern for people but low levels of concern for production. The need to create harmony and avoid conflict thereby allowing subordinates to get on with the job. They would tend to be regarded as *one of the workers* by subordinates.
- Middle of the road management. A medium level of concern for people and production. Keeping everyone happy is a typical approach of such individuals.
- Team management. An equally very high concern for both people and production. Managers with this profile seek to create teams in which both the needs of individuals and the search for output become integrated.

Blake and Mouton found that managers tend to have one dominant style but that many have a backup style if the first proves unsuccessful. They also found that many managers could vary their dominant style to some degree. The factors that influence the style adopted are shown in Figure 14.7.

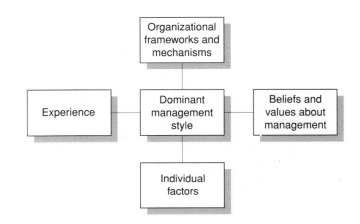

Figure 14.7 Management style determinants.

Hersey and Blanchard's situation approach

This approach was developed by Hersey and Blanchard (1982) and is based on the existence of two different sets of leader behaviour:

- Task behaviour. This approach is based upon the degree to which the leader provides an output focused perspective for the group.
- Relationship behaviour. This approach is based upon the amount of support, encouragement, and two way communication the leader engages in.

There are similarities between this approach and that of Blake and Mouton. The Hersey and Blanchard situation approach adds to those ideas by incorporating additional variables, based on the work of Fiedler. Not all situation variables are included, only those related to the *readiness* of the subordinates to be willing and able to achieve a particular task. From the two basic styles emerge four actual styles when the situation variable of subordinate *readiness* is added to the model (Figure 14.8).

The four actual styles of leadership are:

- Telling. If the subordinates display a low level of readiness to be willing and able to able to achieve the task then the leader should adopt a task oriented style by *telling* subordinates what is expected from them.
- Selling. This style would be most appropriate where the subordinates display moderate levels of readiness towards the task.
- Participating. Where medium levels of subordinate readiness towards the task are found it is possible for the leader to lean towards the relationship aspects of the situation.
- Delegating. With high levels of subordinate readiness there is an opportunity to delegate much of the responsibility for both task and relationship dimensions. The leadership role then becomes facilitation rather than managerial.

There are also similarities between the styles suggested above and those from Tannenbaum and Schmidt described earlier. In practice this model builds on the work of three earlier writers.

There have been a number of criticisms of this model. The theoretical underpinning was argued to be weak because the provision of a rationale for the

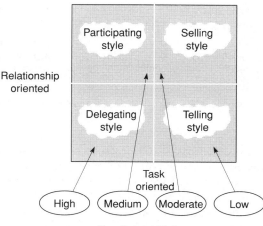

Figure 14.8 Hersey and Blanchard's situation model of leadership (adapted from: Hersey, P and Blanchard, K (1982) *Management of Organizational Behaviour*, Prentice-Hall, New York).

underlying relationships was neglected. The questionnaire used to determine leader effectiveness was also heavily criticized. Nicholls (1985) argues that it breaks the three principles of consistency, continuity and conformity. A revised model is offered which, it is suggested, does not break these principles. Naturally Hersey and Blanchard do not agree with the Nicholls perspective and defended their work in a later publication.

This particular model spans the borderline between style and contingency theories of leadership. It emphasizes style but it also introduces situational aspects into the model.

Contingency theories of leadership

Contingency theory attempts to *add value* by incorporating a wider range of variables into the equation. They suggest that the most appropriate style of leadership is *contingent* upon a range of variables from the context within which the leadership will be exercised. These circumstances could include the expectations of the subordinates, the nature of the task to be achieved or the atmosphere. Management in Action 14.5 reflects the most difficult contingency situation imaginable, a commercial organization attempting to operate during a civil war.

Fiedler's contingency model

This model attempted to identify situational aspects of leadership within a framework that also incorporated effectiveness. Fiedler (1967) brought together three situational aspects for determining the most effective style of leadership. Style was defined as an expression of the leader's personality preferences for either a task or relationship approach. The three situational variables are:

■ Leader–member relationships. It would be reflected in the degree of trust between the parties and a willingness to follow the leader's direction on the part of the subordinates.
■ Task structure. Tasks are either *structured* or *unstructured* in the degree that the task is capable of being achieved through standard procedures. This is similar to the concept of programmed decision making described by Simon.
■ Position power. This construct reflects the degree of authority held by the leader.

The two levels possible for each of these three constructs produces eight situational combinations. These Fiedler combined into three levels of situational favourableness, each linked with either *task* or *relationship* approaches in the behaviour of the leader (Figure 14.9).

Figure 14.9 shows that when the situation is either very favourable or very unfavourable to the leader then a task style is most effective. When the situation is highly favourable to the leader then task orientation ensures that the objectives are achieved. It would be too easy for a 'good time to be had by all' but for nothing to be achieved. When the situation is very unfavourable to the

---

Management in Action 14.5

When managers carry guns

The civil war in Mozambique lasted for 17 years until the signing of a peace accord in October 1992. This deal was largely instigated by 'Tiny' Rowland who arranged the first meeting between the president and the rebel leader. Rowland was at the time head of Lonrho, Mozambique's biggest foreign investor. Lonrho, which had a £53m investment in cotton estates and other businesses, was an obvious target for the rebels during the civil war. In response the company recruited a private army of 1400 men commanded by Gurkhas in order to protect their estates, staff and the flow of cotton. The cost of this was enormous, absorbing up to 30% of the cost of the Mozambique operation.

The rebel forces had crippled much of the economy of Mozambique by blowing up electricity pylons, railway sabotage, the planting of land mines, burning villages and marching the men away into the bush. Lonrho organized its own security. For example, in the Limpopo Valley triple stacks of wire, watchtowers and tanks guarded the perimeter of the company cotton farm. The main buildings were fortresses. John Hewlett, Managing Director of the Mozambique operation, said, 'All our managers were used to farming with a gun on their back. They were mostly Boers or white Rhodesians, and they were excellent at their jobs'.

Every morning tractors on the estate would leave for the fields in columns of five, guarded by 50 members of the security force. Farming was planned with military precision. Routines were changed daily to foil surprise attacks and a constant radio link with headquarters was maintained. Hewlett recalled that several full-blown battles occurred, one resulting in 16 fatalities among the rebel forces.

It was one very large and brutal attack on the farms by the rebels that changed Hewlett's mind about the feasibility of running such operations in the midst of a civil war. About 200 rebels herded cattle at the perimeter fence at dawn one day, raising clouds of dust. A tree was used to fell the barbed wire and cattle stampeded into the compound, followed by the rebels. In a very short period afterwards the rebels blew up about $500,000 of chemicals and irrigation pipes, and set fire to offices and vehicles. The radio operator was burned to death at his transmitter. It was at that point the Hewlett reported back to 'Tiny' Rowland that the war had to be stopped.

In the resulting peace Lonrho made use of its resources in Mozambique to help rebuild the country. It provided former rebels with trucks and office equipment as they attempted to become a respectable political party. The Gurkhas were used as sappers in clearing land mines. Estimates of how many land mines were laid during the civil war ranged from several hundred thousand to several million. Main routes had to be cleared first to allow delivery of humanitarian aid to the stricken population.

Adapted from: Crawford, L. (1994) When managers carry guns. Financial Times, 25 May, p 18.

---

leader then a single-minded, driving approach is necessary in order to achieve the objectives. When the situation is moderately favourable to the leader a relationship approach is necessary in order to gain maximum support for the achievement of the objectives.

In determining the orientation of the leader in terms of *task* or *relationship* behaviour Fiedler developed a test which he called the Least Preferred Co-worker Scale (LPC). Fiedler suggests that these two concepts are personality characteristics and therefore relatively stable leader features. There has been criticism of the research studies that were used to support the development of the model. However there has also been some support for the methodology (Strube and Garcia, 1981).

Leader/member relations	Good				Poor			
Task structure	Structured		Unstructured		Structured		Unstructured	
Position power	High	Low	High	Low	High	Low	High	Low
Situational favourableness	Very favourable			Moderately favourable			Very unfavourable	
Recommended leader behaviour	Task-oriented behaviour			Person-oriented behaviour			Task-oriented behaviour	

Figure 14.9 Fiedler's contingency model of leadership.

Fiedler's work reflects the view that success is a function of the interaction between relationships, task, power and preferred style of the leader. Fiedler suggests that in attempting to optimize effectiveness, organizations should allow managers to maximize the fit between their preferred style and the other variables. This could be achieved through action plans for improving relationships, or perhaps moving key individuals. This approach has attracted some criticism on the basis that they are not consistent with the original model (Jago and Ragan, 1986).

Fiedler subsequently developed his work into a Cognitive Resource Theory (CRT) (Fiedler, 1986). This model attempts to identify the situational circumstances which interact with the cognitive characteristics of the leader and which impact on group performance. As with all research this approach has not been without its critics (Vecchio, 1992). However, it does offer a broader understanding of the interacting variables involved in leadership.

House's path–goal leadership theory

The path–goal model of leadership links leader behaviour with subordinate motivation, performance and satisfaction (House and Mitchell, 1974). This approach is similar to the expectancy theory of motivation. It postulates that subordinate motivation will be improved if the expectation that positive rewards will be forthcoming is likely to be realized. House identified four styles of leader behaviour:

■ Directive leadership. The leader is expected to provide precise instruction on what is required and how it is to be achieved.
■ Supportive leadership. A style that adopts a friendly, concerned approach to the needs and welfare of subordinates.
■ Participative leadership. The leader would seek opinions and suggestions from subordinates before making a decision.
■ Achievement-oriented leadership. The leader is task oriented and sets challenging goals for subordinates.

This contingency approach is based upon the notion that individual leaders are capable of changing their style to match the needs of the situation. The two situational factors are:

- Subordinate characteristics. Leader acceptability depends upon the degree to which subordinates perceive leader behaviour as a source of present of future satisfaction.
- Demands facing subordinates. Leader behaviour motivates performance if the satisfaction of subordinate need is dependent upon performance and other aspects of the environment.

The path–goal model reflects the influence of leader behaviour on subordinate activity as a directional flow towards the goal to be achieved (Figure 14.10).

There have been some attempts to substantiate the model, with mixed results. A paper which reviewed 48 studies demonstrated mixed levels of support for aspects of the model and suggested the continued testing of it (Indvik, 1986).

The Vroom, Yetton and Jago model of leadership

This model was introduced in 1973 by Vroom and Yetton and expanded by Vroom and Jago (1988). Like the other contingency models, it attempts to identify styles of leadership appropriate in particular situations. It presupposes that leaders can vary their style of behaviour and that only some aspects of the situation are relevant. The model postulates that it is the degree of subordinate involvement in the decision making process that is the major variable in leader behaviour. The model is managerial in orientation in that it attempts to offer ways to provide a high-quality decision but at the same time ensure that subordinates actively support the decision.

There are four decision trees offered by the model, two for group problems and two for individual problems. Each pair contains a decision tree for emergency (or time pressured) situations and one for less time sensitive events. The latter variation also allows managers to develop subordinate decision making through their involvement in the process. The decision tree does not provide the answer to the problem itself, but offers a suggestion for a leader style that *should* generate the *best* decision in the circumstances, based on levels of subordinate involvement.

There is a potential difficulty for leaders in being thought inconsistent in their style. For a leader to change style may create conflict, confusion or lower morale and productivity among subordinates. Subordinates may become

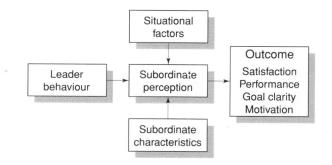

Figure 14.10   Path–goal model of leadership.

accustomed to being involved in decision making or become unsure of the degree of involvement that they will enjoy. That said, there is some research evidence that decisions consistent with the model are more effective than those not consistent with it.

Other approaches to leadership

The vertical dyad linkage model

This approach to leadership was developed by Dansereau *et al*. (1975). It suggests that leaders behave different with different subordinates. Between the leader and each subordinate is an individual relationship, referred to as a vertical dyad. The model postulates that leaders create an *in-group* and an *outgroup* around themselves and that these groups receive different treatments from the leader. The *in-group* are a few special individuals, more trusted, given preferential treatment and special privileges than those not in that elite (see Figure 14.11).

Life-cycle model

Clarke and Pratt (1985) suggest that there are different requirements from a leader during the organization's life cycle. They identify four different leadership patterns:

- Champion. In the formation stages of an organization a leader who can *champion* the new business, win orders, organize a team of employees and display a broad spectrum of managerial ability is required.
- Tank commander. In the growth phase new people will be brought into the organization and departments will be established. An individual to *bulldoze* ideas through and *drive* the organization towards its future is depicted here.
- Housekeeper. The maturity phase tends to require an emphasis on the achievement of cost effectiveness. This is the phase when much activity surrounds the development and application of standard procedures to activity.

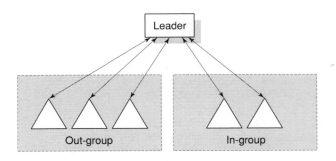

Figure 14.11 The vertical dyad model of leadership.

- Lemon-squeezer. Decline can either result in demise or rejuvenation. A tough leader is required in order to *squeeze* the maximum out of the situation and attempt to inject new life into the organization.

A variation on this approach is that proposed by Rodrigues (1988). This version is based on the premise that the real variation in experience for most organizations is in attempting to continue to function in constantly dynamic context. This carries with it implications for problem solving, implementation and stability in a constantly changing environment.

Transactional and transformational model

Developed by Kuhnert and Lewis (1987) who suggested two types of management activity, each demanding different skills:

- Transactional. This includes the allocation of work, making routine decisions, monitoring performance and interacting with other functions within the organization.
- Transformational. This is about having the skills and personal qualities to be able to recognize the need for change and being able to identify appropriate courses of action.

Bass (1990) identified the characteristics of both types of leader (Table 14.1). He suggests that transactional leaders are a hindrance to change and they foster a climate of mediocrity. Transformational leads on the other hand can produce improved performance in situations of uncertainty and change.

Tepper (1993) found transformational leaders more frequently adopted legitimating tactics. They were also able to achieve higher acceptance of objectives among subordinates than transactional leaders.

Charismatic leadership

House (1977) characterized charismatic leaders as full of self-confidence, with a high level of confidence in subordinates and high expectations for results.

Transactional leaders
1. Contingent reward: Contracts exchange of rewards for effort, promises rewards for good performance, recognizes accomplishments.
2. Management by exception (active): Watches and searches for deviations from rules and standards, takes corrective action.
3. Management by exception (passive): Intervenes only if standards are not met
4. *Laissez faire*: Abdicates responsibilities, avoids making decisions.

Transformational leaders
1. Charisma: Provides vision and sense of mission, instills pride, gains respect and trust
2. Inspiration: Communicates high expectations, uses symbols to focus efforts, expresses important purposes in simple ways.
3. Intellectual stimulation Promotes intelligence, rationality, and careful problem solving.
4. Individual consideration: Gives personal attention, treats each employee individually, coaches, advises.

Table 14.1
Characteristics of transactional and transformational leaders (source: Bass, BM (1990) From transactional to transformational leadership: learning to share the vision. *Organizational Dynamics*, Winter 1990, p 22. Used with permission)

They also have a clear vision of the goal to be achieved, are able to communicate this effectively and lead by example. Charismatic leaders can create problems for organizations. If they do not make effective provision for succession the organization can flounder, illustrated in Management in Action 14.6.

Charismatic leadership could be a function of leader traits and situational variables (Conger and Kanungo, 1988). Traits that may produce a charismatic approach include self-confidence, skills in impression management and social sensitivity. Contextual variables that could encourage the emergence of a

---

Management in Action 14.6

The man at the top is king

What happens when the top manager either dies or leaves the company suddenly? This is an issue that faced the senior executives of Argentine oil giant YPF in 1995 when the light aircraft carrying the company president José Estenssoro crashed into the Andes. It is a particularly difficult situation when the leader is charismatic and the dominant force in the company, as was the case with José Estenssoro. After taking over as company president he saw the state-owned company privatized in 1993 and began the turnaround of the loss-making company into a profitable and expanding business. Employee numbers were cut dramatically from 50,000 to about 6000, yet it managed to achieve membership of the top ten private oil companies measured by reserves through his leadership approach.

Michael J Wolf of management consultants Booz Allen & Hamilton in New York has made a study of charismatic leaders in the media industry. His studies suggest that an inspired succession is crucial, particularly in industries where flair and leadership are key factors for success. However, according to Wolf, 'One of the problems for companies with visionary leaders is that it is often difficult for that person to build a pipeline of talented managers – it's one of the things they tend to ignore'. He goes on to explain that such individuals are frequently reluctant to share their corporate 'gameplan' with the next level of management down. They are often self-obsessed and difficult to work with. 'One of the big questions that companies are facing these days is: do they

have a model that relies on stars, or do they have a pipeline of talent?' he asks.

Ben Morgan of Kleinwort Benson in Buenos Aires said of the situation facing YPF, 'I think they've suffered an enormous shock and they're a little bit directionless as a consequence. Because he was so much the front man and had articulated the strategy so well, there is a worry among institutional investors about whether the business can be made to work without someone of his character'.

Two options face a company in this situation. Firstly, attempt to create a team to take over at the top and develop the management talent lower down the organization whilst holding the situation stable in the short term. Alternatively, some analysts advise, for example Christopher Ecclestone, a broker with Interacciones in Buenos Aires, that an international search should be made for a 'heavyweight' appointment that could step into the vacant position. Someone who could articulate the company strategy and act as front man. This is thought to be particularly important for YPF in Argentina where the corporate hierarchy tends to be more autocratic than in other countries. The argument for this approach being that the day-to-day running of the company was effectively handled by the lower levels of management, and that this had not changed as a result of the death of José Estenssoro. Morgan agreed with this view saying that it was difficult to get collective responsibility right, the squabbling could be destructive and that someone with natural authority was needed to keep the company moving along.

Adapted from: Pilling, D. (1995) The man at the top is king. Financial Times, 15 September, p 12.

charismatic leader include crisis situations and high levels of subordinate dissatisfaction. Howell and Avolio (1992) introduce an ethical perspective, pointing out that it is possible for charismatic individuals to abuse their capabilities to achieve an unquestioning following.

Attribution theory

Individuals observe the behaviour in others and then *attribute* causes to it. The leader observes the behaviour of subordinates, imputes causes to it, and reacts on the basis of those interpretations (Martinko and Gardner, 1987). An employee who is frequently late for work and who will not work flexibly may be *led* as lazy and not interested in the job. One problem is that assumptions made by the leader may be wrong. In addition, the identification of causes of behaviour does not automatically result in behavioural responses. A leader might interpret the cause of employee behaviour as poor working conditions and seek to address those issues rather than changing behaviour.

Leadership substitutes

Kerr and Jermier (1978) suggest three areas where substitution for leadership is possible:

■ Subordinate characteristics. Situations where employees are professionally qualified, highly experienced and very able to undertake the duties expected of them. A subordinate who is indifferent to the rewards that the leader can offer.
■ Task characteristics. Where work is highly routine and contains immediate feedback on performance and achievement.
■ Organizational characteristics. An organization that is highly routinized with little flexibility will have limited need for leader activity as it will almost run itself.

Research suggests that these factors do substitute for leadership. However there may be factors in existence that can influence the level of contribution from a leader.

Leadership as symbolism

It has been argued that it is the symbolism associated with the leadership role that influences subordinate behaviour (Griffin *et al.*, 1987). A head of state has several official duties to perform, signing new laws, opening parliament, welcoming official visitors, etc. In a work context individuals take a lead from the behaviour of their managers. If a leader is thoughtful, caring, concerned and works hard, subordinates will tend to respect that individual and work in a similar manner. The converse is also true.

Leadership – roles and skills

Role theory emerges from the theatre where it is obvious that the actors are performing *roles* as written by the author and as interpreted by the director. The requirements of the part that each actor is performing is set out in the script. There is a requirement that each player will behave as expected for the whole performance to work as intended. The web of expectation that everyone in society will perform as expected in the specific role that they are performing creates stability and predictability in work, recreation and relationships.

Role theory provides individuals with an outline of what is expected of them in undertaking a particular job or function. How to tackle 'problem employees' would be one such example, where individuals are often provided with the opportunity to *role play* particular events and explore appropriate behaviour patterns. The observation that someone is a good (or bad) *role model* is another indication of the value of the concept in *shaping* behaviour.

Zimbardo carried out an experiment in which students took part in the role play of a prison over two weeks. Students were screened for emotional stability and maturity before being randomly allocated to the role of guard or prisoner. A basement was transformed into a prison and the volunteers were dressed appropriately. Guards were instructed to maintain order during their shift and left to arrange things on that basis. Within six days the experiment had to be called off. Both sets of *players* became so integrated into their roles that the well-being of prisoners was at risk. Several explanations have been put forward for this result including the significance of role and its expectations, together with its direct influence on behaviour (Haney *et al.*, 1973).

Considering the notion of role in formal terms there are a number of concepts that need to be examined:

■ Role set. The name given to the group of people with whom a particular person might interact in a particular context. Figure 14.12 is the role set of a personnel manager.

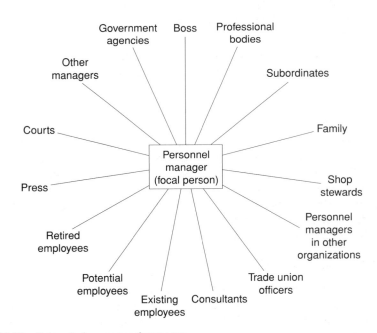

Figure 14.12   Role set of a personnel manager.

- Role definition. The sum of behavioural expectations from the role set surrounding a focal person in a specific context.
- Role ambiguity. Refers to the existence of uncertainty among the role set about the precise role that each is expected to play in a specific context.
- Role incompatibility. Where expectations of members of the role set differ with the focal persons view of their role. Employees may have been used to an open informal style. The appointment of a manager with an authoritarian style produces incompatibility in the expectations.
- Role conflict. Arises with the dilemmas between the roles that individuals are expected to perform in the same situation. In performance appraisal reviews there is often scope for role conflict as a result of the performance and salary requirements.
- Role stress and strain. Pressure arises for individuals as a result of the roles that they are required to undertake in a specific context. Pressure is not of itself a bad thing, but too much can be harmful.

Mintzberg (1973) describes a number of roles undertaken by managers (see Figure 14.13).

More recent studies have introduced different role titles, including visioning and motivator. There has been some support for the use of these concepts and their impact on organizational performance (Hart and Quinn, 1993). However, it has also been suggested that much of this is a reflection of a 'pop-culture' in management – in other words a transient, shallow perspective offering little of substance.

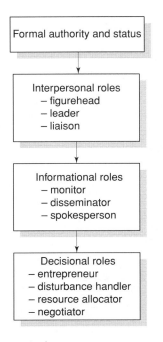

Figure 14.13 Mintzberg's management roles.

International perspectives on leadership

There are tensions inherent in international leadership that do not arise in a single country context. Adler (1991) describes the, '... tensions between one's immediate national concerns and the broader interests of humanity and the future' (p 148). She quotes the work of Levinson on the impact of early culture experience which predisposes individuals to particular ways of relating to other people and power relationships. It is suggested that this in turn conditions particular ways of leading or being led in an organizational context.

Adler also quotes an interesting report by Oh (1976) reflecting the application of Theory X and Theory Y to management in China after the 1949 revolution. It identified that managers allied with the communist ideology tended to adopt the Theory Y perspectives in the belief that they were closely aligned with the philosophy of Chairman Mao. Managers with less skill in the ideological areas tended to adopt Theory X principles. This provides an indication that leadership approach may be influenced by political and economic as well as cultural perspectives.

A US-owned company with a subsidiary in South America is likely to face different leadership scenarios and pressures to an indigenous organization. Equally, a foreign organization in any country in the world led by a national from that country is likely to face different leadership scenarios and pressures to one managed by a parent country expatiate. Figure 14.14 reflects the interaction between the variables active in this context.

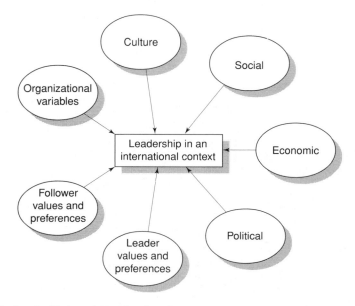

Figure 14.14   Leadership in an international context.

Meetings and humour in management

Meetings are an inevitable aspect of management. The need to involve other people in decision making as well as persuading them to co-operate in specific courses of action are just two of the reasons for their existence. Other reasons for holding meetings include:

- Habit. Holding the regular Monday production meeting, simply because it has always been held, rather than for a specific purpose.
- Political. It is possible for managers to convene a meeting simply to be able to say at some future time that everyone was involved.
- Courage. Managers can lack the courage to take a particular decision on their own.

Meetings can therefore be for rational business-oriented purposes, routine purposes and even defensive or offensive reasons. The existence of a hidden agenda for a meeting can frequently only be guessed at. In addition to formal meetings there are vast numbers of informal discussions in corridors and over coffee that serve much the same purpose. Mackenzie (1972) suggests that many middle managers spend up to 80% of their time in meetings and that approximately 50% of that time may be wasted (p 98).

Humour is a topic that is not formally part of organizational functioning and has therefore been regarded as something incidental to management. It is suggested that organizations are places of rationality and that humour has no place in them. Levity could be a signal that business is not being taken seriously, that there was a lack of respect for the products or senior managers. Humour is generally considered as a trivializing process. However, that is not the only purpose of humour. Consider the use of satire as a means of making political points; such insights are frequently far from trivial.

Barsoux (1993) in a book devoted to a consideration of the links between humour, management and culture, suggests that humour in the workplace, '... is rarely neutral, trivial or random. It is deployed for the achievement of quite specific purposes to do with self-preservation, getting things done or getting one's way' (p vii). Barsoux identifies the three main purposes of humour as being:

- Sword. The *action* aspect of humour. In this it can persuade individuals to particular points of view. It can allow individuals to say those things which otherwise could not be said without causing offence and damage to relationships.
- Shield. The *defensive* aspect of humour. It can be used to make criticism more acceptable (by making a joke out of it) and to enable individuals and groups to cope more easily with failure.
- Values. The basis for *conditioning* individuals into a particular role and the *reinforcement* of organizational values. The use of practical jokes and the use of 'in-jokes' – only understandable to the in-group are the means by which groups can be formed and bonded into cohesive units.

In his book based on a participative research project, Watson (1994) describes a number of aspects of humour during his interviews and observations of managers. In addition to the functions of humour outlined above, he describes the role of humour in relation to communication and control. He describes the communication facilitation provided through a touch of humour in the conversation, 'They [the listener] get something back for giving the speaker their attention' (p 187).

Leadership: a management perspective

That leadership and management are not the same has already been established. Management is the exercise of formal authority in an organizational context, leadership is more to do with performance. It is hardly surprising that managers have for a long time been interested in leadership. Gone are the days when leadership could be assumed as a right of birth – at least in many situations. Managers have an interest in the study of the subject from many perspectives. Firstly, to protect their position. Secondly, managers have an interest in understanding leadership to increase operational effectiveness. Thirdly, it might provide them with a means of dealing more effectively with other managers. The variables associated with the practice of management and leadership include:

- The manager. There are a number of variables that influence the approach to management. They include the personality characteristics of the individual together with the training and experience that they have undergone during their lives and careers. Managers perceptions about the situation and their subordinates also influence how they respond to situations. It should be remembered that managers are also subordinates, with the exception of those that own their organizations. Even the board of directors has to present itself to its shareholders at regular intervals.

- The managed. These are generally mirror images of the previous factors. For example, the personality factors of the subordinates will to some extent predispose them to prefer to be managed in particular ways. Inevitably over time there is a degree of *fit* that emerges between individual and job/organization. Individuals that do not fit into a particular situation either because they think or behave differently tend to leave or are pushed out of the group.

- The context. The industry and organization itself will carry some degree of influence on the nature of management. A context which has been highly confrontational in the past is unlikely to change quickly to one that could support a participative style.

- The situation. The objectives being sought are a feature of the management process. A military leader seeking to win a battle is faced with a different situation to the manager seeking to process thousands of customer accounts. Consequently there will be differences in the way that management would be exercised.

- The task. The work of professional or technical specialists requires different approaches to management than work in a factory. The name *professional* implies a level of capability and an approach to work that implies that management is less to do with the content of the work than development and monitoring performance. Such individuals frequently resent (and resist) direct supervision and control. The importance of the task as well as the technology involved are also variables that could be expected to impact on the management activities. Importance in this context refers to significance for the organization or individuals within it.

Figure 14.15 reflects the linkages between these main variables.

Management and leadership are still problematic concepts. Which of the variables identified in Figure 14.15 are the most important and which the least? How do the variables interact and how do they influence the approach adopted? Does the variation in one variable automatically produce a difference in management? How does management as defined above fit into the concept of leadership? To the practising manager these issues are very real as they attempt to practice the art and science of management. Senior managers have a responsibility to ensure that their organizations are effectively managed, but before they can make provision for that they need to understand the processes involved. They also need to be able to make provision for the selection and development of managers. However, if management reflects a situation specific set of competencies, then a completely different set of criteria apply to the selection, training and careers of managers. Management in Action 14.7 overleaf considers the subject of learning how to be a manager.

It is not possible to offer definitive models that ensure the best match between manager and situation can be provided. It is reasonably safe to assume that the degree of adaptation available through the inherent capabilities of human beings provides a basis for believing that people can learn many of the skills associated with being a manager. Also that they can adapt their behaviour patterns to achieve at least a workable compromise between anarchy and perfection in specific contexts.

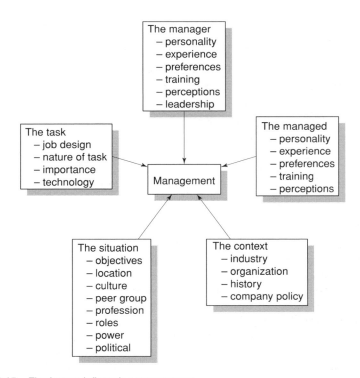

Figure 14.15 The factors influencing management.

Management in Action 14.7

Who taught you to do what you do?

Every manager must learn how to carry out the tasks associated with the job. But how? Ballin and Vincent carried out some research in the steel industry that involved 19 separate businesses and a sample of 245 managers to seek answers to this question. Their research involved a three-stage process. The first was a questionnaire about the experience of the managers in relation to training. The second was a structured 45-minute interview about the experiences of managers in relation to the timing and relevance of training received. The third was another interview process aimed at identifying future training needs and the attitude of managers to training in general.

The results emphasize the role of training in the development of managers rather than specifically who they learn from. It indicated that the training received by most managers was well timed but that learning about people management should come before experiencing it for the first time. There was a general feeling of a lack of structure to the training and development received by managers and that some of the training was too general in content. Equally, managers do not generally place much effort into self development, although they do have some influence over what training they receive. They tend to emphasize formal training courses rather than experiential training for both themselves and subordinates.

Pearn, Honey and Clutterbuck used 250 delegates attending their presentation at the Institute of Personnel and Development annual conference to address the issue of how managers learn. Among the findings of their survey were:

- Peers within the organization were the most popular choice of 'who it was easy to learn from'. This was followed by the line boss and a mentor. Off-line mentors on the other hand were seen as having the most potential for managers to learn from.
- In terms of the learning cycle, most respondents found that 'experiencing' was the easiest part of learning with the 'concluding' aspect being the most difficult.
- Making mistakes represented an important learning opportunity, but the language of talking about mistakes was unpleasant and difficult. It was generally thought that from an organizational perspective the two biggest causes of mistakes were 'blinkered thinking' and 'defining goals'. From an individual perspective the biggest causes of mistakes was 'pressure to act' and 'generalization' (working on partial, untested information and assumption).

Adapted from: Ballin, M and Vincent, R (1995) Who taught you to do what you do? People Management, *30 November, pp 32–3, and Pearn, M, Honey, P and Clutterbuck, D (1995) Learning from the good, the bad – and the ugly mistakes.* People Management, *30 November, p 43.*

Conclusions

This chapter has considered many of the variables associated with the subject of management and leadership. The major theoretical approaches to the study of leadership have been introduced and critically evaluated. In addition we have discussed a number of other approaches to the subject as well as related features of management activity. In this latter category we have considered what it is that managers actually do and the roles that they adopt whilst performing their duties. The subject of international perspectives on leadership were introduced. This chapter ended with a brief consideration of humour in management and the function of meetings which account for much management time.

Discussion questions

1 Define the following key terms used in this chapter:

Management	House's path–goal model
Leadership	Likert's four systems of management
Style	Blake and Mouton's leadership grid
Trait	Hersey and Blanchard's model
Contingency	Role
Vroom, Yetton and Jago's model	Fiedler's model

2 Discuss the differences and similarities between the concepts of management and leadership.

3 Is an attempt to identify the most appropriate management style simply another attempt to identify a formula which is doomed to failure? Justify your answer.

4 Describe Likert's four systems of management and attempt to make a case for system 1 being the most appropriate style in a particular context. What might this imply about the concept of effectiveness in management?

5 'Come the hour, come the leader.' Discuss this statement in the light of the approaches to leadership discussed in this chapter.

6 'There is nothing to choose between the different style theories of leadership.' Discuss this statement.

7 Does humour have any part to play in management? Justify your answer.

8 Fiedler's contingency model suggests that if the situation is very unfavourable to the leader then it is necessary to drive the subordinates towards the objectives by adopting a task oriented style of leadership. Do you agree with this view? Justify your answer.

9 How would you seek to make use of the Vroom, Yetton and Jago contingency model in managing subordinates?

10 'Charismatic leaders are not appropriate in the middle ranks of managerial jobs because they could provide a focus for an organization within an organization.' Discuss this statement.

Research questions

1 Arrange to interview about six different managers from a range of organizations and job functions. Talk to them about their own approach to management. Identify what they consider to be the differences and similarities between management and leadership. Do they consider that management and leadership are skills that can be taught or are they natural talents possessed by some but not everyone? Do they have a particular style of operation or do they change approach to fit the circumstances? Consider the results of the interviews and draw lessons from it with what you have studied in this chapter?

2 For a number of famous business, military or political leaders obtain a copy of their biography or autobiography. What does it tell you about their views of management and leadership, can you reconcile the different views expressed and does the material presented in this chapter accommodate their views (and if not why)?

3   Conduct a library search on the subject of management and leadership. What issues do you think that are relevant to topics that have (or have not) been introduced in this chapter?

Key reading

From Clark, H., Chandler, J and Barry, J. (1994) *Organization and Identities: Text and Readings in Organizational Behaviour*, International Thomson Business Press, London.

- Kanter RM: Men and Women of the Corporation, p 152. Considers the nature of organizations and the impact on the people that work in them.
- Nichols T and Beynon H: The labour of superintendence: managers, p 192. This considers the reality of management in an organization.
- Roethlisberger FJ and Dickson R: Group restriction of output, p 247. Although emphasizing the significance of groups, it also reviews the relationship between managers and subordinates.
- Coch L and French JRP: Overcoming resistance to change using group methods, p 260. Considers a number of aspects of change management, including the strategies adopted by managers.
- Fiedler FE: Leadership: A contingency model, p 272. Part of the original work from this particular writer on the first of the contingency models.
- Needham P: The 'autonomous' work group, p 310. Discusses the nature and role of management within this form of work organization.

Further reading

Berkeley Thomas, A (1993) *Controversies In Management*, Routledge, London. This text concentrates on attempting to understand the complexities associated with the study of management.

Heller, R (1985) *The Naked Manager: Games Executives Play*, McGraw-Hill, New York. The behaviours that managers adopt and the political and business reasons that motivate it are the focus of attention.

Hersey, P and Blanchard, KH (1988) *Management of Organizational Behaviour*, 5th edn, Prentice-Hall, Englewood Cliffs, NJ. This contains a reply to the Nicholls' criticisms of their original model.

Luecke, R (1994) *Scuttle Your Ships Before Advancing and Other Lessons from History on Leadership and Change for Today's Managers*, Oxford University Press, New York. This book takes a look back into history at a number of major events involving management, leadership and change. It then attempts to draw lessons from those episodes that can be of value to managers of today.

Nicholls, JR (1985) A new approach to situational leadership. *Leadership and Organization Development Journal*, 6, 2–7. This offers another view of the Hersey and Blanchard model of management style. It claims to identify major weaknesses in the original and suggests how these can be overcome.

Stewart, R and Barsoux, J-L (1994) *The Diversity of Management: Twelve Managers Talking*, Macmillan, Basingstoke. This book is based around interviews with practising managers. Drawn from a wide range of middle and senior level jobs in diverse industries they provide an introspective account of the nature of their work.

References

Adair, J (1983) *Effective Leadership: A Self-development Manual*, Gower, Aldershot.

Adler, NJ (1991) *International Dimensions of Organizational Behaviour*, 2nd edn. Wadsworth, Belmont, CA.

Ashby, WR (1956) *An Introduction to Cybernetics*, Methuen, London.

Barsoux, J-L (1993) *Funny Business: Humour, Management and Business Culture*, Cassell, London.

Bass, BM (1990) From transactional to transformational leadership: learning to share the vision. *Organizational Dynamics*, Winter, 19–31.

Blake, RR and McCanse, AA (1991) *Leadership Dilemmas – Grid Solutions*, Gulf Publishing.

Clarke, C and Pratt, S (1985) Leadership's four-part progress. *Management Today*, March, 84–86.

Conger, JA and Kanungo, RM (1988) Behavioural dimensions of charismatic leadership. In *Charismatic Leadership: The Elusive Factor In Organizational Effectiveness* (eds JA Conger and RM Kanungo), Jossey Bass, San Francisco, CA.

Dansereau, F, Graen, G and Haga, WJ (1975) A vertical dyad linkage approach to leadership within formal organizations: a longitudinal investigation of the role-making process. *Organizational Behaviour and Human Performance*, **15**, 46–78.

Fayol, H (1949) *General and Industrial Management*, Pitman, London.

Fiedler, FE (1967) *A Theory of Leadership Effectiveness*, McGraw-Hill, New York.

Fiedler, F. E. (1986) The contribution of cognitive resources to leadership performance. *Journal of Applied Social Psychology*, **16**, 532–48.

Griffin, RW., Skivington, KD and Moorhead, G (1987) Symbolic and interactional perspectives on leadership: an integrative framework. *Human Relations*, **40**, 199–218.

Handy, C. (1993) *Understanding Organizations*, 4th edn, Penguin, Harmondsworth.

Haney, C, Banks, C and Zimbardo, P (1973) A study of prisoners and guards in a simulated prison. *Naval Research Reviews*, Office of Naval Research, Department of the Navy, Washington, September, pp 1–17.

Harrison, R. (1994) *Employee Development*, IPD, London.

Hart, SL and Quinn, RE (1993) Roles executives play: CEOs, behavioural complexity, and firm performance. *Human Relations*, May, 543–75.

Hellriegel, D, Slocum, JW and Woodman, RW (1989) *Organizational Behaviour*, 5th edn, West Publishing, St Paul, MN.

Hersey, P and Blanchard, KH (1982) *Management of Organizational Behaviour*, 4th edn, Prentice-Hall, Englewood Cliffs, NJ.

House, RJ and Mitchell, TR (1974) Path–goal theory of leadership. *Journal of Contemporary Business*, Autumn, 81–97.

House, RJ (1977) A 1976 theory of charismatic leadership. In *Leadership: The Cutting Edge* (eds JG Hunt and LL Larson), Southern Illinois University Press, Carbondale, IL.

Howell, JM and Avolio, BJ (1992) The ethics of charismatic leadership: submission or liberation? *Academy of Management Executive*, May, 43–54.

Indvik, J. (1986) Path–goal theory of leadership: a meta-analysis. *Academy of Management Best Papers Proceedings*, 189–92.

Jago, AG and Ragan, JW (1986) The trouble with leader match is that it doesn't match Fiedler's contingency model. *Journal of Applied Psychology*, **71**, 555–59.

Kerr, S and Jermier, JM (1978) Substitutes for leadership: their meaning and measurement. *Organizational Behaviour and Human Performance*, **22**, 375–403.

Kuhnert, KW and Lewis, P (1987) Transactional and transformational leadership: a constructive/developmental analysis. *Academy of Management Review*, October, 648–57.

Likert, R (1967) *The Human Organization*, McGraw-Hill, New York.

Luthans, F (1995) *Organizational Behaviour*, 7th edn, McGraw-Hill, New York.

Mackenzie, RA (1972) *The Time Trap: How To Get More Done In Less Time*, McGraw-Hill, New York.

Martinko, MJ and Gardner, WL (1987) The leader/member attribution process. *Academy of Management Review*, April, 235–49.

Mintzberg, H (1973) *The Nature of Managerial Work*, Harper & Row, New York.

Muczyk, JP and Reimann, BC (1987) The case for directive leadership. *The Academy of Management Executive*, November.

Nicholls, JR (1985) A new approach to situational leadership. *Leadership and Organization Development Journal*, **6**, 2–7.

Oh, TK (1976) Theory Y in the People's Republic of China. *California Management Review*, **19**, 77–84.

Reed, M (1989) *The Sociology of Management*, Harvester Wheatsheaf, Hemel Hempstead.

Rodrigues, CA (1988) Identifying the right leader for the right situation. *Personnel*, September, 43–6.

Rothman, A (1987) Maybe your skills aren't holding you back: maybe it's a birthday. *The Wall Street Journal*, 19 March, 35.

Rowe, C (1993) *The Management Matrix*, Alfred Waller, London.

Scase, R and Goffee, R (1989) *Reluctant Managers: Their Work and Lifestyles*, Unwin Hyman, London.

Stewart, R (1976) *Contrasts in Management*, McGraw-Hill, Maidenhead.

Stewart, R. (1985) *The Reality of Management*, 2nd edition, Pan Books, London.

Strube, MJ and Garcia, JE (1981) A meta-analytic investigation of Fiedler's contingency model of leadership effectiveness, *Psychological Bulletin*, September, 307–21.

Tannenbaum, R and Schmidt, WH (1973) How to choose a leadership pattern. *Harvard Business Review*, May–June, 178–80.

Tepper, BJ (1993) Patterns of downward influence and follower conformity in transactional and transformational leadership. *Academy of Management Best Papers Proceedings*, 267–71.

Torrington, D and Hall, L (1991) *Personnel Management: A New Approach*, 2nd edn, Prentice-Hall, Hemel Hempstead.

Vecchio, RP (1992) Cognitive resource theory: issues for specifying a test of the theory. *Journal of Applied Psychology*, **77**, 375–76.

Vroom, VH and Jago, AG (1988) *The New Leadership*, Prentice-Hall, Englewood Cliffs, NJ.

Watson, TJ (1994) *In Search of Management: Culture, Chaos and Control in Managerial Work,* Routledge, London.

15
Ethics and employee involvement

Chapter summary

This chapter begins with the consideration of the links between ethics and moral philosophy before going on to discuss different approaches to the subject. This will be followed by a review of the major ethical dilemmas facing managers. The chapter will then review the links between participation and control before exploring the relationship between involvement and human resource management. The main forms of employee involvement will also be discussed.

Learning objectives

After studying this chapter and working through the associated Management in Action panels, discussion questions and research activities, you should be able to:

- Understand the basis of ethics and its links with moral philosophy.
- Describe the main forms of employee involvement.
- Explain the different classifications of ethical perspective.
- Outline the links between employee participation, power and control.
- Assess the ethical dilemmas facing managers.
- Appreciate the managerial activity that can be influenced by ethics.
- Discuss the approaches that managers take to resolving the ethical difficulties that they face.
- Detail the options for different forms of employee involvement.

Introduction

Ethical aspects influences both the process involved in making decisions and the criteria used to judge between options. The involvement of employees in decision making also contains ethical perspectives. It is not only managers that face ethical dilemmas. Employees frequently have to make judgements which contain an ethical dimension. For example, what should an employee do when they consider that their organization is cheating customers? There are situations where both managers and employees can collude to defraud other people. Management in Action 15.1 illustrates one such situation, collusion in defrauding the state benefit system. Clearly the ethical and legal implications are being ignored by the individuals involved.

Employee involvement is a difficult area for managers. Employees are human beings and are unlike the other resources available to the organization. Most resources are malleable at the whim of management. Money will go where it is

---

Management in Action 15.1

Employers 'helping workers to claim dole'

The so-called 'Black Economy' provides opportunities for individuals to earn money that is hidden from the state and thereby not liable to taxation. This increases the earnings levels of the individuals in receipt of the money and 'starves' the government of income. It is also a process that allows the employer to save money by not having to pay any company taxation to the state as a result of having someone on the payroll. In addition, it is possible to pay the employee a lower wage because they will not have to pay tax on that income. As a process the black economy works at many different levels. Individual householders may ask a friend with plumbing skills to put in a new shower unit in the bathroom of their house and pay the friend for doing the work. At another level an individual may work for a company at the same time as claiming state benefit for being unemployed.

In the UK the various civil service departments who have a responsibility for paying state benefit to unemployed people have become increasingly aware of the attempts of some unscrupulous people to defraud the system. In a relatively recent trend it has also been found that some employers are actively colluding with employees to allow them to claim unemployment pay as well as wages. This has become so significant that special fraud units have been established to find and prosecute claimants and employers found engaging in these practices. In the year 1992–3, 55 employers were prosecuted and another 71 cases were pending. A total of 264,616 investigations of individuals was carried out which resulted in 2602 prosecutions and another 61,129 people withdrew claims for benefit without being prosecuted.

In some cases employers were found to be allowing employees time off work to claim benefit. In a small number of cases employers actually drove the employee to the benefit office to sign on as unemployed. Typically such employers were very small, with less than 15 workers in total. They also tended to be in the service sector such as mini-cab firms, hotels, catering, casual farm work and amusement arcades. A government minister claimed that such practices were, 'An example of how the black economy corrodes the fabric of our society'. Also that, '... this behaviour gives unscrupulous employers an unfair advantage over their competitors.'

Adapted from: Bennett, W (1993) Employers 'helping workers to claim dole'. The Independent, 11 August, p 4.

---

channelled. Raw material will be worked on and change appearance until it is part of the finished product or scrap. These forms of resource have no choice in how they are used. Human beings do have choice.

To begin with humans decide which organizations to seek to be associated with. They decide when to leave – unless that decision is taken out of their hands through death, illness, accident, retirement or termination of employment by management. Whilst at work there are also many choices available to the human resource. How hard to work; how much effort to put into the job; how conscientious to be in looking after the general interests of the employer; how hard to resist employer demands for more work; how hard to push in seeking to meet their own aspirations for higher pay or shorter hours, etc. These reflect just some of the ways in which human beings can influence events associated with their work experiences.

Managers seek to find ways to *manipulate* the resources under their control in the interests of their objectives. More efficient ways of making products, reductions in waste, and higher productivity are just some of the *manipulations* engaged in. *Manipulation* is frequently regarded as having negative connotations and that can be so in some situations. On the other hand a wood carver can create something of great beauty as a result of the *manipulation* of tools and pieces of wood. The managerial imperative to manipulate is, according to the rational view, intended to harness and direct resources in pursuit of objectives and does not contain a negative connotation. Unfortunately, life is not always so clear and there are frequently hidden agendas being pursued in the dynamic context of an organization. Another way to control employees is to *involve* them in the running of the organization in ways that encourage the creation of empathy with management objectives.

Philosophy and ethics

Ethics is about doing the right thing. Philosophy is about, '... the critical evaluation of assumptions and argument' (Raphael, 1994, p 1). Moral philosophy is a branch of philosophy that takes as its sphere of interest a, '... philosophical inquiry about norms or values, about ideas of right and wrong, good or bad, what should and what should not be done' (Raphael, 1994, p 8). Clearly therefore there are close associations between the study of ethics and that of moral philosophy. Both have an interest in right and wrong behaviour.

Moral philosophy as an approach is able to tease out the underlying assumptions in ethical situations and critically evaluate them. Ethics takes as its focus of interest behaviour that contains rightness, goodness, correct behaviour. Another way of considering the distinction is that ethics is related to aspects of interpersonal behaviour whereas moral philosophy covers a broader range of experiences in the human condition, including beauty and feelings.

The evaluation of behaviour as either good or bad is judged by reference to the norms or values that are generally accepted within a particular context. There are four major approaches to the basis of moral decision making that have emerged over the years, including:

- Naturalism. This view holds that morality can be judged on the basis of human tendencies to adopt a *self-interest* view of behaviour. It posits the view that any particular morality will be situation specific. Being grounded in the species nature of human beings, this approach to morality would be variable depending upon the forces in a particular context.
- Rationalism. This view suggests that there is an absolute truth which underpins ethical standards. The level of knowledge and understanding available in a particular context are a function of the application of reason and logic. Expressed morality can be viewed as an approximation to its real form. As knowledge and understanding develop through logic and reason the expression of morality is refined and comes closer to the ultimate.
- Utilitarianism. This perspective proposes that doing what is *right* promotes happiness. Consequently, the higher the level of practised morality the greater the level of experienced happiness. In that context, morality can be equated with the concept of *goodness*. There are different perspectives on this view of morality. Bentham was the leading nineteenth-century classical

utilitarian who claimed that individuals always act on the basis of achieving maximum personal levels of happiness. The view that all will ultimately benefit from downsizing is an organizational version of this concept and is reflected in Management in Action 15.2.

One of the major difficulties for this approach is that of operationalizing the definition of *goodness*. Goodness (or happiness) are terms that can have multiple and selective impacts at the same time. For example, flogging

---

Management in Action 15.2

The cold war is over and the bosses won

The cold war created many political and military problems for those countries engaged in it. However, it also brought with it a number of benefits. In the USA IT allowed bosses to demonstrate that America had the highest standard of living and lowest levels of unemployment. Bosses were encouraged, as a consequence of the bloated cold war economy, to inflate their payrolls and boast about how many staff they employed. That has all changed.

In the global competition for jobs, first with China and then Russia, US industry is hard pressed. Automation has cut jobs in every industry including banking and finance. Most companies are being downsized, rightsized or re-engineered. The current boast of bosses is of how many people they have fired, forced into retirement before their due date, turned into part-time or contract staff with no fringe benefits at all. Nicholas von Hoffman termed the boss of today as the 'bizbrute'.

The truth behind much of the unemployment faced by today's blue- and white-collar workers is not that poor performance or incompetence causes redundancy. It is the high cost of health insurance, pension plans, and the fact that young people will do the job for half the money that lies behind much of it. For example over the six years prior to 1994 inflation in the USA increased by 27%, but wages only increased by 19%. Manufacturing employees now work 320 hours more than their European counterparts. Over a 10-year period they have added a total of 17 days to the normal work year. Many are burned out as well as disillusioned.

Science PhDs feel the changes more than many. During the 1980s they could expect to walk straight into an affluent lifestyle with an income over $50,000. Indeed, students were actively encouraged to follow this path. With many science and technical jobs moving (with the assembly work) to the location offering the cheapest labour, this is no longer the case. Many well-qualified science and technology students are now lucky to find jobs washing test tubes rather than work as research or development specialists. Prospects for law graduates are the worst for 10 years, with one in six being unemployed six months after graduating in the summer of 1992.

Pringle suggests in rather a cynical way that, 'The key to protecting your job during downsizing is to keep your income low, refuse all raises and other forms of additional compensation. Also, if you're over 40, lie about it'. Pringle illustrates his views with reference to a US sitcom called 'The Larry Sanders Show', which reflects the backstage reality of the late-night talk show. In doing so it also depicts many of the problems facing US employees. Employees harassed by the show's directors are pressured into spending more and more time at work and are carpeted for attempting to deal with the inevitable personal problems that arise from this stress. The show draws a picture of the experience of life within modern organization being nothing more than work and ruthless bosses. A caricature for sure, but with a high degree of reflection of the real life experience for many people.

Adapted from: Pringle, P (1995) The cold war is over and the bosses won. The Independent, 2 January, p 11.

■ Promoting the happiness of other people

■ Refraining from harm to other people

■ Treating people justly

■ Telling the truth

■ Keeping promises

■ Showing gratitude

■ Promoting one's own happiness

■ Maintaining and promoting one's own virtues

Table 15.1
Principles of intuitionism (taken from: Raphael, DD (1994) *Moral Philosophy*, 2nd edn, Oxford University Press, p 44). With permission

individuals convicted of theft might create a feeling of happiness among victims, but at the same time create pain and unhappiness for the criminal and their family. Remember that the family of the thief may have also benefited from the crime in a monetary sense but were not necessarily directly involved in the crime itself. So should the majority rule in the application of rightness? To accept this view could be considered as the basis of justifying the horrors of war, the holocaust and that most recent version of it, ethnic cleansing.

The difficulties faced by utilitarianism in providing an effective basis for understanding morality produced a number of alternative approaches. One of them, referred to as intuitionism, proposed a number of values that stand the test of time and therefore reflect underlying and unchanging principles. Although there are variations in the nature of the principles proposed within this approach, Raphael (1994) identifies eight that cover those most frequently proposed (see Table 15.1).

■ Formalism. It was Kant who described a distinction between categorical and hypothetical imperatives in reaching moral decisions. The hypothetical imperative is based on the pragmatic approach to situations. It considers that actions should be designed to meet some self-interest function of the decision maker. Kant argued that this approach did not explain all circumstances relating to moral decisions and that categorical imperatives reflected circumstances where the means-to-an-end perspective did not apply. For example, giving to charity can be seen in terms of goodness for its own sake and not as a means of providing an indirect benefit to the giver. This provides a *formalized* approach to deciding between courses of action. It requires the individual to apply three filters to the decision (see Table 15.2).

It should be apparent that the perspective adopted in Table 15.2 implies a democratic approach to moral decisions. It can be argued that this

1 Consider you are attempting to create a rule for every individual to follow

2 Consider that the human beings involved are ends in themselves and not a means to some personal gratification

3 Consider that everyone else in society has the same rights and freedoms to act as they see fit and that they should act on the basis of 1 and 2 above

Table 15.2
A simplified form of Kanian ethics (after Raphael, 1994). With permission

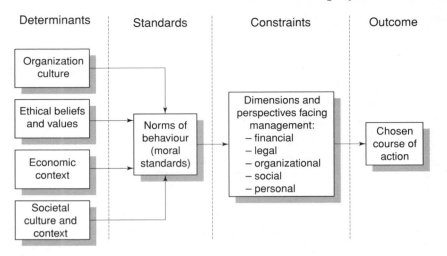

Figure 15.1 Ethical perspectives in management decision making (adapted from: Hosmer, ET (1987) Ethical analysis and HRM. *Human Resource Management*, **23**, 3, 313–30).

approach produces a basis for the regulation of society through the legislative, political and procedural frameworks that are established to provide structure and order. Similar parallels have been suggested to hold in an organizational context. For example, the development of rules and bureaucratic forms of organization as a basis for decision making. Hosmer (1987) describes an approach to management decision making that reflects this ethical perspective (Figure 15.1).

Another way of thinking about the approach adopted by Hosmer is that of a decision-making process influenced by the elements contained in Figure 15.1. The ideas contained in Figure 15.1 can be accommodated into that process as filters for the variables involved. Figure 15.2 attempts to represent this view by reflecting the impact of ethics on the process.

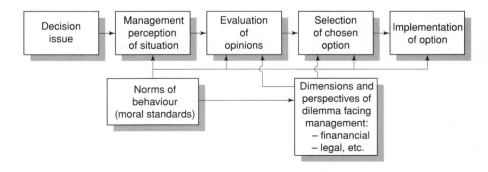

Figure 15.2 Hosmer's ethical model applied to a rational decision-making process.

Ethical perspectives in organizations

Ethical issues are about *rightness*, *wrongness*, *good* and *bad*. This is as much applicable within the sphere of organizational activity as it is in the field of politics or behaviour in society as a whole. Deciding the right thing to do in any particular context can be a demanding task. Consider for example the position of a subordinate who finds out that their manager is falsifying expenses claims. What would be the proper and right course of action for the subordinate to adopt? The choices include:

- Do nothing.
- Report the manager to a more senior manager.
- Let the manager know that they have been found out.
- Send an anonymous letter to the chief executive.
- Report the manager to the subordinates' trade union.
- Write a letter to the press.
- Write a letter to the largest shareholder.
- Report the manager to their professional association (if they belong to one).

Each of the above options has a range of costs and benefits for the individuals involved in the situation. In weighing up the most appropriate course of action the subordinate can adopt one of two approaches. Firstly, they could take the decision based on their judgement of the fundamental rightness or wrongness of the act that they have encountered. In doing so they would be acting irrespective of any consequences for the manager involved, themselves or the organization. Secondly, they could form a judgement based on the possible consequences for the principle stakeholders. For example, if they had an extremely good working relationship with the manager and felt a high degree of personal loyalty towards that individual then an approach which ran counter to that would be likely to cause distress to the subordinate and so be less likely to be adopted.

Cederblom and Dougherty (1990) use the ideas introduced earlier as the basis for deciding between alternative courses of action. They refer to the two approaches as *utilitarianism* and *contractarianism*. Utilitarian approaches are summarized as *benevolence* and contract approaches as about *fairness*. Within each model there are two versions, giving four options to form the basis of choosing appropriate courses of action.

Utilitarian approach

This approach is grounded in the concept of utility or usefulness. In determining the right course of action in any given context a key feature should be the level of valued results produced. The approach to be adopted is one of *benevolence* towards the needs of others in determining one's own behaviour. This approach looks forward in assessing the ethical perspectives in any particular situation. It requires an evaluation of options on the basis of the future impact on those that are likely to effected by the consequences.

- **Act utilitarianism.** This version suggests that every dilemma should be regarded on its own merits. For example, telling a lie could be justified if it created happiness for the people involved. It would appear to run contrary to all the norms of society to be able to justify actions such as lying, cheating and even murder under some circumstances. Given the rise in criminal acts experienced by many over the past few years it would be possible to argue that to allow citizens to murder individuals who threaten them with criminal acts would both save government money and make ordinary people feel happier – but is it right?

- ■ **Rule utilitarianism.** This approach takes the view that applying the principles of act utilitarianism might be a good thing to do in that instance, but still wrong according to the need to operate society in a consistent way. The rule approach to utilitarianism implies that it is necessary to create rule frameworks that would serve as the basis for individuals to identify appropriate courses of action in specific contexts.

Contract approach

This approach to deciding between conflicting courses of action and resolving ethical dilemmas is grounded in the notion that agreements whether they be explicit or tacit should be honoured. In general terms it considers that by virtue of the social environment within which human beings function, co-operation is a major imperative. As a consequence of the web of interaction formed as a result of the co-operative activity many mutual obligations are created. In the execution of these *contractual* relationships individuals are required to apply the general test of *fairness* to their behaviour. Circumstances can create an inequality in the balance of power between the parties to any agreement.

Equally, information can tip the balance one way or the other. Inside knowledge of an impending take-over bid could allow certain individuals to buy shares before they rise sharply when the announcement is made. This would not be fair to those selling shares as they will not gain the benefit that they would have otherwise had. The major difficulty with this approach is that to create a fair set of rules on which to determine contracts individuals would be needed who had no vested interest in the outcome. Cutting a cake is frequently used to illustrate this principle. To be equally fair to all involved the person cutting the cake should be the last person to select a piece to eat. A contract view is one that looks backward at the obligations that have been entered into in the past and assesses the implications of these for future behaviour.

- ■ **Restricted contractarianism.** This approach takes the view that every agreement entered into should be assessed through the *veil of ignorance* (Rawls, 1971). This forces an individual to consider the *rightness* of any arrangement without knowing the impact of the outcome on themselves.
- ■ **Libertarian contractarianism.** This approach holds that the parties should be bound by any agreement voluntarily entered into as long as it does not conflict with the broader rules of a just society or cause harm to others. It is an approach that accepts the limitations on the concept of fairness in the dynamic nature of the social world in which human beings operate. It implies that once a contract is entered into, individuals have an obligation to abide by the terms of that relationship and not to take precipitated action to terminate the contract.

It has already been suggested in many of the chapters in this text that much management activity is associated with making choices or taking decisions. The same is true of many of the non-managerial jobs that exist within organizations.

Manual workers on an assembly line have to make decisions about the quality of work that they are undertaking, administrative employees have decisions to make with regard to dealing with customer queries or complaints and so on. Many of these situations contain ethical dimensions. Leys (1962) produced a diagram in which a number of moral standards are identified and in which conflict with the standards in the opposite side of the model (see Figure 15.3).

This model is useful in identifying many of the conflicts and dilemmas associated with decision making. For example, an employee faced with a boss who is attempting to increase efficiency and reduce the cost of operations will span the dilemmas of loyalty and institutional trends at one side of the model and integrity/self-respect at the opposite side. In such a situation an employee may well feel that *loyalty* to the organization is important and that increased efficiency represents an *institutional trend* that cannot be stopped. At the same time, however, these feeling are likely to be in conflict with the need for personal integrity in performing a good job to high standards of quality and *self-respect* in not being simply a creature of management, subject to every whim of the boss.

This model does not provide a basis for identifying a course of action to resolve the moral dilemma facing the individual. It simply helps to identify some of the conflicting areas of experience. In addition, there are situations which span more than two opposite forces in the model. At best this model should be regarded as a simplification of the complexity of situations involving ethical conflicts. It is, however, a useful starting point for thinking about the issues involved in specific situation.

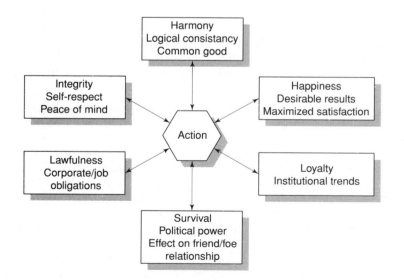

Figure 15.3 Conflicts between moral values (adapted from: Leys, WAR (1962) *The Value Framework of Decision Making*).

Ethical issues in management

There are number of areas of ethical dilemma that face managers in their operational capacity:

Work and society

Work plays a number of important roles in society. It provides the economic basis for individuals to be able to earn money and thereby purchase the goods and services necessary for life and recreation. There are the indirect benefits of work through the payment of taxes so that common services such as health care can be provided. Work also provides individuals with social meaning in their lives through the careers and work activities that they engage in. For example, those with appropriate creative talents could become artists and find ways of expressing their individual identity through their work. It also provides an opportunity for social encounters with other people as employees interact with other human beings.

Should work and the organizations that provide it be seen as the dominant force within society? Should any organization have the power to dictate to the members of a society how they should live and work. How much time should be devoted to work, how much payment should be received and so on? In short, should we as humans work to live or live to work? There are a number of organizations who have an income larger than many of the poorer countries of the world. This could provide opportunities for big business to *arrange* society in a way that supports business objectives, rather than to the benefit of society.

Corporate and public interest

There is a fundamental conflict between organizations and the public at large. In very crude terms, all organizations would like to sell cheap products at a very high prices. Consumers on the other hand would like very expensive products at very low prices. This is a vast simplification of a complex process associated with purchase and ownership. It is well known among marketing people that there are circumstances in which charging low prices actually undervalues the product or service in the eyes of potential customers and therefore make them less likely to buy. This form of conflict can frequently lead to ethical conflicts arising as organizations seek to maximize their profits.

One of the illustrations that can be used to describe potential conflicts in this area is contained in Management in Action 15.3. The conflicts between corporate and public interest in this example are associated with the company need for cheap labour in order to reduce the cost of operations and customer preference for a reasonably priced toy. There are many 'factors' at work in this type of situation. The moral issues associated with this situation include the deliberate payment of low wages (by European standards) as a management policy. There are also issues of customers purchasing products that have not created jobs within their own society and of encouraging cheap labour. Countering this is the provision of economic development in areas that desperately need it. There is also the issue of profit export from, and technology/skill transfer to, areas of cheap labour. This begins to open up economic arguments that are well beyond the scope of this text. Goldsmith (1995) puts forward a spirited defence of his views that by not protecting

Poverty pay of Barbie doll workers

A report produced by the World Development Movement, the Catholic Institute for International Relations, and the Trades Union Congress show that poverty wages are frequently paid to workers in Asia making toys for sale in the West.

The findings of the research indicated that many leading toy companies use sub-contract factories in Asia which fail to meet basic internationally agreed standards. The average person works a shift of at least 10 hours each day for six days per week. For example, Chinese workers were paid less than £2 per day to make Barbie dolls. The Mattel company who make the Barbie doll spend about £1.80 per doll sold on advertising, about the same as the daily wage for each factory worker.

In Bangkok the research team interviewed factory workers and reported the following comments:

> Barbie doll is more expensive than our wages. We lost a lot of sweat to produce those dolls.

Another worker explained that overtime was compulsory,

We have to do it otherwise we would be dismissed. ... One month the management gives 60 dolls for one worker to produce but when we finish the 60 dolls per month they will increase it another 10 to 70 dolls; if we finish 70 dolls they will increase it again.

The group sponsoring the research pressed the British Toy and Hobby Association, which represents companies responsible for 90% of all sales of these products in the UK market, to adopt a new charter in this area. It seeks to establish an independently monitored code of practice for the safe production of toys. It would require companies to undertake spot checks on sub-contractors and to take action if any violations were found.

Mattel as a leading maker of toys welcomed the proposed charter and suggested that it would enhance its own existing code of practice which required sub-contractors to comply with local labour and safety laws. It also required staff to report any violation of the laws.

Adapted from: Garner, C (1995) Poverty pay of Barbie doll workers. The Independent, 23 December, p 2.

jobs and production at home, countries are sowing the seeds of their own destruction.

Obligations at work
There are a number of areas of obligation that impact on employees. Figure 15.4 overleaf attempts to reflect many of these.

Not all of the groupings identified in Figure 15.4 will apply to every employee and there are categories not represented. The ethical dilemmas arising from obligations at work arise as a result of the potential conflicts in demands placed on the individual from the various groupings. For example, balancing the demands of organization and family can create problems in many situations, as can the demands of ever higher productivity on the self-respect of the individual.

Privacy
The right to privacy for the individual has been eroded in a number of areas over recent years and in turn raises a number of ethical dilemmas. For

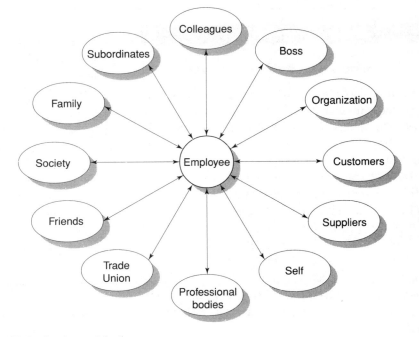

Figure 15.4 Employee obligation map.

example, the use of information technology has created an opportunity to collect and retain information about employees. The organization is able to *know* its employees more fully. However, this should not be overstated as large bureaucracies such as the civil service have had effective and comprehensive personnel files on staff for many years.

Another aspect of privacy in today's world is that associated with medical screening. Testing for drug use and for the existence of the HIV virus are just two of the more recent areas. How far should medical screening go before it moves from being necessary to being intrusive?

Working at home

There are many situations that arise which require the individual to take work home with them. A report may be required at short notice and it may be necessary for a manager to finish it at home in the evening. An employee working on an assembly line may not be able to stop themselves thinking about work when they are at home after management announce that the number of employees is to be reduced.

The ethical issues surrounding the practice of working at home are many and depend upon the circumstances creating the situation. The dilemmas and issues involved in the two examples quoted above are different. In the first case they surround the rights and obligations of both parties. Does a manager have the right to expect subordinates to put in more hours than contractually agreed, particularly at short notice? Equally, does an employee in a senior position have an obligation to 'do what is necessary' in pursuing corporate objectives? In the second case the ethical issues are of a completely different nature as the employee is not being required to think about work at home, it is a result of the threat of redundancy.

Where additional work is required a wide range of ethical issues are involved in addition to those implied in the previous discussion. For example, to refuse to take work home could be regarded as an act of disloyalty and have implications for the career and promotion prospects of the individual concerned. There could also be a number of other employees only too willing to take advantage of the situation as a means of attempting to advance their own careers and promotion. For managers not to accept that they should 'do what is necessary' has implications for their right to be considered leaders and might have a detrimental impact on the well-being of all members of the organization.

Pay, promotion and discrimination

Who should be paid what in an organization? This is a question that also raises ethical issues. It is usually argued that the senior people within an organization should be paid more because they have greater responsibility. However, over recent years organizations have been making strident attempts to delayer themselves and to *empower* employees. It is argued that it is the employees who directly interface with the customer or who actually build the product who can *make or break* the company. If these individuals are so important should they not be paid accordingly – even if it does disrupt the conventional wisdom of pay hierarchies? If the lower level employees do not get *it* right today there will be no tomorrow for managers to plan.

Access to promotion opportunity is another area where there is unequal access for a number of groups. The disadvantaged groups include females, those from ethnic minority groups, disabled people and older workers. There are many forms of the *glass ceiling*, not just that which prevents women from gaining access to the more senior posts. Sexual harassment is another form of discrimination experienced by employees. Again there are ethical issues involved in these areas in attempting to decide what the right course of action should be.

Whistleblowing

Whistleblowing is an act on the part of an employee to bring into the public arena acts that an organization would prefer to keep hidden. Such individuals frequently try unsuccessfully to use internal methods to bring about change within the organization and stop the unethical or illegal activities. In frustration at what they see as the intransigence and wrongdoing of individuals within the organization they find themselves having to go public and *blow the whistle* on the situation.

In whistleblowing the individuals often leave themselves open to retaliation on the part of managers and other employees who think that their job and profit levels might be at risk. They are often dismissed, subjected to abuse and threats of violence to themselves their families or property. When the employer is the government it can also lead to imprisonment for revealing secrets. Codes of practice have been seen as a way of institutionalizing whistleblowing, allowing senior managers to take action on problems as they emerge.

Codes of practice

In an attempt to provide individuals with guidance on ethical standards and behaviour many organizations and professional bodies have produced codes of practice. These can be written in many different forms, but most attempt to establish what the approved courses of action are in particular circumstances, for example, what to do if faced with a demand for a bribe. They also attempt to provide an indication of the procedure to be adopted if a breach of the code is suspected as a result of someone not following established procedures.

The codes of practice for professional bodies only direct themselves to issues associated with that particular area of work and how it should be conducted. There can be occasions when the code of practice for a professional body is in conflict with the practices within the organization employing the member. Such eventualities pose difficulties for the individual in deciding which to follow. For example, a medical practitioner employed by a company may interpret their professional standards as a duty to provide the highest standards of care for employees, but the company may interpret its requirement as to provide the most cost effective level of care.

Power, participation and control

The role of people in an organization is rather ambiguous. What is expected of them by the organization and what they as individuals and groups should expect from the organization is based on a complex wheel of interdependent factors. Figure 15.5 reflects the interaction between these influences and the role of people within the organization.

Another way to express the role of people within an organization is through employee involvement. People are primarily employed by organizations to perform tasks that cannot otherwise be done by machines. As much as technology has developed in recent years it is not yet possible for organizations to function without people to do some of the jobs. Taking the job as the reason for the exis-

Figure 15.5 The wheel of people role determinants within organizations.

tence of employees, it follows that managers seek to make effective use of them. Employee involvement has a part to play in achieving high levels of effectiveness of the human resource.

The major advantage to organizations from the employment of people is the flexibility that they provide. They are cheaper to acquire (no capital costs), can be dispensed with more quickly if necessary, they are adaptable and can solve problems in a dynamic environment. However, there are disadvantages with the employment of people: they are not as consistent in work output or quality as machines; they cannot work every hour that exists without a break; maintenance costs (wages) are high. In addition the major difficulty involved with the employment of people is that they have free will and expectations.

People are not completely malleable at the will of others. Even in the most difficult of circumstances individuals will find ways of expressing individuality and freedom from total domination. The story of Lomax (1995 – identified in the further reading) demonstrates how prisoners of war can maintain some measure of independence even in the most hostile of conditions. From literature, the classic *Brave New World* by Huxley, first published in 1932, provides insights into how a number of the characters are able to resist the all embracing control of society in the future world. From management's perspective the advantages of employing people must outweigh the disadvantages for it to be worth the effort and cost. Therefore ways of directing and controlling the people resource are important aspects of management activity. Managers continually seek devices or techniques to generate additional benefits from the *social capital* that they employ.

From an employee perspective their experience of work includes the ever growing demands of industrialization. Some of these include ever tighter control, reduced ability to adjust the pace of work and subservience to the needs of technology. Mills (1959) described the experience as a number of *traps*, a theme common to many latter sociological studies. Consequently employees actively seek to increase the significance and value from their work responsibilities. Because managers *seek* controlled behaviour from the human resource this does not automatically achieve it. It is not possible to take out the essential nature of human beings simply because management would like to control them.

Alienation was identified as an expression of independence. Management cannot force labour to join in and become part of the system. Compliance is not the same as commitment. It could be argued that the *Fordism* approach was an early attempt to provide control and that because it was largely unsuccessful attempts at *social engineering* replaced it. One aspect of social engineering is to persuade employees to subscribe to the same values as managers through becoming involved in the business.

The more enlightened management approaches recognize that it is not possible to force or restrict the human qualities that employees possess naturally. Indeed, it might even be possible to harness (manipulate) those very qualities to provided added value to the organization. One manager described this as recognizing that with every pair of hands recruited came a free brain. Among the strategies designed to address these issues are those intended to increase employee involvement in the running of the business. Management in Action 15.4 reflects the industrial democracy processes in the John Lewis Partnership, a co-ownership organization in which every employee part owns the business.

Management in Action 15.4

Writing wrongs with democracy

The Gazette is the staff newspaper of the John Lewis Partnership and plays a key role in the way that democracy functions within the organization. Marion Scott, its editor, indicated that it had won an award from the Campaign for Freedom of Information for its contribution to 'free and open debate about both policy and personnel issues of a kind that most companies go out of their way to prevent'.

The history of *The Gazette* goes back to the early days of the John Lewis Partnership when in 1918 John Spedan Lewis set it up as a means of improving communication within the company. The organization is owned by the employees and they expect a significant say in how it is run. Every permanent employee, including part-time staff, are co-owners of the business and entitled to influence the policy and direction of the company as well as share in the profits. Referred to as 'partners' theco-owners are not able to elect managers or interfere with day-to-day operational issues, but they can call into question the actions of managers through the letters pages of *The Gazette*. Only on rare occasions does a letter not appear in print. This decision can only be made by the partnership chairman, and its non-appearance must be justified in *The Gazette*.

Letters published can be anonymous and some contain pointed complaints about the behaviour of senior managers. For example, recent examples have included a complaint about the, 'pathetic use of rudeness and sarcasm' by a senior manager and an observation about the chairman's membership of the Freemasons.

Where a letter requires a reply senior managers are expected to do so. It provides a very tangible measure of the accountability of managers to those that they manage.

The Gazette is not the only form of democracy within the company. Other forms of democracy and involvement engaged in by the John Lewis Partnership include:

- The Central Council. A consultative body that has the ultimate power to remove the partnership's chairman from office.
- Branch Councils. These function rather like a works council in Germany and scrutinize management decisions and actions at local level.
- Committees for Communication. These are the oldest representative bodies. Only open to non-management partners, they meet about six times each year.
- Partners' Counsellor. An ombudsman role within the structure to represent the interest of ordinary partners.

The various representative bodies publish the minutes of meetings to all staff. A virtual plethora of information for all to see, should they wish to do so. One issue of potential difficulty for 'open communication' is that of the commercial sensitivity of some information. This does not appear to have had an adverse effect on the organization in practice or profit levels over the years.

Adapted from Arkin, A (1994) Writing wrongs with democracy. Personnel Management Plus, *April, pp 22–3.*

It is important to recognize that not every employee would wish to become involved with the running of their organization. Some individuals would be happy to simply sell their labour and achieve self-actualization and personal meaning though other routes. A young person may view a job as providing the money to allow them a year out to travel the world. The importance of involvement is that it can meet the needs and expectations of some people and therefore should be available rather than compulsory. In doing so it can improve the quality of working life and provide managers with the potential for better results. Forcing people to become involved simply introduces another form of direct control and is unlikely to have any positive result.

Employee involvement and human resource management

The function with a particular interest in employee involvement is the human resource department. As such these specialists tend to believe in the intrinsic value of involving people at work as intrinsically good (ethical), a means of increasing motivation, tapping into higher levels of commitment and making best use of the human qualities available to the organization.

There are many different views about the nature of human resource management within an organization. Hyman and Mason (1995, chapter 4) provide a comprehensive review of the distinction between the terms *personnel* and *human resource* activities in the context of employee involvement. Among the conclusions is an indication that organizational level employee participation may be intended to impact on employee representation through trade unions.

Marchington *et al.* (1992) suggest that there are four types of involvement:

- Downward communication. Top-down in nature and intended to better inform employees. The purpose being to ensure that employees are aware of what is going on and their part in it. The rationale being that if employees understand the situation they will be willing to play their part more effectively.
- Upwards problem solving. To make more direct use of the skill, ability and ideas of employees in helping managers to solve problems. Based on the view that employees directly involved in the finding of solutions will be more likely to make them work effectively. They may also find other ways to contribute to the smooth running of the organization.
- Financial participation. To give employees a direct stake in the financial performance of their organization. The rationale being that employees who benefit from the performance of the organization will be motivated to search out ways of more effectively meeting customer need and reducing operating costs.
- Representative participation. Not all can become involved in practice (ability, numbers and cost involved) or would want to become involved (interest and tradition). Consequently it is suggested that a number of representatives from among the workforce should become involved with management on behalf of all employees.

There are a number of consequences that arise from the involvement of employees in areas that have been traditionally considered the sole prerogative of managers. Some of the issues include:

- Degree of involvement. Changes to the degree of involvement will disturb existing arrangements. Senior managers and shareholders may have to become accustomed to sharing power with a new group who may have different objectives for the business. Shareholders may want high dividends, while employees seek secure employment and reinvestment of profit. Any form of involvement would need to be agreed by the existing stakeholders.

■ Role of management. Whatever the form of involvement adopted employees will have expectations of increased influence over events in the future. This could be interpreted by managers as an erosion of their function within the organization.

■ Role of trade unions. A trade union might suddenly find itself not the only voice representing employee interest. If it were to consider that it was being marginalized either deliberately or unintentionally it could resist the effective introduction and operation of the selected approach.

■ Management's right to manage. Whilst the term *right* can be questioned in this context and it may not be clear who bestows (or agrees to) that *right*, managers operate on the basis that they are able to exercise it. However, it would not be unusual to find situations in which some employees develop links with senior managers over the heads of their immediate superiors. Under such circumstances it is possible to undermine the position of the superior by threats, real or implied, to go over their head. Employees who become involved in the running of an organization may become party to information that is not available to managers, again a potential source of problems.

■ Rights of involved employees. Do employees become equal partners with the stock owners of the company? Is the limit of their involvement to solve operational problems and to support management in the day-to-day running of the organization? Having experienced minor forms of involvement employees may seek greater levels of it. Employees may think that involvement gives them a greater say in the running of the company than was intended by management, or provided by the scheme.

■ Responsibilities of involved employees. Managers would argue that with involvement comes responsibility. Employees may consider the main benefits of participation are to offset ineffective management. Should involved employees only expect to change those things that others do? Are there responsibilities associated with involvement that require an introspective consideration?

If involvement were to be beneficial in improving operational performance then employees would absorb much of the need for management activity. In so doing involvement could influence the design and structure of an organization. Management in Action 15.5 reflect the experience of two firms in attempting to deal with these issues.

Forms of employee involvement

At the most simple level employees are involved with the organization as a result of the work that they do. There are many informal processes that exist for employee involvement. For example the *grapevine* is usually the quickest way for information to circulate around the company. Gossip and rumour have a higher credibility than formal channels because they are not subject to editing and filtering by managers.

Management in Action 15.5

The bumpy road to devolution

Microsoft's attempt to empower its workforce was launched with great razzamatazz. It was, however, a one-day wonder and collapsed. Employee surveys showed that people did not understand what it meant to them and many dismissed it as yet another management fad. Shaun Orpen, director of marketing services for Microsoft a suggested that, '... there was a genuine feeling in certain areas of the company that people had been given responsibility but not control. They did not know how far their authority went'.

This led the company to rethink what empowerment meant within the organization. The second time there was no high-profile launch. Managers concentrated on how they could realistically devolve both responsibility and authority to staff. For example, the finance director told his staff they no longer needed his authority to take time off, as long as colleagues knew about it and how to contact them. The next phase involved the empowerment of teams and providing people with the necessary skills to exercise discretion.

Linda Holbeche, director of research at Roffey Park Management Institute, suggests that a lack of clarity over roles and responsibilities is one of the major reasons why attempts to empower employees fail. Equally, many managers are unwilling to delegate significant amounts of power to employees. Much of the delegated power remains at the 'ordering of paper clips' level. The existence of a 'blame culture' will quickly discourage the use of initiative and the exercise of judgement.

Holbeche illustrates the effective empowerment of employees in Thresher, the major UK drinks retailer. The company prefer to use the term 'enabling' rather than empowerment. It is about people being given the support to carry out their responsibilities, not simply management abdicating its responsibilities. The exercise began with a combined personnel and operations review of the key operational roles. Having identified what people were expected to do and whether they had the skills to do it, the company set about reviewing the rules and procedures within which people worked. This was followed by structural reorganization at the top of the organization and increased training of the people lower down the organization.

The introduction of self-managed teams in the local areas of the Food and Drinks section of the company encouraged more initiative in running the business to be taken. For example, the development of new staff working models and the local use of incentives. Groups of branch managers meet regularly to share ideas and develop best practice. This also has the benefit of giving shop staff the experience having to take responsibility in the absence of their boss.

An analysis of the company performance showed that in the areas where these changes had been made, performance had improved. Surveys of store and area managers also indicated that they considered the company to be more open, informal and participative. The results have encouraged the company to plan to roll out the process to the rest of the organization. This is anticipated to last about 18 months. It is also anticipated to be a 'bumpy road' by the senior managers as resistance to change is anticipated at all levels. The approach adopted will be one of talking about where the senior managers want the business to go rather than empowerment as such.

Adapted from: Arkin, A (1995) The bumpy road to devolution. People Management, 30 November, pp 34–6.

Downward communication

Downwards communication is intended to inform, to lead opinion and form attitudes that would be considered favourable to management. There is a potential problem to be faced in the use each of the forms of downwards communication available. That is the degree of management bias in the content. Employees may interpret the content as a deliberate attempt to manipulate and adopt a totally different set of attitudes to those intended.

Among the main forms of downwards communication are:

■ Section or departmental meetings. A production department may hold regular weekly meetings to discuss problems and plans surrounding the current production cycle. As part of that process the senior manager may feed back to their subordinates information from the last senior management meeting.

■ Team briefing. The cascade concept of communicating downwards. The senior management team would determine what should form the central core of each briefing session. Each senior manager would brief their immediate team using the core material supported by local information as necessary. Each person would then take the core brief and repeat the process for their own subordinates, repeated throughout the organization. Ramsey (1992) notes general satisfaction with this approach, but points out that success is highly dependent upon contextual features and that commitment to the process needs to be maintained.

■ In-house journal. Company newspapers, journals, magazines and booklets have been in existence for many years. It is also common to find special employee versions of the annual report to shareholders being produced in larger companies. The major difficulties with these forms of journalism are the quality of the publication, generating enough copy to keep the content interesting and preventing the propaganda inclinations of some managers becoming overly assertive.

■ Roadshow. Over the past few years the notion of senior managers going out to meet employees has developed. The three most common forms of this approach are to have a cycle of senior management visits, have senior managers host breakfast (or lunch) meetings or to arrange theatrical style shows at which employees come together in large numbers to experience a *show* put on by management. This last form can be very expensive, involving, lighting, sound, large screen video, fireworks and a well-known personality to lead the presentation.

■ Electronic. In these days of electronic communication the use of e-mail, video and multimedia approaches to communicating form a real possibility. The use of video conferencing provides opportunities for many groups of individual to receive information and interact with others.

Upwards problem solving

This approach allows employees to utilize their skills and knowledge in the search for increased productivity, quality and commitment. This can include:

■ Suggestion schemes. This involves employees identifying ways to improve things and putting forward the suggestion to a committee for consideration. Employees must identify what the problem is, how it can be solved, what the benefits would be expected to be and any problems. If adopted then the person making the suggestion is usually rewarded with a percentage of the saving. It has occasionally been suggested that ideas have been turned down, only to see them implemented a few months later as part of a *normal* change. Managers can feel threatened if it is implied that they should have been able to solve the problem earlier. In most cases the employee only receives a small amount in comparison to the potential saving generated.

■ Quality circles. These originated in Japan after World War II. They were developed by American consultants as a means of improving quality and productivity through employee problems solving (Clutterbuck and Grainer, 1990). Quality circles are voluntary groups of between six and ten employees from a common work area. Members are trained in problem solving techniques and encouraged to identify difficulties in their own work areas and to find workable solutions. The group presents their solution to the management team then implements it. If management decide not to implement the solution they are required to explain their reasons to the circle. Management in Action 15.6 overleaf reflects a similar initiative using project improvement groups.

There was enthusiastic support for this form of employee involvement in the UK in the early 1980s, but problems and difficulties quickly began to emerge (Brennan, 1991; Collard and Dale, 1989). Some first line managers interpreted quality circles as a threat. Some employees were seen as *rising stars*, more able than existing managers. Trade unions sometimes interpreted the establishment of circles as a deliberate attempt to undermine their position and as a means of getting more from workers without extra reward. Circles also found that some of the problems that they attempted to solve were too complex, or that for unclear reasons solutions were not implemented.

■ Total quality management (TQM). It has been suggested that TQM is a philosophy rather than a technique. Flood (1993, p xiii) argues that, 'In reality TQM means a long term, deep involvement of management in partnership with the workforce'. This implies a different approach to managing an organization to that traditionally experienced. The essence of TQM is that the need to pursue excellence and improvement are continual processes. Holden (1994, p 585) provides a useful summary of TQM in relation to employee involvement. TQM is frequently tied into other initiatives such as culture change, worker flexibility and customer care programmes. In that context the emphasis in TQM becomes a management led initiative which, '... with top-down overtones suggests a system whereby worker empowerment is restricted very much within the boundaries set by management' (Holden, p 584).

Also described are increases in worker control and accountability through the increased monitoring and automation of recording and testing procedures. These points are reinforced by other writers (see for example Kerfoot and Knights, 1994). Garrahan and Stewart (1992) describe processes requiring employees to *report* the work failings of others or risk being held accountable themselves. Holden describes evidence that reflects the weaknesses associated with the running of TQM programmes, many of which are similar to those described in relation to quality circles.

■ Group working. It is only in recent years that group working has been systematically developed. The involvement of employees can be increased through the effective delegation to the group of what would otherwise be

Management in Action 15.6

The green shoots of improvement

Jardinerie Garden Centre was started in Cheshire about 12 years ago by three people, Ken Allen, Jon Kitching and Peter Ulyatt. Ken Allen, the chairman of the company, said that, 'We believe that if you get people working together, then profits will come from that energy'. The company quickly grew over 10 years from a single garden centre to 10 garden centres, an interior landscaping business and a staff of about 200 people.

As the organization grew and spread geographically so did the problems of communication. Early in the 1990s Ken Allen met John Teire of Charlbury Consultants, specialists in teamworking and communication training. A senior manager attended one of the programmes provided by Teire and identified ways in which the company could move forward. The programme was made available to the remainder of the management team and adapted for delivery inside the company to members of staff.

The result of the involvement in the programme was that the company were able to use volunteers to set up a 'Pig', or project initiation group, to find ways of establishing active involvement among employees. A number of 'Piglets' (or project improvement groups) of between four and eight people were set up among employee groups and encouraged to find ways of improving their work. Members of the original Pig toured the sites talking to staff and explaining that the Piglets were intended to provide a means of getting things done right first time, making full use of individuals' talents and giving all staff a chance to develop. Staff were encouraged to come up with their own ideas for improvement which in turn were classified under five separate headings:

- Customer care.
- Security.
- Frontage.
- Training.
- Information.

Training was provided for each Piglet under the headings of:

- Learning how to manage the project.
- Learning how to manage the team.
- Learning how to manage the learning so that it became the way things were done in the company.

Unlike many other involvement initiatives, the company has not adopted a 'top-down' approach. It allowed employees to decide for themselves what structures and systems were necessary to be able to deliver teamwork. For example one of the problems faced by the interior landscaping division was that clients moved the plants around. This means that it can be difficult for Jardinerie's staff to find the plants that they are supposed to be caring for. This is even more difficult during holiday periods when substitute staff are sent to client premises. The Piglet examined this problem and developed a simple system of ensuring that information was kept in a way that everyone could access. Another Piglet developed a security system to eliminate the pilferage of plants and other garden material. This area is sensitive as it can involve staff being accused of theft. In this case the staff willingly accepted the system developed by their own members.

Adapted from: Arkin, A (1994) The green shoots of improvement. Personnel Management Plus, May, pp 18–19.

management responsibilities. Work allocation, pace of work, job rotation and work scheduling are examples of the responsibility that can be given to the team. They can become self-managed teams agreeing to deliver a certain end result in return for a particular wage, but being *relatively free* to function in the execution of the process.

■ Project teams. Project teams represent a slightly different form of work group. They provide involvement through involvement in specific exercises. Typical examples of project team activities include the development of a new product, the design of a new workplace layout or the development of a new disciplinary procedure.

Financial participation

Financial participation provides involvement through a monetary stake in the activities of the organization. The main variations are:

■ Co-operatives. This represents a particular approach to the design, structure and ownership of an organization. Essentially the employees own the organization and are therefore directly involved in its financial performance through their decision making. In many of these types of organization the pursuit of profit would not be the main motivation for individuals becoming involved. However, as the owners of the organization they are participating in the financial aspects of the organization as well as the decision making, policy formulation and work.

■ Profit share. This has a long history and there are many examples from the nineteenth century (Church, 1971). The basic model for profit share schemes is that a nominated percentage of the profit generated by the organization would be shared out to employees in the form of a bonus. This form of participation was given a boost during the 1980s in the UK as a result of the beneficial tax treatment for payments resulting from schemes approved by the Inland Revenue. Profits can be distributed either in the form of money or as shares in the company. One of the difficulties associated with profit share is that profit, hard work and effort are not always directly linked. It is difficult to maintain motivation and commitment when that which is intended to facilitate it does not materialize.

■ Share options. Forms of share option include executive schemes and Save-As-You-Earn (SAYE) schemes. The employee is free to keep or sell the shares once the SAYE scheme allows the shares to be purchased. The executive share option allocates shares to an executive perhaps equal in value to a year's salary. The actual involvement is restricted to the channels open to all shareholders, but only once the shares become the property of the individual. At an individual level each shareholding might be small, but taken as a whole they could form a significant block. Over time this could provide the basis for a real power shift within the organization. If a takeover battle occurred it would be possible for the employee shares to play a critical role in deciding the outcome. Management in Action 15.7 overleaf describes an employee share ownership scheme introduced in the bus industry.

Management in Action 15.7

Bus employees take the wheel

In South Yorkshire a progressive public transport policy was operated for 10 years prior to 1986. The major aspect of this policy was that bus prices were heavily subsidised. In 1986 the Conservative government in London forced a change in that policy, bus fares rose by 250% and a process began which led to the management buy-out of the company and a major experiment in employee involvement. The bus company involved in this example employed 2490 people, leased 832 vehicles and had four main garages.

Glasman describes how the new company came into existence thus,

On 16 November 1993 South Yorkshire Transport Ltd. sold all its shares in Mainline Group Ltd. to a new company, Mainline Partnership Ltd., for a nominal £1.

To set up Mainline Partnership Ltd., Mainline Group gave £40,000 to two trusts – Employee Benefit Trust One (EBT1) and Employee Benefit Trust Two (EBT2) – which subscribed for four million shares at the nominal price of one pence per share. Employees received 74% of the shares on the basis of 114 shares for each year of service (with a minimum qualification of two years' service) the remaining 26% were held in trust by EBT1.

The new board consists of four executive directors, led by Peter Sephton, who is both chief executive and chairman. There are four non-executive employee directors, two non-executive community directors (who are district councillors appointed by the management and employee directors), and a non-executive business director (nominated by management and approved by the employee directors).

On some issues, such as a proposal to close a bus garage or to sell the company, the employee directors effectively have a veto. To complicate matters further, the four executive directors have special voting shares which can be used to outvote the ordinary shares, but may not be used for items on which the employee directors have the controlling vote.

One of the issues identified early in the change-over process was the remuneration level for managers. In the resulting adjustment 60 senior managers in the company were offered a share-based bonus scheme. The scheme was based around the allocation of phantom shares to each manager. These are not real shares in the company, but their value reflects the market price of the company's actual shares but they do not convey voting rights. After holding the phantom shares for seven years up to 50% can be cashed in at the prevailing value, the rest only when the manager leaves the company. Obviously the higher the market value of the real shares the larger the bonus. The purpose of the scheme is to attract, retain and motivate senior managers through a loyalty payment process. Managers judged to not be performing could be removed from the scheme.

The possibility of the introduction of a profit-share scheme for other employees which would be intended to allow the payment of an additional sum of money each week was also under discussion. In this case a number of ownership and incentive arrangements have been applied to involve and encourage employees and managers to co-operate in the effective delivery of an important public service.

Adapted from: Glasman, D (1994) Bus employees take the wheel. Personnel Management Plus, May, pp 20–1.

Representative participation

This approach to involvement does not provide involvement for each individual employee. It is a means of becoming involved through some form of representative arrangement. Forms of representative involvement include:

- Collective bargaining. This can be considered a form of employee involvement because it provides the opportunity for employee representatives to explore plans, ideas and options with managers as part of the process. The commonly held view of collective bargaining is that it is intended to provide wage rises for employees. However, it also provides an opportunity for a much broader level of involvement. Trade unions are not able to represent their members effectively during pay negotiations if they do not have an appreciation of management intentions and the financial background to company performance. There are instances in which the level of involvement provided through this medium is prescribed in law. Information required for the interpretation of redundancy proposals must be provided to employee representatives before consultation begins.

- Joint consultation. This implies a regular forum in which managers and employee representatives can meet to discuss issues of common concern. The major difference with negotiation is that management does not have to agree a course of action with employees. The process allows employee opinion and experience to be provided to managers. Managers can then incorporate these into decisions. A Confederation of British Industry (CBI) survey in 1989 reported that 47% of companies had some form of joint consultation. However, it was more likely to be found in the larger organizations. It is not unusual to find joint consultative arrangements falling into disuse if the management do not take them seriously and listen to the views of employee representatives. Management frequently claim that commercial sensitivity restricts what can be included in joint consultation, the argument being that competitors are liable to find out what is being planned.

There are many different approaches and experiences associated with employee involvement around the world. Holden (1994), Hyman and Mason (1995) provides examples from the experiences gained in other countries in this area of work.

Ethics and employee involvement: a management perspective

A considerable proportion of management activity is about taking decisions. Implicit in that view is the notion that managers are faced with options and choices. In many situations facing managers there are dilemmas and conflicts between aspects of the decision facing them. For example, offering a bribe to a potential customer may be against company policy, but it may help to provide jobs in an area of high unemployment, may prevent a company from losing money (if the market is tight) and the product may be the best on the market. Also, competitors may offer bribes to be able to sell inferior products. In addition, just because it is against company policy does not mean that it is against the principles and practices of every country.

This example is just one form of ethical dilemma faced by managers. How should they decide what it is right to do in this and similar circumstance? Equally, it is not only managers that are faced with ethical dilemmas. Employees are also exposed on occasions to decisions that are difficult. What should employees do when they find that an organization has been cheating its customers?

How significant should the cheating be before something is done? There is no single approach that will allow individuals to resolve these types of decision dilemma. This chapter introduced some of the distinctive approaches based on moral philosophy that exist to guide decision making. Each approach offers a particular view of what defines right and wrong in any particular context and against which decisions should be judged.

One area of ethical dilemma for managers relates to the degree and form of involvement that employees should be allowed to have in the running and direction of the business. For at the heart of all capitalist systems is a contradiction, '... the need to achieve both control *and* consent of employees, in order to secure not just the extraction, but the realization of their surplus value' (Legge, 1995, p 175). In most organizations involvement is not undertaken because it is an intrinsically good thing to do. It is done because managers see that it has advantages in helping them to achieve their objectives. The control over the production process and people provided by scientific management has not been able to deliver the desired control and benefits. Consequently the focus has moved in an attempt to *manipulate* the people resource in the search for more effective organizations and higher returns on capital employed. Efforts begun under the human relations umbrella have now become more sophisticated in response to the prevailing circumstances.

At one extreme it could be argued that employees are a resource to be used and that they are paid to do management's bidding. That view, however, misses out on the potential to make use of the mental and intellectual capabilities of employees to contribute to the more effective running of the business. To be able to get employees involved in the business could actually make management activities easier, generate higher profits, improve quality and generally improve operational effectiveness.

The difficulty facing managers is how to identify the most effective means of achieving the objective without creating more problems. The difficulties with employee involvement in practice has been the commitment of managers to make it work. It is easy to understand from a manager's perspective that any form of employee involvement might threaten the position and status of managers. If there were few problems and employees were committed to the aims of the organization to the extent that they were able to organize themselves, what would become of the job of management?

Equally not all employees would wish to become involved in an organization beyond the contractual obligations associated with their job. Consequently, dual levels of involvement have to be catered for. Not all approaches to involvement offer equally effective results, which also complicates the process. As far back as 1975 Poole identified that the intended purpose of involvement would determine which method would be likely to be most effective. On p 164 he indicates that in deciding the form of involvement provided by legislation, lower level forms would be more appropriate if the purpose was to improve efficiency rather than to extend the rights of workers. Deciding what the right thing to do is in this respect an ethical problem as well as a managerial one.

Conclusions

The material included in this chapter provides a basis on which ethical dilemmas can be resolved. It considered the different approaches that have emerged
over the years and how they might link to organizational activity. A number of
the more common areas of conflicting moral obligation were discussed. Just as
important in this light are the areas that have been omitted. For example, giving to political parties and charity is an area that can create difficulties which
must be resolved in a coherent way.

Employees are involved in their organizations as soon as they are recruited.
There is no perfect approach to employee involvement and managers are faced
with different views about what the right thing to do is. The concepts of power
and control have a significant degree of interaction with both ethics and
involvement in organizational activity and will be covered in later chapters.

Discussion questions

1 Define the following key terms used in this chapter:

Utilitarianism	Employee involvement
Joint consultation	Contractarianism
Formalism	Libertarian contractarianism
Ethics	Restricted contractarianism
Rule utilitarianism	Act utilitarianism
Financial participation	Quality circles
Total quality management	Share option
Profit share	

2 'Ethics has no part to play in managerial activities.' Discuss this statement.
3 Discuss employee rights to privacy in the light of management's need to
   maintain good public and customer relations.
4 The primary responsibility of employees is to the organization that pays
   their wages. Whistleblowing should therefore result in the dismissal of the
   employee. Discuss.
5 'Profit share schemes are an attempt to turn employees into capitalists and
   so be sympathetic to management control.' Discuss this statement.
6 Employees put their livelihood at stake by becoming involved with an
   organization and should not be subjected to additional financial risk as a
   result of becoming part of a share option scheme. Discuss
7 'Business is about making money and anything lawful and within reason
   that achieves that objective is ethical.' Discuss.
8 Do you consider that 'upwards problem solving' methods of employee
   involvement would be more effective than 'representative participation'
   approaches? Justify your answer.
9 Do you think that a code of practice could provide adequate guidance for
   individuals in deciding upon the right course of action in any particular situation? Justify your answer.
10 How would you persuade a manager who thought that their job was at risk
    from an employee involvement initiative not to attempt to undermine the
    benefits from the programme?

Research questions

1 Obtain a number of ethics codes of practice from sources open to you. They may be from professional institutions, commercial organizations or government. Compare the approach taken by each example that you find. How similar are they? Do you consider that they offer definite advice on how to resolve dilemmas in the context that they are intended to apply. If not, why? How would you undertake the task of drawing up a code of practice if you were asked to do so?

2 Interview a manager and ascertain their views on employee involvement. Repeat the exercise with a trade union representative, an employee and a shareholder. How do the different views compare? Reconcile any differences and similarities.

3 Identify a company that has an approved profit share scheme under the Inland Revenue regulations. Attempt to identify why they adopted the scheme, how they went about seeking approval, how they communicated with employees, the benefits since its introduction and any reflections on the scheme as a means of involving employees in the business.

Key reading

From Clark, H., Chandler, J. and Barry, J. (1994) *Organization and Identities: Text and Readings in Organizational Behaviour*, International Thomson Business Press, London.

■ Friedman AL: Marx's framework, p 25. This summarizes the Marxist view of aspects of capitalism as the creator of the work organizations within which labour is expressed.
■ Foucault M: Docile bodies and panopticism, p 35. This introduces one aspect of the basis of power and control in a social context.
■ Foucault M: The subject and power, p 43. Another extract from the genius of this writer on the nature and basis of power relationships in society.
■ Bell D: Work and its discontents, p 44. Considers the interaction between politics, ideology and work organization in social evolution.
■ Whyte WH: The organization man, p 149. This considers the relationship between careers and the level of ownership of the individual by the organization.
■ Canter, RM: Men and women of the corporation, p 152. This introduces the idea that work and organizations impact upon the lives of employees and their families in different ways.
■ Tiger L: The possible biological origins of sexual discrimination, p 165. Considers discrimination as a function of biology rather than social forces.
■ Oakley A: Myths of women's place, p 169. Takes a strongly opposite point of view to that of Tiger and describes the labelling of women's work as an attempt to maintain male control.
■ Coch L and French JRP: Overcoming resistance to change using group methods, p 260. Looks at one form of employee involvement.
■ Brunsson N: The virtue of irrationality – decision making, action and commitment, p 294. This considers the rationality of some decision making within organizations and how this relates to an action orientation.
■ Höpfl H *et al.*: Excessive commitment and excessive resentment: issues of identity, p 373. Considers the impact of attempts to change culture on commitment and related concepts.

Further reading

Alatas, SH (1991) *Corruption: Its Nature, Causes and Functions*, S Abdul Majeed, Kuala Lumpur, in association with Gower, London. As the title suggests, this book reviews the history and causes of corruption. It is set primarily within an Asian context and so provides a less-usual reflection on aspects associated with ethics.

Cotton, JL (1993) *Employee Involvement: Methods for Improving Performance and Work Attitudes*, Sage, London. This text provides a comprehensive review of many of the techniques and practices associated with employee involvement. As the title suggests it is firmly rooted in the belief that by providing involvement employees will become more committed to the organization and its goals and that this in turn will create better service and profits.

Hyman, J and Mason, B (1995) *Managing Employee Involvement and Participation*, Sage, London. The text provides a comprehensive review of the basis of employee involvement. It also introduces recent initiatives in this field together with the typical responses by employees, employers and trade unions. It also incorporates experience and examples from Europe and America.

Jamieson, KM (1994) *The Organization of Corporate Crime: Dynamics of Antitrust Violation*, Sage, London. An American review of the illegal and anti-competitive activities of some executives. The writer attempts to place these findings into a theoretical framework.

Lomax, E (1995) *The Railway Man*, Jonathan Cape, London. The true story of a British army officer captured in the fall of Singapore and his subsequent treatment by the Japanese on the infamous Burma railway. It is the story of how the Japanese authorities reacted, the immediate and long-term consequences for the people involved and the ultimate reconciliation of captor and captive.

References

Brennan, B (1991) Mismanagement and quality circles: how middle managers influence direct participation. *Employee Relations*, **13**, No. 5.

Cederblom, J and Dougherty, CJ (1990) *Ethics at Work*, Wadsworth, Belmont, CA.

Church, R (1971) Profit sharing and labour relations in England in the nineteenth century. *International Review of Social History*, No. 14.

Clutterbuck, D and Grainer, S (1990) *Makers of Management: Men and Women Who Changed the Business World*, Macmillan, London.

Collard, R and Dale, B (1989) Quality circles. In *Personnel Management in Britain* (ed K Sisson), Blackwell, Oxford.

Confederation of British Industry (1989) *Employee Involvement: Shaping the Future Business*, CBI, London.

Flood, RL (1993) *Beyond TQM*, John Wiley, Chichester.

Garrahan, P and Stewart, P (1992) *The Nissan Enigma: Flexibility at Work in a Local Economy*, Mansell, London.

Goldsmith, J (1995) *The Response*, Macmillan, London.

Holden, L (1994) Employee involvement. In *Human Resource Management: A Contemporary Approach* (eds I Beardwell and L Holden), Pitman, London.

Hosmer, LT (1987) Ethical analysis and human resource management. *Human Resource Management*, **26**, 313–30.

Huxley, A (1932) *Brave New World*, Chatto & Windus, London.

Hyman, J and Mason, B (1995) *Managing Employee Involvement and Participation*, Sage, London.

Kerfoot, D and Knights, D (1994) Empowering the 'quality worker': the seduction and contradiction of the total quality phenomenon. In *Making Quality Critical* (eds A Wilkinson and H Willmott), Routledge & Kegan Paul, London.

Legge, K (1995) *Human Resource Management: Rhetorics and Realities*, Macmillan, Basingstoke.

Leys, WAR (1962) The value framework of decision making. In *Concepts and Issues in Administrative Behaviour* (eds S Mailick and EH Van Ness), Prentice-Hall, Englewood Cliffs, NJ.

Marchington, M, Goodman, J, Wilkinson, A and Ackers, P (1992) New developments in employee involvement. Manchester School of Management, Employment Department Research Series Number 2.

Mills, CW (1959) *The Sociological Imagination*, Oxford University Press, New York.

Poole, M (1975) *Workers' Participation in Industry*, Routledge & Kegan Paul, London.

Ramsey, H (1992) Commitment and involvement. In *The Handbook of Human Resource Management* (ed B Towers), Blackwell, Oxford.

Raphael, DD (1994) *Moral Philosophy*, 2nd edn, Oxford University Press, Oxford.

Rawls, J (1971) *A Theory of Justice*, Harvard University Press, Cambridge, MA.

16

Japanization and post-Fordism

Chapter summary

This chapter will introduce a number of perspectives on organizations that have emerged over recent years. It was the developments in manufacturing technology first introduced by Ford that allowed a fundamental change to be introduced in the way that work was practised. Since then many other views about the nature and practice of work have emerged and this chapter will review the approaches emerging from Japan, followed by labour process theory and postmodernism. The intention of this chapter is to attempt to place the notion of work into a broader context than the functionalist perspective usually adopted by managers.

Learning objectives

After studying this chapter and working through the associated Management in Action panels, discussion questions and research activities, you should be able to:

- Understand the concept of Fordism as indicative of a particular way of working.
- Describe the main themes associated with the Japanization of work and management.
- Explain what is meant by the labour process approach to work.
- Outline the postmodernist view of work.
- Assess the contribution of labour process and postmodernism to the understanding of work and management.
- Appreciate that there are conflicts and contradictions between approaches to the understanding of work.
- Discuss the distinction between real and pseudo participation as might be experienced in the Japanization movement.
- Detail the management perspectives on the ideas presented in this chapter.

browse this web site

www.itbp.com

Introduction

Over the centuries the control of work and workers by managers has taken many different forms. However, the objective has remained constant: the effective control of organizational activity. The work of FW Taylor on scientific management is frequently regarded as the beginning of modern management practice. It is also regarded as the basis of the deskilled, monotonous, repetitive, alienated work found in many organizations.

Shortly after Taylor began to identify the benefits from his methods the weaknesses also became apparent. Human workers could not be regarded as machines and expected to function in a way where the very qualities of being human were set aside and ignored. Workers, managers and politicians reacted to the changes that were being imposed on the *natural order* of the time and to the scientific management *formula* for work. Consequently other approaches to management and organization began to emerge as the benefits of Taylorism were sought, but in ways that did not create the same problems and loss of potential.

One of the major difficulties created by the market concept of business is that the relentless drive for cost reduction is unstoppable. The market principle sets the scene for high profits to attract new suppliers. Thus anyone who can reduce the cost of operations can force their way into a market through price reduction which competitors would find hard to match. Goldsmith (1995) states that '... 47 workers in the Philippines or in Vietnam can be employed for the cost of a single worker in France' (p 124). This is cost reduction on a grand scale. Western manufacturers were given a significant shock in the 1970s and 1980s with the explosion of high quality Japanese products at low cost on unsuspecting markets. This led to an interest in how this had been achieved, and the term *Japanization* was coined. Reflecting an assumed mixture of management approaches it was thought that an approach vastly different to that developed by Taylor and Ford had been discovered.

Labour process theory and postmodernism are different ways of thinking and theorizing about organizations. They represent relatively recent introductions to the field and attempt to throw light on aspects of organizational activity. Both approaches encounter significant and lively debate among those who consider that they have something to contribute and those that are less convinced.

Fordism and post-Fordism

The development of the factory system of production made available an ever greater variety and volume of manufactured goods. This developed further through the application of *scientific management*. The systematic design and control of work through the activities of people such as Taylor provided employers with the opportunity to both reduce unit labour cost and increase output. The original application of scientific management by Taylor increased output from the 'pig iron' loaders by more than 300% with only a relatively small increase in pay.

The major difficulty in attempting to study organizations in the present is that the events are still in progress and the terminology is unfixed. For example, *post-Fordism* has also been described as *neo-Fordism*. Representing possible distinctions between the adaptation of Fordism or a subsequent movement which changes its fundamental tenets by emphasizing aspects such as flexibility, delayering and empowerment. Management in Action 16.1 illustrates that even Ford itself found it necessary to adapt in the face of significant change.

Fordism

It was the fledgling motor car industry in which the ideas and principles which became known as *Fordism* were first developed. At the turn of the century motor cars were traditionally made by teams of craftsmen. Cars were a product for the rich. The process of manufacture was so detailed that it could take

Management in Action 16.1

Re-fashioning faltering Ford

Ford is no longer able to isolate itself from the impact of other car-makers. Size alone is no guarantee of success. Recent attempts to reorient the company to make it more able to respond to changes in the market place in an increasingly aggressive market environment include:

■ The creation of truly pan-European managers with far wider responsibilities as layers of management are stripped away.
■ New long-term partnership deals with fewer component suppliers.
■ Cutting the product development cycle in half from six to three years.

A number of initiatives have been incorporated into the process for improving productivity and achieving the three objectives indicated above. For example:

■ All employees have been briefed in the factories targeted as the lead factories for particular products.
■ Employees have been interchanged between factories across Europe in order to broaden experience and provide a basis for learning how other people do things.
■ Changes to dealer operations have also been introduced as a means of improving customer service and increasing sales.
■ The introduction of a 30:30:30 initiative. Reductions of 30% in indirect staff levels, 30% reduction in management positions and 30% reduction in levels of foreign service personnel.

These initiatives are in addition to the more direct attempts to reduce the number of component suppliers and reductions in the development cycle.

Adapted from: Lawless, J (1992) Re-fashioning faltering Ford. Management Today, *August, pp 42–7.*

---

anything up to thirteen weeks to complete each vehicle. Even in volume car production there was much skilled work. Partly assembled vehicles remained in one position whilst teams of workers moved around the factory building up the product as they went. This process was relatively inefficient from a number of points of view.

Early attempts to increase productivity included building vehicles on a trestle that could be pushed between teams. This *ad hoc* process was refined into a simple production line in which employees remained in one position and the vehicles moved between workstations. Early attempts required the workers to push each vehicle to the next workstation as they completed their task. This left control over the pace of work to the employee. It was Henry Ford who made a breakthrough in the early years of the twentieth century by mechanically driving an assembly line at a speed determined by management. The breakthrough took three forms. Firstly, mechanically driving the assembly line. Secondly, the continuous movement of the line removed control of activity from workers. Thirdly, the pace of the line became an integral part of the job design process.

The combination of mechanically paced assembly lines, scientific management-based job design and piecework payment was the mixture that managers had been seeking in order to control production. Because of the pivotal role of Henry Ford and the Ford Motor Company in this process it has become

Table 16.1

The effect of an assembly line on car engine production (Ford Motor Company (1918) *Facts from Ford*)

Pre-assembly line	Post-assembly line
1100 men assemble 1000 car engines in a 9-hour day	1400 men assemble 3000 car engines in an 8-hour day
Each engine = 9.9 labour hours	Each engine = 3.37 labour hours
	A reduction in labour content of 6.17 hours or 62.3%

known as *Fordism*. In employee terms it is frequently associated with alienated workers performing boring tasks with no inkling of interest in the end product of their labours. An indication of the benefits of assembly line technology can be found within data published by Ford itself, see, for example, Table 16.1 taken from Ford Motor Company (1918).

It did not take long for the benefits of Fordism to become established across a wide range of industries and countries. The principles were introduced to the manufacturing of a wide range of household goods, including radios and vacuum cleaners. The River Rouge factory of Ford in the USA became the biggest factory in the world, employing some 80,000 people in the assembly of the Model 'T' car. The factory received raw material in the form of metal, rubber and wood and through its own foundries, tyre factories, machine shops and assembly lines a new car was spewed out every few seconds.

However, not everything was perfect. Many employees were not able to tolerate the noise, pace of work, boredom and sheer scale of operation and labour turnover was very high. The response of Ford was to raise wages, thereby retaining labour and allowing employees to become consumers of the goods being produced. It was possible to save for a new Ford through a company savings scheme. Money was used as a *golden handcuff* in an attempt to lock the employee into the company. Ford also engaged a private police force to ensure that workers were committed and did not form or join trade unions. It was in principle and practice very much a *top-down* process with decisions and policies being formulated by managers. Employees were regarded as an extension of the machines that were used to drive the factory system.

The all-pervading significance of Fordism is brilliantly captured in literature in the work of Aldous Huxley (1932). This prescient work pictures a highly stratified society in the future. Everything is provided to each member from cradle to grave by the leader of the world – called the *Great Ford*. There are many aspects of our modern world in this book, including virtual reality machines and social engineering that are quite unnerving given its year of publication. The key to life in this world of Huxley is that one must accept one's place in life and acquiesce to the greater good and insight held by the *Great Ford* as the fount of all knowledge and provider of all bounty. But even in this view of the future not all accepted the dominant view. Some preferred to stay outside of the system, or to leave it.

Managers were not able to realize the full potential from the Fordist approach. The relentless pressure of an assembly line introduced an additional cause of stress into a delicately balanced system. Supervisors were continually pressed for increases in line speed, jobs were deskilled to the level of the banal and the opportunity for social interaction eliminated. The human dimension of the organization was something that Ford actively discouraged: 'A big business is really too big to be human. It grows so large as to supplant the personality of the man' (Ford, 1923, p 263). So conscious was Ford of the need to maintain order and control that several unique features were present in the factories. Under the influence of the sociological department within the company great emphasis was placed on the 'quality' of the working environment. Walls and roofs of factory buildings at the River Rouge factory were painted regularly and windows washed, by the team of 700 cleaners and painters. Welfare provision included school, hospital, cut price shops and a newspaper. However, there was a strong element of paternalism and attempts to achieve control over workers lives through this provision.

Industrial disputes began to emerge as employees found ways of resisting the inevitable control and alienation of work on an assembly line. In structuring production into a stream of activity greater output and reduced cost had been achieved at the expense of vulnerability. A break in any part of the production process brought the entire system to a standstill. This placed a considerable degree of power in the hands of employees. Blauner (1964) describes this in terms of, 'The social personality of the auto worker, a product of metropolitan residence and exposure to large, impersonal bureaucracies, is expressed in a characteristic attitude of cynicism toward authority and institutional systems, and a volatility revealed in aggressive response to infringement on personal rights and occasional militant collective action. Lacking meaningful work and occupational function, the automobile worker's dignity lies in his peculiarly individualistic freedom from organizational commitments' (p 177).

Goffee and Scase (1995) summarize a number of weaknesses associated with the Fordist model (pp 78–9), including:

- **Alienation.** The organizational consequences of alienation can include high labour turnover, absenteeism, the production of poor quality products and even sabotage.
- **Product change.** The original Ford model depended on a single product with no variation. However, with increased competition and customer ability to exercise choice this becomes difficult to sustain in practice. Thus built-in obsolescence is created in any dedicated production system.
- **Managing and doing distinction.** Taylor envisaged a strict distinction between managerial and operational activity. The danger of this view is that it separates parts of the organization that need to co-operate, creating low trust relationships.
- **Inhibition of creativity.** The imposition of managerial control can actively inhibit levels of creativity and desire for change, even among those charged with pursuing them.
- **Potential not fully realized.** Because of the need to plan ahead for specific levels of capacity in production, variation in market demand can frequently lead to an under utilization of resource. In addition, many of the issues discussed above also have the effect of reducing output

These difficulties soon became apparent and led initially to tighter control of the process and work methods in an attempt to *manage* out the undesirable influences. Considerable effort was put into method study and other technique-based approaches in seeking out the problems and solutions.

The post-Fordist model

There are immense benefits to be gained from the application of scientific management to the running of an organization. However, there are a number of forces that conspire to offset these benefits and they are one-off by definition. Once the workers produce a car engine in 3.73 hours instead of 9.9 hours this becomes the *norm* in successive years. Eventually, different approaches become necessary to obtain the *next generation* of leaps in productivity. Management in Action 16.2 provides an indication of the development of Fordism in the car industry.

Post-Fordism attempted to retain the advantages of the original model, but to overcome the major weaknesses. There are three areas in which post-Fordism addressed the difficulties identified:

- ■ Market. Marketing trends demand increasingly fragmented product ranges, updated products and new products, introduced at regular intervals. Whilst there may be arguments about this, it is a fact of life that organizations cannot ignore. Ways have to be found to meet the needs of the market if the organization is to remain in business.
- ■ Methods. The clearest illustration of just how adaptability can be incorporated into production processes comes from the motor car industry. For any of the large car makers consider the number of end product variations within the basic body shell design for any model. The end product range for any model will include engine, styling, colour, upholstery differences and special features or items of optional equipment. This represents a true marvel of modern production technology. Based on the Fordist principles of assembly line production, but cleverly adapted to meet the needs of more sophisticated and complex markets.
- ■ Management. In attempting to overcome the Fordist problems it is managers who must decide what must be done. They need to be prepared to change their own practices to more effectively capture the potential from employees. Ford tried paying higher wages to *handcuff* employees to his factory. This worked for a while, but what was prized and special yesterday does not always work today. Obtaining a job which is highly paid creates a tangible effect in the short term. However, it does not take long for the new conditions to become the norm against which comparisons are made, as well as becoming ordinary by virtue of familiarity. So a circular process is established in which *treats* are necessary on a regular basis to maintain interest. Initiatives in more recent times have attempted to approach this problem from a different direction. Early work from the Human Relations School and the Tavistock Institute began to suggest that employees could usefully become more involved in the activities in which they were engaged. However, to do so contains implications for managers as well as workers. It opened the door for considering a fundamental change in the manager/worker relationship in pursuit of mass production. Developments such as empowerment (delegation of responsibility), delayering and downsizing (reducing the number of levels and people) began to follow as organizations attempted to make more effective use of the *human resource* .

Figure 16.1 on page 494 reflects the phasing process between Fordism and post-Fordism with the three forces outlined above.

Management in Action 16.2

Steering the middle road to car production

The approach to the manufacture of cars in the Saab and Volvo experiments in worker friendly factories was referred to as 'dock assembly'. Groups of workers undertook the final assembly of a motor car in a fixed location (dock). In pure form this approach only lasted a few years. Increases in the number of model variants created complexity and the dock approach was modified to allow the return to line paced assembly organized around teams of workers. Other experiments took place in variants of the original dock assembly. For example the assembly of cars by teams of 10 people was supported by a separate materials centre which prepared the components and transported them to the assembly location at programmed intervals on automated guided vehicles. However, even this initiative only achieved car assembly times of 16 hours per car, compared to the best in Europe of 10.5 hours. The training of operators was also much more complex in dock assembly because of the need to prepare them for up to two hour work cycles compared with a few minutes on a traditional assembly line.

Womack, Jones and Roos from the Massachusetts Institute of Technology conducted a five-year study of the auto industry in the USA, Japan and Europe. Their book on this research titled *The Machine That Changed The World* (published in 1990) coined the term 'lean production' as the way that leading (mostly Japanese) manufacturers operated. There was a very striking 2:1 performance gap in every aspect of the production system between companies that applied lean production compared to those using mass production. Those factories employing lean production engaged in the following practices:

- Just-in-time.
- Zero buffer stocks.
- Quality built into the process.
- Delegation.
- Small lot production batches.
- Problem solving.
- Teamworking.
- Quick set-up times.
- Individual flexibility.
- Individual accountability.
- Individual recognition and reward.

According to Wibberley, lean production uses less of everything to achieve a better product that more closely matches the customer desires. It consists of five main characteristics:

- Lower manufacturing times.
- Devolved responsibility.
- Fewer component suppliers.
- Shorter product development times.
- Twice as many product variants.

This approach to manufacturing emphasizes the people issues to make it work. As Wickens says, 'The mistake is to believe that the production system itself gives the results. What counts is the relationship of people with the process. A controlled Taylorist process need not alienate if the workers are able to contribute, and long-cycle dock assembly will not satisfy if that is all there is (nor will it last if it cannot compete). What we must aim for is lean, people-centred volume production'.

Adapted from: Wickens, P (1993) Steering the middle road to car production. Personnel Management, June, pp 34–8, and Wibberley, M (1993) Does 'lean' necessarily equal 'mean'? Personnel Management, July, pp 32–5.

There are a number of forces that produce a reticence in moving away from the principles embedded in the Fordist approach. As an *ideal type*, the efficiencies available through Fordism retain their attraction. The difficulty is it cannot be achieved in its pure form in the *long run*. Humans are not machines and there are reactions to being controlled by the inflexible assembly line. Roy (1960) describes the rituals and routines of four factory workers over the

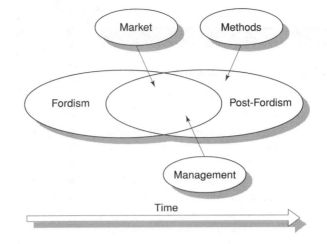

Figure 16.1   The evidence of post-Fordism.

course of a working day as they attempt to cope with the demands of production. Fordist managers would regard such behaviour as deviant and as creating a loss of efficiency for the system and therefore to be eliminated. The underlying problem is that it is not possible to completely separate the individual from the human.

Other pressures in the environment also tend to encourage the retention of Fordist principles, including:

■ Risk. Every person within a Fordist organization is familiar with their role and the types of problem that will be encountered. To introduce change carries with it the risk of unfamiliar events and different behaviour patterns being required. In such situations there is a lower certainty that the events can be dealt with effectively or quickly. There is an inertia in organizations that produces an approach based on incremental improvement rather than adopting more radical change. This reflects a tendency rather than something which would be found in every organization. Many organizations have adopted radical approaches to the activities within them.

■ Training. The training and experience of most managers has been in organizations which originate and espouse the Fordist perspective. Managers make use of what they know and believe in running organizations. It takes time for new ideas, thinking and knowledge to filter through and become an accepted part of their skill base.

■ Systems. The systems and procedures adopted within organizations tend to reinforce the status quo and an incremental approach to managing. The greater the potential risk the greater the required return as justification. In addition, many organizations reward executives based upon short-term financial gains rather than any qualitative measure of corporate performance.

■ Preference. That which could be regarded as radical is frequently seen as deviant and to be avoided. Managers with careers to develop are not likely to deliver things not valued by those in a position to allocate rewards. Also as Kanter (1989) points out, management skills have developed in specific organizational settings and to change these makes many of these skills redundant. The maintenance of the distinction between managed and manager could also be brought into question if radical organizational change were to be pursued. Management in Action 16.3 reflects some of the issues being faced by organizations in the search for flatter structures.

Goffee and Scase (1995) identify a number of distinguishing features which the authors describe as paradigm shifts in management, reflecting the evolution of organizations from Fordist to Post-Fordist models (see Table 16.2).

Management in Action 16.3

Flat season

In these days of flatter organizations a number of problems, real and potential, may arise. Personnel specialists have a vital role to play in helping organizations to come to terms with the demands of the new operating environments. Roffey Park Management Institute have carried out research into how firms are tackling the problems associated with the move to flatter structures and found that although there were many positive signs, a number of problems remained. Among the issues not being effectively addressed by many organizations are the linkage of pay and reward to teamwork performance and team contribution to corporate values. The emphasis remains on short-term performance reward and the payment of market rate levels of salary.

Holbeche provides a number of examples of the changes made by organizations to adapt to flatter structures. They include:

■ British Airways Engineering. The Materials Maintenance and Components Operations Department within the engineering division maintains, supplies and controls all the components needed for maintenance on the company's aircraft and those of other companies for whom it carries out maintenance. It employs about 2300 people, approximately 1200 of whom are in engineering-related positions. The structure of the department was flattened by the removal of one layer of management. The old structure was technician, supervisor, foreman and superintendent. This became technician, cell manager and production manager. Consequently, the ratio of supervisors changed from one supervisor to six staff, to one cell manager to 20 staff. Cell managers were given additional responsibilities, including performance management, identifying training needs, carrying out first stage discipline and managing budgets. This clearly involved considerable training for the people involved. The funding of external courses at masters degree or diploma level for some individuals was also introduced. The major change for the cells was the need to address many issues such as budgetary control that they had previously been sheltered from.

■ Sun Microsoft. The company introduced a programme called 'Managing your career' intended to provide a forum for people to discuss career concerns following a restructuring process. It was intended to demonstrate to, and explore with, employees the alternatives to traditional vertical promotion and career development options.

■ Tektronix. Employees in this computer manufacturer play a significant part in reviewing their own performance across a number of areas, both hard and soft. Goals and objectives are agreed between the manager and employee and a personal growth process is encouraged through the regular review over the year. Job descriptions are only used to recruit people to the organization initially. After that development depends upon the personal growth system. This process ensures that employees can take responsibility for their own development and employability in a rapidly changing work and organizational environment.

Adapted from: Holbeche, L (1995) Flat season. Personnel Today, 25 October, pp 37–9.

	From: Fordist	To: Post-Fordist
Table 16.2 Paradigm shifts in management (taken from: Goffee, R and Scase, R (1995) *Corporate Realities*, Routledge, London, p 83)	■ Precisely-defined job roles ■ Specialist skills ■ Tight control ■ Bounded responsibilities ■ Rules and procedures ■ Closed communication ■ High status differences ■ Low-trust relationships ■ Prevailing custom and practice ■ Colleagues as individuals ■ Invisible management	■ Broadly-defined job roles ■ Transferable skills ■ Loose control ■ Autonomy and discretion ■ Guidelines for behaviour ■ Open/fluid communication ■ Low status differences ■ High-trust relationships ■ Innovation and change ■ Colleagues as team members ■ Visible leadership

Much of this shift can be attributed to the need to create new forms of labour flexibility. The need for a wider, diversified and more frequently changing product range, with shorter lead times and lower costs are frequently behind these moves. It is Japanese companies that have been both the trigger and model for many of these initiatives.

Japanization

That organizations reflect the broader social context in which they exist could not be denied. The difficulty is in delineating the extent of the relationship. These relationships become even more complex when cross-cultural perspectives impinge on the situation. This was highlighted with particular force during the late 1970s and early 1980s when the impact of Japanese manufactured goods suddenly became apparent throughout the Western world. The quality and reliability of Japanese products and the perceived value-for-money decimated the market share of many long established producers. For example, by 1986 Japanese manufacturers held 84% of the world market for 35-mm cameras, 71% of microwave ovens and 55% of motorcycles (BBC/OU, 1986). Oliver and Wilkinson (1992) provide many similar statistics which indicate the significance and magnitude of the Japanese threat. Table 16.3 is a summary of some of these data.

Table 16.3
Japanese and western productivity comparisons (based on: Oliver, N and Wilkinson, B. (1992), Tables 1.2 and 2.1). *The Japanization of British Industry: New Developments in the 1990s*, 2nd edition, Blackwell, Oxford

	Japan	West	America	Toyota
Set-up time (hours)*			6.0	0.2
Number of set-ups per day*			1.0	3.0
Sales per annum per employee†	$150K	$85K		

*Based on the work of Burbridge (1982).
†Based on the work of Parnaby (1987).

The threat to jobs and even whole industries quickly became apparent and a search for an explanation undertaken. The original view was that there had to be a new way of managing to provide such impressive results. It was thought to be a reflection of the Japanese culture and religion as well as the emphasis on the group rather than individual prowess. Oliver and Wilkinson (1992) identify a number of features of Japanese production methods that collectively provide the scale of benefit achieved, including:

- Quality. The view that quality is integral to the entire production process and reduces the cost of operations was generated by US consultants during World War II. There was very little interest in these ideas in the West, but Japanese managers adopted the principles during the rebuilding of the economy in the 1950s. The view of quality in the West was that it was *inspected into* a product after it was made. The quality was checked and repairs carried out if necessary. In Japan, quality was seen as a feature of the manufacturing process and reflecting the level of control within the organization. One of the ways that this can be achieved is by solving problems as they arise rather than tolerating them.

- Just-in-time. This approach requires the elimination of inventory, items needed in production arriving at the point of use *just-in-time*. Inventory is regarded as unnecessary and a means of hiding problems. The traditional Western approach to planning is to *push* items into the system in the belief that if all the parts are available production flow will be maintained. Just-in-time operates on the basis that the needs of assembly should dictate when components are *pulled* forward into the production process. Small frequent deliveries as-and-when needed is the basis of production in this approach. Operating under just-in-time conditions requires inventory levels to be deliberately and progressively reduced. It also requires the problems resulting from the lack of inventory to be dealt with so that they do not continue to restrict operational activity.

- Continuous improvement. The need to improve quality and solve problems associated with just-in-time production require specific programmes. It is never possible to achieve perfection, improvements can always be achieved. This is the philosophy behind continual improvement. It is also part of this approach that improvement can be best identified by the people most directly involved in the work. In the West employees do not traditionally expect to be involved in solving problems and to have their opinions sought by managers. In Japan a culture that expects individuals to participate in these activities (usually in their own time) is the norm. Failure to do so to an acceptable level would be held against an individual in pay and promotion terms.

- Work organization. The use of cellular manufacturing methods and U-shaped production lines allows for greater employee flexibility as well as improved control of the product and process. According to Gaither (1992, p 294) the benefits of a cell approach to production are:
  - Machine changeovers are simplified.
  - Training periods for workers are shortened.
  - Materials-handling costs are reduced.
  - Parts can be made faster and shipped more quickly.
  - Less in-process inventory is required.
  - Production is easier to automate.

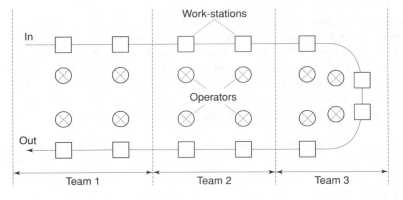

Labour flexibility would exist within each team

Figure 16.2   'U'-shaped assembly line production.

A cell becomes a micro production unit dedicated to the production of a small range of products, thereby allowing a high level of expertise, flexibility and efficiency to develop.

U-shaped assembly lines are assembly lines that have been shaped to encourage a team commitment to develop. In straight assembly lines the linear approach ties workers to specific work stations and their only contact would be with adjacent work activities. U-shaped assembly lines simply bend the straight line to create involvement opportunities. Figure 16.2 shows a U-shaped production line, based upon the principles developed by Toyota.

Teams provide an opportunity for people to work together, help each other with a social perspective to their work. In the Japanese approach this is taken much further. Oliver and Wilkinson (1992) quote Sayer (1986) who indicates that one Toyota worker performed 35 different jobs in one day and walked six miles. Another view of these types of work practice is also quoted by Oliver and Wilkinson referring to Domingo (1985) who suggests that the system deliberately introduces tension into the system which turns every day into a challenge. A negative view of teamwork is provided by Garrahan and Stewart (1992). They describe a control and conflictual perspective on team-based production methods. They suggest that it provides a more effective level of management control and in practice sets one worker against another in the drive to find problems and seek continual improvement. Each worker is expected to report quality problems immediately. Failure to do so makes the individual liable to punishment rather than the 'creator' of the problem.

■ Structure and system. Japanese organization structure was researched by Lincoln and Kalleburg (1990) who show that they generally contained more hierarchical levels and incorporated a greater measure of formality. Oliver and Wilkinson describe the Japanese approach to accounting as providing a strong market focus. The approach adopted being essentially an *outside-in* perspective of identifying a market price and then managing costs within that constraint. The Western approach tends to be based on identifying costs and then attempting to ensure that price can cover these needs, an *inside-out* approach. Similar strengths in product development activities can also be identified. Smaller teams, with greater power and forced by the system to face up to the requirement to *get-it-right-first-time* are able to respond more quickly to changing market forces.

The relationship between buyers and suppliers has been frequently described as an adversarial one in the West. Buyers would frequently have many suppliers and would play one off against the other in terms of price and delivery. The Japanese approach is based upon co-operation and long-term relationships with a small number of suppliers. This leads to an inevitable development of dependence relationships. Neither party can afford to abuse the relationship. The location of suppliers is frequently adjacent to the customer so that just-in-time principles can be better applied, with transport distances being minimized and automated. It is common to find companies part owning their suppliers.

■ Personnel practice. There are many features of personnel practice that have been suggested to differ between the West and Japan. Practices such as life-time employment; high levels of company welfare benefit; selection for employment based on degree of *fit* with company values and norms; promotion and reward based upon seniority and service; and excessively long working hours have all been identified as major points of distinction. However, the experience of employment in Japan would appear to be somewhat more complex. Lifetime employment has not been available to all workers and organizations have made use of large numbers of temporary or short-term contract workers. Management in Action 16.4 on the next page provides a review of the Japanese work ethic.

■ Social, political and economic factors. Organizations and management practice emerge in a specific context, therefore it should not be surprising to discover differences in how organizations are structured and function. It could be argued that much of current management thinking is dominated by Western ideas and that we should not expect to find that these insights offer the only explanations. That said there are a number of features of the Japanese environment that are worthy of note. It is not uncommon to find executives in a Japanese company who have spent time as union officials in that same company as part of their career. The education system is very competitive and forces very young people to study extremely hard for long periods of time. Entrance to the best universities is very competitive and demands considerable sacrifice on the part of students and their families.

The need to work effectively in teams is another feature of Japanese life that is fostered from an early age and which is carried over into working life. The role of the government, particularly the Ministry of International Trade and Industry (MITI), has been crucial in encouraging organizations to develop strategic programmes of overseas trade. Information, financial, administrative and research support are available for particular initiatives involving the development of markets and products, a process that has led to many complaints of state subsidy and manipulating of the market. Companies who do not co-operate in this process are also activity discriminated against.

Fuelled by the inroads made by Japanese products into home markets Western manufacturers have found it necessary to respond or be eliminated. One way of responding is to emulate. It has not always been possible to change

Management in Action 16.4

Sun that never sets

The 'addiction' of Japanese workers to work is legendary and many suggest that this represents the reason for the economic miracle in that country. According to the International Labour Organization the average Japanese works 2100 hours each year, compared to 1650 in Europe. This represents a six-day working week and the average Japanese worker voluntarily gives up half of their annual holiday to attend work. However, there has been some evidence that the Japanese work ethic is dying. The Keidanren, the Japanese business association, surveyed 2125 chief executives and senior managers who claimed that people were generally getting lazier. As individuals have become richer their life goals have changed from 'earning' a living to 'spending' their leisure. In addition, it was suggested that loyalty to the company was also declining.

Roger Goodman, an expert of the Japanese work ethic who has lived there for 10 years, suggests that the workaholic ethos represents a recent phenomenon. At the end of the 1940s Japanese managers faced an unco-operative workforce organized by the Communist All-Japan Congress of Industrial Unions. Industrial unrest was common and the general strike of 1947 was only suppressed with the help of the occupying American military forces. This was followed by a purge of the communist infiltration of industry and the unions together with the introduction of 'softer' industrial relations practices. Legislation at this time introduced life-time employment along with company paternalism, the banning of strikes and an encouragement to work longer hours. The company as 'family' was born and was successful, supported by appropriate seniority based promotion and payment systems.

Economic slowdown is occurring in Japan at the same time as a questioning by unions and employers of the value of such long working hours. The Automobile Workers Union claim that 10,000 people a year die from overwork in Japan, typically working in excess of 3000 hours each year. The report claims that the relationship between employer and employee has become distorted. Employers have been too demanding of employees on the pretext of a common destiny.

Many experts have come out in support of these findings, including Professor Haruo Shimada, an economist from Keio University. The International Labour Office also suggest that average white collar productivity in Japan may not be as high as that in the West. Sony chairman, Akio Morita argued for a reduction in working hours and higher salaries. The government, under pressure from the Europe and America, introduced legislation in 1988 that should see the working week reduce to 40 hours.

However, as Goodman points out, actions speak louder than words. In Europe the working year has been shrinking at the average rate of 0.5% each year since the 1960s, but in Japan there has been no reduction at all during this time. Partly because managers do not cut the amount of work that needs to be done and many shops stay open very late, according to Kenji Saiga, director of Toni & Guy hair salons in Tokyo. Attitudes may be changing, but that does not mean that working habits are.

Adapted from: Durkin, M (1992) Sun that never sets. Personnel Today, *14 July, p 23*.

working practices quickly (or successfully) as employees and trade unions have sometimes perceived initiatives as a threat to established rights and benefits. Most of the major motor manufacturers have experienced years of frustration, negotiation and dispute in order to introduce some of the Japanese practices into UK factories (see, for example, Turnbull, 1986; Giles and Starkey, 1987).

In order to better serve their export markets and to placate any suggestion of unfair competition, Japanese producers began to build factories in the West. Garrahan and Stewart (1992) describe this process in general terms, with particular emphasis on the role of the decision of Nissan to build a car assembly plant in Washington near Sunderland. In this situation there was an opportunity to import Japanese management methods by Japanese companies and to impose them onto *greenfield* sites. The term *greenfield* is used to describe a new location as compared with a *brownfield* site, which already contains an operational unit. Clearly in a greenfield location there are no established practices to change and management have a free hand to set their own agenda without hindrance. This must of course be tempered with the knowledge that there will be the established norms, expectations and behaviour patterns that exist in the surrounding environment. The Garrahan and Stewart text provides a very vivid description of this process and is a useful point of comparison with the authorized management views expressed by Wickens (1987). Wickens was at the time the head of personnel and administration at the company and the first British appointment to be made in the UK operation. A comparison between Japanese and British management training is provided in Management in Action 16.5 on the next page.

The arrival of Japanese companies in the UK provided an opportunity to observe some of the ideas on Japanese management at first hand. Of course many Japanese home country practices could not be translated directly but many of the others were. Essentially, the notion of a flexible workforce committed to teamwork and getting-it-right-first-time were introduced along with single union agreements (the nearest form of enterprise unions that could be achieved in the UK). There is the suggestion that transplanted Japanese operations are little more than warehouses (screwdriver factories) and that the full transfer of all manufacturing activity is far from the intention (Williams *et al.*, 1992). This also has a major impact on the work activities and approach to management adopted by such organizations.

The work reviewed so far clearly reflects that Japanese companies have found ways of organizing themselves that produce very effective organizations. However, there are a number of questions that emerge out of a consideration of this approach to management. First, it is necessary to consider whether or not Japanization reflects an approach to management that is fundamentally different to Fordism and Scientific Management, or whether it simply reflects a high degree of refinement of those principles. Secondly, it raises a question about the purpose of effectiveness. In whose benefit is effectiveness being pursued and why? This in turn leads to a consideration of the purpose of organizations and the goods and services that they produce. Whose benefit are they intended to serve and why? Also emerging are questions related to the purpose of work itself.

It is clear that the purpose of the Japanese approach to management is not intended to be the benefit of the employees. It has been suggested already that stress is a common experience among Japanese workers, to the extent that death is becoming a recognized result. The references already identified indicate the low levels of satisfaction of Japanese workers compared with Western counterparts. The pressure to conform to the needs of the group are considerable and individuality is not encouraged and indeed considered a threat to group cohesion. Therefore one is left with the conclusion that Japanese management practices are grounded in the same principles of power and control as Fordism, but that they are a considerable degree of sophistication more effective from the perspective of management.

Management in Action 16.5

Do the Japanese make better managers?

One early study found that British managers apparently receive more training than their Japanese counterparts. Storey, funded by the Economic and Social Science Research Council, set out to consider some of the issues underlying this. He considered the recruitment, selection, evaluation, reward and related aspects of how management is 'formed' and trained. In setting up the studies four British companies from different sectors were compared with matched companies from Japan. The Japanese companies were only studied in Japan, overseas operations were ignored. The matched samples were Lucas Industries and Sumitomo Electric Industries, Tesco and Jusco, National Westminster Bank and Mitsui Trust and Banking, and finally British Telecom and NTT. In all cases managers were given a detailed self completion questionnaire to complete which was followed up with an interview.

The findings of the study suggested that:

The sectorial differences were sufficiently marked to justify the suspicion that many generalizations about 'Japanese management' are not only superficial but misleading. There were many things in common between the two sets of retail managers which outweighed the 'country effect', and the same could be said about the two sets of bank managers.

Despite the significance of the 'sector effect', the analysis also showed certain broad contrasts between the two different populations of managers. These extend across the full range of dimensions examined in our research, including, for example, careers and career planning, how managers are evaluated and rewarded and how satisfied or dissatisfied they are with various aspects of their employment.

The main conclusion from the study was that Japanese managers treated training and development more seriously than was the case in Britain. Six features differ-

entiated the approach to the training and development of managers between the two countries:

- Higher levels of educational attainment were evident among managers in Japan. Almost 94% of Japanese managers had degrees compared with 42% in Britain.
- British companies were more likely to feel that individuals either have what it takes or not. In Japan continuous development was the norm.
- Japanese companies tended to stay with a broad training and development framework, whereas British companies tended to 'chop and change'.
- Japanese training and development tended to be better integrated into career/HR planning systems. In Japan clear demonstration of involvement in training would be part of the evaluation of a manager's performance.
- The notion of management development is regarded as a much broader concept in Japan than in Britain. In Japan it was seen as more akin to 'capability development'.
- In Japan there is a much stronger expectation that managers will develop their subordinates. This would be a key measure of performance for a manager. They also encouraged on-the-job training to an extent way beyond that which would be found in Britain.

Another important point to note from the research was that the position was not static in either country. For example, quality of working life was beginning to feature more highly in the thinking of many Japanese managers. In the UK the more obvious inclusion of approaches such as mentoring, coaching, personal development plans suggest that it might feature more highly in future management careers.

Adapted from: Storey, J (1991) Do the Japanese make better managers? Personnel Management, *August, pp 24–8.*

Labour process theory

The foregoing discussion of Fordism and Japanese management practices tend to assume a rational and managerial perspective on the design and running of organizations. Contingency theory in relation to organization design posits that environmental forces determine to a significant extent what is created. However, as has already been suggested in this context, it ignores the role of management decision making in responding to the environment. It also ignores the effect of decision variation on environmental success. In a common environment there is not just one response available to managers and variability is possible without *necessarily* adversely impacting upon success. For example Figure 16.3 shows two business cards from rival taxi companies operating in the same rural area. Clearly both offer the same basic service, but one also includes an indication of other possible business opportunities. The two companies are slightly different, but both operate successfully within the same general environment.

Both Fordism and Japanization assume that managers apply a particular *formula* to the organization which in turn produces success. This ignores several features associated with contingency and also the idea of *slack* available within the operational system. Perhaps, therefore, although both views of organization are useful *descriptions* of management practice, they are not effective as *explanations* of organizations.

Labour process theory originated from the Marxist tradition and attempts to explain the nature of work. It has been defined as, 'the means by which raw materials are transformed by human labour, acting on the objects with tools and machinery: first into products for use and, under capitalism, into commodities to be exchanged on the market', (Thompson, 1989, p xv). As an area of study it began with Braverman, who in 1974 published *Labour and Monopoly Capital* which stimulated the rediscovery of the earlier Marxist material on the nature of labour.

Figure 16.3   Taxi company business cards.

There would appear to be five core elements to a theory of labour process and which are identified by Thompson (1989). They are:

■ **Labour as a unique commodity.** In seeking to create profit capitalists acquire a number of resources which they control in pursuit of bringing the goods and services to market. Many of the resources are totally malleable at the discretion of the owner. Raw material will allow itself to be moulded and worked into any shape or product for which it has a capacity to become.

However, the human resource has a high degree of restriction in level of malleability. Humans have free will, they can answer back, they have understanding and communication abilities and most important they can resist management's direction. Many of these human capacities are of potential value to the capitalist. The vast majority of managers are paid employees and are paid to organize, take decisions and use what have been described as the higher level human qualities in support of capitalist objectives. On the other hand, humans employed to produce the goods and services have generally been regarded as a very flexible machine.

Because human labour has the qualities necessary for the achievement of capitalist intentions it is an essential part of the process of converting the other resources into the goods and services intended for sale. However, it is mixed blessing as it automatically brings with it other undesirable qualities and obligations (from a capitalist point of view). For example, a surplus of cash within a capitalist organization has a very different set of connotations and ramifications compared with a surplus of people. It is the range and nature of these relative contrasts between the human and other resources that give it the unique qualities in capitalism.

■ **Labour is a special focus of attention in capitalism.** It is the nature of capitalism to create surplus. The notion of profit is a surplus – the extra obtained through the market system over the cost of production. From that perspective every resource used within the capitalist organization must provide an opportunity for a contribution to the surplus obtained. This is the basis of the concept of added value used in accounting. In the Japanese management approach anything that does not add value represents waste and should be eliminated. Consequently, there is a requirement for labour to create surplus as its basis for existence. In short, labour value must be higher than its cost for it to be viable as a resource. It is argued that this predisposes the participants to a conflictual relationship.

■ **Capitalism forces minimization.** It should be apparent from the previous discussion that there are two pressures in a capitalist system. The first is the notion of surplus as the objective of the whole process. The second is the volatility and unpredictability of the market system. In a truly free market there is no possibility of an individual being able to dictate prices. It is simple economics that high profits attract new supplies and hence price reductions. The converse is also true, the result being that it is not possible to opt out of the process, once begun it is ongoing.

It is the unpredictability of markets that has created attempts to *fix* them in one form or another. Cartels, restraint of trade clauses in employment contracts and holding back supplies are some of the manipulations used to control risk (and keep prices high). The other side of this particular coin is to minimize the cost of operations so that it is possible to achieve the maximum surplus from a particular market price. This is more directly amenable to management action than some of the other options. It also provides a differentiating feature between organizations. Market price affects all suppliers equally, but internal costs influence only one organization. It is also possible to use this approach as the basis of price reduction to force out some of the rivals and achieve a stronger position over market conditions. This invariably forces capitalist organizations into a perpetual search for lower costs and the minimization of disruption to the will of management. Once begun it is a competitive process and functions in a way reminiscent of the concept of perpetual motion; competition forces everyone to minimize or demise.

■ Control is an imperative. There are several perspectives to this feature of the labour process theory. Firstly, in order to ensure that profit is obtained the process must be controlled. If the capitalist does not control the process then one of the other stakeholders will. Secondly, because there are conflicting objectives between the stakeholders in an organization, control is the means by which these are regulated. Thirdly, control is something that is associated with power and the ability to have other people do what the controller wants. It is something that people seek in order to be able to exercise it at a personal level. Fourthly, there are differences between operational and strategic control. Because of the size and complexity of most large organizations the owners of capital delegate much of the operational control decisions to employees designated as managers. By giving employees a financial stake in the performance of the business it is argued that they will be more committed to the objectives of management. However, the proportion of ownership divested in this way tends to be very small in comparison to the total. Consequently, the degree of control devolved is also of little real significance.

■ Institutionalized conflict. The classic Marxist view of the class struggle is also part of the labour process. Much of the foregoing discussion has created a picture of the exploitation of workers. It can be argued that because of the notion of a requirement for added value from every aspect of the resource base it is by nature an exploitative process. Employees are paid less in wages than the true value of their labour. This is the basis of the wage–work bargain much beloved of industrial relations specialists. Managers are permanently attempting to seek better value from the employee resource and employees are attempting to balance the contribution with the reward achieved. This is a low trust approach to organizing and Management in Action 16.6 overleaf provides an outline of it.

Employees are dependent upon the owners of capital for the ability to earn money and acquire the necessities of life. It is therefore a relationship that includes a degree of mutual dependence as well as control. Capitalists need workers to supply their profit. The goods and services produced are sold in a market. But there must be someone to purchase them. Inevitably the goods produced are consumed in some degree by the workers that produce them. It is a feature of modern capitalist organization that as part of the search for minimization much production is carried out in locations remote from consumption. But even in these situations consumerism is beginning to emerge in developing countries to fuel the cycle of dependence.

Management in Action 16.6

Trust: a new concept in the management of people?

Trust does not appear in the management literature very often. There are, however, a small number of works on the subject beginning to appear (see, for example, Kramer, RM and Tyler, TR (eds) (1996) *Trust In Organizations: Frontiers of Theory and Research*, Sage, Thousand Oaks, CA). It is however, a subject that is fundamental to the running of organizations.

Organizations need people to run them. It is not physically possible for any organization to exist without people. Therein lies the basic problem for managers: how far should they trust employees? Consequently how much should they rely on control and audit activities, supported by discipline, socialization and reward to ensure that the managerially determined objectives are achieved? From one perspective trust does not enter into the equation. In a very real and practical sense trust is 'engineered out' of the organizational processes through the management and control procedures adopted. As Handy suggests, organizations don't trust people, except to act on their own short-term interests. Baillie summarizes the work of Handy and Andrews to suggest that this position is becoming increasingly untenable.

Developments such as the creation of the virtual organization create a need to directly confront the issue of trust. As Handy points out, how can people be 'managed' if they are not physically present and can't be seen? Will organizations attempt to develop complex computer-based control systems to monitor and direct such individuals, or will new ways evolve based on trust and different measures of activity? After all some jobs have to rely on high levels of trust. The commander of a nuclear submarine has a high degree of discretion once they have left port and are at sea. Yet ways of ensuring that effective control is retained have been found for such occupations, based on the creation of trust and dependability, supported by appropriate control procedures.

Andrews points out that a lack of trust in employees can seriously undermine attempts by management to introduce empowerment programmes. It is impossible to suggest to individuals that they are being empowered, if at the same time the level of trust is so small that they have no discretion to make decisions. Under such circumstances the lack of trust would ensure that the programme failed. Both Handy and Andrews express similar views in reflecting the need for trust as vital to the effective running of either society or an organization. They also agree that individuals who cannot subscribe to the creation of high trust environments should be removed.

Trust as a necessary part of the way that organizations structure themselves and design their operating procedures is finding its way up the management agenda. Due in no small part to the changes in organizations themselves as a result of the flatter, delayered and re-engineered structures, and managements that invariably claim a commitment to total quality management.

Adapted from: Baillie, J (1995) Trust: a new concept in the management of people? People Management, 31 May, p 53.

As Thompson readily admits, there are many who would argue with the views put forward by labour process theorists. They include those who would see it as moving away from a traditional Marxist view of the common ownership, and those who would prefer to see an emphasis on management study as a traditional social science. It does, however, provide a way of considering the nature of labour in capitalist organizations and perhaps placing Fordism and Japanization into a broader context. It is also an inescapable fact that not all organizations are capitalist, even in a predominately capitalist society. There are the public services, voluntary organizations and charities. Each of these institutions make use of modern management techniques and would be indistinguishable from capitalist organizations apart from the profit motive. So perhaps the labour process approach is fundamentally flawed as a means of being able to provide an all embracing perspective on organizations.

Postmodernism

Another view of organization is provided by the *postmodernist* perspective. In attempting to understand organizations and provide theoretical frameworks many different approaches have been developed. These are frequently given titles as an attempt to both differentiate them from other perspectives and to encapsulate some of the essential essence of the underlying thinking. Another way of considering titles is as a simplifying device, intended as a form of shorthand to compress meaning into *bite-size chunks* of information. For example, scientific management and Fordism are two terms used to describe approaches to organization that are based upon work fragmentation, deskilling, machine paced work and alienated labour. This level of categorization is rather specific but there are terms which attempt to stand further back from the specific. Carter and Jackson (1993) use the terms premodern, modern and postmodern to describe epochs of tendency. The typical basis of organizational rationality in each epoch is identified in Table 16.4

The trend evident in the epochs identified in Table 16.4 is in essence one of an increasing reluctance to accept the given and assumed natural order of things, towards one of uncertainty and an acceptance of a rule of thumb rather than formula management.

It is important to recognize that these epochs or trends are indications of how organizations function and how researchers theorize about them. Research as well as organization is an integral part of the broader social milieu and is as much influenced as influencing within it. Postmodernism is meaningful in terms of its juxtaposition with modernism and it is useful to begin by attempting to provide an indication of the modernist view. Gergen (1992, p 211), identifies modernism as being characterized by:

■ Reason and observation. The basis of understanding and survival emanate from an ability to critically observe, develop testable hypothesis and refine knowledge.
■ Fundamentalism. That there are underlying principles and rules governing the universe and everything in it.

Premodern	Modern	Postmodern
Diagnostic rationality based on theo-logic	Objective rationality based on scientific logic	Subjective rationality based on mytho-logic

Table 16.4
Epochs of organizational rationality (taken from: Carter, P and Jackson, N. (1993) *Modernism, Postmodernism and Motivation, or Why Expectancy Theory Failed to Come Up to Expectation*, p 87)

- ■ Universal design. That there is a growing ability to master the universe through the identification of fundamental principles. Through this improved control will emerge better organizations, societies and standards of life.
- ■ Machine metaphor. Take any machine and consider it as a system. It requires inputs of power, transforms that input into some useful activity or product and spews out the end product back into the environment. Organizations can be described in similar terms, as can people. Therefore if a machine system provides a useful model the metaphor can be taken further and regarded as an essential building block of how things should be.

This rather simplistic view of the universe and how to discover it has been brought into question. For a number of writers the use of language to describe the observations from a modernist perspective became problematic. Even if the *things* being observed and described formed the basis of the essentials of the universe, the language used to articulate them did not. It is the actual pen that creates the writing not the term pen. The term pen conveys nothing about the nature of writing, communication or the intended purpose of the individuals involved. So if there is a distinction between *thing* and *symbol*; how accurate can the symbols be and how accurate can any inferences and conclusions be that are based upon them? Reality and the language used to construct it are in effect separate entities.

Hassard (1993) brings together the work of a number of writers in order to identify the distinguishing features of postmodernism as a basis for understanding organizations. They are:

- ■ Representation. Rather than reflecting facts though language and forming ever clearer understandings, research is suggested to represent several different agendas. For example, it reflects the pre-existing knowledge base used to create understanding and it represents the professional standing of the people involved. Language reflects social, political, personal, access/exclusion and control purposes as well as descriptive needs.
- ■ Reflexivity. The requirement to reflect on the assumptions made as part of the creation of knowledge. If language is not the slave of facts then its use must be questioned on every occasion.
- ■ Writing. It could be assumed that the use of language was to be considered '... as a sign system for concepts which exist in the object world' (p 13). This is not so: postmodernism would see writing as a means by which the symbols of language can be separated from the objects themselves yet remain linked through the spatial and temporal reality of experience for individual people.
- ■ Differance. This concept is related to the need to both separate and join. In postmodernism it is necessary to *deconstruct* knowledge. In the foregoing discussion it is apparent that knowledge is *constructed* from the social context and by the language used. In attempting to create *real* understanding it is first necessary to *deconstruct* these issues.
- ■ De-centring the subject. Most of the knowledge created takes as its basis and perspective the individual. It is the human perspective and interpretation that contains the significant focal direction. That should not be the case, according to postmodernism. Lying on the floor and looking at the world from a child's height would give some impression of a different world to that of the adult for example.

Using the above, postmodernism sets about questioning the place of reason and 'methodological unity' (Hassard, 1993, p 1). From its origins as a perspective on culture and art this perspective has been used in an attempt to provide meaningful interpretation on organizations as they exist in real time and space. Postmodernism would suggest that it is only by facing up to the paradoxes that emerge that the otherwise hidden assumptions begin to emerge.

However, not everyone would support the basic approach suggested by postmodern thinking. It may be interesting to question rationality and to engage in deconstruction, but some experiences are very real no matter how they are described. For example, as Tsoukas (1992) argues, 'It is because actions are not taken and voices not uttered in a vacuum that not all accounts are equally valid. No matter how much I shout at my bank manager he is not likely to lend me money if I am unemployed. This is not a figment of my imagination. Others also tell me they have had similar experience' (p 644). The point being that this experience is common to many people and that as part of organizational activity and the human experience it cannot be explained away as a figment of imagination or language symbolism.

Japanization and post-Fordism: a management perspective

As problem solvers managers seek to find ways of reducing the complexity of the situations that they face and to avoid having to solve the same problem over and over again. This suggests that managers engage in processes of categorization, simplification and the application of procedure in order to carry out their duties. The underlying view implied by this is that rationality pervades the management process. Whilst this may be true part of the time there are also issues such as organizational politics, personal feelings and personality that impact on the work of each manager and organization. Scientific management appeared to provide managers with an opportunity to apply rationality and science to the task of controlling work. It proved to be an elusive but pervasive formula. Problems with industrial relations, quality and commitment very quickly emerged from the application of Taylorism. However, it is deeply entrenched in the management psyche, and is still found in many organizations today.

The use of work study techniques as a means of identifying productivity improvement and of controlling workforce activity can be found in many factory and office sites in many countries. The use of incentive schemes is also very common both in the piecework form advocated by Taylor and in many other disguises. Taylorism is not dead in spite of what many writers might claim. It has, however, been adapted and refined over the years in line with the development of new techniques and the prevailing social conditions. Ford was perhaps only the earliest example of this with the introduction of the moving assembly line.

The concept of Japanization was at first associated with many apparently new and innovative practices that were suggested to encourage employee contribution more effectively. This it was suggested, was achieved by more strongly unifying the interests of employees and management and by encouraging employees to be critical of organizational weaknesses. In return this was rewarded with lifetime employment and other benefits associated with successful companies. However, it could also be argued that these practices are not as they appear at first glance. For example, contribution to problem solving whilst voluntary on the surface is mandatory if the individual wishes to be regarded as an acceptable employee. So perhaps the Japanization process is about being more Taylorist than Taylor, but in more subtle ways. It is also necessary to remember that management practice has a strong cultural element to it and that what works in one place and at a particular point in time cannot be relied upon to have universal appeal. Management in Action 16.7 reflects that perspective.

Management in Action 16.7

Last year's model

Lowe reports some research from the UK suggesting Japanese inward investing companies were having some difficulty in achieving the sort of working practices that they were used to. This was on top of an earlier report that suggested deep concerns among Japanese senior managers about the skill levels in the UK. Eighty-five per cent of personnel managers working for Japanese manufacturers in the North East of England reported that literacy, numeracy and technical skills were in particularly short supply. It was also suggested by Dr Mari Sako, an expert in Japanese industrial relations at the London School of Economics, that as the products produced by Japanese firms became more sophisticated the less the UK had an advantage over other countries.

Other problems emerged from the study, in that Japanese managers identified cultural difficulties between Japanese organizations and the British workforce as an obstacle to success. Different ways of thinking compared to their Japanese employers and the degree of diligence shown towards work were also frequently cited as examples of these cultural differences. The study found that the success of inward investors practising 'Japanese management techniques' had deteriorated over recent years in comparison with UK firms. It has been suggested that the first wave of inward investing Japanese companies were welcomed with open arms because they brought much needed jobs to areas of high unemployment. They also made the effort to develop relationships with trade unions as part of the process of establishing factory operations. Truly 'greenfield' site operations made it easy to import their 'traditional' management practices.

Since then a number of things have happened. Many British companies have made great efforts to introduce 'Japanese management practices' in an attempt to become 'world class'. The learning curve as a result of these changes is now catching up with the Japanese inward investors and so the difference between them is not as obvious as in the past. The recruitment of suitably trained and educated employees remains a problem. The Japanese system of education is regarded as superior and produces employees with the necessary skills to function in organizations. Economic conditions have also changed and it has been suggested that people are less willing to take jobs without question. Some of the Japanese management practices have also received a 'bad press' and so people have become cynical about them.

However, the notion that Japanese management methods are not working as well was thought surprising by many. One large Japanese company in the construction equipment manufacturing business suggested that they had only found it necessary to drop one element in their usual practice, and that was the early morning exercises. Single status contracts, the use of the advisory council and other aspects of Japanese management practice had been in place from day one. So change might be happening but it is not clear what might be causing it, or how much is actually changing.

Adapted from: Lowe, K. (1993) Last year's model. Personnel Today, *14 September, pp 37–8.*

It could be argued that labour process theory and postmodernism have little to offer practising managers. However, as attempts to throw light on the underlying processes they offer an insight into aspects of the management process. This line of argument is based on the view that before being effective in managing others it is first necessary to understand oneself as both an individual and manager. It also allows the behaviour of others to be placed into a context of their own assumptions and belief systems.

Conclusions

This chapter has attempted to provide an introduction to a number of the more recent perspectives on the work of Taylor and its impact on organizational activity and management. It attempts to demonstrate how some of the approaches post Taylor have adopted particular views of the benefits of scientific management in an attempt to avoid the negative results, thereby obtaining the maximum benefit on behalf of management. In effect, by attempting to humanize Taylorist ideas an ability to control the organization and its activities more effectively is achieved. The result of this means that managers are controlling the workforce more effectively than would have been possible under more direct approaches. The next chapter develops this notion of power and control in management.

Discussion questions

1 Define the following key terms used in this chapter:

Fordism	Postmodernism	Alienation
Post-Fordism	Just-in-time	Empowerment
Japanization	Golden handcuffs	Ideal-type
Labour process theory	Top-down management	

2 Why do you think that Japanese organizations would be happy to allow Western managers to study and understand their 'secrets of success'?
3 Postmodernism is of no relevance to the study of modern organizations. Discuss.
4 Fordism is a necessary approach to organizational activity if people are to have goods and services that they can afford. To what extent would you agree with this view and why?
5 Japanization is nothing more than 'old wine in new bottles'. Discuss this statement.
6 Can a capitalist system ever hope to overcome alienation among workers. Justify your answer.
7 To what extent do you agree with the view that FW Taylor was the founder of modern management practice?
8 Approaches such as just-in-time place absolute power in the hands of the workers. Managers must, therefore, find new ways to offset this potential threat to production. Do you agree and how might this be achieved?
9 Does labour process theory provide an explanation of why alienation and poor industrial relations have pervaded much organizational experience over the past hundred years? Justify your answer.

10 To what extent do you consider that post-Fordism is different to Fordism in any meaningful degree?

Research questions

1 Find a number of books or articles that refer to Japanization and compare them with the practices described in the Garrahan and Stewart (1992) text identified in the reference section. How far do the views expressed about work under Japanese designed management practices complement and contradict each other? Why do you think that is so?
2 Prepare a summary of the labour process theory and postmodernism. Describe them to a manager. Having done so ask for their opinion on the value of these ideas for their work. Based on their views consider the implications for the development of theory in management and organization issues. Also, what are the implications for the content of academic and training courses in management and business?
3 Discuss the concepts of Fordism, post-Fordism and Japanization with a trade union official. What are their views about the advantages and disadvantages of these approaches and how do they impact on the jobs of workers? Compare and contrast this with the views of a practising manager. What do the differences and similarities in these views tell you about the different perspectives of the individuals, the jobs that they do and the nature of work?

Key reading

From Clark, H., Chandler, J. and Barry, J. (1994) *Organization and Identities: Text and Readings in Organizational Behaviour*, International Thomson Business Press, London.

■ Coyle K: Post-modernism, p 58. Considers the essence of post-modernism in the context of a critique of post-Fordism.
■ Mackenzie G: Class, p 189. Reviews the Marxist view that the division of labour might be abolished with the introduction of automation.
■ Cockburn C: Male domination and technical change, p 197. Demonstrates how the social context within work organization and structure should be viewed.
■ Illich I: Disabling professions, p 207. Introduces the view that it is individual in positions of power that attempt to manipulate events to their own advantage.
■ Thompson EP: Time and work – discipline, p 216. This describes a historical review of work patterns and time intended to control worker activity in pursuit of higher output.
■ Weber M: Bureaucracy, p 225. This classic work reflects the view that management and social control are deeply linked.
■ Taylor FW: Scientific management, p 231. Taylor sets out his views on work and how it should be organized.
■ Hobsbawm EJ and Rudé G: Early forms of worker resistance – swing riots, p 317. This reviews the reaction of workers who felt themselves threatened by events around them in relation to work.
■ Hill S: The nature of total quality management (TQM), p 367. A short article that introduces the main elements of TQM as an approach to work.
■ Hill S: Why total quality management might succeed, p 369. Based on field studies this article reviews why TQM initiatives appeared to be successful in particular situations.

Further reading

Doray, B. (1988) *From Taylorism to Fordism: A Rational Madness*, Free Association Books, London. Translated by David Macey. This book is about the development and implications of Fordism from the perspective of a psychiatrist. It is based on survey material gained from French industry and brings together a Marxist and individual orientation in identifying the consequences of this approach.

Oliver, N and Wilkinson, B (1992) *The Japanization of British Industry: New Developments in the 1990s*, 2nd edn, Blackwell, Oxford. This text covers a broad spectrum of management, social and organizational perspectives on the encroachment of Japanese management practices on companies. It includes case study and survey material in support of the discussion as well as discussing the policy and practice implications for British organizations.

Pascale, RT and Athos, AG (1981) *The Art of Japanese Management*, Simon & Schuster. The original review of Japanese management practice which attempted to identify why it was that these organizations were so successful. It was based on an in-depth review of the Matsushita Electric Company.

Suzuki, Y (1991) *Japanese Management Structures, 1920–1980*, Macmillan, London. This text provides an in-depth insight into many aspects associated with the management and organization of Japanese companies over a 60-year period. Written by an eminent Japanese scholar, it provides a measure of well-informed historical understanding against which to judge the many other views found in the literature bout Japanese companies.

Thompson, P (1989) *The Nature of Work: An Introduction to Debates on the Labour Process*, 2nd edn, Macmillan, London. This provides a concise overview of the history and evolution of labour process theory. In doing so it encompasses consideration of other topics such as Japanese management practices and Fordism.

Whitaker, A (1992) The transformation in work: post-Fordism revisited. In *Rethinking Organizations: New Directions in Organization Theory and Analysis* (eds M Reed and M Hughes), Sage. This chapter reviews much of the debate surrounding the notion of post-Fordism in its broader social and organizational context.

References

BBC/Open University (1986) Strategies for change: the task force. PT 611: The structure and design of manufacturing systems. Open University/BBC production, course film.

Blauner, R (1964) *Alienation and Freedom: The Factory Worker and his Industry*, University of Chicago Press, Chicago, IL.

Braverman, H (1974) *Labour and Monopoly Capital: The Degradation of Work in the Twentieth Century*, Monthly Review Press, London.

Burbridge, J (1982) Japanese kanban system. *International Journal of Production Control*, January/February, 1–5.

Carter, P and Jackson, N (1993) Modernism, postmodernism and motivation, or why expectation theory failed to come up to expectation. In *Postmodernism and Organizations* (eds J Hassard and M Parker), Sage, London.

Domingo, R (1985) 'Kanban': crisis management Japanese style. *Euro-Asia Business Review*, 4, 22–4.

Ford, H (1923) *My Life and Work*, Heinemann, London.

Ford Motor Company (1918) *Facts From Ford*, Detroit, MI.

Gaither, N (1992) *Production and Operations Management*, 5th edn, Dryden Press, Fort Worth, TX.

Garrahan, P and Stewart, P (1992) *The Nissan Enigma: Flexibility at Work in a Local Community*, Mansell, London.

Gergen, KJ (1992) Organization Theory in the Postmodern Era. In *Rethinking Organization: New Directions in Organization Theory and Analysis* (eds M Reed and M Hughes), Sage, London.

Giles, E and Starkey, K (1987) From Fordism to Japanisation: Organizational Change at Ford, Rank Xerox and Fuji Xerox. Paper presented at a conference on the Japanisation of British Industry, UWIST.

Goffee, R and Scase, R (1995) *Corporate Realities: The Dynamics of Large and Small Organizations*, Routledge, London.

Goldsmith, J (1995) *The Response*, Macmillan, London.

Hassard, J (1993) *Postmodernism and Organizational Analysis: An Overview. In Post-modernism and Organizations* (eds J Hassard and M Parker), Sage, London.

Huxley, A (1932) *Brave New World*, Chatto & Windus, London

Kanter, RM (1989) The new managerial work. *Harvard Business Review*, **67**, No. 6.

Lincoln, JR and Kalleburg, AL (1990) *Culture, Control and Commitment*, Cambridge University Press, Cambridge.

Oliver, N and Wilkinson, B (1992) *The Japanization of British Industry: New Developments in the 1990s*, 2nd edn, Blackwell, Oxford.

Parnaby, J (1987) A systems engineering approach to fundamental change in manufacturing. Paper presented at the Ninth Industrial Engineering Managers' Conference, New Orleans, 9–11 March.

Roy, D (1960) Banana time: job satisfaction and informal interaction. *Human Organization*, **18**, 158–68.

Sayer, A (1986) New developments in manufacturing: the just-in-time system. *Capital and Class*, **30**, 43–72.

Thompson, EP (1989) *The Nature of Work: An Introduction to Debates on the Labour Process*, 2nd edn, Macmillan, London.

Tsoukas, H (1992) Postmodernism, reflexive rationalism and organization studies: a reply to Martin Parker. *Organization Studies*, **13**, 643–49.

Turnbull, PJ (1986) The Japanisation of British industrial relations at Lucas. *Industrial Relations Journal*, **17**, 193–206.

Wickens, PD (1987) *The Road to Nissan*, Macmillan, London.

Williams, K, Haslem, C, Williams, J, Adcroft, A and Johal, S (1992) Factories or warehouses: Japanese manufacturing foreign direct investment in Britain and the United States. Occasional Papers on Business, Economy and Society, Number 6, University of East London.

Part VII

The dynamics of the work environment

Power and politics

browse this web site
www.itbp.com

Chapter summary

This chapter will begin by considering the related concepts of power, influence and authority and then go on to examine what generates power as used by individuals and groups within an organization. Power is frequently described as an influence on decision making and this forms the next focus. Political behaviour is examined in relation to attempts to influence the power balance already in existence. The chapter ends with consideration of how political behaviour can be managed.

Learning objectives

After studying this chapter and working through the associated Management in Action panels, discussion questions and research activities, you should be able to:

■ Understand the nature of power as experienced within an organization.
■ Describe the sources of power within an organization.
■ Explain the relationship between power and decision making.
■ Outline the concept of organizational politics.
■ Assess the differences and similarities between the concepts of power, influence and authority.
■ Appreciate how political behaviour is used by individuals within organizations.
■ Discuss how political behaviour can be managed within an organization.
■ Detail the value of power and politics to the running of an organization.

Introduction

The notion of power is endemic in organizational relationships. Managers exercise power over subordinates in directing their endeavours towards the objectives being sought. Industrial relations activity within organizations is largely directed towards a redistribution of the prevailing power balance between managers and employees. The annual negotiation over wages is an attempt to influence the otherwise unilateral management determination of the distribution of company finances.

Politics reflect processes found in the behaviour of individuals in the workplace. *Politicking* is frequently described as behaviour outside the accepted procedures and norms, intended to further the position of an individual or group at the expense of others. As such it is frequently identified with undesirable behaviour not intended to advance the interests of the organization. It is most often associated with the attempts of individuals to advance their own careers, or to undermine the status and reputation of other departments and people to their own advantage.

Both concepts of power and politics contain positive aspects. For example, an effective power balance between capital and labour should allow both to function effectively without damage to the interests of either. Political activity can be of benefit to the organization. If through the *politicking* of the marketing manager product changes are brought about which in turn provide commercial gains for the organization, then it could be argued that such behaviour was of benefit.

Power, influence and authority

Power is a concept related to manipulation. In that sense it is a process of being able to *influence* the behaviour of others. It is also something that is an accompaniment to the concept of *authority*. Generally, those in authority would be expected to have power. However, this is relative as there are those with power irrespective of position. The elected prime minister of a country has considerable power by virtue of the electoral mandate. They are able to ensure that particular legislation is enacted and enforced. However, they are also at the whim of the population when it comes to election time. The *victims* of the power displayed by politicians hold the power to take away the position that is the source of power. Management in Action 17.1 outlines how influence can be achieved when authority (power) is absent.

Power has been defined in many different ways. Perhaps the most effective definition is that provided by Pfeffer (1992) who brings together a number of views as, '... the potential ability to influence behaviour, to change the course of events, to overcome resistance, and to get people to do things that they would not otherwise do' (p 30). In this definition the linkage between power and influence is evident.

Within an organizational context it is easy to envisage the linkage between power, influence and authority. There is no purpose to the position of a line manager unless it is the exercise of authority over others. However, some management positions exist because of the high technical skill and status necessary to undertake the job and the direct management of others may not be a major activity. However, by virtue of position within the hierarchy, authority and the ability to influence others will still exist.

There are also positions that do not have any formal authority yet the individuals are able to exercise considerable influence. The secretary or personal assistant to a chief executive is frequently in such a position. *Having-the-ear* of the person with formal authority allows considerable influence. In a very real sense they are gatekeepers and the power behind the throne.

Authority has been described as the legitimate expression of power (Handy, 1985, p 119). In this context it reflects power used by someone who is accepted as having the legitimate right to exercise it in that context. Employees generally accept the rights of managers to exercise authority over their activities and behaviour by virtue of the position conveyed formally by the organization. The work of Milgram (1965), introduced in an earlier chapter, is important in this context. His experiments with fake electric shocks demonstrated just how far people can be pushed and why individuals tend to comply with those in authority.

Management in Action 17.1

Influence without authority

Cohen and Bradford describe that, 'the crutch of authority' is missing from modern organizations. However, that does not mean that management action is unnecessary – things still have to be done. The inhabitants of modern organizations need to be able to influence others. This not only applies in top-down situations, where managers may have larger spans of control as a consequence of delayering, and may be responsible for areas in which they have no personal expertise. It can include the need for subordinates to influence superiors and/or equals who may be busy and not have the time or inclination to offer assistance. Managers who are under considerable pressure to achieve results may show a marked reluctance to take actions involving more work for themselves or adding more change to an already overburdened system.

Influence is not a new organizational skill. Cohen and Bradford remind us that it was the snake in the Garden of Eden who first demonstrated the possibility of gaining advantage through it. The eating of the apple by Eve and then her influence on Adam speaks volumes for the significance of the concept in organizational terms.

Northrop, an American aircraft manufacturer, decided that manufacturing specialists should be involved from the beginning of the design process, the intention being to improve the ability to build aircraft more efficiently and with fewer problems. The cost and time involved in making engineering changes whilst in production were excessive and reduced the commercial viability of the company. The ability of the manufacturing people to veto the design engineers specifications at first caused some problems and resentment. However, when the benefits became obvious in the form of fewer in-process problems

it began to function more easily. The results speak for themselves in that 97% of all parts fitted perfectly first time (the previous best was 50%) and engineering changes were reduced to one-sixth of their previous levels, and were implemented five times faster. The same applies in many service sector companies, including banks, who must share information between separate parts of the organization to target customers more effectively. In the days of electronic information flows it is less easy for managers to control access to information. Restricting its availability is less practical, thus encouraging co-operation based control processes.

Effective influence begins with the ways that individuals think about the people that they must influence. Regarding them as a partner or strategic ally involves a different approach to working relationships. It moves away from the old win–lose approach to interpersonal relationships with an emphasis on obligations and exchange. After all the person that wants help from you today might be in a position to help you next week. It matters little if they are your boss or a subordinate, the network of relationships is about mutual benefit. Cohen and Bradford make the following suggestions for individuals seeking to achieve influence over others:

■ Mutual respect. Assume that others are competent and smart.
■ Openness. It is not possible to know everything, so sharing information helps you as well as 'them'.
■ Trust. Assume that individuals will not purposely hurt or undermine you and so there is no reason to hold back information.
■ Mutual benefit. Plan win–win strategies.

Adapted from: Cohen, AR and Bradford, DL (1993) Influence without authority. World Executives Digest, *December, pp 28–32.*

It was Chester Barnard who was among the first to write about the notion of authority in an organizational context. In 1938 he describes authority in the following terms, '... the character of a communication (order) in a formal organization by virtue of which it is accepted by a contributor to or "member" of the organization as governing the action he contributes; that is, as governing or determining what he does or is not to do so far as the organization is concerned' (p 163). Barnard goes on to explain that a requirement to act in a particular way is evaluated by the recipient in terms of its legitimacy. Acceptance of the requirement to follow the order also acknowledges the authority of the giver of that order. Conversely, denial of the order also denies the legitimacy of the giver to issue it. So, much as those in authority might deny it, the classification of an order as legitimate or otherwise is not in their gift, it is for the recipient to decide. This is what Luthans (1995) describes as an *acceptance theory* of authority intended to support group cohesion and goals.

The inability of those in authority to guarantee that subordinates accept every instruction as legitimate remains a potential source of difficulty. There have been many disciplinary cases based on the refusal of an employee to carry out what was classified by managers as a reasonable instruction. Inevitably, whatever the context, the refusal to obey a reasonable instruction (as defined by management) would be regarded as a threat to the established order and as such something to be dealt with severely.

Influence is an interesting word in English and Handy (1985) introduces it as both noun and verb to explain some of the confusion with power. He attempts to clarify its use by restricting it to use as a verb in the sense of, '... the use of power' (p 119). In that connection power is but one of the sources of the ability to influence others. Influence can therefore be regarded as a *broader* concept than power. Influence is also a *softer* term than power. It implies a willing acquiescence on the part of the subject and more subtle processes at work than would be expected if power was being applied. Influence implies persuasion, co-operation and relationship-based mechanisms for achieving the desired behaviour.

It would be tempting to restrict the distinction between power and influence to this rather cosy view of persuasion. However, these terms are more complex than that would allow. Overt attempts to use power and force are likely to be met with resistance. Consequently it is not uncommon to find more subtle mechanisms being used in order to obtain compliance with the will of another. For example, by allowing employees to become shareholders they might find it easier to accept the perspectives of managers by working flexibly and lowering pay expectations, this could be interpreted as a cynical attempt to manipulate employees into a position where the exercise of naked power by managers became unnecessary. Rothschild and Miethe (1994) (quoting Forsyth, 1990) identify, in the context of whistleblowing, a number of influence strategies that they suggest are used in order to obtain compliance from employees. These are identified in Table 17.1.

Eight of these nine tactics, bullying being the odd one out, represent indirect applications of practices intended to persuade the individual to offer compliance to the will of the perpetrator. In each of these cases it could be suggested that a deliberate attempt to avoid resistance is being attempted and hence the underlying notion of power is being hidden or disguised.

Where power is a feature of a particular relationship there is also *dependency*. Power can be exercised if there is no dependency present but it achieves *compliance* at best. In an organization, if an individual does not value money, promotion or any of the other 'benefits' provided there is little *dependency*

Promising	to do something for the individual in the future	
Bullying	the use of threat (real or implied)	
Discussion	the use of rational argument and explanation	
Negotiation	making compromises	
Manipulation	the use of lies and deceit	
Demand	insistence on compliance	
Claiming expertise	reliance on superior knowledge or skill	
Ingratiation	reliance on flattery	
Evasion	avoidance of revealing aspects of the situation	

Table 17.1
Influencing tactics, From: *Group Dynamics*, GDR Forsyth. Copyright © 1988, 1990, 1993 Brooks/Cole Publishing Company, Pacific Grove, CA 93950. A division of International Thomson Publishing Inc. By permission of the publisher

present and the opportunity for power to be used as a source of influence is strictly limited. In effect managers have few *levers* (influencing tactics) with which to control and direct the behaviour of the individual.

Sources of power

Power is invisible. It has never been seen, it cannot be held, touched, and it is not detectable by any sensor. It is important to distinguish between power and the associated trappings which are detectable. For example, wealth is frequently associated with power. Stereotypic assumptions lead to implying that an individual holds power simply because they dress in expensive clothing or behave as if they were superior. False claims to power through such outward signs if uncovered can leave the individual concerned subject to ridicule or marginalization.

Power is something that only lives in the minds, attitudes, behaviours, expectations and perceptions of individuals. Of course there are situations where direct force (or the threat of it) is used to obtain results, but this represents the application of a particular form of power. In organizations it is employee acceptance of the fact that managers have the power to direct endeavours that allows managers to exercise power. If the employees were not willing to accept management direction then managers would have no ability to influence events. This is the dependency aspect of power described earlier.

If power is not a tangible entity and is dependent upon the recipients to create its significance where does it originate? French and Raven (1968) identified a number of sources of power within a social context including:

■ Coercive power. This form is based on the ability of the power holder to enforce the threat of direct control. In the mind of the receiver of this form of power is the fear that they may be punished if they do not comply with the directions of the power holder. An organizational example of this is provided in Management in Action 17.2 overleaf, which illustrates the power of frozen food manufacturers over small shops.

In an organization there is a degree of coercive power implied in the managerial relationship with subordinates. Historically, this power source was much stronger than it is today. The emergence of trade unions,

---

Management in Action 17.2

Ice-cream makers caught in cold war

The provision of freezers to shops by ice-cream and frozen-food makers has been used over the years to provide a means of controlling the market. Essentially, a large frozen-food manufacturer would agree to give the shopkeeper a freezer cabinet, as long as only that company's products were kept in it. Sales staff from the manufacturer would check the cabinets during their regular calls on each shop. From the shopkeepers perspective the advantage was access to a 'free' freezer that was designed to house particular products. The advantage to the frozen food manufacturer was that they were able to restrict consumer access to their competitors products – the size of small shops prevents the use of a wide range of display cabinets.

Another side effect of this practice was the restriction of access to the market by small manufacturers who could not afford to subsidize shops as a means of acquiring vital shelf space. Pendleton's Ices in Merseyside was one such company. After a year of financial problems, closure, insolvency and industrial action by employees, new hope of it remaining in business arose. Grants were made available from the government and the local council,

Nestlé (who bought the factory) donated equipment worth £500,000 and a local businessman invested £150,000. These actions allowed the company to restart operations. 51% of the shares in the company were held by the employees.

The troubled history of the plant had not daunted the will of the employees to keep the business afloat. However only about 27 of the company's 75 member workforce had been re-employed by the summer of 1993. This was due in no small part to the 20% shortfall in revenue compared to that anticipated in the business plan. This shortfall was largely due to the inability of the company to find outlets for its products as a result of freezer cabinet restrictions. However, Co-operative supermarkets had agreed to take the product and other potential customers were being pursued with high quality products. The company was also intent on complaining to the Monopolies and Mergers Commission about the freezer practice. Employees and managers were hopeful of improvements in sales despite the restrictions imposed as a result of restrictive practices by the large manufacturers.

Adapted from: Foster, J (1993) Ice-cream makers caught in cold war. The Independent, *10 August, p 5.*

---

improved management practices and employment legislation have all provided counterbalancing to the freedom of managers to take unilateral action.

◼ Reward power. Managers have the power to award pay increases, promote and otherwise reward individuals who perform as desired. In most organizations there are limitations on the opportunity for individual managers to control a broad range of rewards. Individual managers do not totally control all aspects of reward such as promotion. Company procedures are designed to limit the ability of individual managers to create inconsistencies in reward allocation across the organization.

Managers can easily send the wrong signals about what behaviours are valued by inadvertently rewarding inappropriate behaviours. Paying considerable attention to difficult or troublesome employees can indicate to good employees that it does not *pay* to be well behaved. Managers who occasionally allow poor quality work to be despatched clearly indicate that good quality is not always important. In general terms such inadvertent rewarding of undesirable behaviour reinforces the idea that individuals should *play the system*, taking an instrumental view of work.

■ Legitimate power. In an organization most people accept that managers have legitimate authority to exercise power. There are three main sources of authority (Luthans, 1995, p 323). Firstly, the accepted social structures within a society provide certain groups with a legitimate basis for exercising power. It might be a ruling family or a class of people that perform that role. Secondly, cultural values can also create a basis for claiming legitimate power through the veneration of particular classes or individuals. For example, old people often become significant leaders or men play a dominant role in society. Thirdly, legitimate power can be delegated. Managers are acting on behalf of the owners of an organization in running the business on their behalf.

   Handy (1985) suggests that holding legitimate power provides automatic access to three invisible assets. Firstly, information, which as a commodity can be directed, channelled and traded by power-holders. Secondly, rights of access to a number of different networks. The significance of networking cannot be underestimated. Heald (1984) examines many different networks along with the principles and practices that guide them. Thirdly, the right to organize. With legitimate power comes the right to decide what and how things should be done. Management in Action 17.3 overleaf illustrates some of the implications of legitimate power in the sometimes uneasy relationship between academics and the organizations that fund jobs within universities.

■ Expert power. This originates from the knowledge, skill and expertise of the holder. The pilot of an aeroplane is the one with the appropriate skills to fly it and consequently everyone goes where the pilot decides. Within management, technical specialists often have greater knowledge than the line managers that they are supposed to be supporting and so have considerable influence. Claims to be an expert are subject to validation by the group over whom the expertise is being claimed. Failure to deliver the results of claimed expertise can be dealt with severely by the group who will feel that their trust has been violated and that they have been conned.

■ Referent power. This is about the characteristics of an individual. It could be that the individual is of celebrity status and so attracts others to surround them and follow their wishes. Religious and political leaders are frequently charismatic and so attract many follows only too willing to follow every word and instruction. Advertisers continually utilize this perspective in using models, stars and personality figures to sell products.

There is also a sixth form of power that is different in nature to the others, but can have a significant impact on events (Handy, 1985, p 127):

■ Negative power. This form of power impacts through not doing something that should be done. For example, a post-room employee who is dissatisfied with their job could quickly cause confusion throughout the organization by deliberately misdirecting the post for a few days. It is the ultimate revenge of the *little people* within the organization.

Management in Action 17.3

Dons learn that 'freedom' has a bottom line

It is common practice for academic posts to be sponsored by commercial organizations. Most of the time this does not pose a problem for any of the parties involved, university: sponsor, the individual academic or the wider community. However, there have been occasions when this set of relationships has been put at risk for various reasons. Perhaps not surprisingly this has been most keenly observed among accounting academics. Jack provides several examples of what can happen when 'the world outside intersects with university life'.

In one example Mr Prem Sikka, from the University of East London, wrote to the Chartered Association of Certified Accountants questioning the voting procedures for an election in which he was unsuccessful. The correspondence between the two grew to an amazing half-inch thick. However, most significantly the Association wrote to the Vice Chancellor seeking to find out if the University endorsed Mr Sikka's views. This was seen by Mr Sikka as an attempt to put pressure on him from above. Mr Anthony Booth, Director of Standards for the Association, explained that, had the institution endorsed Mr Sikka's views then a review of the accreditation of courses offered by the University might have taken place, as these depended to a significant extent on trust between the parties.

Another case described by Jack was that of Professor David Cooper, one time Price Waterhouse Professor of Accounting at UMIST. In 1984, during the year long national miners' strike in the UK, he published an article alleging 'misinformation' in the National Coal Board's assessment of the viability of its coal mines. One member of the board expressed indignation and the editorial practice of the journal in question was reviewed. Cooper also claims to have been telephoned by one of the partners at Price Waterhouse (they had also been appointed sequestrators to the National Union of Mineworkers). Cooper recalls the conversation with the partner thus, 'He screamed at me about causing the firm severe embarrassment and how could we bite the hand that fed us and how Price Waterhouse would continue to fund the chair over his dead body'. The partner concerned (by now retired) was asked for a response by Jack and he said, 'I did have words. It was an irritation. We were just concerned that he didn't start impinging on our activities. We were trying to keep a low profile'.

This is not a problem unique to the UK. In the USA Abe Briloff, Emeritus Professor of Accounting at Baruch College in New York, faced a defamation suit brought against him in 1976 by Saul Steinberg. The Professor had written a critical article about Steinberg's work as a corporate raider. Most academics would claim to adopt a responsible attitude to such matters. For example, Christopher Nobes, Coopers & Lybrand Professor of Accounting at Reading University, indicated, 'Maybe sometimes a professor might feel constrained from saying things because they are worried what the firm or its clients might think, or the professor doesn't like what the firm says. I have sometimes not done things because of my link with Coopers. I have never said something I don't believe. Sometimes I have not said things I do believe. That's merely being responsible'.

Adapted from: Jack, A (1993) Dons learn that 'freedom' has a bottom line. Financial Times, 9 December, p 14.

These sources of power provide the basis of the ability to influence the behaviour and actions of others. What they do not do is provide an indication of how that power is converted into influence. It is the mechanisms or tactics described in Table 17.1 that provide the operationalization of power.

Power and decision making

Decision making and politics are inextricably entwined within organizational activity. Many decision-making approaches assume rational behaviour on the part of the participants. Politics also influences the ability to implement a solution. Former President of the United States of America Richard Nixon wrote in 1982, 'It is not enough for a leader to *know* the right thing. He must be able to *do* the right thing. ... The great leader needs ... the capacity to achieve' (p 5).

Being able to ensure that a particular course of action is followed requires both power and political expertise. This is most clearly identified in the sphere of national and local politics. The hugely successful British television series and books under the title of '*Yes, Minister*' and '*Yes, Prime Minister*' found much of their appeal in illustrating the political management of the elected politicians by civil servants. After the British election campaign of May 1997 much debate centred on the ability of the newly elected Labour government to implement its election promises irrespective of opposition through the scale of its majority in the House of Commons. This despite any experience of real political power for the previous 18 years whilst they were in opposition.

Pfeffer (1992) identifies three aspects of decision making that provide for the concept of power to be incorporated into the processes. They are:

- Decisions change nothing. Taking a decision does not automatically imply that it will be acted upon. New Year resolutions are a clear example of decisions to take actions in one's own life which invariably last about one week. In addition to a *decision science* it is necessary to understand *implementation science*.
- Decision quality requires retrospective assessment. It is not possible to judge the value of a decision until after the event. It is only with the benefit of hindsight that any realistic evaluation can be made.
- Significance duration. Pfeffer points out that the impact of any decision invariably lasts longer than the time taken to reach the decision in the first place. This perspective has led some psychologists to suggest that human beings are rationalizing rather than rational (Aronson, 1972). It also provides a link with cognitive dissonance as discussed in an earlier chapter.

One of the consequence of this perspective on decision making is that it reflects a stream rather than discrete processes. A decision is taken and then implemented. Consequences then flow from that. Some of the results will be desired, others will be undesirable or were not anticipated and so further decisions are required. In addition, circumstances around the decision could also change, or the decision could have been wrong in the first place. Whatever the cause, there are many reasons which require decision making to be regarded a continuous process.

So far this discussion has been about *decision science* aspects and has largely ignored the *implementation* issues. Within commercial organizations it is largely assumed that power is directly correlated with level in the hierarchy. Whilst that may be true to some extent it reflects a vast oversimplification of the nature of organizational power and its practice. The trade union representatives in some organizations hold more power than many of the line managers, at least reflected in the ability to influence employees. The other sources of power identified also form part of the dynamic of organizational behaviour and its influence on decision making. For example, managers rarely work in isolation, it is necessary for other people to be involved on many occasions. For instance, an accounting department may create a policy on expense claims, but it is other individuals who must comply with the system if it is to work. Management in Action 17.4 illustrates this and the use of negative power with regard to the completion of expense claims within one large organization.

Managers must engage in co-operative behaviour in ensuring that their decisions are acted upon. The personnel department of a company would find it hard to implement a new remuneration system if other managers refuse to allow employees time to attend meetings to evaluate jobs or to write job descriptions. Competing priorities are frequently cited as the reason for one department or manager not being able to help another, the net result being that a particular decision may not be implemented, irrespective of the intentions of senior managers. An opposing view is that managers should always follow orders, as in the military. However, what if the *orders* are deficient? The danger in highly centralized structures in which real power is restricted to a few people at the top of the organization is that it can be abused. The late Robert Maxwell was an illustration of the ability of one individual

---

Management in Action 17.4

Reasonable expenses

This is a true story that has been changed slightly to protect both the organization and its employees. The essential facts, however, remain the same. The company concerned was in the service sector and employed several hundred field-based staff. The primary duties of these staff involved travelling to client organizations and carrying out work at those locations. This could involve a short visit of about two hours or anything up to two weeks of travelling daily to the same location. Clearly this process involved considerable amounts of travelling and high levels of expense claim.

The company concerned paid staff a mileage allowance for each mile travelled on company business. The distance used as the basis of payment was the smaller of either the actual distance travelled, or the distance to the visit from the office at which the member of staff was based. This was generally regarded as a fair system by staff as it allowed for the normal travel to work distance each day.

In an attempt to save money senior management

decided that any distance travelled to visit a client which involved the individual travelling over part of the normal route to the office would also be discounted for expense purposes. This was seen as both complex and unfair by the staff concerned. It also involved keeping more records of distance and routes travelled.

As a consequence staff adopted a number of strategies in response to this instruction. One of the most effective was to find and use minor roads when visiting clients in areas near to the normal route to the office. Another involved changing visiting routines to find reasons to attend the office when visits involved distances which would be longer than if done directly form home. Managers became confused about the new rules and would sign expense claims only to have them rejected by the accounts department on a technicality. This led to severe delays in payment as queries were resolved.

Very quickly it was recognized that the cost of administration of the scheme was increasing rapidly, as was the level of expense claim. Eventually the old rule was reinstated. In other words, by following the new scheme and using some ingenuity employees were able to exercise negative power and frustrate the intentions of senior management.

1.	Decide what your goals are, what you are trying to accomplish.
2.	Diagnose patterns of dependence and interdependence; what individuals are influential and important in your achieving your goal?
3.	What are their points of view likely to be? How will they feel about what you are trying to do?
4.	What are their power bases? Which of them is more influential in the decision?
5.	What are your bases of power and influence? What bases of influence can you develop to gain more control over the situation?
6.	Which of the various strategies and tactics for exercising power seem most appropriate and are likely to be effective, given the situation you confront?
7.	Based on the above, choose a course of action to get something done.

Table 17.2
Power and decision making
(taken from: Pfeffer, J (1992)
Managing with Power, Harvard
Business School Press, p 29)

to use various forms of power and bullying to centralize control for their own purposes.

Pfeffer (1992) identifies seven decision issues that should be considered as part of the process of decision making. These are included as Table 17.2. Of course not every decision requires the exercise of power in order to be successfully implemented. If the contributors are actively in favour of the decision or even if it is within their *zone of indifference* it is unlikely to require much application of power to influence events. The zone of indifference refers to an area of impact on an individual below the threshold at which they will respond negatively.

There have been attempts to create a contingency model of power by bringing together the work of French and Raven as described above and the work of Kelman. Luthans (1995) brings together these ideas in a model, to which has been added the levels of analysis perspective of Fincham (1992). The resulting contingency model is reflected in a simplified form in Figure 17.1.

In the contingency approach to power there exists a relationship between the sources of power and the responses generated as a consequence of specific conditions and motivation to respond in particular ways. For example, with a power source based on reward, a compliance reaction is likely to be created

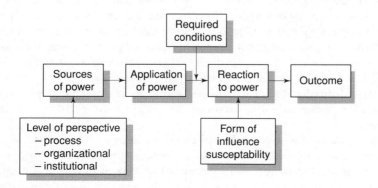

Figure 17.1   Contingency model of power.

if the target person seeks to avoid punishment or to make a favourable impression. To be successful the power holder must have the ability to deliver the reward as well as the punishment for failure.

It was argued in Chapter 15 that empowerment and other forms of involvement contain elements of power and control. One possibility in situations where power is an obvious element within the employment relationship is that employees will simply comply or conform. In Etzioni's (1975) terms they might adopt an *alienative* or *calculative* (instrumental) response. Clearly in today's world of lean, delayered and high performing organizations these responses are not desirable. Empowering and otherwise involving employees can be a way of encouraging them to *buy-into* or *adopt* the underlying values of management. Employees with the same value set as managers would be easier to manage and would think in the same terms as managers. This can be thought of as eliminating the need for power in the employment relationship. Equally, it can be described in terms of substituting internalized forms of self-control for the less effective outward forms. In effect, relying on covert rather than overt forms of power application – power by socialization.

Power as part of the decision-making process is frequently associated with political behaviour. Individual managers frequently seek power as a means to further their careers and enhance the position of their departments. This relationship was also identified in the work of McClelland on motivation. This was reviewed in an earlier chapter when the nPow concept associated with the need for power within the individual was discussed. The acquisition of power is something that some managers seek and is associated strongly with a tendency to function politically.

Politics within organizations

The quotation from Richard Nixon earlier indicated that an effective a leader must be able to implement the decisions made. In doing so the political perspectives become apparent. There are two different perspectives on organizational politics. One views politics as a negative process that actively inhibits the effective running of an organization. The other views it in a more positive light, viewing politics as an inevitable mechanism of conflict resolution and a process geared to reaching compromise.

It is not possible to offer a definitive view of all political behaviour, it can only be judged on a case by case basis. For example, managers who seek to advance their own careers by engaging in *politicking* might engage in some unpleasant tactics. However, assuming that they subsequently perform very well as senior managers, how should they be judged? Of course there are a range of criteria that could be used to evaluate this situation and the material on ethics has relevance. The difficulty is that it is not possible to know what might have happened under different circumstances in order to use that as a basis of evaluation.

One of the earliest works on the subject of politics was that of Machiavelli on the subject of serving princes and other rulers. His work titled *The Prince* was written in the period of fifteenth-century Renaissance Italy when politics was frequently a life or death business. Essentially, the argument put forward by Machiavelli was that the ends justified the means and anything was acceptable in the pursuit of the protection of the state. In short, it reflected how to obtain and hold onto power through political actions.

The negative view of politics imposes a definition that considers it to be outside normal practice, used to enhance existing power or to offset the power of another, the purpose being to increase the certainty that a particular and preferred course of action (as defined by the person engaging in politics) will be followed (Mayes and Allen, 1977). The difficulty in practice is that it is not always possible to categorize acts of political behaviour as clearly as this definition might imply. Imagine a situation in which a manager attempts to influence a forthcoming decision by lobbying for support for their preferred plan. Just how far this should go before it would be considered wrong is a difficult matter to judge, particularly if the result were beneficial to the organization.

The more positive view of political behaviour regards it as an inevitable part of the need for individuals and groups to function in a collective context. Organizations are run by a mixture of individuals, departments and interest groupings. Whatever the nature of the job it involves interaction with other people and politics is a means of achieving collaboration between them and other subunits within the organization. Every individual is part of a number of formal and informal groups within the organization. There are professional as well as friendship and departmental groups to identify just some of the more obvious ones. Each of these *levels* within the organization will have objectives to achieve and preferences for how the organization should function. For example, the marketing department frequently finds itself in conflict with the production department of the organization because of the different perceptions of how best to run the company. However, co-operation is needed between these groups when it comes to product planning and so a political balance must be struck.

Split departments are another level of grouping within organizations that can become part of the political process. The manufacturing division of a company might include a personnel department which is technically separate from the head office personnel function. However, it is not uncommon in these situations to find that a divisional personnel department identifies more strongly with the plans and objectives of its manufacturing division than with its professional grouping in head office.

As a positive process politics allows for these groupings to find ways of accommodating each other's perspective in a competitive framework which limits real damage to the individuals or the organization. Underlying this model of political behaviour is its association with success and failure. Imagine a situation in which a manager presses for a preferred course of action which is followed but which is not successful. The perceived status if not the actual job or status of the individual would be severely reduced.

Most managers recognize the dual nature of politics within an organization. They intuitively understand that it contains elements of both good and bad and that it can be an important, indeed inevitable part of the experience of work. Gandz and Murray (1980) carried out a survey among over 400 managers in an attempt to identify how managers perceived politics in their working lives. Table 17.3 reflects some of the more interesting findings.

It is clear from the findings illustrated in Table 17.3 that politics is regarded as common, more prevalent in senior positions and linked with success and promotion. It is also regarded as something that individuals undertake if they

Table 17.3
Perceptions about politics among managers (source: Gandz, J and Murray, V (1980) The experience of workplace politics. *Academy of Management Journal*, June 1980, p 244)

Statement		Strong or Moderate Agreement %
(a)	The existence of workplace politics is common to most organizations	93.2
(b)	Successful executives must be good politicians	89.0
(c)	The higher you go in organizations, the more political the climate becomes	76.2
(d)	Only organizationally weak people play politics	68.5
(e)	Organizations free of politics are happier than those where there is a lot of politics	59.1
(f)	You have to be political to get ahead in organizations	69.8
(g)	Politics in organizations are detrimental to efficiency	55.1
(h)	Top management should try to get rid of politics within the organization	48.6
(i)	Politics help organizations function effectively	42.1
(j)	Powerful executives don't act politically	15.7

have no other source of power and is the cause of inefficiency and unhappiness. These findings reflect the duality of politics in its positive and negative connotations. These findings have broadly been confirmed by later studies, Ashforth and Lee (1990) for example.

The positive view of organizational politics suggests that it will be rewarded if it is linked to success for the organization in some way. Imagine that a marketing manager were to set out to change the existing power balance of the organization from one which favoured the production department to one which favoured marketing. The strategies adopted might include attempting to *get close* to the chief executive, using every opportunity to make adverse comment about problems in production and indicating how competitors were gaining market share through the adoption of marketing strategies. Strengthening alliances with departments that might be favourable to the cause of marketing would also be another likely strategy. As a consequence of these strategies further imagine that a change in the power of the production department occurred as the company became marketing driven. If as a result the company found its reputation, market share and profits rose then it is likely that the company would pay more attention to advice from the marketing department in the future and less attention to the needs of production. That is until the marketing department succumbed to the political activity of other departments or failed to deliver success. This can be reflected in diagrammatic form (see Figure 17.2).

The point made by Figure 17.2 is that from an organizational point of view rewarding political behaviour if it delivers success encourages functions to compete without harming the whole. In effect this approach allows for a process of providing an effective match between the needs of the market and

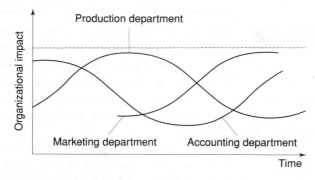

Figure 17.2 Organizational politics: impact and success.

the capability of the organization. Political activity that helps the organization ultimately benefits everyone and should be allowed free rein. It is the harsh world of the market that is the ultimate judge of politics, not the impact on particular individuals or groups. If the market reacts badly to the consequences of political behaviour then one way or another *punishment* of the perpetrators will follow.

This view of political behaviour would be criticized because it ignores the personal and ethical perspectives on why people engage in it. It is clear from the negative perspective on it that there are individuals who use it for their own ends, rather than for the benefit of the organization. It can be used to help or harm individuals just as it can be a process of attempting to acquire power to enable decisions to be implemented.

Using and managing political behaviour

The use of power within an organizational setting involves adopting one of three strategies. They are:

■ Offensive. These political strategies are effectively initiating behaviours. They represent the attacking behaviours that are intended to gain advantage over another individual or group. In military terms these are the equivalent of one army going on the offensive and attacking another before it has time to marshal its defences. An example of this form of political behaviour is described in Management in Action 17.5 overleaf.

Frequently political behaviour contains a high degree of *normal* or *allowable* behaviour but applied in ways that produce a particular end result. In Management in Action 17.5 it can reasonably inferred that James' manager wanted rid of him as he was perceived to be a threat to the manager's position. However, prioritizing work and reallocating resources are all perfectly legitimate practices in running a department. It is the intent behind such actions that indicates a political motive. In reality James was set up to fail by his boss who used practice and procedure in a way which cloaked the real intention.

There is another type of offensive strategy based on the view that, 'If it is not possible to look good oneself, then make the others look bad.' This is an *undermining* strategy. It covers many different types of behaviour all

Management in Action 17.5

Getting rid of a subordinate

This is a true story, according to the individual who told it to me during an interview. Only the details and names have been changed to protect the individuals and the organization.

James was an experienced manager and had a particular expertise in personnel management, having worked for a number of years with one of the large consultancies. He was recruited by a large manufacturing company to act as deputy manager in the Personnel Department in preparation for the departmental manager being promoted to a more senior position about six months later. The existing departmental manager had not worked in any other organization since leaving university some 15 years earlier.

Shortly after James joined the company it became apparent that the company was entering a difficult period and that restructuring was a real possibility. It was at that time that the departmental manager began to adopt an

offensive political campaign against a number of people including James. James had been recruited to take over from his manager and it was becoming apparent that this would not happen. The department manager was not going to be promoted in the restructuring. James was therefore a potential threat to his manager's position.

The political campaign included deliberately holding back the start date for jobs that James was to undertake and reallocating staff and other resources away from supporting him. Performance was, however, still to be judged against the original objectives and timescales for the work allocated to James. Eventually, after about seven months it was time to review the salary of James. His manager produced an annual report that claimed that James was underperforming, incompetent and should be downgraded perhaps even dismissed. Such performance certainly did not justify receiving any pay increase that year. James, having suspected what was to happen, had found another job and tendered his resignation on the spot.

---

intended to weaken the position of another individual or group. Examples include making disparaging comments about the target at either a personal or professional level. It can involve recalling with gusto any past mistakes as evidence of continued weakness. This can also lead to *whispering campaigns*. The spreading of rumour without evidence can be a very effective means of undermining other people without the need for evidence to support the assertions.

- ■ Defensive. Defensive strategies are those that are not intended to harm others but are destined to prevent harm being done by them. In Management in Action 17.5 James decided not to defend himself as such but to find another job and leave. He could have attempted to fight fire with fire and engage in a range of political behaviours to protect himself. For example, he could have made a number of alliances with more senior managers who may have been prepared to defend him against his boss. He could have set out to undermine the position of his boss with other managers. James could also have attempted to set his manager up for a fall by deliberately doing something wrong that would directly reflect on his boss. It should not be inferred that defensive political behaviour is weak or less aggressive than the offensive form. It can be just as effective and equally nasty in execution. It is the intention, not the content that differentiates it.
- ■ Neutral. This approach to political behaviour reflects a stance that does not actively engage in it for either of the two purposes so far described. It

reflects an actively protectionist approach to politics. It is an approach that attempts to keep out of political battles but one which will defend itself if absolutely necessary. It is an appeasing approach to the existence of politics. It is easiest to use offensive politics against a neutral strategy as it takes considerable pressure to begin to retaliate. James could be described as adopting a neutral strategy in response to his manager's attack. He did not defend himself other than by attempting to do the best job that he could and by attempting to be considered as a non-threatening subordinate by his manager. In the end rather than *take on* his manager in a battle, he sidestepped the problem by leaving the organization.

Some of the tactics that are used politically within an organization are identified in Table 17.1 as influencing tactics. Behaving politically is a process of attempting to influence other people towards a decision, viewpoint or course of action favoured by the initiator. Consequently many of the strategies adopted can be categorized under the headings in that table. Other researchers have identified categories that are framed slightly differently. For example, Yukl and Falbe (1990) identified the tactics described in Table 17.4.

It can be seen by comparing Tables 17.1 and 17.4 that although the terms used are different, they are broadly similar in flavour and content. Moorhead and Griffin (1992) bring together the work of a number of other writers in order to identify the main techniques associated with political behaviour. Table 17.5 overleaf lists the main techniques identified.

Tactics	Description
Pressure tactics	The use of demands, threats, or intimidation to convince you to comply with a request or to support a proposal.
Upward appeals	Persuading you that the request is approved by higher management, or appealing to higher management for assistance in gaining your compliance with the request.
Exchange tactics	Making explicit or implicit promises that you will receive rewards or tangible benefits if you comply with a request or support a proposal, or reminding you of a prior favour to be reciprocated.
Coalition tactics	Seeking the aid of others to persuade you to do something or using the support of others as an argument for you to agree also.
Ingratiating tactics	Seeking to get you in a good mood or making you think favourably of the influence agent before asking you to do something.
Rational persuasion	Using logical arguments and factual evidence to persuade you that a proposal or request is viable and likely to result in the attainment of task objectives.
Inspirational appeals	Making an emotional request or proposal that arouses enthusiasm by appealing to your values and ideals, or by increasing your confidence that you can do it.
Consultation tactics	Seeking your participation in making a decision or planning how to implement a proposed policy, strategy, or change.

Table 17.4

Political tactics (adapted from Yukl, G and Falbe, CM (1990) Influence tactics and objectives in upward, downward, and lateral influence attempts. *Journal of Applied Psychology*, **75,** 133). Copyright © by the American Psychological Association. Adapted with permission.

Table 17.5
Political techniques (adapted
from: Moorhead, G and Griffin,
RW (1992) *Organizational
Behaviour*, 3rd edn, Houghton
Mifflin). p 303–6

- Controlling information
- Control of communication channels
- Using outside specialists
- Control of the work and/or meetings agenda
- Game playing
- Impression and image management
- Creating coalitions
- Control of decision making criteria

Considering briefly each technique in turn:

- Control of information. There is a saying that information is power. The ability to determine who has access to what information provides a particularly powerful opportunity to influence events. Decision making requires information. The individual with access to the best range and quality of information is the one most likely to be in a strong position to plan effective strategies for the future. In relation to the stock market, access to inside information on company plans could make anyone privy to it rich as they could either buy or sell shares at the most advantageous price. That is why *insider dealing*, as it is called, is regarded as a serious offence and market authorities are constantly monitoring market activity to detect and prevent it.

- Control of communication channels. The control of who has access to whom, who communicates with whom, etc. can significantly influence events. During the 1960s, 1970s and early 1980s most trade unions regarded communication with employees as their prerogative. In situations where particularly militant trade union representatives were present threats of strike action would be used if managers proposed addressing their workforce directly. In such situations whoever actually communicated with the workforce was likely to put their particular perspective on the message being communicated. This control of the communication channels within organizations is now rare and more joint or parallel processes exist. However, there are many examples that can be found within the management levels of an organization. Simple examples include who is invited to attend particular meetings and who might be left off the distribution list for a report.

- Use of outside specialists. The use of external specialists can be a powerful lever to ensuring that one's point of view is favoured. The selection of a particular consultant or expert is a difficult process as there are many thousands of potential candidates available. It is relatively easy to select one who might be expected (or told) to support a particular point of view. This lends weight to the insiders who also lean towards that particular viewpoint, as outside experts are supposed/assumed to be independent.

- Control over work and meeting agendas. Being able to influence events directly is another useful political technique. The individual who determines the agenda for a meeting determines what can (and frequently of more significance what cannot) be discussed. This allows the direction of decision making to be determined and channelled to the advantage of the person setting the agenda. A related political technique is to accept responsibility for writing the minutes of meetings. Very few meeting records are verbatim and so the writer has considerable discretion over what is recorded and more importantly how the record should be phrased. Naturally it is usual for the minutes to be verified at a subsequent meeting but a skilled political operator would not find that a particular problem.

■ Game playing. There are individuals who appear to enjoy the sport of playing politics just to see what happens and to demonstrate their ability to control events. Management in Action 17.5 described the events surrounding James and his eventual departure from the organization. The department manager in that situation was playing games in that he was using established procedure and practice to achieve a particular objective that would not have been officially sanctioned. At least two of the books identified in the Further Reading section below contain material relevant to game playing.

■ Impression and image management. This represents a less direct approach to politics as it involves creating an image that in turn could be expected to influence events. Simple examples include attempting to become associated with successful projects or to distance oneself from failing ones. It is not unusual for a manager to sit on the sidelines of a particular programme of work and to suddenly seek to take a high profile near to completion when success is more certain. Claiming major involvement in particular projects is another common example of overstating activity in order to enhance one's reputation. Of course this must be done carefully as a number of people will know the truth on such claims. Once exposed as false claims they can undermine every other claim made by that individual. Bromley (1993) provides an analysis of many aspects of impression management which collectively demonstrate the complexity of these psychological constructs.

■ Creating coalitions. Political alliances are another means of achieving desired objectives. Imagine a situation in which a personnel manager wishes to introduce a new payment system into a company. The sales manager may not see any benefit or problems with such a scheme and so may be neutral towards it. The production manager may be in favour if higher productivity and reduced cost is possible. The finance director may be openly hostile towards the idea as it would create additional work for his department. The employees may also be against the idea because higher productivity may result in job losses and having to work harder. Clearly the personnel manager needs to ensure that all the managers are supportive of the plan before attempting to convince the employees of its merits. The finance director is presumably more senior to the other managers and as a result would carry 'more weight' in collective decision making. Perhaps if the sales manager could be persuaded to actively support the scheme and ways could be found to lessen the burden on the finance department then open hostility might be reduced. The personnel manager would probably begin to lobby the sales manager for support, perhaps using the argument that the higher productivity achieved would benefit the sales department though pricing and delivery benefits. This together with a scheme redesign might be enough to sway the finance director in a meeting.

Taken to extreme this approach to political behaviour can be little more than horse trading. Attempting to operate on the basis of buying co-operation for past favours or support for promises of future help on matters of value to the courted individual. At an organizational level this approach reflects the cartel approach to fixing markets in favour of particular suppliers.

■ Control over decision-making criteria. It is sometimes possible for a manager to set down the criteria against which decisions will be made and in so doing they do not have to be directly involved in order to influence events. It is not uncommon for industrial relations specialists facing the annual negotiation round with the trade unions to initially hold meetings with other managers to determine the negotiating strategy. In doing so it can happen that a chief executive will set out in very clear terms what they expect to happen and in effect to write the script for the negotiators. Clearly in this situation very little scope is available to the negotiation team to respond creatively to the dynamics of the situation and create a settlement acceptable to all sides. The 'dead hand' of the chief executive rests over the situation and effectively controls events in absentia. In a more general context such approaches can allow a leader to claim non-involvement in a situation whilst in reality controlling events. They are able to distance themselves from events both physically and psychologically whilst retaining control in reality.

The degree to which it is possible to manage political behaviour in others is difficult to specify. It depends upon so many factors. For example, the style of management within the organization can determine the level and volume of politicking that takes place. The personality of the individual is likely to influence their predisposition for playing games and other forms of politics. The skill level and networks of the individuals concerned can also influence events.

Managers are inevitably in competition with each other for resources and power. There is never enough resources to meet every possible demand within an organization. Every manager could make a positive contribution to the organization given a completely free hand in spending unlimited amounts of money. It is just not possible for any organization to be in that position and therefore a process of rationing must exist. Rationing implies deciding between competing ways of allocating scarce resource and in finding ways to prioritize alternative options. This creates a context where managers must justify proposed actions and find ways to gain support for their plans. Politicking can be used to influence these processes and increase the probability of success.

In order to attempt to control and minimize the harmful effects associated with politics it is necessary to find ways to encourage competition without allowing hidden agendas to flourish. Specifying in advance how decisions will be made and by not allowing power to become a means of acquiring resources are just some of the ways that this can be encouraged. By separating the evaluation of resource allocation from issues associated with performance evaluation and promotion some control of politics can also be achieved. The sending of very clear signals that politicking will not be tolerated by dealing severely with obvious cases and encouraging examples to be openly discussed is another means of minimizing its impact.

Power and politics: a management perspective

The nature of power and politics within an organizational context is very complex. Power and authority are closely aligned concepts and are integral to aspects of management. With organizational status and position in the hierarchy comes the right to have others follow your instructions. Managers without power are likely to have little influence on the organization for which they work. It is the close relationship between power and influence within a management context that provides a perfect breeding ground for the political behaviour that formed the second major theme of this chapter. The use of political behaviour can enhance the level of power and influence held by an individual or group, thereby increasing their status and perhaps career prospects.

Etzoini (1975) first provided a categorization for the basis of power as normative (based on legitimacy of authority), utilitarian (based on the payment of inducements) or coercive (based on the ability to apply sanction). It is through the application of the latter two categories that the potential for the misuse of power and political behaviour is created. The complex interlinkage between power and politics in an organizational context is reflected in the example described in Management in Action 17.6 on the next page.

However, it is also important to recognize that there are three caveats to the use of power in an organization. They are:

- Balance. Only on very rare occasions is there a complete imbalance in the power held between the parties to a particular situation. Pushed too hard employees may feel that they have nothing to lose by withdrawing their labour by going on strike or seeking alternative work. The degree of care and attention that an employee pays to their work is largely a matter for them to decide. Managers are not in a position to control every aspect of work all of the time. Employees who feel they have no stake in a situation are likely to apply negative power to the disadvantage of management.
- Domain. Few sources of power are likely to be valid across time and in every context. An employer may be able to force down the price of labour when there is little alternative work for employees. However, employers are generally unable to restrict the movement of jobs to areas as a consequence of cheap labour. As a result labour costs will inevitably rise and employees will follow the economic principles by moving employers.
- Relativity. The application of power is only possible if the source is of value to the target person or group. For example, an organization that does not value personnel management skills is unlikely to listen to the advice offered by such specialists and therefore the function would have little power in that situation.

Kotter (1977) identified a number of characteristics shared by those managers who were able to use and manage power effectively, including:

- Sensitivity. They are able to understand the feelings of others as to how power is obtained and used.
- Intuitive. They have an intuitive feel for how to acquire and use power across a wide range of contexts. They also recognize that in making use of power that it is people that are influenced by it, not just objects.

Management in Action 17.6

Mexican union cries foul at paper's tactics

The Union of Newspaper Hawkers has 17,000 members in Mexico City along with the exclusive rights to sell newspapers in the city. However, even with a population of about 8 million people only around 500,000 daily newspapers are sold. There are 32 different daily newspapers in Mexico city and nearly all charge the same price (60 US cents) per copy. Into the fray a new newspaper (*Reforma*) has emerged and it wants to dictate when and how its papers are sold. The union does not want to go along with that and sees it as a direct challenge to its position.

It is the Union of Newspaper Hawkers which dictates where and when all of the newspapers are sold. News-stands do not open before 8 am and they are invariably loaded down with papers that will not be sold. The publishers of about half of the daily papers are not too concerned about volume of sales as most of their income is derived from flat-fee government advertising. Private advertising, which is dependent upon volume of sales, does not contribute much to the income of most of the publishers. *Reforma* has been in a continuous battle with the union since it sought to control where and when

its papers would be available. It wanted to target the more affluent areas, but could not do so through the union distribution system.

The distribution of *Reforma* was done through a motley salesforce of journalists, students, politicians and housewives who suffered violent attacks and theft over the initial weeks of its existence. In a twist of tactics, the publishers of *Reforma* sent its own vendors out onto the streets on the Sunday that Mexico celebrates its revolution. It is one of only five days in the year when the union does not work and so newspapers are not normally available. Union leaders claim that *Reforma* is attempting to destroy the union, which it argues provides a service to many publications. The government also regard the union in a friendly light having used it in the past as a last stand against renegade or independent publications. However, the publishers of *Reforma* have appealed to the Federal Competition Commission to be allowed to distribute the paper themselves, and have ignored negotiations at the Interior Ministry which is responsible for regulating the media.

Adapted from: Bardacke, T (1994) Mexican Union cries foul at paper's tactics. Financial Times, *22 November, p 22.*

- **Repertoire.** They have a wide repertoire of power sources on which to call.
- **Career.** Some jobs are naturally more powerful than others and they gravitate towards these positions by actively seeking them out.
- **Investment.** Managers who are able to make effective use of power tend to regard it as an investment. It is not a static resource, it can be grown, harvested and squandered. Through careful husbandry all the resources available to an individual can be used to grow the power available to them.
- **Maturity.** The naked use of power and crude attempts to acquire it are quickly transparent to most, who then resist it. To be most effective power needs some support (or at least little resistance – the zone of indifference) from those exposed to it and so a mature approach to it is more likely to produce positive results for the individual practising it.

Politics on the other hand can be seen as a means of sharing power among a number of interested groups and individuals. At an organizational level it can provide a mechanism for allowing the relative power of the various departments and subsidiary companies to rise and fall without adversely effecting the structure and performance of the overall organization. However, just as power can be misused so can political behaviour. It is possible for political behaviour to be used to the personal advantage of those perpetrating it. In such situations it is not uncommon to find the existence of special interest groups that are informal, perhaps temporary, but definitely outside the formal organizational framework.

Cliques are one form of group whose prime motivation is the defence of the members against the interests of other groups and individuals. Trade unions exist to advance and protect the interests of members against the inevitable power imbalance in the employment relationship. Another example would be a coffee break group that attempted to provide member support against the behaviour of a dictatorial and inconsistent boss. Cabals are another form of group that attempt to take the initiative within an organization to the positive advantage of its members. The phrase *Young Turks* is frequently use to describe the activities of young executives who attempt to force the organization to adopt policies supportive of their wishes. In that sense it represents a proactive approach to the acquisition and use of power through political means.

Political behaviour is encouraged to exist in situations where the formal roles and authority are unclear. If the designated roles and lines of authority are clearly specified then it is easy for breaches and deviations to be identified. In addition it is also easy to appeal to the formal structural mechanisms as ways of combating the politicking.

There are a number of issues that emerges from this view of political behaviour and organizational informality or lack of clarity. A number of new structural forms of organization attempt to take out the formality and rigidity of structure originating from bureaucracy. The informality and lack of clear role definition implied by these recent innovations could provide the very basis on which political behaviour flourishes. It is possible that without very clear attempts to manage out these aspects of organizational activity they could offset the advantages available through the informality and ability to respond rapidly to market conditions.

There are also managerial benefits from being political. Over the past few years organizations have been delayering and downsizing, all of which impacts directly on the number of management jobs available. This has had a major impact on management careers and job opportunity. No longer can managers expect to be protected from the harsh realities that have faced many other occupational groups. As a consequence they find it necessary to take a more active role in managing their own careers and survival. This can lead to political behaviour as a means of influencing decisions about job security and career development. Being considered a good employee is now as important for every manager as it is for every other employee. Politics can be used to enhance the probability of success by tipping the balance one way rather than another. Trust and loyalty between employer and employee has always been part of this non-political equation and yet in this new world of personal careers writers such as Charles Heckscher suggest that it should be eliminated. This view is outlined in Management in Action 17.7.

There is also a link between the type of organization and the form that politics takes within it. For example, in bureaucratic organizations it is the audit functions that enjoy a high degree of power and influence. The predominance of rules and procedures encourages the policing role in an attempt to prevent fraud. In organic types of organization it is the advisory functions that have most power as they attempt to maintain consistency of operation across a range

Management in Action 17.7

The importance of stamping out loyalty

In a book review of *White Collar Blues: Management Loyalties in an Age of Corporate Restructuring* (1995) by Charles Heckscher, published by HarperCollins, Jackson identifies some interesting ideas. In the USA, middle managers account for 8% of the workforce, yet between 1988 and 1993 they accounted for 19% of the job losses. The old middle-class ethos of commitment to the organization was based on a two-way commitment. In return for security, managers worked extra hours, took risks and allowed inroads into their personal lives. Heckscher suggests (as have others) that this two-way commitment has been broken by employers and so they cannot expect middle managers to continue to support a one-sided deal.

The existence of communal trust and loyalty between the members of an organization developed as a means of allowing the bureaucratic forms of organization to function effectively. However, Heckscher argues that this is now too rigid and does not allow change to happen at the necessary rate. Heckscher goes on to argue that it should not be a question of how to regain the loyalty of middle managers, but how to firmly stamp it out. While managers cling to the debris of the old order, fundamental change cannot happen and continuous decline becomes inevitable. This creates a cycle of yet more drudgery, further resentment and less likelihood that change will be successful.

Some of Professor Heckscher's work has found that change was least successful in organizations in which loyalty was strongest and managers were most overworked. Conversely, change was most effective in those organizations in which the level of loyalty was the weakest. A different form of loyalty is proposed by Heckscher, that of loyalty not to the organization, but to the project on which the individual is working. This may last for three to five years and then the individual moves on to another project, perhaps even with a different company.

There are of course many implications of this form of working. Individuals would have to accept greater levels of responsibility for their own career, job networking and training. Equally, organizational issues such as pension portability and commitment to making individuals more marketable on a wider scale would need to be introduced. But for those organizations and individuals who have been able to make this change the benefits in being more relaxed and confident about the future and their place in it are available.

Adapted from: Jackson, T (1995) The importance of stamping out loyalty. Financial Times, 30 March, p 18.

of relatively segregated operating units. In this type of situation the organizational politics would tend to be aimed at holding or changing the power balance between line and staff functions.

Conclusions

Power and politics are important aspects of organizational behaviour. They are inseparable from the needs of organization and the needs, aspirations and inclinations of the individuals that work within them. There are individuals who introduce an element of game playing intended to enhance their power base and as a means of making work more interesting. They can also introduce a source of fun and enjoyment in observing the behaviour of others. They are also the basis of much conflict within organizations.

Discussion questions

1 Define the following key terms used in this chapter:

Zone of indifference   Politics   Referent power
Power   Political strategies   Expert power
Authority   Cliques   Legitimate power
Influence   Cabals   Reward power
Coercive power   Negative power

2 Compare and contrast the influencing tactics identified in Table 17.1 with the political techniques identified in Table 17.5.
3 Is power and politics linked to organizational design? Justify your answer.
4 It is suggested that there is an inevitable power imbalance in the employment relationship and that this can lead to the development of self-defence groupings such as trade unions. Why might this power imbalance exist, is it inevitable and can it be limited?
5 Describe the main sources of power and provide examples of each from an organization.
6 Managers must compete for scarce resources. Political behaviour can influence decisions. In what ways might it be possible to encourage competition whilst minimizing the potentially harmful effects of political behaviour?
7 Identify the differences and similarities between the concepts of power and influence.
8 Why is the 'zone of indifference' important to the notion of how power and politics operate within an organization? Justify your answer.
9 'Politics is a process which cannot be eliminated from an organization therefore it should be ignored in running a business.' Discuss this statement.
10 Management is ultimately about acquiring and using power successfully. The best leaders are successful politicians. Reconcile these two statements.

Research questions

1 In the library find six different journal articles associated with power and politics. What are the different points of view expressed in these papers about these concepts and how do they support or contradict the discussion in this chapter? In addition attempt to find any books on the subject of how managers should gain and use power and/or politics. How do the views expressed in these books differ if compared with the academic papers that you identified?
2 Speak to a number of practising managers about the subjects of power and politics. How do they describe these terms and how significant do they consider them to be in practical management activities? Do the different types of organization or industry have an impact on the perception of the managers about these subjects? Do the interviewees consider that politics can be controlled, if so how?
3 Interview a cross-section of people from different levels of organizational life. Attempt to incorporate individuals from manual, clerical, administrative, specialist/technical as well as a range of management jobs. Attempt

to identify how each group views power and politics; who engages in it and why; is it beneficial or harmful to the individuals, organization and customers? Compare and contrast the views of each group and draw any general conclusions from the results. How do your results compare with the material contained in this chapter?

Key reading

From Clark, H, Chandler, J and Barry, J (1994) *Organization and Identities: Text and Readings in Organizational Behaviour*, International Thomson Business Press, London.
- Foucault M: Docile bodies and panopticism, p 35. This offers insight into the forms of social control employed by managers to achieve their objectives
- Foucault M: The subject and power, p 43. This short extract considers the relationship between power and freedom.
- Bell D: Work and its discontents, p 44. Time as money, which can be wasted, are examples of how control is related to the experience of capitalism.
- Hobsbawm EJ and Rudé G: Early forms of worker resistance – swing riots, p 317. Considers the early attempts of workers to resist the power of managers in the early 1800s.
- Taylor L and Walton P: Industrial sabotage, p 321. Sabotage can take many forms, all disruptive, some dangerous or humorous (usually to colleagues or outsiders).
- Hyman R: The power of collective action, p 322. A consideration of the nature of collective action in its various forms as compared with individual action.

Further reading

Heller, R (1985) *The Naked Manager: Games Executives Play*, McGraw-Hill, New York. Considers a broad range of the games that are played within organizations. They are not directly political in the negative sense of the term. Nevertheless it is possible to gain a flavour of the complexity and subtlety of much of this activity.

Jay, A (1987) *Management and Machiavelli*, revised edn, Hutchinson Business, London. A humorous text which considers many aspects associated with power and authority in management. It does not take Machiavelli's work specifically as its basis, but his spirit is evident. A recent translation of Machiavelli's original work, which is very accessible and available as a 1981 Penguin book, is also well worth reading.

Jermier, JM, Knights, D and Nord, WR eds (1994) *Resistance and Power in Organizations*, Routledge, London. Provides a review of how attempts to use power as a basis of control inevitably leads to resistance in one form or another. It is grounded in the labour process perspective and attempts to interpret the arguments from the perspectives implied by that model.

Matthews, R (1989) *Power Brokers: Kingmakers and Usurpers Throughout History*, Facts On File, Oxford. Although not a business or management book this text provides a brief insight into the way that power, its acquisition and use has been used by those who would aspire to be political leaders.

Monks, RAG and Minow, N (1991) *Power and Accountability*, HarperCollins, London. This book attempts to show some of the consequences of power when large organizations can operate without the effective means of holding them accountable for their actions. As such it is a chilling reminder of the many ways that power can be abused and trust violated.

Pfeffer, J (1992) *Managing With Power: Politics and Influence in Organizations*, Harvard Business School Press, Boston, MA. This text provides a comprehensive review of the use of power and politics within modern organizations. It considers the organizational, personal and career aspects of these concepts as well as their association with decision making.

References

Aronson, E (1972) *The Social Animal*, WH Freeman, San Francisco, CA.

Ashforth, BE and Lee, RT (1990) Defensive behaviour in organizations: a preliminary model. *Human Relations*, July, 621–48.

Barnard, CI (1938) *The Functions of the Executive*, Harvard University Press, Cambridge, MA.

Bromley, DB (1993) *Reputation, Image and Impression Management*, John Wiley, Chichester.

Etzioni, A (1975) *A Comparative Analysis of Complex Organizations*, The Free Press, New York.

Fincham, R (1992) Perspectives on power: processual, institutional and internal forms or organizational power. *Journal of Management Studies*, **29**, No. 6.

Forsyth, D (1990) *Group Dynamics*, 2nd edn, Brooks-Cole, Belmont, CA.

French, JRP and Raven, B (1968) The bases of social power. In *Group Dynamics: Research and Theory*, 3rd edn (eds D Cartwright and AF Zander), Harper & Row, New York.

Gandz, J and Murray, V (1980) The experience of workplace politics. *Academy of Management Journal*, June, 237–51.

Handy, CB (1985) *Understanding Organizations*, 3rd edn, Penguin, Harmondsworth.

Heald, T (1984) *Old Boy Networks: Who We Know and How We Use Them*, Ticknor & Fields, New York.

Kotter, J (1977) *Power, Dependence and Effective Management*.

Luthans, F (1995) *Organizational Behaviour*, 7th edn, McGraw-Hill, New York.

Mayes, BT and Allen, RW (1977) Toward a definition of organizational politics. *Academy of Management Review*, **2**, 672–7.

Milgram, S (1965) Some conditions of obedience and disobedience to authority. *Human Relations*, **18**, 57–76.

Moorhead, G and Griffin, RW (1992) *Organizational Behaviour*, 3rd edn, Houghton Mifflin, Boston, MA.

Nixon, RM (1982) *Leaders*, Warner, New York.

Pfeffer, J (1992) *Managing With Power: Politics and Influence in Organizations*, Harvard Business School Press, Boston, MA.

Rothschild, J and Miethe, TD (1994) Whistleblowing as resistance in modern work organizations: the politics of revealing organizational deception and abuse. In *Resistance and Power in Organizations* (eds JM Jermier, D Knights and WR Nord), Routledge, London.

Yukl, G and Falbe, CM (1990) Influence tactics and objectives in upward, downward, and lateral influence attempts. *Journal of Applied Psychology*, **7**, 132–40.

18
Conflict and control

███ browse this web site ███

www.itbp.com

Chapter summary

This chapter begins with an introduction to the concepts of conflict and control. Conflict then becomes the focus of attention in attempting to identify its sources, forms and consequences. The forms and characteristics of control are examined before the strategies for using it are introduced. The chapter concludes with a consideration of the management perspectives on the topics discussed.

Learning objectives

After studying this chapter and working through the associated Management in Action panels, discussion questions and research activities, you should be able to:

■ Understand the nature and impact of control within organizations.
■ Describe the sources and forms that conflict can take.
■ Explain the characteristic features of control systems.
■ Outline the major conflict handling strategies.
■ Assess the relative strengths and weaknesses of the various conflict handling strategies.
■ Appreciate that conflict is not automatically negative in its impact.
■ Discuss the management perspectives on conflict and control.
■ Detail the control strategies available to organizations.

Introduction

Conflict frequently arises when the *differences* between two or more groups or individuals become apparent. In industrial relations situations this might occur if a trade union makes a demand for a 10% pay increase and management make an equally forceful case for a 2% increase. The normal use of the term conflict implies a negative and openly hostile situation. Indeed, the first definition of the term in *The Pocket Oxford Dictionary* is, 'trial of strength between opposed parties or principles'. In an organizational context it is perhaps more appropriate to consider conflict in terms of its *potential* or as a *scale of activity* . In industrial relations terms the need to take into account the potential for conflict can lead to anticipatory behaviour (thus avoiding open conflict) as well as strikes and other industrial action intended to force a change in behaviour in the other party.

A concept that has strong association with conflict is that of control. This can be used to refer to a range of actions, including the rational procedures associated with the control of machine processes. It can also refer to the management of the organization on behalf of the principle stakeholders. However, it can also be used to reflect more sinister processes. It can be taken to reflect the *manipulation* of employee behaviour by managers. There are many examples where managers resort to bullying tactics in order to force subordinates to comply with their wishes. These intentions may not only reflect the need to provide job instruction but also the desire of some individuals to exercise control in its broadest sense (Adams, 1992).

Conflict: sources and forms

Conflict can be considered as something that disrupts the normal and desirable states of stability and harmony within an organization. Under this definition it is something to be avoided and if possible eliminated from the operation. However, it is also possible to consider conflict as an inevitable feature of human interaction and perhaps something that if managed constructively could offer positive value in ensuring an effective performance within the organization.

Fox (1966) describes three major perspectives on organizations that each have a different perspective on the nature of conflict:

- Pluralism. This holds that an organization comprises a collection of groups each with their own objectives, aspirations and agenda to follow. Inevitably, the diversity of groups involved will have divergent interests. Employees seek to maximize earnings and organizations seek the lowest labour cost. These different perspectives are irreconcilable and are therefore a basis for conflict between the groups involved. However, such differences do not automatically result in a failure of the ability of the organization to function. All of the groups recognize that compromise is essential if they are to stand any chance of partially achieving their objectives.

  Conflict provides an indication of the issues on which there are fundamental differences between the groups. In effect it provides a relationship regulation mechanism, preventing major fracture which would be to every group's disadvantage. However, as Management in Action 18.1 shows there are situations in which the opportunity to bridge the gap in seeking a resolution simply does not exist.

- Unitarianism. This suggests that the whole is the natural unit of consideration. The organization is frequently likened to a family unit in which different branches and factions might exist but the family unit is the unit of concern for all members. Conflict in that sense is something that reflects a major breakdown in the *normal* state of affairs. In that perspective conflict is suggested to reflect something that should be avoided if possible and eliminated. It is viewed as emanating from members classed as deviant, so they should be dealt with severely as they put at risk the overall harmony of the group.

- Marxist. The radical perspective as it is sometimes called suggests that conflict is an inevitable function of capitalism. Employees are exploited by the controllers of the means of production. One of the consequences of this is resistance to the will of management in the form of conflict. Not only is this inevitable but desirable in the Marxist tradition as it assists the breakdown of capitalism in the revolutionary creation of socialism.

A boss's life at the sharp end

Life for Alberto Morales, General Manager of the Gillette manufacturing subsidiary near Seville in Spain, changed completely on 18 March 1994 when he told the works council that the company had decided to close the factory. Since then his home has been put under 24-hour guard, he is always accompanied by two bodyguards and he no longer leaves his office to walk around the factory.

About 250 people are employed at the factory, but the parent company wants to concentrate European razor-blade manufacture in England and Germany. Reaction to the proposed closure was strongly hostile at a number of levels. The regional government challenged the decision in the courts and the industry minister for the country described the move as 'a provocation' for example. Even a boycott of Gillette products was suggested in reaction to the closure. Spanish labour law allows for collective redundancy on certain grounds, including the reorganization of production. However, these were intended to cover situations within Spain, not the cross-border transfers of work. Globally Gillette was seeking to realign its operations, which involved the loss of about 2000 jobs, mostly outside the USA, and the creation of new jobs

in countries such as China, Russia and Poland where new ventures were planned. The justification for the factory closure according to Morales, 'is not that it is unprofitable, but that it is superfluous'.

To avoid lengthy administrative procedure, Spanish employers frequently offer the maximum redundancy compensation of 45 days' pay for each year of service. Morales suggested that the company might even go beyond that level in order to achieve a negotiated settlement. The works council at the Seville factory would not listen to the initial offer from management for two months. This consisted of a retirement plan, outplacement services and a range of insurance policies. Future negotiations were also likely to be 'conflictual' in nature. The future for Morales at a personal level was also bleak. He was aged 54 and had been at the factory for 20 years, the last six as general manager. He felt that there were not many suitable alternative positions for him within the company. As a factory manager, the possible locations were likely to be India or somewhere like it. Not a prospect that he relished, and once the factory was closed down he expected to be out on the street just like the other workers.

Adapted from: White, D (1994) A boss's life at the sharp end. Financial Times, *8 June, p 20.*

Sources of conflict

There are six major areas within an organization that can give rise to conflict (see Figure 18.1).

Taking each of the sources of conflict in turn:

- ■ Intrapersonal. This represents the conflicts that arise within the individual. The ethical dilemmas facing individuals through work were discussed in Chapter 15. These represent one potential area of conflict for the individual to resolve within themselves.
- ■ Interpersonal. Whetten and Cameron (1991) identify four sources of interpersonal conflict. They are:
  1 Personal difference. No two people are exactly alike. It is not possible to like everyone with whom one works and personalities frequently clash.
  2 Role incompatibility. The functional nature of work activity creates very real potential for interpersonal conflict. For example, a personnel manager may seek to organize training courses for employees. However, an

Conflict: sources and forms

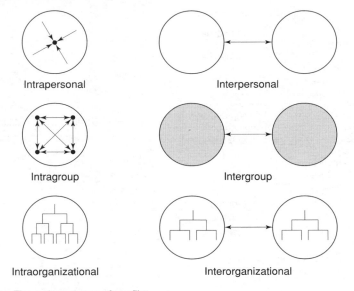

Figure 18.1   The major sources of conflict.

operations manager with tight production schedules to meet and with no spare labour may resent the efforts of the personnel manager.

3 Information deficiency. An individual with access to information is better able to perform more effectively. Therefore information can provoke conflictual relationships between individuals. The quality of information provided to a computer system designer could easily become the subject of conflict if the system does not meet expectations.

4 Environmental stress. Conflict can become more likely in times of competitive pressure. Most organizations have been going through significant periods of downsizing, re-engineering and change over the past decade. As a consequence individuals can find that their ability to retain a job and career is continually under threat. If most individuals within the organization feel similarly the environmental conditions exist for fractious relationships and open conflict.

■ Intragroup. One particular context within which interpersonal conflict can be found occurs within a group. The models proposed by Belbin and Margerison and McCann, discussed in the chapters dealing with groups, offer a basis for minimizing the potential for harmful conflict between group members. Group activity inevitably brings the characteristics, attitudes and opinions of individual members into focus. The interaction of these variables on the group process and conflict can be reflected in a diagram (Figure 18.2 overleaf).

■ Intergroup. There are many different groups that exist within an organization and inevitably they will experience differences and conflict at some point in time. Employees seek to earn as much money as possible, employers on the other hand want labour to be as cheap as possible. There is an inherent basis of conflict in this situation. Marketing departments may press hard for a diversified product range with regular changes in order to compete in turbulent markets. The production department may demand stability in order to achieve economies of scale.

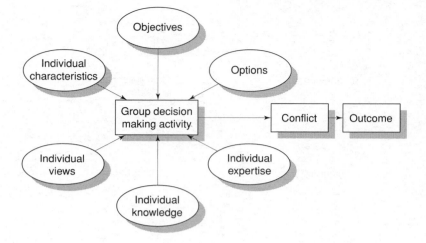

Figure 18.2 Group decision making and conflict.

- **Intraorganizational.** Individuals and groups play such a significant part in organizational activity that they inevitably account for much of the incidence of conflict. However, there are other features of organization that favour the emergence of conflict (see Figure 18.3).

  The physical realization of an organization in terms of structure, hierarchy, information flows, together with career development, rewards, information flows are all ways of *compartmentalizing* activity. Link these with the inevitable limitations of resource availability and a basis for competition is created. There is a very narrow line between competition and conflict. If one party considers that it has not been fairly treated in the competitive process or attempts to influence outcomes in its favour then conflict can arise. There are also propensities to conflict in the nature of

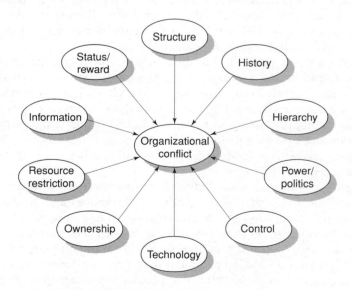

Figure 18.3 Organization and the determinants of conflict.

organizational ownership and the relative exclusion of employees. The impact of technology on jobs linked to the concepts of power, control and politics are other endemic features of organizational functioning that allow conflict to emerge.

- Interorganizational. Markets provides a scenario in which organizations are inevitably in conflict with each other. All of the competitors in a particular industry attempt to meet the needs of the customer in such ways as to maximize profit and market share for themselves. The unfair use of state subsidy can support otherwise uneconomic organizations to the disadvantage of organizations that do not have access to those funds. There is considerable unease in some quarters at the potential for conflict of interest within the large accountancy practices offering a wide range of services. The essence of this debate is reflected in Management in Action 18.2 on the next page.

Forms of conflict

This reflects the way that conflict can find expression within an organizational setting. Disagreement that escalates to the level of conflict could be anticipated to find expression in forms of argument, adversarial, antagonistic and other forms of hostile behaviour for example. Within an organization there are two distinct forms of classification for differentiating the form that conflict can take. They are the individual and group levels of analysis.

Conflict from a managerial perspective has the potential to create disruption within the organization and hence lower output levels, quality and profit. As a result most organizations attempt to institutionalize the mechanisms for dealing with it. These issues will be discussed further below, taking each class of conflict expression in turn in order to examine some of the forms that it can take.

Individual

Some of the ways that conflict can find its way into observable behaviour include:

- Sabotage. The deliberate interruption of company operations is the broad definition of sabotage. At one extreme it involves causing machines to breakdown by deliberately causing a malfunction. At the other extreme it is simply not working as effectively as would be considered reasonable by management. Sabotage arises through the deliberate intent to damage the interests of another by an individual who considers that they have some reason to feel aggrieved by the actions of that party. Sabotage is not part of the conflict itself, but it reflects an attitude and an attempt to *get even* with the target.
- Ethical dilemmas. The existence of an ethical dilemma is an example of a conflict, usually between alternative courses of action. For example, should an individual *whistleblow* on their boss who has been deliberately over claiming expenses?
- Interpersonal disputes. It is just not possible for all human beings to live in peace and harmony all of the time. Much as we might strive for such an ideal and even function as if it were the norm, the weight of history and human nature would suggest otherwise. For example, a manager may

Management in Action 18.2

For what we are about to receive

Many large accounting practices have a range of services that they offer to clients. Such firms claim that there are 'Chinese walls' between the various component parts of the practice, particularly in the sensitive areas of audit, support and insolvency. However, not everyone is convinced that the inevitable tensions are dealt with as they should be. This situation becomes even more complex when the role of bankers in company financial management is taken into account.

Jack describes one case that illustrates some of these potential conflicts. It involves a north London textile company, a bank, the accountants that it hired and the eventual fall into receivership of the business. In 1992 the company lost its largest customer. The bank pressed the owner of the business to consider the implications of this loss of revenue and he agreed to pay £18,000 to a large firm of accountants to write a report on the viability of the company. As a result of the report all parties agreed that the company should stay in business, but that the position should be reviewed six months later. During that time the business paid the accountants £3000 each week to monitor the financial health of the company.

At the end of the six months the company overdraft had been reduced to within a few thousand pounds of the owner's forecast. The owner and his independent auditors made repeated proposals for the restructuring of the company which were turned down by the bank and the accountants. Instead the bank appointed the firm of accountants as receivers and closed the business down. The underlying issue from this case (and many others) is the probity of banks using the same accountants to investigate troubled companies as would be appointed as receivers should the company fail. The potential conflict of interest that arises in these situations emerges from the pressure on the accountants to generate fee earning opportunities. There is a danger that the information on a company may be 'slanted' to 'encourage' its closure in order to gain the additional fees for the accountants if it were appointed as receiver.

Not all firms of accountants undertake insolvency work as some believe that the potential for a conflict of interest does not serve their clients well. Mr Michael Snyder, senior partner at accountants Kingston Smith indicated that they did not conduct any insolvency work because he believed that it did not sit happily with its work as investigating accountants. He went on to say, 'What is required is a wholly independent review. The investigators appointed [from large firms] are most likely to be insolvency experts with the prospect of a future receivership in their minds'.

However, not surprisingly these claims are vigorously denied by the large firms. Mr Allan Griffiths, a partner with Grant Thornton and Vice President of the Society of Practitioners of Insolvency, said, 'It's a bit hard to stomach people doubting my professional integrity. I get my enjoyment from saving companies, not closing them down'. He also suggested that most of the companies that he is asked to investigate emerge intact with existing management in place and with the creditors none the wiser. He also pointed out that to appoint another firm as receivers would add to the cost as they would have to learn about the business. Word would spread and the value of the remaining assets would drop further. The banks are also divided on the issue. The Royal Bank of Scotland has taken positive steps to control the situation by reducing the number of people that can approve receivership from 300 to three. By this action and deliberately not appointing investigating accountants as receivers it claims to have greatly reduced the number of companies put into receivership.

Adapted from: Jack, A (1994) For what we are about to receive. Financial Times, 24 June, p 18.

perceive that a subordinate is lazy and inefficient. They may react by making life difficult for that individual as an encouragement to leave. This would inevitably create a conflictual and antagonistic relationship between them.

- Work manipulation. It is not unknown for new work procedures to be followed to the letter by those onto whom they have been forced, even though they recognize that problems will occur. The intention being to exact a measure of revenge on the managers concerned.
- Misuse of resources. The appropriating of resources for personal use can be rationalized by individuals on the basis of correcting a perceived injustice and by so doing reduce the possibility of conflict. Many organizations now consider such theft as a major cost and attempt to clamp down on it. The procedures involved have included random searches of people and property, which can create new opportunities for conflict to emerge!
- Choice. Virtually limitless opportunities for choice exists within an organization. Promotion; access to career development opportunities; pay increases; interesting work; the giving or withholding or friendship; co-operation and assistance are just some of the more obvious. For example, to fall out with a boss may result in open conflict over duties, or it may result in certain opportunities not being made available. Discrimination in all its forms falls clearly into this type of behaviour.
- Politicking and power. There is an ability to experience conflict through power and political behaviour. For example, the personal conflict between two managers could lead to an attempt by one to undermine the position and authority of the other through political activity.
- Rumour and gossip. This can be regarded as a milder form of political behaviour and power. That is not to suggest that rumour and gossip in themselves are mild. There are occasions when they form very powerful and damaging weapons in their own right. The creating and spreading of rumours about someone with whom one is in conflict can represent effective ways of undermining their position and credibility. Management in Action 18.3 overleaf describes the impact of one such situation.
- Attitude. It is possible to identify how attitudes can be influenced by conflict and indeed vice versa. Individuals who experience conflict and for whom it is not effectively resolved retain a sense of grievance and hostility towards the other party. In that context attitudes towards and about that person are formed.
- Absence and leaving. In extreme instances conflict can result in one or more party withdrawing from the situation. This can result in absenteeism or in leaving the company, as was the case in Management in Action 18.3.

Group

Some of the forms of conflict identified under the *individual* classification can also find expression at the *group* level. The major forms of group conflict include:

- Strikes and lock-outs. The withdrawal of labour by employees or the prevention of work activity by management are two sides of the same coin. During a collective dispute between managers and trade unions the final lever that either party hold is to restrict the activities of the other. If all employees go on *strike* they effectively prevent management from running

Getting rid of the boss

This event was described to me by the personnel director of the organization concerned. It is a real story and only the names and incidental details have been changed.

There was one small department within a large company that dealt with a single product for a particular market. This department was for all practical purposes independent of other activities within the company. Over the years it had gained the reputation for being a problem area, containing difficult staff, and ineffective management. The standard of service was continually slipping downwards. Eventually the manager was moved sideways and replaced by one of the staff, who up to that point had enjoyed a good reputation for attempting to do things correctly.

Unfortunately this action created a number of additional and unforeseen problems within the department. The previous boss resented being moved to another job. The staff began to see that change was about to be forced upon them and began to side with the old boss. The new manager was not experienced, neither did he receive any training. Senior managers did not make any obvious attempt to ensure that everyone would take the new situation seriously. The result was an escalating cycle of resentment, frustration, a sense of grievance and unresolved conflict at a personal and job level.

Eventually, rumours began to spread about the new boss and staff would not talk to directly the individual. In short life became difficult, a hostile (bad) atmosphere developed and work began to suffer even more. After some time anonymous letters were sent to senior managers purporting to demonstrate the wild excesses in behaviour and general lack of ability of the boss. Investigations failed to reveal the source of these letters, but the situation continued to deteriorate. Eventually after about one year the boss asked to be moved to another job and this was done. After another three months the boss resigned and left the company altogether.

A new boss was recruited from outside of the organization but he was not given the resources necessary to change the situation. Things did not deteriorate much further, but neither did they get any better. The department did not develop the full potential of its product and market and was eventually closed down.

the business. If managers *lock out* the workers they prevent them from earning any wages. The intention of both courses of action is to force one side to concede to the demands of the other, or at least to negotiate further to find an acceptable compromise.

■ Work-to-rule. The loss of income is significant even if it is only for a brief period. It is clearly more effective to attempt to find ways of putting pressure on an employer without the consequent loss of income. One way of achieving this is through the notion of a work-to-rule. The rationale of such a course of action is that managers inevitably encourage employees to go *beyond the contract* in work activities. Although extending the contract is claimed to be a feature that distinguishes human resource management from personnel management (Legge, 1995), it has a long history in practice. If it were not so then the practice of working-to-rule would not have carried any impact. To go beyond the contract is an attempt to obtain more value for money from the labour resource it represents an attempt to exploit. However, given the complexity of organizational activity it is impossible to specify in detail every element of the work relationship with its rights and responsibilities.

Even unskilled workers hold the power to frustrate the efficiency and profitability of the organization by failing to co-operate actively in the work process. The required level of co-operation needs to go beyond mere compliance with rules if work is to be performed efficiently. Indeed, a common form of worker insubordination is 'working to rules', whereby employees are able to undermine the manufacturing process or quality or service provided merely by doing exactly and precisely as they are required (rather than exercising a level of discretion not covered by the rules). Essentially, then, management want workers to follow the spirit, not the letter of the rules (Blyton and Turnbull, 1994, p 31).

It is interesting to contemplate why it is that organizations are making themselves increasingly vulnerable to this form of action through delayering and empowering employees. Clearly the greater responsibility that is delegated to employees the greater the risk of susceptibility to action of this type should conflict erupt. This is perhaps why many organizations seek to adopt what have been described as progressive personnel policies in an attempt to reduce (through socialization and association) divergence of attitude between managers and workers. It is a trend that parallels the diminution in the power to influence events of the trade union movement since the late 1970s as a result in political and economic forces.

- Work restriction. Groups are capable of determining the level of effort that they are prepared to invest on the employers behalf. A frustrated group of employees who feel some sense of grievance with an employer are not likely to perform at their best.
- Factionalism. There are a wide range of means by which groups can affect some degree of expression of conflictual relationships with other groups. The circumstances that gave birth to the British tradition of trade unions being occupationally based also gave rise to strategies that attempted to protect the interests of those groups against the interests of others. This created a number of opportunities to display factional behaviour including demarcation disputes between unions and employers and membership disputes between unions.

Conflict: the consequences

There are a number of consequences that arise from the existence of conflict. The potential for conflict between individuals and groups in the work context produces a situation in which co-operation cannot be taken for granted. Everyone within the organization must work on the quality of relationships or conflict is likely to arise. That is not to suggest that conflict can be eliminated completely. There will always be individuals who do not get along at a personal level. Equally, the motivations that cause one group to act in a particular way are subject to different perceptions and interpretations by another. However, to minimize conflict (assuming that represents a desirable state) is something that requires positive action rather than passivity.

Conflict is a concept that can be argued to be either a negative or positive force. Interpreted as a negative force and therefore something to be driven out (or at least minimized) conflict is regarded as something that disrupts effective operation. If it follows, the employees can be persuaded, or forced to see things as managers do then the conflict would disappear. As a positive force, it can be described as a means of challenging the *status quo* and of forcing all parties within an organization to seek the most effective compromises in pursuit of objectives.

Another viewpoint suggests that conflict represents a force that can either be negative or positive depending upon the circumstances. Too much or too little conflict is harmful. However, just the right amount of conflict can actually aid in optimizing performance. This view is represented in Figure 18.4.

Essentially in this view conflict is being defined as a pressurizing force. Using the analogy of a domestic water pipe, too little pressure in the system and no water will come out of the tap. Too much pressure and the pipe is likely to burst. Just the right mount of pressure is needed in order to make the system function effectively as intended.

Conflict in this model is regarded as a force that can be harnessed to ensure that *slackness* is kept out of the workings of the organization. For example, if management cannot take for granted the loyalty and commitment of employees they will find it necessary to ensure that they keep in touch with the thinking and aspirations of the workers. In so doing a continual reassessment of the working relationship will be undertaken and the potential for major conflict minimized.

With no conflict in existence a form of amnesia would result. People and groups would begin to act as if they were operating on *automatic pilot*, simply going through the motions of work without thinking about them. In this view such a organization would become *slack and desensitized* to the activities going on around it. Equally, at the other extreme excessive conflict, for example a protracted labour stoppage, would bring the organization to a standstill and thereby reduce performance to zero.

In practice there are a number of consequences of conflict within an organization. They range from the harmful to the beneficial. Not all would be active in every situation. They include the items identified in Figure 18.5.

Most of the consequences identified in Figure 18.5 are self-explanatory, but some need further elaboration. Items such as stress, high labour turnover and difficult relationships can easily be understood as a direct consequence of conflict. However, items such as training and involvement should be considered further:

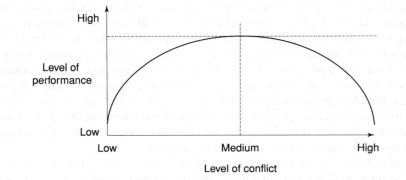

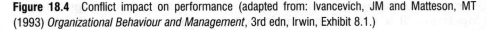

Figure 18.4 Conflict impact on performance (adapted from: Ivancevich, JM and Matteson, MT (1993) *Organizational Behaviour and Management*, 3rd edn, Irwin, Exhibit 8.1.)

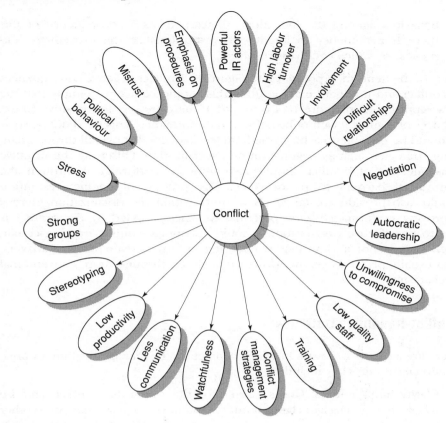

Figure 18.5 Some consequences of conflict.

■ Training. Where conflict is a real possibility training and other *exposure* activities can be effective means of exploring and resolving the difficulties. Training can therefore emerge as a direct consequence of the perceived conflict.

■ Autocratic leadership. There is a view that conflict represents an unwillingness to compromise and a direct challenge to authority. Therefore one consequence could be to become autocratic in management style, thereby eliminating the opportunity and desire to compromise. This view can be based on the assumption that conflict emerges as a result of perceived weakness and willingness to compromise under pressure. Making the leadership position clear and strong eliminates conflict as subordinates recognize that it is pointless. The counter argument is that such approaches *bottle up* resentments that find expression at some point in time.

■ Low quality staff. There are organizations who have a reputation for autocratic management and conflictual working relationships. Consequently in a local labour market potential employees tend to regard such employers as a last resort and only remain until something better comes along.

■ Less communication. When people are in conflict the level and quality of communication drops. This can be seen in any industrial dispute. There are also consequences such as the emergence of strong groups and political behaviour among the individuals concerned. As a consequence of this there is a tendency to attempt to institutionalize the procedures and process by which conflict is resolved.

Many of the items incorporated into Figure 18.5 reflect negative consequences of conflict and it might be argued that this should be taken to imply that the view represented in Figure 18.4 is invalid. If there are very few positive consequences of conflict it cannot be helpful to performance. This need not be so as it should be possible to achieve medium levels of conflict overall through handling strategies such as negotiation and socialization. Offsetting the negative consequences of conflict should also improve performance through the removal of barriers to performance. The process of conflict resolution should also provide greater levels of unity within the organization thereby improving performance. One potential weakness implied by Figure 18.4 is that to be effective organizations should encourage conflict up to a certain level. This is not a view that would sit comfortably with many managers, who usually prefer to see performance achieved through more conventional mechanisms.

Conflict-handling strategies

There are a number of ways in which conflict can be managed within an organizational setting. They include:

■ Clarity and openness. This is based upon the notion that conflict can arise where there is a lack of clarity about the intentions of management or other people. For example, when managers suddenly spend considerable amounts of time away on business and groups of visitors are shown around the facilities it is only natural that doubts about the future of the company will emerge. A commitment to ensure a clarity and openness within the organization can go some considerable way to provide a climate of trust which in turn minimizes the possibility for misunderstandings and conflict.

■ Signals. The signals that managers and other individuals within the organization give also contribute to the likelihood of conflict breaking out. For example, if managers only speak to employees when there is a real threat of industrial action taking place, then they are sending out a clear signal of how they deal with workers. It becomes apparent that the only way to attract the attention of management is to threaten to take industrial action. Appropriate signals can be used to encourage different behaviour patterns. For example, it would be possible to encourage openness and discussion by involving employees on a regular basis. This would also signal that it was not necessary to threaten conflict in order to gain attention.

■ Training and socialization. The development of training courses can help to reinforce a management perspective. For example, a training course on customer care is a signal that managers are interested in customers, as well as providing an opportunity to explain why managers adopt those views and thereby providing staff with an opportunity to internalize those same views. This provides an opportunity to be *socialized* into particular behaviour patterns and beliefs as defined by management, thereby reducing the potential for conflict.

Employees are selected for training and for promotion or career development. Employees who display inappropriate behaviours are less likely to be allowed to develop or gain access to training. Consequently development depends upon delivering appropriate behaviours and generally meeting management expectations. Part of this involves not engaging in behaviours that would be classed as undesirable, including conflict.

■ Style and structure. Autocratic managers with dictatorial styles are more likely to create resentment and hostility. Employees inevitably seek the means to deal with this and collective action may be the result. The structure of an organization can also encourage conflict if there are unclear boundaries between job and decision-making responsibilities. For example, if it is not clear that the sales department must agree any urgent delivery orders with the production department before they are confirmed then a basis for conflict exists.

■ Procedure. There are many different forms of procedural mechanism that can be utilized to either prevent conflict from arising or to minimize its potential for disruption and negative effect. Among the more common procedural devices used are:

  – Operating policy and procedures. Every organization requires policy and procedural frameworks to guide its functioning. The purpose being to provide clarity of operational responsibility, prevent duplication of effort and to establish *ground rules* for activity. In many large, complex organizations such policies and procedures would be committed to writing in the form of procedures manuals. However, in smaller companies they may be more informal and reflected in the organization structure, job descriptions and the normal ways of carrying out the work required.

  – Communication and consultation procedures. Conflict can arise through a lack of knowledge or the misunderstanding of the actions and intentions of others. Communication and consultation between the various groups that exist within an organization should facilitate an improved level of understanding and knowledge which in turn should reduce the prospect of conflict.

  – Decision-making practices. The processes adopted with regard to decision making can also be used to reduce the opportunity for conflict and assist with its resolution. For example, a department that is involved in a decision will have little scope for subsequently engaging in conflictual behaviour with regard to the outcome. Of course this point of view assumes that the decision-making process is both rational and fair. In most organizational decision-making situations there is a degree of power and political behaviour present and if not kept in check these in themselves can create scope for parties feeling aggrieved and conflict arising.

  – Negotiation. This was a topic covered in detail in Chapter 8 (along with decision making). Negotiation provides a process by which individuals and groups can directly resolve their differences. It is a process of reaching an accommodation that is acceptable to all parties to the process. However, it assumes that all parties are prepared to negotiate and reach a compromise which although less than ideal would be acceptable.

  – Discipline and grievance procedures. Torrington and Hall (1991) introduce the notion of *organizational justice* in relation to discipline and grievance procedures (p 542). The employment contract determines the duties and responsibilities to which both employer and employee commit themselves during the employment relationship. The discipline and grievance procedures are the vehicles through which both parties have the opportunity to ensure satisfaction with the execution of the contract. For example, if an employee arrives late for work the employer is not receiving the input of time required by the contract. One way to redress this conflict is through the application of the disciplinary procedure by management. Equally, if an employee feels that they are being discriminated against by a manager (perhaps not being given an opportunity to work overtime) they have the grievance procedure to seek redress for this conflict.

– Industrial relations procedures. One definition of industrial relations is that it, '... is concerned with the formal and informal relationships which exist between employers and trade unions and their members.' (Armstrong, 1991, p 667). In the same source, p 665 indicates that, 'The primary aims of [industrial relations] policies and procedures are to improve co-operation, to minimize unnecessary conflict, to enable employees to play an appropriate part in decision making, and to keep them informed on matters that concern them'.

Disputes between employers and trade unions are a major reflection of the existence of a state of conflict within an organization. However, to retain an ability to continue operations and earnings levels both parties need to achieve a workable compromise. It is in this area that the process of negotiation plays a part. However, if it is not possible to achieve a resolution of the conflict through direct negotiation there is the opportunity to invoke the services of the Advisory, Conciliation and Arbitration Service (ACAS) who have at their disposal specialists in dealing with conflict situations. The aim of ACAS is to assist the parties to find solutions to what are very often intractable and deep rooted conflictual situations.

The above strategies provide an indication of the devices that are available through which to manage conflict but not how to respond to it in behavioural terms. Thomas (1976) identified five generic conflict-handling styles based upon the balance between two dimensions of the need to satisfy the concerns of the *self*, 'self-assertion' and the *other party*, 'co-operation' involved. This model is reflected in Figure 18.6.

The five conflict-handling styles identified in Figure 18.6 are:

■ Smoothing or accommodating. This approach reflects a style that would allow the other party to achieve what they desire from the situation. It is an attempt to maintain unity and harmony though subjugating one's own wishes. This could be as a consequence of indifference towards any needs other than those of the other party. It could also reflect a degree of fear of the consequences of failing to allow the other party to have their way.

■ Avoidance. This style reflects a minimalist approach to the situation. It constitutes a desire to ignore the problem and hope that it will go away. Common responses include ignoring the problem, evading specific attempts to deal with it and elongating any procedural devices invoked

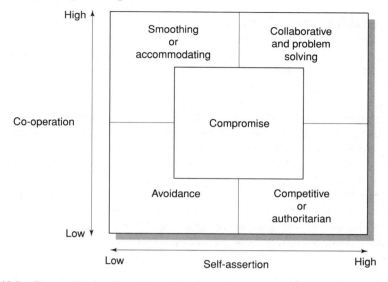

Figure 18.6 Five conflict handling styles (based on: Thomas, K (1976) Conflict management. In *Handbook of Industrial and Organizational Psychology* (ed MD Dunnette), Rand McNally.)

to deal with it. This is the active avoidance of any open confrontation or hostility.

■ Collaboration and problem solving. This approach represents the *maximize* approach to conflict situations. It reflects the *win–win* approach to negotiation and problem solving (Fisher and Ury, 1986). This style gives equal recognition to the need to resolve conflict through meeting the objectives and desires of both parties if a lasting settlement is to be achieved. Leaving one party disadvantaged is a recipe for future conflict. That is not to say that every party can expect to achieve everything desired as a result of conflict resolution.

■ Competitive or authoritarian. This style reflects the *win-at-all-costs* approach to conflict resolution. It contains no consideration of the other parties' interests in the situation and simply concentrates on the desires of the *self* in the process. In negotiation terms it represents the view that anything conceded is something lost.

■ Compromise. This is the search for the *acceptable*. It represents the *satisficing* approach to conflict resolution. It is the search for the acceptable middle ground between two points of view so that no one completely wins or loses.

The style adopted in a particular conflict situation will be a reflection of a number of forces. The preferences of the individuals will play a part. Prior experience will also create a tendency towards a particular style. For example, a trade union which has encountered an aggressive manager during previous negotiations is more likely to begin by using that style in future. In an emergency situation, where little time is available to seek mutually acceptable solutions, it is more likely that a directive/authoritarian style would be adopted.

Control within organizations

There are many definitions of control. One of the simplest is that provided by Dunford (1992), in which it is described as a process which, '... involves attempts to bring about desired outcomes' (p 243). Within an organization there are two distinct and opposite aspects to the existence of control. Firstly, it provides the basis of order and predictability in operational activity. Processes need to be *under control* if the product or service is to be delivered consistently to the customer with acceptable quality and at a realistic price. This is the view of control which defines the responsibilities of senior managers described in Management in Action 18.4.

Opposing that perspective is the view that control is restrictive, lacks flexibility, is manipulative and greedy with regard to the abolition of personal freedom. It could be argued that many initiatives on employee involvement and participative management are covert attempts to find ways of retaining control within an illusion of freedom for the individual. These initiatives are frequent-

---

Management in Action 18.4

Tightening the reins on risk

The collapse of Barings Bank resulting from the actions of one trader in an office on the other side of the world which brought down the whole group is every manager's nightmare. It was an event which forced the issue of control and risk assessment to the forefront of management thinking. There have been a number of committees that have considered the issue of corporate control and most have suggested (among other things) that its review and development should form part of the board's responsibility on a regular basis. In these days of flatter and leaner organizations it is not uncommon to find managers seeking to effectively replace formal control systems with 'appropriate' and 'responsible' forms of employee behaviour.

There are not as many people within organizations these days and inevitably control systems are not regarded as 'added value' activities and so can be regarded as a potential source of saving. It is sometimes argued that if employees and managers had the 'right' values and attitudes (whatever they may be) then they would effectively self-control. For example, some surveys have shown that the morale of managers could have a material impact on the level of fraud within a company. If

this 'appropriate behaviour' could be achieved and assuming that the form of self-control was in alignment with what management wanted, then the need for formal control systems would be eliminated, or at least severely reduced. However, a number of people argue that this is not practical or viable as a basis of protecting the organization from fraud or simple bad decision making. Sensible control processes are needed which balance the need for employees to be able to apply common sense with the need to protect the business.

Risk assessment is the emerging discipline which specializes in the identification and evaluation of the possible dangers that exist in and around the organization. The application of scenario planning which asks the question, 'what would happen if ...' is the basis of this approach. However, to apply it effectively needs a thorough understanding of the business and its operations. It also needs to be applied across all aspects of the business, not just at the level of, 'what would happen if the electricity supply to the computers was interrupted?' It also requires directors to question what they are told and not just assume that everything is as it appears.

Adapted from: Atkins, R. (1995) Tightening the reins on risk. Financial Times, 22 March, p 12.

ly expressed as an encouragement to go beyond the contract and enjoy a new partnership with managers in developing a mutually prosperous and fulfilling future. The net effect, however, being the exercise of more subtle forms of control intended to minimize the risk of conflict and maximize contribution.

It has been suggested by Huczynski and Buchanan (1991, p 579), that control has three connotations. Firstly, it is necessary as an *economic* activity, critical to the success of the organization. Secondly, it represents a *psychological* necessity in order to eliminate the ambiguity, unpredictability and disorder that would prevent individuals from operating effectively within the organization. Thirdly, it represents a *political* process in which some individuals and groups are able to exercise control over less fortunate groups. It possible to identify a fourth purpose that control serves in addition to the three identified above: *physical*.

- ■ Physical. At the detailed control level jobs, processes and machines need to be organized and controlled effectively if they are to combine to produce the goods and services required (Edwards, 1986). Frequently the physical level of control involves record keeping, measuring activity and checking actual performance against that intended.

- ■ Economic. As an economic process control is geared towards achieving the financial objectives of the organization. It is not just the detailed control described above. It represents the micro-level co-ordination and planning of activity along with the macro-level directional planning necessary to achieve the financial returns to ensure that investors remain satisfied.

- ■ Psychological. This process represents both the need among individuals to function within a predictable environment and the need that some individuals have to either control or be controlled. In its broadest sense management can be described as a controlling activity. That some individuals seek elevation to these positions can be taken as evidence of their desire to exercise control over resources. There are individuals who for many reasons do not gain promotion within organizations. Some do not have the opportunity, others do not have the confidence or the inclination. Still others perceive promotion as selling out to the owning 'classes' or perhaps they achieve fulfilment through other aspects of their life. Whatever the reason subordinates psychologically accept the right to be controlled by others.

- ■ Political. Control provides the means by which existing structures and social conditions can be reinforced. Owners of capital insist on their pre-eminent right to ultimate determination of organizational existence. If an organization does not make money then the owners, creditors and banks retain the right to liquidate the assets irrespective of the impact on the non-owning stakeholders. That represents the ultimate political control. Of course accountants would argue that an uneconomic business must fail, but this represents the exercise of a particular perspective and the case could be argued otherwise. A different economic picture would emerge if the social costs of closure were to be taken into account, for example.

There are other political perspectives to control. For example, through the exercise of political skill a departmental manager may be able to increase their own significance and importance within an organization, thereby being able to exercise control over a greater range of resources. Management in Action 18.5 illustrates this and other aspects of control.

Thou shalt not cook the books

The finances of English cathedrals provides a fascinating opportunity to study accountancy practice. The Cathedrals Measure of 1963 required the accounts of the 42 Anglican cathedrals to be published each year. However, it provided little guidance on the form that the accounts should take and the Church Commissioners do not examine them in any detail. Most cathedrals operate as charities and need considerable sums of money to maintain them. But as Mr Malcolm Hoskins of Touche Ross suggested, 'like any other charity, if anything the incentive is not to appear too financially healthy'. He should know, he has audited cathedral accounts and serves on a working party set up by the Association of English Cathedrals to identify how to present financial information fairly and consistently.

One member of a commission set up in 1992 by the Archbishop of Canterbury to examine the management of church resources said, 'Cathedral accounting is disgraceful. It's a fascinating aspect of medieval life. They get up to every trick in the book'. He described the use of off-balance sheet finance and concealment in undeclared trusts the true wealth of cathedrals from the church hierarchy. Deans and canons are in an impregnable position in a cathedral as once appointed they become a 'corporation spiritual' and immune to any other earthly power but God. Perhaps, that is, until the controlling power of the accounting profession reaches out and lays its hand on them!

Adapted from: Jack, A (1993) Thou shalt not cook the books. Financial Times, 17 December, p 9.

Control: form and characteristics

Control and organization are inextricably linked. It has been argued (Thompson, 1989) that it was a desire for increased control by owners that formed a significant part of the movement towards the factory system of production in the eighteenth century. Under the *putting-out* system owners could not directly control the activities of workers (Table 18.1) and the development of the factory system was intended to change that situation.

Although the control *levers* indicated in table 18.1 would appear to provide a sound basis for the effective operation of a business this is not so compared with factory-based systems of production. A factory system provided the owners with an opportunity to exercise an immediate *in-process* level of control. For example it became possible to break the manufacturing process down into small parts and to create jobs requiring low skill levels. Lower skill levels are directly associated with cheaper labour and reduced unit labour costs. Equally

Table 18.1	**Allocation**	– the ability to allocate or withhold work.
Control under the 'putting-out' system	**Price**	– the ability to reduce the price paid to workers in order to pressure them into producing more in order to maintain earnings.
	Quality	– the ability to reject (and therefore not pay) for work not of an acceptable standard.
	Machine	– in some instances owners provided workers with the equipment necessary to perform the tasks and so controlled production methods.

the pace and methods of work could be directly controlled in a factory, increasing the output per worker and reducing labour costs.

Very little control takes the overt form of force or pressure. It is usually incorporated into the fabric of the organization, management practice and indeed society. Becoming part of the experience of what would be considered *normal* it is not subjected to question by those to whom it is being applied. If control is defined in terms of the ability to determine the behaviour of others it makes sense to exercise it in such a way that obviates the likelihood of conflict. Creating an acceptance of the normality and necessity for control mechanisms is one way of achieving this. The main forms of organizational control are:

■ Output control. This is based upon the premise that if the output achieved is as predicted, then the *system* is under control. It is the *management-by-exception* process that posits that managers should function on the basis of defining in advance what should occur, provide the resource to deliver that requirement and subsequently manage the deviations from that intention. It is argued that it is a waste of valuable time and resource to monitor and review things that are going according to plan.

■ Process control. This form of control reflects the mirror image of the previous approach in that it relies on monitoring and controlling the *means rather than the ends*. It is premised on the view that it is necessary to control the detail and process aspects of operational activity in order to ensure that the objectives are achieved. It represents the traditional bureaucratic approach to organizational activity. Procedures determine in detail what should be done within the *system* and yet more procedures determine and report on events as they occur.

■ Work design. In terms of the ability to control activity in the workplace the design of jobs is a key determinant. The way that the tasks to be undertaken are clustered together into jobs reflects many facets of organizational life. However, it is also a reflection of the intentions of management in relation to how they view the business and the need to *control* activity in relation to the desired objectives. For example, the specialization of work into such categories as nursing, physiotherapy, hotel services and administration allows high skill levels to be developed across a relatively narrow range of tasks. Thereby productivity can be achieved in a *factory* type of hospital configuration. As such it provides the possibility of tighter control of the overall process and its associated cost.

■ Structure. Much of the work design issues follow from and contribute to the way that the organization is structured. It is the *compartmentalization* of activity that provides the opportunity to control through specialization. It also allows managers to be able to simplify complex activity into meaningful and understandable units. For example, the creation of an accounting department provides the opportunity for the development of efficient, specialized accounting control systems as a consequence of grouping together experts in a particular field. It also provides the more senior managers with the knowledge that accounting issues are the responsibility of that department and that they have (in theory) no bias towards other functions in reporting accounting data. The *compartments* provide a clarity in relating to the complexity of organizational activity, particularly from a *top-*

down perspective. Consider the difficulty of attempting to understand and manage a university if it were not compartmentalized into student records, library, teaching, etc.

■ Hierarchy and authority. The owners of the capital are held to be the people who have the ultimate right to determine what happens within an organization. Much of that right is delegated to the board of directors. In large organizations some form of delegation must be introduced. In practice a power sharing process must be entered into in order to define the relationships between the principle players. As a consequence of these processes a hierarchical arrangement of responsibility and control is introduced into the organization. Individuals explicitly acquiesce to these arrangements when they agree to join the organization. Managers know that they have certain rights to exercise control over their subordinates, again subject to policies and procedures. They are part of a complex web of hierarchy and authority that allows control over activity to be exercised in support of the objectives being sought. This view is reflected in the description of activity in Management in Action 18.6.

Management in Action 18.6

Employers cast as partners in crime

Lorenz reports on an article in the *Harvard Business Review* (March/April, 1994) on the nature of ethical behaviour in organizations. It was titled 'Managing for organizational integrity' and was written by Professor Lynn Sharp Paine from Harvard. In the article she argues that corporate misconduct is not usually the result of individual flaws or problems. Unethical business practice she argues more frequently reflects the values, attitudes, language and behavioural patterns that define an organization's operating culture.

Paine describes a rush towards 'compliance-based ethics programmes' in order to meet the requirements of US legislation. The magnitude of fines for unlawful conduct partly reflect the degree to which companies have tried to prevent such misconduct. The provision of a rule-book, a code of ethics and training is unlikely to be sufficient on it own to prevent such practices according to Paine. She suggests that appropriate behaviour will only be encouraged when organizations take an 'integrity-based' approach to ethics. This approach encourages the development of guiding values, aspirations and patterns of thought which support ethically sound behaviour; in addition a sense of shared accountability between employees is needed.

One example given by Paine which demonstrates the lack of an integrity-based ethics approach is that involving a car service offshoot of Sears Roebuck in America. The company was accused of misleading customers and selling them unnecessary parts and services. Sears' chief executive accepted management's responsibility for the problem as a result of introducing pay and target setting processes which encouraged over-selling.

This is contrasted with the case of Johnson & Johnson in which all levels of the company quickly and automatically withdrew a particular painkiller from the market after batches were found to have been poisoned. Paine suggests that without a shared set of values and the guiding principles that were ingrained throughout the organization the response would not have been the same.

Adapted from: Lorenz, C (1994) Employers cast as partners in crime. Financial Times, 4 March, p 14.

It has long been recognized that the direct exercise of authority is not always the most effective way to achieve the desired result. It can create a *compliance* and *dependence* culture. Being *conditioned* to expect that someone in authority will direct every move can result in individuals failing to exercise discretion and common sense in performing their duties. An employee who continued to produce faulty components knowing them to be sub-standard because they had not been told to stop would serve as an example.

Unless it is a specific requirement then the exercise of direct authority is likely to be resented by subordinates and produce a compliance response (or conflict). It is therefore desirable to avoid the undesirable consequences by softening the application of authority based control. There are many ways of attempting to achieve this, for example the use of training courses allows managers to inculcate employees with the *preferred value and attitude sets*, thereby internalizing the managerial norms that underpin control. Employees consequently become self-regulating. Only if employees show dissent would it be likely that formal authority (direct control) becomes the means of achieving the desired result.

In commercial organizations it is increasingly being claimed that with *every pair of hands recruited comes a free brain*, and that this represents the most valuable of the human assets. To capitalize on this managers need to ensure that individuals are liberated from constraint and prepared to contribute to the maximum of their capability. This was introduced in Chapter 15 as employee involvement. Under such operational situations the direct application of control is likely to be counter-productive. It is hardly surprising that middle managers have not been enthusiastic supporters of employee empowerment as it can be described as undermining their traditional authority base. It is also possible that increased control can be achieved by accident. If employees push for greater involvement and as a consequence become more understanding and amenable to management perspectives, greater managerial influence (control) over events will have been achieved (Fells, 1989).

■ Skill. There are many other jobs in which skill or professional status provides an opportunity to exercise control in one form or another. To *know more* than others in the same context is a basis for acquiring power and exercising control. Only chartered accountants are able to sign the audit of a set of company accounts. This requirement is intended to provide confidence to investors that the accounts are a true and realistic reflection of the financial position of the company.

■ Technology. Machines can work at a predictable and stable pace until they breakdown or are switched off. People are not so programmable. As a consequence of the desire of managers to justify the introduction of technology humans are frequently relegated to second place in consideration. It is the technology that *determines* (controls) the human participation in the production process. The work that humans undertake is determined by what the technology cannot tackle and by what is needed to service the ability of the technology to maintain continuous production. This is very real form of control over human endeavour.

It is not just factory work that has been subjected to the influence of control through technology. Clerical, administrative, technical and managerial

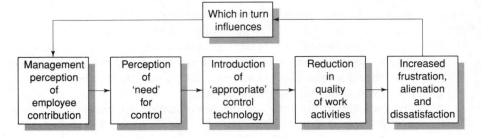

Figure 18.7 Vicious cycle of control (adapted from: Clegg, S and Dunkerley, D (1980) *Organizational Class and Control*, Routledge & Kegan Paul).

work has all been influenced and are therefore subject to different forms of control than previously. For example, in customer service teams it is common to find that the technology providing improved ability to serve the customer also provides the opportunity to more effectively manage the performance of staff. Telephone calls are recorded for subsequent analysis, call rates and queue waiting statistics are automatically generated.

■ Social control. There are many forms of social control, including those institutions provided by the state, the police, law and other government agencies being some of the examples. In addition, and of particular relevance to an organizational setting are institutions such as the education system which is intended to prepare children and young people for the world of work. Within an organization there are the induction, training, development, performance appraisal, pay, promotion and career development activities which all provide a basis for shaping behaviour patterns in one way or another.

Clegg and Dunkerley (1980) describe the impact of control as provoking a vicious circle reinforcing the need for ever tighter means of control. This arises as a consequence of the continually constricting influence of control on employees and of their reaction in terms of increased dissatisfaction thereby reinforcing the perception of managers and creating the need for more direct control. Figure 18.7 reflects the essence of their model.

It is the danger of creating the downward spiral of ever tighter control leading to less real contribution from employees that leads to organizations attempting to introduce involvement strategies. The hope being that involved employees would internalize the need for the control being sought by managers and so respond positively.

Conflict and control: a management perspective

It has been argued (Braverman, 1974) that the organizational history of the twentieth century can be described in terms of increasing management control and the potential for conflict and alienation that flows from it. This neatly encapsulates the fundamental dilemma that exists from a management perspective. The scale of international business, the level of competition, the differential costs of operations around the world and many other forces all create conditions in which there is continual pressure for improved organizational performance. Inevitably this dynamic leads managers to seek ever greater levels of control over every aspect of the enterprise in order to achieve greater value for money from it. Braverman makes it clear that the price for this increased control is that employees experience greater levels of alienation. They are increasingly treated as just one of the resources available to managers and consequently subject to manipulation.

For managers control contains different connotations depending upon such factors as the seniority and job function of the individual. For example, a chief executive should not be concerned with control over the purchase of pens. They should, however, assure themselves that someone is exercising control over the purchase and use of consumables. A production supervisor would be expected to exercise detailed control over day-to-day production activities. They would not be expected to opine on the strategic direction of the business, that would be regarded the preserve of senior managers. Control in an organization is a fragmented function, distributed across the members according to level and function. This could be taken to imply a rational and planned process, determined by some all-seeing and omnipotent senior manager applying appropriate models to achieve effective control. Indeed such models do exist; Figure 18.8 is representative of this view, based upon Dent and Ezzamel (1995).

However, even within models such as included as Figure 18.8 there is limited recognition of the realities of organizational life. The data essential for control purposes is not always available, accurate or available at the appropriate time. The style of management and decision making are also variables that influence control activities. In addition there are the power and political processes that operate which can influence not only the control processes but the interpretation of the data emerging from them. Like all aspects of management the design of control systems and the exercising of the consequences of the information provided from them are social processes. Management in Action 18.7 overleaf describes one such situation in which there were a number of forces, not all rational, acting upon a particular situation.

There are different views about the impact of the existence of conflict within an organization. The response to the existence of real or potential conflict

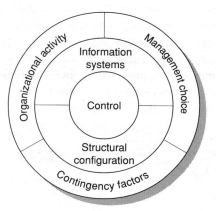

Figure 18.8 The organizational control 'onion' (adapted from: Dent, J and Ezzamel, M (1995) Organizational control and management activity. In *Performance Measurement and Evaluation* (eds J Holloway *et al.*), Sage).

Management in Action 18.7

Controlling the invisible

This story describes real events that occurred only the names and location have been changed to protect the individuals concerned. The process involved the butchery of pig carcasses into pork joints and for curing as bacon. The management accountant was responsible for the determination of product costing and required a full breakdown of material and labour data for each process. The work study department were tasked with the job of obtaining and collating the wide variety of data needed for this. A number of studies were undertaken to determine the time taken to perform the work and product weight was checked at each stage of the process. The data collection phase of this exercise lasted for several weeks.

The data was collated and among the various findings was the rather surprising one that each carcass lost weight at each stage of the butchery process. Each carcass was weighed before each process and all processed meat was also weighed (including the small trimmings, bones, etc.). There was always a slight difference between the after processed weight and the original weight. When this was first discovered it was thought to be due to careless weighing. Considerable effort was made to tighten up on the weighing process and this was eventually discounted. An invisible loss as it became known had been identified. Everyone on the project team was satisfied that this loss (of about 4% of total weight on average) was probably due to moisture leaching out as the meat was being cut. This was included in the findings presented to the management accountant.

The accountant was not happy with the idea of having something that could not be properly accounted for and even worse with no physical evidence to see. This went against every belief and professional training for the accountants and he refused to accept the work as the basis of costing product. Something had to be wrong,

meat just did not become invisible. Of course the fact that meat is a valuable commodity and the temptation to steal it is an ever-present risk in the trade was another factor in the thinking of the accountant. He was being asked to price the company product on the basis that some 4% was disappearing. Over a full year that represented a considerable volume and value of meat. The accountant created a scene within the senior management of the company and demanded that the data be rejected and more tests be done. He even refused to believe the evidence of his own eyes when he was present at a demonstration of the effect.

Clearly there was a problem associated with the ability to control the processing of meat within this factory that needed to be addressed. It was at this stage that the politics and relative power of the key players began to influence events. The management accountant was not popular as an individual and had upset the production director in the past. He was considered to be pedantic, rude, unhelpful and not part of the senior management team, and that was on a good day! The finance director was a quiet individual who did not have high levels of charisma or other natural or status sources of power and influence. So the stage was set for a battle of who would win the argument about the invisible loss. The accountants had a natural advantage in this situation as they had to satisfy the board of directors that the company was being well run. They also determined the product costing upon which sales prices and production costs depended. But the management accountant was in a difficult political position as he had alienated the key players from the operational functions and did not have strong support from his own superior.

After considerable lobbying by all concerned and discussion with various other organizations in the meat industry the management accountant was overruled and the invisible loss became a feature of the costing process.

would depend in part on the view about its role within the organization. Against this backdrop much management activity over the past few years has been an attempt to reframe organizational reality for employees so that effective (and tighter) control can be exercised but in ways that minimize the risk and consequences of conflict.

Drawing on the earlier work of Edwards (1986), Blyton and Turnbull (1994) identify the major problem for employers in relation to the *wage–work* bargain with employees. It is the last vestige of the ability of employees to resist the attempts of employers to exercise absolute control and to be able to adjust the level of effort expended in the service of the master. The extended tea break, pace and diligence of work are some of the variables at the disposal of the employee in demonstrating independence from total subjugation to the will of another. Recent managerial approaches can be categorized as attempts to delegate control in such a way as to provide the illusion of independence and encourage self-control. Torrington and Hall (1991) use a hierarchical model of discipline in an organizational context to describe the level of responsibility for ensuring appropriate behaviour, Figure 18.9.

There are many implications that emerge from considering the nature of discipline as described in Figure 18.9. Defined in terms of behaving in expected ways, discipline can be seen as a means of control. Management discipline is behaviour control achieved thorough a superior, team discipline is achieved through group norms and influence and self-discipline is achieved through accepting and internalizing the desired behaviours. At the self-discipline level of the hierarchy very little management effort is required as employees effectively *police* themselves by delivering that which is expected of them automatically. If this level of the hierarchy can be achieved then the benefits to managers in terms of the reduced cost of management, an improved performance from employees and reduced levels of conflict are considerable. From this perspective it is hardly surprising that managers have made considerable efforts to ensnare employees into adopting self-managed practices across a wide range of facets of employment. It also leads to the accusation of deceit and manipulation by those who interpret such events as a cynical attempt to take advantage of employees in the pursuit of higher profit levels.

Figure 18.9 The discipline hierarchy (adapted from: Torrington, D and Hall, L (1991) *Personnel Management: A New Approach*. 2nd edn, Prentice-Hall, Figure 30.1).

Conclusions

This chapter has attempted to consider the related topics of conflict and control. These subjects have strong links with negotiation, power and politics which were introduced in previous chapters. Both conflict and control can be argued to be endemic to organizational life. They are necessary in that control is needed to ensure that objectives are met. However, as with most other aspects of organizational behaviour they contain the seeds of danger and risk that can cause damage to either individuals or the organization if they are not handled carefully and with respect.

Discussion questions

1 Define the following key terms used in this chapter:

Conflict	Wage–work bargain
Control	Conflict handling styles
Organizational justice	Vicious cycle of control
Compliance culture	Socialization
Sources of conflict	Sources of control
Forms of Control	Forms of Conflict

2 What are the major forms of conflict that might be expected to arise in a group context? How do these differ from the individual expressions of conflict?
3 Can compliance as an employee response to employment ever form a basis for the creation of an effective organization? Justify your answer.
4 'Control does not exist in reality. Ultimately everyone is subject to some form of control by others. Consequently it is a device that provides an illusion of order and structure.' Discuss.
5 Describe the various sources of conflict that exist within an organizational context. To what extent can any of them be eliminated?
6 'The trick in management is to find ways of control that are socially acceptable.' Discuss.
7 Identify and provide an analysis of the procedural devices that can be used to minimize and resolve conflict within an organization.
8 'Conflict management represents the biggest challenge for every manager.' To what extent and why do you agree with this statement?
9 Identify the different forms that control can take within an organization. Evaluate each in terms of the value to management as a means of improving organizational performance.
10 'Participation is nothing more than the worst type of confidence trick, played on people who have no opportunity to resist by those who have everything to gain.' Discuss this statement.

Research questions

1 Examine the national press, magazines and journals for as much information as you can find on a particular industrial dispute. Put together an

analysis of the situation in terms of the material presented in this chapter and the previous one (Power and Politics). In your analysis specifically consider how the dispute arose and developed; could it have been resolved earlier and why was it not handled in that way; who stood to gain most from the situation being handled in the way that it was and why; how have events developed since the dispute was resolved?

2 Seek to interview a cross-section of practising managers and trade union officers about the subject of conflict and control. How do these groups see the concepts and issues differently and what divergence of opinion is there within each group. Attempt to explain these differences in terms of the material covered in this chapter.

3 Identify a range of journals and books from disciplines that might be expected to have some views about conflict and control. These might include management, sociology, psychology, criminology, politics, military studies and law. How do each of these disciplines treat these concepts and what are the differences and similarities between them? What organizational and managerial implications exist from the range of views identified?

Key reading

From Clark, H, Chandler, J and Barry, J (1994) *Organization and Identities: Text and Readings in Organizational Behaviour*, International Thomson Business Press, London.

- Kanter RM: Men and women of the corporation, p 152. This considers issues associated with experience within an organization that contain both conflict and control.
- Nichols T and Beynon H: The labour of superintendence: managers, p 192. Considers how the social construction of working relationships and the attitudes taken by members of the hierarchy influences the freedom to act.
- Cockburn C: Male dominance and technological change, p 197. This extract considers how male dominance can be reaffirmed through the application of technology.
- Illich I: Disabling professions, p 207. Reflects on control associated with the existence of professional groups.
- Thompson EP: Time and work – discipline, p 216. Considers the nature of time and its ability to control much human experience of work.
- Taylor FW: Scientific management, p 231. Introduces some of Taylor's ideas on the way that work should be organized and controlled.
- Roethlisberger FJ and Dickson WJ: Group restriction of output, p 247. This identifies the way that employees manipulated events in an attempt to ensure that they were not at the whim of management.
- Hobsbawm EJ and Rudé G: Early forms of worker resistance – swing riots, p 317. This extract demonstrates that those subjected to direct forms of control are liable to resist if they feel that they have nothing to lose.
- Taylor L and Walton P: Industrial sabotage, p 321. This provides another example of employee reaction to strong control.
- Hyman R: The power of collective action, p 322. Reflects on the role and value of collective action as a means of resolving conflict.
- Höpfl H *et al.*: Excessive commitment and excessive resentment: issues of identity, p 373. This attempts to reflect on how the concept of commitment was used by one very large organization as a means of introducing change across a wide range of work aspects.
- Braverman H: The degradation of work, p 385. This considers the effects of control and conflict on individuals through the emergence of degradation.
- Marx K: Alienated labour, p 387. Introduces some of Marx's views on alienation and its roots in the capitalist nature of work.

■ Fromm E: Alienation, p 391. This introduces another perspective on how work is managed. Implicit are the notions of control and conflict underpinning much management practice.

■ Wright Mills C: The cheerful robot, p 396. This material considers the concept of freedom of the individual in the context of the needs of organization.

Further reading

Adams, A (1992) *Bullying At Work: How to Confront and Overcome It*, Virago, London. This review of the experiences of individuals at work being bullied provides an insight into the darker side of control. The book is written as a guide to the subject and also offers some advice on how to deal with the subject of being bullied at work.

Caws, P ed (1989) *The Causes of Quarrel: Essays on Peace, War, and Thomas Hobbes*, Beacon Press, Boston, MA. This book provides a philosophical and political review of many aspects associated with conflict and control in an international context. Although not directly intended as an organizational text, it does incorporate a wide range of parallels.

Edelmann, RJ (1993) *Interpersonal Conflicts at Work*, British Psychological Society, Leicester. This small book is intended to help the reader to understand the causes of a range of interpersonal conflicts that can arise in a work setting and to be able to develop strategies to cope with them more effectively.

Gunn, C (1992) *Nightmare on Lime Street: Whatever Happened to Lloyd's of London*, Smith Gryphon, London. This book is based in the world of the insurance market. In describing and analysing the events surrounding three years of disastrous losses for the investors of Lloyds it becomes clear that there are many issues associated with conflict and control.

Kolb, DM and Bartunek, JM eds (1992) *Hidden Conflict in Organizations: Uncovering Behind-the-Scenes Disputes*, Sage, Newbury Park, CA. This book provides an insight into a wide range of dispute and conflict situations that are not at first glance formally part of organizational life. The book surfaces many otherwise hidden or cloaked features of conflict and its resolution.

Pascale, RT (1991) *Managing on the Edge: How Successful Companies Use Conflict to Stay Ahead*, Penguin, London. This book takes the view that conflict is an aspect of human behaviour which is to be welcomed within an organizational setting. It encourages a healthy tension between the individuals and functional groupings which can be used to the benefit of the business through the synergy generated.

References

Adams, A (1992) *Bullying At Work: How to Confront and Overcome It*, Virago, London.

Armstrong, M (1991) *A Handbook of Personnel Management Practice*, 4th edn, Kogan Page, London.

Blyton, P and Turnbull, P (1994) *The Dynamics of Employee Relations*, Macmillan, Basingstoke.

Braverman, H (1974) *Labour and Monopoly Capital: The Degradation of Work in the Twentieth Century*, Monthly Review Press, New York.

Clegg, S and Dunkerley, D (1980) *Organization, Class and Control*, Routledge & Kegan Paul, London.

Dent, J and Ezzamel, M (1995) Organization control and management activity. In *Performance Measurement and Evaluation* (eds J Holloway, J Lewis and G Mallory), Sage, London.

Dunford, RW (1992) *Organizational Behaviour: An Organizational Analysis Perspective*, Addison-Wesley, Sydney.

Edwards, PK (1986) *Conflict at Work: A Materialist Analysis of Workplace Relations*, Basil Blackwell, Oxford.

Fells, RE (1989) The employment relationship, control and strategic choice in the study of industrial relations. *Labour and Industry*, **2**, 470–92.

Fisher, R and Ury, W (1986) *Getting to Yes: Negotiating Agreement Without Giving In*, Penguin, New York.

Fox, A (1966) Industrial sociology and industrial relations, Royal Commission Research Paper, Number 3, HMSO, London.

Huczynski, AA and Buchanan, DA (1991) *Organizational Behaviour: An Introductory Text*, 2nd edn, Prentice-Hall, Hemel Hempstead.

Legge, K (1995) *HRM, Rhetorics and Reality*, Macmillan, London.

Thomas, K (1976) Conflict management. In *Handbook of Industrial and Organizational Psychology* (ed MD Dunnette), Rand McNally.

Thompson, EP (1989) *The Nature of Work: An Introduction to Debates on the Labour Process*, 2nd edn, Macmillan, Basingstoke.

Torrington, D and Hall, L (1991) *Personnel Management: a New Approach*, 2nd edn, Prentice-Hall, Hemel Hempstead.

Whetten, DA and Cameron, KS (1991) *Developing Management Skills*, 2nd edn, Harper-Collins, New York.

19

Managing change

```
▣▣ browse this web site ▣▣
www.itbp.com
```

Chapter summary

This chapter will consider the nature and impact of change on organizations and the people that are employed within them. The chapter will introduce some of the forms that resistance to change can take, as well as some of the reasons for it. This will be followed by a consideration of the major approaches to the management of change and the role of innovation as a coping and accommodating strategy. The chapter will conclude with a consideration of change from a management perspective.

Learning objectives

After studying this chapter and working through the associated Management in Action panels, discussion questions and research activities, you should be able to:

- Understand the range of forces that impact on an organization and which can require change to be made.
- Describe the organizational development approach to change management.
- Explain the difference between and significance of planned and unplanned change.
- Outline the association and implication between politics, power and change.
- Assess the value of managing innovation as part of a change strategy.
- Appreciate why people frequently resist change.
- Discuss the mechanisms through which managers attempt to control change.
- Detail the contingency and systems approaches to change management.

Introduction

The world in which we live is changing, as are the organizations and the work within them. The world has always changed and people, plants and animals have evolved and adapted to new circumstances. Failure to adapt effectively has been punished very severely – by the death or demise of the individual or species. However, the rate of change that is being experienced now is much greater than ever before. To demonstrate the rate of change together with some of the ways in which it can influence the working environment Table 19.1 has been extracted from Pritchett (1994).

Given that change has always existed and that it requires adaptation among those exposed to it, it should be a feature of life that humans can cope easily with. This is not so. Resistance and reluctance to adapt to change appear to be normal. There would appear to be a desire, if not a predisposition among

1	The number of mobile telephones sold was zero in 1982 and 4 million in 1995.
2	The cost of computing power drops approximately 30% every year and microchips are doubling in performance power every 18 months.
3	The first industrial robot was introduced during the 1960s. By 1982 there were approximately 32,000 in use in the USA. Today there are over 20 million.
4	Of the largest 100 UK companies in 1965 only 32 remained in that list by 1995.
5	In 1954, 45% of UK employees worked in manufacturing. Now it accounts for less than 22%.

Table 19.1
Twelve changes over recent years (taken from: Pritchett, P (1994) *The Employee Handbook of New Work Habits for a Radically Changing World*, Pritchett & Associates)

significant numbers of humans to remain with the familiar and to avoid the ambiguity or uncertainty that accompanies change. Predictability in life appears to be a valued condition for many people. There are likely to be many reasons behind this response. It is because of the dilemma created by the requirement to change and a resistance to adopt it that managers must pay special attention to the subject.

Pressure for change

For organizations there are particular *events* and *experiences* that are the instigators of change. Some of these forces arise from outside the organization and some from inside it. These forces can be changes by the organization or events to which the organization must respond by making changes. Management in Action 19.1 on the next page illustrates that some changes originate in the political, cultural and fashion connotations of management.

Change can affect the individual, for example a change to the methods of work. It can affect a group through the introduction of teamwork. It can also affect the entire organization, for example the development and introduction of a new product range. There are also changes that impact on society and which in turn cascade back into organizations. The taxation levels applied to products such as alcohol and tobacco are designed to influence consumption rates and consequently the organizations producing these products experience reductions in business. There is another factor to be taken into account when considering the complexity inherent in change, that of random or chance factors. In some parts of the world earthquakes and storms are natural hazards. An earthquake could physically destroy buildings and disrupt communications in seconds, the effects of which could last for months.

Forces acting upon organizations

There are many and varied forces acting upon organizations which create, directly or indirectly, the need for change. There are many ways that these forces can be classified; one is to categorize them as originating from either outside or inside the organization. Table 19.2 represents some of the external sources of pressure for change (Open University, 1990).

Management in Action 19.1

Off with their overheads

Cutting the number of employees may be a necessary course of action in difficult situations but can potentially damage future prospects. As Trapp says, 'It is not a lesson that British or US managers have yet fully learned. The cut, cut, cut mentality is now deeply embedded in Anglo-Saxon corporate culture – every company says people are its greatest asset, but when life starts to get tough, again and again those 'assets' are unceremoniously heaved over the side.'

Fortune magazine suggested in the early 1990s that companies were caught in the grip of 'wee-ness envy'. An envy and desire to emulate other companies who were smaller than themselves. Russell Baker commented that the scale of dismissals by a manager was a measure of the right to membership of the CEO club. Two examples of the cut, cut, cut mentality identified by Trapp include:

■ During 1995 British Gas experienced 150% increase in complaints. At the same time it was in the process of shedding 25,000 jobs.

■ Ever Ready the battery manufacturer was acquired by Hanson in the early 1980s. It shed 900 of the 2900 jobs the R & D centre. This began what one commentator described as an attempt to make the decline of the company as long and profitable as possible. When it was sold in 1993 its market share had dropped from 80% to 30%. Its technology was by then 10 years behind the industry.

Professor Gary Hamel, Visiting Professor of International and Strategic Management at London Business School, compiled a 'Downsizing Hall of Fame' which included such names as Westinghouse, Kodak, General Motors, Union Carbide and DuPont. All of which had aggressively reduced the numbers employed over recent years. In the UK, companies such as Hanson, GEC, British Coal (which cut itself out of existence) and the clearing banks would all appear on the list. This has produced a generation of what Hamel describes as 'lowest common denominator managers' in the USA and the UK. Managers who are able to delayer, downsize, declutter and divest better than managers in other countries. As evidence of this, from 1987 to 1991 (a period of economic growth) more than 85% of the *Fortune* 500 companies reduced the size of their white collar staff. Hamel describes the process as one of 'corporate anorexia' – leaner companies are not necessarily fitter.

Business Process Re-engineering (BPR) has most frequently been linked with downsizing and has largely been discredited as a consequence. It has been suggested that some 75% of all attempts to apply BPR fail. The main intention behind BPR to focus the business on what it should be attempting to achieve has been overshadowed by it potential to cut cost and numbers of employees. Surveys in the USA have shown that only 22–34% of companies that restructure increase productivity to their satisfaction. This invariably leads to a downward spiral of cutting and failure to achieve success. Similar results on profitability have also been observed. In a survey of 210 companies not one reported a post-redundancy profit performance that matched the previous figures.

Hamel suggests that companies continue to adopt the cutting approach because it has become an organizational norm. Organizations are 'forced' by various means to follow the conventional wisdom of the day. This includes pressure from institutional shareholders, following the fashions of the moment, pressure from city analysts, a desire to be like other organizations and a wish to follow the lead of those organizations that are regarded as the most prestigious in their industry. It does not, however, guarantee commercial success or benefit for customers or society.

Adapted from: Trapp, R (1995) Off with their overheads. Independent on Sunday, *Business Section, 10 December, pp 1–2.*

In addition to these sources of change, Hellriegel *et al.* (1989) identify the following:

■ Rapid product obsolescence. This refers to the increasing rapidity of product change necessitated by fashion and technology, etc. It reflects the pace of change.

■ Knowledge explosion. Information and knowledge are rapidly becoming commodities in their own right. This creates new organizations and impacts on those not directly involved in the *creation of information*. This can impact on an organization in many different ways, one of which is the current trend to *benchmark* as a means of judging performance against nominated targets, see Management in Action 19.2 on the next page.

■ Demographics. The demographics and nature of both customers and the workforce is changing. Education levels are rising as are the expectations about the role of work in people's lives.

The internal forces for change include:

■ Efficiency. There is an ever present drive for *minimalism* in organizations. The increased level of competition forces every organization to enter a spiral of cost reduction. The finance markets seek ever higher profit levels on behalf of investors. Managers themselves have careers to *manage* through being *better* than their peer group. Better in this context implies being able to demonstrate that they can deliver that which more senior managers expect – minimalism!

■ Fashion. Change for the sake of change is another force acting upon internal change processes. There are organizations (and managers) who pride themselves on being *leading edge* in this respect. This creates a pressure for change as others follow and adopt yesterday's innovation.

Source of change	Examples
Market demand	Decline in demand for particular products/services, for example, monochrome television sets
Market supply	Mergers in retail companies
Economic	Overall fall in retail companies; changes in exchange rates
Social	Changes in taste, for example, increase in health consciousness in 1980s
Technological	Increased availability of new production technologies and information systems
Political	Change in leadership of local authority or government
Chance	Earthquake, fire, flood, storm

Table 19.2
External pressure for change (taken from: *Managing Change*, Book 9, B784, The effective manager, Open University)

Management in Action 19.2

A measure of success

Benchmarking is a process intended to provide a basis of comparison. It allows an organization to identify others against which it can measure its own performance and from whom it can learn new ways of improving its effectiveness. For example:

- South-West Airlines in the USA studied the performance of the pit crews at the Indy 500 motor car race and learned how to reduce the turnaround time of its aircraft at an airport gate from 30 minutes to 15.
- The Granite Rock Company studied the use of ATMs in banking. Its own loading procedures required accurate figures and records along with simple and convenient use. The upshot being that the company introduced a system of ATM-like cards for its drivers to make the weighing and record keeping simpler, faster and more reliable.

Benchmarking is not new, it has, however, taken off as a necessary management technique over the past few years. It could be argued that it was Walter Chrysler who began the idea when he bought and stripped down an Oldsmobile. He was intent in finding out what went into the competitor's car, how it was made and how much it cost to make. It was during the early 1990s that renewed and large-scale interest in the technique emerged. It is frequently seen alongside business process re-engineering and total quality management as a trilogy of efficiency improvement techniques.

The British government also uses the technique as part of its market-testing programme for public-sector efficiency.

In a survey of the top 10,000 UK companies by Coopers & Lybrand and the Confederation of British Industry it was revealed that 66% of the respondents across all sectors practised benchmarking and that 85% felt that it had been successful. Of the *Fortune* 500 companies, 80% use the technique and 60% intended to increase investment in its application. In the early 1980s it was Xerox that began to use benchmarking to seek ways of combating competition from the Far East in copier products. In doing so it recognized that to identify the best ways of doing things it was not essential to copy from one company. It is possible to identify parallels in other sectors against which to measure oneself against and then learn from their experience.

In recent times the emphasis has moved away from performance measurement and concentrated on what gives leading companies their competitive edge. The emphasis should not be 90% on the development of measurements and 10% on change, but the other way around, according to Victor Luck, head of commerce and industry consulting services at Coopers & Lybrand. Arthur Andersen, an international accounting and consultancy firm, has invested over £6.4m in developing the Global Best Practices Knowledge Base. This represents its proprietary benchmarking database, built up from a wide variety of sources and intended for use by its consultants in helping clients. Clearly benchmarking as a technique is likely to be around for some considerable time to come.

Adapted from: Dickson, T (1993) A measure of success. Financial Times, *5 May, p 14.*

- Control. New managers frequently make change simply to demonstrate that the previous incumbent has gone. Employees frequently refer to, 'The way it has always been'. This might be accurate, but it also represents an attempt to socialize the new manager into employee preferred work practices. Employees have the upper hand in such situations as they inevitably know the established ways better than the new manager. If the new manager changes everything around then it neutralizes that potential benefit.

■ Internal pressure. Change can be forced on an organization as a result of the internal pressure from various stakeholder groups. For example, changes to the wage structure and working practices could be brought about as a result of industrial action by the workforce.

Stewart (1991) identifies a number of changes that influence managerial careers. They include, in addition to the points already made:

■ Business structure. This category would include more frequent changes in business ownership; growth in multinational and foreign ownership; privatization of the public sector and the globalization of business activity.
■ Business functioning. The growth of flexibility as a means of matching resources to requirement through self-employment, contracting and the need to seek new business opportunities.

This discussion has demonstrated that a wide range of forces act upon organizations and directly or indirectly result in change. It is now appropriate to consider how these are experienced within an organization. There are four different ways in which change can be experienced by an organization, dependent upon the scale of change and the degree of planning involved. Figure 19.1 illustrates this process.

Each of the four cells in Figure 19.1 reflect different response scenarios. As such they provide a basis for identifying management strategies. The axes of the model will be discussed in the following sub-sections, but it is appropriate to briefly consider each of the cells in turn at this point:

■ Surprise. This reflects situations that are both unplanned and relatively minor in nature. Interest rates might unexpectedly change and require the finance managers of a company to adjust loan repayment schedules.
■ Incremental. This could reflect situations which are anticipated yet relatively minor in nature. For example, the implementation of quality circle recommendations.
■ Crisis. This represents both the unexpected and the serious. An extreme example might be the destruction of a factory as the result of a gas explosion or terrorist attack. It contains the potential to destroy the organization unless the response is appropriate and effective.

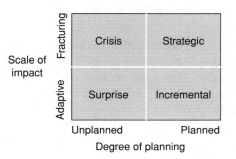

Figure 19.1 The change matrix.

Launching a new tradition in a Clyde shipyard

The shipbuilding industry in the UK once led the world in its field but had the reputation of poor management and conflictual industrial relations. Working practices were inflexible and investment was very low. Not surprisingly, shipyards in Asia soon overtook the UK in terms of delivery, cost and innovation.

Of the few remaining shipyards, Kvaerner Govan, owned by a Norwegian shipping and engineering group and located on the river Clyde, is a notable exception. Showing losses of £45m in 1988 when it was taken over by Kvaerner it turned in a profit of £1m in 1994 and had forward orders for at least two years. In the past the company suffered a serious lack of investment and poor working practices. For example, absenteeism was running at 23% and productivity was low, taking 2.5 times as many hours to build a ship as its competitors. The turnaround in the company fortunes had been achieved through several initiatives running in parallel:

- £31m investment in new plant and machinery.
- Recognition that 35% of costs were associated with 'making' each ship and it was therefore an added value company.
- Identification of 'lost time' of 240,000 hours per year. The major reasons being:
  - Average working week of around 29 hours compared with the paid hours of 39. The causes being concessions to the workforce on breaks, stopping and starting times to encourage new work practices.
  - 60,000 hours each year spent by union representatives on union business.
  - 70,000 hours lost each year through accidents and injuries.
  - Inefficient shift pattern organization and restrictive practices also accounted for a high number of hours lost.
  - Absenteeism accounted for 440 of the yard's 2000 employees being off work at any one time.

- The unions were told of the findings and that if the company was to survive it had to become profitable. It was also made clear that the processes to be changed would be agreed and that training would be provided for employees to enable them to work in the ways required.
- New welding techniques were needed for an order and so training was begun and a bonus of 5% paid to those who passed the course.
- The absence problem was tackled head-on. Employees were visited at home to find out if they were fit to return to work. Individuals were told that their sick pay would be stopped and their jobs were in jeopardy. The absence rate fell sharply to 10% and then again to 5% when overtime pay was restricted to only those who had worked 37 hours or more in a week.
- The changes were introduced in two phases. The working week was reduced to 37 hours but the various concessions were eliminated. The number of shop stewards was cut to 20 and they were allowed one hour each day for union duties. Petty demarcations between jobs were eliminated. The second phase followed a year later. It involved the changing of shift patterns. Shop-floor resistance to these changes led to a strike as shiftwork had previously been optional and controlled by the unions. The strike ended when the company sent letters to all employees telling them that they would be sacked the following week if they did not return to work. Several layers of management and supervisory jobs were also eliminated during this phase.

The result of these changes brought the number of hours to build a ship down to almost the same as its competitors and returned the yard to profit.

Adapted from: Hodges, C. (1994) Launching a new tradition in a Clyde shipyard. Personnel Management Plus, April, pp 20–1.

■ Strategic. This represents major planned events that attempt to position the organization more effectively in relationship to its environment. For example, a company making manual typewriters anticipating the growth of computer-based systems may seek to acquire a business systems or computer division. Management in Action 19.3 reflects another form of strategic change, the desire for survival.

Adaptive change

The vertical axis of Figure 19.1 represents a scale of change impact. Those categorized as adaptive are relatively small in scale and which as a consequence can be accommodated without major disruption and danger to the organization. It represents the many thousands of small *adaptive* movements in absorbing and responding to day-to-day events, balancing and integrating operations with the environment within which they takes place.

There are many possible examples of this type of change that exist. For example, a flu epidemic occurs and the level of sickness absence suddenly and unexpectedly rises. This type of change can be accommodated relatively easily, but not without some measure of increased cost. Employees at work could be asked to stay behind and work overtime. Alternatively, temporary labour could be hired to cover for the absent employees. Allowing production to fall behind schedule is another option. These represent the tactical levels of decision that line managers engage in all the time in responding to the ever changing circumstances that they are exposed to.

Other *adaptive* changes are more permanent, but nevertheless minor in scale. For example, minor modifications to the external features of product design on an annual basis. The intention being to keep it fresh in appearance and to respond to marketing initiatives among competitors. The introduction of a new computer package for personnel records would serve as another example. The new system might require changes to the design of a number of personnel forms and procedures as well as the transfer of much existing data from one computer system to another.

Fracturing change

This scale of change impact (Figure 19.1) represents the major events that occur within the experience of all organizations. The scale of change represented by this category is very large and of a significance that could seriously damage or destroy the organization. It has the potential to *fracture* or break it.

Products and services are all designed to meet particular needs among their consumers. There is always a danger that these needs can be met in different ways and thus eliminate the market for a particular product. In recent years the changes to political structures have fundamentally changed the military balance that existed for the previous 40 years. The so called *peace dividend* has produced a number of major changes, including the possibility for a massive reduction in work for those companies making military equipment. Such organizations have had to adjust rapidly to this dangerous (for their survival and profit) situation or face severe contraction or even demise.

Another example of the possibility of fracturing change would be the natural disasters that can strike any organization at any time. For example, a gas explosion could destroy a building and so potentially destroy the company. A major area of managerial responsibility over recent years has been the field of risk and disaster planning in an attempt to minimize the consequence of such events.

There is a scale of magnitude reflecting the level of real or potential threat to the organization. Equally, some issues which might be major in one context may be considered minor in another. For example, in a company with a poor industrial relations record frequent strikes may be the norm. Therefore it may be part of the management planning process to build an allowance into their operations, schedules and costs to reduce the impact. Also, there are situations in which relatively minor events can slip out of control and become life threatening if they are not handled effectively. For example, the new computerized personnel system referred to in the previous sub-section could be inappropriate or faulty in some respect. Its introduction could be resisted by personnel staff. Employees could also interpret its introduction as an attempt by managers to tighten control and intrude into their lives. The consequences of any of these could be a slide into a major disaster for the organization.

Planned change

The horizontal axis of Figure 19.1 reflects the degree of planning that can be brought to bear on the situation. It is about the level of anticipation concerning the events which are forcing change to occur. Planned change represents those events that management intend to occur, for which they can provide a predetermined response.

There are many examples of planned change. Management may identify that its ability to retain market share is being threatened by competitors with much lower labour costs. Consequently a package of measures could be developed including the introduction of automation and high technology; the development of flexibility and teamwork practices among the workforce; the linking of wages to performance; the redesign of the product to make it more attractive to the customer; the development of a range of customer inducements and support measures.

It also represents the strategic moves made by organizations in order to position themselves to minimize the overall impact of declining markets and to capture the potential of expanding businesses. This refers to the merger, acquisition and divestment strategies that many large organizations engage in as they search for higher returns. Planning for the many small changes that occur is part of normal managerial experience. For example, the introduction of quality circles is an attempt to capture continuous improvement.

Unplanned change

This category represents the unexpected events that can never be completely eliminated. Parts of California are known to be subject to earthquakes as they lie along faults in the earth's crust. Knowing this, measures can be taken to minimize the consequences through building design and emergency planning. However, it is not yet possible to predict with any certainty when or how strong a particular tremor will be. They remain random factors and so when they occur pre-prepared recovery plans must be activated. It can be argued that it is one of the primary responsibilities of management to anticipate events and to minimize the possibility of the unexpected arising. Also they have responsibility for the development of plans for dealing with such eventualities that cannot be eliminated or totally harnessed. This contingency planning approach to change attempts to scan the internal and external environment and develop response scenarios for what might be expected to occur.

Over recent years many organizations have engaged a reductionist approach to managing. The ability to cut back the numbers of employees and to rationalize operational activity has been a much prized skill (Management in Action 19.1). This is achieved by eliminating *slack* from the system and by concentrating on *doing* rather than *thinking*. One of the potential dangers of this *minimalist* approach is that it removes the ability to *anticipate and plan* as a result of the emphasis on producing in the current time period. The inherent risk in this approach is that higher degree of missed intelligence creates more unplanned events with a consummate risk of *crisis* being higher. Crisis in Figure 19.1 being the least desirable and most dangerous cell in the matrix carries with it the greater risk for the survival of the organization.

Resistance to change

The starting point for considering *resistance to change* is the image conjured up by the phrase itself. It implies that an individual or group have determined to frustrate the intentions of another to implement a particular course of action. In a managerial context that inevitably reflects the decision of the employer to *change* some aspect of the organization and in so doing influence the work activities and/or employment of employees. Kahn (1982) suggests that resistance behaviour during times of change is frequently indistinguishable from normal behaviour patterns. The difference being a function of the perspective of the person classifying the behaviour rather than the behaviour itself.

The following material has been compiled from a number of sources including Kotter and Schlesinger (1979); Kanter (1983); Plant (1987); Hellriegel *et al*. (1989); Moorhead and Griffin (1992); Armstrong (1995) and Mullins (1996).

Individual resistance to change

Individuals resist change for a number of reasons, including those indicated in Figure 19.2.

Many of the reasons indicated in Figure 19.2 are self-explanatory and easily understood. For example, fear of the unknown infers that the individual would prefer to remain with existing arrangements. Change can be a negative experience for many employees. Organizational experience soon indicates that managers do not always have the best interests of employees at heart, particularly when cutbacks are the norm! However, some of the reasons identified in Figure 19.2 need further explanation:

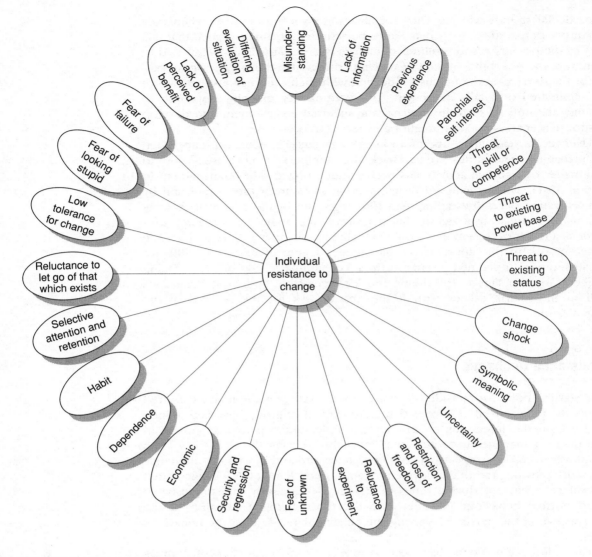

Figure 19.2 Individual reasons for resisting change.

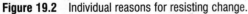

- Symbolic meaning. The entitlement to benefits such as a company car or the use of a private office rather than an area separated by partitions all provide symbols of status within the organization. Changes which impact on such visible signs can be fiercely resisted even if they are incidental.
- Change shock. The previous routine will have been familiar, individuals will have known instinctively what they were supposed to do. Change can destroy that level of familiarity and create situations in which less is predictable.
- Selective attention and retention. Individuals define *reality* for themselves based upon their understanding of the world as they experience and understand it. Change can call into question these frames of reference and

as a consequence be rejected. Individuals have a tendency to only pay attention and retain that information which supports their existing world views which can lead to resistance.

- Dependence. Students are dependent upon lecturers for their intellectual development. However, taken to extreme, dependence can become a force which resists change as security is threatened. Dependence can also place significant power in the hands of those who are relied upon. Management in Action 19.4 overleaf reflects how ICL communicated in order to minimize the possibility of negative dependence and at the same time raised awareness of the positive side of change.

- Security and regression. The need for security can lead to a search for the past when things appeared simpler and more familiar. This *regression* on the part of such individuals is a clear force for resisting change.

Group and organizational resistance to change

Resistance to change at a group or organizational level comes in many forms (see Figure 19.3).

Most of the categories of resistance identified in Figure 19.3 are self-explanatory, but a few could benefit from some explanation:

- Misinformation. Control over communication provides opportunities for a group to impart particular interpretations to information and so engineer resistance.

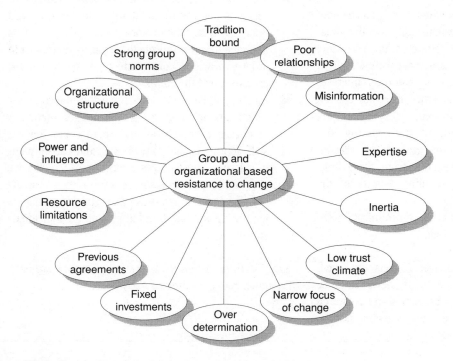

Figure 19.3　Group and organizational reasons for resisting change.

Management in Action 19.4

Network support

ICL, the computer company transformed itself in 1990 from making and selling its own hardware to offering a wide range of value added services. As a consequence the company had to develop completely new ways of operating and of communicating with employees. Half of the staff within the company now work for subsidiaries and the head office has been reduced in size from 750 people to just 50.

Any change that is planned by management should be communicated as quickly and thoroughly as possible was the view expressed by Mr David Wimpress, the group Personnel director for the UK. These principles were applied when the company needed to tell its employees that a pay freeze was being implemented and that the staff numbers would have to be reduced by 4% in 1993. The information was quickly cascaded throughout the company by management using the established mechanisms.

Subsidiary companies have their own management teams and their first line of responsibility is to that organization and its performance. However, the personnel specialists of each company also meet with Wimpress each month to discuss items of 'common interest'. In addition each of the head office directors sits on the board of subsidiary companies. For example, Wimpress acts as chairman of the training and office design companies in the group. The breadth and depth of involvement resulting from these links helps to bind together the separate aspects of the business.

A number of different forms of communication are used by the company. They include:

- Team briefing. Each manager collects their staff together and 'briefs' them on whatever is to be communicated. Questions are asked and answered within the meeting. The essential message is then used as the basis of subsequent briefings by each subordinate to brief their own staff. Information, reactions and responses can also be communicated back up the line within this framework.

- Electronic mail is used by the company to cascade information throughout the organization quickly. Being a computer organization almost everyone has access to a terminal and so this option becomes feasible.

- Audio cassette based briefings on specific aspects of company policy are issued to staff on a regular basis.

- An annual company attitude and opinion survey is undertaken across the whole company. There are a common set of questions but subsidiaries are allowed to incorporate specific issues if necessary. Topics include an evaluation of management effectiveness, team briefing processes and the setting and clarity of objectives.

- A company handbook of policies is common to all subsidiaries.

- A document called *The Management Framework* sets out the commitment to customer care and issues such as how to word a job offer letter. It is intended to communicate to managers how to act in order to provide a consistently high quality outward appearance of the company.

- Investing in People is a scheme within the company which among other things encourages managers to engage effectively in performance pay, regular staff appraisals, objective setting and career planning issues. These processes encourage the effective use of the people resource within the company and provide a two-way dialogue on what is happening and how it will impact on the individuals concerned.

Adapted from: Williams. M (1993) Network support. Personnel Today, 23 March, p 41.

- Organization structure. The bureaucratic form of organization was designed to deliver consistency and predictability of operations. Consequently it is a structure that does not cope easily with change.
- Previous agreements. Arrangements entered into with another group or organization are designed to control events in the future. This restricts the ability to make changes over the period of such agreements.
- Fixed investments. The investments that an organization makes in buildings, land and equipment place considerable restriction on what can be done in the future. In practice they limit the ability to change because they represent assets that are not easy to liquidate in the short term.
- Overdetermination. The systems and procedures that organizations create to provide control can also restrict the ability to introduce change.
- Narrow focus of change. In considering change an organization very often takes the immediate zone of impact into account. It is possible for situations to arise in which groups not immediately affected by change resist involvement and so limit the benefits ultimately gained.

Managing organizational change

It has already been established that change is both endemic to management and an issue which can generate resistance from a wide range of sources. The major responsibility of managers is to enable the organization to function effectively and so it is they who have a prime responsibility for both creating change and responding to it in pursuit of their objectives. Management in Action 19.5 on the next page illustrates that not all large scale change can be planned   and that even senior managers have to respond to the situations that they find themselves in.

One model of an organization, the work of Leavitt (1965), attempts to reflect the constituent parts of an organization within its environment as a basis for change management (see Figure 19.4).

Leavitt argues that change can affect any of these variables, alternatively they can be changed individually in an attempt to influence other elements within the organization. Because of the integrated nature of these elements changes to one of them will have consequential effects on the others. For example, a

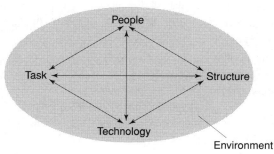

Figure 19.4 Leavitt's organization variables. (Huczynski, A and Buchanan, D (1991). *Organizational Behaviour*. Prentice Hall, Hemel Hempstead.)

Management in Action 19.5

Shake-up inspires new state of mind

On 5 July 1995 the UK government decided to merge the employment and education departments. The justification for this move was that the overlap between education and training provision was not effectively served by the separation of the two main civil service departments responsible for them. The scale of the integration was to bring together two distinctly different organizations with vastly different traditions and functions, and as a consequence create a single entity that could improve services to the nation. The numbers employed by these two departments of state were, employment 50,000 people and education 1700. Many of the employment department's staff (45,000) were engaged in front line duties associated with the employment service (job centres, etc.). The education department was much more policy based in its function and many of its staff worked through public bodies such as the Further Education Funding Council.

The merger, for that is what it was, was always going to be difficult and complex. There were a number of sub-departments that would not easily fit into the new structure. For example, the division that dealt with industrial relations policy development was transferred to the Department of Trade and Industry. The Health and Safety Executive (about 4300 staff) was transferred to the Department of the Environment. The merger was extraordinary for three principle reasons:

- Speed. The two secretaries of state responsible for the departments (the senior politicians) and the two permanent secretaries (the senior civil servants) did not know of the planned change until one hour before it was announced.
- Culture. The cultures of the two organizations were completely different.
- Leadership. It was initially decided that both senior civil servants would be retained. However, since then one of them (Sir Tim Lankester) left to take up the position as director of the School for Oriental and African Studies.

The senior managers quickly determined that they would adopt a holistic approach by focusing on the five ingredients necessary for success:

- Clarity of values.
- Clarity of aims and objectives.
- A structure that facilitated the achievement of values, aims and objectives.
- Processes that supported the achievement of values, aims and objectives.
- People who felt comfortable with the values and who had the necessary skills.

A transitional board was established to develop the mechanisms for integration and by mid-September an integrated set of aims for the new Department for Education and Employment was published. They were to:

> Support economic growth and improve the nation's competitiveness and quality of life by raising standards of educational achievement and skill and by promoting an efficient and flexible labour market.

By Christmas 1995 the senior 110 positions had been filled and work began on other aspects of the change. This involved restructuring the work of the departments and of introducing common systems of recruitment, appraisal, training and promotion. Communication was used constantly to keep staff informed and involved in the change process. Bichard explained that he tried to ensure that information was honest, never hiding bad news, ensuring that fairness would be a key criteria and wherever possible an outcome with which the staff would be comfortable. The next stage was to move people's attention from looking backwards to looking toward the future.

Adapted from: Bichard, M (1996) Shake-up inspires new state of mind. People Management, 8 February, pp 22–7.

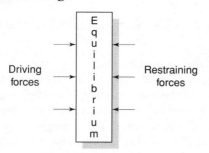

Figure 19.5 Lewin's forcefield analysis model.

change to some of the key managers in an organization could well create a number of subsequent changes to the structure of the organization, its technology and some of the tasks.

Another feature of the management of change is the role of *change agents* in the process. A change agent is someone who plays a leading part in sponsoring the need for change or in its implementation. There have been a number of frameworks describing the forms of change agent activity. One of the more recent is that of Ottaway (1982) who produced a taxonomy linked to a particular model of change – that of Lewin (1951). This model states that any situation exists as the result of a balance between the forces acting upon it. These forces occur in opposing directions, some *driving* for change whilst others are *restraining* that change by pressing in the opposite direction. It is known as the *forcefield analysis model*, intended to guide the identification of the forces acting upon the situation (see Figure 19.5).

The model is very simple to understand and can easily be applied to a wide range of situations. The current level of absence within a company might be 500 hours per month. An analysis of the situation might reveal the *driving* and *restraining* forces indicated in Table 19.3.

The absence level of 500 hours per month is the balance point between the sum of driving and restraining forces. It follows that if a change is desired in that situation then either the magnitude of the driving forces needs to be increased, and/or the magnitude of the restraining forces reduced.

Driving forces	Restraining forces	
Management need for higher productivity	Laziness	**Table 19.3**
Need to reduce high levels of payment for sickness absence	Past practice	Examples of driving and restraining forces acting upon absence levels
Management desire for control	Boring and monotonous work	
Employee commitment to the company	Lack of car ownership	
Employee travel to work distance	Poor public transport	
Employee loss of income	Road congestion	
Employee desire to do a good job	Domestic difficulties	
Career development and promotion desire	Illness	
	Inconvenient work starting time	
	Habit	

Lewin identified three stages of change associated with his forcefield analysis model:

- Stage 1 – Unfreezing. The first stage requires the current situation to be *unfrozen*. The current level of absence is frozen at 500 hours as a result of the balance between the two opposing forcefields. A desire to change that requires the current situation to be unfrozen in preparation for change to be made. It is a difficult period in any change process as the intentions for the future become clear and when resistance to that intention surfaces. In the example used, this could involve a statement by management of the problems associated with absence and the beginning of negotiations with the trade unions on how to deal with the problem.
- Stage 2 – Changing. Having unfrozen the situation it is then time to make appropriate *changes*. This could involve introducing mandatory counselling after every period of absence; changing the working hours; introducing flexi-time; introducing nursery provision and many more initiatives. These changes could be in both driving and restraining forces. The level of absence should be seen to reduce if the changes have been successful.
- Stage 3 – Refreezing. The change process is one of movement. The third stage of the Lewin model requires the changes to be *refrozen* or consolidated in a new state of balance. If this is not done then the balance will not be fixed and it will *slip* back to its previous position. Refreezing implies that the changes made become the new norms for that particular situation.

Ottaway's taxonomy is based on this model of change. Three types of change agent are identified:

- Change generators. These are linked with the unfreezing process. They are the individuals or groups who identify areas of potential change and convince others of the need to take action. This could include a charismatic leader who is able to create a movement willing to adopt the changes expressed in the leader's vision. It could also include a special project team who are give the task of reviewing a particular aspect of company operations.
- Change implementors. These deliver actual change to the organization. They can be charismatic leaders who are able to persuade subordinates to accept change. They can be sponsors from senior management who lend their position to the call for change and so encourage others to see it as important or inevitable. They can be industrial relations specialists who have the task of making agreements with employee representatives and thereby operationalize change proposals.
- Change adopters. These represent the *refreezing* stage of the Lewin model. They are the individuals who make the changes work in practice and by so doing ensure that they become the norms within that particular context. They are inevitably the line managers, supervisors and employees who get on with the job and make sure that it does not slip back to what existed before.

In seeking to manage change Plant (1987) advocates *Key Relationship Mapping* in attempting to identify appropriate change strategies. The model requires consideration of four key elements associated with change: winners, losers, power and information (see Figure 19.6).

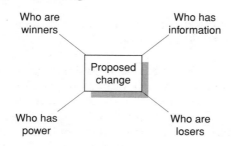

Figure 19.6   Key relationship map (taken from: Plant R (1987) *Managing Change and Making It Stick*, Fontana, p 24).

Winners would not normally be expected to resist proposed changes, whereas losers would. If a company reorganizes the wage structures those employees who receive a pay rise are likely to consider it a good scheme and those who lose money would consider it a bad scheme. The power balance between management and unions might be important in the identification of likely courses of action. A company with a seasonal product cycle would be at a political disadvantage if it sought to introduce change at the time of peak production. Those who hold or have access to information also have the potential to help or hinder change. In considering these four elements it is possible to identify the *key relationships* between them and to plan networking strategies in support of the change process.

In managing change it is necessary to utilize aspects from each of the models so far described. Not to do so would be likely to reduce the effectiveness of the change strategy adopted. The following sub-sections consider a number of specific perspectives on managing the change process.

Organizational development and change

Organizational development (OD) can be defined as, 'a systematic application of behavioural science knowledge to the planned development and reinforcement of organizational strategies, structures, and processes for improving an organization's effectiveness' (Cummings and Worley, 1993, p 2). The strands of theory and practice within OD include:

- T-groups. Small unstructured groups meet and by exploring the interactive behaviour of the group learn about their own behaviour.
- Survey feedback. The findings from attitude or similar surveys need to be communicated to the participants in a way that create learning opportunities.
- Action research. This reflects an active and iterative approach to research and change. It is based upon a cyclical process beginning with research into identified problems. This in turn leads to conclusions and the development of action plans. Opportunities for further study and problem solving are also identified, and so the cycle begins again.
- Quality of working life. The quality of working life (QWL) movement has already been discussed in an earlier chapter and it has been incorporated into the OD practitioners toolkit.
- Strategic change. An attempt to integrate all organizational variables into a common purpose. A vision or strategy is needed for this and the change

perspective arises through the consequence of the integration of all activity into a cohesive (*strategic*) whole.

The basis and practice of OD has been criticized for a number of reasons. It is a practice that assumes incrementalism as the best way to achieve change. This is fine as long as the organization is at a high level of effectiveness to begin with. Dunphy and Stace (1988) argue that not all situations allow for the slow process of evolutionary change. Time and the political climate may be against the approach. OD as a process requires participation which, as Stephenson (1985) suggests, is not the panacea often claimed. Individuals or groups intent on resisting change, perhaps as a consequence of being disadvantaged by the outcome, may not be persuaded by involvement and might slow down the process itself. Involvement can expose but not necessarily solve problems. Compromise may not be the best option and changing opinions may not deliver as intended. A company faced with a competitor's product that serves as a replacement for their own may not have the time or financial resource to allow an OD approach to finding a solution.

Figure 19.6 makes specific reference to the notion of power as part of the change process. This is lacking in the classic OD approach. Recognizing this weakness Schein (1985) makes several suggestions for including a power and political perspective to OD interventions. Identifying with powerful stakeholders and attempting small projects first to gain credibility before tackling the more complex and risky projects, for example. The OD approach to change management can be seen in the following example of change in the Rover Group over a five-year period, described in Management in Action 19.6.

Power, politics and change

There are two major ways in which power and politics interact with change:

- Process. If change is to be successful support and commitment must be maximized whilst resistance and opposition are minimized. Power and politics can be used to facilitate this. For example, offering to provide help in the future in return for support now would constitute a recognition of the political dimension to decision making.
- Purpose. There is a saying about not getting mad but getting even as a means of extracting revenge. Change can therefore be used as the means to achieve another purpose. For example, the management of a company might 'engineer' the need for a redundancy in order to be able to dismiss particular employees. The implication being that it would be possible to 'create' a reduction in the number of employees and then to 'engineer' the means of selecting particular employees classified as undesirable.

Stephenson (1985) identifies the following tactics useful in the introduction of change:

- Simple first. 'Nothing succeeds like success.' Beginning with small projects that are successful creates confidence and encouragement to go on and tackle more difficult problems.
- Adaptation. Being flexible and adaptable in modifying planned changes improves the chances of success. It provides a means of meeting unplanned events and of dealing with resistance.

Management in Action 19.6

Changing Rover Group through its employees

In 1988 the Rover Group set out a corporate mission, key actions and an operating philosophy to secure its long term viability. This began a series of initiatives:

- Stage 1. 1988. Rover defined its mission and critical success factors as:

  'Rover group will be internationally renowned for extraordinary customer satisfaction.' This involved activity across each of the following themes:
  - Delight the customer.
  - Move up market.
  - Export more.
  - Reduce costs.
  - Success through people.

- Stage 2. Formation of product supply – 1990. This stage involved the combination of previously separate engineering and manufacturing organizations into five core businesses. It saw the introduction of a uniform for managers across the company and the blurring of traditional work roles. More empowerment and changes to the culture by the introduction of upward appraisal and TQM owned by managers also encouraged a new emphasis.

- Stage 3. Rover tomorrow – the new deal – 1992. Cell manufacturing methods had been introduced but more was needed if single status and multiskilling was to have any real impact. The new deal was developed which included a 'jobs for life' element. With this Rover took responsibility for people's employment until they wished to leave the company. This did not imply a particular job, or a type of job or even a job within Rover. What it did mean was that the company took responsibility for the future employability of people through their skill level.

- Stage 4. The quality strategy. Encouraging high levels of employee involvement, self development and job flexibility which impacted on the bottom line was the intention of this phase. The purpose was to improve the business, including the management of people, logistics, manufacturing, planning and product improvement through quality.

A number of features have been incorporated into these staged initiatives which in turn provide the basis for improvement, change, empowerment and employee involvement. They include:

- Culture. The ways that things get done needed to be addressed as a means of increasing the commitment and contribution from employees.
- Involvement and corporate learning. Rover set out to improve the use and effectiveness of involvement and change.
- Quality circles and discussion groups. The company introduced informal quality circles and continuous improvement groups.
- Organization. The organization of employees in work groups of 10–15 with a team leader selected jointly by managers and the team introduced the potential for employee self-development.
- Creating the environment for involvement. The feedback of company performance relative to competitors in simple language such as cars produced per employee encouraged a broader perspective to creep into the thinking of all concerned. Rover provided assistance for training initiatives by allowing each associate £100 towards the cost of course fees, the intention being to encourage people back into learning as a continuous process

The company intended to manage change from two parallel perspectives. The first was the formal change model of plan, communicate, implement and record. The second was a notion of 'Copy Plus'. This attempted to offset the natural tendency to create every idea from scratch. It was about learning from experience and past effort.

Adapted from: Stephenson, A (1994) Changing Rover Group through its employees. Management Services, *February, pp 6–10.*

- Incorporation. People feel less threatened and more comfortable with minor change. Consequently incorporating as much as possible from an existing situation in a change programme gives the appearance of continuity and stability.

- Structure. Political persuasion can be used to influence attitude through the structural and physical aspects of change. Product and service quality ultimately comes down to employee commitment. This reflects underlying attitudes to a significant extent. By changing working practices through training, reward systems, etc. quality is addressed directly and changes in attitude brought about over time. Eventually the changed attitude supports the higher quality without the need for *structural props*.

- Ceremony. The use of ceremonial events provide a clear signal of what defines success in a particular context. It also has the effect of institutionalizing change through the ceremonies attached to it. The razzamatazz around new product launches are as much about rewarding the changes in bringing them about as they are marketing initiatives.

- Assurances. How people perceive that they will be treated as the result of change is important to how they react to it. Previous experience of the value of assurances (on say fair treatment) are an important part of creating future responses.

- Timescales. As a general rule the more time available to make change the more likely it is to be successful. However, there are situations in which time is not available and rapid change must take place. Crises can become a focus for successful change.

- Support. Adapting to change causes stress and individuals often feel threatened. This requires support in order to maintain momentum and to avoid encouraging resistance.

- Transition. There are three different contexts active at the same time in change processes. The existing situation, the desired situation and the transitional situation. They are not discrete categories of event. This creates uncertainty, ambiguity and complexity, all of which must be managed.

- Unexpected. Unexpected things can and will occur. Some preparation for these situations can be done and not all are hostile to change.

Another way of considering the political and power dynamics associated with change were identified by Nadler and Tushman (1988). In this view there are three mechanisms required to manage the problems associated with the power, anxiety and transitional situations found in all change situations:

- Mobilizing political support. This mechanism is all about preparing the ground for the change process. It involves gaining the support of key sponsors and of forming supportive alliances with those likely to be influential in or affected by the process. It is about attempting to maximize support and minimize resistance to the proposed changes.

- Encouraging supportive behaviour. This mechanism uses a variety of devices to build support among those more directly involved with the change. For example, the participation of employees in designing changes to working practices might help them understand existing problems and identify appropriate alternatives.

- Managing the transitional process. Having identified what is to be done, it then has to be achieved in practice. The difficulties associated with transition are the uncertainty of the new state – because it has not yet arrived; the familiarity of the old – because it has not yet gone; and the complexity of temporary arrangements – designed to facilitate movement from one situation to another. The transition period is a dangerous one for any change process as things can go horribly wrong and threaten the achievement of the ultimate objective.

The political and power dimensions associated with change can be inferred from the merger and acquisition activity described in Management in Action 19.7 on the next page.

Whilst power and politics are very important aspects of any change process they do not provide the only basis for managing them. Indeed, it could be argued that by acting in an overtly political way management could be encouraging others to act in a similar way, creating a deteriorating cycle of behaviour into a pit of intrigue and politics. In this situation power and politics become the masters, not the servants.

Contingency approaches to change

Contingency approaches to change incorporate a broader range of elements into the process than political or OD perspectives. They represent a directly managerial approach to the subject of change compared with OD, which tends to be directed at incremental and self-directed methods. However, under the OD methodology managers still retain control of the agenda and context. It could therefore be argued that it also represents a manipulative device intended to find ways of achieving acceptance of managerial perspectives.

One of the earlier approaches to the contingency view of change is reflected in the work of Kotter and Schlesinger (1979). They identified a number of change management strategies along with the contexts to which they could be applied (see Table 19.4 on page 597).

Taking each of the strategies for change in turn:

- Education plus communication. This strategy represents an approach to change based on understanding and rationality. If employees can be shown the reason behind a proposed change they are more likely to accept the need for it and support the programme. It is a slow process and can provide potential opposition through access to information.
- Participation plus involvement. This strategy is based on the notion that if people are actively involved in change they will go along with it. It can be useful where resistance is likely to exist. Also by working together improvements to interpersonal relationships could occur and the ground prepared for more effective change in the future. There is a danger of participation producing inappropriate outcomes if a new power balance emerges.
- Facilitation plus support. This would be suitable in situations where the difficulty was one of being able to cope with the change process or the new situation. It is an approach in which the strategy is one of providing an opportunity to come to terms with the change and to grow in confidence during the transition.
- Negotiation plus agreement. Negotiation is a strategy aimed at resolving difference though agreement. It is usually associated with problem solving

Management in Action 19.7

Executive action for acquisition success

Angwin describes a number of changes that surround the take-over process. He suggests that as many as one in seven executives will experience a take-over during their working lives and that this might be expected to be higher for MBA qualified managers. He also points out that most take-overs fail (about 44% subsequently split-up) and that many of those involved find it a negative experience. In America consultants recommend a formal grieving period for staff in the acquired company, even including mock funerals and coffins on occasions!

The research conducted by Angwin suggests that immediately following the take-over a high level of change related initiatives occur and that this quickly tails off. He reports levels of 500 changes initiated in the first month following a take-over dropping steadily to less than 50 changes by month 19. This process reflects the new owners being seen to 'take control' and making everyone in the company see that they 'mean business'. The speed of making such changes is a little surprising given that the new owners cannot know everything about the acquired company before they take charge. It might be expected that extensive pre-take-over planning would identify

what changes were to be made following acquisition. Angwin's research, carried out in conjunction with Ernst & Young, did not find this in practice. Many executives described the process as running into a 'wall' as senior managers who instigated the deal frequently go on to complete new deals and the running of the acquired company falls to executives not involved in the negotiations.

Some of the immediate change can be accounted for as a result of the need to introduce standardized procedures and practice in the finance areas. Equally there

is the 'expectation' on senior executives that change will be made and so already planned or considered change might be implemented when this was not possible under the old regime. If a senior executive is appointed from outside to run the company then they will wish to 'stamp' their authority on both the old and new companies. Doing nothing was not regarded as a realistic option by the respondents in Angwin's study.

The research shows that not all changes are introduced in the relatively short time after a take-over. This is noticeable at the end of the first year with the initial thrust on finance and marketing being replaced by human resource issues coming to the fore. This was suggested to be a necessary refinement on what inevitably was a crude process immediately following a take-over. The subsequent changes also tend to be more complex and difficult to achieve. Perhaps the skeletons in the cupboard of the acquired company have finally come to light and need to be dealt with. The post take-over period is highly stressful for everyone concerned, particularly because job security is always at risk. It is not uncommon to find that companies put together teams of opposite numbers from each company to integrate activity. Over the period of the integration it becomes apparent which of the pair will be 'released'.

After an acquisition there can be strong feelings of 'winners and losers', but it is frequently forgotten that it can be a two-way process. The acquiring company can also be changed as a result of exposure to the purchased one. This interactive development is the very best possibility to emerge from a take-over and can be a driver for strategic renewal. However, for this to be achieved, take-overs are a change process that need careful, sensitive management.

Adapted from: Angwin, D (1996) Executive action for acquisition success. Warwick Nexus, *Spring, pp 4–5.*

Approach	Commonly used in situations	Advantages	Drawbacks
Education + communication	Where there is a lack of information or inaccurate information or inaccurate information and analysis	Once persuaded, people will often help with the implementation of change	Can be very time consuming if many people are involved
Participation + involvement	Where the initiators do not have all the information they need to design the change, and where others have considerable power to resist	People who participate will be committed to implementing change, and any relevant information they have will be integrated into the change plan	Can be very time consuming if participators design an inappropriate change
Facilitation + support	Where people are resisting because of adjustment problems	No other approach works as well with adjustment problems	Can be time consuming, expensive, and still fail
Negotiation + agreement	Where someone or some group will clearly lose out in a change, and where that group has considerable power to resist	Sometimes it is a relatively easy way to avoid major resistance	Can be too expensive in many cases if it alerts others to negotiate for compliance
Manipulation + co-option	Where other tactics will not work, or are too expensive	It can be a relatively quick and inexpensive solution to resistance problems	Can lead to future problems if people feel manipulated
Explicit + implicit coercion	Where speed is essential, and the change initiators possess considerable power	It is speedy, and can overcome any kind of resistance	Can be risky if it leaves people mad at the initiators

Table 19.4
Methods of managing change (Kotter, JP and Schlesinger, CA (1979) Choosing stategies for change. *Harvard Business Review*, March/April, p 111)

and situations in which a trade-off possibility exists. Changing working patterns in return for higher pay, for example.

■ Manipulation plus co-option. The political aspects of change provide a clear indication of situations in which some form of *arranging* of events and alliances are undertaken in order to make more certain a particular outcome. In a very real sense this represents a *manipulation* of events. Co-option can be used as a means of diverting resistance through direct involvement. For example, the promotion of an active trade union representative to a supervisory position might reduce conflict and allow a more moderate individual to take over the trade union position. The major problems with manipulation and co-option are in being discovered, or misinterpreted.

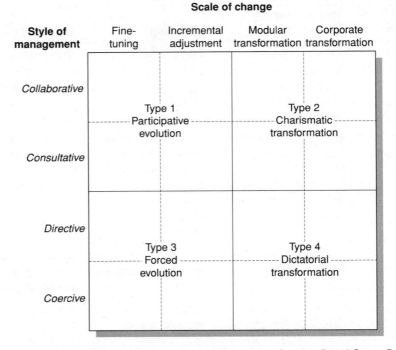

Figure 19.7   Dunphy and Stace's change strategies (taken from: Dunphy, D and Stace, D (1990) *Under New Management: Australian Organizations in Transition*, McGraw-Hill, Sydney, p 82).

■   **Explicit plus implicit coercion.** This strategy towards change is all about force and threat. It is not intended to create commitment, it is intended to achieve compliance. It is a 'take it or else' approach. As an example it is the strategy that makes it quite clear that the company will relocate to areas of cheap labour unless the workforce accept lower wages and higher output targets. Implicit coercion is a more subtle form of that force. As a strategy this can offer success for a while – as a result of the compliance achieved. For example the threat to close a factory if employees do not accept low pay might work for a while but as soon as higher paid work becomes available they will leave. The quality and quatity of output might also be expected to drop, or if the spending power of the employees becomes very low they may call the bluff of managers and strike.

Dunphy and Stace (1990) introduce a two-dimensional matrix as another way of identifying strategies for the management of change. One axis describes the *scale of change* involved and the other the *style of change management* in the situation (Figure 19.7).

   The four change strategies in Figure 19.7 are as follows:

■   **Participative evolution.** This strategy involves relatively small changes achieved through involvement.
■   **Forced evolution.** This strategy forces change onto the participants, but the changes themselves are relatively small.
■   **Charismatic transformation.** This strategy is used for large-scale change of a one-off nature. Frequently such changes are initiated and driven by a charismatic leader or sponsor.

■ Dictatorial transformation. This strategy relies on force or coercion to make large-scale changes of a one-off nature. This could be most successful as a one time emergency response to a crisis. Here time is of the essence and significant resistance might be expected.

Each of the contingency models reflect a *simplification* of the complex circumstances that exist at the time of change. Simplification represents a mechanism for aiding understanding and therefore the ability to control. It is searching for and imposing the familiar onto stimuli to create meaning. In doing so the signals can be misinterpreted, clues missed and inaccurate interpretations made. Inevitably if this happens as part of a change programme there is a danger of a failure in the process, or of the ability to generate the result intended.

The potential limitations in contingency models have been recognized by a number of writers and Dunford (1992) reviews some of them in relation to the Dunphy and Stace model outlined in Figure 19.7. Examples include the complexity of the organization and environment relationship and the political nature of managerial self-interest. Managers have particular ways of relating to organizations, works and the rights and responsibilities of the stakeholder groups. This leads to the creation of particular *interpretative schemes*, the existence of which play a determining role in strategy formulation. So as with all aspects of management, caution in accepting any model of change management is necessary.

Systems perspectives on change

There are a number of systems approaches that would have something to offer as a basis for problem solving. One approach is specifically worthy of mention in the context of managing change. *Total Systems Intervention* (TSI) is grounded in the philosophy of *critical systems thinking*. This philosophy is itself based upon three principles: complementarism, social awareness, and human well-being/emancipation. These principles reflect the view that techniques should be selected according to their appropriateness, that the social context plays a major part in determining the approach adopted and that the human dimension to work should contribute to the process of problem solving. The original source for this perspective is Flood and Jackson (1991). A more recent review of this subject (Flood, 1996) is referenced as Further Reading.

The TSI approach is a problem solving approach and has a wider application than the management of change. It is included here because of its relevance to managing some change processes. TSI comprises three phases:

■ Creativity. 'The task during the creativity phase is to use systems metaphors as organizing structures to help managers think creatively about their enterprises' (p 50).

■ Choice. 'The task during the choice phase is to chose an appropriate systems-based intervention methodology (or set of methodologies) to suit particular characteristics of the organization's situation as revealed by the examination conducted in the creativity phase' (p 51).

■ Implementation. 'The task during the implementation phase is to employ a particular systems methodology (systems methodologies) to translate the dominant vision of the organization, its structure, and the general orientation adopted to concerns and problems, into specific proposals for change' (p 52).

Although there are three stages to the TSI methodology it is intended to function as an iterative process with movement back and forth through reference to earlier and later stages during the process. Within the TSI approach there is the opportunity to utilize one or more specific systems methodologies. Each of the systems methodologies available are claimed to be of benefit in particular contextual conditions.

The benefits of the systems approaches are that a range of techniques can be accessed that offer the opportunity to tailor actions to locally defined analysis. It offers the ability for wide involvement in creating a creative picture of the situation and of finding mechanisms for resolving the competing points of view about those situations, in the process finding ways of surfacing and managing the power and political aspects of change.

Innovation as a change strategy

Innovation and change are areas of activity that are strongly tied together. One dictionary definition of innovation is to bring in novelties and to make changes. This conveys a feeling of something that is frivolous, not to be taken seriously and of little importance. Nothing could be further from the truth about the experience of innovation in many organizations. The need to be able to stay ahead in an increasingly competitive world is something that many management writers draw attention to. Tom Peters, for example, has produced a stream of books that began with *Thriving On Chaos* published in 1988. All intended to drive a message home about the need for continual revolution in responding to the operating environment, the basic message being innovate or die.

It is in this context that innovation and change are strongly linked together. The degree of innovation demanded by such writers as Peters requires nothing less in the running of organizations than a total and complete revolution on a continuous basis. Change on a large scale, permanently. The line of argument being that competition poses such a dramatic and global threat that if Western companies do not completely revolutionize their strategies and operational activities they will not be able to compete with companies who make those changes and who operate from a base with natural advantages.

Innovation carries with it a measure of risk because it involves doing things differently. Consider the decision to innovate through the introduction of high technology to perform part of the assembly process for a particular product. The equipment will be expensive; it may not have been used for that particular application before; employees may see it as a threat to their future employment; and it will take time to commission the equipment to an acceptable standard of reliability. Each of these features caries with it a measure of risk which when combined produces an even higher danger of failure. There are some industries that are particularly prone to the risks associated with innovation. For example, restaurants and clothing are subjected to rapid and frequent changes in fashion and taste. Unless they continually innovate and update their offerings to the market they will lose trade. The risk for these organizations is that their offerings will not be found *attractive* by potential customers.

Just as with change itself, innovation is an issue that finds resistance in many organizations for a number of reasons. There is a significant degree of inertia built into most organizations. Control and operational effectiveness comes from the predictability, repeated practice and consistency available through standardized products and services. Changing anything can create uncertainty, unfamiliarity and problems. Pascale (1990) points to a number of organizational features that restrict the ability to innovate and change (see Table 19.5). These arose from a comparison between Honda and General Motors.

There are different forms that innovation can take. Betz (1987) identifies three levels of innovative activity:

■ Radical. This represents the invention of something new. This is frequently the application of fundamental science. It carries with it the greatest level of risk, highest cost and longest timescale for development.

■ Systems. This level represents the application of existing science and technology in a novel way. It tends to be the combination of radical level innovations once they become established and less vulnerable to failure. The combination of the internal combustion engine and carriage building technologies to create the motor car for example. The timescales involved in the introduction of innovations at this level are shorter.

■ Incremental. This level of innovation represent the adaptation of existing technologies and products, etc. It is the fine tuning of that which already exists. It is the easiest form of innovation to make use of, along with being the cheapest and least vulnerable to failure.

In parallel with the risks, costs and timescales associated with each of these three levels of innovation the scale of benefit runs conversely. The possible returns from the radical level of innovation are much higher than at the incremental level. Risk and return are strongly correlated: the higher the risk the higher the potential return. This dilemma makes innovation management such a problematic issue. The upgrading of existing technologies can more easily demonstrate a return, whereas the return from R&D is at best at some unspecified time in the future.

There is no aspect of an organization that is not amenable to innovative activity. The Leavitt model of an organization identified in Figure 19.4 identifies the

Finances hegemony	–	the pre-eminence of one function (finance) with a restricted perspective
Learned helplessness	–	simultaneous pressure to show initiative whilst undermining examples of it by senior managers
Rituals of humiliation	–	the socialization process of conformity as the basis of promotion
Rituals of avoidance	–	the internal company realities of how conflict and difference are dealt with
Privilege and reward	–	the rights and rewards of senior executives in comparison with the lower levels and the history of compliance with authority
Empowerment	–	the lack of any real delegation of power and decision making ability
Reinforcing folklore	–	the traditions and usual ways of doing things are continually passed down and reinforced in stories

Table 19.5
Examples of the restrictions on innovation and change (taken from: Pascale, R (1990) *Managing on the Edge: How Successful Companies use Conflict to Stay Ahead*, Penguin, London, pp 237–44)

four defining features of an organization as *people*, *technology*, *task* and *structure*, surrounded by the *environment*. Each of these features can sustain innovation in one form or another. Innovation is a process that is only dependent upon the ingenuity of the human resource within the organization. It is limited only by their creativity and willingness to engage in it.

Another way of conceptualizing an organization is the model that has become known as the *Seven S Framework*. Originally developed for use by the McKinsey consulting firm in 1979 by individuals such as Richard Pascale, Anthony Athos, Robert Waterman and Tom Peters it attempts to capture the most important features of activity for managers (see Figure 19.8).

Pascale (1990) revisits this model in the context of a discussion of stagnation and renewal as a cyclical process. Innovation and change are not single events that can be adopted once and then forgotten. They represent dynamic processes in which change is followed by a period of stagnation as the benefits are harvested. This in turn produces a resistance to seek continuous change and so a disjointed process is generated. The Seven S Framework provides a basis for managers to consider each of the important elements of the organization on a regular basis and so limit the negative effects of stagnation.

Having identified that innovation is an important part of the change process it is useful to consider how it is harnessed to the benefit of the organization. Schermerhorn (1993) identifies five elements of the innovation process:

- Internal organizational sensitivity. Reflects the ability to be aware of the need for innovation and how to harness effort in support of it.
- Idea creation. This stage involves generating new ideas and finding ways of adapting existing methods and procedures.
- Initial experimentation. This reflects the development of prototypes and testing the ideas generated in the previous stage.

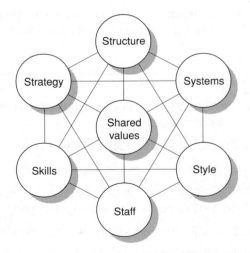

Figure 19.8 The McKinsey 7-S framework (taken from: Peters, TJ and Waterman, RH (1982) *In Search of Excellence*, Harper Collins).

- Feasibility determination. The determination of the practicality of an innovation involves checking the financial viability, practicality and operational benefits to be gained.
- Final application. This stage represents the commercialization of ideas and their adoption within the organization. In a perfect world it would lead to further ideas creation as a consequence of the internal sensitivity to the need for innovation.

Change: a management perspective

It was suggested earlier that management and change are closely linked and that change is an ongoing feature of organizational life. That must be the starting point for any consideration of a management perspective on change. It can be argued that management is a process of seeking a balance between change and stability. Stability is necessary in order to achieve the economies of scale in mass production and services. Change on the other hand is necessary because of the need to keep ahead of the competition and to ensure constantly reducing cost. It can be argued that the success of Japanese management methods is in being able to provide the means of effectively harnessing these conflicting requirements.

Too much change it can be argued is bad for operations, leads to confusion and reduces efficiency, quality and morale. Too little change results in stagnation with no ability to adapt to changing circumstances. Many recent developments in management practice have been designed to allow ever greater levels of change to be adopted without loss of control over operations; just-in-time, teamwork, empowerment, quality circles and the other planning and control techniques all offer some ability to adapt operational activity to changes in product, technology or environment.

Another way of looking at change is that is a natural part of life. The problems arise from stability, not from change. The changing seasons, weather, ageing, birth and death, sickness and health and family responsibilities represent just some of the ways in which change manifests itself in the life experience of human beings. Consider the changes in the range of skills and abilities of a human being between the ages of three and twelve. Under these circumstances it is not stability that is the norm, it is change. Yet there is something that happens to human beings when they become adult and part of an organization that seeks to create security, stability and predictability. This resists change. Perhaps it is the human experience of organizations that creates this 'change' in people? It is the responsibility of management to develop the structural, procedural and cultural arrangements that encourage the expression of human talents desirable in a change environment.

What to change is one of the major difficulties faced by management. Everything and continuously would appear to be the advice offered by many of the writers on the topic. But for practising managers knowing what to change is frequently a difficult decision. How far change should go is another difficult decision area, as resistance and cost inevitably increase with the degree of change. The process of change is another area with a number of dangers attached to it. The end result, once achieved, may not meet the expectations predicted and fail to deliver the intended benefits. This exposes management to additional cost and loss of credibility as they seek to remedy the deficiency. So from a management perspective change is a dangerous practice that it is not possible to avoid and yet it carries all manner of personal, professional and organizational risks. An exiting aspect of management!

Conclusions

This chapter has analysed the nature of change and assessed the ways in which it impacts on organizations and management. The reasons for change were examined as were the forms of resistance to it. Change management approaches were evaluated as was innovation as part of the change process. Every aspect of an organization is subject to and involved with change in some way or other. From that perspective every other chapter in this book contains some aspect of change, its origins, impact and interacting variables. It is for that reason that change is a suitable conclusion for the book.

Discussion questions

1 Define the following key terms used in this chapter:

   Forcefield analysis model   Organizational development
   Planned and unplanned change   Individual resistance to change
   Leavitt's organizational variables   Innovation
   Dunphy and Stace's change strategies   Change agent
   Fracturing and adaptive change   Total Systems Intervention

2 Describe the McKinsey Seven S Framework and explain how it could be used to inform a change management programme.

3 Outline the links between power, politics and change and explain why they are necessary to the management of a change programme.

4 Provide a brief explanation for each of the individual reasons for resisting change identified in Figure 19.2.

5 Distinguish between planned and unplanned change, adaptive and fracturing change. What are the consequences of these distinctions?

6 What are the main reasons for resistance to change and how can they be overcome?

7 Describe the contingency approach to organizational change and distinguish it from the OD approach.

8 Provide a brief explanation for each of the group and organizational reasons for resisting change identified in Figure 19.3.

9 'The true skill in management is to keep change happening so that everyone has to pay attention to what they are doing and they do not have any spare time to cause trouble for managers.' Discuss this statement.

10 Describe the stages of innovation from creating the climate to implementation. What are the risks associated with change and how do they link with the levels of innovation?

Research questions

1 In small groups of five, seek out an organization that has just gone through a major change of some description. This might be the introduction of a new product, a significant reduction in the number of employees or the amalgamation with another company. Arrange to discuss the changes made with a cross-section of managers and employees. Identify how the need to change was detected, how it was planned and implemented and if it has been successful. Compare what you find in terms of the different opinions expressed and methods used with the material introduced in this chapter. Explain the differences and similarities that you find.

2 Conduct a forcefield analysis of a situation in your life. It could be the number of times that you miss lectures or the number of times that you phone parents or friends. Attempt to identify factors that might drive you to attend lectures (or phone) more frequently and those that encourage you to do it less frequently. Draw a diagram of this particular forcefield. Attempt to identify a change programme for the situation using the three stages in the Lewin model. Attempt to implement your analysis and after two months review if you were able to refreeze your behaviour at the desired level. Explain why or why not. What does this teach you about managing change?

3 Trawl through books and magazines for examples of change that were successful and examples that failed. Attempt to identify what created the conditions for success and failure in the examples that you find. Reconcile the findings of your work on this with the material contained in this chapter.

Key reading

From Clark, H, Chandler, J and Barry, J (1994) *Organization and Identities: Text and Readings in Organizational Behaviour*, International Thomson Business Press, London.

■ Campbell B *et al.*: The manifesto for new times, p 49. This considers the changes facing Britain as a capitalist society entering the 1990s.

■ Cockburn C: Male dominance and technological change, p 197. Considers the impact of changing technology in the printing industry on the work of both men and women.

■ Roethlisberger FJ and Dickson WJ: Group restriction of output, p 247. Part of the famous Hawthorne studies, this demonstrates that change is endemic to organizations and that employees do not always react to it in ways anticipated by managers.

■ Coch L and French JRP: Overcoming resistance to change using group methods, p 260. This is a research-based examination of change and its consequences within one manufacturing establishment.

■ Hobsbawm EJ and Rudé G. Early forms of worker resistance – swing riots, p 317. This attempts to reflect the experience of workers attempting to influence (change) aspects of their working life.

Further reading

Cummings, TG and Worley, CG (1993) *Organization Development and Change*, 5th edn. West Publishing, St Paul, MN. A text dedicated to the review of the subjects indicated in the title and how they impact on organizational activity and functioning. In that sense it is a standard textbook in this field.

Flood, RL (1996) *Solving Problem Solving*, John Wiley. This text takes a new look at a number of systems approaches to problem solving and updates the approach to the TSI perspective introduced earlier. In that context problem solving is being equated with the management of change. It should be recognized that there are distinctions between these two concepts in particular situations.

McCalman, J and Paton, RA (1992) *Change Management: A Guide to Effective Implementation*, Paul Chapman, London. As the title suggests, this book is about how to manage change processes. In doing so it concentrates on the two approaches to managing change, the systems approach and the organizational development model.

Morgan, G (1993) *Imaginization: The Art of Creative Management*, Sage. Although not about change directly, this book provides a whole set of ways to develop new perspectives on thinking about organizations and management. In practice this represents an invitation to *change* our thinking about organizations and what we do within them. If this approach is to be of any value then it should also change organizations as a consequence.

Oswick, C and Grant, D (eds) (1996) *Organization Development: Metaphorical Explorations*, Pitman, London. This text attempts to provide a basis for the critical evaluation of organizational development, rather than the more usual practitioner perspective. It also uses the metaphor as a basis of enhancing understanding of organizational development in general and specific terms.

References

Armstrong, M (1995) *A Handbook of Personnel Management Practice*, 5th edn, Kogan Page, London.

Betz, F. (1987) *Managing Technology*, Prentice-Hall, Englewood Cliffs, NJ.

Cummings, TG and Worley, CG (1993) *Organization Development and Change*, 5th edn, West Publishing, St Paul, MN.

Dunford, RW (1992) *Organizational Behaviour: An Organizational Analysis Perspective*, Addison-Wesley, Sydney.

Dunphy, D and Stace, D (1988) Transformational and coercive strategies for planned organizational change: beyond the OD model. *Organization Studies*, **9**, 317–34.

Dunphy, D and Stace, D (1990) *Under New Management: Australian Organizations in Transition*, McGraw-Hill, Sydney.

Flood, RL and Jackson, MC (1991) *Creative Problem Solving: Total Systems Intervention*, John Wiley, Chichester.

Hellriegel, D, Slocum, JW and Woodman, RW (1989) *Organizational Behaviour*, 5th edn, West Publishing, St Paul, MN.

Kahn, EF (1982) Conclusion: critical themes in the study of change. In *Change in Organizations* (eds PS Goodman and associates), Jossey-Bass, San Francisco, CA.

Kanter, RM (1983) *The Change Masters*, Allen & Unwin, London.

Kotter, JP and Schlesinger, LA (1979) Choosing strategies for change. *Harvard Business Review*, March/April.

Leavitt, HL (1965) Applied organizational change in industry: structural, technological and humanistic approaches. In *Handbook of Organizations* (ed JG March), Rand McNally, Chicago, IL.

Lewin, K (1951) *Field Theory in Social Science*, Harper & Row, New York.

Moorhead, G and Griffin, RW (1992) *Organizational Behaviour*, 3rd edn, Houghton Mifflin, Boston, MA.

Mullins, LJ (1995) *Management and Organizational Behaviour*, 4th edn, Pitman, London.

Nadler, D and Tushman, M (1988) *Strategic Organizational Design*, Scott, Foresman, Glenview, CO.

Open University (1990) Book 9, *Managing Change*. Course B784 The Effective Manager, Open Business School, Milton Keynes.

Ottaway, RN (1982) Defining the change agent. In *Changing Design* (eds B Evans *et al.*), John Wiley, Chichester.

Pascale, R (1990) *Managing on the Edge: How Successful Companies Use Conflict to Stay Ahead*, Penguin, London.

Peters, TJ (1988) *Thriving on Chaos*, Random House, New York.

Plant, R (1987) *Managing Change and Making it Stick*, Fontana, London.

Pritchett, P (1994) *The Employee Handbook of New Work Habits for a Radically Changing World*, Pritchett Associates, Washington, Tyne & Wear.

Schein, VE (1985) Organizational realities: the politics of change. *Training and Development Journal*, February, 37–41.

Schermerhorn, JR (1993) *Management For Productivity*, 4th edn, John Wiley, New York.

Stephenson, T (1985) *Management: A Political Activity*, Macmillan, Basingstoke.

Stewart, R (1991) *Managing Today and Tomorrow*, Macmillan.

Index